Curriculum Books

"An essential scholarly tool for anyone who works in curriculum. The bibliography itself is the most valuable reference source yet published on the history of the field, and [the] commentary adds an incisive and comprehensive interpretation of twentieth-century developments in curriculum."
—*George Willis, Professor of Education, University of Rhode Island*

"Students in the curriculum field and those engaged in curriculum development will find this book filling the void of understandings about the...development of curriculum theory and practice."
—*Ralph W. Tyler, Center for Advanced Study in Behavioral Sciences*

"*Curriculum Books* is monumental in scope—the most helpful feature of the commentaries given in each decade is the grouping of books that followed similar appraoches...."
—*Edmond C. Short, Professor Emeritus, Pennsylvania State University*

"...a very useful tool. An excellent addition to the professional literature of the curriculum field."
—*Paul R. Klohr, Professor Emeritus, Ohio State University,*
Excerpt from The Journal of Curriculum Theorizing

"Should be at the elbow of every curriculum scholar and in every professional library. It is a valuable reference work in graduate courses and seminars."
—*George S. Tomkins, Professor, University of British Columbia*

"A unique compilation and analysis, useful for all serious, advanced students."
—*Daniel Tanner, Professor, Rutgers University*

"An outstanding contribution to curriculum studies. The bibliography and commentary complement one another perfectly...a basic handbook for anyone interested in the history of education in general and of curriculum in particular."
—*David Pratt, Professor, Queen's University*

"More than...a guide to curriculum thought and literature; ...[*Curriculum Books* provides an] interpretation of trends and directions...and reveals many insights."
—*Educational Leadership*

Curriculum Books

Studies in the
Postmodern Theory of Education

Joe L. Kincheloe and Shirley R. Steinberg
General Editors

Vol. 175

PETER LANG
New York • Washington, D.C./Baltimore • Bern
Frankfurt am Main • Berlin • Brussels • Vienna • Oxford

William H. Schubert, Ann Lynn Lopez Schubert,
Thomas P. Thomas, Wayne M. Carroll

Curriculum Books

The First Hundred Years

Second Edition

PETER LANG
New York • Washington, D.C./Baltimore • Bern
Frankfurt am Main • Berlin • Brussels • Vienna • Oxford

Library of Congress Cataloging-in-Publication Data

Curriculum books: the first hundred years / William H. Schubert ... [et al.].— [2nd ed.].
p. cm. — (Counterpoints; v. 175)
On previous edition Schubert's name appears as the first of two authors.
Includes bibliographical references and index.
1. Education—United States—Curricula—Bibliography.
I. Schubert, William Henry. II. Counterpoints (New York, N.Y.); v. 175.
Z5815 .U5 S34   016.375'00973—dc21   2002004066
ISBN 0-8204-5192-4 (paperback)
ISBN 0-8204-6211-X (hardcover)
ISSN 1058-1634

Die Deutsche Bibliothek-CIP-Einheitsaufnahme

Curriculum books: the first hundred years / William H. Schubert ... [et al.].— [2nd ed.].
−New York; Washington, D.C./Baltimore; Bern;
Frankfurt am Main; Berlin; Brussels; Vienna; Oxford: Lang.
(Counterpoints; Vol. 175)
ISBN 0-8204-5192-4 (paperback)
ISBN 0-8204-6211-X (hardcover)

Cover design by Joni Holst

The paper in this book meets the guidelines for permanence and durability
of the Committee on Production Guidelines for Book Longevity
of the Council of Library Resources.

© 2002 Peter Lang Publishing, Inc., New York

Printed in the United States of America

TABLE OF CONTENTS

ACKNOWLEDGMENTS

(From the First Edition)

Most lovingly, I wish to thank my wife, Ann, for her constant encouragement of my work. Her unwavering assistance in research, typing, discussion of ideas, and reading made this work possible.

I also wish to thank a number of scholars at other institutions who have encouraged the work by their comments, suggestions, and sharing of information. They include: Michael Apple of the University of Wisconsin, George A. Beauchamp of Northwestern University, O. L. Davis of the University of Texas, John I. Goodlad of the University of California at Los Angeles, L. Thomas Hopkins of Columbia University, William Pinar of the University of Rochester, Gerald Ponder of North Texas State University, George Posner of Cornell University, J. Harlan Shores of the University of Illinois at Urbana, Edmund Short of Pennsylvania State University, Charles A. Speiker of the Association for Supervision and Curriculum Development, Kate Strickland of the University of Texas at San Antonio, Daniel Tanner of Rutgers University, Laurel Tanner of Temple University, Ralph W. Tyler of Science Research Associates, Max van Manen of the University of Alberta, and George Willis of the University of Rhode Island.

Many colleagues at my current institution, the University of Illinois at Chicago Circle, are also acknowledged for their encouragement and suggestions, especially Maurice J. Eash, Harriet Talmage, Herbert Walberg, William Ernst, Joy Johnson, David Miller, Julius Menacker, Van Cleve Morris, Edward Wynne, David Wilson, Ernest Pascarella, Susanna Pflaum, Neal Gordon, Robert Crowson, Larry Nucci, Eugene Cramer, Edward Haertel, Geneva Haertel, and Sue Rasher.

Appreciation is extended to Madeline Schubert for helpful comments on an earlier version of the manuscript. Many thanks are also extended to Karen and Elaine for being thoughtful during their visit when we worked on this book.

Two professional associations are thanked for helping to make this work known among fellow scholars: The American Educational Research Association Special Interest Group on the Creation and Utilization of Curriculum Knowledge, and the Society for the Study of Curriculum History.

Evelyn Pope is thanked for her many hours of effort in typing the manuscript. I am particularly grateful to Catherine Terdich for her editorial assistance.

Special appreciation is extended to J. Harlan Shores for his gift of more than 200 curriculum books and monographs. Finally, Pearl Kanaley, my great-aunt and first-grade teacher, is thanked most kindly for supporting this project.

ACKNOWLEDGMENTS

(From the Second Edition)

The above-mentioned acknowledgments for the first edition are intended to maintain historical continuity. I think this is especially appropriate for a book that is historical in character. Hence, those "thank-you" remarks stand today as during the preparation of the first edition.

We appreciate many who provided valuable commentary on the first edition and encouraged the long process of developing the second edition. The many students who used the book, colleagues in curriculum (and related fields), and members of the Society for the Study of Curriculum History, Professors of Curriculum, and the American Educational Research Association Special Interest Group on Creation and Utilization of Curriculum Knowledge (now the Special Interest Group on Critical Issues in Curriculum). Special thanks in the curriculum field is extended to Craig Kridel, Bill Ayers, Dan Marshall, Bill Watkins, Bob Morris, Janet Miller, Edmund Short, Bill Pinar, George Willis, Mike Apple, Max van Manen, Elliot Eisner, Paul Klohr, Ralph Tyler, William Connell, Dorothy Huenecke, David Pratt, Antoinette Oberg, Harro Van Brummelen, George Tomkins, Robert Zais, Michael Belok, David Silvernail, and J. Harlan Shores. Among faculty at the University of Illinois at Chicago I also thank Vicki Chou, Don Hellison, Bernardo Gallegos, Michelle Parker, Carole Mitchener, and Mary Ann Koch for her secretarial assistance.

At Peter Lang Publishers, we thank Christopher Myers, Lisa Dillon, Joe Kincheloe, Shirley Steinberg, Stephanie Achard, others in the editorial and production departments for their thorough attention to detail. Facilitating the invitation and opportunity to do a second edition with them is much appreciated.

Ann Lopez Schubert and I thank Heidi and Henry for their interest in this aspect of their parents' work and for their insights about curriculum matters. Madeline Schubert is again thanked for her support and interest. Tom Thomas extends special thanks to Claudia Thomas and their family and

Wayne Carroll extends special thanks to Jane Carroll and their family; I, too, thank them for their understanding and support. We all thank other members of our families and friendship circles, for it is their encouragement that helps us to move ahead. This includes, again, the many students, former students, and colleagues who make up such an important part of our lives in the curriculum world.

Finally, we dedicate this work to those who have already carried on with it and to those who will do so in the future, i.e., educators (in and out of schools) who build upon the past scholarship to provide a brighter future.

William H. Schubert

PREFACE

Many fields today realize the necessity of searching for their historical roots. Scholars who discourse in mathematics, biology, chemistry, and physics are increasingly curious about the ideas of their intellectual ancestors. For too long it was assumed that the sciences and their technological derivatives in medicine, industry, transportation, communication, and so on, were nearly perfect evolutionary systems. That is to say, they automatically expurgated inert thoughts and perceived little need to probe their archaic past. Today, this position is recognized for its puerility. Much of importance can be gleaned from the thought patterns and techniques, if not from the substantive knowledge, expressed in works by those who forged the origins of many a scholarly domain. To be ahistorical is indefensible.

This is the case for the study of curriculum in the field of education.[1] Curriculum scholars, administrators, and teachers have come to see themselves as part of an evolving historical context. They need to know about the insights, foibles, and achievements of those who faced similar problems in other times and circumstances. Many do recognize this need. Yet historical awareness cannot be achieved by desire alone. The centralization of literature about curriculum is a necessary prerequisite to knowledge and analysis of its origins. To know one's origins is to know one's present and to be able to create one's future.

PURPOSE AND ORGANIZATION

This book provides a chronology of curriculum books that appeared in the United States from roughly 1900 to 2000. Thus, it is designed for anyone whose interests and professional pursuits deal with education. It portrays a stream of books used to educate school administrators, teachers, aspiring educators, educational scholars, and the wider public about curriculum for the past century. It is not a history book in a technical sense; rather, it is a chronology of books with commentaries. Each chapter treats a decade for which background of two kinds is provided. The first consists of reminders about and reflections on sociocultural, intellectual, artistic, and scientific developments. The second is discussion of major curriculum movements, trends, books, and authors. These context-setting sections are followed by yearly bibliographies of curriculum books published in the decade.

As an attempt to provide a comprehensive resource on curriculum books published in English, this book is designed to ease curriculum scholarship which can lead to improved curricular decision and action. The categories used to discuss curriculum contributions in each chapter are not always uniform because events are quite different from decade to decade. Uniformity is, however, provided by continuing reference to schools of curriculum thought; namely, *experientialists, intellectual traditionalists*, and *social behaviorists*. These schools are characterized in the first chapter. These orientations to the curriculum are joined with the appearance of a fourth perspective, the *critical reconstructionist*, in the 1980s. There will also be the appearance of important scholars who attempted to find points of agreement among these various perspectives (here noted as *conciliarists*) and scholars who found that they could not speak authentically in any of the dominant options and brought in new perspectives on the curriculum from other discourses.

Since this work is an attempt to help the curriculum field become less ahistorical, the following is a bit of the history that prompted the writing of the first edition of this volume: *Curriculum Books: The First Eighty Years*.

HOW THE FIRST EDITION DEVELOPED: A NARRATIVE RECOLLECTION BY BILL SCHUBERT

During my first year of doctoral study I pondered possible directions for my curriculum research. As I pursued my coursework, one need in particular became indelible in my mind: the need for a comprehensive bibliography of curriculum studies. I experienced great difficulty in locating bibliographies of curriculum works. I suspected that other students had similar difficulty. Soon I realized that this difficulty was shared by scholars in the field, even eminent ones. I felt that this might well be a productive problem to remedy, especially since I already had started a citation collection. Early in my doctoral study at the University of Illinois, my mentor, J. Harlan Shores, wisely suggested that as I study I should keep a card file of all sources encountered. At the conclusion of the program I had accumulated cards on approximately 600 books, articles, miscellaneous papers, and other materials.

Stocked with these cards, I estimated that I was in a position to propose a paper for presentation at the 1976 American Educational Research Association Annual Conference. Brashly, I proposed to centralize and categorize all of the curriculum development literature from 1900 to 1976. Thankfully, I had the sense to limit the kinds of citations by using a system of rules. Essentially, the rules confined the study to curriculum books written in English. The proposal was accepted, and as the task evolved it seemed increasingly insurmountable. Yet it is surprising what one can accomplish when one intentionally overcommits oneself. I at least had to approximate the proposed task.

It was at that point that my travels began, both actually and figuratively. I toured major curriculum text books and their bibliographies. One need only sample the elaborate citations in Caswell and Campbell (1935), Smith, Stanley, and Shores (1950), Stratemeyer, Forkner, and McKim (1947), Seguel (1966), Trillingham (1934), and Taba (1962) to empathize with the magnitude of the task.[2] Numerous other texts were surveyed as well. My paper, *The Literature of Curriculum Development: Toward Centralization and Analysis,* was presented in San Francisco in April 1976.[3] It included a bibliography of 753 curriculum publications, mostly books. In the paper, citations were categorized in three ways: (1) their tendency to be prescriptive or descriptive treatments of curriculum; (2) disciplinary orientation of the authors; and (3) principal sub-areas of education that the books treated. Although tendencies emerged in these areas, I learned that productive analyses should be considerably more complex and often specific to historical situations.

Following the presentation, considerable positive commentary was received through letters and personal contacts, all of which encouraged continuation on a larger scale. Since sources listed in bibliographies of curriculum texts had a frequent habit of conflicting with one another, the next venture was to check citations with standard reference collections. The following were among the most helpful, both in checking citations and augmenting the bibliography for the first edition:

> *Books in Print* (Past and present editions, particularly the subject guides). New York: R. R. Bowker Company.
>
> Broudy, H. S., et al. (1967). *Philosophy of education: An organization of topics and selected sources.* Urbana: University of Illinois Press. (with 1969 & 1971 supplements, curriculum sections).
>
> Columbia University. (1970). *Dictionary catalogue-Teachers College Library.* Boston: G. K. Hall. (and available supplements from subsequent years)
>
> Harvard University Library, Widener Library Shelflist Service. (1968). *Education* (Two Volumes). Cambridge, MA: Harvard University Press.

Library of Congress Catalog-Books: Subject indexes. (1943-present). Washington, DC: Library of Congress.

United States Department of Health, Education, and Welfare. (1965) *Subject catalogue of the department library* (Volume Four). Boston: G. K. Hall.

Even these formative reference works proved incomplete and sometimes inaccurate. I therefore determined that libraries must be visited. During the next year several library collections were surveyed. This endeavor prompted a good deal of study of curriculum literature, not merely citations alone. The following libraries were an immense assistance, even though the librarians likely have no remembrance of my being there.

- ❖ University of Illinois—Urbana, Illinois
- ❖ Northwestern University—Evanston, Illinois
- ❖ National College of Education—Evanston, Illinois
- ❖ University of Illinois at Chicago Circle—Chicago, Illinois
- ❖ University of Chicago—Chicago, Illinois
- ❖ Chicago Public Library—Chicago, Illinois
- ❖ Washington University—St. Louis, Missouri
- ❖ University of Rochester—Rochester, New York
- ❖ Waterloo University—Waterloo, Ontario
- ❖ Johns Hopkins University—Baltimore, Maryland
- ❖ University of Houston—Houston, Texas
- ❖ Teachers College, Columbia University—New York, New York
- ❖ Pennsylvania State University—University Park, Pennsylvania
- ❖ Stanford University—Palo Alto, California
- ❖ Ontario Institute for Studies in Education—Toronto, Ontario

A presentation of the updated findings was made at the 1977 American Educational Research Association Annual Conference in New York City.[4] This resulted in the request by the AERA Special Interest Group on the Creation and Utilization of Curriculum Knowledge for permission to copy and distribute the bibliography to its membership. The slightly revised version, *A Chronology of Curriculum Development Literature*,[5] was disseminated in 1977 and for several subsequent years. The response from scholars from many parts of the United States and world indicated the desire for a more substantial publication that portrayed the growth of curriculum thought during the twentieth century. Hence, the impetus for the first edition of this book.

REVISING *CURRICULUM BOOKS*:
A COMMENTARY BY TOM THOMAS

The revision of the text was discussed as early as the mid-1980s. The positive reception to the volume in sales (in academic circles, at any rate) and in the kind remarks by various curriculum scholars provided the impetus to think about revising and updating the text at the end of the 1990s. Among the comments and criticisms of the first edition, views that inspired the second edition of this work were the following:

Edmund Short contended, "The most helpful feature of the commentaries given in each decade is the grouping and citation of books that followed similar approaches or subject matter." Short also stated his approval for the classifying orientations in a review for *Educational Leadership* (39:1, 79–80). He wrote, "While one familiar with the range of curriculum thought and with many of the particular books and writers might argue with Schubert's choice of categories and occasionally with his placement of particular writers within them, nevertheless, his analysis is largely correct and reveals many new insights."

George S. Tomkins, writing in the *Newsletter of the Canadian Association for Curriculum Studies* (November 1982), noted the value of research on texts from early in the twentieth century. He wrote, "Small though the numbers are for the earliest decades, Professor Schubert has unearthed a number of titles hitherto little known, if known at all, to most of us and thereby served his major aim of furthering historical consciousness for curriculum inquiry." He summarized, "*Curriculum Books* should be at the elbow of every curriculum scholar and in every professional library. It should also find use as a valuable reference work in graduate courses and seminars."

In the *Phi Delta Kappan* (63:6, 423) David Silvernail concluded,

> Educators will find this clear, concise overview of curriculum history a valuable addition to their professional libraries. The book helps readers to better understand the evolution of the curriculum in recent decades. Discussing books and curricular trends in the context of cultural events and major perspectives in education thought risks oversimplification. Nonetheless, this is valuable technique for giving readers some insight into the saga of curriculum development in the 20th century.

Rob Walker in the *Journal of Curriculum Studies* (15:3, 350) contended that the book did not demonstrate an "intimate" knowledge of the literature and that the historical reminders are presented rapidly and without development. Nonetheless, he favorably opined,

> Curriculum is a field in which changing fashion closely mirrors changes in other aspects of the culture as well as preceding in terms of its own unfolding logic. Those of us caught up in the academic pursuit of the field lose sight of these interconnections with the culture too easily and too readily and this book does a valuable job in reminding us of the fact. Despite its faults, this is a book with a vision, a vision of a 'curriculum of curriculum' and as such it may well mark a coming of age for the field as well as establishing one scholar's contribution to it.

William F. Connell (*Curriculum Perspectives* 2:3, 93) contrasted the limited treatment of general context with the curriculum analyses, which he characterized as a "useful summary of trends." Connell contended that the curriculum perspective classification employed to organize writing about the curriculum "works reasonably well up to about 1930 partly, perhaps, because it is a rather loose one."

In his review in the *Journal of Curriculum Theorizing* (1981, 3:2, 229–230), Paul Klohr recognized the work as "A very useful tool for teaching and scholarly work. It has been much needed…an excellent addition to the professional literature of the curriculum field." He also recognized that new directions in curriculum thought would challenge the three orientations used to categorize writing on the curriculum. He wrote,

> Insights from psychoanalysis, political theory, and gender analysis—to name only several sources significant in the work of some of the reconceptualists—clearly differ markedly from the common sources under-girding the thinking of most of those Schubert calls experientialists. The problem for curriculum theorists is even more complex than a confrontation between experimentalism and existentialism, but that is part of it. I view this issue as the most pressing matter curricularists face in the 1980's as their field continues to mature.

When Bill Schubert and Ann Lopez Schubert set about collecting citations for the revision of the volume, historical research was coupled with the demands of being contemporary chroniclers of the rapidly expanding field of curriculum scholarship. The technology of publishing made it possible to produce small runs of a book and turn a modest profit. This was a boon to scholars looking for acceptance of a text with a limited audience. In addition, the explosion of texts that looked at curriculum from a critical reconstructionist or other "reconceptualist" perspectives (using a term offered by William Pinar that proved useful in the 1980s) augmented the continued production of books that addressed curriculum development in its more conventional discourse. This vastly expanded the number of works that addressed curriculum.

To assist in bibliographic research, Bill Schubert asked graduate research assistants to help in the task beginning in the late 1980s. Marcia Chaimowitz, Michael Costigan, Shannon Hart, Leslie Herzog, Anne Isaacson, Fred Klonsky, Patty McGuiness, Jackie Pawelek, Bonnie Strykowski, Dana Welte, and Norman Weston assisted with bibliographic research. Patrick Roberts is thanked for his careful proofreading and thoughtful comments on the recent drafts. Two of the research assistants, Wayne Carroll and Tom Thomas, were subsequently asked to aid in the compiling and editing of citations, participating in revision of the original chapters and writing historical contexts for the 1980s and then the 1990s.

Locating citations for the bibliography took the researchers back to the library, but with the advent of the Internet, new methods of locating books were employed. It is now possible to locate books across Illinois and the nation from the personal computer. On-line bookstores provided surprisingly useful information. Publisher web sites began to appear in the 1990s, providing yet another avenue for discovering new texts. Information could be checked against the Library of Congress database. The catalogs sent by publishing houses that specialize in education texts were a valuable resource, and the annual meetings of AERA and ASCD found Bill busy making the rounds of publishing houses, searching for brochures and new titles. Finally, the research that Tom Thomas conducted in the completing of his dissertation on the moral constructs that underlie curriculum thought in the first two-thirds of the twentieth century uncovered new authors and titles.

Ann became delightfully occupied with home schooling in the 1990s and unfortunately has also experienced numerous chronic health problems. Thus, she assumed a less involved role in the revision. The task of writing the first draft of commentary on curriculum books for these periods eventually became Thomas's responsibility. Carroll helped to revise and update the historical context sections and took on the monumental task of revising the indexes. Bill assumed the role of principal author, editor, and sage, being final redactor for the entire work and providing a new conclusion to the text.

ON CITATION SELECTION

As the original book took shape, guidelines for inclusions and exclusions became defined. Explicating rules for citation selection is a difficult task. Using any set of rules, even rigorous legalistic ones, involves sizable portions of human judgment. That is the case here; nevertheless, rules enhance potential for replicability.

It was decided for the original text that inclusions be limited to curriculum books published in English, including monographs and yearbooks, but excluding dissertations, research reports, and curriculum guides having limited distribution, unless these are formally published and have national or international distribution. This rule was maintained for this revision. Journal articles are excluded, unless they appear in books of curriculum readings. In rare instances educational journals devoted entire issues to curriculum matters and are included. (Several issues of the *Review of Educational Research* are cases in point.) This does not refer, however, to curriculum journals, for example, *The Curriculum Journal, Educational Leadership, Curriculum Inquiry* (formerly *Curriculum Theory Network*), *The Journal of Curriculum Studies, Journal of Curriculum and Supervision,* or *The Journal of Curriculum Theorizing* (later renamed *JCT*). These publications normally devote their space to curriculum matters.

The central criterion that guided the selection of citations was the question: What twentieth century books contributed substantially, *directly or indirectly*, to curriculum thought? The decision to include works of influence that may not directly address curriculum but nonetheless came to be a part of the conversations about curriculum resulted in a much longer listing of texts, but, we would argue, a more valid portrait of the discussions that were occurring. Commentary sections were guided by the question: How do these books portray a saga or heritage of ideas and emphases in curriculum thought? Responses to these questions must, of course, be built on certain clarifications in terminology and decision mechanics.

Books were judged as suitable for inclusion if they deal with curriculum, that is, the substance or subject matter of educational activity. More specifically, they are included if they describe, prescribe, and/or discuss questions such as the following: How do or how should people determine what to teach others? How do they defend or justify it? What issues are involved in deciding what to teach or learn? How do we and how should we study such matters? Essentially, the root, *curriculum*, is honored: What is/should be the nature of the course or journey on which we take those whom we teach? Generally, such works pertain to schooling, since the study of curriculum formally evolved to satisfy pressures for universal schooling. However, the growth of attention to popular culture, the curriculum of media and technology, and to the nonschool curriculum has brought in new insights and more titles. An author's own categorization as indicated by a work's title is accepted, that is, if *curriculum* appears in the title, the book is included. However, books with *curriculum* in the title are usually excluded if they deal primarily with a specialized subject area, such as mathematics curriculum, physical education curriculum, special education curriculum. The growth of attention to content standards and disciplinary statements in the past decade, however, has caused us to relax this restriction for the sake of being authentic to what is happening in writing about curriculum. Then there are certain books that do not have *curriculum* in the title, although they deal directly with the above questions and have exerted influence on books labeled *curriculum*; therefore, they are included.

Finally, it is emphasized that several excluded categories are not deemed irrelevant; they were eliminated from this listing because of the authors' lack of resources, time, and expertise. Surely, for example, non-English curriculum writings are needed for thorough perspective on curriculum issues, yet many are not translated into English. Although the volume strives to consider writing about the curriculum outside of the United States and Canada, it is conceded that these perspectives are underrepresented in this volume. Excellent contributions are available in journal articles, dissertations, and narrowly disseminated research reports, but they are not a part of this study. Consideration of non-English and journal sources is imperative to the provision of defensible curriculum perspectives in the future.

Nevertheless, serious study of books provides a quite thorough exposure to the heritage of curriculum literature. Most influential curriculum articles, reports, and papers eventually make their way into books. A question that is likely to arise for some readers is whether the authors read all of the books that are written about in the interpretive overviews. We did not, but we did read lots and lots! Some of the commentary is admittedly based on either a cursory reading of the text or a consideration of the interpretations of others. In the end, it is possible that we have not represented, underrepresented, or misrepresented an author's position. We are confident that we have been responsible in our research but are also open to correction. In compiling the bibliography, we attempted to be comprehensive and accurate. Scholars have and undoubtedly will again dispute the selection of inclusions and exclusions, even when utilizing the guidelines described above. They may also differ as to our choice of books for commentary and the nature, classification, and scope of commentary. We renew the invitation extended in the first edition to interested others to add information and interpretation. It is only through collaborative efforts that consciousness of the curriculum heritage can grow. Criticism as well as agreement can stimulate serious study, speculation, and research. To these ends this book is again offered.

INTRODUCTION

Note: Rather than substantially revise the body of the original text, we have decided to have Tom Thomas offer commentary on what Bill and Ann wrote 20 years ago in light of the changes in thinking about life and curriculum that have transpired in the past two decades. His commentary follows each paragraph or section with text printed in italics.

CURRICULUM STUDY: SETTING THE STAGE

The kinds of concerns that stir the interests and efforts of curriculum scholars and practitioners are immensely important concerns. Although differences of persuasion abound in the curriculum field, those who devote careers to curriculum share a common concern about the substance of education. They address directly the issue of what is learned and why it should be learned. To be quite literal, curricularists are concerned with the human journey that results in learning. What, they ask, are the life excursions that bring persons to certain feelings, knowings, and doings? What do learners need? Why do they need it? Through what kinds of content or activity can they acquire experiences that result in productive growth? What is productive growth and how can it be recognized?

These considerations pertain to, but are deeper and more pervasive than, concerns about curriculum guides, courses of study, course syllabi, and daily lesson plans. At best, such documents reflect shadows of ideas, knowledge, feelings, attitudes, skills, concepts, behaviors, and interrelationships that are learned and prescribed for learning. Fundamentally, these domains are the focus of curriculum study. Such study can take many forms; it can probe the limits of meaningful inquiry and action.

The use of open-ended questions as an approach to writing and engaging conversation about curriculum remains a key feature of Bill Schubert's writing and teaching. The series of questions asked in this paragraph continue to be asked and highlight the notion that good teaching is not about providing clever answers but rather posing meaningful points of inquiry.

CURRICULUM AS AN INFORMAL AREA OF INQUIRY

According to the above characterization, informal curriculum study has occurred as long as humans have sought ways to induct their young into an accumulated heritage. Adults in prehistoric tribes made decisions about what children needed to learn to become members of the social group. As civilizations evolved along major river valleys, individuals began to specialize. They no longer needed, nor were they able, to amass all of the knowledge of the social group. As adult roles began to specialize, children could no longer glean a holistic sense of the ways of their culture by following parents in daily activities. Therefore, specialists or teachers were needed to introduce the young to essentials in their heritage. Specialists were also designated to teach knowledge of specific roles in which learners would later participate. Although many of the early civilizations provided education that was mainly technical and concrete rather than abstract and formal, their efforts were quite clearly curricular. They made decisions about what the substance of learning should be. Usually, these decisions were implemented in institutions akin to schools. Cultural histories, histories of education, and biographies reflect much about the form and impact of schooling from ancient times to present.

When it is suggested that early societies were "technical and concrete," rather than engaged in abstraction, is very much like applying Piaget's developmentalism to the history of humankind. The articulation of myth by ancient societies, a generation ago considered a simplistic way of trying to explain natural phenomena, is now recognized as a remarkable, enduring, and certainly abstract and formal consideration of human nature and the cosmos. Although young people in these ancient societies were taught practical skills, so too were they were invited to learn the prayers, chants, poetry, and the central narratives of their culture. This is a significant curriculum that often continues to be passed over as "unscientific" or "primitive." A postmodern perspective on knowledge and learning challenges the ready dismissal of these contributions.

The advent of Western philosophy in ancient Greece ushers in another phase in the evolution of curriculum thought. Philosophical discourse about the substance and contribution of education emerged and subsequently appeared in great normative treatises for centuries. Writings by Plato, Aristotle, Plutarch, Quintillion, Saint Augustine, Luther, Bacon, Descartes, Locke, Rousseau, and Kant are prime exemplars. Such writings had profound impact on the curriculum promoted in schools for generations and on educational thought as well.

One can turn to another source, the idealistic and existential portrayals of human experience in poetry, plays, novels, biography, journals, diaries, stories, and the arts. These embody insight into ways humans respond to the learning substance of living, that is, to the curriculum of life itself. Think of the portrayals provided by such authors as Homer, Sophocles, Aristophanes, Dante, Goethe, Milton, Shakespeare, Donne, Blake, Pope, Dickens, Tolstoy, Dostoevski, Twain, Chekhov, Cervantes, Balzac, Faulkner, Steinbeck, Hesse, Joyce, Kafka, Ibsen, Vonnegut, Chaucer, Whitman, Dickinson, and a host of others. They have taught and continue to teach about the curriculum of learning from life's experiences. Such authors contribute as much to what Mortimer Adler calls the "Great Conversation"[1] as do philosophers, scientists, and social scientists. In all of their writings great literary figures address the sources and substances of human knowledge, feelings, and actions. Sometimes they critically portray school as systematic attempts of societies to reproduce and dispense their heritage of values, beliefs, skills, and alleged facts. In the richness of their art lies a seldom tapped reservoir of illumination about the substance of learning amid the tragedies, comedies, predicaments, and glories of human experience. Those who want to study curriculum should not pass by these portrayals of the curriculum of humankind.

In both the philosophical and the literary sources, however, curriculum is treated as an outgrowth or side effect of something larger. Curricular recommendations, for example, are offered as minor parts of elaborate philosophical systems. Curricular criticisms are offered as episodes in a character's action and feeling or as an author's personal commentary. These are useful to the study of curriculum, but alone do not legitimate curriculum as a professional area of study in its own right.

Although the authors of this book have a long-standing debt in the development of their own thinking on curriculum to the experientialist orientation established by John Dewey, this paragraph demonstrates an equally deep appreciation for the humanist origins promoted by intellectual traditionalists. The work of Robert Ulich (1954) is an enduring source of inspiration on how the humanities craft a worthwhile curriculum. In recognizing this contribution, however, the paragraph is open to the same criticism often made against intellectual traditionalists. The listing of authors, with the exception of the chaste Emily and the irreverent Kurt, is DWWM (dead, white, Western males). There are numerous other authors who can be added to this list of important writers. The writings of women (from Sappho and Hildegard of Bingen to the Brontës and George Eliot to contemporary writers such as Barbara Kingsolver, Laura Esquivel, Toni Morrison, Maya Angelou, Jamaica Kincaid, Louise Erdrich, and Alice Walker), and men from marginalized and repressed cultures (e.g., Mohandas Gandhi, Black Elk, Richard Wright, Jorge Luis Borges, Gabriel Garcia Marquez, N. Scott Momaday, Chinua Achebe, Claude McKay) should certainly be recognized.

Such legitimization began to evolve with the advent of scholars who wrote almost entirely about the subject of education, for example, Comenius, Pestalozzi, Herbart, and Froebel. Curriculum, however, remained conflated with the whole topic of education. It was a consequence of the educational ideology advanced by a given scholar. Educational scholarship evolved rather fully as a separate academic domain in the early to middle 1800s. Pestalozzi's famed demonstration center at Yverdon, begun in 1804, exemplified a zenith in the European tradition of teacher education. Even Tolstoy was influenced by Yverdon. His travels to learn about schooling in Switzerland, France, and Germany resulted in his liberal redesign of elementary schools in his Russian hometown of Yasnaya Polyana in 1861. Horace Mann, noted initiator of universal, nonsectarian, free, public education, organized the first three normal schools for the education of American teachers in 1839–40. Not only teacher education, but also the specialized study of education as a separate academic domain, spread across the United States and Europe in the second half of the nineteenth century. In 1902, John Dewey published *The Child and the Curriculum*. This book represented a synthesis of his scholarly work in establishing the Department of Pedagogy at the University of Chicago with his practical experience in developing the Laboratory School there. It also represented an initial appearance and legitimization of curriculum as an area of study. In the same decade, the study of curriculum started to form as a distinct sub-field of educational scholarship.

For these early curriculum proposals, the flow is typically from the statement of an educational ideology based on a sympathetic if not scientific understanding of the nature of learners and their place in the world and the cosmos to the proposing of curricula that invites the learners to explore their world. It is undoubtedly true that in style and in incidentals, the writing of these pioneers in educational thought is anachronistic. Their writings retain, however, a loveliness that can be of benefit to reflection on the central questions of curriculum thought: What is worth knowing, sharing, being, and becoming? Horace Mann, by contrast, does not fare as well historically. His missionary zeal ("nonsectarian" education for Mann meant that he could abide only the various versions of Protestant Christianity in the curriculum of the public school) for the Americanization of immigrant populations is a questionable agenda both in hindsight and today.

CURRICULUM AS A FORMAL AREA OF INQUIRY

No longer was all curriculum study a mere offshoot of philosophy, literature, social science, and more recently educational theory. In the beginning of the twentieth century the attention of certain educators centered directly on curriculum questions. In time, they came to be known as curriculum scholars. Shortly, too, administrators in schools began to differentiate line and staff positions as curriculum supervisors, coordinators, and consultants. Both scholars and practitioners directed their attention to the question of what should be taught in schools. Proposed and actual activities of schooling became their direct concern. This was due in no small measure to the ever-evolving emphasis on universal schooling. With increased focus on schooling, alternative curriculum viewpoints were aired and debated. The assumptive roots of alternative arguments were explored more deeply. Curricularists had, perhaps unwittingly, carved out a new version of the perennial question about the substance of education. In essence, they now wanted to know how curriculum should be developed *for schools*. Thus began the era of curriculum development as a separate sub-area of specialization within the study of education.

The growth of the public school as the expected social institution for all young people in the United States from 1870 to 1920 is remarkable. Before 1870, only two states (Massachusetts in 1852, Vermont in 1867) and the District of Columbia (1864) had enacted compulsory education laws. Between 1870 and 1918, all existing states adopted a compulsory education law. This unprecedented acceptance by policy makers gave rise to the enthusiastic consideration of possibilities by scholars and school people. What needs to be remembered, however, was that schools were not a new social invention, they were the expansion of a way of organizing and evaluating young people that had been in place for many years in some parts of the country (notably the northeastern United States). A curriculum was assumed with the identity of the institution and it was a curriculum that emphasized disciplinary knowledge (language arts, mathematics, and history initially, later including geography, science, and the fine arts). The curriculum was given legitimacy through school people such as William Torrey Harris. Harris's involvement in the development of the American common schools, beginning as superintendent of the St. Louis schools in 1867 and progressing to his tenure as United States Commissioner of Schools from 1889 until 1906, positioned him as a preeminent voice on the business of schooling. He served on the National Educational Association's Committee of Ten for the revision of the secondary school curriculum in 1893 and was chair of the Committee of Fifteen report on elementary education in 1895. It was generally conceded among contemporaries that Harris controlled the identity of the NEA as long as he was alive and that the association was largely made in his image and likeness (Leidecker, 1946, 527).

Through the influence of Amos Bronson Alcott, Harris was converted to German idealism after a brief affiliation with American transcendentalism early in his scholastic career and labored long years as the primary American disciple of Frederick Hegel. Although a writer and lecturer of wide reputation, Harris produced only one book-length manuscript. Published in 1898, late in his career, The Psychologic Foundations of Education *serves as a compendium of his thinking on education. Harris argued that schooling, through the forming of right habits and a liberal arts curriculum, should serve as an introduction to the wisdom of the ages. The "five windows of the soul," as Harris referred to the essential disciplines of culture, provide avenues of illumination for the individual to cultural heritage and provoke insight. The five disciplines were advocated as keys to intellectual development. They are (1) grammar, being the technical and scientific study of language, (2) literature and arts, (3) mathematics and physics, (4) biology, and (5) social studies, geography, and history. Here are the subjects that endow the mind with intellectual tools and knowledge—the legacy of civilization. Harris contended that learned people act virtuously and intelligently because they are one with the highest aspirations of the cultural epoch.*

Prior to the dawning of cultural enlightenment when an individual can be "self-active" in morality, the society's duty is to control the behavior of the person not only for the well-being of society but, of necessity, for the benefit of the individual. While opening the five windows, teachers were to train students in the "four cardinal duties." The aim of this disciplining of habit was to teach "self-control" by the "subjugation of the will" (Harris in McMurry, 1897, 59). The four duties to be promoted were (1) regularity, (2) punctuality, (3) silence, and (4) industry (Harris in McMurray, 1897, 60). Each virtue, in its own fashion, reminded students that they are subject to the will of a larger institution (see end-of-chapter bibliographies for parenthetical references).

Harris served as a powerful apologist for a curriculum that was already implemented in piecemeal fashion in many of the public schools. This is not to say that Harris's curriculum was in place; what is contended is that most existing schools were teaching curricula compatible with Harris's academic discipline proposal. This was a curriculum theory that was within their sphere of practice. Harris's achievement was to give academic legitimacy to the institutional status quo. All efforts to re-vision schooling ran up against an intellectual traditionalist curriculum understood to be the identity of legitimate school practice. The reports of the Committee of Ten and the Committee of Fifteen were the National Education Association's imprimatur on this institutional curriculum.

Two aspects of this emphasis are worth noting in a bit more detail. Macro- and microperspectives both have advantages and limitations in any scholarly domain. Curriculum study is no exception. Prior to the twentieth century, curriculum was treated indirectly as a rather small portion of a larger scheme that was dominantly philosophical, sociological, historical, psychological, and literary. As such, curriculum was examined in a broad contextual framework or macro perspective, rather than with the kind of microscopic detail that frequently accompanies specialized study. Macroperspectives, particularly those of a literary nature, probed into the substance of learning without necessarily relating it to schooling. Demerits of macroperspectives obviously reside in lack of detailed analysis of topics for study within a delimited field. As education became differentiated from literature, social sciences, and philosophy, certain hazy boundaries began to identify educational inquiry during the nineteenth century. Curriculum study developed a similar differentiation in the twentieth century. Thus, a microperspective appeared and persisted. Curriculum was studied in more detail relative to schooling, but less as the journey of life's education.

The debate on the value of micro and macroperspectives on curriculum continues between those who continue to work within the parameters of curriculum development, the academic craft that emerged to serve the school in the beginning of the century (Pinar and colleagues named this participation "institutional discourse" [Pinar, Reynolds, Slattery, and Taubman, 1995]) and those who sensed that the perspective was constricting and ill-suited to their interests and their passions for inquiry. To escape the microperspective, they assumed discourses that they had adopted through participation in other academic disciplines (literature and philosophy reemerged, joined by critical social inquiry) or social identities (ethnic, gender, sexual orientation, ableness). Pinar and his colleagues argue cogently that the microperspective no longer dominates scholarship in curriculum and that the macroperspectives, having established viable platforms for curriculum scholarship, will eventually reconstruct school practices. This worthwhile discussion persists.

Books identified by their authors as curriculum books were virtually non-existent prior to 1900. Exceptions did occur; to wit, Claude Fleury's *The History of Choice and Method of Studies*, perhaps the earliest curriculum book.[2] A case may also be made that Frank and Charles McMurry and other Herbartians wrote about curriculum in the late 1800s, though they usually called it *method*. This point is not argued; the evolution of the curriculum field was gradual, not abrupt. Twenty-four citations are quite evenly distributed from 1900 through 1917. These books predated the 1918 appearance of Bobbitt's *The Curriculum* and the *Cardinal Principles of Secondary Education*, two sources most frequently recognized as the Adam and Eve of curriculum works.

Harris's Psychologic Foundations *can also be considered an early work on curriculum. Another scholar who should be counted as both a direct and indirect influence on curriculum is G. Stanley Hall, whose contribution is discussed in the first chapter.*

Thus, the early twentieth century brought a gradual growth in curriculum books that portrayed the evolution of curriculum as a separate sub-field within the overarching study of education. With this evolution came the emergence of unwritten standards for becoming a legitimate member of the expanding curriculum coterie. For example, to have a curriculum scholar as one's mentor enhanced one's chances of becoming a recognized curriculum scholar or practitioner. One became known as a curriculum authority if one published books or articles with *curriculum* in the title. In 1929, the *Curriculum Journal* emerged and flourished until 1943, when it joined forces with *Educational Method*, forming *Educational Leadership*, the flagship publication of the Association for Supervision and Curriculum Development. Questions about the substance of education became increasingly specific in books and articles that focused on schooling. Emulation of methods of inquiry that fostered successes of natural sciences occurred in the social sciences and education, and concomitantly in curriculum. Detailed analyses of curriculum ideas took place. This is not intended to indicate that uniformity of language resulted. On the contrary, there were perhaps as many ways of discussing curriculum as there were scholars, a problem that has plagued the field throughout its existence. With analysis, however, came the propensity of curricularists to seek causes and to provide defensible explanations. The latter took the form of attempts to provide justifiable bases for curriculum inquiry and proposals.

At least three dominant schools of thought vied for supremacy. We shall call them the *intellectual traditionalists, social behaviorists,* and *experientialists.* Disagreement might exist about the terms, but they are convenient categories for early curriculum thought as well as for many of the variations that evolved during the first eight decades of the twentieth century. More will be said about each in Chapter One. In addition to the emphasis on scientific analysis, another feature of the microperspective should be noted. As specialization increased, and as pressures to perpetuate universal education mounted, the study of curriculum became relegated to the purposes of schooling rather than the consideration of education at large. It had been the latter under the macro-orientations of previous centuries. In the conclusion of this book I argue that the study of curriculum will not productively survive if it does not directly embrace several non-school spheres of learning that profoundly influence the growth of children and youth in pluralistic cultures: for example, homes, peer cultures, media, and work. The kind of inquiry needed is both macro and micro, an integration of specialized perspectives that focuses directly on curricular problems.

The substance of this argument is maintained. The curricular orientations suggested in the original edition have been widely adopted by other scholars and Bill Schubert employed them effectively in his curriculum text Curriculum: Perspectives, Paradigms, and Possibilities *(Schubert, 1986). Here, we amend these three perspectives with a position that Tom Thomas labeled as* conciliarist,[3] *where scholars sought to fuse two or more of the dominant orientations and the emergence of the critical reconstructionist position in the 1980s.*

Differences that occur because scholars speak from their individuality or by employing a meaningful discourse to unveil a dimension of curricular thought or practice are all to the good. Similarly, when these differences result in points of contention either within a discourse or across discourses, they can be a strong catalyst for conversation. When difference creates division or derision and there is no effort toward resolution, conversation about the curriculum is injured. Curriculum study is, by our account, more than curriculum development for schools, certainly more than content standards, more than the academic disciplines continually reconfigured, reified, or refried. But it must, in part, be a consideration of these proposals as well as much larger visions of what curriculum is or should be.

In the relatively short time that curriculum study has existed, a great deal had been written and too much has been lost or obscured in dark corners of university libraries, tattered and scattered bibliographies, and fading memories. Much that makes up the heritage of curriculum study in the twentieth century is well worth studying, both for relevance to current problems and for historical illumination. During the past 20 years perceptive curriculum scholars admonished members of the curriculum field to become increasingly conscious of their historical ancestors. Surprisingly, curriculum writers of the 1950s and 1960s seldom cited sources of works that were written between 1900 and 1940, with the exception of a dozen or so of the field's classics.[4] In 1974, Ponder[5] used the term *ahistorical* to characterize this state of the field. The sentiment was not without precedent.[6] During the 1970s the number of articles, professional papers, and portions of curriculum texts devoted to curriculum history increased. To this end the Society for the Study of Curriculum History was established in 1977 under the guidance of Laurel Tanner and other founding members. The Society meets each year prior to the Annual Meeting of the American Educational Research Association. Its members engage in the presentation and discussion of contributions to curriculum history.

This book is offered to further historical consciousness for curriculum inquiry. It is primarily an attempt to whet curricular appetites and inspire further study. Such study may corroborate or it may dispute commentary contained herein, but the major point is to augment curriculum as a scholarly enterprise grounded solidly in its history. Therefore, the book is intended as a resource for anyone who wishes to learn more about the richness of curriculum literature. Designed as a companion reference to facilitate the work of students who pursue advanced graduate degree programs in curriculum,[7] it is offered to scholars whose necessary but seemingly endless library searches could, in part, be avoided. Of utmost importance is the hope for indirect value that this book might have for children and youth, the new members of societies who must be inducted into the social life that has evolved from the dawn of humankind. As I look at W. E. Smith's moving photograph (on my office wall) of a boy and girl walking hand in hand, anxious, self-assured, excited, curious, and vulnerable into a forest, I think of curriculum. To me the forest represents the life ahead of them. Curriculum is the attempt of educators to help their journey. What do they need to know, feel, and do? Why do they need it? What do they learn about living and from what sources? What should they learn about living and from what sources? What should be provided by those specialized agencies called schools that are set aside by advanced industrial societies to teach that which children need but do not receive from everyday living?

One hundred years of effort to answer these and related questions is charted in more than 3,000 books[8] by curriculum scholars and practitioners. It is incumbent upon current and future curriculum scholars and practitioners to know the heritage of their field. It is their responsibility to build on, criticize, and renew that heritage.

A look at the interpretations of curriculum books for the 1980s and 1990s indicates that curriculum history has, fortunately, emerged as a vital discourse for curriculum study in the past two decades. The original volume was accepted as one of the first efforts to establish a historical context for the contemporary discussion of curriculum. One of the open questions is whether there will continue to be writing history about curriculum in the next decade or whether the expansion of scholarship away from specialized institutional curriculum development will result in curriculum history being subsumed into the larger categories of histories of education or social histories. Ivor Goodson has proposed an interesting method of inquiry to usefully engage in historical study of the curriculum by localizing its institutional expression. Whether histories of curriculum thought will even be possible in the twenty-first century is open to speculation.

CHAPTER ONE

Curriculum Literature and Context
1861–1909

CONTEXTUAL REMINDERS

The first decade of the twentieth century signaled the ascendance of the progressive reform movement in the United States, a social vision with a lasting impact on American politics, culture, and education. Americans were in an optimistic mood. The economy had shrugged off the depressions of the 1890s and had engaged in imperial expansion with the conquest of Hawaii and victory in the Spanish-American War. Theodore Roosevelt, who had become president upon the assassination of William McKinley, personified this optimism. Progressive reformers aspired to broaden economic opportunities by imposing tougher government regulation of the railroads, oil companies, and public utilities, and they argued for political change to diminish the power of city machines such as that of New York's Boss Tweed. Journalists and social workers labored to remedy unsafe and unsanitary working conditions in the mines, mills, and slaughterhouses and led the fight to expand suffrage to women and to preserve the nation's natural resources. In its political and social embodiments, the progressive movement targeted the special privileges doled out by the government between the Civil War and the turn of the century. In other respects, it was a movement geared toward emancipation from entrenched and traditional ways of behaving and believing.

At least three social dynamics help provide an explanatory context for events during this decade. One dynamic sought to preserve and maintain the power and prestige the United States had gained in the nineteenth century. A second hoped to gain efficiency, expansion, and then perhaps even equity, through a real or imagined "scientific" approach to life management and problem solving. The third aspired to expand freedom for the individual and the group, by rejecting traditional or sometimes prescribed ways of thinking in favor of more creative, if experimental, ways of expression, power sharing, and decision making.

The United States had achieved industrialization. A significant portion of the American population was literate and growing in political sophistication. Fortunes had been amassed by a relatively small percentage of citizens who had dominated American political, social, and economic institutions. The reform activity of the early twentieth century was as much about demands for equitable distribution of wealth and the elimination of special privilege as it was about political corruption in the boroughs of the cities and filthy working conditions in the nation's plants and factories. A group of social critics gave voice to progressive sentiments and turned a disparaging label into a badge of pride. Perhaps best known among the works of the muckrakers were Frank Norris's *The Octopus*, Ida M. Tarbell's *History of the Standard Oil Company*, and Upton Sinclair's *The Jungle*. To this reformist literature were added Jack London's *The War of the Classes*, Ray Stannard Baker's *Following the Color Line*, and Lincoln Steffens's *The Shame of the Cities*, works that drew attention to the abuse of power and the reality of racial prejudice and discrimination. The Ku Klux Klan, Jim Crow laws, and the terror of lynching maintained a system of injustices against African Americans. W. E. B. Du Bois, author of *Souls of Black Folk*, was a key participant in the Niagara Movement, precursor to the National Association for the Advancement of Colored People and a clarion call for promotion of civil rights for African Americans. The NAACP was founded in 1908 in the wake of tragic race riots in Atlanta, Georgia, and Springfield, Illinois.

The women of Hull House gained status approaching that of folk heroes, at least for certain disenfranchised, abused, and maltreated groups. Jane Addams, Ellen Starr Gates, Frances Kelley, and numerous other young women established the profession of social worker and in the process helped to redefine what constituted meaningful education for immigrant populations. Frances Willard campaigned for better working conditions for women and passage of stricter child labor laws, and she championed constitutional amendments for prohibition and suffrage. This was the decade during which Robert La Follette of Wisconsin, Joseph W. Folk of Missouri, and Hiram Johnson of California led successful attacks on the political machines that had dominated their states.

America was not unique among the emerging industrial powers. Conditions were remarkably similar in Great Britain, France, Germany, Russia, and Japan, all of which sought to bolster their industrial base by maintaining and expanding imperialist influences and, to one extent or another, adopting militarism as a tool of foreign policy. Witness, as examples, the intervention by U.S. and European forces to put down a rebellion by Chinese opposed to Western imperialist influences (referred to as the "Boxers") in 1900, the British defeat of the Dutch in the Boer War in 1902, the American acquisition of the Panama Canal Zone in 1903, the Russo-Japanese War of 1904, the Austrian annexation of Bosnia-Herzegovina in 1908, or the Japanese annexation of Korea in 1910. Europe was a hotbed of nationalist, ethnic, and religious strife. Tensions existed between Magyars, Austrians, Croats, Serbs, and a dozen other groups. Both the Russian pogroms of 1903 and 1905 and the court-martial of Alfred Dreyfus served as visible proof of the blatant anti-Semitism prevalent in Europe.

As in the United States, working men and women in Great Britain fought for higher pay and safer conditions. In Great Britain the Labour Party was founded in 1900 by Keir Hardie and in 1906 the victory of the Liberal Party made possible a major reform to improve the lot of the working class. Emmeline Pankhurst founded the Women's Social and Political Union and moved toward female suffrage. The unwillingness of Kaiser Wilhelm to address demands for political reform as well as to moderate his adventuresome foreign policies served to increasingly isolate Germany and helped to bring about the alliance system that would shortly prove so tragic. The Social Revolutionary Party was founded in Russia in 1901, the same year in which Victor L. Berger and Eugene V. Debs founded the American Socialist Party. In those nations with hereditary monarchs, public sentiment was highly critical of the corruption, waste, and abuse of the royal families. Following upon the record-breaking reign of Queen Victoria, the Edwardian Age represented the last waltz for a class of wealthy individuals who appeared romantically transfixed, unable to perceive the imminent collapse of a tradition, if not a hegemony, that stretched back almost a millennium. Royal assassinations were the order of the day and included King Carlos of Portugal, Humbert I of Italy, Emperor Ito of Japan, and a host of lesser-known figures.

The decade, however, certainly cannot be characterized by battles, annexations, trials, murders, and revolutions alone; it was a time when the arts, sciences, and other scholarly activities flourished with a special fervor. A young painter named Pablo Picasso experimented with unusual styles of painting that would bring cubism to full fruition, at least symbolizing the possibility of multiple perspectives on the world. Paintings by Derain, Rousseau, Matisse, Monet, Gauguin, and Cezanne that today grace our galleries were created during this period. It was the time of Puccini's *Tosca* and *Madame Butterfly*, and of the impressionistic compositions of Debussy. Both the triumphant impressionism and the emergent abstract experimentation depicted art's move into the human psyche, with its portrayals of complexity in feelings and unpredictable responses to life's impossible dilemmas. Such inner mysteries of human personality were given an impetus toward becoming explainable in 1900 by Sigmund Freud in *The Interpretation of Dreams*. In 1910 Auguste Rodin cast his classic bronze figure, *The Thinker*, in a pose as if he were pondering the events of the decade.

Strides in the sciences brought breakthroughs that pushed back the wall of mystery even further and increased our perhaps naive confidence in the probability of causal explanation: Marie and Pierre Curie won the Nobel Prize for Physics in 1903 for their pioneering work in radioactivity, and a year later Ivan Pavlov won the Nobel Prize for his research on the conditioned reflex. Walter Reed's discovery of transmitting agents that caused yellow fever; Jokichi Takamine's isolation of adrenaline; the discovery of secretin by Ernest Starling and William Maddock Bayliss; Paul Ehrlich's synthesis of salversan, a cure for syphilis; and Frederick Hopkins's discovery of vitamins are among the most prominent advances. The practical results of scientific investigation were accentuated in such technological inventions as Marconi's wireless; the Wright brothers's airplane; Wilhelm Einthoven's electrocardiograph; de Forest's triode electron vacuum tube; the building of the Panama Canal; color photography via the autochrome plate by the Lumiere brothers; the first operation of the Trans-Siberian Railroad; the opening of the New York subway system in 1904; Leo Baekeland's invention of Bakelite, the first plastic polymer; and the construction of the HMS *Dreadnought*.

The immediate advantage of such technological achievements may have influenced the patience exercised to develop the vast potential of such artistic scientific imaginings as Max Planck's development of quantum theory in 1900 and Albert Einstein's publication of the special theory of relativity in 1905. During this decade the human spirit's desire to probe the unknown was evidenced in the quest to reach the North Pole by Robert E. Peary in 1909. The long lost Code of Hammurabi was discovered in Iran, and Sir Arthur Evans uncovered archaeological evidence for the existence of the mythical Minoan culture at Knossos. Frontier territories within the human brain opened for exploration as Harvey Cushing studied the pituitary gland. Yet unknown potential vistas of energy sources, possibilities for both reconstruction and destruction, were released with Rutherford's publication of *Radio Activity* in 1904. In 1905 Alfred Binet developed the IQ test.

In the literary world, authors depicted the perils and ill-fated treatments of everyday strivings. The tragedies of those who strove for success were depicted in works by Samuel Butler, Anton Chekhov, Henry James, Theodore Dreiser, Maxim Gorki, Auguste Strindberg. Joseph Conrad exposed the thin veneer of twentieth-century civilization in his *Heart of Darkness*. It was a time, also, of subtle, sophisticated humor from O. Henry; pervasive scientific imagination from H. G. Wells; mystery, heroics, and the application of deduction from empirical evidence from Sir Arthur Conan Doyle; and the epitome of glorious moments in human evolution from G. B. Shaw's *Superman*. The first decade of the twentieth century brought a golden age in children's classics: Rudyard Kipling's *Just So Stories*, Beatrix Potter's *Peter Rabbit*, James Barrie's *Peter Pan*, L. Frank Baum's popular *Oz* series, and Kenneth Grahame's *The Wind and the Willows*. The long history of striving for equal rights on racial, sexual, and economic bases was nudged a bit further by the reluctant acceptance of the United States' Jack Johnson as the first African American world heavyweight boxing champion. In popular music, Scott Joplin's syncopated ragtimes were fueling the sales of sheet music and piano rolls.

CURRICULUM THOUGHT AND LITERATURE

Although it is impossible to draw direct lines of cause and effect between the activities described above and educational developments in the same decade, it is certain that the latter were influenced by many combinations of the former.[1] Science, technology, and industrialization profoundly affected education and all avenues of life. With increased urbanization came changes in home, work, recreation, and all social institutions. Pressures to provide, coupled with the "rapid is better" ethic in the factory model of production, influenced the creation of schools. Like factories, schools were sturdy, large, cubical buildings with compartments for like parts. One of the main compartmental parts was comprised of students, mined like raw material from the streets and workplaces to satisfy a strange combination of legal, economic, and humanitarian purposes. Students were grouped by age and were given age-graded textbooks. Clearly, despite the rapidity of these changes, some worthwhile substance had to exist in these books and, more importantly, had to be perceived in the experiences that students had in the schools.

It became equally clear, to some at least, that no one had a monopoly on the best knowledge of how to determine this "substance" for school learning. Surely, the problem had been dealt with before, but not on such a massive scale.

The need for full-time experts to engage in specialized decision making was a frequent occurrence in many occupations. The emergence of an area of specialization within education, an area known as curriculum development, was thus no surprise. Full-fledged curriculum developers were not yet recognized, although they were on the horizon and would quite fully present themselves in the next decade. Nevertheless, their ancestors were very much making a contribution to the field.

These curricularists forged the rudiments of distinct schools of thought, advocating distinct curricular philosophies. Each curricular orientation, of course, was reputed to have certain important benefits for the creation of learning substance for students. As noted earlier, the labels *intellectual traditionalists, experientialists,* and *social behaviorists* will be used to discuss general orientations. The labels are not sacrosanct; they are provided to ease communication and to convey a framework for discussion of curriculum as an area of study. Evolving versions of each orientation or school of thought are discussed throughout the remainder of the book.

As was suggested in the introduction, *intellectual traditionalists* have been with us the longest and were the commonly recognized institutional curriculum of schooling at the turn of the century. Their position stems from ancient Greece and Rome and the Classical tradition. They hold that certain subject areas (namely, grammar, mathematics, music, speaking, exposure to great literature, and finally [if the student is able to master the prerequisites] philosophy, that paragon of all studies) cultivate the mind, harvest virtue, and reap the full person. In the Middle Ages the emphasis was on the classical *trivium* and *quadrivium* that made up the Seven Liberal Arts. The *trivium* consisted of grammar, rhetoric, and dialectic; the *quadrivium* was composed of arithmetic, geometry, astronomy, and music (Wagner, 1983). Schools throughout the intervening centuries to 1900 catered to the economically advantaged and persisted in this tradition with a few exceptions. With the universal schooling movement in the nineteenth and twentieth centuries, more social classes were served. Reading, writing, arithmetic, a bit of history or civics, and little else were primary constituents of early curriculum for children. In later schooling, reading took the form of great literature (Latin, English classics, and sometimes Greek); writing evolved into essays and was often combined with the later stages of reading; and arithmetic evolved into algebra and geometry. These subjects were deemed basic to all living. It was assumed that they molded character, developed sharp logical thinking, and were generally applicable to any respectable domain of living.

An interestingly strange amalgam emerged in the early 1900s. It was the joining of this classical tradition with elements of a branch of psychology known as "faculty psychology." Briefly, faculty psychologists likened the mind to muscles that could be developed with practice in subjects of the classical curriculum. For example, it was held for some time that mastery of subjects such as Greek, Latin, and geometry built the faculty of reasoning or logical thinking. Similarly, particular kinds of "exercises" were thought to develop such faculties as observation, perception, imagination, and memory, though the types of faculties to be developed differed depending on who wrote about them. Nonetheless, it was clear that throughout most of the nineteenth century and much of the twentieth, the predominant "curriculum theories," especially those practiced, were built around the notion of habits to be cultivated. These came to be known as mental disciplines. Concerned, thus, with developing powers of the mind (intellectual powers) through exercises largely drawn from liberal arts that had "stood the test of time" (tradition), proponents of this view may be fairly labeled *intellectual traditionalists.*

The influence of the intellectual traditionalists was altered, however, in the early twentieth century, due to a combination of intellectual and social changes. Renowned scholars such as William James and Edward L. Thorndike, imbued with the methods of science, decided to test the assumptions of faculty psychology. James, in the 1890s, concluded that the faculty of memory did not improve with practice. Later, while James turned to philosophic pursuits, Thorndike's inquiries caused him to decide that subjects such as Latin and mathematics did not improve the mind more than did less traditional subjects. These studies had an impact on the decline of classical subjects from the curriculum.

As great an impact may be attributed to increases in education for all, not merely for the elite. With universal education came heightened interest in the practical results of schooling, results that called for curriculum that did more than make the mind a touted instrument to be used in circles that valued high culture. Socioeconomic pressures demanded results of schooling that demonstrated upward mobility relative to social class, job acquisition, and capacity to handle the practical demands of everyday living. As represented in the literature and arts of the decade, the public was no longer content with the belief that intellectual life alone sufficiently guided the complex process of living. The time was ripe for a revival of the broader perspective epitomized in the title of Herbert Spencer's (1861) book, *Education: Intellectual, Moral, and Physical.*

People looked at their everyday experience and the problems, feelings, and satisfactions derived from it, and concluded that worthwhile schooling could not ignore life as they knew it. Thus, the intellectual traditionalist position evolved to include a wider array of subject emphases. These emphases were, however, spearheaded by a commitment to a mental discipline style of thought. They were summarized in the work of the Committee of Ten and Committee of Fifteen in the late 1890s.[2] Composed primarily of college faculty members, the committees influentially promoted a subject-oriented curriculum. Though the subjects differed somewhat from their classical ancestors, the idea that certain subjects are basic to proper human growth was clearly iterated.

William Chandler Bagley (1905) and Herman Horne (1906) are exemplars of two enduring variants of intellectual traditionalism. Herman Horne was, like W. T. Harris, a disciple of Hegelian idealism. Promoting an educational philosophy he labeled "theistic idealism," Horne was not compelled to exemplify the contemporary relevance of those traditional disciplines that feed the will and the mind of human beings. For Horne, the disciplines were correct because they spoke to the essential character of human nature. W. C. Bagley's argument for the value of the traditional disciplines was based on their relevance to contemporary social needs. The "socially efficient" person was that individual, according to Bagley's evaluation, who had attained competence in the standard disciplines. Bagley's (1905) treatment of the educative process was not nominally a curriculum book, but was sufficiently comprehensive to have a major effect on curriculum and other educational thought of its day. Bagley's "essentialist" argument for the intellectual traditionalist orientation epitomized a profound and lasting difference of assumptions with proponents of the experientialist and social behaviorist proposals.

Before dismissing the proposal of intellectual traditionalists as socially conservative, one should consider the argument of W. E. B. Du Bois (1903) in a chapter from his classic work, *The Souls of Black Folk*. Engaged in debate with Booker T. Washington on the most appropriate curriculum for African Americans, Du Bois rejected Washington's contention that the practical social benefits of vocational education were to be advanced in African American schools. Du Bois called for a rigorous liberal arts curriculum that would challenge the thinking of African Americans and also identify and educate a "talented tenth" of the African American population, a professional class capable of confronting the systematic injustices of a racist society. Du Bois, a product of liberal arts education, believed that the denial of this curriculum to any group of people is an invitation to domination by the privileged.

The acceptance of a set of beliefs that stemmed from the work of Johann Friedrich Herbart would provide a common background to two other orientations. Although Herbart died in 1841, American advocates of his line of thinking (e.g., Charles and Frank McMurry, Charles De Garmo, and C. C. Van Liew) built a Herbartian conception of curriculum development at the turn of the century. Essentially, this position, taken from earlier educational theorists such as John Locke and Johann Pestalozzi, held that the mind is a *tabula rasa* to be given form and substance by experience. As experience and knowledge accumulate, they form an aperceptive mass, or stored repertoire through which the world is perceived and interpreted. Learning takes place only as outside knowledge and experience relate to the aperceptive mass. A major curricular implication of this view was that method was of utmost importance. Method was considered the necessary process of organizing the content or substance of learning in order to make it relevant to students' aperceptive masses. The study of child development was deemed invaluable to constructing methods that brought desired curricula to students. Heretofore, few educational theorists had given the study of child development a primary emphasis in their thinking about the curriculum.

It is in the "proper" understanding of the "scientific" study of children that the two orientations, social behaviorist and experientialist, emerge at the beginning of the twentieth century. The social behaviorist's approach to "scientific method" is modeled after the techniques of the natural sciences. The scientist is a dispassionate researcher discerning generalized principles through the objective, analytic interpretation of technical observation. This follows from research of natural phenomena where the researcher patiently contrives isolated studies of refined problems, subjects the study to observation of effect through a valid and reliable instrument, and then quantifies the results so that a statistical generalization can eventually be established. Statistical analysis is a most forceful tool for argument. If, then, one wishes to know how a child thinks, what material is most age-appropriate for the developing learner, or what curriculum is most relevant for the learner, application of this research model will yield an answer.

An early proponent of social behaviorism, American psychologist Granville Stanley Hall was a student of Wilhelm Wundt. Wundt established the first laboratory for the study of psychological behavior in Leipzig and used "introspection" as a method of inquiry. The portrayal by American Herbartians of child development as analogous to cultural epochs in the evolution of the human race (labeled the "recapitulation theory") became a basis for G. S. Hall's proposal. A curricular application of this notion was included in the *Third Yearbook of the National Herbart Society* in 1897. A large contingent of writers on education, contemporaries of Hall, gave currency to the cultural epochs notion and developed curriculum models appropriate to the theory. Charles and Frank McMurry, Charles De Garmo, Colonel Francis Parker, and even John Dewey for a time gave deference to the notion of cultural epochs in child development. Hall, however, offered perhaps the fullest explanation of the recapitulation process and its promise for a new educative age, one based on child study rather than philosophical assumptions. Based on what Hall claimed was grounded research in child study, a compelling theory of child development was articulated (Hall, 1905) that served as a paradigm for curriculum organization until it was challenged by behaviorist psychologists and activity analysts. Hall wrote, "In general, nearly every fact, sensation, feeling, will, and thought of the young child tend to be paleophysic just in proportion as the child is let alone or isolated from the influence of grown ups whose presence always tends to the elimination of these archaic elements....Thus, from one point of view, infancy, childhood, and youth are three bunches of keys to unlock the past history of the race" (Hall, 1965, p. 46-47).

To declare the infant an animal, the child a savage, the adolescent a primitive was not metaphor in G. S. Hall's terminology. These were descriptors of the stages of development of the young person as she/he slowly emerges into the present stage of civilized human life.

The cultural epochs model is the cornerstone to effective education and prescribes an appropriate curricular scope and sequence. Through mental measurement, Hall contended, it was possible to reveal nature's intended social pattern. Mental testing was capable of determining the stages of development and identifying those who will not rise to full civilized human development. The social order can prepare those less developed for a social role commensurate with capability. For some, this meant that compulsory universal schooling was counterproductive to their needs. Hall declares, "There are many who ought not to be educated and who would be better in mind, body, and morals if they knew no school. What shall it profit a child to gain the world of knowledge and lose his own health?" (Hall, 1965, p.116).

Hall's adamant faith in the behavioral sciences (psychology and sociology) as the foundation of meaningful scholarship in education, albeit science that was as much romance as it was authentic investigation, was precursor to a curricular orientation that contended it was possible to construct a curriculum scientifically by attending to the principles of contemporary behavioral science. Though puerile by today's standards in educational psychology, Hall reflected a desire among some educators at the turn of the century to make child study central to the process of curriculum construction.

One aspect of empirical scientific research that social behaviorists were particularly eager to emulate was the use of technological instruments to facilitate accurate scientific observation and measurement. Joseph Mayer Rice became one of the first widely recognized educational reformers when his articles, based on careful observations of contemporary school practices, were published in *The Forum*. These articles evoked widespread public response and were published as a book in 1893. Rice's faith in the power of testing to indicate educational quality was put into practice when he administered a battery of spelling tests around the nation in order to determine, through "scientific" means, which spelling programs were most efficient and effective. Although the results of Rice's endeavor proved inconclusive (Rice, 1913), the notion that good scientific instruments can provide guidance for effective educational practice became a commonplace conviction. In this vein, Alfred Binet and Theodore Simon developed the first test that claimed to determine intelligence in 1906, perhaps the single event of long-term impact that best epitomized the growing deification of science in education.

It did not take long to shift scientific focus from child study for effective instruction to the statistical study of society to determine the most efficient and relevant curriculum. A sentiment emerged from educational theorists such as Hall and Rice that curriculum for schools should be determined "scientifically." This paved the way for Franklin Bobbitt to call for the detailed observation and careful analysis of the usual activities of ordinary adult life. Youth are then inducted into society by teaching them specific tasks involved in such activities. This process of curriculum-making is frequently referred to as "activity analysis" or "scientific curriculum-making" (see Bobbitt, 1915, 1918, 1922, 1924). As an orientation to curriculum construction, this process is sometimes placed within the social efficiency movement. Because it purports to mold or engineer behavior in certain socially acceptable ways, the label of "social behaviorists" is used. Social behaviorists possessed a special appeal both for those who desired to emulate successes of natural sciences and technology and for those who desired to prepare for the necessities of life in a businesslike fashion. More is said about this group in the next chapter.

The five stages of method (preparation, presentation, comparison, generalization, and application) that the Herbartians derived from Johann Herbart's writings on method had paramount impact on interpretations of instructional strategies throughout the century. It is interesting to note that these stages were not mere prescriptions about the way that curriculum should be developed for schooling. Instead, they were primarily interpretations of stages in the process of knowledge acquisition by the aperceptive mass during ordinary life experience.[3] The assumption here is critical. Learning that occurs during ordinary life experience provides great insight into the way that learning should be developed for students in schools. Implicit in Herbart's position was that the end of learning should be ethically good.

That education must embrace the ethical is central to the third school of curriculum thought, the experientialist position. The work of John Dewey continued, elaborated, and reconstructed this humanistic dimension of the Herbartian position. Child study was to be "scientific" but in a more practical, socially invested, problem-solving manner than the perspective of social behaviorists. The question an educator needs to ask is not limited to only *how* children learn, but should also consider questions like *why, where, what,* and *with whom* they learn. Children's intellectual development is intimately related to an understanding of the interests of the learner. Similarly, the social order must be referred to in a "scientific" inquiry to determine what "lessons" are best suited to the child's cultural progress. Noteworthy at this point is Dewey's *My Pedagogic Creed*, first published in 1897. It is available in numerous curriculum anthologies and provides a good brief introduction to Dewey's early thought on education. The student who wishes to acquire a broad understanding of the curriculum field should consider the study of several of Dewey's works indispensable. More will be said about them throughout the discussions of the literature that follow. At this point it is enough to note that Dewey and those who advocated his ideas were a mainstay of experientialist curriculum thought for several decades to come.

With publication of *The Child and the Curriculum* (1902a), Dewey etched his place in curriculum archives for all time. In this book, he related both theory and practice as synthesized in the activity of the laboratory school at the University of Chicago. Dewey presented three conceptual models for determining curriculum. The first option was the discipline-centered approach Dewey labels the "Old Education." Against this model Dewey described a perspective on education he calls the "New Education," a model for education predicated on the interests of the child. Old Education matches well the orientation labeled "intellectual traditionalism" above. New Education was the Herbartian school, represented in the writing of Charles McMurry and Hall. Dewey declares himself distinct from both discipline-centered and interest-centered pedagogues. John Dewey's thinking on education evolved as he served as head of the University of Chicago Laboratory School. Influenced by Ella Flagg Young, Jane Addams, and Alice Chapman Dewey (his wife) in school practices and William James, Lester Frank Ward, and Albion Small in social thought, Dewey promoted a new understanding of education: the "experiential." This work, together with his *The School and Society* (1900),[4] laid the groundwork for several interpretations of the experientialist line of thought that reached a stage that might be called its "golden age" in the Progressive Education era of the 1920s and 1930s.

Dewey's treatment of a practical art/science of problem solving that attends to specific circumstances is portrayed in a lesser-known work, *The Educational Situation* (1902b). At the risk of oversimplification, the line of thought in these books perceives humans as biological/social organisms who possess the potential for growth by using their intelligence to adapt to and live in balance with the environment. Throughout history, humans acquire experience in this process. Such experience must then be passed on to subsequent generations. The responsibility of the schools is to provide experiences that cannot be enacted in an educational context outside of schools. Learning does not occur by didactic transmission of adult-organized reservoirs of knowledge. Although it is desirable to obtain the knowledge and skills organized in the academic disciplines, the best means to their attainment is psychological, that is, through building from the genuine interests of students. Problem resolution can frequently be best obtained by the exercise of communication or group study through which transaction of experience occurs among persons. This might more simply be called democratic living based on mutual regard. The labels "child-centered curriculum" and "education of the whole child" came to be attributed to Deweyan thought. So, too, evolved "problem solving" and "learning by doing." The latter was evident in descriptions in *The Child and the Curriculum* and *The School and Society* of children learning about past human problem-solving by reenacting activities such as tool making and spinning thread. The contributions of Dewey are far too extensive to summarize here; we will consider the development of his proposal in the next decade and his response to the experientialist tradition he founded in the 1930s.

Those who are interested in arguments against the experientialists should consult writings of William C. Bagley, Charles H. Judd, Herman Horne, and Henry C. Morrison as well as others throughout the next three decades. John Dewey remained active as teacher and discussant of the experientialist movement for 50 years and was arguably its most significant contributor to contemporary curriculum theory.[5] Dewey will assume the role of critic to new movements in curriculum. Although virtually all writers will be succeeded by other voices in their respective educational positions, Dewey is never superceded as spokesperson. Even today, he retains his posture as the single most significant voice of the experientialist perspective.

Hopefully, enough is said throughout this book to provoke curiosity and build a context for the study of curriculum literature produced during the first decade of the twentieth century. Three lines of thought have been developed: the intellectual traditionalists, the social behaviorists, and the experientialists. Descendants of each are traced in subsequent decades.

Let us now glance at the kind of books that appeared before curriculum study is usually thought to have begun. The 19 books that appeared in the 1900–09 decade illustrate that the term *curriculum* at that time was sufficiently widespread to merit inclusion in book titles. Heretofore, it had been used in conjunction with books on education, and then sparingly. Columbus Bowsher's text of 1900 is the first book found to use *curriculum* in its title. Apparently, it had small distribution and little impact. Bowsher developed curricular prescriptions from a philosophical worldview, an infrequent occurrence even today. American texts, presumably used to train teachers in normal schools and/or to influence curriculum developers and school administrators, mainly presented conceptions of what should be taught and guidelines for determining content. A book of influence at the time for school people was C. Hanford Henderson's *Education and the Large Life* (1902), a proposal which contains much the same criticism of the Old Education that Dewey was advancing in his writings. Books that appeared in Britain during this time, exemplified by Thompson (1905), treated curriculum as a matter of debate. Eight of the 19 books emphasized curriculum at the elementary or primary levels. The text by Meriwether (1907) was a historical treatment.

The curriculum books that had lasting impact, evidenced by their continued reference by scholars beyond the decade, were written by Dewey (1900, 1902), McMurry (1906), and Bagley (1905). Du Bois's volume, while not specifically curricular, must be acknowledged for its continual influence on curriculum thought and the education of marginalized peoples. Charles McMurry, a prominent neo-Herbartian at the turn of the century, placed primary emphasis on method. As seen in his title, the term "course of study" is used instead of "curriculum." This is, perhaps, a remnant of the word's etymology from Latin, meaning a "chariot course." The analogy is that of a neophyte guided by one who is experienced as they tour the land of accumulated wisdom of the human race. McMurry, therefore, outlines recommendations and discusses issues about essential human experience during the first eight grades. It is interesting to note that "course of study" was used frequently throughout much of the twentieth century as a near synonym for "curriculum," especially in informal discourse.

In concluding this discussion of the first decade, it is recalled that 1918 is often given as the birth date of the curriculum field. If this developmental metaphor were elaborated, it could be fairly argued that the first decade was an advanced embryonic stage. As noted in the introduction, the time from conception to birth was indeed extensive. It was conceived when humans first thought of teaching others and was born shortly after 1915. (This makes the gestation period of curriculum compared to that of even elephants seem analogous to that of elephants themselves compared to fruit flies.) The point is heartily emphasized that serious study of curriculum roots must probe into the thought, art, and action of the distant human past to the earliest attempts of humans to introduce their young to living.

BIBLIOGRAPHY OF CURRICULUM BOOKS 1900–1909

Significant contributions: 1860–1899

Spencer, H. (1861). *Education: Intellectual, moral, and physical.* New York: D. Appleton & Co.

National Education Association Committee of Ten on Secondary School Studies. (1893). *Report.* (Chaired by C. Eliot). Washington, DC: Government Printing Office.

Rice, J. M. (1893). *The public school system of the United States.* New York: The Century Company.

Parker, F. W. (1894). *Talks on pedagogics.* New York: E. L. Kellogg.

De Garmo, C. (1895). *Herbert and the Herbartians.* London: Heinemann.

National Education Association Committee of Fifteen Report. (1895). *Addresses and proceedings.* (Chaired by W. T. Harris). Washington, DC: The Association.

National Education Association. (1895). *Report of the committee of fifteen on elementary education.* New York: American Book Company.

Dewey, J. (1897). My pedagogic creed. *School Journal, 54* (3), 77–80.

McMurry, C. (Ed.). (1897). *Third yearbook of the National Herbart Society for the Scientific Study of Teaching.* Chicago: University of Chicago Press.

Harris, W. T. (1898). *Psychologic foundations of education.* New York: D. Appleton and Company.

James, W. (1899). *Talks to teachers on psychology; and to students on some of life's ideals.* New York: W. W. Norton.

1900

Bowsher, C. A. (1900). *The absolute curriculum*. Champaign: The University of Illinois.

Dewey, J. (1900). *The school and society*. Chicago: University of Chicago Press.

1901

Weet, H. S. (1901). *The curriculum in elementary education*. Rochester, NY: University of Rochester Press.

1902

Dewey, J. (1902a). *The child and the curriculum*. Chicago: University of Chicago Press.

Dewey, J. (1902b). *The educational situation*. Chicago: University of Chicago Press.

Henderson, C. H. (1902). *Education and the large life*. Boston: Houghton Mifflin.

1903

Du Bois, W. E. B. (1903). *The Souls of Black Folk: Essays and sketches*. Chicago: A. C. McClurg & Company.

1904

Columbia University Press. (1904). *The curriculum of the elementary school*. New York: Author. (Also reports intermittently to 1915).

1905

Bagley, W. C. (1905). *The educative process*. New York: Macmillan.

Hall, G. S. (1905). *Adolescence*. New York: Appleton.

Lodge, O. J. (1905). *School teacher and school reform: A course of four lectures on school curriculum and methods*. London: Williams and Norgate.

Payne, B. R. (1905). *Public elementary school curricula*. New York: Silver Burdett.

Thompson, H. M. (1905). *Essays in revolt; being a discussion of what should be taught at school*. London: J. M. Dent.

1906

Dodd, C. (1906). *The child and the curriculum*. London: S. Sonneschein.

Horne, H. (1906). *The philosophy of education*. New York: Macmillan.

McMurry, C. A. (1906). *Course of study in the eight grades (Vols. I and II)*. New York: Macmillan.

1907

Meriwether, C. (1907). *The colonial curriculum 1607–1776*. Washington, DC: Capital.

1908

Horace Mann School. (1908). *The curriculum of the elementary school of Horace Mann School.* New York: Teachers College, Columbia University.

1909

Hayward, F. H. (Ed.). (1909). *Primary curriculum.* London: Ralph.

CHAPTER TWO

Curriculum Literature and Context
1910–1919

The second decade of the twentieth century is best remembered for the tragedy of the First World War, a historical event that is commented on at some length in due course. This decade is also most frequently acknowledged as having given birth to the curriculum field. It was a decade of transitions and newfound realities.

In Britain, Edward VII died, succeeded by George V. The Edwardian age had itself been a period of transition between the uneasy stability of the Victorian age, when Western imperial powers dominated the Southern Hemisphere of the planet, and the uncertain possibilities offered by the new century of relativism. Two signs of change were the Union of South Africa becoming an independent dominion under Great Britain and Portugal's revolution resulting in the declaration of a republic, both in 1910.

The United States was politically uncertain about its role as an imperial power. Assertive in its own hemisphere, the U.S. government was reluctant to become embroiled in the violent chaos that was enveloping Europe. To maintain domination, U.S. Marines landed in Cuba, in Nicaragua, and then in Haiti, where they remained for 20 years. Woodrow Wilson was first elected U.S. president in 1912, the same year the Balkans erupted in war. This mounted tensions throughout Europe, marked by increased naval strength and strategic military location on the part of Germany, France, and England. It is remarkable that, given the many international crises, world war did not break out sooner.

Discovery and scientific advancement were hardly at a standstill. Bertrand Russell and Alfred North Whitehead produced the landmark study

Principia Mathematica between 1910 and 1913, continuing the previous decade's propensity to probe and explicate fundamental principles in many areas of scholarship. In the same year, Marie Curie isolated radium, an event that might be said to have unleashed a chain reaction of other events that ushered in the era of atomic power. The next year, for example, Ernest Rutherford continued his explication of atomic theory, and in the United Kingdom, in 1913, Frederick Soddy discovered isotopes. Stature was achievable through scientific discovery, and it did not always accrue via laudable measures, as evidenced by the finding of the hoax-riddled Piltdown Man's remains in 1912, the year that Alfred Wegener formulated his theory of continental drift. Roald Amundsen reached the South Pole in 1911, followed by Robert F. Scott the following year; Scott lost his life in the attempted return to England. Perhaps the most memorable tragedy in ocean travel occurred in this same year when the "unsinkable" *Titanic* rammed an iceberg and sank with 1,595 fatalities.

Developments in science and technology intensified public faith in this mode of human creation. In 1913, Hans Geiger invented his now well-known radiation detector. The Panama Canal was opened for shipping. In 1914, medical science was advanced by Edward Kendall's discovery of thyroxine. The trans-Atlantic Canadian railway was completed. In 1915, while in New York, Alexander Graham Bell asked Mr. Watson to come to him. Watson's reply from San Francisco was distinct, demonstrating the potential of transcontinental telephone communication. This same year Albert Einstein published his general theory of relativity. The next year brought the addition of electron valency to the growing atomic theory of matter and energy. Astrophysicist Karl Schwarzschild developed the black hole theory. Despite the scientific advances achieved since the turn of the century, an estimated 22 million people died from the influenza epidemic that broke out in 1918. New explanations for unconscious functioning were published by personality theorist Carl Jung, bringing marked departures from Freudian thought with a theory of archetypes in the collective unconscious.

The labor movement also gained momentum across the globe, in both local and global contexts. The Industrial Workers of the World (the IWW or "Wobblies") aspired to form working people into one great union to confront the increased centralization of industrial capitalists. At the same time, unions were formed to address the specific concerns of an industry (garment workers, mine workers). The Triangle Shirtwaist Factory fire of 1911, a sweatshop operation whose unsafe conditions trapped 146 working women and doomed them to death, brought national recognition to the desperate conditions of immigrant women. Nonetheless, the power of the police was with the factory, mill, and mine owners, and time after time union organizers such as Mother Jones and

Bill Thompson faced hostility and arrest. The remarkable success of the Bolsheviks in Russia in 1918 under V. I. Lenin posed new worries for capitalists across the globe. It gave rise to the charge that unionists were "reds" seeking the ultimate overthrow of the U.S. economic and political system. When steel workers in Gary, Indiana, sought to unionize in 1919, the result was a bloody confrontation with federal troops.

The grim head of prejudice arose again with an international profile in the field of sports. Olympian Jim Thorpe, a Native American, lost his trophies in the decathlon and pentathlon on what many considered extreme technicalities accusing him of professionalism. Questions of equality arose on other issues as well. Suffragettes demanded the right to vote in Britain in 1913, the same year that Mahatma Gandhi was arrested in India for exercising civil disobedience. D. W. Griffith's *The Birth of a Nation*, a remarkable film that vilified African Americans while portraying the Ku Klux Klan as saviors of the South, led to violent race riots in several large cities after it was shown in theaters in 1915. Violent confrontations between whites and African Americans took place throughout the summer of 1919 in Norfolk, Virginia; Washington, D.C.; and Chicago, where 31 people were killed and more than 500 injured.

The rights of women were on the public mind in both the United States and England. In 1916 Margaret Sanger was arrested for opening the first birth control clinic in Brooklyn. In 1918, a woman was elected to Parliament and the vote was secured for women over age 30 in England. This event, as well as the election of Jeannette Rankin as the first U.S. congresswoman (a Republican from Montana) evinced growing support for suffrage for all women in the United States.

Dissonance in many varieties—political, social, and cultural—was in the air. It was given artistic expression through Stravinsky's *The Firebird*, a ballet that, together with his *The Rite of Spring* in 1913, increased awareness of the value of dissonance in musical composition. The next year provided visual dissonance in painting as well, bringing even more of a view of the inner workings of the human spirit through the Russian Vassily Kandinsky's colorful compositions and Franz Marc's Blue Rider group in Munich. In 1912 Vaslav Nijinsky won fame by choreographing and then dancing in *The Afternoon of the Fawn*. Marcel Duchamp solidified the ascent of artistic expressionism in painting with his *Nude Descending a Staircase*. At the opening of John M. Synge's *Playboy of the Western World*, audience members hurled objects on stage and rioted.

Novels by Marcel Proust, D. H. Lawrence, and James Joyce continued the previous decade's probe into the human psyche with their existential portrayals of absurdities and predicaments in the human condition. Franz Kafka wrote *The Metamorphosis* in 1915. George Bernard Shaw, however, extended his praise of the "superman" in *Pygmalion* and *Androcles and the Lion*. The popularity of *Tarzan of the Apes* by Edgar Rice Burroughs in 1914 further attested to hope in the ideal of a superior natural goodness and strength in humankind with the disquieting qualification that the countenance of this strength was white. Somerset Maugham portrayed the plights and delights of human interchange in *Of Human Bondage* (1915) and *The Moon and Sixpence* (1919). Henri Matisse, Jean Renoir, and Picasso continued to provide impressionistic and expressionistic insights on canvas. At the same time, architecture embarked on a revolutionary thrust spearheaded by Frank Lloyd Wright's Imperial Hotel in Tokyo (1916) and Walter Gropius's Bauhaus School at Weimar, Germany, established in 1919, emphasizing functional design that is consonant with the construction medium.

Motion pictures were another literary medium that ascended to popularity and sophistication during this decade. The very best, exemplified by D. W. Griffith's *Intolerance* (1916) and Charlie Chaplin's *Shoulder Arms* (1918), became works of art appreciated across social class barriers. Irving Berlin's *Alexander's Ragtime Band*, a popular adaptation of African American jazz, tapped a new source of American musical sentiment. George M. Cohan was the celebrated musical entrepreneur of the decade, however, particularly when he wrote the score for U.S. involvement in World War I with "Over There."

Undeniably the most significant event of the decade was the First World War. The 1914 assassination of Austria's Archduke Franz Ferdinand unleashed other mounting tensions and armed conflict rapidly overwhelmed Europe. Although the United States remained neutral for the first three years of the conflagration, war was declared on Germany in 1917. The U.S. military initiative was supported by new financial strength derived from a 1913 constitutional amendment introducing the graduated income tax and motivated by both a zealous press and financial interests favoring British victory. In preparation for entry into the war, the first Selective Service Act in U.S. history was passed in law. A succession of Allied victories deflated German and Austrian powers, bringing the war to an end in 1918.

The years between 1910 and 1920 might be considered the most significant of this century. The problems that gave rise to the First World War and new problems that resulted from this conflict have in many ways continued to influence our lives to the present time. Some refer to the period between 1914 and 1945 as the "Second Thirty Years' War," a historical event similar to the First World War in its magnitude of far-reaching effects. With the collapse of the Hohenzollern, Hapsburg, Romanov and lesser dynasties in Europe (and we might also bear in mind that the Chang dynasty had fallen in China the previous decade), it was not clear what new form of governmental and economic systems would best serve the peoples of these new nations. Even in victorious countries, radical movements and ideologies were present; in all the nations, governments were destined to play increasingly greater roles in the lives of common people. It was indeed the end of an era best précised by Lord Gray's remark, "The lamps are going out all over Europe; we shall not see them lit again in our lifetime." The full impact of these tragic events would become apparent in the following decade. The foci of power and wealth would move away from the nations of empire across the ocean to America.

Europeans and Americans both were shocked by the carnage of trench warfare and by the wanton use of weapons of mass destruction, from dirigibles to mustard gas, which made no distinction between soldiers and noncombatants. As an example of the carnage, the Battle of the Somme alone resulted in 700,000 wounded or killed. Western civilization had not seen loss of life on this scale since the Thirty Years' War of the seventeenth century. Uncivilized warfare had supposedly been outlawed following that conflict with the publication of Hugo Grotius's *On the Law of War and Peace*. The resulting cynicism toward traditional institutions—religious, political, economic—was of course most profound in Europe, but even in America, the idealism symbolized by President Wilson quickly was transformed into an isolationist reaction symbolized by the U.S. Senate's rejection of the League of Nations.

The United States emerged from the war a transformed nation. This was the result of many factors, including the exposure of American males, many from rural areas, to European culture and atrocity; the entrance of women into the wartime work force; and the crude but highly successful home front scramble by some entrepreneurs to profit from the war. It is no coincidence that the incidence of venereal disease following the return of the doughboys from the war became epidemic and resulted in legislation by many states requiring blood tests before civil marriage licenses were issued. It is to this unsettled decade that the emergence of curriculum as a formal study is most frequently attributed.

CURRICULUM THOUGHT AND LITERATURE

The social behaviorist school of curriculum thought, taking its cue from further successes in the natural sciences, advanced to prominence under the influence of publications by Franklin Bobbitt. Not only did the tenor of the times promote a scientific and technological approach to determining what was taught in schools, it demanded observable practical consequences from public education offered in schools. A 1913 conference in Cleveland gave social behaviorists both power and promise. Under the leadership of E. L. Thorndike, C. H. Judd, and W. S. Gray, the Cleveland Conference became an annual event that promoted the scientific study of curriculum.[1]

Franklin Bobbitt assumed that the material necessary to teach in the schools was virtually identical to the tasks performed by adults in society. Therefore, he introduced "activity analysis," a procedure by which life's activities were analyzed in minute detail. Activities, particularly those most frequently needed in productive and efficient living, were carefully cataloged and translated into learning experiences for students in schools. Obviously, assumptions had to be made about the nature of efficient, successful, and productive living. This fact constituted a major seedbed of subjectivity in what was being presented as a process of objectively oriented curriculum development procedures. In *What the Schools Teach and Might Teach* (1915), Bobbitt addressed the question of "is" versus "ought," though this book is deemed less important than his *The Curriculum* (1918), a work often considered the first major modern book on curriculum. Bobbitt's 1915 book, however, illustrated a development in curriculum thought that began to bud in the second decade of the twentieth century, that is, the propensity for prescribing or forecasting that which should be, often contrasting it with that which is. Both the prescriptive and descriptive views presumed the existence of schooling on a large scale.

Gray (1911) was concerned with revisions at the secondary level. Gilbert (1913) overtly probed into reasons behind values implicit in decisions to teach selected subject matter at the elementary level. Weeks (1913) projected into the future, attempting to advocate curricula consistent with economic democracy. The pre-1900 trend of linking method with curriculum prevailed in Heckert's 1917 emphasis on explicating relationships between the organization of instructional materials and elementary school curriculum. Later, organization became a permanent curricular concern; similarly, the relationship between curriculum and instruction became a perennial debate.

The experientialist school of curriculum thought was given solid roots in John Dewey's educational magnum opus, *Democracy and Education* (1916). Though not exclusively a curriculum book, this work set curriculum issues in a political, scientific, philosophical, psychological, and educational context. Its direct and indirect impact on curriculum thought and action was monumental. By relating the ordinary-life functioning of individuals to the social quest for problem resolution, Dewey wove a democratic conception of education from which aims emerged as a continuous flow of consequences of intelligent action. Growth and direction, he argued, were achieved through a kind of situational scientific inquiry. This process of "reflective thinking" was described for educators and the general public in his text *How We Think* (1910). Dewey contended that empirical/rational/democratic deliberation, characteristic of effective logic, comes to full power when it fully engages prior knowledge, play, curiosity, meaning-construction in language, system, judgment, as well as conjecture, intellectual rigor, critical observation, control of data, and verification of results. This expansive notion of deliberation placed in consideration of issues of social significance was more comprehensive and more compelling than conventional, restricted, technical notions of scientific thinking. By arguing for a transacting mutuality of seeming opposites—for example, interest and discipline, independence and dependence, work and play, experience and reflection, labor and leisure, the intellectual and the practical, and interest and need—Dewey provided the basis for a conception of curriculum that united school with life and preparation with living.

In 1918, William Heard Kilpatrick began his ardent crusade to propagate his interpretation of Dewey's proposal, specifying its implications for method and curriculum. His "project method" became widely known among curriculum scholars and practitioners. In the brief 1918 reprint of his 18-page article, Kilpatrick promoted the idea that learning activities should be built around the hub of shared student interest, and that all subject areas could be related to and integrated into that central interest. A work by Mendel Branom produced in 1919 was a first effort to integrate the method into existing school practice. Some scholars accepted this method as a consistent extension of Deweyan thought; others heatedly disputed it. The latter may have favored the interpretive records of the Horace Mann School (1913 and 1917) as more genuine expressions of experientialist thought, since this renowned laboratory school at Columbia's Teachers College was thoroughly rooted in experience and reflection on it. Dewey's own review of settings that enacted aspects of experientialist educational theory is contained in the volume he authored with his daughter, Evelyn, *Schools of Tomorrow* (1915).

Reflecting their growing influence on policy and school practices, the ideas of women educators about curriculum were first published as books in this decade. Maria Montessori, an Italian physician, had established herself as a major figure in educational reform in Europe with a remarkable record of success in educating children who were designated as mentally incompetent. Her methods were in the developmentalist tradition of Johann Pestalozzi, Fredrich Froebel, Jean Itard, and Edouard Seguin but were adapted to her own particular theoretical structure. Montessori's stature grew when she was given the opportunity to work with the children of the poor in the San Lorenzo slums of Rome, the Casa dei Bambini. The clamor for training in facilitating the individual developmental activities of young people that characterized the Montessori approach resulted in the production of her first statement of philosophy and practices, *The Montessori Method* (1912). One of the earliest U.S. enthusiasts and promoters for the Montessori method was Helen Parkhurst. When Montessori visited the United States in 1913, Parkhurst became her translator and collaborator and assumed leadership of the movement in the United States. Montessori was heralded as an inspiration for the reform of education by Alexander Graham Bell (Bell's wife would be a cofounder of the Montessori Education Association) and Thomas A. Edison. Montessori spoke to the NEA, visited the White House, and lectured at Carnegie Hall. The popular press carried articles about this new phenomenon for child education. Montessori followed up her initial work with *The Advanced Montessori Method* (1913), applying the method to standard academic subjects and a training manual (1914). Montessori's popularity dovetailed with the increased acceptance of public funding for kindergartens. The Congress of Mothers lobbied state legislators for the extension of education before the age of six.

The Montessori reform, however, took on the characteristics of a fad. By 1918, the Montessori Education Association was dissolved, Montessori had left the United States never to return, and Montessori's methods remained an option primarily for private education. There are various reasons suggested for why the method did not endure in the United States as it did in Europe. Montessori's writing style was flowery, indirect, abstract, and repetitive, making her works an effort for all but the true believer to struggle through. Maria Montessori insisted on maintaining direct control of the propagation of the method, making it expensive to implement and limited in scope. Undoubtedly the non-U.S. origins of the proposal placed it in suspicion, particularly when there were various alternatives being promoted that were "made in America." Finally, the method was strongly criticized by W. H. Kilpatrick as contrary to the social orientation of progressive education and failing to address the social needs of young people.[2] As an alternative, the proposal of Patty Smith Hill (1915) for an experimental kindergarten included an emphasis on social interaction and was deemed more commensurate with experientialist or progressive ideals.

The name of Alice Barrows is not as well known as Maria Montessori and certainly she leaves no legacy for contemporary schooling, but in her time she was an active school reformer who believed that all students could benefit from broad vocational training. She is best known for the work that she did in implementing the platoon system in the Gary public schools, a hybrid of social efficiency engineering and progressive notions on curriculum.[3] Her opposition to defining vocational education in a narrow and specialized fashion, and her argument instead for general and conceptual instruction in various industrial activities, are demonstrated in her work *Report of the Vocational Guidance Survey* (Barrows, 1912).

Study of prevailing curriculum in schools provides ample evidence that the intellectual traditionalist line of thought was far from dormant during this decade. In the practices of the classroom teacher in determining appropriate

curriculum material, particularly on the secondary level, intellectual traditionalism influenced the minds and practices of most teachers. In curriculum thought,
William Chandler Bagley (1910) continued his effort to develop a practical
apologia for intellectual traditionalists. At the same time, it was recognized that
in the debate over how to make a curriculum, intellectual traditionalism was
perceived as the "old education" and was in need of updating. The National
Education Association assembled a committee of educators (both from higher
education and school administrators) to update their policy on a relevant curriculum for the high school.

The *Cardinal Principles of Secondary Education* (1918) heralded a new perspective on curriculum thought. Rather than fomenting controversy, the document
was an amalgam of current perspectives, reflecting an effort in curriculum
thought toward consensus, a movement that would be as important in the
development of curriculum thought as the three orientations described previously. Many of the lines of distinction drawn carefully by Dewey, Bobbitt, and
Bagley were blurred or ignored. As a political statement, this work served to
promote the cause of compromise by providing a broad conception of goals to
which it would be difficult to deny allegiance, regardless of one's school of
thought. Who, for example, would want to go on record as having opposed any
of the following: (1) health, (2) command of fundamental processes, (3) worthy
home membership, (4) vocational preparation, (5) citizenship, (6) worthy use of
leisure time, and (7) development of ethical character?

Such principles or general goals were not without precedent. They can be
traced to the National Education Association Committee of Ten pronouncements of 1893, led by Charles Eliot's indefatigable admonition for an education
that embraced both pure and applied sciences, modern languages, and mathematics, that is, practical studies having practical results. This was followed by
the report of the Committee of Fifteen that focused on elementary education.
Both were highly subject-oriented.[4] The Seven Cardinal Principles can be
traced with even greater ease to Herbert Spencer's (1861) five educational
categories that lead to full living: (1) direct self-preservation, (2) necessities of
life, (3) rearing offspring, (4) proper social and political relations, and (5)
gratification of tastes and feelings. It requires no great intellectual contortions to
see direct connections between these highly influential documents. Further, it is
quite evident that such statements are open to extraordinarily broad interpretation, thus making them quite similarly acceptable to any of three orientations to
curriculum. If, for example, the list appears to exclude traditional subjects of
study, the authors of the *Cardinal Principles* assured intellectual traditionalists
that they had no reason to be concerned. The authors indicated how each
discipline could be applied to these aims. Social studies should emphasize the

history of vocations, of family life, of civic duty. The English literature teacher can show how literature suits well the worthy use of leisure, or literature can be an instrument to build ethical character or promote wholesome family life. The authors of the report, which included educational practitioners and administrators as well as academicians, sought to integrate the multiple perspectives currently in discussion in curriculum and fashioned a document ensuring all perspectives are represented. The result is a conciliar document where all voices work toward harmony.

This effort to harmonize the three orientations, finding helpful commonalities that could be translated to educational policy and practice, established an eclectic, fluid curriculum perspective labeled here as "conciliar." The conciliarists should not be dismissed as without influence in the educational community, nor should they be regarded as writers lacking substance. Conciliarists cannot be summarily dismissed as shallow thinkers or compromisers simply for the sake of politeness or lack of understanding of the debate. Conciliarists maintained a commitment to form a plan of action in curriculum development that was consonant with other dimensions of the emerging identity of the American public schools. These writers were not seeking an educational revolution; they aspired to infuse conceptions of a quality curriculum into an existing institution's practice with consideration of instructional method, operational structure, and community expectations.

The end of the second decade of the twentieth century brought a kind of solidarity in recognizing curriculum as a viable area of study. It was, however, an area of study fraught with controversy. It was, perhaps, curricularists' overarching concern for the substance of learning in schools that contributed to the longevity that this area of study has thus far attained. Playing no small role in sustaining that longevity was the *Cardinal Principles of Secondary Education*, a document that found more than a modicum of acceptance in the worlds of both scholarship and practice, a kind of unifying power without which the separate schools of curricular thought may have splintered, atrophied, and faded away.

Bibliography of Curriculum Books 1910–1919

1910

Bagley, W. C. (1910). *Educational values*. New York: Macmillan.

Dewey, J. (1910). *How we think: A restatement of the relation of reflective thinking to the educative process*. New York: D. C. Heath.

1911

Gray, E. D. McQ. (1911). *How the curriculum of the secondary school might be reconstructed*. Albuquerque, NM: University of New Mexico Bulletin.

1912

Barrows, A. (1912). *Report of the vocational guidance survey*. New York: Public Education Association.

Montessori, M. (1912). *The Montessori method: Scientific pedagogy as applied to child education in "the children's houses" with additions and revisions by the author*. New York: F.A. Stokes Company.

Smith, T. L. (1912). *The Montessori system in theory and practice*. New York: Harper and Brothers.

1913

Dewey, J. (1913). *Interest and effort in education*. Boston: Houghton Mifflin.

Gilbert, C. B. (1913). *What children study and why: A discussion of educational values in elementary course of study*. New York: Silver Burdett.

Greenberg, D. S. (1913). *Socialist Sunday school curriculum*. New York: Socialist Sunday Schools Publishing Association.

Horace Mann School. (1913). *The curriculum of the Horace Mann elementary school*. New York: Teachers College, Columbia University.

Montessori, M. (1913). *The advanced Montessori method*. New York: F. A. Stokes Company.

Rice, J. M. (1913). *Scientific management in education*. New York: Nobel and Eldridge.

United States Bureau of Education. (1913). *Report of the committee of the national council of education on economy of time in education*. Washington, DC: United States Government Printing Office.

Weeks, A. D. (1913). *The education of tomorrow: The adaptation of school curricula to economic democracy*. New York: Sturgis & Walton.

1914

Davis, C. O. (1914). *High school courses of study*. Yonkers-on-Hudson, NY: World Book Company.

Montessori, M. (1914). *Dr. Montessori's own handbook*. New York: F. A. Stokes Company.

1915

Bobbitt, F. (1915). *What the schools teach and might teach.* Cleveland, OH: The Survey Committee of the Cleveland Foundation.

Dewey, J. (1915). *The school and society* (Revised edition). Chicago: University of Chicago Press.

Dewey, J. & Dewey, E. (1915). *Schools of tomorrow.* New York: E. P. Dutton.

Hill, P. S. (1915). *Experimental studies in kindergarten theory and practice.* New York: Bureau of Publications, Teachers College, Columbia University.

1916

Dewey, J. (1916). *Democracy and education.* New York: Macmillan.

1917

Heckert, J. W. (1917). *Organization of instruction materials, with special relation to the elementary school curriculum.* New York: Teachers College, Columbia University. (AMS Reprint Available)

Horace Mann School. (1917). *The curriculum of the Horace Mann elementary school.* New York: Teachers College, Columbia University.

1918

Bobbitt, F. (1918). *The curriculum.* Boston: Houghton Mifflin. (Reprint 1972 by Arno Press and Norwood Editions)

Commission on the Reorganization of Secondary Education. (1918). *Cardinal principles of secondary education.* Washington, DC: Government Printing Office.

Judd, C. H. (1918). *The evolution of a democratic school system.* Boston: Houghton Mifflin.

Kilpatrick, W. H. (1918). *The project method.* New York: Teachers College, Columbia University (Reprinted from the Teachers College Record, 19(4), 18).

1919

Branom, M. (1919). *The project method in education.* Boston: R. G. Badger.

Richmond, K. (1919). *The curriculum.* London: Constable & Company.

CHAPTER THREE

Curriculum Literature and Context

1920–1929

It has been called the "Roaring Twenties," "the Decade of Wonderful Nonsense," "the Jazz Age," "the Ballyhoo Years," and "The Age of Disillusionment." The Great War was over. Despite immediate food shortages after the signing of the Armistice, prosperity was established once again. This, at least, was the landscape in the United States, where the detached perspective provided by the Atlantic's vastness suggested to Americans a finality to European conflict brought by the Treaty of Versailles. A need for some sort of internationalism evolved, conceived by Woodrow Wilson as a League of Nations. Though this sentiment was shared throughout much of the world, the United States chose to isolate its interests. The United States of America, banker to the Allies and first among victors, now possessed the majority of the world's gold bullion in her vaults. Like a not quite mature adolescent given a bequest on reaching legal age, the vision of many in the United States became myopic, focused on short-range goals and self-gratification. Maturity exacted a heavy price.

Peace in Europe was followed in the United States by a short-lived depression and a series of labor actions including the Boston police strike, the UMW coal strike led by John L. Lewis, the AFL steel strike, and a rail strike. When the Boston police commissioner, after riots and looting had been put down by National Guard troops, refused to allow the striking police to return to their jobs, he was supported by Governor Calvin Coolidge, who declared, "There is no right to strike against the public safety by anybody, anywhere, anytime."

In the previous chapter we commented on reactionary responses to social-ism by Western nations following the Russian Revolution. In the United States, a Red Scare convinced the federal government to keep in effect the Espionage Act passed during the war. This act legalized arrests and deportations of those who expressed unpopular political or economic views. Another right-wing response was the renewed popularity of hate groups like the Ku Klux Klan. The governor of Oklahoma was removed from office after he tried to use his office to fight the KKK in 1923. The exclusion of Japanese from immigration to the United States strained relations between these two countries. The arrest, con-viction, and execution of anarchists Nicola Sacco and Bartolomeo Vanzetti became a national symbol of the capitalist oppression and xenophobia.

Republican victories in 1918 and 1920 were as much signs of voter dis-pleasure with Wilson and Democratic progressivism as a symbolic attempt to return to the "good old days" before the war. But times had changed and there was no turning back the clock. U.S. involvement in the war had brought about fundamental changes in American society and culture, demonstrating that even victors suffer from their accomplishments in war. Within a few years the econ-omy recovered, and under the succeeding administrations of Harding, Coolidge, and (briefly) Hoover, many Americans experienced unprecedented prosperity, a prosperity that, coupled with the disillusionment of the war, in no small meas-ure contributed to the collapse of a dominant moral tradition. When Tennessee passed a law prohibiting the teaching of evolution, young biology teacher John Scopes openly challenged its authority over science. The law symbolized the attempt of policy makers to keep modernism under control. Although Scopes lost in his trial, the acceptance of modern ideas and the prosperity that they were bringing were claiming the nation.

In 1926 Herbert Hoover declared that Americans were enjoying the highest standard of living in U.S. history. He had good reason to make this boast. Unemployment was down and goods were never more affordable. An example is the automobile. Henry Ford phased out the Model A, commonly known as the "Tin Lizzie," after producing over 15 million autos. It was a car for every-one. Its replacement, the Model T, was accepted enthusiastically. In the United States, there were over 9 million autos on the roads when Herbert Hoover accepted the presidential nomination of the Republican Party in 1928. Hoover proudly contended, "We are near the final triumph over poverty."

The 1920s was a decade of scandal, easy money, and low margins. Although farmers and many working people did not share in the prosperity, others grew wealthy by legitimate—or in the case of organized crime or scandals like Teapot Dome—illegitimate means. Hypocrisy became increasingly fashionable as Americans ignored the passing of Prohibition and frequented new business establishments called "speakeasies." The behavior of bourgeois young adults with relaxed attitudes toward sex and authority in this decade of the "flapper" evidenced that a new era of excess and consumption was emerging in the United States. Their hairstyles, fashions, music, and fascination with new dances (inspiring the bizarre phenomenon, the dance marathon contest) raised eyebrows and emptied pocketbooks. Organized crime emerged as a highly successful, albeit dangerous, enterprise supplying Americans with things illegal but desired, including alcohol, prostitutes, gambling, and drugs. Even after the repeal of Prohibition in 1933, organized crime remained an enduring dimension of American culture.

During the 1920s, "time and motion studies" sought to increase efficiency of the assembly line and mass production. Business owners began to use cost accounting techniques. Clarence Birdseye introduced the quick-freezing technique for preserving food. Urbanization arrived. According to the 1920 census, more Americans lived in cities and towns than in rural areas. School enrollments increased dramatically. Rising industrial wealth made possible the construction of new schools, purchase of equipment, and increases in teachers' salaries. Vocational and trade schools became more popular, and the curriculum included courses in industrial training, home economics, and commercial subjects. Extracurricular activities such as honor societies, student councils, and team sports also became commonplace in high schools throughout the United States.

Great Britain and France paid for their success in the war with their own "lost generation": young people lost not to material excess but to the battlefield. Their economies were in shambles and their cultures in turmoil. Their postwar treatment of Germany assured a legacy of bitter feelings and a desire for revenge. With hindsight, it is clear that the British victory came at the cost of an empire. Britain's colonial dominion gradually disintegrated with the 1922 independence of Egypt, the 1921 creation of the Irish Free State, and continued protest in India led by Mohandas Gandhi.

This was a decade for acquiring social equality in several spheres. The Nineteenth Amendment to the U.S. Constitution gave women the right to vote in 1920. Women were also awarded degrees at Oxford University in Britain. Now a familiar part of the workforce, over 8 million women working out of the home and farm (although 87% of the jobs were as teachers or secretaries). Texas elected the first female governor. Charlotte Perkins Gilman, representing the "new woman," led a powerful feminist movement. The International Court of Justice was established at The Hague in the Netherlands. After 500 years, Joan of Arc was transformed from witch to canonized saint; in 1923 George Bernard Shaw helped immortalize this new interpretation with *Saint Joan*. British women were accorded the vote at age 21 in 1928.

Internationally, however, political equality and social freedoms were disappearing. In the year 1922, as Mussolini marched on Rome and took over the Italian government, Josef Stalin became Secretary-General of the Communist Party in Russia. The nation's status became the Union of Soviet Socialist Republics in the following year, the world's first major Communist national power. Vladimir I. Lenin, the leading figure in the Bolshevik revolutions of 1905 and 1917, warned before his death in 1924 that Stalin could not be trusted. Revolutionary leader Leon Trotsky was expelled from Russia by Stalin and took refuge in Mexico, later to be defended by John Dewey, among others. In 1927, Stalin gained full political control of the USSR.

For many nations it was a decade of turmoil. Consider Mexico and China. Mexico remained in political upheaval with a succession of violent political overthrows and assassinations. Sun Yat-sen, president of China, died in 1925, an event that was followed by confusion and civil war, eventually leading to the ascension of Chiang Kai-shek in the south, with the support of Western powers, and Chang Tso-Lin in the north. The communist party in China held its first meetings in the 1920s and quickly came to be a factor in the national turmoil. By the end of the decade, the Japanese were also expanding their military onto China's mainland.

When the Kellogg-Briand Pact was signed by dignitaries from 65 nations in 1928, it was a day of great optimism. The nations agreed to principles for peaceful settlement of international disputes and the prohibition of war. The entire proceedings were placed on sound motion pictures, perhaps the only lasting legacy of this failed political agreement.

During the 1920s the arts continued their turn inward to souls fraught with confusion by the perceived absurdities of life, bureaucracy, and human suffering. Sinclair Lewis produced *Main Street* in 1920, followed by *Babbitt* in 1922. D. H. Lawrence's *Women in Love* was published in 1921. John Galsworthy continued the *Forsythe Saga*. Though hope of a realized dream permeated F. Scott Fitzgerald's *The Great Gatsby*, it was a hope of false illusion anchored in a naiveté from a past that existed only in the over-idealistic imagination. That innocence seemed exorcised by the existential "realities" that mocked the acquisition of dreams built on dignity, honor, and enlightenment, as portrayed in James Joyce's *Ulysses*, Eugene O'Neill's *The Emperor Jones*, T. S. Eliot's *The Wasteland*, e. e. cummings's *Enormous Room*, Thomas Mann's *The Magic Mountain*, Theodore Dreiser's *An American Tragedy*, and culminating in Franz Kafka's *The Trial* in 1925.

It was a time when literature simultaneously conveyed that luck could overpower despair and inner sensitivity could be dulled to submission by the eroding wheels of human power and the blights of unexpected tragedy in Shaw's *Back to*

Methuselah, André Gide's *The Counterfeiters*, Upton Sinclair's *Oil!* and *Boston*, Willa Cather's *Death Comes to the Archbishop*, Virginia Woolf's *To a Lighthouse*, Sinclair Lewis's *Elmer Gantry*, Aldous Huxley's *Point Counter Point*, and Erich Maria Remarque's *All Quiet on the Western Front*. The sparse, direct writing of Ernest Hemingway and the rich psychological portraits of William Faulkner contributed to introspection on the human drama. *The Gypsy Ballads* announced the talent of the Spanish author Frederico Garcia Lorca in 1928. The Harlem Renaissance, a flowering of literary and artistic production by African Americans, was enriched by the contributions of Countee Cullen and Claude McKay.

Expressionism continued to dominate contemporary painting. Picasso executed a variety of works, including the famed *Three Musicians*. Klee, Miro, and Chagall explored new dimensions of abstraction and entry into surrealism, offering contrast with the stark realism of Grant Wood. George Grosz's "dadaism" established what he termed the "new machine art." The varied musical compositions of Prokofiev and Copland, Weill's *Threepenny Opera*, Coward's *Bitter Sweet* operetta, and Gershwin's *Rhapsody in Blue* portrayed dream-seeking amid dissonance in this era.

Americans were treated to daily news reports, popular dramas, mysteries, action-suspense, jazz, and classical and popular music sung by "crooners" with the appearance of commercial radio. In 1920 the first commercial radio station, KDKA, began broadcasting. By the end of the decade over 600 stations were in operation and one in every three homes had a radio. Will Rogers, the Oklahoma humorist who had made a big splash in Ziegfeld's Follies on Broadway, became one of the first stars of radio. The broadcasting of popular music was a boon to the livelihood of jazz musicians. Although Paul Whiteman was the standard-bearer for white audiences, it was the inventions of King Oliver and his young trumpeter, Louis Armstrong, as well as the first offerings of Washington, D.C.'s "Duke" Ellington that were establishing a new musical language.

Motion pictures had become a commonplace form of entertainment internationally and had also matured as an international art form. Sergei Eisenstein's *Potemkin* and Robert Weine's *Cabinet of Dr. Caligari* remain outstanding contributions to the cinema. Charles Chaplin's *The Kid* and *The Gold Rush* were his most popular feature-length productions. The comedy of Buster Keaton and Stan Laurel and Oliver Hardy may have lacked some of the complexity of Chaplin, but they were inventive and insightful in their own right.

The expansion of use of technology took a leading role over the invention of new technology or scientific endeavor in this decade. The extension of the quantum theory of Max Planck by Neils Bohr of Denmark and Einstein's work on a unified field theory were publicly recognized but seldom comprehended. On the other hand, everyone was excited to see science applied. Whether it was

H. O. D. Segrave's jaunt across Daytona at 203 miles per hour in his Sunbeam speedster for a new land speed record or Charles Lindbergh's cross-Atlantic flight, people were anxious to hear of the new limits set by machinery.

And there was time to play. Baseball became a national pastime and the New York Yankees with Babe Ruth and Lou Gehrig became immortal in baseball legend. Bobby Jones, an amateur golfer and attorney, attracted national attention to his sport. Knute Rockne gave college students and their wealthy onlookers at Notre Dame something to do on Saturday afternoons, despite the protest of the American Association of University Professors that football was a cultural and academic abomination.

The unpredictability of dire human predicaments depicted in the existential literature of this decade was corroborated by major natural disasters and in the rapid economic decline at the end of this era. High winds in Florida and flooding in the Mississippi would be remembered as tragic natural disasters, but when over 300,000 persons died and half a million were injured in the 1924 earthquake in Japan, there was no comparison to the immensity of this catastrophe. When the Deutsche mark became worthless and the German economy fell in 1927, the racist and repressive speeches of Adolf Hitler found a wider audience. This unemployed Austrian painter had been arrested in 1923 for his participation in a coup attempt against the German government. While in prison, he had penned his disturbing anti-Semitic manifesto, *Mein Kampf*. The next year Brazil's economy collapsed. Economic crisis plagued the globe with the U.S. stock market crash of 1929, three years after John Maynard Keynes wrote *The End of Laissez-Faire*. A decade that had ascended to new vistas in prosperity and excess had spiraled into depression and despair.

CURRICULUM THOUGHT AND LITERATURE

The air of prosperity in the early 1920s was also present in the curriculum domain. One hundred twenty-seven books appeared in this decade, compared with a total of 48 in the two previous decades combined. Curriculum began to emerge as an area of study with an increasingly distinct and productive identity. In 1920, Frederick Bonser characterized curriculum as experiences that students are expected to have in school, and detailed the sequential order of such experiences (1920, p. 1). This characterization set the stage for years of subsequent writing and activity by other curriculum scholars. Curriculum scholars studied the experiences that students were expected to have in schools. Moreover, the primary interpretation that dominated the literature was prescriptive rather than descriptive. Curriculum scholars advocated, even proselytized, for that which they thought schools should provide—that is, the nature and order of learning experiences—much more frequently than they attempted to describe what the schools actually did provide. The portrayal of practice was not entirely absent, however, from early curriculum writing, as evidenced by Dewey's description of the University of Chicago Laboratory School and the three book-length reports by the Horace Mann School during the first two decades of the century. Added to these in 1920 was *Studies in Education*, prepared by the Francis W. Parker School faculty in Chicago. It might be expected that these particular writings would be largely descriptive; description, however, constituted only a portion of the works. Even these books were prescriptive in the sense that they emerged from an interactive process of actually running a school. This was particularly the case for schools that engaged in aspects of progressive education. The experientialist school of curriculum thought, although not as prominent as social behaviorism in its impact on scholarship in the 1920s, was clearly moving into what might be called its "golden age." The 1920 book by the faculty of the Francis Parker School is a good example of child-centered experientialism, emphasizing attention to individual students, tailoring curricula to their needs and interests.

The trend to make recommendations for curriculum for particular institutional levels (elementary, junior high, or secondary) was continued and expanded in the 1920s. In previous decades some books were geared to the secondary schools and others to the elementary schools. In the 1920s the junior high school was considered as a separate area of concern in books by Koos (1920, second edition, 1927b), Glass (1924), Hines (1924), the American Association of School Administrators (1927), the National Education Association Department of Superintendence (1927a), the National Education Association (1928a), and Cox (1929). A book by Gray (1929) appeared on the junior college curriculum, a new institutional approach to accommodate the growing market demand for post-high-school education. There was a clear institutional focus to many curriculum texts, addressing curriculum to the various levels of schooling established in the previous generation.

Several books emphasized curriculum applicable to the kindergarten and early primary school years: the International Kindergarten Union (1922), Burke and associates (1923), Salisbury (1924), Keelor (1925), Carmichael (1927), and Skinner and Chappell (1929). Books on the secondary curriculum continued to flourish; representatives include Stout (1921), Clement (1923), Cox (1925), Counts (1926), Morrison (1926), Davis (1927), Koos (1927a), Uhl (1927), Monroe and Herriott (1928), and the National Education Association (1929). The collection of books on the elementary school curriculum was also augmented by Bonser (1920), Meriam (1920), Wells (1921), Phillips (1923), National Education Association (1924), and the faculty of the Lincoln School of Teacher College (Columbia University, 1927), among others.

Two other thrusts in the curriculum literature of the twenties are worth special note: the study of school practices and attempts to provide guidance to practitioners. In contrast to the notion that earlier curriculum writers lived in ivory towers, unaware of the curriculum practices of their time, a number of books suggest the contrary. Examples include *A Look at Themselves* by the Francis Parker faculty through a treatment of their mechanisms of adaptation (1920); Stout's (1921) survey of curriculum development in the North Central states; Bobbitt's (1922) Los Angeles study; Collings's (1923) experiment with project-oriented curricula; Glass's study of intermediate and junior-high curriculum practice (1924); Keelor's (1925) study of curriculum in the second grade; a California curriculum study by Bagley and Kyte (1926); Bobbitt's (1926) investigations, previously noted; the Lincoln School staff's elaborate self-study (Columbia University, 1927); a review of practical curriculum applications by the Sisters of the Order of Saint Dominic (1929); and of great importance, the excellent survey of innovative curricula presented in Part I of the *Twenty-sixth Yearbook* of the National Society for the Study of Education (1927a).

The second thrust, that of writing to practitioners in ways that speak to their needs, presented a special problem. Perceived needs had to be addressed. Practitioners did not have time to pore over detailed intellectual treatises. They needed to make curricula and implement them with the students who sat in the classrooms. Recipients of the technology of mass schooling, these students sat there "right now." One response to this need was to simplify and distill. Lists of what came to be known as "principles" for curriculum development appeared in the twenties and flourished in later decades. This approach, a "recipifying" of curriculum knowledge, has roots in the following: Clement (1923), Bobbitt (1924), Herriott (1926), Monroe (1925), Craig (1927), Harap (1928), Acheson (1929), and Wisehart (1929). Among these, special note should be given to Henry Harap, a skilled conciliarist, acknowledged by L. Thomas Hopkins as one who made great strides to explicate curriculum for practitioners. Hopkins considered this an important, and certainly not a pejorative, development in curriculum literature. Hopkins wrote, "All books written up to 1928 were too long on theory and too short on its application in practice. Harap made the first real attempt to bridge this gap. He combined theory and practice into a series of steps to be followed by the curriculum maker in relating educational aims to the construction of units of instruction."[1] Surely problems can arise due to the brevity and standardization of such recipe-like orientations. The implications can indeed be deleterious. Nevertheless, books like those authored by Harap met the increased practitioner demand for how-to formulae. The value of such works to practitioners should not be overlooked.

Although curriculum studies grew at least partially out of the Herbartian emphasis on method, curricularists often maintained a rather sharp (albeit artificial) line of demarcation between the domains of curriculum theory and curriculum practice. Phillips (1923), however, symbolized a reunion of curriculum and method that appears frequently throughout the subsequent literature and is simultaneously no small cause for the perennial debate about the relationship between curriculum and instruction.

Henry Cope, editor of the journal *Religious Education*, established a theist approach to democratic life in his work *Education for Democracy* (1920). Advancing the union of liberal Protestantism with the ideals of communal living in love and service, the aspiration of democracy, Henry Cope proposed that the way democracy could most effectively be taught in the public schools was through the "pathway of directed experience." Two actions teach democracy to young people: (1) Ideal enterprises, collective undertakings to pursue some social good, and (2) democratic self-control, the willingness to allow young people the power to control group activities. Agnes Burke and her colleagues (1923) also addressed the time-honored concerns about student behavior and the role of schools in moral development. A monograph written by Carmichael (1927) was a product of the University of Iowa's Character Education project headed by Edwin Starbuck.

When consumerism was at high tide, a few years before the stock market crash, Henry Harap (1924 and again in 1927) became known for his emphasis on consumer education through curriculum materials development. A number of books, exemplified by Bower (1925), Betts (1924), and Acheson (1929), focused on the topic of curriculum in religious education. Flanders (1925) and Hamilton (1927) substantiated the fact that any kind of advocacy, including curriculum books, invariably involves legal issues. Similarly, it is patent that whenever generally stated ideas are offered to practitioners in books, they must be tailored to fit situations. Thus, in this first decade that witnessed a flourishing of curriculum books, problems in application were noted (e.g., Sharp, 1925 and Briggs, 1926), and the need to adjust to unique needs was perceived (e.g., Cox, 1925).

The *1926 Yearbook of the National Education Association Department of Superintendence* emphasized public roles in the development of public school curriculum. Stratemeyer and Bruner (1926) provided a book-length realization of the fact that if objectives are made, and if curriculum is created and implemented based on those objectives, then the courses of study need to be evaluated. Though slow to start, this means-ends technology of accountability remains pervasive in schooling, especially in calls for curriculum alignment today. It comes as no surprise that special emphasis on curriculum study would result in a plethora of curriculum materials. Knox (1927) was convinced that practitioners needed to be aware of such materials and of the various activities that they facilitate, as evidenced in his sizable compendium on that topic.

Throughout the 1920s one-room schoolhouses were in decline. Nonetheless, they remained the lived experience of schooling for many rural communities for another generation. The new emphasis on curriculum presented the special problem of determining how thoroughly curriculum was developed and implemented in each of the thousands of little red or white schoolhouses that dotted the American countryside. Holloway (1928) addressed this issue and advocated the need for inclusion of supervision within the curriculum arena, or at least as a very close relative. The idea of supervision was developed further in a group of essays edited by William Burton (1929).

Although the intellectual traditionalists continued to dominate practical school activity, experientialists and social behaviorists grew in number and influence through consulting to school districts and as instructors in colleges of education. The social behaviorist treatments of specific curricular objectives continued to be produced, sometimes as book-length concerns. In some ways, this trend stemmed from the goal statements by such groups as the Committee of Ten and the Commission on Reorganization of Secondary Education, noted in previous chapters. They were given a new twist in the work of David S. Snedden (1921) who advocated placing students in what he called "case groups" based on their particular biographical data, thus differentiating curricula appropriate to student background and ability. Educators recommended the rigorous sorting of students, labeling them by the use of sociological data, thus solidifying conceptions of their potential and limiting their future lines of endeavor in occupational and educational domains. Bobbitt continued his methods of activity analysis, this time by application, described in *Curriculum Making in Los Angeles* (1922). W. W. Charters set his name in curriculum fame with *Curriculum Construction* (1923), setting forth perhaps the most defensible theoretical framework in early social behaviorist writing. Charters contended that the starting point for curriculum construction should be analysis of the ideals of a skill or knowledge base, not characteristics of existing activities. In 1924, Bobbitt produced a more practice-oriented text, *How to Make a Curriculum*, focusing on prescription of the means for actualizing the orientations advocated in the 1918 work. Bobbitt further elaborated on actual applications of his social efficiency approach to curriculum making by school personnel in *Curriculum Investigations* (Bobbitt, 1926). David Snedden (1927a) provided a thorough interpretation of the sociological underpinnings of curriculum making. By the end of the decade,

Snedden's (1921) emphasis on objectives was amplified with Cox and Peters (1929) to produce a major statement that gave increased perspective to the role of the objective in education generally, and curriculum in particular. The above developments may give evidence of early stitches in what is now referred to as the "patchwork" curriculum.

New areas of curriculum inquiry emerged, areas that may have appeared to be mere trends in the 1920s, but actually accumulated to bolster the curriculum domain. Hartman (1923) treated curriculum in the context of home and community life, moving a bit beyond the frequent propensity to focus on curriculum within schools as segmented from the rest of student life. Charles A. McMurry (1923) emphasized the organization of learning experiences as a major element of curricular concern. The scientific reverence for facts gave impetus to an early fact-finding mission on curriculum by the National Education Association (1923).

The life of the child became an imperative concern of the experientialist educator as evidenced by Meriam (1920) and the Rugg and Shumaker classic of 1928, *The Child-Centered School*. Harold Rugg and Ann Shumaker provided incentives as well as background to many a scholar and practitioner who possessed even an inkling of the progressive inclination. Continuing the experientialist line of thinking, with his own unique style, L. Thomas Hopkins attempted to fuse a Deweyan interpretation of curriculum with the requests for principles and procedures in his 1929 publication of *Curriculum Principles and Practices*. Particular note should be given to his table of contents, which was organized according to major and supporting questions that pervaded curriculum concerns of that era. It is interesting, moreover, to consider the relevance of those concerns to the kinds of questions being asked by today's curricularists.

An elaborate rendition of method was produced by Kilpatrick (1925). In this work he laid the foundations of much of the progressive thought and action to be realized in the years that followed. In the late 1920s the activity curriculum became a full-blown feature of the progressive school. The first large-scale description of its curricular features was provided by Ferriere in 1928. One can see the emergence of the project method, heralded by Kilpatrick (1918), in the work of Wells (1921) and Collings (1923 and 1926). McMurry's (1923) emphasis on organizing the curriculum evolved from his sturdy Herbartian roots. Salisbury's (1924) and Ferriere's (1928) treatments of the activity curriculum represent a topic long associated with Deweyan thought and the experientialist traditions. George S. Counts, later to be nationally acknowledged for his promotion of political activism as an integral dimension of progressive education, should be mentioned here for his early work on the high school curriculum (1926).

For progressive educators, child study was a purposeful activity. By learning about the lives of young learners, the curriculum could be responsive to their development. Agnes Burke and her collaborators (1923) prescribed a conduct curriculum that addressed the interests and needs of children in kindergarten. Carolyn Pratt (1924) edited a volume that described experimental curricula for elementary school students. Works also appeared in translation by a little-known Swiss child psychologist. While Jean Piaget's theories on the development of language (1926), reasoning and judgment (1928), and cognition (1929) did not impact curriculum thought for over a decade, his ideas first became available to English-speaking scholars in the 1920s. A poor surrogate for Piaget's child development theories, the fascination with the pseudo-science of social recapitulation was kept in academic currency, evidenced by Joseph Lee's (1921) advocacy for playful activities in the curriculum that relate to the cultural ages of humankind. The importance of adolescence, stressed for some time by educational psychologists, also appeared in the curriculum literature of this decade (e.g., the National Education Association, 1928a and 1928b; Owen, 1929).

As mentioned earlier, the 1920s saw the formidable emergence of progressive education in both literature and school practice. Thus, a dominant brand of experientialist thought, as characterized here, flourished in a variety of shapes and sizes. One can read literature produced directly out of the practical experience in schools, such as that produced by the faculties of Francis Parker School in Chicago, and Lincoln and Horace Mann Schools at the Teachers College at Columbia University in New York (Craig, 1927; Columbia University, 1927). Helen Parkhurst's design for contract learning to address the needs of the individual child was an evolution of her earlier work as a devotee of Montessori. Parkhurst's model was called the "Dalton Plan" after the Massachusetts town where the concept was first implemented. Parkhurst (1922) contended that children needed to learn responsibility in an environment of freedom. Fixed allotments of time were eliminated in favor of learning centers and monthly contracts that teachers negotiated with students. Students earned grades by demonstrating both quantity and quality in their work. Although represented as an expression of progressive education, the Dalton Plan implemented few changes in the subject-centered and textbook-driven character of schooling.

Establishing new directions in education for women was the work of Willystine Goodsell. A graduate of and professor at Columbia University (John Dewey was chairperson of her dissertation committee), Goodsell (1923) argued against the popular perception and the scholarly opinion of E. L. Thorndike and G. S. Hall that the intellectual abilities of women were substantively inferior to the capacities of men. The most insidious aspect of this theory was the proposal that excessive scholarship would result in a woman's infertility. She contended that women should be provided with an education of quality and equity.

It is somewhat ironic that as the stockpile of literature authored by both experientialists and social behaviorists grew, [and as descriptors such as *modern* (Phillips, 1923), *keeping pace* (National Education Association Research Division, 1925), and *evolving* (Davis, 1927) invoked an air of rapid innovation] most schools reflected an intellectual traditionalist character—an orientation intelligently articulated by William Bagley (1925) and Bertrand Russell (1926). It seems clear, however, that many schools felt pressured to provide the appearance of the projects and activities of progressivism or the scientific analysis of social efficiency. This is not to say that schools ignored social behaviorist or experientialist proposals. Progressive education, in particular, had a large number of followers. Though not large by comparison with those who perpetuated the intellectual traditionalist position, it was large enough to persuade scholars that they were influencing practice.

Perhaps the best treatment of the diverse orientations toward curriculum thought was presented by Boyd H. Bode in *Modern Educational Theories* (1927). The first half of this work is devoted to an analysis of the assumptions that undergird the numerous orientations to curriculum thought. Although Bode's categorization of the schools of thought that pertain to curriculum differs somewhat from the one used in this book, it remains a sound and well-defended construct for understanding curriculum theory in the 1920s.

Alfred North Whitehead's *The Aims of Education and Other Essays*, first published in 1929, remains a classic in education literature. Though Whitehead did not intend this work specifically for curriculum scholars, it is often cited in curriculum literature. Many of the ideas advanced are of an experientialist flavor, for example, an emphasis on the interdependence of knowledge, a belief that education is the art of using knowledge, a disdain for inert ideas, and a concern for interest and development implicit in his idea of rhythms of education. It would be a mistake, however, to classify Whitehead as a devotee of experientialism. His emphasis on the "religious" character of education and the encouragement of exploring the profound in education places Whitehead in a unique orientation. Whitehead belongs to that significant group of curriculum theorists who are not aligned with any of the dominant curriculum orientations and are not advancing a synthesis of these orientations. These writers ponder deeply the philosophical, social, and psychological issues that consideration of the curriculum can evoke. Their contribution is a refreshing and provocative alternative to the three curricular orientations (intellectual traditionalist, social behaviorist, and experientialist) as well as to the conciliarists, who aspired to harmonize and make these perspectives relevant to school practice.

At least temporarily, the conclusion seemed to be reached in the late 1920s that the influence of curriculum theory could be augmented if a consensus were achieved among scholars. Thus, under the leadership of Harold Rugg (1927), a leading experientialist, Part II of the *Twenty-sixth Yearbook* of the National Society for the Study of Education was created to make visible a composite statement by curriculum scholars from differing persuasions. The book began with the posing of 18 questions deemed central to the foundations of curriculum making. These were followed by a 17-page composite statement signed by William C. Bagley, Franklin Bobbitt, Frederick Bonser, W. W. Charters, George S. Counts, Stuart Courtis, Herman Horn, Charles Judd, Frederick J. Kelly, William H. Kilpatrick, Harold O. Rugg, and George A. Works.

In his 1975 critical appraisal of the *Twenty-sixth Yearbook*, Decker Walker referred to it as "a unique record of the thinking and of the hopes and fears of the founders of the curriculum field."[2] It represented the product of two and a half years of deliberation by these founding scholars of the curriculum field. Their general statement is followed by particular opinions of the scholars individually. The *Twenty-sixth Yearbook* thus exemplifies tendencies toward each of the three schools of curriculum thought set forth in this book: the experientialists, the social behaviorists, and the intellectual traditionalists. Moreover, the perennial nature of the questions discussed by these founding scholars of curriculum is attested to by a personal note. We have found that if we present excerpts from the composite statement to curriculum students, they are almost invariably surprised that the publication date is 1927 rather than today. Readers should not infer from the above that we believe that this early statement is beyond reproach. The desire to achieve a semblance of consensus is always accompanied by certain portions of diluted ideas that are more productive when taken separately. Walker's criticism (also note 1) of the composite statement is recommended to allay the propensity to deify this contribution to curriculum thought. Nevertheless, it is an important statement, a necessary one for understanding curriculum development just prior to the 1930s. Perhaps of even greater importance than the statement's content is the precedent that its creation sets forth for interdependent efforts by major curriculum scholars to work together, a precedent seldom utilized in the years that followed, certainly not with similar magnitude of effort.

BIBLIOGRAPHY OF CURRICULUM BOOKS 1920–1929

1920

Bonser, F. G. (1920). *The elementary school curriculum.* New York: Macmillan. (Also 1921, 1922, 1923, 1927, and a 1978 reprint by Telegraph).

Cope, H. (1920). *Education for democracy.* New York: Macmillan.

Francis W. Parker School (Faculty). (1920). *Studies in education: The individual and the curriculum: Experiments in adaptation.* Chicago: Author.

Koos, L. V. (1920). *The junior high school.* New York: Harcourt, Brace and Howe, Inc.

McMurry, C. (1920). *Teaching by projects: A basis for purposeful study.* New York: Macmillan.

Meriam, J. L. (1920). *Child life and the curriculum.* Yonkers-on-the-Hudson, New York: World Book.

Parker, S. C. (1920). *Methods of teaching in high schools* (Revised edition). New York: Ginn.

Stockton, J. L. (1920). *Project work in education.* Boston: Houghton Mifflin.

1921

Bode, B. H. (1921). *Fundamentals of education.* New York: Macmillan.

Lee, J. (1921). *Play in education.* New York: Macmillan.

Snedden, D. S. (1921). *Sociological determination of objectives in education.* Philadelphia: Lippincott.

Stout, J. E. (1921). *The development of high school curricula in the North Central states from 1860–1918 (Monograph Number 15).* Chicago: University of Chicago Press.

Wells, M. E. (1921). *A project curriculum, dealing with the project as means of organizing the curriculum of the elementary school.* Philadelphia: Lippincott.

1922

Bobbitt, F. (1922). *Curriculum making in Los Angeles.* Chicago: University of Chicago Press.

Bonser, F. G. (1922). *The elementary school curriculum.* New York: Macmillan.

International Kindergarten Union. (1922). Bureau of Education Committee. *A kindergarten-first-grade curriculum.* Washington, DC: Government Printing Office.

Parkhurst, H. (1922). *Education in the Dalton Plan.* New York: E. P. Dutton.

Strayer, G. D., & Norsworthy, N. (1922). *How to teach.* New York: Macmillan.

1923

Burke, A., Conrad, E. U., Dagliesh, A., Hughes, E. V., Rankin, M. E., Thorn, A. G., & Garrison, C. G. (1923). *A conduct curriculum for kindergarten and first grade.* New York: Charles Scribner's Sons.

Charters, W. W. (1923). *Curriculum construction.* New York: The Macmillan Company. (Also 1924, 1925, 1929, 1938; and 1971 by Arno Press, New York).

Clement, J. A. (1923). *Curriculum making in secondary schools.* New York: Henry Holt & Company. (Also 1924, 1927).

Collings, E. (1923). *An experiment with a project curriculum.* New York: Macmillan.

Goodsell, W. (1923). *The education of women: Its social background and its problems.* New York: Macmillan.

Hartman, C. (1923). *Home and community life, curriculum studies for the elementary schools.* New York: E. P. Dutton.

McMurry, C. A. (1923). *How to organize the curriculum.* New York: The Macmillan Company.

National Education Association. (1923 November). *Facts on the public school curriculum.* Research Bulletin.

Phillips, C. A. (1923). *Modern methods and the elementary curriculum.* New York: Century. (Also 1931).

1924

Betts, G. H. (1924). *The curriculum of religious education.* New York: Abingdon.

Bobbitt, F. (1924). *How to make a curriculum.* Boston: Houghton Mifflin. (Also Norwood Editions).

Collings, E. (1924). *An experiment with a project curriculum.* New York: Macmillan.

Glass, J. M. (1924). *Curriculum practice in the junior high school and grades five and six.* Chicago: University of Chicago Department of Education Supplementary Educational Monographs, Number 25.

Harap, H. (1924). *Education of the consumer: A study in curriculum material.* New York: Macmillan.

Hines, H. C. (1924). *Junior high school curricula.* New York: Macmillan.

Kilpatrick, W. H. (1924). *Sourcebook in the philosophy of education.* New York: Macmillan.

National Education Association. (1924). *The elementary school curriculum: Department of Superintendence second yearbook.* Washington, DC: American Association of School Administrators.

Pratt, C. (Ed.). (1924). *Experimental practice in the city and country school.* New York: E. P. Dutton and Company.

Salisbury, E. (1924). *An activity curriculum for the kindergarten and primary grades.* San Francisco: Harr Wagner Publishing Company.

Smith E. E. (1924). *The heart of the curriculum.* New York: Doubleday, Page, & Company.

Spain, C. L. (1924). *The platoon school.* New York: Macmillan.

Stormzand, M. J. (1924). *Progressive methods of teaching.* Boston, MA: Houghton Mifflin.

1925

Bagley, W. C. (1925). *Determinism in education*. Baltimore: Warwick and York.

Bower, W. C. (1925). *The curriculum of religious education*. New York: Charles Scribner's Sons.

Collings, E. (1925). *An experiment with a project curriculum*. New York: Macmillan.

Cox, P. W. L. (1925). *Curriculum adjustment in the elementary school*. Philadelphia: J. B. Lippincott.

Flanders, J. K. (1925). *Legislative control of the elementary curriculum*. Contributions to Education Number 195. New York: Bureau of Publications, Teachers College, Columbia University.

Herriott, M. E. (1925). *How to make a course in arithmetic*. Urbana: University of Illinois.

Keelor, K. L. (1925). *Curriculum studies in the second grade*. New York: Teachers College, Columbia University.

Kilpatrick, W. H. (1925). *The foundations of method*. New York: Macmillan.

Monroe, W. S. (1925). *Making a course of study*. Urbana: University of Illinois.

National Education Association. (1925). *Research in constructing the elementary school curriculum: Department of Superintendence third yearbook*. American Association of School Administrators. Washington, DC: Author.

National Education Association, Research Division. (1925 September and November). *Keeping pace with the advancing curriculum*. Research Bulletin, 3.

Sharp, L. A. (1925). *Problems in curriculum construction*. Boulder, CO: University Extension Division.

1926

Bagley, W. C., & Kyte, G. C. (1926). *The California curriculum study*. Berkeley: University of California Printing Office.

Bobbitt, F. (1926). *Curriculum investigations*. Chicago: University of Chicago Press. (Also 1927).

Briggs, T. H. (1926). *Curriculum problems*. New York: Macmillan.

Collings, E. (1926). *An experiment with a project curriculum*. New York: Macmillan.

Counts, G. S. (1926). *The senior high school curriculum*. Chicago: University of Chicago Press.

Herriott, M. E. (1926). *How to make a course in reading*. Urbana: University of Illinois.

Herriott, M. E. (1926). *How to make a course in social studies*. Urbana: University of Illinois.

Hosic, J. F., & Chase, F. E. (1926). *Brief guide to the project method*. Yonkers-on-Hudson, NY: World Book.

Kilpatrick, W. H. (1926a). *Education for a changing civilization*. New York: Macmillan.

Koos, L. V. (Ed.). (1926). *Part II, Extracurricular activities—25th Yearbook*. Bloomington: National Society for the Study of Secondary Education.

Morrison, H. C. (1926). *The practice of teaching in the secondary school*. Chicago: University of Chicago Press.

National Education Association. (1926). *The nation at work on the public school curriculum*: Department of Superintendence Fourth Yearbook. Washington, DC: Author.

Piaget, J. (1926). *The language and thought of the child*. London: Kegan Paul, Trench, Trubner.

Pratt, C., & Stanton, J. (1926). *Before books*. New York: Adelphi.

Russell, B. (1926). *Education and the good life*. New York: Boni and Liveright.

Stratemeyer, F. B., & Bruner, H. B. (1926). *Rating elementary courses of study*. New York: Teachers College, Columbia University.

Yearbooks of the Department of Superintendence. (1926). *The nation at work on the public school curriculum—Fourth yearbook*. Washington, DC: National Education Association.

1927

American Association of School Administrators. (1927). *The junior high school curriculum*. Washington, DC: The Department of Superintendence of the National Education Association of the United States.

Bode, B. H. (1927). *Modern educational theories*. New York: Macmillan.

Carmichael, A. M. (1927). Moral situations of six-year old children as a basis for curriculum construction. Studies in Education: University of Iowa, 4(6).

Columbia University, Teachers College, Lincoln school. (1927). *Curriculum making in an elementary school*, by the staff of the elementary division of the Lincoln School of Teachers College. Boston: Ginn.

Craig, G. S. (1927). *Certain techniques used in developing a course of study in science for the Horace Mann elementary school*. New York: Teachers College, Columbia University.

Davis, C. O. (1927). *Our evolving high school curriculum*. New York: World Book.

Denver Public Schools. (1927). *The Denver program of curriculum revision*. Denver, CO: Board of Education.

Douglas, A. A. (1927). *A secondary education*. Boston: Houghton Mifflin.

Freeland, G. E., Adams, R. M., & Hall, K. H. (1927). *Teaching in the intermediate grades: A study of curricula and methods of teaching in grades four, five and six*. Boston: Houghton-Mifflin.

Hamilton, O. T. (1927). *The courts and the curriculum. Contributions to Education Number 250*. New York: Bureau of Publications, Teachers College, Columbia University (AMS Reprint Available).

Harap, H. (1927). *Economic life and the curriculum*. New York: Macmillan.

Knox, R. B. (1927). *A guide to materials and equipment for elementary schools*. School Activities and Equipment. Boston: Houghton Mifflin.

Koos, L. V. (1927a). *The American secondary school*. Boston: Ginn and Company (Reprinted by Norwood).

Koos, L. V. (1927b). *The junior high school*. (Second edition). Boston: Ginn and Company.

National Education Association. (1927a). *The junior high school curriculum: Department of Superintendence Fifth Yearbook*. Washington, DC: Author.

National Education Association, Research Division. (1927b). *Creating a curriculum for adolescent youth*. Research Bulletin Number 5.

National Society for the Study of Education. (1927a). *Curriculum making: Past and present. Twenty-sixth Yearbook, Part I (Harold O. Rugg, Chairman)*. Bloomington, IL: Public School Publishing Company. (Also published in 1969 by Arno Press, New York).

National Society for the Study of Education. (1927b). *The foundation of curriculum making. Twenty-sixth Yearbook, Part II (Harold O. Rugg, Chairman)*. Bloomington, IL: Public School Publishing Company. (Also published in 1969 by Arno Press, New York.)

Smith, M. (1927). Education and the integration of behavior. Contributions to Education, No. 261. New York: Teachers College, Columbia University.

Snedden, D. S. (1927a). *Foundations of curricula: Sociological analysis*. New York: Columbia Teachers College, Columbia University.

Snedden, D. S. (1927b). *What's wrong with American education?* Philadelphia: J. B. Lippincott.

Uhl, W. L. (1927). *Secondary school curricula*. New York: Macmillan.

Yearbooks of the Department of Superintendence. (1927). *The junior high curriculum — Fifth yearbook*. Washington, DC: National Education Association.

1928

Cocking, W. D. (1928). *Administrative procedures in curriculum making for public schools*. New York: Teachers College, Columbia University. (Also published in 1972 by AMS Press, New York).

Ferriere, A. (1928). *The activity school*. New York: The John Day Company.

Harap, H. (1928). *The techniques of curriculum making*. New York: Macmillan.

Holloway, W. J. (1928). *Participation in curriculum planning as a means of supervision in rural schools*. New York: Teachers College, Columbia University.

Lewis, M. H. (1928). *An adventure with children*. New York: Macmillan.

Monroe, W. S., & Herriott, M. E. (1928). *Reconstruction of the secondary school curriculum: Its meaning and trends. Bureau of Educational Research, Number 41*. Urbana: University of Illinois.

National Education Association. (1928a). *The development of the high school curriculum: Department of Superintendence Sixth Yearbook*. Washington, DC: Author.

National Education Association, Research Division. (1928b). *Creating a curriculum for adolescent youth*. Research Bulletin Number 6, January.

Naumburg, M. (1928). *The child and the curriculum: Dialogues in modern education*. New York: Harcourt, Brace, & Co.

Piaget, J. (1928). *Judgment and reasoning in the child*. New York: Humanities Press (1962 reprint).

Rugg, E. *Curriculum studies in the social sciences and citizenship*. (1928) Greeley, CO: Colorado State Teachers College.

Rugg, H. O., & Shumaker, A. (1928). *The child-centered school*. Yonkers, New York: World Book.

Williams, L. A. (1928). *The making of high-school curricula*. New York: Ginn.

Yearbooks of the Department of Superintendence. (1928). *Development of the high school curriculum — Sixth yearbook*. Washington, DC: National Education Association.

1929

Acheson, E. L. (1929). *Construction of junior church school curricula*. New York: Teachers College, Columbia University.

Bower, W. C. (1929). *Character through creative experience*. Chicago: University of Chicago.

Burton, W. H. (Ed.). (1929). *The supervision of elementary subjects*. New York: Appleton.

Cox, P. W. L. (1929). *The junior high school and its curriculum*. New York: Charles Scribner's Sons.

Cox, P. W. L., Peters, C. C., & Snedden, D. (1929). *Objectives of education*. New York: Teachers College, Columbia University.

Dewey, J. (1929). *The sources of a science of education*. New York: H. Liveright.

Gray, W. S. (Ed.). (1929). *Junior college curriculum*. Chicago: University of Chicago Press.

Hopkins, L. T. (1929). *Curriculum principles and practices*. New York: Benjamin H. Sanborn & Company.

Indiana Department of Public Instruction. (1929). *Guiding principles of elementary curriculum revision for the state of Indiana*. Indianapolis, IN: Department of Public Instruction.

National Education Association, Research Division. (1929). *Vitalizing the high school curriculum*. Research Bulletin Number 7, September.

Owen, R. A. D. (1929). *Principles of adolescent education*. New York: Ronald Press.

Palmer, A. H. (1929). *Progressive practices in directing learning*. New York: Macmillan.

Piaget, J. (1929). *The child's conception of the world*. Totowa, NJ: Littlefield, Adams, and Co.; New York: Humanities. (1960 reprint)

Sisters of the Order of Saint Dominic. (1929). *Curricular studies: Practical application of the principles of Catholic education*. New York: Macmillan.

Skinner, M. E., & Chappell, E. P. (Eds.). (1929). *A curriculum study for teachers of beginners: A manual for use in standard training courses*. Nashville, TN: Cokesbury Press.

Whitehead, A. N. (1929). *The aims of education and other essays*. New York: Macmillan.

Wisehart, R. P. (1929). *Guiding principles of elementary curriculum revision for the state of Indiana: Bulletin Number 107*. Indianapolis, IN: Department of Public Instruction.

CHAPTER FOUR

Curriculum Literature And Context

1930–1939

In contrast to the 1920s, the 1930s began in caution, despair, and neediness. Bank failures deprived many Americans of their life savings; millions lost their jobs and homes and became destitute searching for shelter and food. President Herbert Hoover reflected the pessimism of the time when he remarked at the end of his term, "We are at the end of our rope." By the time of the presidential inauguration of Franklin D. Roosevelt in 1932, industrial production was at 50% of what it had been before the Depression. With wages reduced by more than half for those who could find work, about 12 million people were unemployed. Farmers burned their harvests to keep warm. Veterans marched on Washington demanding their "War Bonuses" be paid in advance and living in makeshift tents. Hoover's response was to send in federal troops to rout the veterans, contending that they had been infected by communists and socialists.

Lives changed for many. More Americans stayed home; borrowed more books from the libraries; repaired clothing, appliances, and automobiles to make them last longer; and took up hobbies, card games, and new board games like *Monopoly*. The radio became as integral to daily life as television is for our own generation. As many Americans turned with glib evasion from the mounting turmoil that brewed in Europe and Asia, some measure of hope, confidence, and prosperity began to emerge by the end of the decade, attributed largely to President Franklin Roosevelt's New Deal policies of direct government intervention.

Yip Harburg's 1932 song, "Brother, Can You Spare a Dime?" characterized the times. Protest marches by the unemployed amassed thousands in most U.S. cities, eventually leading to legislation that spawned the House Un-

American Activities Committee. In such a context it was not difficult to perceive injustice as pervasive. A best-seller implying that President Harding's death was caused by poisoning at the hands of his wife; the exposé of horrendous prison abuses via the 1931 film *I Am a Fugitive from a Chain Gang*; the decade-long imprisonment of the nine "Scottsboro Boys," nine young African Americans falsely accused of raping two white women; and the conviction of Bruno Hauptmann for the kidnapping of Charles Lindbergh's son, all reflect social tensions of the times. Countless other expressions of frustrations of "having not" involved diverse avenues of society, for example, anti-prohibitionists, labor unions, tar paper shack dwellers, veterans, communists, miners, and students—many of whose protests were met with violence. The news media of 1933 carried stories about homeless children wandering the New York streets in numbers upwards of 70,000.

Roosevelt led Democrats back to leadership of the federal government at the height of the Great Depression in 1933. The desire to conquer the Depression and its haunting accoutrements at the expense of other important social issues can be understood, if not condoned, in the face of the economic dilemma. To combat continued unemployment, Roosevelt promised a "New Deal." He authored the short-lived National Recovery Act (declared unconstitutional by the U.S. Supreme Court), and established the Tennessee Valley Authority, the Civilian Conservation Corps, and the Public Works Administration to combat unemployment, aid farmers, and remedy the Depression. Roosevelt's agenda was decried by some on both the right and the left as an insufficient response. The Communist Party remained an active critic of Roosevelt's program, contending that only the nationalization of essential industries could effect a change in the economy. From a different perspective, a Roman Catholic priest in Royal Oak, Michigan, gained a national radio audience with his reactionary attacks against Roosevelt. Later in the decade, Fr. Charles Coughlin would rail against Jews and communists. Senator Huey Long became, for a brief time, the "dictator" of Louisiana, promoting a populist program that was designed to selectively abolish large corporate control of industries in his state. Long was assassinated at the height of his political power.

Economic and political crisis was not particular to the United States. Europe continued to be mired in economic depression and new and dangerous political leaders gained support. Benito Mussolini, regarded by many sophisticated people as more buffoon than threat, provoked concern with his expansion of Italy's military and the repression of dissenters. When, on the pretext of incursions by the Ethiopian military into the Italian colony of Somaliland, Italy invaded Ethiopia and unseated Haile Selassie as emperor, it became evident that there was no cause for laughter. Meanwhile, the increased political stature of the National Socialist or Nazi Party in Germany posed an even greater threat. The Nazi Party became the largest party in Germany. By mid-decade Adolf Hitler had become chancellor of Germany and was, after the death of President von Hindenburg, granted dictatorial powers. Within days of assuming control, actions were taken against all those who were perceived as enemies of the party, with deliberate action taken against the Jewish people. Albert Einstein and others seeking political and intellectual freedom took up residence in the United States. In 1936, Hitler and Mussolini announced the Berlin-Rome Axis, consolidating the fascist identity. In Asia, Japan capitalized on the political chaos in China. The Japanese military moved quickly into Manchuria and established a base of operations on the Asian continent. When the League of Nations condemned this action, Japan withdrew its membership.

In contrast to the expansion of the military by Germany, Italy, and Japan, Great Britain, France, and the United States were focused on economic recovery, hopeful that negotiations could forestall international aggression. Josef Stalin was also preoccupied domestically, consolidating his power base through a series of brutal pogroms of the opposition. A major naval disarmament treaty was signed by France, the United States, Japan, and Great Britain; the United States and the Soviet Union established diplomatic relations and joined in world disarmament talks in Geneva. Agreements were made between Italy and France, between Germany and England, between Russia and Germany.

It was increasingly clear that the sun was setting on the British Empire. By 1931, after abandoning the gold standard, Great Britain recognized dominions of the Empire as sovereign states. The continued nonviolent protests of the Indian people, organized by Mohandas Gandhi, signaled the failure of colonial rule. Germany's refusal to adhere to disarmament clauses of the Treaty of Versailles was denounced but no action was taken. In the midst of this turmoil, Edward VIII abdicated the English throne to marry Mrs. Wallis Simpson, concluding an issue that had raised no small measure of constitutional crisis in Great Britain.

Military turmoil and uprising also impacted the lives of people in Brazil, Peru, Colombia, and Bolivia. The Balkan countries of central and eastern Europe braced themselves for the brewing conflict that seemed all too imminent. Civil war in various forms beleaguered Spain throughout the decade. The battle lines became well defined, however, when defenders of the Spanish republic were confronted with a fascist coalition under the direction of Francisco Franco. Germany and Italy overtly assisted Franco's reactionary forces in the civil war, using this conflict as a training ground for the next theater of war. The horrors of that war, and of wars in general, were preserved by Picasso in *Guernica*, his depiction of the German bombing of the Basque people.

Other developments in the arts and sciences in the decade reflect dimensions of the social crisis. In 1932 Erskine Caldwell portrayed dilemmas of the times in the controversial *Tobacco Road*, while Aldous Huxley projected future perils in *Brave New World*. Although the mounting strife in central Europe quelled artistic endeavor in some respects, artistic acuity often stems from the depths of tragic perception. In 1935, T. S. Eliot created *Murder in the Cathedral* in Britain, and John Steinbeck published *Tortilla Flat* in America. A different sense of life came from Harlem with the powerful poetic testimony of Langston Hughes. That film could portray a literary masterpiece was demonstrated in 1935 by Clarence Brown's *Anna Karenina*, in which "haves" and "have nots" were vividly juxtaposed. Frank Capra, initially successful in the vein of madcap comedy, shifted to populist political themes in the late 1930s (*Meet John Doe, Mr. Smith Goes to Washington*). King Vidor's *Our Daily Bread* offered a powerful and explicit message on humaneness and economics. Margaret Mitchell's *Gone with the Wind* (1936) warned of the tragedy that war can bring to all. Sinclair Lewis, an author recognized for his strong social commentary, became the first American to win the Nobel Prize in literature in 1930. A Sinclair Lewis title had captured a pervasive public hope among peoples who seemed beyond the vibrations of escalating war: *It Can't Happen Here*. In America, many people wanted to believe that the secrets to success had unfolded before them, evidenced by the demand for Dale Carnegie's best-seller, *How to Win Friends and Influence People* (1936). Hemingway, immersed in the Spanish Civil War, portrayed the state of affairs that war accentuates with his 1937 title, *To Have and Have Not*. If this were not vivid enough, French philosopher-novelist Jean-Paul Sartre captured the feeling of absurdity implicit in war and suffering with *Nausea* (1937). Folklorist Zora Neale Hurston captured the culture and drama of African Americans living in the South in *Their Eyes Were Watching God* (1937). Steinbeck continued to portray the plight of accumulated circumstance among the less fortunate in *Of Mice and Men* (1937) and *The Grapes of Wrath* (1939).

There were also personal dramas. Though not nominally existentialist, Thornton Wilder accented absurdities and compassion in small towns everywhere in the flow of routine and facade, striving and provincialism, passivity and dream, and the seemingly invincible wall of death in *Our Town* in 1938. The next year James Joyce concretized the existential predicament in his modern literary classic, *Finnegan's Wake*. The arts were not all unrelinquished despair in the thirties. There was certainly room for escape in literature, on the stage, and at the movies. Young persons of every age experienced delight and empathetic trepidation as they viewed Disney's *Snow White and the Seven Dwarfs*. Somerset Maugham published *Cakes and Ale*, and playwrights George Bernard Shaw and Noel Coward produced *The Apple Cart* and *Private Lives*, respectively. A year later

Pearl Buck published *The Good Earth*. The music of Cole Porter remained delightfully playful, personal, and at times, sensual. Music continued to vary during the latter half of the decade; Gershwin's *Porgy and Bess*, Rachmaninov's *Rhapsodies*, Copland's *Billy the Kid*, Richard Strauss's *Daphne*, and Bartok's experimental dissonance symbolized this diversity. The variety of artistic styles might well be symbolized in the musical compositions of Stravinsky, just as the desire for calmness, stability, and contentment was epitomized in Hilton's *Lost Horizon*, that is, of a Shangri-la in the glimmering hope of everyone. There was, however, an underlying political sensibility in what could appear on the surface as the most uncontroversial content. Was *The Adventures of Robin Hood*, starring Errol Flynn, mere swashbuckling entertainment or was it a reminder of the need for vigilance against legal tyranny? Was the advent of the horror film, whether the sophisticated production of *M* by Fritz Lang or the more popular films *Dracula, Frankenstein*, and *King Kong* appealing to audiences only because of their novel camera work and special effects or did the public view social metaphors in these cinematic monsters? Was *The Wizard of Oz* spectacle or a reflection of the aspirations of the next generation? Children were given hope in the victory of goodness; Peter was victorious against the wolf in the story of Prokofiev's composition. Was Chaplin solely hoping to entertain when he presented the audience with the Little Tramp's many dilemmas in *Modern Times*? Why was the music of Benny Goodman considered a defilement of Aryan youth in Nazi Germany? Is it perhaps because all art is, inevitably, political?

Artistic expression in the 1930s often demanded the attention of the observer, a call to alertness. This was the intent of the Dutch painter Piet Mondrian, with his mathematically derived compositions that he labeled "abstraction-creation." Those who were even mildly interested in art during the early thirties will recall being awestruck by the Empire State Building, a monument to engineering and to artdeco. Equally compelling were the detailed renderings of nature by Georgia O'Keefe. The appearance of such stark realism as Grant Wood's *American Gothic* and Edward Hopper's *Route 6* were juxtaposed to the abstractions of Picasso, Matisse, Kandinsky, and Klee. The "workers' art" produced under New Deal Civil Works Administration remains on the walls of schools, post offices, and other public buildings throughout the United States. The murals of Diego Rivera creatively expressed the class struggle. Sculpture took a new turn with Henry Moore and his topological use of space within pieces often displayed in natural settings.

This far-off and detached perspective of the imagination was, in a sense, corroborated in the world of science through the discovery of yet another planet, Pluto, by Clyde W. Tombaugh in 1930. Looking inward at the micro "solar systems" of the atom, John Cockcroft and Ernest Walton smashed atoms apart, developing an electrostatic accelerator, while Ernest Lawrence invented the cyclotron to enable further insight in high energy physics. Two years later, discoveries of the neutron by James Chadwick, the positron by Carl Anderson, and the element deuterium by Urey added to the repertoire of understanding about the constitution of matter and energy. Otto Hahn and Strassmann bombarded atoms of uranium, successfully splitting the atoms and producing 200 million volts of energy. They provided evidence that they had effected fission. The ramifications of this experimentation were not lost to the military minded.

In readily observable technology, humans plunged into new vistas of distance, height, speed, and depth. In 1930 Amy Johnson flew solo from London to Australia. In 1931 August Piccard entered the stratosphere by balloon. In 1933 Wiley Post made the first solo flight that circumscribed the globe, and in 1934 William Beebe descended 900 meters below the sea's surface in his bathysphere. The fuel that propels humans themselves was understood a good bit more as well, with the identification of Vitamin A by Paul Karrer in 1931 and the synthesis of Vitamin C by Tadeus Reichstein in 1934, both of Switzerland, and the isolation of the elusive Vitamin E crystals from wheat germ in 1935.

In science and technology in the late thirties, Robert Watson-Watt developed radar, Britain began public television service, Frank Whittle advanced jet engine research, and Howard Aiken began work on digital computers. DDT was developed by Paul Muller. Of widespread note in everyday life was Georg Biro's introduction of ballpoint pens.

The interests of ordinary citizens were seen clearly in increased demands for desired equalities. Whether internationally or in the United States, human rights were won only through hard struggles. Violent reprisals to worker strikes, assisted by government agents, continued through the decade, whether at the Peabody Coal Company in Harlan County, Kentucky, or Republic Steel in Chicago. In 1935 the Wagner Act was passed to ensure the right of U.S. workers to collective bargaining. In the same year John L. Lewis orchestrated the merger of eight labor unions in a unit called the Committee for Industrial Organization as a part of the American Federation of Labor. In 1938 the Committee for Industrial Organization changed its name to the Congress of Industrial Organizations and became a rival of the AFL. In his presidential acceptance speech in 1937, Franklin D. Roosevelt warned of a kind of "government" that might evolve as a result of increased corporate power.

In the struggle for civil rights, two events have symbolic importance. In 1936, American black athlete Jesse Owens riled Hitler at the Olympics in Berlin by winning four gold medals from the highly publicized Nazi athletes there. In 1939, when black contralto Marian Anderson was barred from appearing in Constitution Hall by the Daughters of the American Revolution, she was, instead, welcomed by Eleanor Roosevelt and 75,000 citizens at the Lincoln Memorial.

Under Hitler's direction in 1938 and 1939, German forces converged on Austria, Czechoslovakia, and Poland. Italy conquered Albania. In 1939 Britain and France declared war on Germany. Likewise the Soviet Union, seeking its share of Poland, invaded that nation from the east and then entered Finland. The world was plunging into a starless night.

The thirties, a decade that began in economic strife and political uncertainties, resisted the efforts of legislation, hope, and hard work. By 1939, Europe was in war, Japan was expanding across China, the Philippines, and the Pacific, and in the United States, the unemployed still numbered 10 million. With only a spark of hope kindled, the United States and other non-European nations were understandably fearful and resistant to the impending flow of war that was to engulf all major nations of the planet.

CURRICULUM THOUGHT AND LITERATURE

The substantial contributions in the 1920s to curriculum thought were not easy acts to follow. The social behaviorist line of thought was staked out by Bobbitt, Charters, Snedden, Finney, and others. Dewey, Kilpatrick, Counts, Rugg, Shumaker, and others defined the experientialist school. Intellectual traditionalists were cogently defended by Bagley, Morrison, Horne, and Russell. What is more, curriculum thought of the 1920s was capped with a monumental attempt by curriculum scholars from many persuasions to produce a unified statement, that is, Part II of the *Twenty-sixth Yearbook* of the National Society for the Study of Education. It is interesting to note that the central concern of the authors of that yearbook was curriculum development for schooling in contrast with that of other educative forces. This symbolized the contention that curriculum studies largely emerged to support and augment schooling.

It should also be reemphasized that curriculum thought of the twenties, and subsequently of the thirties, was markedly influenced by three publications that were not overtly curricular but nonetheless had important curricular implications. The first was a 1918 reprint of an article by W. H. Kilpatrick, from Teachers College Record, entitled "The Project Method." It had practical value for certain lines of experientialist thinking evidenced by titles bearing the term "project" in the twenties. The next two publications appeared in 1925 and 1926: H. C. Morrison's *The Practice of Teaching in the Secondary School*, a practical rationale for the curriculum structured on academic disciplines, and Kilpatrick's

Foundations of Method.[1] The influence of these works is fully alive in the curriculum books of the thirties.

The thirties provide a body of literature that joined instructional methods with curriculum theory, creating the process known as "curriculum development." Some titles in 1930 began to utilize the term "program" in lieu of "curriculum," for example, Caswell (1930) and Harrington (1930). More books dealt with curriculum in reference to particular states or cities. The emphasis on both program and increased specification bypassed unresolved questions about assumptions that were illustrated by Hopkins (1929) and the *Twenty-sixth Yearbook* (1927). More emphasis was placed on the procedural, as epitomized by Harap (1928). Other examples include: Broady, Platt, and Bell (1931), Lide (1933), North Carolina (1934), Woody (1934), Draper (1936), Stigler (1936), and Shearer (1937).

Treatments of assumptions behind procedures were, however, not absent from the literature. McCall (1930) reviewed conceptual bases in curriculum literature from 1900 to 1930. F. G. Bonser (1932) described curriculum that fostered education based on a conception of life needs. Milligan (1937) probed the relation of professed philosophy to curricular content and proposed learning activities. Patty (1938) took an extended look at the mechanics of educational advocacy in theory and practice, a study that posed particular implications for curriculum even though it treated the topic of mechanism in relation to education generally.

Integration took on another quite different meaning as well in curriculum thought of the thirties. A propensity to decompartmentalize curriculum thinking and to view heretofore separate categories as interrelated wholes evolved in the literature in a variety of ways. The notion of integration stemmed from the work of Dewey and other experientialist educators. One interpretation emphasized statements about the need to relate one subject to another. It is interesting to note that Dewey's insistence on unifying intellectual divisions and his expressed desire to integrate school life with nonschool experience was often interpreted as an admonition to join academic subjects together. This tendency is illustrated by Tuttle (1935), the National Council of the Teachers of English (1936), Connole (1937), Oberholtzer (1937), and Weeks (1938).

Jones (1939) advocated the notion of correlation as a means to integration, while promoting unit construction as a mechanism for actualizing the process. The thematic unit, very familiar today, is a conciliar adaptation of Kilpatrick's project method, with an appeal to traditional teachers and others who desired the appearance of systematization associated with science and technology. Now, often regimented and distant from its Deweyan origins, the unit appealed more to the social behaviorist and intellectual traditionalist than to the more learning community interests approach of experientialists. This interpretation of units is in great kinship with a regimented, statisticized, positivist notion of science espoused by educational researchers who ironically justify their work by appealing to the free-flowing, situation-oriented, instrumentalist, and practical problem-solving advocated by Dewey in his *Sources of a Science of Education* (Dewey, 1929). The curriculum work of the thirties that provides the most accurate interpretation of integration related to the ideas of Dewey was produced by Hopkins (1937) and stands toward the opposite end of the continuum from a hobbled joining or correlation of subject areas.

Thus, curricular concerns varied markedly from the philosophical to the procedural, interpretative, and action-oriented. This variety, coupled with such influences as Morrison's emphasis on teaching and Kilpatrick's emphasis on method, contributed to the growing parameters of that which was accepted as curricular. Thus, the purview of curriculum literature embraced additional categories: teaching, instruction, methods, guidance, materials, administration, organization, and extracurricular activities. Examples included Phillips (1931) on methods; Stratemeyer (1931) on materials; Brewer (1932) on guidance; Trillingham (1934) on organization and administration; Jones (1935) and McKowan (1938) on extracurricular activities; Staley (1935) on sports; Wynne (1937) on teachers; Hopkins (1938) on pupils and teachers; University of Michigan (1938) on pupils; Melvin (1939) on teachers and curriculum committees; and Stretch (1939) on the child. As the areas of inclusion in the curriculum literature were augmented, the pervasive nature of curriculum inquiry was clarified but the definition of curriculum as an area of study was clouded. A persistent dilemma, curriculum study could not be extricated from conflation with educational studies in general. This matter of definition is far from resolution.

Categorization of curriculum literature according to level of schooling continued from the previous decade and was extended to greater inclusiveness in the thirties. Elementary schools continued to be treated separately by some authors, for example, Caswell (1930), Northern Ireland (1931), Phillips (1931), Stevens (1931), Caswell (1932), Woody (1934). Secondary curriculum continued as a special focus of attention. Examples include Lull (1932), Weersing and Ricciardi (1932), the North Central Association (1933), the NEA's Society for Curriculum Study (1938), and Prosser (1939). The junior high emphasis kindled in the previous decade was continued by Harrington (1930). Curriculum construction at the college and junior college levels was given extended attention in the 1930s. Prominent illustrations were a conference at Rollins College chaired by John Dewey (1931), Deyoe (1934), Headmasters' Conference

(1935), Rugg et al. (1935) on teacher education, Heaton and Koopman (1936), Colvert (1937), Minnesota (1937), and Colvert (1939).

Another interesting category of schooling given considerable emphasis during the 1930s was small schools (though quite different, not without precedent for the small schools movement today). Noteworthy sources in this area are: Caswell (1930), Broady, Platt, and Bell (1931), Caswell (1932), National Education Association (1933), and Broady (1936).

A sizable number of curriculum books focused on curriculum development in particular locales. In a sense these might be forerunners of current case study approaches. Examples include Houston (1930), South Dakota (1930), Rollins College (1931), Jacob (1932), National College of Education (1932), Columbia University Teachers College Survey of the Schools of Chicago (1932), Wright (1932), Adams (1934), Sanguinet (1934), North Carolina (1935), Heaton and Koopman (1936), Pennsylvania (1936), Henderson (1937), Glencoe (1938), and of special note, Spears (1937), who drew on administrative experiences in curriculum development to delineate strategies for curriculum building.

Miscellaneous areas of emphasis appeared in curriculum literature in this decade and should be noted due to the fact that some later became more widespread. Ricciardi described a conference method for curriculum construction. In the same year the common school was emphasized by Reisner (1930). Noting the governance of curriculum materials, Stratemeyer (1931) advocated their study for effective use. Similarly, Ruth Andrus and associates (1936) emphasized the study of curriculum guides. McKowan (1938), Jones (1935), and Staley (1935) argued in favor of curricular roles for extracurricular activities. Broady, Platt, and Bell (1931), the National Education Association (1934), and Broady (1936) focused on the need for enrichment provisions in the curriculum. The National Society for the Study of Education (1937) stressed international cooperation as a worthy end for curriculum. Marshall and Goetz (1936) treated curriculum-making relative to one subject area—social studies. The topic of curriculum laboratories was elaborated by Leary (1938) in a series of bulletins that extended from 1934 to 1938.

The increased numbers of approaches to curriculum thought and practice being reported reflected a desire to discover more widespread information. To this end special studies and surveys were instituted to make curriculum knowledge more readily available. Examples that focused on schools include Caswell (1930), Conference on Curriculum-making and Revision (1931), Langvick (1931), Caswell (1932), Columbia University's Teachers College Survey of the Schools of Chicago (1932), the California Elementary School Principals' Association (1937), Milligan (1937), and Shearer (1937).

The curriculum survey provided a perspective on current school policies and practices. This information was provided in the *Thirty-third Yearbook* of the National Society for the Study of Education on the activity movement (1934); and the 1935 University of Michigan surveys of curriculum relative to innovative practices, social trends, and state and national trends. Surveys of curricular research and thought are exemplified by McCall (1930), special issues of the *Review of Educational Research* (1931 and 1934), Trillingham (1934), and the Caswell and Campbell (1937) collection of readings on curriculum. The latter was the first of a kind that many would later emulate in the long saga of books that came to be known (both praisefully and pejoratively, depending on quality) as books of curriculum readings.

In the midst of this multitude of new dimensions in curriculum literature, a bit more should be said about the three schools of curriculum thought discussed in earlier chapters. Although the decade produced works by Snedden (1931), a sociological philosophy of education by Ross Finney (1933) with curricular recommendations, a treatise by Judd (1934), a revision of Charters's *Curriculum Construction* in 1938, and one of the first "life adjustment" curriculum proposals for secondary education by Charles Prosser (1939), the social behaviorist line diminished in overt number of publications, at least temporarily. It might be more accurate to say that it became more fully integrated into the fabric of the conciliarists that dominated practice. Thus, its proponents no longer needed to draw separate attention to themselves.

Intellectual traditionalists continued to proclaim the news that the standard disciplinary curriculum was not outmoded; in fact, it had scarcely been promoted effectively. Herman Horne produced a critical exegetical response to Dewey in *The Democratic Philosophy of Education* (1932), a companion to his more general and accessible criticism of social behaviorism in *The New Education* (1931). Bertrand Russell's *Education and the Modern World* (1932) called for a conservative direction in education for the good of society while simultaneously promoting radical controversial attitudes toward sexual conduct and religious allegiance. Bagley (1934) convened a committee of intellectual traditionalists to post a manifesto in 1938 that directly confronted the advances of progressive education. "The Essentialist's Platform for the Advancement of American Education" instituted a new label for Bagley's argument for the practical value of intellectual traditionalism. Henry C. Morrison's (1934) influence was maintained through the decade with his revision of instruction of disciplinary knowledge into unit constructions.

The experientialists produced a plethora of literature during the thirties, making this decade the most influential and the most varied in the century, although much of experientialist writing was quite different from Herbartian and Deweyan origins. Those who wrote about the activity curriculum promoted it in the name of progressivism, as had many of those who promoted correlated curricula, projects, and units. That which fell in the category of activity curriculum usually had something to do with Dewey's notion of learning by doing, either in a substantive way or perhaps only nominally. An exception is Maria Montessori's activity curriculum (1939), but her individual developmental activity curriculum continued to be out of place with the dominant curriculum orientations. This form of experientialism was interested primarily in progressive instructional methods rather than the whole curriculum picture.

Works by William Heard Kilpatrick, Harold Rugg, and L. Thomas Hopkins were among the most significant contributions to experientialism in the decade. Kilpatrick (1936) produced a small book advocating a remaking of curriculum in his interpretation of Deweyan pedagogy. Kilpatrick's interpretation of Dewey had great impact on many who read his work and listened to him speak, but it was also a popularization that some criticized for oversimplification and lack of social dimension. Illustrative of the range of interpretations in this variety of experientialism are Clement (1931), Stevens (1931), Hissong (1932), Adams (1934), National Society for the Study of Education (1934), Sanguinet (1934), Melvin (1936), and Mossman (1938). A careful attempt by Dewey to clarify his position was entitled *The Way Out of Educational Confusion* (1931), but it received considerably less attention.

In 1932, G. S. Counts extrapolated the Deweyan idea of reconstruction to ask his famed question that served as his book title, *Dare the School Build a New Social Order?* This paved the way to an interpretation of experientialist curricular purpose focused on social transformation with an emphasis on the expansion of democracy to economic institutions, a stance that became known as a social reconstructionist position. Highly critical of social and economic injustices, Counts's work was a forerunner of what we label the "critical reconstructionist" orientation, an understandinding of curriculum that emerged in the 1970s and strengthened as the century progressed. Jesse Newlon (1939) and Charles Beard (1937) wrote persuasively in the same perspective, supporting a social mission for the schools. A highly respected treatment of social ideas of key American educational theorists was published by Merle Curti in 1935. A remarkable contribution by African American scholar Carter G. Woodson delivered an enduring challenge. Arguing that an oppressed people can be "miseducated" to become participants in their own domination, he promoted a curriculum that would advance the civil rights and economic power of African Americans. Widely known among African American educators, the book regrettably received little attention in the mainstream white curriculum field—a fact that underscores the racial, political, and economic injustices that Woodson (and Counts) decried. *The Miseducation of the Negro* (Woodson, 1933) remains in print, recognized as a classic early statement on the education of the oppressed.

A variety of other approaches to experientialism emerged in the decade, variously approaching the Dewey construct. George Coe (1932) approached experientialism from a liberal Protestant perspective, largely compatible with the ideas promoted by William Clayton Bower (1929). Pickens Harris's (1937) argument for a socially and individually relevant education was an intelligent extension of Dewey's thought, but it was not a widely recognized contribution.

Boyd Bode offered a distinct understanding of experientialism, reflected in his thorough criticism of various curriculum proposals of the decade (1938). A professor at Ohio State University, Bode might be considered a synthesis of William Bagley's style and John Dewey's philosophy. Dewey himself acknowledged that among experientialists Bode best understood his proposal for education. This did not mean, however, that Bode was Dewey's disciple. Rather, Bode established his own conception of what democratic education should be, deviating from Dewey in some critical aspects.

A most incisive critic from the experientialist perspective, paralleling Bagley's role for intellectual traditionalists, Bode's writings emphasized the philosophical shortcomings of other proposals. The Deweyan character of his writings is demonstrated in his unreserved passion for democracy as the end of education and creative reflection as the means to realize this social aspiration. Whereas John Dewey, however, contended that the process of philosophy and the process of science were a unified deliberation directed to different phenomena, Bode asserted that philosophy and science were different modes of thinking, one being a social and political argumentative process, the other a technical process. Thus, democracy for Bode was a belief system constructed through philosophical dialogue; science, in contrast, was a process of thinking that empowered individuals and societies that aspire to democracy to realize their vision. Dewey, on the other hand, viewed democracy as corporate scientific deliberation. Bode maintained that education in "scientific method" left education without an articulated end or purpose. Democracy is the appropriate end of education because it is the pursuit of the ideal social order (Bode, 1937). Bode's emphasis on the compatibility of democracy as end and science as means established a philosophy that guides the work of education. Bode contended that what was needed in the schools was a "gospel of democracy" that could be lived and taught (Bode, 1938, pp. 58–59). Bode, therefore, established a basis for democracy that left continual room for the expansion of the concept so that the meaning reveals itself in conduct (Bode, 1938).

Bode contended that education fails when it teaches any rule, law, or standard as a fixed belief, or promotes an institution, even one that purportedly is democratic in structure, as a moral ideal. Thus, the promotion of patriotism, a code of ethics, or unreflective moral training is contrary to democratic education. "Sound education does not seek to prescribe belief or conduct, but to provide for the creation of new standards in accordance with new conditions and new needs" (Bode, 1938, p. 234). With the world itself in continual readjustment, the student of this world must be ready to rethink solutions that culture has endowed with sanctity. "In the democratic social order," Bode writes, "the schools have a distinctive obligation to provide for the continuous examination of traditional beliefs and practices, on the ground that 'time makes ancient good uncouth'" (Bode in Alberty & Bode, 1938, p. 5).

Bode argued that any of the so-called "scientific approaches" to education are self-contradictory if they prescribe educational outcomes before the educative experience is undertaken. In his analysis of Bode's career and thought, Chambliss (1963) emphasized that Bode considered the traditional distinction between pure and applied science to be a critical demarcation in determining what constitutes teaching scientific inquiry to students. Bode, in *Modern Educational Theories* (1927), highlighted this difference in contrasting the work of the chemist and the plumber. The chemist doing research works with hypotheses to seek and determine whether the hypothesis will assist in understanding the phenomenon investigated. A plumber is taught technical skills to resolve standard problems (i.e., applied science). To be scientific in conduct, Bode contended, training students in applications will not satisfy; educators must involve learners directly in resolving problems that lack a specified technical procedure for resolution.

For Bode, making the adjustment from study of natural phenomena to consideration of human dilemmas was simple. In all scientific inquiry, an openness to consider fully all dimensions of the interaction is critical. In human conduct, the demand is imagination and sympathy guided by intelligence to determine which conclusions are in the best interests of the participants. This is democratic resolution. It is not a search for truth, it is inquiry for meaning.

In addressing current educational practice, Bode was better able to provide criticism of current theory (e.g., Bode, 1927, 1938) than formulate, in light of his educational philosophy, a program for action (it could be argued that Harold Alberty will provide this dimension to Bode's proposal in the next decade). His persistent criticism was of social behaviorists, but Bode recognized particular failings in the proposals of some experientialists and intellectual traditionalists as well.

The social behaviorists were opposed by Bode, since they lacked an articulated philosophy and misinterpreted science while claiming the high road in scientific inquiry. This avoiding of the questions that philosophy asks leads inevitably back to an affirmation of the status quo. In this regard, social behaviorists, rather than riding the wave of the future, are retrogressive in determining their curricular policies. If civilization is to progress, people must continually rethink problems scientifically. Learning techniques of the present social order enables the learner only to maintain that which already is (Bode in Kilpatrick, 1933).

Bode also found intellectual traditionalists to be limiting. Although not lacking in philosophy, intellectual traditionalists so deify their philosophical conclusions as to prohibit further growth in thought. The intellectual traditionalists, in particular Morrison, also promoted disciplinary compartmentalization, which Bode rejected as pigeonholing knowledge. Traditional academic disciplines, according to Bode, both allow ideas to be contradictory (since they are not placed against each other) and make them impractical, since they are not related to the integrated life experiences of the students.

In *Progressive Education at the Crossroads*, Bode critiqued weaknesses in experientialist theory and practice. With their limited focus on making instructional methods more child-centered, Bode argued, some experientialists did not critically assess whether the curriculum progressives now teach with these new methods is truly democratic. Bode wrote,

> Progressive education is confronted with the choice of becoming the avowed exponent of democracy or else of becoming a set of ingenious devices for tempering the wind to the shorn lambs. If democracy is to have a deep and inclusive human meaning it must also have a distinctive educational system. (Bode, 1938, p. 26)

Bode was concerned that some progressive educators had turned from the absolutism of intellectual traditionalists to a new kind of absolutism: one of slavishness to the nature of the child. "Instead of turning to the ideal of democracy for guidance, it has all too often turned to the individual" (Bode, 1938, p. 40).

Bode upheld an educational system that is democratic in aspiration, confronting contemporary problems with an intelligent scientific perspective, a disposition toward a resolution that was progressive and that satisfied the conditions of an articulated educational philosophy. That Bode never became precise in his description of what the democratic schools should look like was due to his preoccupation with reestablishing the importance of philosophy in educational theory. Each individual is held to be important to this process of education since each person can contribute, through his or her own uniqueness, to the resolution of a stated problem. Bode viewed specialized education that does not ultimately contribute back to the life of the social group as a deception. People have intrinsic worth because they are a gift to the community in their individual potential. To dismiss this potential or to allow this potential to be self-serving is detrimental to democratic aspirations.

Other attempts to translate Deweyan philosophy of education into advice for experientialist curriculum developers and teachers include *American Life and the School Curriculum* (1936) by Rugg, Axtelle, Caswell, and Counts; Hopkins's (1937) explanation of the meaning and application of integration; the *Thirty-eighth Yearbook* of the National Society for the Study of Education (1939), a volume devoted to investigating relationships between child development and curriculum stemming from Herbartian roots; and the *Third Yearbook* of the John Dewey Society (1939), a publication that addressed the relationship between curriculum and democracy. The *Thirty-third Yearbook* of the National Society for the Study of Education, Part II (1934) includes pieces that are quite admirable attempts to explicate dimensions and extensions of Deweyan philosophy.

All this writing was quite serious, perhaps as it should be, but levity and satire can influence at times when serious argumentation falls short. It was Harold Benjamin, under the pseudonym of J. Abner Peddiwell, who in *The Saber-Tooth Curriculum* (1939) contributed markedly to the experientialist desire to rid the curriculum of the intellectual traditionalist propensity to emphasize instrumental skills and concepts that have atrophied beyond their utility. Posing as a researcher of prehistoric curricula, he lectured on the continuance of such curricular inclusions as "saber-tooth tiger chasing with fire" and "fish grabbing with the bare hands," long after glaciers had frozen both fish and streams and had chased the tigers southward, because major prehistoric curricularists deemed them inherently beneficial to the fully educated caveman.

The above authors variously approached and differed from the unique contribution of John Dewey. It should be stressed, however, that it is no mean task to educate en masse vast numbers of curriculum practitioners in a perspective as complex as Dewey's. Joseph Schwab, for example, wrote persuasively in 1959 about the difficulty of being a progressive teacher, not to mention educating progressive teachers and curriculum developers. [2]

That there is no better source of interpretation of a line of thought than its creator cannot be denied. To wit, Dewey must have been offended at some of the trends that attempted to emulate his thought. In *Experience and Education* (1938) he attempted to clarify misinterpretations of his thought. After concentrating his efforts primarily in philosophy for over 20 years since the production of his magnum opus, *Democracy and Education* (1916), Dewey returned to educational writing in an effort to clarify his orientation. Since he accepted education as a kind of testing ground for philosophy, he clearly had not lost touch with educational endeavors through philosophic pursuits in the intervening years.

Instead, he had strengthened his position. Dewey's *Art as Experience* (1934) is arguably among his most insightful statements on education in the broadest sense, through it is usually relegated to the realm of aesthetics. Philip Jackson (1998) recently interpreted valuable lessons for educators provided by art, derived from *Art as Experience*, which indicate a more extensive concept of education (and thus of curriculum) than that which pertains to schooling alone.

Many consider *Experience and Education* (1938) to be Dewey's most concise statement of his educational thought. It is Dewey's attempt to succinctly clarify his ideas on educational practice offered to his well-meaning and often creatively perceptive followers. Study of both contemporary and subsequent developments in curriculum thought and action reveals a state of affairs that fell far short of bringing, in Dewey's words, "the way out of educational confusion," the title of his 1931 book. This is not intended as a disparaging commentary on the field; rather, it is simply evidence that pointing the way, though difficult in itself, is often a less complex task than actualizing the vision. John Dewey's *Experience and Education* captured the essence of his response to the raging altercations of both traditional educators and zealous but sometimes superficial interpreters of his position in the following passage:

> It is the business of intelligent theory of education to ascertain the causes for the conflicts that exist and then, instead of taking one side or the other, to indicate a plan of operations proceeding from a level deeper and more inclusive than is represented by the practices and ideas of the contending parties. (p. 5)

In *Experience and Education*, Dewey spelled out the tenets of such a theory, carefully restating central threads from *Democracy and Education*. The reader should note the relevance of arguments advanced in *Experience and Education* on battles between progressive and traditional education of the thirties to similar debates that occurred later, for example, open versus traditional education in the late 1960s, humanistic versus "back to basics" orientations of the 1970s, and *A Nation at Risk* versus *Our Children at Risk* debate of the 1980s as well as current debates about the values of state goals, standards, curriculum standardization, and testing.

The influx of new topics in the curriculum domain coupled with the barrage of experientialist literature contributed to an interesting new phenomenon in curriculum literature of the thirties; namely, the propensity of authors to emphasize the trends, modernity, revision, and rapid pace of curriculum thought and activity. Titles portray well an underlying assumption that curriculum thought and practices were advancing with tremendous rapidity. One gets the distinct impression that if an educator was not a voracious reader, she/he would soon be left behind in the dust of curricular progress. Examples include *The Evolution of the Common School* (1930) by Reisner; *The Case for Curriculum Revision* (1932) by Browne; *The Selection and Organization of Personnel for Curriculum Revision* (1932) by Flavius; *High School Curriculum Reorganization* (1933) by the North Central Association; three reports on innovations and trends by the University of Michigan (1935); *Curriculum Trends* (1935) by Zirbes; *The Changing Curriculum* (1937) by Harap; *The Curriculum and Cultural Change* (1937) by Harris; *The Changing Curriculum* (1937) by the National Education Association and the Society for Curriculum Study; *Procedures in Curriculum Revision Programs of Selected States* (1937) by Shearer; and *A Challenge to Secondary Education: Plans for the Reconstruction of the American High School* (1938) by the Society for Curriculum Study.

Purposes were addressed as being prior to procedures in a 1938 statement of the Educational Policies Commission entitled *The Purposes of Education in a Democracy*. Although not a statement that probed democracy in relation to education in great depth, it represented at least three salient developments in curriculum writing. First, it at least covertly recognized the accumulating impact of experientialist thought, particularly of Dewey's *Democracy and Education* (1916), on curriculum thought. Second, it represented a growing tendency to consider purposes as being contingent on socio-political values. Third, it was an attempt to integrate disparate lines of educational thought. In this manner it was reminiscent of the 1918 statement of the Commission of the Reorganization of Secondary Education and that of the National Society for the Study of Education Twenty-sixth Yearbook Committee (1927). The Educational Policies Commission (1938) publication listed forty-three objectives that the well-educated person in American democratic society should strive toward. These are categorized under four headings: self-realization, human relationships, economic efficiency, and civic responsibility. It is a fine example of how conciliarism varies through the decades, emphasizing the curriculum orientations that have greater contemporary academic currency. The 1930s was the decade of experientialists, and conciliar writings reflect their significant influence.

Finally, a new form of curriculum book emerged during the thirties. It was, in no small measure, a response to the proliferation of trends and the emphasis on the need to keep pace with modernity. It must have been felt that a mechanism needed to be developed that could embrace all of the evolving components of the curriculum mosaic at once—the trends, the survey results, the array of experimentalist literature, the descriptions of happenings in specific locales, the emphasis on integration in its various modes, the inclusion of administration, instruction, evaluation, methods, teaching, materials, guidance, pupils, etc., in the curriculum domain, and the miscellany of subtopics of curricular concern. All of these needed to be communicated to anyone who wanted to know about

and effectively participate in the curriculum field. Books were written responding to this felt need, serving as compendia, encyclopedic portrayals of an ever-
increasing stockpile of curricular knowledge. A major function of such books
was to introduce new members to the curriculum field. Monumental examples
were *Foundations of Curriculum Building* (1936) by Norton and Norton, and
Curriculum Development (1935) by Caswell and Campbell. In their 1935 text,
Caswell and Campbell treated the following as major topics: the school in
contemporary life, the social responsibility of the school, influences on curriculum, principles for curriculum development, curricular aims and scope, pupil
purposes, activities to develop purposes, subject matter selection, grade placement and time allotment, teaching procedures, evaluation, organization, instruction, units, courses of study, and administration. This was all supplemented by a
vast list of references for further study. Two years later the text was further
supplemented by *Readings in Curriculum Development* (1937), providing convenient exposure to articles considered central to a variety of curriculum concerns.

It should be noted that the use of the term *curriculum development* became
highly prominent during the next two decades, becoming almost synonymous
with curriculum study at large. As the reader will discover, books that followed and dominated the field for the next three decades took on the encyclopedic character exemplified by these works. They were the major kinds of
writings that socialized curriculum workers (be they professors, administrators, consultants, or teachers) to the work that they pursued. In subsequent
chapters these books are referred to as "synoptic texts."

BIBLIOGRAPHY OF CURRICULUM BOOKS 1930–1939

1930

Caswell, H. L. (1930). *Program making in small elementary schools*. Nashville, TN: George
   Peabody College.

Counts, G. S. (1930). *The American road to culture*. New York: John Day.

Garretson, O. K. (1930). *Relationship between expressed preferences and curricular abilities of ninth
   grade boys*. New York: Columbia University, Teachers College (Reprinted by AMS).

Harrington, H. L. (1930). *Program making for junior high schools*. New York: The Macmillan
   Company.

Houston, Texas Independent School District. (1930). *Curriculum revision and development in Houston, Texas, 1924–30, Part II*. Houston, TX: Board of Education.

McCall, W. M. (1930). *A critical review of various conceptions underlying curriculum-making since 1900*. Columbia: University of Missouri.

Peters, C. C. (1930). *Objectives and procedures in civic education*. New York: Longmans, Green.

Reisner, E. H. (1930). *The evolution of the common school*. New York: Macmillan.

Ricciardi, N. (1930). *The application of the conference method to curriculum making*. Bulletin Number G-5. Sacramento: California Department of Education.

South Dakota. (1930). *Preliminary reports of approach to and theories regarding curriculum construction, general aims and guiding principles of education for the state of South Dakota*. Bulletin Number 1. Pierre, SD: State Department of Education.

1931

American Educational Research Association. (1931, January). *The curriculum*. A special issue of the *Review of Educational Research*. Washington, DC: Author.

Bonser, F. G. (1931). *The effective use of curriculum materials*. New York: Teachers College, Columbia University.

Broady, K. O., Platt, E. T., & Bell, M. D. (1931). *Practical procedures for enriching the curriculum of small schools. University of Nebraska Publication Number 84*. Educational Monographs Number 2. Lincoln: University of Nebraska.

Clement, J. A. (1931, February 24). *Progressive trends in the external organization and in the curriculum content of our schools*. Urbana: University of Illinois Bulletin Number 54.

Conference on Curriculum-making and Revision. (1936, October 30–31). *Curriculum-making in current practice*. Evanston, IL: Northwestern University.

Dewey, J. (1931). *The way out of educational confusion*. Cambridge, MA: Harvard University Press. (Also printed by Greenwood Press, New York, 1970).

Horne, H. H. (1931). *The new education*. New York: Abingdon.

Langvick, M. M. (1931). *Current practices in the construction of state courses of study*. Washington, DC: U.S. Government Printing Office.

Morrison, H. C. (1931). *Practice teaching in the secondary school* (Revised edition). Chicago: University of Chicago Press.

Northern Ireland. (1931). *Committee of inquiry on the program of instruction in public elementary schools*. Belfast, Northern Ireland: Her Majesty's Stationery Office.

Phillips, C. A. (1931). *Modern methods and the elementary curriculum (Revised edition)*. New York: Century.

Rollins College. (1931). *The curriculum for the liberal arts college, being the report of the curriculum conference held at Rollins College, January 19–24, 1931*. (John Dewey, Chairman, together with the reports of Rollins College committees on curriculum.) Winter Park, FL: Rollins College.

Rugg, H. (1931). *Culture and education in America*. New York: Harcourt, Brace.

Scottish Council for Research in Education. (1931). *Curriculum for pupils of twelve to fifteen years (advanced division)*. London: University of London Press.

Snedden, D. S. (1931). *Cultural education and common sense: A study of some sociological foundations of education designed to refine, increase, and render more functional the personal cultures of men*. New York: Macmillan.

Stevens, M. P. (1931). *The activities curriculum in the primary grades*. Boston: D. C. Heath.

Stratemeyer, F. B. (1931). *The effective use of curriculum materials*. New York: Teachers College, Columbia University. (Reprinted in 1972 by AMS, New York).

1932

Bonser, F. G. (1932). *Life needs and education*. New York: Bureau of Publications, Teachers College, Columbia University.

Brewer, J. M. (1932). *Education as guidance; an examination of the possibilities of a curriculum in terms of life activities, in elementary and secondary school and college*. New York: Macmillan.

Browne, G. S. (1932). *The case for curriculum revision*. Melbourne, Australia: Melbourne University Press.

Caswell, H. L. (1932). *Program making in small elementary schools. Field Studies Number 1* (Revised edition), Division of Surveys and Field Studies. Nashville, TN: George Peabody College for Teachers.

Coe, G. (1932). *Educating for citizenship*. New York: Charles Scribner's.

Columbia University, Teachers College, Institute of Educational Research, Division of Field Studies. (1932). *The curricula of the schools*. Report of the Survey of the Schools of Chicago, Illinois, Volume III. New York: Bureau of Publications, Teachers College, Columbia University.

Counts, G. S. (1932). *Dare the school build a new social order?* New York: John Day. (Reprinted by Arno Press, 1969).

Flavius, L. D. (1932). *The selection and organization of personnel for curriculum revision*. Cleveland, OH: Western Reserve University.

Hissong, C. (1932). *The activity moment*. Baltimore: Warick & York.

Horne, H. H. (1932). *The democratic philosophy of education*. New York: Macmillan.

Jacob, T. N. (1932). *The reconstruction of the curriculum of the elementary schools of India*. Calcutta, India: Association Press, Y.M.C.A.

Lide, E. S. (1932). *Procedures in curriculum making. National Survey of Secondary Education, Bulletin Number 17, Monograph Number 18*. Washington, DC: Government Printing Office.

Lull, H. G. (1932). *Secondary education: Organization and program*. New York: W. W. Norton.

Meiklejohn, A. (1932). *The experimental college*. New York: Harper and Brothers.

National College of Education. (1932). *Children's School Staff*. Curriculum records of the Children's School, National College of Education. Evanston, IL: Bureau of Publications, National College of Education.

Russell, B. (1932). *Education and the modern world*. New York: W. W. Norton.

Virginia State Board of Education. (1932). *Study course for Virginia State Curriculum Program*. Richmond, VA: Division of Purchasing and Printing.

Weersing, F. J., & Ricciardi, N. (1932). *Curriculum making in secondary schools. Syllabus for course in Education 254B*. Los Angeles: University of Southern California.

Wright, L. E. (1932). *Units of work. A first grade at work; a non-reading curriculum*. New York: Bureau of Publications, Teachers College, Columbia University, for Lincoln School of Teachers College.

1933

Dewey, John. (1933). *How we think: A restatement of the relation of reflective thinking to the educative process*. (Revised edition). Chicago: D. C. Heath.

Finney, R. L. (1933). *A sociological philosophy of education*. New York: Macmillan.

Kilpatrick, W. H. (Ed.). (1933). *Educational frontier*. New York: D. Appleton Century Co.

Lide, E. S. (1933). *Procedures in curriculum-making*. Washington, DC: U.S. Government Printing Office.

National Education Association of the United States. Department of Rural Education. (1933). *Organization of curriculum for one-teacher schools*. Washington, DC: National Education Association.

North Central Association of College and Secondary Schools. (1933). *High school curriculum reorganization*. The North Central Association of Colleges and Secondary Schools. Ann Arbor, MI: Author.

Woodson, C. G. (1933). *The miseducation of the negro*. Washington, DC: Associated Publishers.

1934

Adams, F. (1934). *The initiation of an activity program into a public school. Contributions to Education Number 598*. New York: Bureau of Publications, Teachers, College, Columbia University.

American Educational Research Association. (April, 1934). *Review of educational research, the curriculum*. Washington, DC: National Education Association.

Bagley, W. C. (1934). *Education and emergent man*. New York: T. Nelson and Sons.

Counts, G. S. (1934). *The social foundations of education*. New York: Charles Scribner's Sons.

Dewey, J. (1934). *Art as experience*. New York: Minton, Balch & Co.

Deyoe, G. P. (1934). *Certain trends in curriculum practices and policies in state and normal schools and teachers colleges*. New York: Teachers College, Columbia University.

Judd, C. (1934). *Education and social progress*. New York: Harcourt Brace.

Morrison, H. C. (1934). *Basic principles in education*. Boston: Houghton-Mifflin.

National Education Association of the United States. Department of Rural Education. (1934). *Economical enrichment of the small secondary-school curriculum*. Washington, DC: Department of Rural Education, National Education Association.

National Society for the Study of Education. (1934). *The activity movement: Thirty-third Yearbook, Part II* (Lois C. Mossman, Chair). Bloomington, IL: Public School Publishing Company.

North Carolina. (1934). *Suggested procedures for curriculum construction and course of study building, 1934–1935. Publication Number 179*. Raleigh: State Superintendent of Public Instruction.

Sanguinet, E. H. (1934). *An approach to curriculum construction based on a child activity survey in the Philippine Islands*. Manila, Philippine Islands: Philippine Teacher's Digest.

Stanford Education Conference. (1934). *Curriculum and instruction*. Stanford, CA.

Stewart H. H. (1934). *Comparative study of the concentration and regular plans of organization in the senior high school*. New York: Columbia University, Teachers College. (Reprinted by AMS).

Trillingham, C. C. (1934). *The organization and administration of curriculum programs*. Los Angeles: University of Southern California Press.

Woody, C. (1934). *Syllabus for the construction of the elementary school curriculum*. Ann Arbor, MI: Brumfield & Brumfield.

1935

Caswell, H. L., & Campbell, D. S. *Curriculum development*: New York: American Book Company. (Reprint by R. West 1978).

Curti, M. (1935). *Social ideas of American educators*. New York: Charles Scribner's Sons.

Jones, G. (1935). *Extra curricular activities in relation to the curriculum*. New York: Teachers College, Columbia University (AMS reprint available).

Michigan, University of. (1935a). *Innovative practices in the curriculum*. Ann Arbor, MI: School of Education.

Michigan, University of. (1935b). *Social trends and curriculum revision*. Ann Arbor, MI: School of Education.

Michigan, University of. (1935c). *State and national trends in education*. Ann Arbor, MI: School of Education.

New York (State) University. (1935). *Secondary school curriculum reorganization. Suggestion relative to sequences.* Albany: The University of the State of New York Press.

North Carolina Department of Public Instruction. (1935). *A study in curriculum problems of the North Carolina public schools. Suggestions and practices.* Raleigh: North Carolina State Superintendent of Public Instruction.

Rugg, E. U., Peik, W. E., Foster, F. K., John, W. C., & Raup, B. R. (1935). *Teacher education curricula.* U.S. Department of the Interior, Harold L. Ickes, Secretary. Office of Education, George F. Zook, Commissioner. Washington, DC: U.S. Government Printing Office.

Staley, S. C. (1935). *The curriculum in sports.* Philadelphia: W. B. Saunders. (Also by Stipes Publishing Company, Champaign, Illinois).

Standing Joint Commission Committee of the Headmasters' Conference and Incorporated Association of Preparatory Schools. (1935). *Curriculum for the preparatory schools; being the report of the Standing Joint Committee of the Headmasters' Conference and Incorporated Association of Preparatory Schools.* Winchester, England: Warren & Sons, Ltd.

Tuttle, F. P. (1935). *Correlated curriculum activities.* Mankato, MN: Creative Educational Society.

Zirbes, L. (1935). *Curriculum trends: A preliminary report and challenge.* Washington, DC: Association for Childhood Education.

1936

Andrus, R., and Associates. (1936). *Curriculum guides for teachers of children from two to six years of age.* New York: Reynal and Hitchcock (A John Day Book).

Broady, K. O. (1936). *Enriched curriculum for small schools.* Lincoln: University of Nebraska.

Bruner, H. B. (1936). *A tentative list of approaches to curriculum and course of study construction with selected bibliographies.* New York: Teachers College, Columbia University.

Draper, E. M. (1936). *Principles and techniques of curriculum making.* New York: D. Appleton-Century.

Hanna, P. (1936). *Youth serves the community.* New York: D. Appleton-Century.

Heaton, K. L., & Koopman, G. R. (1936). *A college curriculum based on functional needs of students; an experiment with the general curriculum at Central State Teachers College, Mount Pleasant, Michigan.* Chicago: University of Chicago Press.

Kilpatrick, W. H. (1936). *Remaking the curriculum.* New York: Newson and Company.

Marshall, L. C., & Goetz, R. M. (1936). *Curriculum-making in the social studies.* New York: Charles Scribner's Sons.

Melvin, A. G. (1936). *The activity program.* New York: Reynal and Hitchcock.

National Council of the Teachers of English. (1936). *A correlated curriculum.* New York: D. Appleton-Century.

Norton, J. K., & Norton, M. A. (1936). *Foundations of curriculum building.* Boston: Ginn and Company.

Pennsylvania Department of Public Instruction. (1936). *Suggestions for the development and use of curriculum materials in the elementary school.* Harrisburg: Pennsylvania Department of Public Instruction.

Rugg, H. O., Axtelle, G., Caswell, H., & Counts, G. S. (1936). *American life and the school curriculum: Next steps toward schools of living.* New York: Ginn and Company.

Stigler, W.A. (1936). *Handbook for curriculum development.* Austin: Texas State Department of Education.

1937

Beard, C. A. (1937). *The unique function of education in a democracy.* Washington, DC: Educational Policies Commission.

Bode, B. H. (1937). *Democracy as a way of life.* New York: Macmillan.

California Elementary School Principals' Association. (1937). *Current curricular practices in elementary education.* Los Angeles: Elementary School Principals' Association.

Caswell, H. L., & Campbell, D. S. (Eds.). (1937). *Readings in curriculum development.* New York: American Book Company.

Colvert, C. C. (1937). *A critical analysis of the public junior college curriculum.* Nashville, TN: George Peabody College for Teachers.

Connole, R. J. (1937). *A study of the concept of integration in present day curriculum thinking.* Washington, DC: Catholic University of America.

Harap, H. (Ed.). (1937). *The changing curriculum.* New York: D. Appleton-Century.

Harris, P. E. (1937). *The curriculum and cultural change.* New York: D. Appleton-Century.

Henderson, H. R. (1937). *A curriculum study in a mountain district.* New York: Teachers College, Columbia University.

Hoban, C. F., Hoban, C. F. Jr., & Zisman, S. B. (1937). *Visualizing the curriculum.* New York: Cordon. (Also reprint by R. West).

Hopkins, L. T. (1937). *Integration, its meaning and application.* New York: D. Appleton-Century.

Joint Committee on Curriculum of the Department of Supervisors and Directors of Instruction of the National Education Association and the Society for Curriculum Study. (1937). *The changing curriculum.* New York: D. Appleton-Century. (Reprinted in 1972 by AMS, New York).

Milligan, N. G. (1937). *Relationship of the professed philosophy to the suggested educational experiences; a study in current elementary school curriculum making.* New York: Teachers College, Columbia University. (Reprinted in 1972 by AMS, New York).

Minnesota—University Committee on Educational Research. (1937). *The effective general college curriculum as revealed by examinations.* Minneapolis: University of Minnesota Press.

National Society for the Study of Education. (1937). *International understanding through public school curriculum (I. L. Kandel and G. W. Whipple, Editors). Thirty-sixth Yearbook.* Bloomington, IL: Public School Publishing Company.

Oberholtzer, E. E. (1937). *Integrated curriculum in practice. Contributions to Education Number 694.* New York: Teachers College, Columbia University. (AMS reprint available).

Shearer, A. E. (1937). *Procedures in curriculum revision programs of selected states.* Nashville, TN: George Peabody College for Teachers.

Spears, H. (1937). *Experiences in building a curriculum.* New York: Macmillan.

Wynne, J. P. (1937). *The teacher and the curriculum.* New York: Prentice-Hall.

1938

Alberty, H., & Bode, B. H. (Eds.). (1938). *Educational freedom and democracy: The John Dewey Society second yearbook.* New York: Appleton, Century, Crofts.

Bode, B. H. (1938.) *Progressive education at the crossroads.* New York: Newson.

Charters, W. W. (1938). *Curriculum construction* (Revised edition). New York: Macmillan.

Dewey, J. (1938). *Experience and education.* New York: Macmillan.

Educational Policies Commission. (1938). *The purposes of education in American democracy.* Washington, DC: The Educational Policies Commission of the NEA and AASA.

Glencoe Public Schools. (1938). *A guide for curriculum planning.* Glencoe, IL: Board of Education.

Hopkins, L. T. (1938). *Pupil-teacher learning.* Wilmington, DE: The Delaware Citizens Association.

Leary, B. E. (1938). *Curriculum Laboratories and divisions: Their organization and functions in state departments of education, city school systems, and institutions of higher education. Surveys of courses of study and other curriculum materials—A series (1934–1938) of bulletins.* Washington, DC: Office of Education.

McKowan, B. C. (1938). *Extra-curricular activities.* New York: Macmillan.

Michigan, University of. (1938). *Pupil development and the curriculum.* Ann Arbor, MI: School of Education.

Mossman, L. C. (1938). *The activity concept.* New York: Macmillan.

Ohio State University, Columbus. University School. (1938). *Were we guinea pigs? By the Class of 1938, University High School, the Ohio State University.* New York: H. Holt and Company.

Patty, W. L. (1938). *A study of mechanism in education*. New York: Bureau of Publications, Teachers College, Columbia University. (Reprint 1972, AMS, New York).

Society for Curriculum Study. (1938). *A challenge to secondary education: Plans for the reconstruction of the American high school (Samuel Everett, Editor)*. New York: D. Appleton-Century.

Weeks, R. M. (1938). *A correlated curriculum. Report of the National Council of Teachers of English*. New York: Appleton-Century-Crofts.

1939

Benjamin, H. (Peddiwell, J.A., psuedonym). (1939). *The saber-tooth curriculum*. New York: McGraw-Hill. (Also 1959 reprint).

Colvert, C. C. (1939). *The public junior college curriculum; an analysis*. Baton Rouge, LA: Louisiana State University Press.

Department of Elementary School Principals. (1939). *Enriching curriculum for the elementary school child. Eighteenth Yearbook*. Washington, DC: National Educational Association.

Dix, L. (1939). *A charter for progressive education*. New York: Teachers College, Columbia University.

Heffernan, H. (Ed.). (1939). *Newer instructional practices of promise*. Washington, DC: Association for Supervision and Curriculum Development.

John Dewey Society. (1939). *Democracy and the curriculum*. Third Yearbook. New York: D. Appleton-Century.

Jones, A. J. (1939). *Principles of unit construction*. New York: McGraw-Hill.

Melvin, A. G. (1939). *Activated curriculum: A method and a model for class teachers and curriculum committees*. New York: John Day Company.

Montessori, M. (1939). *The secret of childhood*. New York: F. A. Stokes Company.

National Society for the Study of Education. (1939). *Child development and the curriculum (Guy Whipple, Editor). Thirty-Eighth Yearbook, Part I*. Chicago: University of Chicago Press.

Newlon, J. (1939). *Education for democracy in our time*. New York: McGraw-Hill.

Prosser, C. A. (1939). *Secondary education and life*. Cambridge, MA: Harvard University Press.

Rugg, H. O. (Ed.). (1939). *Democracy and the curriculum: The life and program of the American school*. New York: D. Appleton-Century.

Stretch, L. B. (1939). *The curriculum and the child*. Minneapolis, MN: Educational Publishers.

Thayer, V. T., Zachry, C. B., & Kotinsky, R. (1939). *Reorganizing secondary education*. New York: D. Appleton-Century.

CHAPTER FIVE

Curriculum Literature and Context
1940–1949

CONTEXTUAL REMINDERS

The second act of the firestorm first ignited in 1914 spread again to a global arena. Nazi and Fascist forces controlled most of Western Europe. France would fall in 1940 and the Battle of Britain would commence in preparation for the planned invasion by Hitler's forces. Italy sought to consolidate control in Albania, Ethiopia, and Libya. Japanese troops had captured Peking, China, and were advancing on the colonies of the western powers in Southeast Asia. As a result of its nonaggression pact with Germany, the Soviet Union eventually gained control over Finland, Estonia, Latvia, eastern Poland, and Bessarabia. Despite strong sentiment in the United States to remain neutral, President Franklin Roosevelt made clear this nation's commitment to its former European allies and prepared the nation for war through such measures as the Two-Ocean Navy Act, the Selective Service Act, and the Lend-Lease Act. In addition, pressure on the Japanese to halt their Asian expansion resulted in the eventual freezing of Japanese assets and an embargo on Japanese trade.

In December 1941, German and Italian forces were joined by the Japanese, who, under the direction of General Hideki Tojo, launched a surprise bombing attack on the U.S. naval base at Pearl Harbor in Hawaii. The United States declared war on Japan and its allies, Germany and Italy, the following day. In 1942 German and Italian expansion continued in Africa and Europe but slowed when German forces attempted to seize Stalingrad. Although the toll in human suffering was tremendous (over 19 million died), Soviet resistance proved a major setback for the German master plan. Japan continued to expand in the Pacific by capturing the Philippines and Hong Kong. U.S. forces entered North

Africa, repeatedly bombed Germany and occupied France, and blocked Japanese offensives at Guadalcanal, Midway, and the Coral Sea. In 1943, the tide of Axis expansion was quelled. Allied troops forced Axis withdrawal from North Africa. The Italians surrendered unconditionally to the Allies, and the Nazi armies besieging Stalingrad surrendered to the Soviets. Marshall Tito initiated a Balkan offensive against a weakened Germany. Allied landings in Normandy came on D-Day in 1944. Charles de Gaulle set up a provincial government in Paris. Russia invaded Bulgaria, Rumania, and Hungary. Germany began rocket attacks on Britain, but despite introduction of these "wonder weapons," Nazi power was broken. May 8, 1945, was named Victory in Europe (VE) Day by President Harry S. Truman. Italians executed Mussolini. In Germany, Hitler was reputed to have committed suicide. The full immensity of the tragedy was known with the liberation of the death camps by Allied forces. The horror of the Nazi Holocaust shocked the world. At the concentration camp in Auschwitz alone over 3 million people were put to death. In 1946 the Nuremberg Tribunal passed death sentences on 12 Nazi leaders for genocide and other war crimes.

The war in the Pacific ended with a U.S. victory at Okinawa, followed by the controversial atomic bombing of Hiroshima and Nagasaki. These weapons of mass destruction, the practical results of decades of research by physicists, forever changed the meaning of being human on this planet. Victory for Allied forces came on VJ Day, August 14, 1945. In the same year, Churchill, Attlee, Truman, and Stalin met at Potsdam to determine Germany's future and to divide the defeated nation into Allied occupation zones. Albania, Czechoslovakia, Hungary, Poland, Bulgaria, Rumania, and Yugoslavia came under Soviet control. Europe would be divided until 1990 into Soviet and Allied camps by a series of walls, watchtowers, electrified fences, and mine fields that Churchill called the "Iron Curtain." In 1949 Mao Tse-tung was able to declare the People's Republic of China under Communist control by forcing Chiang Kai-shek's corrupt and unpopular Nationalists off the mainland onto Taiwan. This further increased the fears of the U.S. politicians and military leaders of a "Domino Effect," with nations succumbing to communist governments. Under U.S. military occupation, General Douglas MacArthur administered the rehabilitation of a vanquished Japan that included renouncement of the emperor's divinity and the adoption of a new constitution.

The world at war both inhibited and stimulated artistic and scientific contributions; scientists, artists, and technologists inevitably worked in the context of war: its tragedy, horror, and intimations of glory. In literature, Hemingway's *For Whom the Bell Tolls*, Graham Greene's *The Power and the Glory*, and even Chaplin's film *The Great Dictator*, all appearing in 1940, reminded their audiences that all human drama takes place in a political context. Desire to escape is understandably prevalent in such times, and opportunity to do so was provided through the music of Stravinsky, Britten, Bartok, and Shostakovich, as well as by the perennially popular Disney film *Fantasia* and the peaceful New England landscapes of Grandma Moses. Painter Paul Nash depicted the war in *Bombers over Britain* in 1941, the same year that Russian Ilya Ehrengurg wrote about *The Fall of Paris*. The power and portent of rugged individualism were brought to question in Fitzgerald's *The Last Tycoon*, and in film by Orson Welles's *Citizen Kane*, both in 1941. This theme contrasted with that of *Casablanca* and *Mrs. Minniver*: putting aside personal interests to confront impending present evils. The painters John Piper, Stuart Davis, Marc Chagall, and Graham Sutherland, as well as the sculptor Henry Moore, continued to work throughout the forties. Frank Lloyd Wright's design of the Guggenheim Museum, revealed in 1946, was another reinventing of his architectural genius.

The literary scene, as in the thirties, provided readers and audiences with works by Noel Coward, T. S. Eliot, and C. S. Lewis. Amid the disillusionment and alienation that accompanies war, there evolved a kind of literature that described the lack of purpose in the slice of life accorded to ordinary living. Portrayals varied widely, from the existentialism of Albert Camus in *The Stranger* in 1942 to the operatic depiction of inherent injustices in Benjamin Britten's *Peter Grimes* in 1945. In 1944, Somerset Maugham interpreted the inner and outer portions of human conflict in *The Razor's Edge*, while Tennessee Williams portrayed accumulated inwardness and retreat in *The Glass Menagerie*. Each of these works of art, in its own special uniqueness, conveyed the plights of human existence on this planet as greatly outweighing the delights. Similarly, the injustice of misplaced concentrations of political power was made vivid by Robert Penn Warren's fact-based novel of 1946, *All the King's Men*. An allegoric, satirical warning of unrestrained power was presented by George Orwell in his unforgettable *Animal Farm* (1945). In quite a different manner, the potential to rise to the top via sexual exploitation shocked the readers of Kathleen Windsor's *Forever Amber* in 1944. The demand for this best-seller, combined with paper shortages, resulted in the expansion of paperback books. The literary reflection of public sentiment and action, however, was not exclusively dedicated to portraying the world as absurd and chance as winning in the end. One can recall the popularity of *Oklahoma*, the famed 1943 musical by Richard Rodgers and Oscar Hammerstein III. Providing counterpoint to this uplifting quality of tribute to the heartland was Dylan Thomas's consideration of mortality's mystery in *Deaths and Entrances* (1946).

In the technological realm, in addition to the proliferation of war materials, the early forties initiated the era of wonder drugs. Australian-born Howard Florey advanced the discovery of Alexander Fleming some 12 years earlier by isolating and purifying penicillin in 1940, and in 1943 Selman Waksman of the United States developed streptomycin. In 1941, the apparel industry was introduced to dacron, the first polyester fiber. DuPont replaced silk stockings with nylon, the invention of Wallace Carothers, in 1940. The micro-world was increased in both clarity and perceived complexity with the 1940 invention of the electron microscope by Ladislaus Morton. In 1946 the ENIAC computer of J. Presper Eckert and John Mauchly at the University of Pennsylvania ushered in a revolution in the art of calculation. The forties also brought the tubeless tire, the electric blanket, the helicopter, the drive-in bank, seeding of clouds, supersonic flights, the 33 1/3 rpm record, solar heating, cortisone treatment for rheumatism, and the invention of the transistor by John Bardeen, Walter Brattain, and William Shockley.

The unconscionable atrocities of World War II, including the extermination of over 6 million Jews and Poles, the horror of combat and bombing on all sides, the death marches, and the separation of grief-stricken loved ones, magnified the necessity of developing a world that could more fully provide the four freedoms articulated by Franklin Roosevelt in his 1941 inaugural address (freedom from want and fear, and freedom of religion and speech). The postwar creation of the United Nations was an attempt to move in the direction of these aspirations through international deliberation. The United Nations was formally created in 1945 and found a permanent residence in New York City the following year, on a site donated by John D. Rockefeller, Jr. In its first two major efforts at global reconciliation, the assembly learned that it would take more than good will to avert violence. Indonesians resumed fighting in a quest for independence from the Dutch. This action was quelled by a UN call for a cease-fire in 1947 but remained unresolved. With assistance from Great Britain and the UN, Jewish peoples proclaimed a national homeland, the State of Israel, in 1948; the displacement of the Palestinian peoples to establish this new state sparked generations of conflict. In the same year, India and Pakistan were divided to accommodate the political demands of Hindus and Moslems following their independence from Great Britain. An opponent of the partition assassinated the spiritual leader of the independence movement, Mohandas Gandhi.

The extent to which the United States was willing to fully support this human quest for equality and well-being stated in the aforementioned four freedoms was an open question. The U.S. government, fearing espionage, sabotage, and collaboration with the enemy, ordered the internment of over 100,000 Japanese Americans through World War II, contending that these citizens constituted a security risk. Similarly, one could challenge the commitment to equality when African Americans remained segregated in society and in the military. Richard Wright's powerful portrait of a young African American male,

Bigger Thomas, in *Native Son*, exposed the structural racism of the "land of the free." To be sure, there continued to be signs of changes to come after the war: Jackie Robinson was signed by the Brooklyn Dodgers in 1947, breaking the color barrier in major league baseball. The University of Oklahoma law school was required to accept a qualified African American student. President Harry Truman, who succeeded Roosevelt on his death in 1945, spoke in public opposition to the Jim Crow laws. Nonetheless, the "curtain of color" remained firmly in place in the United States.

The United States was one of a few nations that retained their industrial capacity in the aftermath of the war. The later years of the 1940s brought a surge of hope for prosperity, not wholly unlike that which occurred in the wane of World War I. The demands of rebuilding the national and global economy were immediate priorities. A certain degree of atonement for suffering incurred by U. S. veterans, as well as an attempt to stave off postwar unemployment, was provided by the GI Bill of Rights in 1944, enabling veterans to receive vocational and educational benefits more readily. In a sense, the GI Bill marked the opening of higher education to the middle and lower middle classes. In 1946, the Atomic Energy Commission was established to foster the peaceful development and application of atomic energy. The Marshall Plan provided over $100 billion in foreign assistance in 1948.

Although the end of the war inspired hopes for freedom and cooperation, it also aroused distrust accompanied by sharpened security. The Smith Act of 1940 required all aliens to undergo a fingerprinting process and outlawed organizations that advocated the overthrow of the American government. Following the war, President Truman issued an Executive Order that all federal employees be required to undergo a loyalty investigation. Part of this 1947 procedure involved the listing of "security risks." In the same year the House Un-American Activities Committee (HUAC) commenced files on persons suspected or verified as potentially subversive. Among the many who were scrutinized by the federal government were educators John Dewey, George S. Counts, and Harold O. Rugg.[1] Suspicion ran rampant. Indeed, microfilm evidence hidden in a pumpkin at a Maryland farm was brought to the attention of the House Un-American Activities Committee by *Time* magazine editor Whittaker Chambers in 1948, implying that former State Department official Alger Hiss had communist affiliations. The Hiss investigation served as a springboard for the political aspirations of Richard Nixon. Other Californians, screenwriters with connections to socialist ideologies, were offered as sacrificial lambs to the HUAC by the Screen Actors Guild to quell charges that Hollywood had "gone red."

At the international level, in 1947 Bernard Baruch warned that the United States was in the midst of "cold war," a year after Churchill's noted remark that an "iron curtain" was present on the European continent. By 1948, the USSR had withdrawn from the Allied Control Commission and began a blockade of West Berlin. The Western nations responded with a massive airlift of supplies. In the same year North and South Korea were established as rival governments. In 1949, on the other side of the globe, the blockade of Berlin by the Soviets was ended, and West and East Germany were separated into democratic and communist nations. The predicted cold war had descended. The United States joined Canada and 10 Western European countries in signing the North Atlantic Treaty Organization (NATO) pact, agreeing to mutual defense in the event of armed attack in 1949. The world was stunned when the Soviet Union announced that it also had atomic weapons.

Nevertheless, the public hope for an era of prosperity was not wholly unwarranted. Economic conditions improved with the 1947 General Agreements of Tariffs and Trades, involving 23 nations. Aid from the United States and other sources provided temporary respite for the war-torn nations. Rations were terminated in most of the destroyed areas of Europe and Britain, and much rebuilding was accomplished through great perseverance.

The arts experienced a renewal, though surely not one that forgot the war, as illustrated by the posthumously published *Diary of Anne Frank*. The architecture of Le Corbusier grew in prominence. The painting of Jackson Pollock, Fernard Leger, and Picasso accentuated the medium and left the message open for interpretation by the viewer. The music of Richard Strauss, Cole Porter, and Leonard Bernstein brought at least a modicum of peacefulness to war-eroded souls. Radio provided a full slate of entertainment from variety shows like *The Kraft Music Hall*, vaudevillian entertainment from Abbott and Costello, Edgar Bergen, and Jack Benny, and the development of the popular short story form for broadcast media in comedy (through situation comedies such as *The Great Gildersleeve* and *The Life of Riley*) and in drama (*Suspense* and *Inner Sanctum*). Still, slice- of-life literature carried frequent reminders that it is through challenge to spirit, mind, body, and expectations that we experience knowledge of our aliveness, as provided by Eugene O'Neill's *The Iceman Cometh* (1946); William Wyler's (1946) film classic *The Best Years of Our Lives*; Tennessee Williams's *A Streetcar Named Desire* (1947); Norman Mailer's *The Naked and the Dead* (1948); Alan Paton's *Cry the Beloved Country* (1948); T. S. Eliot's *Cocktail Party* (1949); and Arthur Miller's *Death of a Salesman* (1949). Ancient literature also stirred up intellectual and emotional turmoil when a Jordanian shepherd boy discovered baskets of scroll fragments that dated from the first century C.E. The Dead Sea Scrolls would prove a boon to historical and biblical scholarship.

A decade that began with war and division ended with a world newly divided. People were getting accustomed to living in an ever-present state of tension centered in cold war and the threat of nuclear annihilation. Feelings of contentment co-existed with those of personal nihilism. It was a time that was ripe for the warning signaled by George Orwell in *1984*.

CURRICULUM THOUGHT AND LITERATURE

The economy's servitude to World War II, not dissimilar in many respects to that during World War I, quelled growth in many areas, including education and its several subdivisions. Of 102 curriculum books that appeared during the forties, only 21 were published during the middle years, 1943–45. The 1940s represented a turning point in the history of the United States and a turning point in the curriculum field as well. Whereas curriculum studies in the 1920s were dominated by social behaviorists and the 1930s gave prominence to the ideas of experientialists, the 1940s cannot be characterized as being led by any one curricular orientation. Social behaviorism merged with child-centered experientialism to fashion curriculum proposals labeled either as "life needs" (predominantly experientialist in influence) or "life adjustment" education (predominantly social behaviorist). Intellectual traditionalists found a new voice in the Thomistic viewpoint of Jacques Maritain. Experientialism was extended by Earl Kelley's call for a thoroughly relativized education and Theodore Brameld's first articulations of education for social reconstruction. Conciliarists exercised their talent through the vehicles of committee reports and the synoptic text. It was a decade with important individual contributions, whether due to or in spite of the lack of a dominant perspective. It was apparent, however, that experientialism's relationship with liberal democracy was a political risk, a target for red-baiters during the advent of the Cold War.

The reconsidering of educational purposes took place in 1940 as the American Council on Education reassessed what it deemed ought to be taught by secondary schools. A 1940 White House Conference addressed purposes of schooling for children. Progressive educators' emphasis on democracy seemed to permeate this statement's interest in democracy relative to child growth. Experientialist thought continued to be well represented in many curriculum books, for example, Kilpatrick's (1940) promotion of a method of education as the forerunner of cooperative education; Wood's (1940) treatment of curriculum as an interplay of school with community life; and Goggans's (1940) stress on units and interest centers as curriculum organizing factors. However, it is emphasized that many of the sources from this decade provided an integration of contemporary perspectives and thus are best classed as conciliar in orientation, weaving together ideas from the three orientations. An example of the conciliar approach, Harold Spears (1940) offered his experience as a school administrator as foundation for a modest reform proposal for the high school curriculum. Later in the decade, Hollis Caswell (1946) influenced curriculum thought by treating the responsibility and promise of the American high school.

J. Murray Lee and Doris May Lee (1940) produced their first edition of an enduring synoptic text for elementary education. Their proposal borrowed from Henry Morrison and William H. Kilpatrick, and even recognized Jean Piaget's contribution to an understanding of a child's development of judgment. The central point of the text, however, is its indebtedness to *The Purposes of Education in American Democracy* from 1938. The authors were child-centered in the Kilpatrick tradition, encouraging a curriculum where the child's nature is the principal referent for developing curriculum, but they were inclusive of other perspectives.

A new variation on the experientialist theme was advanced by Lorenzen (1940), advancing a core curriculum that integrated subject areas to serve the study of social problems. A central feature of the core curriculum, heavily emphasized for the next 15 years, was the integration of social problems with child interest or perceived problems. A problem that could be defended for both social and student-oriented relevance would serve as the core or center of inquiry that enabled students to expand their interests and simultaneously consider problems from a combination of subject matter perspectives. The justification of a Deweyan theory of knowledge was often used in defense of this approach. Such experientialist thought, however, became increasingly integrated with the universal education thrust often promoted as America's great educational contributions stemming from the legacy of Horace Mann and Thomas Jefferson.

The study of curriculum as a dimension in the broad Deweyan interpretation of education had become largely restricted to the study of curriculum as bounded by the limits of schooling. This was the particular emphasis for Henry C. Morrison (1940) whose intellectual traditionalist orientation guided his treatment of the common school curriculum as an agency to promote study of fundamental "universal institutions," the constituent elements of civilization. These are bodies of thought, plans of action that embody (1) intelligence, (2) conscience, and (3) taste. Three essential disciplines can convey these institutions: the humanities, the sciences, and language arts. This treatment dealt with the development of these disciplines of civilized nurturance from the early primary years through junior college.

Robert Ulich (1940) produced a text that set forth a philosophy he coined "self-transcendent empiricism." While giving recognition to John Dewey and

William James, Ulich also appropriated elements of intellectual traditionalism and is a kindred spirit with A. N. Whitehead. Ulich argued that education has the responsibility for engaging people in conversation about that which is most profound and challenging about being human, pondering questions of meaning and purpose across time and cultures. This can best be done by surrounding the learner with people excited about being or becoming philosophers, poets, mystics, and scientists, eager to share ideas and discoveries.

Franklin Bobbitt, a foundational social behaviorist, produced *The Curriculum of Modern Education* (1941), a lesser-known work that seems out of character with his works of two or three decades earlier. Epitomizing his apparently altered viewpoint is a statement that appears on page 298: "Curriculum 'making' belongs with the dodo and the great auk." This carries a bit of irony when juxtaposed with his 1924 title, *How to Make a Curriculum*. Nevertheless, the point becomes clearer when it is realized that (1) Bobbitt treated education as substantively much more than schooling, a perspective not shared by most earlier social behaviorist literature and (2) he criticized any curriculum that did not seek to undertake a scientific examination of the intellectual and dispositional readiness of the learner. Packaged curriculum proposals must give way: "Current curriculum discovery, one for each child and youth, takes its place." Bobbitt acknowledged that children are educated by many personal and social forces that shape unique individuals; generalized curriculum-making misses much of that uniqueness. Individualized but still scientifically determined curricula needed to be developed. The impact, if any, that Bobbitt had on the individualization movement and the appearance of life adjustment and life needs education in the 1940s is not easy to document; however, because of his general notoriety in the field, it seems plausible to attribute some importance to this, his final book contribution.

Charles C. Peters also revised his earlier writing using a language that was more accommodating to experientialists, arguing that specific blueprints are needed to provide effective "instruction on democratic behavior" (Peters, 1942, p. 130). Whereas experientialists shift to greater specificity by the end of the decade (e.g., Stratemeyer, Forkner, and McKim, 1947, discussed below), Peters emphasized social skills rather than personal development. Peters is devoted to "life adjustment," a curriculum that directs children into the life of a democratic (and capitalist) society, not the social practice of democracy in learning communities.

In 1941, L. Thomas Hopkins was again quite visible, this time publishing *Interaction*, a book that discussed the role of democratic processes in education. Much was to be written for many years to follow on the kind of group deliberation that best contributed to sound curricular decisions. Noteworthy in this regard is J. Galen Saylor's appearance on the scene. He studied factors that are associated with participation in cooperative programs of curriculum development, and he continued to stress democratic curriculum planning in his contributions, which were destined to span the next three decades. Cooperative planning was treated in published form also by the National Commission on Cooperative Curriculum Planning, their title noting the emphasis given to this idea in 1941. The work of this group gave special consideration to the subject fields; thus, it accented a separate subject orientation that experientialists went to great length to fuse, correlate, integrate, and "core-ify." Thus, cooperation and interaction pertained both to subject matter and to the process determining it.

Analyses of actual school curricula were not absent in the first years of the forties. Bruner, Evans, Hutchcroft, Wieting, and Wood (1941) attempted to discover what schools were teaching through analyses of courses of study in social studies, science, and industrial arts. J. C. Morrison (1941) surveyed examples of activity curricula in New York City elementary schools. The National College of Education (1940) provided another book that recorded developments of their Children's School.

Results of the most massive curriculum-oriented study of the first half of the twentieth century, the Eight Year Study (circa 1933–1941), were published in 1942. This study, commissioned by the Progressive Education Association, compared traditional and progressive schools using a variety of evaluation techniques and instruments under the direction of Ralph Tyler and was presented in a five-volume set. Aikin (Volume I) provided an overview of the Eight Year Study, Giles et al. (Volume II) looked at the thirty schools involved in the study from the stance of curriculum consultants, and Smith and Tyler (Volume III) discussed evaluation methods and results.

Interpretations of the data vary, but in general the comparisons of college work of some 3,000 high school students (paired for such factors as race, family background, age, sex, and test scores) indicated that those from experimental schools (schools that used interpretations of progressive theories and practices and did not have to utilize usual college entrance requirements such as grades, class rank, required courses, etc.) did as well or better in college (relative to grades, extracurricular activities, judgment, critical thinking, and knowledge) when compared with those who attended traditional schools.

One major problem with the Eight Year Study was that programs were often dissimilar among the experimental schools; the experiences of experimental students were quite diverse, making it difficult to generalize about the best curriculum organization, design, or development. What seemed quite clear, however, was that the more novel the curriculum, that is, the further it was from tradition, the more successful the students were in college. The most novel curricular orientations involved students in community settings, made extensive use of community volunteers in schools, provided large amounts of individual contact between teachers and students, and involved peer teaching, integration of subject areas, and problem solving. Many of the progressive curriculum plans and instructional activities developed by Eight Year Study schools were the foundation for Thayer, Zachry, and Kotinsky's (1939) proposal for the redesign of secondary schools. Incidentally, the Eight Year Study extensively used portfolios with students demonstrating their work in lieu of traditional grades and test scores.

The students of Ohio State University Laboratory School offered their own personal perspective on their involvement with the Eight Year Study in *Were We Guinea Pigs?* (1938). An interesting follow-up study was reported by Willis (1961). She studied graduates from the class of 1938 of the Ohio State University Laboratory School, a novel experimental school in the Eight Year Study. These graduates were judged as highly successful in life according to questionnaire results that revealed considerable self-satisfaction, stable family situations, and contributions to professional leadership. Furthermore, they were compared with Terman's subjects in his renowned study of geniuses, and were rated higher on the above characteristics than Terman's subjects.

Other previously emphasized categories of curriculum literature were bolstered in 1942. Stephen Corey provided a treatment of general education relative to the secondary school. Parker, Menge, and Rice also dealt with secondary education relative to curriculum. The idea of developing curriculum, previously accented by Caswell and Campbell (1935), was perpetuated by Pierce in his book on the high school. J. Minor Gwynn, highly prominent in curriculum and supervision during subsequent decades, initiated his extensive contributions to curriculum and supervision literature with *Curriculum Principles and Social Trends* (1943). In doing so he capitalized on several of the burgeoning attributes of curriculum literature. His book was synoptic in the Caswell and Campbell vein, it espoused principles of Harap's "how-to" variety, and it perpetuated the notion of modernity with extensive treatment of curriculum revision and change. Gwynn's overall proposal, however, accepted H. C. Morrison's "unit method." Morrison thus provided an approach to intellectual traditionalism that most conciliarists could readily accommodate because it had such strong connections to the "unit method" in current school practice.

Particular locales produced statements that usually paralleled the standard trends and cloudy technical language of emerging synoptic texts. Examples include Lawson (1940) on city schools as contrasted with the small school thrust of the previous decade; National College of Education's (1940) *Children's School Staff Report*; the California Elementary School Principals' Association statement on school environment in reference to curriculum (1941); the Santa Barbara Schools' discussion of developmental curriculum (1941); the Universities of Florida and Oregon report on cooperative school projects (1942); and a guiding principles statement by the New York City Department of Education (1943). This emphasis on curriculum in specified locales was given international attention as well. Statements about standards by the Ministry of Education in China (1942, 1944, and 1946a and b), and a treatment by the British Secondary School Examinations Council (1943) on curriculum and examinations serve as examples of this emphasis.

Two contributions from the first half of the 1940s that moved curriculum thought in new directions were provided by Doane (1942) and Burton (1944). Doane's work was an early example of needs assessment of youth to enable more effective setting of purposes. Burton dealt with the role of teacher interaction or intervention in tailoring curriculum or learning experiences to the needs and interests of children. He included examples that point to the necessity of continuous monitoring of student interaction with their schoolwork in an effort to determine the extent to which they comprehend material rather than merely learn to produce requested results.

Two texts from 1943 give an indication of variation in intellectual traditionalist thought. Isaac Leon Kandel's criticisms of experientialism in *The Cult of Uncertainty* were a direct offspring of W. C. Bagley's essentialist movement. Jacques Maritain, in contrast, based his proposal, *Education at the Crossroads*, on a contention that there are fundamental qualities to the human character that are responsive to a meaningful education. Maritain called for a modernization of the liberal arts, the Trivium and the Quadrivium, as that curriculum which best fostered these common human attributes.

Herbert Read's classic work, *Education through Art*, first appeared in Great Britain in the midst of the Second World War. Read produced a work remarkable for its anticipation of the concept of multiple intelligences and its insightful understanding of child development through the maturation of the aesthetic sensibilities. Read is one of the first writers on education to advance the ideas of Carl Jung in his proposal. He argued that elementary education should not be about the accumulation of facts; rather, it should respond to the sensibilities of the child by fostering her or his capacities for self-expression. The integrative center of education is located through craftwork (a construct derived from Edmond Holmes and John Dewey) with visual, musical, plastic, kinetic, verbal, and constructive artistic endeavors. He wrote, "Education is the fostering of growth, but apart from physical maturation, growth is only made apparent in expression—audible or visible signs and symbols....The aim of education is therefore the creation of artists—of people efficient in the various modes of expression" (Read, 1943, p. 11).

A major extrapolation of Horace Mann's notion of the common school took place in the mid-forties under the rubric of "general education." The central concern was that if the ideal of the common school exists in the United States, if almost all children and youth attend school, what is the common core of knowledge, skills, and attitudes that they should acquire for intelligent citizenry? Stemming from their *Purposes of Education in American Democracy* of 1938, the Educational Policies Commission of the National Education Association devised a postwar canon of common learning and stated them as imperative needs of youth in *Education for All American Youth* (1944), a statement endorsed by the National Association of Secondary School Principals. The 10 imperative needs dealt with salable skills, health, competent citizenship, good family membership, defensible consumerism, scientific methodology, aesthetic appreciations, wise use of leisure time, democratic values, and rational thought. Even a cursory look at this statement of imperative needs would enable the curriculum student to note the implicit synthesis of schools of curriculum thought. Examples that prevailed included the addressing of both contemporary needs by the social behaviorist and the time-honored virtues of intellectual traditionalists. The lack of emphasis on experiential thought, an important part of the 1938 statement, indicates how policy, a conciliar product, was sensitive to the contemporary discussions. Such statements seemed to be developing a tendency to amalgamate, whether this attempt to synthesize diverse perspectives produced statements that were greater than each constituent school taken separately or whether they were attempts to placate proponents of each school by granting inclusion of some of their views. To consider a curriculum proposal predicated on an experientialist interpretation of the needs of contemporary adolescents in a democratic society, the earlier work of Thayer, Zachry, and Kotinsky (1939) provides contrasting points of emphasis.

In 1945, the Harvard Committee on the Objectives of a General Education in a Free Society (1945) published their summary report. While conceding that three-fourths of high school graduates did not attend college, the Committee rejected the notion that there should be curricular specialization demarcating college preparation from workplace readiness. The Committee suggested that all high school students should be provided with a general background in English (at least three years), social sciences (at least two years), natural sciences, and mathematics (at least three years). This general education should be provided in ways that are tailored to methods of learning and abilities that fit less gifted and less academically oriented students as well as the general population and the exceptional learner. These areas, they argued, should be presented in such a manner that would enable students to think effectively, communicate well, make relevant judgments, and develop values. The fine arts, physical education, and health were recognized as important aspects of education, but the statement offered no specific curricular guidelines. Elective coursework, the Committee suggested, permitted college-bound students to specialize more deliberately in academic coursework and also afforded opportunity for students who did not plan on continuing into higher education to acquire vocational training. The end result of the proposal was closely aligned to existing practices in many high schools in the United States, authorizing the status quo. The 1946 republication of the 1938 Educational Policies Commission statement of purposes in a larger document called *Policies for Education in American Democracy* further bolstered the argument for general education.

The creation of new options for education in the postwar era was variously interpreted. In 1944, the Association for Supervision and Curriculum Development (ASCD) produced *Toward a New Curriculum* as their yearbook. In the same year, Offner treated the matter of change relative to curriculum in teachers' colleges. In Great Britain, too, the Council for Curriculum Reform (1945) pushed for change toward the novel, labeling it "reform." Similarly, the National Society for the Study of Education's *Forty-fourth Yearbook, Part I* (1945) called for curriculum reconstruction in American education of the postwar period. A number of scholars contributed to this work were highly influential in curriculum literature during the next several decades. Notable in this regard were Ralph Tyler, a key evaluator in the Eight Year Study, and Hilda Taba, who laid groundwork for her later work in a chapter entitled "General Techniques of Curriculum Planning" (pp. 80-115). The above interest in novelty and change was combined with another interest from the thirties, that of decision making. A synthesis of both foci is evident in the 1946 treatment of curriculum change by Alice Miel. She saw curriculum decision making as more than an exercise of rationality; it was also a social process. Although her book had considerable impact, much time elapsed before curricularists again expressed the import of the message she advanced. Storen, however, produced an ASCD publication in the same year that called for lay participation in curriculum planning as a social process.

Perhaps the most radical proposal of the decade came from Theodore Brameld of the University of Minnesota (Brameld, Hovet, O'Shaughnessy, & Traphagen, 1945). In collaboration with a school administrator and two teachers from the Floodwood Minnesota High School, they reported on an experiment in democratic education that put into practice social reconstructionist principles. George Counts, having received a political rebuking for his perspectives on the social purpose of the American curriculum, also persisted in promoting a curriculum for social reform (1946). Sidney Hook (1946), writing from a perspective more directly aligned with Dewey's proposal for education, suggested a curriculum that provided students with the opportunity to critically evaluate current social problems.

Among the miscellaneous, though not less significant, contributions to curriculum literature of the mid-forties are Baker's (1945) report on curriculum planning based on questions asked by children; Martens's (1946) call for curriculum adjustments for gifted students; and a Pennsylvania (1946) plan for local participation in curriculum revision. Several new treatments of perennial curriculum topics were made in the mid-forties: Fleming (1946) contributed to the relation of research and curriculum; Cole (1946) provided a text on elementary school curriculum with specific emphasis on subject areas; and Jersild (1946) drew on his extensive background in child development, advancing curriculum implications.

The last years of the 1940s brought another in the line of synoptic or comprehensive curriculum books, that is, books that presented several curriculum orientations in encyclopedic fashion, and from them derived guidelines for curriculum developers to follow. In 1947, a synoptic text produced by Florence B. Stratemeyer of Teachers College, Hamden Forkner, and Margaret McKim added new dimensions to the evolution of that kind of text. The notions of development and of modernity were stressed throughout. The authors discussed bases and sources of curriculum development, its purpose and strategies, and disclosed a greater array of persons who contribute to curriculum development processes than were conventionally treated in the literature. They interpenetrated most of the book with continual emphasis on the role that childhood activity should be given in the curriculum development process. Namely, curriculum experiences should be drawn from analysis of persistent life situations faced by children and youth. Nearly 200 pages of specific examples were provided to indicate the implementation of a "persistent life needs" curriculum. The elaborate lists and directions provided by the authors are as complex as anything produced in the heyday of social behaviorists with their detailed objectives. Stratemeyer, Forkner, and McKim argued, however, that learners should have a primary role in developing curricula, and the actual teaching-learning situation should itself be considered curricular.

A contrasting perspective on an education for contemporary living, derived from a social behaviorist platform, was provided by the Federal Security Agency (FSA, 1947). *Life Adjustment Education for Every Youth* was an extension of a speech given by Charles Prosser at the 40th Annual Meeting of the American Vocational Association. Prosser argued that although educational institutions were currently prepared to address the lives of the 20% of adolescents who went on to college and the 20% who go on to skilled trade as a result of vocational education, 60% of young adults were not being served. The document called for a renewed commitment to the curriculum promoted in the *Cardinal Principles* and in subsequent Educational Policies Commission documents. The emphasis is clearly on vocational preparation. In a work coauthored with Thomas Quigley (Prosser & Quigley, 1949), Prosser argued that rearing democratic citizens requires that society prepare students for industry and also prepare industry for an intelligent work force. Educators need to set aside aristocratic notions of education for leisure and train youth to contribute to social institutions. Their conclusion: "the more democratic a society, the more industrial its civilization" (Prosser & Quigley, 1949, p. 16).

Other variations on the synoptic text that had considerable enduring influence were introduced in the forties. One major type began with a comprehensive overview of the field and then moved toward specialization in either secondary or elementary curriculum. J. P. Leonard's *Developing the Secondary School Curriculum* (1946) is an example. The work began with historical perspectives that set schooling and curriculum in historical context and continued by providing discussions of trends, theoretical perspectives, and evaluation. Following these considerations, Leonard focused on secondary school curriculum by relating the core curriculum idea to the units of work, and considering means for revision and modernization.

In 1947, Harl R. Douglass edited a collection of articles on secondary curriculum that, by their organization, first established perspectives relative to society and schooling and moved into treatments of general curriculum development issues and specific subject areas at the secondary level. In the same year, Harold Alberty published *Reorganizing the High School Curriculum*, a book that was dedicated to and in many ways emulated Alberty's mentor, Boyd H. Bode. Alberty discussed curriculum foundations, moved to design and implementation, and treated planning and the process of deliberation extensively. Alberty proposed a "resource unit," a carefully designed curriculum for the secondary school that critically examines contemporary social problems. Alberty's "resource unit" gained great popularity as a tool to be used by the second generation of social reconstruction experientialists in the 1950s (e.g., Smith, Stanley, and Shores [1950] and Theodore Brameld [1956]). Harold Spears added to the growing line of comprehensive texts, providing a distinctive practice-oriented flavor in his revision of *The Emerging High School Curriculum and Its Direction* (1948).

The late forties also brought its share of miscellaneous topics, some of which would prove quite influential in subsequent curriculum literature. The topic of organization was given increased attention relative to elementary schools by the Association for Supervision and Curriculum Development in 1947. Noar's (1948) emphasis on units and the Bathurst, Blackwood, Mackintosh, and Schneider (1949) treatment of the place of subject areas in the curriculum reflect this interest. A review of curriculum laboratories in the United States by Drag (1947) shows a concern for actual cases. So do reports on development in particular locales, for example, California (1948), Loftus (1948), the NEA (1948), Tasmania (1948), Wisconsin (1948), New York (1949), and Ohio State (1949).

The desire to know what had occurred in certain spheres of curriculum development was responded to in 1949 by Harlan Shores, who critically reviewed research from 1890 to 1949 on elementary school organization. Postwar reflections brought realization that the armed services had, in fact, developed curricula to prepare members of the military for war and the concomitant conclusion that such curriculum development could be studied for its implications for schools. Goodman (1947) pursued such investigations. In 1948, the Association for Childhood Education accented this action-oriented dimension of curriculum construction by examining a very different form of curriculum practice.

Postwar sentiments also contributed to the decline of progressive education. It became apparent that reflection on the war, combined with evolving conservatism as seen in the quests for performers of un-American activities, provided escort service for a not-so-gradual exit from the curricular scene by progressive education. The influential status of progressive education prior to World War II established it as a convenient scapegoat for societal ills that surrounded the times. The growth of experientialist curriculum thought was temporarily halted. This was accompanied by an emerging attentiveness to the "nuts and bolts" of education, that is, basic skills instead of progressive intangibles. This kind of reaction frequently accompanies the "let's get back to business" response that follows wars. Such was symbolized in Hildreth's (1947) *Learning the Three R's* and Mortimer Smith's (1949) *And Madly Teach*. A conservative's curricular consciousness-raising about the purpose of knowledge itself was provided by Lynd in *Knowledge for What?* (1948). No small part of the return to basics was inherent in the problem of providing general education. The Educational Policies Commission spelled out the priority as revealed in the title of its 1948 publication, *Education for All American Children*.

The debate about purposes for American education was seriously pursued at length by Harold Rugg (1947), continuing to work from an experientialist orientation. Carolyn Pratt, a dedicated early childhood teacher, later professor, in the first half of the twentieth century titled a book *I Learn from Children* (1948). The work is a refreshing practitioner's perspective on the successes that result from building a curriculum *with* learners rather than *for* children. Harold Benjamin's cautionary tale of the "animal" school, offered in his Inglis Lecture and published as *The Cultivation of Idiosyncrasy*, is a delightful reminder that education must build on the strengths of each student. He rejected the popular calls to general education as a trimming down of the gifts of individuality for the sake of convenience and conformity. Also swimming against the tide of prevalent opinion was Earl Kelley. His *Education for What Is Real* (1947) argued for a total individualization of the curriculum to coordinate with the realization that all reality is a personal construct. Based on the research on perception by Adelbert Ames at the Hanover Institute, Kelley concluded that educators cannot "teach" knowledge, only the tools of critical perception. The work stands somewhere between experientialism and existentialism, hinting at themes that would be developed by postmodernists a generation later.

Finally, and of immense influence not only in the forties but in the whole of curriculum literature, was the 1949 appearance of Ralph Tyler's *Basic Principles of Curriculum and Instruction*. It was originally created as a course syllabus for Education 360 at the University of Chicago. Although this book raised issues considered by Dewey, Bobbitt, Harap, Hopkins, Charters, Caswell, Bode, Stratemeyer, and others who published earlier, they were rationally organized and concisely stated, making them compelling vehicles for thinking and learning about the elements of curriculum and instruction. Essentially, Tyler raised four categories of consideration that he claimed were basic to curriculum development: purposes, experiences, organization, and evaluation. In suggesting these topics he provided the following: (1) sources and procedures that schools could use to determine purposes; (2) principles and illustrations for studying and developing learning experiences that enable the attainment of the purposes; (3) considerations for organizing the learning experiences; and (4) procedures for evaluating the effectiveness of the learning experiences. The format of numerous curriculum guides, teachers' editions of schoolbooks, lesson plan books, evaluation instruments by accrediting agencies, course syllabi, and many curriculum books that appeared in the next 30 years are organized around Tyler's four topics.

Like others who have had impact on curriculum study, Tyler's work has not been immune to criticism. One type of criticism, however, erroneously assumes that Tyler intended that his questions be rigidly pursued in step-wise fashion. This kind of faulty interpretation was anticipated and countered by Tyler in the final chapter of his book. He unambiguously stated that the sequence of considerations is flexible and contingent on a multiplicity of situational attributes. Other criticisms contend that he overemphasized rationality as contrasted with political, social, and economic conditions. These human conditions often call for other categorical systems to map curricular phenomena. One point is clear, however: The curriculum student who looks carefully at the literature of the next three decades will recognize the vast influence of Tyler's *Basic Principles of Curriculum and Instruction*. Tyler might best be characterized as a moderator of the curriculum discussion. While not articulating direct allegiance with any of the three curriculum orientations, Tyler did not hold the philosophic interests of Whitehead or Ulich, nor did he desire to locate practical approaches in the midst of theoretical debate, the ambition of conciliar writers. Tyler framed the discussion of all orientations for the coming generation in an elegant structure that any of the orientations could employ. It is a disservice to dismiss or misrepresent this outstanding intellectual contribution to the field.

As a footnote in their study, curriculum students would do well to keep in mind Tyler's advocacy of a unified view of curriculum and instruction. He apparently assumed that the same or similar principles apply to both. The relation of curriculum and instruction, as noted earlier, is a topic about which no small debate has raged in curriculum circles. Thus, the curriculum literature of the 1940s bolstered the character of the field by providing: (1) a strong precedent for curriculum research; (2) a tendency to centralize curriculum knowledge and priorities through the work of associations and commissions; (3) a continuation of synoptic curriculum texts; and (4) a concise formulation of categories that established boundaries of curriculum literature for at least a generation.

BIBLIOGRAPHY OF CURRICULUM BOOKS 1940–1949

1940

American Council on Education, American Youth Commission. (1940). *What the high schools ought to teach; the report of a special committee on the secondary school curriculum* (Ben G. Graham, Chairman; Thomas H. Briggs, Will French, et al.). Washington, DC: American Council on Education.

Ch'en, T. H. (1940). *Developing patterns of the college curriculum in the United States*. Los Angeles: The University of Southern California Press.

Dale, E. (1940). *Building a learning environment*. Bloomington, IN: Phi Delta Kappa Educational Foundation.

Goggans, S. (1940). *Units of work and centers of interest in the organization of the elementary school curriculum*. New York: Teachers College, Columbia University, (Reprinted by AMS 1972, New York).

Kilpatrick, W. H. (1940). *Group education for a democracy*. New York: Association Press.

Lawson, D. E. (1940). *Curriculum development in city school systems*. Chicago: University of Chicago Press.

Lee, J. M., & Lee, D. M. (1940). *The child and his curriculum*. New York: Appleton-Century-Crofts.

Lorenzen, S. (1940). *Planning a core curriculum*. Bulletin Number 9. Connecticut Curriculum Center. Storrs: Connecticut Curriculum Center.

Morrison, H. C. (1940). *The curriculum of the common school, from the beginning of the primary school to the end of the junior college*. Chicago: University of Chicago Press. (Reprinted by Folcroft, 1977).

National College of Education, Children's School Staff. (1940). *Curriculum records of the children's school, National College of Education*. Evanston, IL: Bureau of publications, National College of Education.

Spears, H. (1940). *The emerging high school curriculum and its direction*. New York: American Book Company.

Ulich, R. (1940). *Fundamentals of democratic education*. New York: American Book Company.

Umstattd, J. G., & Hammock, R. (1940). *Proceedings of the 1939 curriculum conference and study group*. Austin: University of Texas.

White House Conference on Children in a Democracy. (1940). *Final Report*. United States Children's Bureau. Washington, DC: Government Printing Office.

Wood, H. B. (1940). *The school curriculum and community life*. Eugene: University of Oregon.

1941

Bobbitt, F. (1941). *The curriculum of modern education*. New York: McGraw-Hill. (Also Norwood Editions).

Bruner, H. B., Evans, H. M., Hutchcroft, C. R., Wieting, C. M, & Wood, H. B. (1941). *What our schools are teaching: An analysis of the content of selected courses of study with special reference to science, social studies, and industrial arts*. New York: Bureau of Publications, Teachers College, Columbia University.

California Elementary School Principals' Association. (1941). *The elementary school environment and the modern curriculum*. Los Angeles: Elementary School Principals' Association.

Hopkins, L. T. (1941). *Interaction: The democratic process*. Boston: D. C. Heath.

Morrison, H. C., et al. (1941). *The activity program: A survey of the curriculum experiment with the activity program in the elementary schools of the city of New York*. Albany, NY: State Department of Education.

National Commission on Cooperative Curriculum Planning. (1941). *The subject fields in general education*. New York: D. Appleton-Century Company, Inc.

Santa Barbara (California) Schools. (1941). *Developmental curriculum*. Bulletin Number One, Revision Number One, November.

Saylor, J. G. (1941). *Factors associated with participation in cooperative programs of curriculum development*. New York: Bureau of Publications, Teachers College, Columbia University. (Reprinted by AMS, 1972, New York).

1942

Aikin, W. M. (1942). *The story of the eight year study*. New York: Harper and Brothers.

Chamberlin, C. D., Chamberlin, E. S., Drought, N. F., & Scott, W. E. (1942). *Did they succeed in college? The follow-up study of the graduates of the thirty schools*. New York: Harper and Brothers.

Chinese Ministry of Education. (1942). *Curriculum standards for the elementary school*. Shanghai, China: Cheng Chung Book Company.

Corey, S. M. (1942). *General education and the American high school*. Chicago: Scott Foresman.

Doane, D. C. (1942). *The needs of youth: An evaluation for curriculum purposes*. New York: Teachers College, Columbia University. (Reprinted by AMS, 1972, New York).

Educational Policies Commission. (1942). *A war policy for American schools*. Washington, DC: National Education Association.

Eight Year Study. (1942). *Adventures in American education series, volumes I-V*. New York: Harper Brothers. (Volume I, by W. M. Aikin, cited above; Volume II, by H. H. Giles, S. P. McCutchen & A. M. Zechiel, cited below; Volume III, by E. R. Smith, R. W. Tyler, and the Evaluation Staff, cited below; Volume IV, by D. Chamberlin, E. S. Chamberlin, N. F. Drought & W. E. Scott, *Did they succeed in college?*; and Volume V, by the thirty schools, *Thirty schools tell their story*.)

Florida, University of, & Oregon, University of. (1942). *Cooperating school projects as a technique of curriculum improvement*. Gainesville, FL: University of Florida.

Giles, H. H., et al. (1942). *Exploring the curriculum: The work of thirty schools from the viewpoint of curriculum consultants*. Eight Year Study, Volume II. New York: Harper and Brothers.

Parker, J. C., Menge, W., & Rice, T. D. (1942). *The first five years of the secondary schools curriculum, 1937–1942*. Lansing, MI: Michigan Study of the Secondary School Curriculum. State Board of Education.

Peters, C. C. (1942). *The curriculum of democratic education*. New York: McGraw-Hill.

Pierce, P. R. (1942). *Developing a high school curriculum*. New York: The American Book Company.

Smith, E. R., Tyler, R. W., & the Evaluation Staff. (1942). *Appraising and recording student progress*. New York: Harper and Brothers.

1943

Berkson, I. B. (1943). *Education faces the future*. New York: Harper and Bros.

Britain Secondary School Examinations Council. (1943). *Curriculum and examinations in secondary schools*. London: Her Majesty's Stationery Office.

Educational Policies Commission. (1943). *Education and the people's peace*. Washington, DC: National Education Association.

Gwynn, J. M. (1943). *Curriculum principles and social trends*. New York: Macmillan.

Kandel, I. L. (1943). *The cult of uncertainty*. New York: Macmillan.

Maritain, J. (1943). *Education at the crossroads*. New Haven, CT: Yale University Press.

New York City Department of Education. (1943). *Guiding principles in curriculum development*. Brooklyn, NY: Department of Education.

Norwood, C. (1943). *Curriculum and instruction in secondary schools*. London: His Majesty's Stationery Office.

Read, H. (1943). *Education through art*. New York: Pantheon.

Thirty Schools. (1943). *Thirty schools tell their story*. New York: Harper and Brothers.

1944

Association for Supervision and Curriculum Development. (1944). *Toward a new curriculum*. 1944 Yearbook. Washington, DC: Author.

Burton, W. H. (1944). *The guidance of learning activities*. New York: D. Appleton-Century.

Chinese Ministry of Education. (1944). *A plan for the six years' curriculum standard in secondary schools*. Shanghai, China: Cheng Chung Book Company.

Educational Policies Commission. (1944). *Education for all American youth*. Washington, DC: National Education Association.

Indiana Department of Public Instruction. (1944). *A good start in school; a curriculum handbook for primary teachers*. Indianapolis, IN: Department of Public Instruction.

Offner, H. L. (1944). *Administrative procedures for changing curriculum patterns for selected state teachers colleges; with special reference to New Jersey, New York and Pennsylvania*. New York: Bureau of Publications Teachers College, Columbia University.

1945

Baker, E. V. (1945). *Children's questions and their implications for planning the curriculum with special reference to the contribution of the natural and social sciences in the intermediate grade curriculum*. New York: Teachers College, Columbia University.

Brameld, T., Hovet, K., O'Shaughnesey, D., & Traphagen, D. (1945). *Design for America: An educational exploration of the future of democracy for senior high schools and junior colleges*. New York: Hinds, Hayden and Eldridge.

Council for Curriculum Reform. (1945). *The content of education; proposals for the school curriculum, being the interim report of the Council for Curriculum Reform*. Bickley, Kent: University of London Press, Ltd.

Harvard Committee on the Objectives of a General Education in a Free Society. (1945). *General education in a free society*. Cambridge, MA: Harvard University Press.

National Society for the Study of Education. (1945). *American education in the postwar period: Curriculum reconstruction*. (N.B. Henry, Ed.). Forty-Fourth Yearbook, Part I. Chicago: University of Chicago Press.

1946

Caswell, H. L. (Ed.). (1946). *The American high school: Its responsibility and opportunity* (Eighth Yearbook of the John Dewey Society). New York: Harper and Brothers.

Chinese Ministry of Education. (1946a). *Curriculum standards for the normal school*. Shanghai, China: Cheng Chung Book Company.

Chinese Ministry of Education. (1946b). *Revised curriculum standards for junior and senior high schools*. Shanghai, China: Cheng Chung Book Company.

Cole, L. (1946). *The elementary school subjects*. New York: Rinehart and Company, Incorporated.

Counts, G. S. (1946). *Education and the promise of America*. New York: Macmillan.

Educational Policies Commission. (1946). *Policies for education in American democracy*. Washington, DC: The Educational Policies Commission of the NEA and the AASA.

Fleming, C. M. (1946). *Research and the basic curriculum*. London: University of London Press.

Hook, S. (1946). *Education for modern man*. New York: Dial Press.

Jersild, A. T. (1946). *Child development and the curriculum*. New York: Teachers College, Columbia University.

Leidecker, K. F. (1946). *Yankee teacher: The life of William Torrey Harris*. New York: Philosophical Library.

Leonard, J. P. (1946). *Developing the secondary school curriculum*. New York: Rinehart and Company.

Martens, E. H. (1946). *Curriculum adjustments for gifted children*. Washington, DC: U.S. Office of Education.

Miel, A. (1946). *Changing the curriculum: A social process*. New York: Appleton-Century.

Pennsylvania Department of Public Instruction. (1946). *Local participation in state-wide revision of the elementary school curriculum*. Harrisburg: Pennsylvania Department of Public Instruction.

Storen, H. F. (1946). *Laymen help plan for the curriculum*. Washington, DC: Association for Supervision and Curriculum Development.

1947

Alberty, H. (1947). *Reorganizing the high school curriculum*. New York: Macmillan.

Association for Supervision and Curriculum Development. (1947). *Organizing the elementary school for living and learning*. Washington, DC: National Education Association.

Benjamin, H. (1947). *The cultivation of idiosyncrasy*. The Inglis Lecture, Cambridge, MA: Harvard University.

Douglass, H. R. (Ed.). (1947). *The high school curriculum*. New York: Ronald Press.

Drag, F. L. (1947). *Curriculum Laboratories in the United States*. San Diego, CA: Office of the County Superintendent of Schools.

Federal Security Agency. (1947). *Life adjustment education for every youth*. Washington, DC: Federal Security Agency.

Goodman, S. M. (1947). *Curriculum implications of armed services education programs*. Washington, DC: American Council on Education.

Hildreth, G. H. (1947). *Learning the three R's* (Second edition). Minneapolis, MN: Educational Publishers.

Kelley, E. C. (1947). *Education for what is real*. New York: Harper and Bros.

Rugg, H. O. (1947). *Foundations for American education*. Yonkers-on-the-Hudson, NY: World Book Company.

Stratemeyer, F. B., Forkner, H. L., & McKim, M. G. (1947). *Developing a curriculum for modern living*. New York: Bureau of Publications, Teachers College, Columbia University.

1948

Association for Childhood Education. (1948). *Curriculum at work* (F. Mayfarth, Ed.). Washington, DC: Association for Childhood Education.

California Elementary School Principals' Association. (1948). *Principal and curriculum building*. Twentieth Yearbook.

Chu, Chih-hsien. (1948). *Curriculum for elementary schools*. Shanghai, China: Commercial Press.

Educational Policies Commission. (1948). *Education for all American children*. Washington, DC: National Education Association.

Loftus, J. J. (1948). *The story of how a great school system developed a new educational program*. Chicago: F. E. Compton.

Lynd, R. S. (1948). *Knowledge for what?* Princeton, NJ: Princeton University Press.

National Education Association of the United States, Department of Secondary School Principals. (1948). *Curriculum trends in the secondary school: A series of articles that describe curriculum provision and developments for youth in many sections of the country.* Washington, DC: National Association of Secondary School Principals.

Noar, G. (1948). *Freedom to live and learn: Techniques for selecting and developing units of learning in the modern classroom.* Philadelphia: Franklin.

Pratt, C. (1948). *I learn from children.* New York: Harper & Row.

Spears, H. (1948). *The emerging high school curriculum and its direction* (Second edition). New York: American Book Company.

Tasmanian Education Department. (1948). *Curriculum for primary schools.* Hobart, Tasmania: H.H. Pimblett, Government Printer.

Wisconsin Cooperative Educational Planning Program. (1948). *Underlying principles and implementations.* Madison, WI: State Superintendent, J. Calahan.

1949

Bathurst, E. G., Blackwood, P. E., Mackintosh, H. K., & Schneider, E. (1949). *The place of subjects in the curriculum.* Educational Bulletin Number 12. Washington, DC: Office of Education.

Central New York Study Council Committee on Flexibility. (1949). *Toward a more flexible elementary school curriculum: A second report* (Prepared by Arthur E. Smith). Syracuse, NY: Central New York School Study Council.

Montessori, M. (1949). *Education and peace.* Chicago: Henry Regnery Company.

New York City Board of Education. (1949). *Source materials in curriculum development.* Brooklyn, NY: New York City Board of Education.

Ohio State University College of Education. (1949). *How to develop a core program in the high school* (Directed by H. Alberty). Columbus: Ohio State University, College of Education.

Prosser, C. A., & Quigley, T. H. (1949). *Vocational education in a democracy.* Chicago: American Technical Society.

Shores, J. H. (1949). *A critical review of the research on elementary school curriculum organization 1890–1949.* Urbana, IL: College of Education, Bureau of Research and Service, University of Illinois.

Smith, M. (1949). *And madly teach: A layman looks at public school education.* Chicago: Henry Regnery.

Tyler, R. W. (1949). *Basic principles of curriculum and instruction.* Chicago: University of Chicago Press.

CHAPTER SIX

Curriculum Literature and Context
1950–1959

CONTEXTUAL REMINDERS

The victory of the Second World War positioned the United States as an unquestioned world leader militarily, economically, and in social influence. The postwar recession had been averted by a rapid transition to production of consumer goods. Impatient from wartime shortages, Americans busied themselves with procuring all the economic benefits of living in a superpower nation, creating huge suburban sprawls in places like Levittown, Pennsylvania, and Park Forest, Illinois, purchasing new, faster, more powerful automobiles representing a different kind of freedom ("See the USA in your Chevrolet," Dinah Shore reminded the American people).

Gathering in one of 10 million neighbors' homes to watch Milton Berle, *Your Show of Shows*, *The Big Top*, *The Lone Ranger*, *I Love Lucy*, and *Gillette's Cavalcade of Sports*, it was difficult for the viewers to imagine the impact that television would have on culture. It was the decade of *The Man in the Gray Flannel Suit*. Many Americans were quite content with the status quo as long as they could pursue their individual economic ambitions. Even though they eschewed the notion that they exerted power over much of the globe, Americans delighted in fronting larger-than-life icons to represent their social ideals. Like the twenties, there was a general relaxation of sexual mores in the fifties. Hugh Hefner's *Playboy* magazine could be seen on coffee tables in middle-class homes, depicting the ideal nude form (female, white, young, middle class, with plans). Marilyn Monroe represented sexuality; James Dean represented rebellious, misunderstood youth; Mickey Mantle and Johnny Unitas represented athletic prowess. In fiction, the popularity of the Cold War anti-hero was evidenced by the appearance of Ian Fleming's James Bond in his first novel, *Casino Royale*. Fidelity was down, divorce was up, tranquilizers were in. Before the decade ran its course, America would have the TV dinner, rock 'n' roll, the beginning of the interstate highway system, and two new states, Alaska and Hawaii. In contrast to the laissez-faire twenties, Americans in the fifties were more purposeful and, having known the Depression and World War II, more intent on personal and financial security.

On the one hand, it seemed like a time of peace with potential for prosperity. On the other hand, it appeared that the entire world stood on the brink of destruction. Isolationism was never an option. The war, it seemed, had only succeeded in redefining global power relationships and some influential U.S. citizens found it easier to understand this world in as few a number of divisions and with the least number of major players as possible. The persistent tension and hostility between the Soviet and U.S. camps, the Cold War, made for the least complex division and perhaps the least accurate.

The world could never forget the devastating power of atomic warfare that ended the war with Japan. Both communist and democratic powers possessed an ever-increasing stockpile of weapons that, by comparison, dwarfed even those that had destroyed Nagasaki and Hiroshima. The fear that world war was now equal to world obliteration was real, not wholly unwarranted, and contributed to both fatalistic thinking and paranoid action. Fear prompted the search for spies. Klaus Fuchs was convicted in England for giving secrets on the atomic bomb to the Soviets. He was sentenced to 14 years in prison. In the United States, Ethel and Julius Rosenberg were convicted of sharing secrets on the making of nuclear weapons. The charge of high treason carried the death penalty. Their executions were viewed by some as victimization to national hysteria. This fear was manifested in the spirit of inquisition that seized the nation when Senator Joseph McCarthy of Wisconsin led the House Un-American Activities Committee on a hunt for communists throughout the United States. When McCarthy, apparently invincible, contended that the Truman administration had been rife with communist influence and that the Army was also infected, his bravado had finally exceeded what even conservatives considered useful to their interests. Edward R. Murrow, a highly respected CBS newsperson, conducted a successful media campaign to expose McCarthy. Combined with a challenge by the Army, McCarthy was censured by the Senate in 1954 and this tragic dimension of domestic Cold War politics ended.

In 1950 the Korean War began. United Nations forces helped South Korea under the leadership of General Douglas MacArthur, and North Korea was aided by the People's Republic of China. For many who wavered on the issue of the reality of the Cold War, Korea legitimated the warning of a communist threat, warranted or not. In 1951, the fervor of the "beat the Communists" attitude was reduced a bit by President Truman's removal of MacArthur in an effort to quell the desire kindled by the general to expand the war by attacking North Korean supply depots across the Yalu River in China. Peace negotiations, dampened by Chinese accusations that the United States was using germ warfare in Korea, continued throughout 1952. In the same year the war ended with the signing of an armistice at Panmunjon. South Korea and the United States signed a mutual defense treaty in the same year. Indo-Chinese forces gained independence from the French for Vietnam, Cambodia, and Laos at the Battle of Dien Bien Phu. A very unstable treaty accepted the separation of Vietnam into a northern sector under the leadership of Ho Chi Minh and a southern sector that remained up for exploitation.

Changes in leadership of the two major world powers occurred in 1952 and 1953. Hero of the Second World War's European campaign General Dwight D. Eisenhower, campaigning against a bloated and out-of-touch federal government that "bungled" the Korean War, became U.S. president in a sweeping Republican victory over Adlai Stevenson. The death of Josef Stalin resulted in a high stakes power play for Soviet leadership. Nikita Khrushchev emerged as Soviet premier in 1958, ousting Nikolai Bulganin.

In 1954, the USSR rejected Western suggestions that Germany be reunited; the occupation of West Germany by Britain, France, and the United States was terminated, although a divided Berlin remained. West Germany became a member of NATO. Other alliances evolved to prevent military aggressions between the major powers of the free and communist worlds. In 1954, Japan and the United States established a mutual defense agreement. In the same year the Southeast Asian Defense Treaty was actualized by Australia, Britain, France, New Zealand, Pakistan, the Philippines, Thailand, and the United States. The Warsaw Pact was signed in the following year, initiated by the USSR to offset NATO in the continual press of the major powers to tip the scales in the balance of power. The effort to control through alliance was continued in 1955 at a Geneva conference, attended by 72 nations, to discuss peaceful uses of atomic energy. Under the leadership of Dag Hammarskjöld, who succeeded Trygve Lie as secretary-general, the United Nations made notable strides, but was also impeded by the major powers, who increasingly controlled international decisions and actions, both economically and politically.

Meanwhile in Europe, economic cooperation was on the upswing. In 1950 West German Chancellor Konrad Adenauer proposed cooperation between France and Germany, and in 1951–1953 the European Coal and Steel Community was planned, actualized, and implemented. In Britain, after a brief interlude in which Clement Attlee served as prime minister, Winston Churchill recaptured that role in 1951. In 1952 King George VI died and was succeeded by Queen Elizabeth II.

Much of the world was dominated by political strongmen from either the left or the right. Single names were recognized as powerful, stable, and often ruthless managers of their nations, for example, Tito of Yugoslavia, Franco of Spain, Mao in China. A neocolonial relationship of southern hemisphere countries with industrial powers was under construction. In western Asia, the nationalization of the oil industry in Iran, controlled by Reza Pahlevi, the Shah of Iran, led to altercations with Britain in 1951 and 1952. King Faisal II controlled Iraq through much of the fifties, but was overthrown in a coup in 1958. Jordan's king was assassinated in Jerusalem, but his son, Hussein, assumed power and quickly evidenced his skill in maneuvering through troubled political waters.

When Gamel Abdel Nasser assumed direction of Egypt in 1952, the country became a republic with dictatorial overtones. Egypt began to exert its independence by repealing treaties with Britain and demanding control of the Suez. In 1954, Egypt and Britain agreed to the evacuation of British troops from the Suez Canal Zone. This action was followed in 1956 by Egypt's seizure of the canal from French and British commercial interests. French, British, and Israeli forces invaded the Canal Zone in Egyptian territory, at which point the USSR threatened to intervene. United Nations forces entered, and France and Britain withdrew. In 1957, Egypt reopened the canal.

Colonialism came under attack throughout Africa, notably in Morocco in 1953, Malaya and the Gold Coast in 1954. Although Britain was resigned to redefining its relationship with its former colonies, it sought to control this transition. For example, Jamo Kenyatta, president of the Kenya Africa Union, was arrested by the British for supporting Mau Mau terrorism. Algeria began a movement to free itself from French control. India and Pakistan, having moved beyond colonial control, continued to be locked in a hostile dispute over control of Kashmir.

Nations under the influence of the United States were also subject to tyranny. Fulgenzio Batista reestablished his cruel dictatorship in Cuba in 1952, spawning a revolutionary movement under the direction of Fidel Castro and Che Guevara. In Nicaragua, a long-term dictatorship was established by Anastazio Samoza. François ("Papa Doc") Duvalier took control of Haiti. In 1954, the United States directly intervened on behalf of the United Fruit Company to oust the elected president of Guatemala, Jacobo Arbenz Guzman, to install a military dictatorship more amenable to U.S. corporate interests.

While peaceful coexistence was actively sought through organized effort, international conflicts in the mid-fifties provided seedbeds of international strife for many years to follow. Uprisings continued in Greece and Turkey over the rightful ownership of Cyprus. Revolts in Argentina forced the exile of Juan Peron. In Hungary, Imre Nagy was ousted by the Communist Party, leading to the revolution of 1956. Under Nagy's direction, a coalition government was quickly formed and Hungary withdrew from the Warsaw Pact. The Soviet invasion of Hungary resulted in Nagy's death, much killing and injury, the escape of nearly 150,000 refugees, and the restoration of Communist rule. In Africa, Tunisia, Morocco, and Sudan gained independence by 1956.

In the world of art, under the modern masters such as Picasso and Chagall, abstract expressionism flourished in the 1950s. Picasso produced the timely *Massacre in Korea* in 1951, and Salvador Dali unleashed his often morose brand of surrealism on the world. Jackson Pollock mass-painted a sort of media unencumbered by the human psyche, standing on stepleaders and squeezing tubes of paint on canvases which were then cut to size according to the patron's wishes. Jasper Johns and Robert Rauschenberg were experimenting with pop art. In England, the abstractions of Barbara Hepworth, Reg Butler, and Lynn Chadwick were the style of the day, but there were "realist" exceptions; Sutherland's portrait of Churchill and Annigoni's portrait of Queen Elizabeth II are particularly notable. The organic architecture of Eero Saarinen demonstrated the aesthetic quality of art remaining true to its medium, perpetuating Louis Sullivan's ideal that "form ever follows function."

Musicals such as Frank Loesser's interpretation of Damon Runyon's *Guys and Dolls* (1950) and Julie Styne's *Wonderful Town* (1953) offered alternatives to Rodgers and Hammerstein's dominance of Broadway with *Carousel*, *The King and I*, and the Pulitzer Prize–winning *South Pacific*. The Hollywood musical achieved its apogee with Gene Kelly's inventive productions *Singin' in the Rain* and *An American in Paris*, along with Fred Astaire's strongest vehicle since the 1930s, *The Band Wagon*. Popular music audiences were exposed to the contemporary folk music of Huddie Ledbetter (Leadbelly) and Woody Guthrie through the unlikely matching of orchestra arranger Gordon Jenkins with the Weavers, a musical group that fell victim to blacklisting by mid-decade. A number of operas appeared that were usually based on famous literary themes, for example, Menotti's *The Consul*, Britten's *Billy Budd*, Vaughn Williams' s *A Pilgrim's Progress*, Stravinsky's *Babel*, Martinu's *What Men Live By*, and Milhaud's *David*.

In literature, as in the visual and performing arts, authors continued to express inner dilemmas caused by external circumstances. Examples include Ezra Pound's *Seventy Cantos*, Hemingway's portrayal of the relationship of an old fisherman and a young boy in pursuit of a great fish in *The Old Man and the Sea*, Herman Wouk's probe of the disturbed authoritarian psyche in *The Caine*

Mutiny, J. D. Salinger's own version of the absurd in his social critique through the mind of an institutionalized teenager in *The Catcher in the Rye*, Steinbeck's gripping saga of a family in turmoil in *East of Eden*, Beckett's existential classic play, *Waiting for Godot*, and Arthur Miller's bold indictment of the McCarthy era by retelling the Salem witch trials in *The Crucible*.

Humphrey Bogart and Katherine Hepburn dominated both nature and the Nazis in John Huston's *The African Queen.* Stanley Kramer's film *High Noon*, starring Cary Cooper, was released in 1952. Now considered the quintessential western, it served as a metaphor for the rugged individual who, faced with a moral dilemma, emerges victorious by strength of conviction and use of force.

Science, technological invention, and discovery expanded in multiple directions in the early fifties. New elements were added to the periodic table in chemistry. Thor Heyerdahl let the world know about his Kon Tiki expedition. The first jet airliner was produced in Britain, and atomic power was used to produce electricity in the United States. The prehistoric was found to be alive and doing well when the coelacanth was discovered off the African coast in 1952. This was the same year that an atomic-powered submarine was designed and a hydrogen bomb was exploded, both under U.S. jurisdiction. The next year brought a Soviet H-bomb explosion. In 1953 Hillary, Norgay, and Hunt climbed the summit of Mount Everest "because it was there," and James Watson and Francis Crick proposed the double helix structure of DNA. B. F. Skinner's *Science and Human Behavior* appeared in 1953, a central text in the behaviorist interpretation of human nature. In mid-decade Dr. Jonas Salk developed a polio vaccine. The first induced pregnancy was successful and many were stunned when it was announced that Christine Jorgensen had undergone the first sex change operation.

Meyrin, Switzerland, became an international center for nuclear research, and Mount Wrangell in Alaska became the residence of an observatory to study cosmic rays. By 1955 it was discovered that radio waves emanate from Jupiter. The ion microscope, with its magnification of 2.75 million; the discovery of the neutrino; and a visual telephone all appeared in the same period. The last three years of the fifties ushered in a new technological age, the Space Age. The world, especially the United States, reacted in disbelief when the Russians launched *Sputnik I*, the world's first unmanned spacecraft, in 1957, followed by *Sputnik II*, with a canine passenger, later the same year.

Concern about the Space Age was, however, not the primary concern everywhere in the last years of the 1950s. In Cuba, Fidel Castro was successful in overthrowing Batista. The revolutionary force took control of sugar firms and, to the surprise of many Americans who supported his liberation efforts, instituted a communist government in 1959. In 1958, Egypt and Syria joined together to create the short-lived United Arab Republic. Martial law was initiated in Jordan; U.S. troops were called to maintain order in Lebanon while British troops were requested to do the same in Jordan.

In 1959, Charles de Gaulle came out of retirement and became president of the Fifth Republic of France. He attempted to resolve the long-lasting French conflict in Algeria by declaring that Algerians should be granted autonomy. International alliances continued to mold the picture of economic and political conditions: the European Economic Community (an alliance of Belgium, France, West Germany, Italy, Luxembourg, and the Netherlands); the Baghdad Pact or Central Treaty Organization (an alliance of the United States, Turkey, Iraq, and Iran); and the European Free Trade Association (Austria, Britain, Denmark, Norway, Portugal, Sweden, and Switzerland). The quest for human rights and freedom resounded in the 1950s in the already mentioned independence achieved by many Third World nations that had formerly been colonies. By the end of the fifties, Cyprus and Mali joined the list of newly independent former colonies, with the Belgian Congo the next likely candidate.

Colonial freedom was not the only kind of liberty pursued. The subjugation of native Africans in South Africa became an international symbol of racism. By 1959 the United Nations General Assembly had issued a condemnation of both racial discrimination generally and apartheid in particular. Strides were made in freedom from racial discrimination, and at no small price either. In the United States, racial segregation in the public schools was declared unconstitutional by the Supreme Court in its landmark 1954 decision in *Brown v. Board of Education of Topeka*. The practical implementation of this decision, however, at Little Rock High School in Arkansas in 1957, required President Eisenhower to enlist the National Guard to protect the lives of the brave young women and men who sought to exercise their constitutional rights. In the following year Dr. Martin Luther King, Jr. led a nonviolent campaign of civil disobedience in Montgomery, Alabama, in order to secure civil rights for dominated peoples in the United States. The Civil Rights Act of 1957 established a commission to investigate the violation of civil rights.

The important contributions of African American women were being recognized. Marian Anderson became the first African American to perform in the Metropolitan Opera House. In 1959 Lorraine Hansberry's *A Raisin in the Sun* was the first play authored by an African American woman to be performed on Broadway. Althea Gibson vaulted the color barrier in professional tennis for the first time. Autherine Lucy demanded entry to the University of Alabama. Although she was subsequently expelled on spurious charges, she pioneered the efforts to desegregate colleges and universities.

Unemployment rose distinctly in the late fifties, but through the merger of the American Federation of Labor (AFL) and the Congress of Industrial Organizations (CIO) the power of unionized laborers was considerably increased. With this greater power came charges that major unions, most notably the Teamsters, had allied with organized crime.

The arts continued to portray the times. The popular Leonard Bernstein musical *West Side Story* suggested to non-urban America something of inner-city life. Some attribute the birth of rock 'n' roll to the 1955 hit by Bill Haley, *Rock Around the Clock*. In that year the young actor James Dean was killed in an automobile crash. In the next year, Elvis Presley had his first hit record, "Heartbreak Hotel." Literature varied greatly, from the penetrating insight into human feeling of Faulkner, to the sensible nonsense of Dr. Seuss, the philosophical stories of Iris Murdoch, the absurd realities of William Saroyan's plays, and the characterization of the searching quests of the Beat generation by their own Jack Kerouac in *On the Road* (1957) and *The Dharma Bums* (1958). *Lord of the Flies* (1954) by William Golding shocked its readers by suggesting that civilization or perhaps capitalism were thin veneers masking the truly savage nature of humankind. Less noted at the time was the release of J. R. R. Tolkien's chronicle of Middle Earth, the *Lord of the Rings* trilogy.

Urban flight was already well under way even before being given fresh impetus by the desegregation of public schools. The deteriorating conditions of America's cities and the changing nature of the problems in urban schools were the subject of Evan Hunter's *The Blackboard Jungle* (1954). The film version, starring Glenn Ford, presented moviegoers with a violent portrait of the urban school. The artistic films of Ingmar Bergman, and David Lean's *Bridge on the River Kwai*, another tale of conviction and rugged individualism, illustrate the range of high quality work in that medium. Technological advances gave rise to the monster movie genre in Japan, where Godzilla met Rodan and every other conceivable destroyer, all spawned by nuclear fears. In the United States, Cinemascope and special effects provided sufficient equipment to rival Yahweh's accomplishments with Cecil B. DeMille's production of *The Ten Commandments*.

The new school of architecture, one characterized by functionalism, glass and steel, and cantilever construction, was furthered by LeCorbusier's Tokyo Museum, Niemeyer's Presidential Palace in Brasilia, Mies van der Rohe's Seagram Building in New York, and Wright's Guggenheim Art Museum, also in New York. Henry Moore contributed sculpture and Jean Miro offered murals to the UNESCO Building in Paris. The compositions of artists as varied as Paul Hindemith, Cole Porter, Buddy Holly, and Little Richard, among many others, brought enjoyment to what Rubinstein labeled a "sixth sense." On

Broadway, Lerner and Loewe had translated Shaw's *Pygmalion* into *My Fair Lady* and Rodgers and Hammerstein told the story of the Trapp Family Singers in *The Sound of Music*. Variety in literature was exemplified by the appearance of Pasternak's *Doctor Zhivago*, Capote's *Breakfast at Tiffany's*, Huxley's repeated warnings in *Brave New World Revisited*, Pinter's *The Birthday Party*, and J. Edgar Hoover's *Masters of Deceit*, all appearing in 1958. And in 1959 diversity continued with Faulkner's *The Mansion*; Mailer's *Advertisement for Myself*; Bellow's *Henderson, the Rain King*; Wesker's play *Roots*; and Ionesco's *The Rhinoceros*, a classic example of the theater of the absurd.

Science and technological wizardry, supported by the public's fascination with science fiction, were propelled by the national desire to embark on the conquest of space. At the end of the fifties the competition for prowess in space between the United States and the USSR was keen. In 1958 the United States launched *Explorer I*, among other satellites, and Russia launched *Sputnik III*. James Van Allen discovered a radiation belt around the Earth. Russia's *Lunik II* and *III* reached the moon in 1959; the latter returned with photographs of the moon's other side.

Thus, the fifties ushers in several new "ages." The Space Age had begun; the Nuclear Age swelled with potential for both progress and peril; there was national recognition that international alliance was necessary for economic and social growth. It was also an age of emergence for the oppressed—be it on racial, colonial, sexual, ethical, political, or economic grounds—to assert their humanity forcefully and unambiguously and demand their liberation. The journey of the maturing processes for all of these "ages" was indeed arduous, yet the potential for human growth in each would be great enough to rekindle human imagination and productivity to reach new plateaus.

CURRICULUM THOUGHT AND LITERATURE

The curriculum literature of the fifties, comprising 142 books, continued the kind of curriculum writing that had evolved in the previous decades, particularly the synoptic text. It might even be said that the fifties were the heyday of this type of curriculum book, a contribution to the literature that, though sometimes faulted for both superficiality and hodgepodgedness, implanted in the minds of many the idea that curriculum study was a viable specialization within educational studies. The synoptic text portrayed a body of literature that aided the justification of curriculum as a field of inquiry. Although it is impossible to measure the impact of this type of book, it was an indisputable contributor to the solidification of curriculum's place in educational literature. The synoptic text was a major instrument used to prepare both practitioners and scholars in

educational occupations; thus, it contributed markedly to the production, nature, and sustenance of curriculum roles in school systems. Such roles as the
curriculum superintendent, director, and consultant were prevalent in schools of
the 1950s.

With the exception of Harold Alberty and, to a lesser extent, Florence
Stratemeyer and associates, the synoptic text was primarily a tool of conciliarists
through the 1940s. With its emergence as a major vehicle for curriculum discourse, proponents of the various curriculum orientations began to explore the
synoptic text's possibilities for effectively expressing their perspective. The
popular synoptic text *Fundamentals of Curriculum Development* by B. Othanel
Smith, William O. Stanley, and J. Harlan Shores first appeared in 1950 and
was revised in 1957. Not only did this text provide an encyclopedic background
on the curriculum field, the authors added several dimensions that were to
become mainstays of curriculum literature for some time to come. Curriculum
development was set in a sociocultural context by tying curriculum issues to the
following: an interpretation of the meaning and structure of culture, community
changes, economic considerations, and social values. The authors expanded the
ideas of development and principles that were basic to the curriculum literature
of the 1930s by explicating criteria for determining objectives, subject matter or
experiences, content, sequence and grade placement, and time allotment and
distribution. Three alternatives for curriculum organization (the subject, activity, and core curricular patterns) were presented, and characteristics, problems,
practices, and criticisms of each were discussed.

One can perceive similarities between categories of curriculum discussion
used by Smith, Stanley, and Shores with those used by Tyler (1949), i.e., purpose, experiences, organization, and evaluation; however, the kind and degree
of elaboration within each category sets the Smith, Stanley, and Shores effort
apart. This text devoted considerable attention to the role of human relations
and interpersonal politics in curriculum change, revision, and decision making.
Finally, the authors identified and discussed alternative viewpoints on theoretical curriculum issues. These discussions, though somewhat general by comparison with the conceptual analysis prevalent in curriculum theory today, were
nevertheless more solidly grounded in philosophy than the recipe-orientation to
treatments of "principles" evident in many synoptic texts. The authors referred
to their discussion of issues as theoretical (especially Part Five, 1957), doubtless
an attempt to inspire other curriculum writers to probe assumptions when
dealing with curriculum-related problems. Authors of many subsequent texts
took this cue and devoted sections to what they labeled "curriculum theory."

These contributions to the genre were remarkable, but equally worthy of
note is that the authors promoted in the construct of their exposition a curricu-

lum orientation that is allied with the social reconstructionist perspective of experientialism. The synoptic text was no longer an effort to synthesize competing viewpoints on curriculum and instruction. Smith, Stanley, and Shores explicate and evaluate current options to argue for critical analysis of a curriculum that critically analyzes social problems using the "resource unit" proposed by Harry Alberty.

The attempt to inspire theory development in curriculum was pursued at a 1947 conference on curriculum theory at the University of Chicago. The conference convened under the leadership of Virgil Herrick and Ralph Tyler, who subsequently published the conference proceedings (Herrick & Tyler, 1950). Actually, the conference participants (B. Othanel Smith, Herman Frick, George E. Barton, Virgil Herrick, Gordon Mackenzie, Ralph Tyler, J. Paul Leonard, Edgar Dale, G. Max Wingo, William M. Alexander, Hollis L. Caswell) hoped for a more ambitious outcome than just inspiration. According to his reflection some 30 years later, Ralph Tyler[1] indicated that their intent had been to develop tenets of theory that could more effectively explain and defensibly propose curriculum activity and research. Tyler expressed some satisfaction that the conference resulted in statements of conviction about what a sound curriculum theory should embrace, but he lamented that the desired theoretical formulations were beyond attainment at that conference.

Thus, 1950 brought both a synoptic text that was thought to be exemplary by many, and a set of admonitions designed to inspire, if not exemplify, the development of curriculum theory. In view of these two contributions alone the field was given momentum, although it must be acknowledged that considerable diversity exists among curriculum scholars about the worth of these and most other pieces of curriculum literature.

As great as their impact was on other authors, these two contributions were not alone in 1950. Other formidable contributions in that year helped to initiate the work of the remainder of the decade. First among these were revisions of previously published texts. The demand for new editions indicates a fairly widespread assessment of usefulness of a text and its ideas. Jersild (1950) and Lee and Lee (1950) produced revisions of their texts that stressed the relationship between understanding children and the development of curricular experiences. Both could be considered as giving support to experientialism, with their emphases on child study as a prime basis for curriculum development. J. M. Gwynn (1950) revised his *Curriculum Principles and Social Trends*, helping to perpetuate both the earlier notion of principles and the emphasis on modernity of curriculum thought. Another synoptic text, *Curriculum Planning* (1950), was produced by Edward A. Krug, who tailored his treatment toward local situations by dealing with the relation of purposes to all-school programs, curriculum guides, creation of specific teaching-learning aids, relationships between curriculum development and the teaching-learning process, and specific suggestions for organizing curriculum development in local school systems.

Despite the school-specific orientation mentioned above, broader considerations of curriculum were also prevalent. National impetus to provide education for all, not just for the college-bound, led to concern for the utility of curriculum. The U.S. Office of Education continued to promote a life adjustment education in efforts to offset the almost exclusive college and vocational orientation to high school curriculum that characterized the previous generation. An example of this movement's continuance in the fifties was the support it received in a 1950 statement by the National Association of Secondary School Principals.

Cooperative endeavors in curriculum development emerged in the literature of the late forties. These were furthered by Taba (1950) and Evans (1950); the former focused on intergroup relations in the elementary school and the latter treated cooperation in research and programs of improvement. Together the two illuminated a considerable range within the sphere of that which was considered curricular advocating reform through cooperative organization.

Although much of the literature produced in 1950 proposed or prescribed more often than it described, the precedent for research on contemporary school practices that prevailed in the forties was kept alive by Caswell and Associates (1950). Their survey provided: (1) perspectives for evaluating cases in curriculum improvement; (2) reports on a wide range of curriculum programs; and (3) a report on curriculum materials. Their descriptions and accompanying discussions of actual curriculum cases represent a major contribution to the literature that analyzed extant curriculum practice.

Variations on the core curriculum, considered by many a more characteristically Deweyan interpretation than the activity or correlated curricula of years gone by, were given marked impetus by Smith, Stanley, and Shores (1950 and 1957), G. S. Wright (1950 and 1958), and Ovsiew (1951). Considerable elaboration was provided by Faunce and Bossing (1951 and 1958). It may be that the core represented an attempt to correct pervasive misinterpretations of Dewey in practitioner-oriented literature. It may be that a new label was needed to relieve the taint of postwar association with the life activity curriculum. In any event advocates of the core emphasized a closer relation between student interest and interdisciplinary knowledge. This helped to correct the misperception that progressive educators were preoccupied with the caprice and whims of young people.

The Association for Supervision and Curriculum Development continued to emphasize curriculum revisions, calling them "improvements." Their 1951 *Yearbook* and annual conference highlights of that year illustrate this thrust, and their publication on funds and time indicated practical considerations for getting the job done. Harold Hand added to the movement by advocating a program that could be applied to enhance improvement (1951). Toward the same end, but with greater thoroughness than any of the above, Benne and Muntyan wove the idea of improvement, christening it "change," with the idea of human relations implicit in the literature on cooperative endeavors in curriculum development. Their book of readings, *Human Relations in Curriculum Change* (1951), can be viewed as a forerunner of contemporary ideas associated with organizational development. It provided an important linking contribution to change-literature and curriculum literature.

Sometimes the curriculum literature on change, innovation, modernity, and related areas smacked of riding the bandwagon, that is, a desire to "keep up with the times" regardless of need. In response, Shane and McSwain provided *Evaluation and the Elementary Curriculum* (1951), stressing the need to carefully assess existing curriculum and the values they embodied as a prerequisite to defensible change or revision. Their text provided two other contributions that should be noted: It represented a tailoring of the synoptic text idea to elementary curriculum and evaluation, and it provided separate sections on subject matter areas within an evaluation context. The latter accepted a given from intellectual traditionalist thought, namely, that the separate subject areas were treated as "givens." This combined with the linear and systematic thought implicit in the "business" of social behaviorist evaluation technology. It also combined with a humanist experientialism that lingered from the progressive era. Taken together, the three emphases represented a coming-of-age, a composite of curriculum knowledge that was assumed applicable to any educational level or subject area.

The synoptic text was a preferred vehicle for conciliarists eager to find a harmonization of the multiple perspectives on curriculum thought discussed in the previous two decades. During the fifties these texts became the acknowledged preserver and conveyer of curriculum knowledge. Surely one can see differences of orientation that roughly parallel the three schools of curriculum thought within the general category of synoptic curriculum texts. Nevertheless, with few exceptions, an amalgamation of the intellectual traditionalist, social behaviorist, and experientialist schools was quite evident in most synoptic texts. Depending on one's personal orientation, one might tend to view this amalgamation as largely productive and refer to it as an eclectic synthesis, or conversely, as largely antiproductive and think of it as a watered-down oversimplification of each of the topics and positions on them. Such texts were no doubt offered to consolidate the diversity of school and classroom needs, that is, to reach common goals. What was lost was the structured and sustained argument in defense of a particular curricular orientation.

Some authors, however, did remain consistent with an established curriculum orientation. One example is Carlton Washburne's (1952) elaboration on the character of child-centered experientialist education. Other books of the first half of the decade that defended a specific curriculum orientation were written by Arthur Bestor (1953, 1955), Robert Maynard Hutchins (1953), and Earl Kelley and Marie Rasey (1952). L. Thomas Hopkins produced an opus on child-centered experientialism (1954), and Theodore Brameld (1955, 1956) framed a reconstructionist proposal.

Arthur Bestor, a history professor at the University of Illinois, attacked colleges of education and curriculum specialists as being responsible for creating "educational wastelands." Bestor argued that the best kind of education is one that is constructed by scholars of the disciplines and that those disciplines that should be taught in the schools are those that are most useful to a society's aspirations. Bestor's work enjoyed wide popularity, prompting his proposal for *The Restoration of Learning* (Bestor, 1955). Bestor was joined by other conservative critics (e.g., Lynd [1953] and Flesch [1955]) in arguing that life needs and life adjustment curricula were promoting illiteracy.

Robert Maynard Hutchins, president of the University of Chicago, penned a critical assessment of contemporary educational philosophies (1953). Working from an Aristotelian-Thomist viewpoint, Hutchins declared that the purpose of education was primarily to prepare students with the competence to consider the great ideas of human history (Hutchins, 1952). The Great Books curriculum, still much in vogue, was tied to this classical intellectual traditionalist perspective. An admirable connection to this "great ideas" orientation is Robert Ulich's (1954) collection from philosophical and religious classics that serve as great ideas about education.

Earl Kelley and Marie Rasey amplified the individual interpretation of experientialism that Kelley had introduced in his earlier text (1947). With Dewey's approval, they drew progressive implications from contemporary biological, psychological, and other scientific research. Kelley's practical application of his ideas is provided in his description of the workshops that he conducted with teachers (Kelley, 1951). Kelley noted that the workshop as a professional development activity usually involved training teachers on the use of some instructional tool to apply to the classroom. In contrast, Kelley encouraged teachers to adopt the workshop process itself, encouraging participants to contribute their talents and life histories to the construction of new knowledge.

The Emerging Self in School and Home (1954) by L. Thomas Hopkins explicated a curriculum that he contended resonates deep within the fabric of human
experience. Hopkins contended that, analogous to the biological development of
the cell, all human growth (e.g., intellectual, social, emotional, moral) proceeds
through phases of expansion, differentiation, and integration—making the home
as viable a space for education (thus expanding the notion of curriculum) as the
school. This work is Hopkins's definitive statement, bringing together his 1929,
1937, and 1941 classics, as well as other works.

Theodore Brameld (1955) used the synoptic philosophy of education text,
stylized by Kilpatrick and John Brubacker, to argue for a curriculum designed
to create a new social order. Working primarily with the secondary school and
junior college curriculum, Brameld suggested a social problems core much like
that proposed by Alberty. The difference was that the examination of social
problems was not an intellectual exercise, it was a political dynamic intended to
conclude in social action. This program was detailed with greater precision than
the proposal of George Counts. Brameld (1956) claimed it was a "post-
progressive" reconstruction. The popular acceptance of Brameld's text, like the
synoptic curriculum work of Smith, Stanley, and Shores, is remarkable given
the strong social commentary supported by the authors and the political tenor of
the times.

The appearance of Sharp's *Curriculum Development as Re-education of the
Teacher* (1951) Spears's *The Teacher and Curriculum Planning* (1951), Stratemeyer's (1952) provision of guides to supplement and concretize her own 1947
text, and Ragan's (1953) synoptic treatment of curriculum at the elementary
level all acknowledged the importance of teachers in curriculum actualization.
Ragan's work signaled a significant departure. The text offered subject matter
perspectives on curriculum development and attempted to empower teachers as
curriculum creators. The risk of oversimplification by providing a single exposure of teachers to curriculum was significant, but so was the alternative of no
exposure at all.

Books appeared that extended the subject orientation exemplified by Ragan, that is, entire books that introduced teachers at the secondary or elementary levels to mathematics curriculum, or language arts curriculum, or social
studies curriculum, or science curriculum, and a host of other specialized areas.
These books usually dealt with methods and subject matter more extensively
than they did curriculum development. Therefore, they are omitted from the
present discussion unless they are considered to represent a special advance in
the way that curriculum can be viewed or studied. A noteworthy exception was
Meier, Cleary, and Davis's (1952) treatment of citizenship education. Even
though this is a topic that would seem to fall wholly within social studies, the

text addressed citizenship as a basis, substance, and outcome, as well as a deliberative process in curriculum development. The same kind of exception can be made for Henry Harap's (1952) book that used social living as an organizing theme or core from which to derive, implement, and judge curricula, not merely as a certain body of knowledge to be amassed along with appropriate pedagogical techniques.

The emphasis on democratic deliberation that characterized the above-mentioned books was not only advocated by scholarly circles, it was sometimes practiced. Exemplary here was a faculty committee (representatives were from Andover, Exeter, Lawrenceville, Harvard, Princeton, and Yale) assembled to make recommendations about the issue of general education in schools and colleges. Not only was the value of cooperative decision making given credence by their efforts, the cooperation was international as well, resulting in a publication entitled *General Education in School and College* (1952). In the same year the first volume of the *Fifty-first Yearbook* of the National Society for the Study of Education provided explorations into the meaning of general education in the context of the fifties, a time of great postwar influx into educational institutions. Although no patented conclusion was accepted by all, questions about the nature of an education that would best produce an enlightened citizenry were given considerable scrutiny beyond dimensions that focused solely on vocational preparation and readiness for further education. The theme of general education was explicitly stated in many of the books on secondary curriculum in the first half of the fifties, a time when the synoptic text came to fruition in secondary education. Briggs (1951), and Hand (1951) to a slighter extent, paved the way.

In 1953, revised editions of Harry Alberty's *Reorganizing the High School Curriculum* and J. P. Leonard's *Developing the Secondary School Curriculum* furthered the influence of synoptic texts. Beck, Cook, and Kearney did the same at the elementary school level with the publication of *Curriculum in the Modern Elementary School* (1953), as did the aforementioned *Modern Elementary Curriculum* by Ragan in the same year. In that year synoptic books by McNerney and by the American Association of School Administrators provided encyclopedic backgrounds and treatments of issues that were designed to apply to curriculum development at all levels of schooling.

Organization was a common area of study for synoptic texts dating from writings by Harap (1928), Hopkins (1929), and Caswell and Campbell (1935) to Gwynn (1943), Tyler (1949), and Smith, Stanley, and Shores (1950 and 1957). The issue of how to organize curricular experiences for effective learning was addressed at book length in the fifties by Krug, Liddle, and Schenk (1952) and Doll, Passow, and Corey (1953), helping to solidify it as a problematic area for curriculum inquiry. In 1956 Herrick, Goodlad, Estvan, and Eberman introduced the idea that curriculum development and design should have an "organizing center," i.e., a central idea or hub around which curriculum organization and instruction turned.

Democracy was another issue that received considerable attention in the mid-fifties. The perceptions of democratic curriculum were subject to several quite different interpretations. One of these was the community school, a thoroughly grounded integration of the school functioning in the community (Olsen, 1953; NSSE, 1953 a and b), an idea promoted in the 1930s by Kilpatrick. These sources expressed democratic interpretations of schooling that included deliberation and cooperative action, as repeatedly emphasized in many curriculum books. Action research, mentioned at some length in synoptic texts of the fifties, can be seen as another extension of democracy into curricular endeavors by giving teachers and other school personnel the opportunity to conduct educational research specific to their own settings. Stephen Corey (1953) authored a pioneering book-length discussion of action research as an important prerequisite to curricular revision. In 1955, Corey joined efforts with Passow and Miles in a call for a type of cooperative research that could unite workers in different roles within curriculum scholarship and practice. This focus on specific educational settings had potential for providing clearer visions of the characteristics and needs of children and youth. It clearly related to the first volume of the *Fifty-second Yearbook* of the National Society for the Study of Education (1953), which was devoted to the idea of adapting curricula to young people rather than molding them to a desired end, an experientialist perspective.

The manifold list of developments in curriculum literature of the early fifties led to publications that discussed trends. Noting that mid-century is a good time to reflect on progress, Henry Harap (1953) produced a book on this topic, arguing for a conciliar curriculum emphasizing a "balanced school life." Campbell (1953) reflected on trends in Canadian curriculum, and the Association for Student Teaching (1953) discussed curriculum trends relative to teacher education. Koos analyzed trends in the development of junior high schools (1955), trends that he had often initiated or influenced. An analysis of curriculum guides by Merritt and Harap appeared in the same year. Harold Shane's editorship of the *Thirteenth Yearbook* of the John Dewey Society (1953) provided reflections on curriculum by several prominent educators (e.g., John Childs, Arthur Foshay, Henry Otto, Edgar Dale, Walter Moore, Celia Stendler) on past developments and challenges that these provided for the future.

In 1954, the reappearance of Adams's *Educating America's Children* illustrated the appeal of the growing reunion of curriculum and methods that was furthered by Ragan and other authors. In the same year two attempts were made to explain how to develop curriculum for adolescents, one by Romine and the other by the Association for Supervision and Curriculum Development. Of paramount impact that year and for many years hence, in its numerous revitalizations, was *Curriculum Planning for Better Teaching and Learning* by Saylor and Alexander. This text, both synoptic and oriented to the preparation of curriculum-minded teachers and administrators, was used widely in the education of curriculum specialists. Books by Kirk (1953) and Columbia University (1955) were marketed as descriptions of the tasks of curriculum specialists in schools, further advancing the identity for this administrative functionary.

Curriculum books in the second half of the fifties continued discussion of curriculum topics that emerged during or prior to the first half of the decade. Otto (1955) considered curriculum enrichment for gifted students within the regular elementary school classroom. Relations between curriculum and guidance were explored by Kelly (1955) and by the 1955 ASCD *Yearbook*. Jackson (1956) and Lurry and Alberty (1957) sustained the proposal for a core curriculum, the former focusing on staff perceptions and the latter on the secondary school. Hoppe (1957) advanced the core curriculum at the junior high school level. The revised edition of *Developing the Core Curriculum* by Faunce and Bossing and Wright's *Core Curriculum Development*, both in 1958, sustained promotion of this experientialist project throughout the 1950s.

The predominant form for books on curriculum from 1955 through the remainder of the decade was the synoptic text in several variations. Examples include Fitzgerald and Fitzgerald (1955), Beauchamp (1956), Hurley (1957), and Shane and McSwain (1958) at the elementary school level; Douglass's second edition of *The High School Curriculum* (1956) and Venable (1958) at the secondary level; and Krug, et al. (1956) at the level of administrative planning. Other authors offered a general perspective on curriculum development instead of specifying an institutional level. Examples include Anderson (1956); the revised edition of Smith, Stanley, and Shores (1957); the revised edition of Stratemeyer, (1957); and Krug's 1957 revision of *Curriculum Planning*.

The 1956 ASCD Yearbook addressed purpose relative to high school education by venturing responses to the question of what high schools should teach. Nisbet (1957) produced one of the first major British curriculum books to have international impact since the early years of the century. His book focused entirely on conceptions of purposes or ends of education conveyed by the curriculum.

But it was consideration of the form of educational purpose, more so than the content, that caught and retained scholars' attention. The learning objective, a grammatical design in consideration of curriculum purpose, has had lasting impact, continuing to be a staple of pre-service teacher education. Foremost among contributions to this grammar was the 1956 taxonomical classification of cognitive objectives produced by Benjamin Bloom and others. This book's influence provided at least rival competition to the impact of Tyler (1949) in both scholarly citation and in the rhetoric of educational practice. Countless practitioners were exposed to Bloom's taxonomy and its six cognitive levels (memory, interpretation or comprehension, application, analysis, synthesis, and evaluation). Applications were indeed prodigious as applied to many areas: lesson planning, the writing of course or school curricula, questioning techniques, and skills management systems. Clearly, not all of the uses were anticipated or condoned by the authors, but these applications did elevate the work to the status of an icon in educational theory and practice.

While interest in precision in stating educational purposes was capturing the interests of scholars, the 1957 Russian launching of *Sputnik* brought on a public outcry for a much more dramatic reexamination of educational purposes. Many interpreters of the event held that this technological achievement proved the educational superiority of the USSR over the United States and other nations. Thus, widespread criticism of American education, including the influential scolding of Admiral Hyman Rickover (1959), coupled with anguished hopefulness gave hasty birth to programs called "curriculum projects," a mainstay of curriculum development in the 1960s. In their infancy many of these programs were presented in journals and at conferences. Proposals that had been considered un-funded eccentricities before *Sputnik* were awarded massive funding by both governmental and private sources that catered to the expediency of "political necessity." The increasingly acknowledged perennial lag between social pressure and educational change prevented the immediate emergence of major curriculum projects. As a result, post-*Sputnik* curriculum projects initiated in the late 1950s did not come to be realized until the beginning of the next decade.

Other issues shared the spotlight in curriculum books for the remainder of the fifties. Let us review some of these to round out the decade. Edwards (1956) evaluated a cooperative secondary curriculum development program. French and associates (1957) provided one of the first book-length treatments of behavioral goals in education since those presented by the social behaviorists early in the twentieth century, though this interpretation was quite different from the notions of the behavioral objectives movement that swelled in the late sixties and early seventies. Spears (1957) noted the import of in-service programs in curriculum development, a phenomenon that characterized the widespread funding of new programs in the sixties. The United Nations brought an international flavor to curriculum literature. Examples often appeared under the auspices of UNESCO and include Olson's (1957) emphasis on psychological foundations; Lourengo's (1957) treatment of primary curriculum in Latin America; a comparative study of primary curriculum by the Conference Internationale (1958); and UNESCO's book on research and revision of curriculum (1958). The 1958 ASCD Yearbook treated the topic of continuity in school programs from level to level. An alternative solution to this organizational issue was offered by Goodlad and Anderson (1959). Their plan for the elimination of grades by chronological age stirred much scholarly and practical thought and action. Both, however, were interpreted with great ambiguity. The relationship between curriculum and the school plant itself constituted an organizational issue treated by Helen Heffernan and Charles Bursch (1958). In the same year, the National Society for the Study of Education rekindled the organizational pattern of integrating educational experiences advanced by Hopkins and others in the thirties. This was another variation on the topic of organizational patterns for curriculum.

Curricularists themselves became the subjects of their books at times. It was not difficult to detect that many factors provided impediments to the work of the ever-increasing occupational role known as the curriculum consultancy. In her concern for this problem, Lawler (1958) addressed factors that contributed to the successes of curriculum consultants. The emergent issues and topics in curriculum were numerous indeed, a state of affairs that sparked Alcorn and Linley to edit a book of articles on curriculum issues in 1954 and again in 1959. Their books represent a thorough sampling of the hot topics of the times, and they exemplify the many collections on contemporary curriculum debates that would follow. The existence of curriculum as an area of study for half a century prompted historical portrayals as well as collections. Such was the response of the ASCD (though later historical analyses would be more thorough) in their discussion of improvements from 1857 through 1957 (ASCD, 1957). When these contemporary classics are coupled with Ulich's (1954) collection of classic excerpts on education, one possesses a kind of synoptic sketch of the vast history of curriculum thought (i.e., conceptions of what's worth knowing).

Laura Zirbes's final book was an invitation to consider curriculum as living creatively with learners in contrast to speaking in the less organic processes of "construction" or even "development." Zirbes contended,

> Creatively considered, a curriculum is an ongoing continuity of situational "school" experiences—flexible, vital experiences—in which teachers are interacting educatively with learners in terms of the needs, potentialities, and propensies of those learners, on the one hand, in terms of the cultural conditions, resources, and interactive processes by which learners are actively challenged and zestfully involved, so that they live to take it unto themselves in their own becoming, and use it as a medium in their own creative individual and group endeavors, drawing from it, but

also identifying with its values in ways which carry those values forward to fruition in their own lives. (Zirbes, 1959, pp. 90–91)

Spurs to Creative Teaching has a conversational tone, almost as though Zirbes is speaking personally to her reader, engaging in the process of curriculum co-creation that she encouraged in her text. Enacting curriculum and instruction as one fluid process, Zirbes reflected on each of the standard academic subjects, offering ideas on how to creatively engage students in the continual imagining and active invention of learning.

Dynamics of Curriculum Improvement (1959) by P. T. Pritzkau is difficult to classify, perhaps because the work has a strong relationship with existentialism, a philosophic position then uncommon to curriculum discourse. Pritzkau's work was a departure from the usual generalizations found in many of the synoptic texts, especially those that utilized the guideline or recipe notion of "principles." He did attempt to structure the decision-making process but acknowledged the need to attend to the essential uniqueness of each situation, making his treatment complex and lacking the kind of quick answers that some practitioners desired and often demanded. This orientation to situational complexity was not without precedent; there was Dewey, of course. Further, the interested reader should wait patiently, for there is more that is similar in Phenix and Schwab in the 1960s and the "reconceptualists" and others in the 1970s and beyond.

Finally, the fifties ended with a book that was instrumental in creating the institutional and curricular character of the high school in subsequent years. With considerable backing from the Carnegie Foundation, sufficient to supply many school boards with copies of his book, James Bryant Conant produced *The American High School Today* (1959). In it, he outlined a kind of high school curriculum, complete with college preparatory, vocational, and general dimensions, that has come to be popularly accepted as the perennial character of the U.S. high school. The number of credit requirements or Carnegie units of mathematics, English, languages, science, social science, humanities, etc., which now seem so commonplace were in no small measure perpetuated by the impact of Conant's work. He recommended school consolidation and thereby the reduction of numbers of small schools. He advocated counseling systems, individualized program scheduling, required courses and electives, ability grouping by subject, transcripts, special emphasis on English composition, as well as an overall emphasis on marketable skills. Other features included prerequisites for advanced courses, honors lists, six- to eight-period days, increased emphasis on foreign language and science preparation, courses that enhanced the vocational preparation and home skills needed by girls, and the study of American government in the twelfth grade. High schools were to be more academically rigorous for all. What was particularly timely about the proposal was that Conant advocated the identification of student ability and the programming of curriculum by aptitude. While including the recommendation of special programs for slow readers, much of the consolidation of resources was overtly designed to accommodate special programs for academically talented and extra provision for highly gifted students. It was a common perception that the schools had for too long held back the initiative and ability of the most talented. By ensuring that each school had the technological resources to advance the most able, the United States would foster its intellectual leadership for the next decade. In short, Conant promoted the development of the comprehensive high school designed to facilitate general education, college preparation, and the gamut of vocational education simultaneously, with special attention to cultivating the most able.

In the fifties we have seen a pinnacle in production of synoptic texts, a call for theoretical soundness of purpose, a continuation of the core curriculum, a call for curriculum evaluation, an expansion of the domain of curriculum considerations, and a continuation of concern for social adjustment. Many of these topics were deemphasized amid frustrations to equalize status with the Soviets. But this was more of a problem for the sixties. The continuation of the synoptic text as the dominant form of curriculum writing in the fifties, coupled with the uniquely American rise of the comprehensive school, further solidified the amalgamation of schools of curriculum thought. Thus, while not wanting to understate the existence and worth of varied tendencies within both curriculum literature and practice, it seems safe to assert that an assumption underlying both was that most things necessary for the education of most persons could be contained within one source. In other words, that which curriculum decision-makers needed could be presented in the synoptic text, and that which students needed could be presented in the comprehensive schools. Benefits of this tendency to mass-produce knowledge and disseminate it efficiently must be weighed against the debits of uncritical synthesis, inordinate pigeonholing of ideas, simplification of guidance, the rhetoric of having provided more substance where less is justifiable, and the tendency of such syntheses to propagate the values and activities of the most powerful social groups in a society.

BIBLIOGRAPHY OF CURRICULUM BOOKS 1950–1959

1950

Bathrust, E. G. (1950). *Where children live affects the children. Educational Bulletin Number 7.* Washington, DC: Government Printing Office.

Caswell, H. L., & Associates. (1950). *Curriculum improvement in public school systems.* New York: Teachers College, Columbia University.

Columbia University Teachers College. (1950). Institute of Field Studies. *Public education and the future of Puerto Rico, a curriculum survey 1948–1949* (Gordon N. Mackenzie, survey director). New York: Bureau of Publications, Teachers College, Columbia University.

Conference on Problems of Curriculum Development. (1950). *Problems of curriculum development.* Salem, OR: Author.

Evans, H. M. (Ed.). (1950). *Cooperative research and curriculum improvement.* New York: Bureau of Publications, Teachers College, Columbia University.

Featherstone, W. B. (1950). *A functional curriculum for youth.* New York: American Book Company.

Gwynn, J. M. (1950). *Curriculum principles and social trends* (Second edition). New York: Macmillan.

Herrick, V. E., & Tyler, R. W. (Eds.). (1950). *Toward improved curriculum theory. Supplementary Educational Monographs.* Chicago: University of Chicago Press.

Jersild, A. T. (1950). *Child development and the curriculum.* New York: Teachers College, Columbia University.

Jobe, E. R. (1950). *Curriculum development in Mississippi public white high schools, 1900–1945.* Nashville, TN: Bureau of Publications, George Peabody College for Teachers.

Kobayashi, T. (1950). *Our curriculum.* Ikarashi, Japan: Niigata University, Department of Education, Elementary School.

Krug, E. A. (1950). *Curriculum planning.* New York: Harper and Brothers.

Lee, J. M., & Lee, D. M. (1950). *The child and his curriculum* (Second edition). New York: Appleton-Century-Crofts.

Mitchell, L. S. (1950). *Our children and our schools.* New York: Simon and Schuster.

National Association of Secondary School Principals. (1950). *Life adjustment in the secondary school curriculum. Number 171.* Washington, DC: Author.

Rasey, M. I. (1950). *This is teaching.* New York: Harper and Brothers.

Scottish Education Department. (1950). *The primary school in Scotland: A memorandum on the curriculum.* Edinburgh, Scotland: Her Majesty's Stationery Office.

Smith, B. O., Stanley, W. O., & Shores, J. H. (1950). *Fundamentals of curriculum development.* Yonkers-on-the-Hudson, New York: World Book Company.

Taba, H. (Director). (1950). *Elementary curriculum in intergroup relations*. Washington, DC: American Council on Education.

Tennessee Department of Education, Division of Public Schools. (1950). *Curriculum planning for our schools; a unified plan for curriculum improvement developed during the summer of 1949 by workshop groups at the University of Tennessee and the A and I State College*. Nashville, TN: Department of Education.

Western Illinois State College, Macomb. (1950). *Curriculum revision for more effective living*. Macomb, IL: Western Illinois University.

Wright, G. S. (1950). *Core curriculum in public high schools: An inquiry into practices, 1949*. Washington, DC: Government Printing Office.

1951

Association for Supervision and Curriculum Development. (1951a). *Action for curriculum improvement*. 1951 Yearbook. Washington, DC: Author.

Association for Supervision and Curriculum Development. (1951b). *Curriculum improvement in the world crisis; highlights of the 1951 ASCD convention, sixth annual meeting, February 10–15, 1951, Detroit, Michigan*. Washington, DC: Author.

Association for Supervision and Curriculum Development. (1951c). *Time and funds for curriculum development*. Washington, DC: Author.

Benne, K. D., & Muntyan, B. (1951). *Human relations in curriculum change: Selected readings with special emphasis on group development*. New York: The Dryden Press.

Briggs, T. H. (1951). *The secondary school curriculum: Yesterday, today, and tomorrow*. New York: Teachers College, Columbia University.

Burton, W. H. (1951). *The guidance of learning activities (Second edition)*. New York: Appleton-Century.

Faunce, R. C., & Bossing, N. L. (1951). *Developing the core curriculum*. New York: Prentice-Hall.

Hand, H. C. (1951). *How the Illinois secondary school curriculum program in basic studies can help you improve your high school*. Springfield, IL: Superintendent of Public Instruction.

Harap, H. (Ed.). (1951). *Preparation of teachers in the area of curriculum and instruction (monograph number two)*. Austin (University of Texas): National Society of College Teachers of Education.

Harvard University. (1951). Graduate School of Education Center for Field Studies. *Pittsfield junior high school; stages in curriculum design, 1951–1960*. Pittsfield, MA: Harvard University.

Kelley, E. C. (1951). *The workshop way of learning*. New York: Harper and Row.

Ovsiew, L., & a Committee of Teachers from Elizabeth, New Jersey schools. (1951). *Making the core work*. New York: Metropolitan School Study Council.

Parkhurst, H. (1951). *Exploring the child's world*. New York: Appleton.

Shane, H. G., & McSwain, E. T. (1951). *Evaluation and the elementary curriculum*. New York: Bureau of Publications, Teachers College, Columbia University.

Sharp, G. (1951). *Curriculum development as re-education of the teacher*. New York: Teachers College Press.

Spears, H. (1951). *The teacher and curriculum planning*. Englewood Cliffs, NJ: Prentice-Hall, Inc..

Tannenbaum, S. (1951). *William Heard Kilpatrick: Trail blazer in education*. Columbus: Ohio State University Press.

1952

Association for Supervision and Curriculum Development. (1952a). *Bibliography on supervision and curriculum development (prepared by Thelma Byars and others)*. Washington, DC: Author.

Association for Supervision and Curriculum Development. (1952b). *Time and funds for curriculum*. Washington, DC: Iowa Association chapter.

Blackmer, A. R. (Chairman). (1952). *General education in school and college*. Cambridge: Harvard University Press.

Committee on General Education. (1952). *General education in school and college: A committee report by members of the faculty of Andover, Exeter, Lawrenceville, Harvard, Princeton, and Yale*. Cambridge: Harvard University Press, 1952.

England, Ministry of Education, Welsh Department. (1952). *The curriculum and community in Wales*. London: Her Majesty's Stationery Office.

Harap, H. (1952). *Social living in curriculum: A critical study of the core in action in grades one through twelve*. Nashville, TN: George Peabody College for Teachers.

Hutchins, R. M. (1952). *The great conversation*. Chicago: Encyclopedia Britannica.

Jones, L. (1952). *Curriculum aids in continuation education*. Sacramento, CA: California Department of Education. Bulletin V 21, Number 12.

Kelley, E. (1952). *Education and the nature of man*. New York: Harper and Bros. (1970 Edition with Marie Rasey).

Krug, E. A., Liddle, C. S., & Schenk, Q. (1952). *Mutiple period curriculum organization in Wisconsin secondary schools*. Madison, WI: University of Wisconsin.

Meier, A. R., Cleary, F. D., & Davis, A. M. (1952). *A curriculum for citizenship*. Detroit, MI: Wayne State University Press (Reprinted by Greenwood Press, New York, 1969).

Miel, A., & Associates. (1952). *Cooperative procedures in learning*. New York: Bureau of Publications, Teachers College, Columbia University.

National Society for the Study of Education. (1952). *General education. Fifty-First Yearbook, Part I*. Chicago: University of Chicago Press.

National Union of Teachers, London. (1952). *The curriculum of the secondary school; report of a consultative committee appointed by the Executive of the National Union of Teachers*. London: Efans Brothers.

Piaget, J. (1952). *The origins of intelligence in children*. New York: Norton and Company.

Rugg, H. O. (1952). *The education of teachers*. New York: Harper and Brothers.

Stratemeyer, F. B., Forkner, H. L., & McKim, M. G. (1952). *Guides to a curriculum for modern living*. New York: Teachers College, Columbia University.

Washburne, C. (1952). *What is progressive education?* New York: John Day Company.

1953

Alberty, H. (1953). *Reorganizing the high school curriculum (Second edition)*. New York: Macmillan.

American Association of School Administrators. (1953). *American school curriculum*. Washington, DC: National Education Association Yearbook.

Association for Student Teaching. (1953). *Curriculum trends and teacher education. 1953 Yearbook* (J.A. Bond and J.A. Hockett, Eds.). Lock Haven, PA: Author.

Beck, R. H., Cook, W. W., & Kearney, N. C. (1953). *Curriculum in the modern elementary school*. Englewood Cliffs, NJ: Prentice-Hall.

Bestor, A. (1953). *Educational wastelands*. Urbana: University of Illinois Press.

Campbell, H. L. (1953). *Curriculum trends in Canadian education*. Toronto: W. J. Gage.

Corey, S. M. (1953). *Action research to improve school practices*. New York: Bureau of Publications. Teachers College, Columbia University.

Doll, R., Passow, H., & Corey, S. (1953). *Organization for curriculum improvement*. New York: Bureau of Publications, Teachers College, Columbia University.

Harap, H. (1953). *Curriculum trends at mid-century*. Cincinnati, OH: Southwestern Publishing Company.

Hutchins, R. M. (1953). *The conflict in education in a democractic society*. New York: Harper and Bros.

Kearney, N. C. (1953). *Elementary school objectives: A report prepared for the mid-century committee on outcomes in elementary education*. New York: Russell Sage Foundation.

Kirk, D. L. (1953). *The role of the curriculum director of administration of American public school programs*. Austin: School of Education, University of Texas.

Leonard, J. P. (1953). *Developing the secondary school curriculum*. (Revised edition). New York: Rinehart and Company.

Lynd, A. (1953). *Quackery in the public schools*. Boston: Little, Brown.

McNerney, C. T. (1953). *The curriculum*. New York: McGraw-Hill.

National Society for the Study of Education. (1953a). *Adapting the secondary school program to the needs of youth. Fifty-Second Yearbook, Part I.* Chicago: University of Chicago Press.

National Society for the Study of Education. (1953b). *The community school. Fifty-Second Yearbook, Part II.* Chicago: University of Chicago Press.

Olsen, E. G. (Ed.). (1953). *The modern community school.* New York: Appleton-Century-Crofts.

Ragan, W. B. (1953). *Modern elementary curriculum.* New York: Holt, Rinehart and Winston.

Shane, H. G. (Ed.). (1953). *The American elementary school. Thirteenth Yearbook of the John Dewey Society.* New York: Harper and Brothers.

Western Illinois State College. (1953). *Curriculum revision and development.* Macomb, Illinois: Western Illinois State College.

1954

Adams, F. (Greene). (1954). *Educating America's children; elementary school curriculum and methods (Second Edition).* New York: Ronald Press Company.

Alcorn, M. D. & Linley, J. M. (Eds.). (1954). *Issues in curriculum development.* New York: World Book Company.

Association for Supervision and Curriculum Development. (1954). *Developing programs for young adolescents; a booklet prepared for ASCD by the Department of Supervision and Curriculum Development of the Florida Education Association.* Washington, DC: Author.

Cassidy, R. F. (1954). *Curriculum development in physical education.* New York: Harper.

Hopkins, L. T. (1954). *The emerging self in school and home.* New York: Harper and Brothers. (also 1970).

New York (State) University, Bureau of Elementary Curriculum Development. (1954). *The elementary school curriculum; an overview.* Albany, NY: New York (State) University.

Ohio State University, University School. (1954). *A description of curricular experiences: the lower school...kindergarten through grade six.* (Revised Edition). Columbus, OH: Ohio State University.

Romine, S. (1954). *Building the high school curriculum.* New York: Ronald Press.

Saylor, J. G., & Alexander, W. (1954). *Curriculum planning for better teaching and learning.* New York: Holt, Rinehart and Winston.

Ulich, R. (Ed.). (1954). *Three thousand years of educational wisdom.* Cambridge: Harvard University Press.

1955

Association for Supervision and Curriculum Development. (1955). *Guidance in the curriculum.* Yearbook. Washington, DC: Author.

Bestor, A. (1955). *The restoration of learning.* New York: A. Knopf.

Brameld, T. (1955). *Philosophies of education in cultural perspective*. New York: Holt, Rinehart and Winston.

Columbia University Teachers College. Seminar in Supervision and Curriculum Improvement. (1955). *The work of the curriculum coordinator in selected New Jersey schools; a report to the New Jersey curriculum coordinators*. New York: Bureau of Publications, Teachers College, Columbia University.

Fitzgerald, J. A. & Fitzgerald, P. G. (1955). *Methods and curricula in elementary education*. Milwaukee, WI: Bruce Publishing Company.

Flesch, R. (1955). *Why Johnny can't read: And what you can do about it*. New York: Harper.

Kelly, J. A. (1955). *Guidance and the curriculum*. Englewood Cliffs, NJ: Prentice-Hall.

Koos, L. V. (1955). *Junior high school trends*. New York: Harper and Brothers.

Lee, J. M. (Ed.). (1955). *Selected bibliography for curriculum workers*. Washington, DC: Association for Supervision and Curriculum Development. (Briefer versions were published in 1953 and 1954 under similar titles.)

Merritt, E., & Harap, H. (1955). *Trends in the production of curriculum guides*. Nashville, TN: George Peabody College for Teachers.

National Council of Churches. (1955). *A guide for curriculum in Christian education*. Chicago: Division of Christian Education, National Council of Churches.

Otto, H. J. (Ed.). (1955). *Curriculum enrichment for gifted elementary school children in regular classes*. Austin, TX: University of Texas.

Passow, A. H., Miles, M. B., & Corey, S. M. (1955). *Training curriculum leaders for cooperative research*. New York: Teachers College, Columbia University.

1956

Anderson, V. E. (1956). *Principles and procedures of curriculum improvement*. New York: Ronald Press.

Association for Supervision and Curriculum Development. (1956). *What shall high schools teach? 1956 Yearbook*. Washington, DC: Author.

Beauchamp, G. A. (1956). *Planning the elementary school curriculum development*. New York: Allyn & Bacon.

Bloom, B. S. (Ed). (1956). *Taxonomy of educational objectives, handbook I: Cognitive domain*. New York: David McKay & Company.

Brameld, T. (1956). *Towards a reconstructed philosophy of education*. New York: Dryden Press.

Douglass, H. R. (Ed.). (1956). *The high school curriculum* (Second edition). New York: Ronald Press.

Edwards, T. B. (1956). *The regional project in secondary education; evaluation of a program of cooperative curriculum development*. Berkeley: University of California Press.

Herrick, V. E., Goodlad, J., Estvan, F. J., & Eberman, P. W. (1956). *The elementary school.* Englewood Cliffs, NJ: Prentice-Hall.

Hoppe, A. A. (1956). *Students help improve the curriculum in Indiana.* Bloomington, IN: Division of Research and Field Services, Indiana University.

Jackson, D. M. (1956). *Staff perceptions of developing core programs.* Chicago: University of Chicago.

Krug, E. A., et al. (1956). *Administering curriculum planning.* New York: Harper and Brothers.

1957

Association for Supervision and Curriculum Development. (1957). *One hundred years of curriculum improvement, 1857–1957.* Washington, DC: Author.

French, W., et al. (1957). *Behavioral goals of general education in high school.* New York: Russell Sage Foundation.

Hoppe, A. A. (1957). *The core in junior high school.* Bloomington, IN: Division of Research and Field Services, Indiana University.

Hurley, B. J. (1957). *Curriculum for elementary school children.* New York: Ronald Press.

Krug, E. A. (1957). *Curriculum planning.* New York: Harper and Brothers.

Lourengo, M. B. (1957). *Primary school curricula in Latin America.* Paris: UNESCO.

Lurry, L., & Alberty, E. J. (1957). *Developing a high school core program.* New York: Macmillan.

Nisbet, S. D. (1957). *Purpose in the curriculum.* London, England: University of London Press.

Olson, W. C. (1957). *Psychological foundations of the curriculum.* Paris: UNESCO.

Smith, B. O., Stanley, W. O., & Shores, J. H. (1957). *Fundamentals of curriculum development* (Revised edition). New York: Harcourt, Brace and World.

Spears, H. (1957). *Curriculum planning through in-service programs.* Englewood Cliffs, NJ: Prentice-Hall.

Stratemeyer, F. B., Forkner, H. L., McKim, M. G., & Passow, A. H. (1957). *Developing a curriculum for modern living* (Second edition, revised and enlarged). New York: Bureau of Publications, Teachers College, Columbia University.

1958

Association for Supervision and Curriculum Development. (1958). *A look at continuity in the school program.* 1958 yearbook. Washington, DC: Author.

Bereday, G. Z. F., & Lauwerys, J. A. (Eds). (1958). *The secondary school curriculum: The yearbook of education.* New York: Harcourt, Brace, Jovanovich.

Conference Internationale De L'Instruction Publique. (1958). *Preparation and issuing of the primary school curriculum: A comparative study.* Paris: UNESCO.

Cummings, H. H., & Mackintosh, H. K. (1958). *Curriculum responsibilities of state departments of education*. Washington, DC: U.S. Department of Health, Education, and Welfare, Office of Education.

Faunce, R. C., & Bossing, N. L. (1958). *Developing the core curriculum (Second edition)*. Englewood Cliffs, NJ: Prentice-Hall.

Heffernan, H., & Bursch, C. (1958). *Curriculum and the elementary school plant*. Washington, DC: Association for supervision and Curriculum Development.

Lawler, M. R. (1958). *Curriculum consultants at work: Factors affecting their success*. New York: Teachers College, Columbia University.

National Society for the Study of Education. (1958). *The integration of educational experience. Fifty-seventh Yearbook, Part III*. Chicago: University of Chicago Press.

Shane, H. G., & McSwain, E. T. (1958). *Evaluation and the elementary curriculum (Revised edition)*. New York: Henry Holt.

UNESCO. (1958). *Curriculum revision and research*. Paris: UNESCO

Venable, T. C. (1958). *Patterns in secondary school curriculum*. New York: Harper.

Wright, G. S. (1958). *Core curriculum development: Problems and practices*. Bulletin Number 5. Washington, DC: U.S. Office of Education.

1959

Alcorn, M. D., & Linley, J. M. (Eds). (1959). *Issues in curriculum development*. Yonkers-on-the-Hudson, NY: World Book Company.

Conant, J. B. (1959). *The American high school today*. New York: McGraw-Hill.

Frederick, R. W. (1959). *The third curriculum: Student activities in American education*. New York: Appleton-Century-Crofts.

Goodlad, J. I., & Anderson, R. H. (1959). *The nongraded elementary school*. New York: Harcourt, Brace and World.

Pritzkau, P. T. (1959). *Dynamics of curriculum improvement*. Englewood Cliffs, NJ: Prentice-Hall.

Rickover, H. (1959). *Education and freedom*. New York: Dutton.

Zirbes, L. (1959). *Spurs to creative teaching*. New York: G. P. Putnam

CHAPTER SEVEN

Curriculum Literature and Context
1960–1969

CONTEXTUAL REMINDERS

For the United States, the 1960s would be one of the most domestically tur-bulent decades of the century. The decade began in economic recession, with public concerns that the United States could not compete, at least technologi-cally, with the Soviet Union. In the 1960 presidential election, the charismatic John Kennedy and his New Frontier agenda narrowly defeated Richard M. Nixon, representing the Republican administration of Dwight Eisenhower after having been in power for eight years. Kennedy's leadership as president inspired in many an air of determination and confidence in the ability of U.S. citizens to solve chronic problems domestically and abroad. President Ken-nedy established the Peace Corps in 1961 to meet the need for skilled people in Third World nations, and the VISTA program followed shortly thereafter as a resource to enable the rural poor of the United States. In the same year, Kennedy proposed to place a man on the moon by decade's end. With the help and later leadership of Lyndon B. Johnson, social ills would be confronted through a War on Poverty and Great Society legislation. By the decade's end, however, the aspirations of the Kennedy era (a period which came to be called Camelot, a name borrowed from a popular Broadway play of the same time period) had largely vanished. The nation had witnessed three major assassina-tions, experienced unprecedented race violence, and found itself bitterly divided over a distant and highly controversial war.

Many "baby boomers," despite having benefited from the economic ex-pansion and political stability of the fifties, were increasingly preoccupied with forcing the attention of the older generation on the inequities of U.S. social, economic, and political life. The boomers as well as many older individuals who shared their social concerns were idealistic, energetic, and impatient; many questioned the authority of age, establishment, and tradition. Some dropped out, choosing to follow alternative lifestyles and goals. Use of marijuana and other mind- and mood-altering drugs increased dramatically. Despite the ability to place a man on the moon, the United States grappled with but did not resolve the plethora of domestic problems against which numerous and diverse groups protested.

Flashpoints served as reminders of the ongoing Cold War. U.S.-USSR relations were strained in 1960 by the shooting down of an American U-2 spy plane piloted by Gary Powers over Soviet territory, making ineffectual the planned Paris summit meeting between Khrushchev and Eisenhower. The most terrifying confrontation came as a result of Cuba's alignment with the Soviet Union. Cuba had been recently liberated from the dictatorship of Batista and from organized crime by guerrilla forces under Fidel Castro, but U.S. interests were angered by seizure of its private property in the island nation. In turn, Cuba appealed to the United Nations for assistance in dealing with U.S. "aggression." In 1961 the United States supported the Bay of Pigs invasion by Cuban exiles, a fiasco organized during the Eisenhower administration for which Kennedy accepted responsibility. In 1962, Cuba and Russia signed a trade agreement and a Russian fishing base was established in Cuba. This agreement somehow evolved into a missile base that would place Soviet nuclear weapons within striking distance of U.S. targets. This threat prompted Kennedy to order a U.S. blockade of Cuba. The Cuban Missile Crisis brought the superpowers to the very brink of war and served as a sober reminder of the potential for nuclear catastrophe unless more peaceful means could be found to settle international disagreements.

By 1963, relations between the United States and the USSR seemed to be on the road to improvement with the establishment of a telephone "hot line" between Moscow and Washington, D.C., providing immediate communication between leaders in the event of military calamity. This easing of tensions was then accentuated by an above ground nuclear test ban treaty signed by the United States, the USSR, and 114 other nations. Crises in leadership, however, stalled further negotiations. In November 1963, President John Kennedy was assassinated in Dallas and was succeeded by Lyndon B. Johnson. Controversy concerning causal factors in the Kennedy assassination was left unresolved by the findings of a federal commission chaired by Supreme Court Chief Justice Earl Warren.

The Soviets exerted efforts to contain their own sphere of influence. The Berlin Wall was built overnight to halt the flow of refugees into the West. Albania was ousted from the Communist bloc due to its support of the People's Republic of China. The Soviet Union was in a stormy relationship with its communist neighbor. China under Mao denounced Russian relations with the West on numerous counts. The Chinese Red Guard was begun in 1966 to activate a cultural revolution designed to recreate a Chinese identity purged of Western influence. In Russia, Khrushchev was replaced by the leadership of Premier Kosygin and President Brezhnev. This was followed by Brezhnev's assertion that Mao's policies posed a threat to the Communist movement throughout the world.

The United Nations suffered its own crisis of leadership in the 1960s. Dag Hammarskjöld, killed in a plane crash, was succeeded by U Thant as UN secretary-general. When war in Cyprus reignited between Turkey and Greece, the United Nations peacekeepers found themselves in the midst of armed conflict. Memories of Nazi Germany were rekindled with the discovery, trial, and execution of Adolf Eichmann by Israel, assuming authority that some considered to be within the province of a world court.

In South Vietnam, war with the Vietcong, supported by North Vietnam, quickly escalated at mid-decade. Martial law was instituted after the assassination of President Dinh Diem, and the U.S. military established an advisory command in South Vietnam during the Kennedy administration. When U.S. and North Vietnamese forces came into open conflict in 1965, American involvement in Vietnam escalated, with Johnson sending in 180,000 troops. Opposition to the war by Senators Gruening and Morse in 1964 marked the participation of high-ranking governmental officials in the student-dominated protests over U.S. involvement in Vietnam. The Gulf of Tonkin Resolution, used subsequently in lieu of a declaration of war, enabled President Johnson to order military action in Vietnam. Students, frequently investigated for subversive activities, staged protests of governmental interference in their lives and activities and in those of others. The AFL-CIO pledged support of U.S. halting of communist aggression in Vietnam, isolating labor from its traditional association with liberal intellectuals. The step-up of the military draft led to increased protest and a law forbidding the destruction of draft cards. This law proved an ideal symbol of governmental control for protestors; two Roman Catholic priests and brothers, Daniel and Philip Berrigan, became infamous when they poured human blood and napalm on draft records.

The demand to be heard crossed ideologies, cultures, and boundaries. Recognizing the need for reform of the justice system, worldwide protest accompanied the execution of seemingly rehabilitated convict Caryl Chessman, including appeals for his life by Albert Schweitzer, Aldous Huxley, and Pablo Casals. In 1960, the first female prime minister took office in Ceylon. Contraceptive pills were approved for sale by the Federal Drug Administration. Pat Robertson founded the Christian Broadcasting Network. Powerful voices were heard across the United States in the struggle for civil rights by African Americans. The "sit-in" was initiated as a protest of the Jim Crow laws prohibiting blacks from receiving full service at lunch counters in many southern states. In less than a year, eating establishments became integrated in well over a hundred major U.S. cities. A year later "Freedom Riders" traveled in buses and trains throughout the South, testing desegregation laws, encountering violence, finally being aided by the protection of federal marshals. In 1962 James Meredith became the first black student to attend the University of Mississippi, assisted by U.S. Marshals on his fifth try for admission. Reaction included riots, two deaths, and well over 100 injuries.

Another kind of freedom, freedom from suffering the unchecked effects of technology and industrialization, was vividly brought to public attention by Rachel Carson's *Silent Spring*, a book that did much to stir ecological awareness. This work articulated a growing suspicion that human rights were indeed threatened by the use of excess power by major corporations. In 1961 nearly 30 electrical companies were found guilty and sentenced fines by the U.S. government for rigging bids and fixing prices in the sale of heavy electrical equipment. In 1962 President Kennedy publicly took on big steel and encouraged the awarding of a $5 million Defense Department contract to a small steel firm to prevent U.S. Steel and other major companies from actualizing a large price hike.

By 1963 civil rights advocates protested segregation, brutality, and job discrimination; these issues soared to a high pitch with the killing of Medgar Evers, a black civil rights leader from Mississippi. August of the same year culminated in a march on Washington by over 200,000 civil rights proponents, and a meeting of black leaders with President Kennedy during which Dr. Martin Luther King Jr. lyrically called for all humans to share his dream and "let freedom ring." Massive school boycotts protested *de facto* segregation in major U.S. cities in 1964. Half a year later President Johnson signed the most all-inclusive civil rights legislation in U.S. history. It called for integration of public accommodations; forbade job discrimination by employers and labor unions on the grounds of race, sex, or religion; and included provisions for education, elections, federal funding, and legal protection of the discriminated. The Civil Rights Act of 1964 was tested amid much turmoil, often resulting in major violence, looting, and protesting throughout the nation, the most dramatic being the outbreak of violence in the Los Angeles neighborhood of Watts. In the same year, Dr. Martin Luther King Jr. received the Nobel Peace Prize for his leadership in the civil rights movement and for his promotion of nonviolence. The remarkable journey of Malcolm X came to a tragic and untimely end by assassination.

African Americans who attempted to register to vote in Alabama were violently resisted and had to be assisted by federal troops. When Dr. King led a voting rights march from Selma to Montgomery, it captured the attention of the U.S. media.

Protests against inequality were certainly not isolated to the United States. Third world peoples demanded basic political freedom and economic self-determination. As the sixties progressed and as limited but profound wars developed and lingered in many parts of the world, dissent was voiced by political, racial, ethnic, consumer, poverty-stricken, environmental, and intellectual groups of citizens. Demands were directed to authorities, both economic and governmental, calling for conceptions of equity on multifarious grounds. Inquisitions of leadership came from the grassroots as well as from the top down.

As colonialism disappeared, 14 African countries became independent in 1960. Turmoil and revolution plagued Zaire and Ethiopia. Uganda and Algeria achieved independence. In Ethiopia, the Organization of African Unity was formed in 1963 to advance the shared agenda of these emerging nations. Demonstrations against apartheid were met with repression by the South African government. A protest in Sharpesville ended tragically with 56 people killed. The African National Congress (ANC) responded with violence; the South African premier barely survived an assassination attempt. Nelson Mandela was sentenced to life imprisonment in South Africa for his anti-apartheid activities. The world community spoke against this oppression when a leader of the ANC, Albert John Luthuli, was awarded the Nobel Peace Prize. Across the Atlantic, the dissolution of the West Indies Federation gave independence to Jamaica and Trinidad and Tobago. In 1965, U.S. Marines were sent to quell an uprising in the Dominican Republic and remained in charge on the questionable premise that communists would take control in their absence.

Literature in the first half of the sixties signaled the need for human rights. In 1960 Lionel Bart's *Oliver*, a musical adaptation of Dickens's *Oliver Twist*, reiterated the perennial disparities between rich and poor. William Shirer chronicled the relationship of Nazi power to human freedoms in *The Rise and Fall of the Third Reich*. Vance Packard began his crusade against exploitation by those who disseminate the rampant flow of technological products in *The Waste Makers*. In his play *A Man for All Seasons*, Robert Bolt showed the intolerance suffered by those who stand in moral opposition to political expedience through the character of Thomas More. In much different settings and with different media, the novel *To Kill a Mockingbird* by Harper Lee and the film *Exodus* by Otto Preminger portrayed the ugliness of prejudice, the physical and emotional uprooting that it can engender, and the strength that can overcome it.

The futility of hope in an everyday life that was subject to bureaucracy, power, accident, and ignorance often caused the cry of injustice to wane into detachment. This detachment was depicted in the plays of Edward Albee (*Who's Afraid of Virginia Woolf?, A Delicate Balance*), in Joseph Heller's *Catch-22*, and Tennessee Williams's *The Night of the Iguana*. In 1962, Ken Kesey sensitized his audiences to the life of those unfairly labeled "insane" in his novel *One Flew Over the Cuckoo's Nest*. The same year brought Solzhenitsyn's *One Day in the Life of Ivan Denisovich* and Pasternak's *In the Interlude. The Making of the President, 1960* by T. H. White constructed a popular form of political analysis. Literature of the following year reflected the increased liberation in morals and living situations that was altering the society at large and was derived from the ideas of the so-called new left; illustrations include Mary McCarthy's novel *The Group*; Ionesco's play *Exit the King*; and the film interpretation of Henry Fielding's novel *Tom Jones*. Although there was still box office for the spectacle films that had dominated Hollywood in the fifties (e.g., David Lean's *Lawrence of Arabia*) intimate human dramas such as *A Taste of Honey* and *The Loneliness of the Long Distance Runner* also found audiences. Alfred Hitchcock shocked audiences with his exploration of human violence in *Psycho*.

Concern for the effects of uncontrolled power was a theme in many artistic creations of 1964: Jerry Bock's musical *Fiddler on the Roof*; Stanley Kubrick's film *Dr. Strangelove;* Peter Brook's film adaptation of Golding's novel *Lord of the Flies*; C. P. Snow's novel *The Corridors of Power*; and Gore Vidal's novel *Julian*. Literature from diverse cultures was being sampled through translation. The writing of Yukio Mishima of Japan, Ernesto Sabato of Argentina, and Heinrich Boll of Germany expanded human understanding personally, culturally, and internationally.

The same time period was a coming-of-age for television as a new form of public literature in which the good were victorious and the admirable were successful. This development did much to confirm the sentimentality lurking in the souls of a seemingly detached and suspicious populace. The western and detective genres were ideally suited to promoting this vision. Protest was not commercially successful as entertainment. Lenny Bruce's comedy was relegated to the nightclub circuit and then was banned even from this limited venue when his act was declared obscene. In an era of protest, some of the fine arts remained characteristic of former days. Even the avant-garde of the near past was not immune to tests of the establishment. Thus, while the operas of Britten and Barber, the tone poems of Stravinsky, the compositions and interpretations of Bernstein, and electronic music of Cage and Stockhausen contributed to the musical advancement of the times, it was an emergent pop music group named the Beatles and the new folk music of Bob Dylan that moved the masses.

Herein, calls for social change met the public more fully than through television. Gradually pushing aside songs about first loves and novelty dances like the twist, creative new species of message, bearing musical expression—combining jazz, folk, non-western, electronic, croon, band, orchestral, and rock 'n' roll— were being fashioned by young voices.

Architecture was furthered by Saarinen and Le Corbusier, and painting by Picasso and Miro. Jean Dubuffet's puzzle-like intertwining of humans and objects challenged the viewer. Salvador Dali ventured into the realm of mysticism. A showing of pop art by such artists as Rauschenberg, Johns, and Warhol at a 1963 exhibition at New York's Guggenheim Museum that abstraction began to blend with realism, the bizarre with the ordinary, and the arts of painting, sculpture and architecture began to fuse. James Rosenquist was also noted for his contributions to pop art. These musical and artistic amalgamations exemplified a more pervasive tendency to synthesize in many domains; curriculum was no exception, as is illustrated by the synoptic text.

The first half of the sixties occasioned its share of developments in science, technology, and discovery. Most of these related to the space and armaments races. Americans developed the laser beam and the French tested a nuclear bomb in 1960. In the following year the USSR sent the first person into space (Yuri Gagarin, in the spaceship *Vostok*) shortly before Alan Shepherd made similar history for the United States. In 1962 three U.S. astronauts orbited the earth. *Telstar*, a communications satellite was developed and put in operation and an unmanned spacecraft named *Ranger* successfully reached the moon. In 1963, Valentina Tereshkova became the first woman to orbit the earth as a Russian cosmonaut. The next year U.S. *Ranger VII* photographed the moon, and *Mariner IV* began its journey to do the same on Mars, succeeding in 1965. In the same year, Soviet cosmonauts and American astronauts walked together in space. At the same time that the space race was flourishing, Jacques Piccard and Don Walsh, with support from the U.S. Navy, descended to an unprecedented 36,000 feet by bathysphere in the Pacific.

In the life sciences, Crick and Watson confirmed the double helix structure of DNA in 1961, opening the way for future quantum jumps in the genetic sciences and related areas. Science also pointed out negative phenomena. In 1962 scientists discovered that thalidomide caused deformities in babies. In 1964 the official surgeon general's report that linked smoking and cancer was issued. In 1965 President Johnson signed a law requiring that a health warning be printed on cigarette packages, thus contributing to the right to knowledge that influences health.

By mid-decade international developments were many, varied, and often heated. Indonesia withdrew from the United Nations. West Germany initiated diplomatic relations with Israel. France withdrew from NATO. Disputes between India and Pakistan, centered on control of Kashmir, were temporarily quelled by the Tashkent Declaration. In a different realm, the Roman Catholic Church concluded its deliberations at the Second Vatican Council, issuing a series of declarations and constitutions that would reshape the identity of this denomination and foment internal division.

World leadership underwent marked changes as well: Lyndon B. Johnson was elected to his first full term as U.S. president, resoundingly defeating Barry Goldwater in 1964; Charles de Gaulle was re-elected president of France; Podgorny was named president of the USSR; South African Prime Minister H. F. Verowerd was assassinated, succeeded by B. J. Vorster. Indira Gandhi became prime minister of India. In 1967 Greek army officers seized power, forcing the exile of King Constantine and resulting in the emergence of George Papadopolous as leader of the military government. The Rhodesian declaration of independence was met with British animosity, U.S. trade bans, and sanctions by the United Nations.

In 1967, tensions mounted and fighting erupted between Israel and Arab nations over the Gulf of Aqaba, the Gaza Strip, the Golan Heights, and Jordan territories. By order of the United Nations, a cease-fire was achieved. The next year the U.S.S. *Pueblo* was seized by North Korean forces and was later returned amid strange diplomatic circumstances. The same year Soviet and other Warsaw Pact troops invaded Czechoslovakia to depose Alexander Dubcek and to quell freedoms initiated by him as the newly named Communist Party leader. The Nigerian civil war continued, resulting in the secession of Biafra amid great suffering. In Northern Ireland, eruptions over rights of Roman Catholic minorities involved British troops by the end of the decade. Conflict between Arabs and Israelis resumed with the 1968 hijacking of an Israeli airplane by Arabs. In 1969, Golda Meir became Israel's prime minister and appealed to the United States for military aid. By the decade's conclusion, de Gaulle resigned and was succeeded by Pompidou in France, and in Spain, Franco designated Juan Carlos as his successor.

Meanwhile, in the United States, the last half of the sixties was fraught with increased protest and dissension on issues of race and involvement in Vietnam. Dramatic inroads were being made in African American leadership. The Supreme Court ruled that the Georgia legislature must seat black legislator Julian Bond. Robert Weaver was the first black appointed to the U.S. presidential cabinet, Edward Brooke became the first African American U.S. senator; Bill Russell was the first African American to be named head coach of a National Basketball Association team. Sidney Poitier, the first African American to receive an Academy Award for best actor, was featured in the social drama, *In the Heat of the Night*. Civil rights organizations, however, were in disunity. As leaders of the Student Nonviolent Coordinating Committee, Stokely Carmichael and H. Rap Brown shifted emphasis from civil rights to black power. This stance was accepted by the Congress of Racial Equality (CORE) but not wholly endorsed by the NAACP and the Southern Christian Leadership Conference (SCLC). Dr. Martin Luther King Jr., head of the SCLC, was educating the public on connections between economic structures, U.S. involvement in Vietnam, and institutional racism, distancing himself from the more limited agenda of the NAACP. Racial violence in 1967 occurred in well over 100 cities, most notably Newark and Detroit. By 1968, FBI Director J. Edgar Hoover called for a counterintelligence program to prevent the formation of a coalition of militant black nationalist groups. In April of 1968 Martin Luther King Jr. was assassinated in Memphis, an act that led to violent rioting in most U.S. cities and the use of federal troops and National Guard forces to control outbreaks. The next year Chicago Black Panther leader Fred Hampton was killed by police acting under orders from the FBI.

Protests against the Vietnam War grew. By 1967, a women's peace group, several thousand scientists, Martin Luther King Jr., and huge numbers of students demonstrated for an end to the war. Dissent focused on the draft, and several persons self-immolated as suicide protests. Muhammad Ali was stripped of his title of World Heavyweight Boxing Champion for refusing military induction on the grounds of being a conscientious objector. Massive demonstrations occurred frequently in protest of the U.S. government's excessive involvement in foreign and private matters, accusing the government of coalition with the bastions of economic power. Famous persons from many walks of life—folk singer Joan Baez, pediatrician Dr. Benjamin Spock, Harvard biologist George Wald—joined in sympathy with many elements of the protest arguments.

The 1967 film *The Graduate*, starring Dustin Hoffman, expressed the younger generation's perception of hypocrisy and deceit in the older generation. The anti-establishment hippie musical *Hair* opened to packed theaters. A new form of music, derived in part from the use of hallucinogenic drugs and labeled "psychedelic," was born in San Francisco by the Grateful Dead, Jefferson Airplane, and others.

By 1968 America had a half million troops in Vietnam; Senators Eugene McCarthy and Robert F. Kennedy denounced the war, challenging President Johnson's renomination by the Democratic Party. Traditional Southern Democrats found allegiance with the campaign of George Wallace, governor of Alabama. Johnson withdrew from the race, recognizing that the war had made him a political pariah. In the same year Robert Kennedy was assassinated after winning the California primary election. The Democratic convention in Chicago is less remembered for Hubert Humphrey's being named the Democrats' presidential candidate as it is for the unleashing of violence in the streets with "yippies" and police in direct confrontation. Humphrey was closely defeated in the presidential race later in the year by Richard M. Nixon. The decade ended with publications about the My Lai massacre, countless demonstrations in small towns and cities, and a culminating march of 150,000 protestors to Washington in 1969.

The late sixties also brought the emergence of Ralph Nader's "raiders," who alleged economic and consumer injustices. Jimmy Hoffa was reelected Teamsters Union president, despite his conviction for having used union funds for bail money. Reports appeared that the National Student Association received several million dollars worth of support from the CIA through fictitious foundations. Widespread air hijackings, the Woodstock music festival, the Paris Peace Talks, the Pope's ban on all artificial forms of birth control, and the establishment of Medicare to provide health care for the elderly indicate the discordant tenor of the times.

Simultaneous with the advance of the Vietnam War and the movement for racial equality, the effort to reach the moon continued. *Luna 9* and *Luna 13* made soft unmanned landings on the moon's surface in 1966. In the same year two U.S. spacecrafts joined together while orbiting Earth. The 1967 tragedy when *Apollo 3* exploded on the launch pad, killing three astronauts, did not deter the resolve to achieve the mission. A year later, *Apollo 8* took three astronauts in orbit around the moon. Finally, the great culmination of the first phase of space explorations took place in 1969. While millions watched on television, Neil Armstrong became the first man to walk on the moon, followed by Edwin (Buzz) Aldrin, while Michael Collins piloted their orbiting craft, *Apollo 11*. Soon afterward, *Apollo 12* successfully transported astronauts to obtain lunar samples.

Scientific and technological advance was by no means deterred by the concentration on space exploration. Offshoots occurred in many domains, some of which were highly unexpected. Notable in this regard were the use of plastic hearts in surgery by U.S. physicians in 1966; South African Dr. Christiaan Barnard's first heart transplant in 1967; the 1968 discovery of pulsars by astronomer Martin Ryle; the discovery of the molecular structure of hemoglobin by Max Pertutz, also in 1968; the 1969 discovery of oil in Alaska; and the flight of the French supersonic Concorde airliner in 1969. By the end of the sixties, both China and France had exploded hydrogen bombs.

In 1967, Francis Chichester entered the annals of both exploration and knighthood by circumnavigating the globe in his yacht, while an era of lavish sea travel was closed and another opened with Britain's replacement of the *Queen Mary* with the *Queen Elizabeth II*.

The aesthetics of space technology provided widespread evidence of the too often unrealized union of art and science. Great scientists and artists of any era join together in sophisticated image-making and intuitive empiricism, as is apparent in their work from daVinci to Chagall, and from Archimedes to Einstein. In the late sixties, the art of technology may have overshadowed the formal arts, but there is a large sense in which both illustrated the growth of human imagination pulled by an aesthetic drive to produce the functional. Marc Chagall's mural *The Triumph of Music*, created for the New York Metropolitan Opera House, and the release of the Beach Boys' *Pet Sounds* combined with literary works by Graham Greene (*The Comedians*), Truman Capote (*In Cold Blood*), and William Manchester (*The Death of a President*) to illustrate samples of artistic endeavors in the limelight by 1966. In the same year major artistic masterpieces were destroyed in the floods of Florence. The minimalist sculpture of Donald Judd initiated a new form in this medium. Edward Kienholz used assembly art to create environments with a strong social message. In 1967, pressures associated with racial integration were made vivid in film by Stanley Kramer's *Guess Who's Coming to Dinner?* Desmond Morris tuned the American public to anthropological perspectives with his *Naked Ape*, and Ira Levin horrified many with *Rosemary's Baby*. The Beatles revolutionized popular music with the innovative *Sgt. Pepper's Lonely Hearts Club Band*. The arts of 1968 were represented in the work of Mies van der Rohe in architecture, Gian Carlo Menotti and Jimi Hendrix's frenetic electric guitar in music, Arthur Miller on stage, and new novels by Gore Vidal, Iris Murdoch, and Alexander Solzhenitsyn. In the same year John Updike's *Couples* portrayed the continuing sexual revolution as it moved from the communes of those who "went to San Francisco" to the beginnings of sensitivity and encounter movements that brought sexual openness to life in suburbia and other "established" spheres of society. The neo-folk movement was given voice in Crosby, Stills, and Nash. Sculpture by Calder and music by Stockhausen, Tippet, and Berio characterized artistic expression in 1969. Olivier Messiaen's *The Transfiguration* placed contemplation in a contemporary musical setting. Literary contributions included James Gould Cozzens's *Morning, Noon and Night*, Philip Roth's insight into American Jewish life and feeling in *Portnoy's Complaint*, and Mario Puzo's inside look at the Mafia through, powerful fictitious family of Sicilian background in *The Godfather*. International attention was being given to the writing of Mario Vargas Llosa of Peru, Octavio Paz of Mexico, Gabriel Garcia Marquez of Colombia, and Andre Malroux of France.

Film had also become an international medium in the decade through the proliferation of art cinemas in most urban areas. Audiences were being exposed to the work of Federico Fellini (*8½; La Dolce Vita*), Lucino Visconti, and Michelangelo Antonioni (*Blow Up*) of Italy; Francois Truffaut and Jean Luc Goddard of France; the Czech filmmaker Milos Foreman; Costa Garvas; and Roman Polanski (the latter three all later came to work in the United States). The tone of despair that concluded the films *Midnight Cowboy* and Dennis Hopper's *Easy Rider* challenged the hedonistic optimism of the "flower children" to consider the realities of the contemporary world. Finally, capturing the space conquest and pointing to new directions and possible perils as science fiction writers have often done, Stanley Kubrick helped conclude the decade with his film *2001: A Space Odyssey*.

With a major phase of space exploration completed in 1969, some questioned future government allocations of funding, contending that other social programs demanded attention. The quest for racial equality was pushed forward at great cost to many committed to it, and the future direction was unclear. The media exposed no small level of public disenchantment with the power of business and government, focusing on the war in Vietnam, the domination of the consumer, and the devastation of the environment. Far from resolved, these issues, combined with mushrooming technological achievement and budding commitment to fight poverty in urban areas, set the stage for the emergence of the seventies.

CURRICULUM THOUGHT AND LITERATURE

If the production of curriculum books in the fifties was prolific as compared to previous decades, this propensity for production was magnified in the sixties. During this decade over 180 more books were published than in the fifties. This can be attributed, in part, to vast increases in educational funding. As a response to *Sputnik,* the funds provided through the National Defense Education Act of 1958 reached fruition in the early sixties. In 1965, the Elementary and Secondary Education Act provided additional funding opportunity. The increased attention to education by the media, the widespread granting of funds for educational research and development from both private and public sources, and a naive faith in the schools as a solution to poverty, all combined to usher in an era of unprecedented financial support for education. If the twenties belonged to social behaviorists, if the twenties and thirties were the golden age for progressive curriculum, and if the fifties were a golden age for synoptic texts and curriculum specialists in schools, the sixties was literally the age of "gold" for curriculum projects. These projects were most often conceived as highly structured sets of procedures and materials, usually designed by specialists in the academic disciplines dominated by the sciences, mathematics, and languages.

Funding for curriculum projects was often derived from the aforementioned federal programs; derivative programs that stemmed from them; numerous sources within the Department of Health, Education, and Welfare; and/or sources such as the National Science Foundation, the National Endowment for the Humanities, as well as private foundations such as Carnegie and Ford. A covert if not overt hope of many project authors was to produce "teacher-proof" materials, that is, materials that would achieve goals without distortion by teacher implementation. Given the constitutional decentralization of educational policy making to states and local governments, federal funding of education would have been considered less than constitutionally correct. Justification was achieved by claiming that the funding of education was for purposes of national defense.

Cognitive psychological theories were often drawn upon to design the organizational properties of such projects. Jean Piaget and Jerome Bruner were most often referenced. Piaget was cited for his theories of a developmental structure implicit in the growing mind of the child (Piaget, 1929, 1952; Piaget & Inhelder, 1969). Many advised that his stages of cognitive development should establish the sequence for ordering learning experiences. Bruner advocated a related conception, a structuralist position known as the "structure of the discipline" approach. In his highly influential book *The Process of Education* (1960, reissued with a new preface in 1977), Bruner argued that each discipline possessed an inherent structure that, when understood, opened the door to provide the learner with an essential ability to piece together elements of that discipline with relative ease. Whereas Piaget studied the learner, Bruner studied the organization of the academic discipline to determine the learning experiences most appropriate to the learner's cognitive development. Academic subjects would be revisited in a regular pattern, sometimes labeled a "spiral" curriculum, since students expand and deepen understanding with each successive exposure to the academic discipline. Both theories accepted Dewey's dictum to move from the "psychological to the logical," but established different research agendas based on this agreement. Piaget and Bruner, along with Dewey and Herbart, assumed the primacy of child interest and activity in interacting with an environment to experience constructions of knowledge that eventually lead to the fund of knowledge organized in the growing disciplines of academe.

The complexity of this argument and the necessity to mass-disseminate educational insight often worked at odds with one another. It seemed impossible to convey such complicated ideas in meaningful ways to hundreds of thousands of practitioners in brief periods of time. It is little wonder why authors of curriculum projects of the sixties provided rigorously structured materials that were not to be altered relative to teacher and student needs and interests. While the design of some projects was admirable, and while the assumption that instructional materials are a prime source of content for the curriculum was surely warranted, later studies point to marked discrepancies between design and implementation.[1] Schaffarzick and others pointed out that the comparisons of the results of the new curriculum project with those of traditional curricula are dependent on the tendencies of evaluation instruments themselves toward the newer or the traditional curricula. One can find descriptions of the curriculum projects in numerous sources, including the synoptic texts of the 1960s and 1970s. For more detailed treatment one may refer to original project documents, journal articles, research reports, and books such as Heath (1964).

A central point drawn from the above bears heavily on the state of schools of curriculum thought that were developed during preceding chapters. In the fifties the popularity of presenting curriculum literature in the synoptic text tended to favor the conciliar fusing of experientialist, social behaviorist, and intellectual traditionalist thought. One effect of this fusion was that it promoted a unified appearance to curriculum literature and helped curriculum scholarship assert a tighter grip as a recognized domain of inquiry. At the same time, it tended to dilute each of the three positions. It could be argued that unification had a positive influence, that is, it reduced the pejorative tendency to myopically cling to one school of thought or another. Alternatively, it could be argued that unification brought undue simplification; an attempt to provide eclecticism where the pieces could not defensibly be fit together.

During the early fifties, curriculum implementation in schools largely rejected the essential life needs variant of experientialism when it came under attack by a series of popular authors. Although progressivism was manifest in the literature from the late 1920s to the mid-1940s, it always embodied an experientialist curriculum that took a back seat to the intellectual traditionalists in practice. Granted, during the Progressive era practice did sway in the experientialist direction for numerous high profile schools and school districts. Despite the results of the Eight Year Study, the curriculum pendulum in the early fifties swung away from the experientialists. The social behaviorist flavor of precision, efficiency, and prepackaging inched its way into practice in the fifties. These characteristics became major features of the curriculum project movement.

Propelled by the space race, proponents of this orientation leaped onto the curriculum project bandwagon and stayed there in the sixties. Oddly enough, they embodied quite different versions of structure as compared with the "structure of disciplines" approach that was a central feature at the movement's start. Drawn from Dewey, Piaget, and Bruner, and illustrated by Elam (1964) and Ford and Pugno (1964), the structure of the disciplines was learned through interaction and discovery. It was connoted that the organization of knowledge would develop through transactions among the learners, the society, and the environment, and would not be imposed by an outside expert. Despite this orientation, however, the spontaneity of discovery and the emergence of objectives through collaboration gave way to a social behaviorist's interpretation. This interpretation emphasized a means-ends rationale with predetermined objectives that governed, or at least rationalized, systematically designed learning activities. Such a turnabout was promoted in many synoptic texts. If it was not conveyed overtly, it was done covertly by the brevity implicit in vast coverage. The result embodied the technology of behaviorism and systems applications. It ushered in a new version of social behaviorism and systems applications. With growing demands for government accountability in society at large came increased demands for curricularists to pre-specify what they planned to achieve, to directly strive to obtain it, and then to prove that they had. Hence, behavioral objectives arrived on the curricular scene. It was a social behaviorism that differed from the aims of Bobbitt's and Charters's behaviorism. Focus was on disciplinary knowledge, not occupations or ideal adult activities. Intellectual traditionalists and social behaviorists had found each other, reconciled by their shared interpretation of the insightful construct of Jerome Bruner. Bruner's conciliarism, perhaps the most intelligent synthesis of the three perspectives in the century, was translated into a technician's dream, an intellectual's puzzle, and for many teachers, an administrative burden.

Robert Mager, a popular promoter of behavioral objectives, attacked the use of general or global objectives that pervaded educational literature. Global objectives were found to lurk in many a curricular corner; examples include vague pronouncements by zealots of Progressivism, writers of "principles" in synoptic texts, and statements of goals by governmental commissions and educational associations such as the National Education Association. As an alternative, Mager and others called for businesslike specification of objectives stated in terms of observable behavior, with time limits for actualization and criteria to evaluate accomplishment. It is interesting to note that Mager's humorous and sensible but rather simplistic explanations, for example, *Preparing Instructional Objectives* (1962), were designed to move those who wrote objectives away from the use of vague terms with multiple interpretations. The immense popularity of the above book, however, produced staunch proponents of this new approach, who rejected goal statements that had even a tinge of vagueness, lacked time specifications, lacked definitive criteria for evaluation, or failed to specify results in observable (and hopefully reasonable) behaviors.

Taken in moderation, the idea, not particularly novel to curriculum literature, provided useful clarification, but in exaggerated interpretation it became
ludicrous, superficial, and cumbersome. One could imagine teachers agonizing
about the observable behaviors that indicated appreciation of Beethoven's Sixth
Symphony, or committees deliberating for years about all of the prerequisite
specific behaviors needed to learn matrix algebra. The dilemma was that no one
had time to thoroughly perform these tasks, but accountability pressures said
that they had to be carried out. So they were done superficially. Some publishers capitalized on this problem and provided stockpiles of behavioral objectives,
sometimes known as performance objectives. Schools that had neither the time
nor the desire nor the ability to comply with these demands to produce objectives could simply purchase the kind and number of objectives that met their
requirements.

A variation within the movement included the specification of competencies
assumed to equal proficiency in mastering course content. Sometimes competencies became substitutes for objectives. In some cases, thousands of competencies were identified for certain aspects of curriculum, for example, in a
teacher education curriculum. Hence, effective teaching was equated with
demonstration of a certain number of competencies.

Just as the first social behaviorists, such as Bobbitt, Charters, Snedden, and
G. S. Hall before them, sought to emulate the science and technology of their
day, many proponents of behavioral objectives in the sixties couched their
pronouncements in the rhetoric of systems analysis and behaviorist psychology.
Their justification of results with complex psychometrics is not an unfamiliar
practice today. This, however, was apparently enough to satisfy many government agencies, which were increasingly oriented to the language of business and
technology. Governmental mandates to justify programs with quantitative
portrayals of success often required work based on an epistemology that only
admitted evidence of achievement or worth relative to prespecified ends. Thus,
the increased involvement in curriculum projects by behaviorist psychologists
and other social scientists brought with it their methodology, which fit, or
created, the desire for quantitative assessment of means-ends productivity.
From this time well into the 1980s, curriculum research was dominated by social
science methodology. Subsequently, quantitative competence increased markedly; requirements in doctoral programs fostered it. It is interesting to note that
this movement was born in the social expediency of a space race permeated by a
means-ends model of production and accountability.

Both behavioral objectives and curriculum evaluation through quantitative
assessment are clearly a part of the social behaviorist tradition. Both are quite
different from the experientialist epistemology on which the curriculum projects

movement was initiated. Experientialist assumptions about an internal structure of knowledge, the importance of child study, student interest, experience, and genuine discovery faded into routinization and mass production. Proper form, behavioral objectives, and their accoutrements became the emphasis rather than justifications for learning activities and curricular proposals. Focus on the problem of whether the means brought prespecified ends became so central that it obscured deliberation about the worth of purposes and their assumptions.

The above background facilitates the review of the categories of curriculum books that appeared in the sixties. Given this setting, we will now consider the kinds of curriculum books that were produced.

A major category of curriculum text that appeared in the sixties consisted of newer editions of earlier synoptic texts. Both those of the general variety and those that focused on elementary or secondary levels continued to appear in revised form. Examples include Beck, Cook, and Kearney (1960); Gwynn (1960) and Gwynn and Chase (1969); Lee and Lee (1960); Ragan joined by Stendler (1960, 1966); Alberty and Alberty (1962); Burton (1962); Douglass (1964); Saylor and Alexander (1966, with considerable changes from the 1954 version, including title changes); Van Til, Vars, and Lounsbury (1967); Sowards and Scobey (1968), and Tyler (1969, representing one of several reprintings). The appearance of reprints, new editions, and substantial revisions attests to the relevance attributed to certain texts. Sales provide evidence of demand for more of the same or similar; and sales are dependent on the judgments of curriculum scholars who order books for courses that they teach. Thus, a sort of refereeing system is at work in producing the demand for subsequent editions of texts.

The refereeing process, no doubt, reminds readers of journals. Since this book directly treats only special journal issues (as described in the introductory sections), salient journal articles are included in this book indirectly due to the widespread emergence of another kind of curriculum book: namely, books of readings on curriculum topics. Such collections often provide seminal journal articles as well as original selections. Thus, the salient role of journal articles is not omitted from this exhibit of curriculum thought. Although collections of readings can be traced in the curriculum literature to Caswell and Campbell (1937), it wasn't until the sixties that such collections were commonly published. Examples of books that provided original pieces and/or those selected from journals include Passow (1962), Sowards (1963), J. R. Wright (1963), Chasnoff (1964), Douglass (1964), Ether (1964), Huebner (1964), Passow (1964), Passow and Leeper (1964), Rosenbloom (1964), Hass and Wiles (1965), Leeper (1965a), Leeper (1965b), Unruh (1965), Callaway (1966), Halverson (1966), Leeper (1966), Macdonald and Leeper (1966), Martin and Pinck (1966), Robison (1966), Alexander (1967), Alpren (1967), Berman (1967), Leeper

(1967), Heller and Rosenthal (1968), Kerr (1968), Kopp (1968), Leeper (1968), Short and Marconnit (1968), Steeves (1968), Unruh and Leeper (1968), Witt (1968), Bar (1969), Dragositz (1969), Frazier (1969), Guttchen and Bandman (1969), Hamilton and Saylor (1969), Jones (1969), Rubin (1969), and Vars (1969). Surveying journals, of course, can prove very valuable to curriculum students and scholars. Direct study of journals can provide a context of historical perspectives and a flavor of that which was deemed important in a particular time period.[2]

New variations on the synoptic text and new types of curriculum contributions appeared in the sixties. Chief among the latter are books that dealt with varieties of organizational patterns and their curricular implications. The literature was by no means confined to these areas. Philosophical analyses, practical proposals, historical inquiries, and an array of other variations appeared. So many were the varieties and so defiant are they of categorization that the remainder of the contributions made in the 1960s will be discussed on a yearly basis.

New general synoptic treatments in 1960 included Brown's *Curriculum Development* and Wood's *Foundations of Curriculum Planning and Development*. Synoptic books that appeared at the elementary level were *Elementary School Curriculum* by Jameson and Hicks and *Curriculum Development in the Elementary School* by Rucker. Published at the secondary level were Krug's *The Secondary School Curriculum* and *Preparation of Secondary School Curriculum* by UNESCO's International Bureau of Education. McNally, Passow, and Associates produced *Improving the Quality of Public School Programs* (1960), a book that provided an overview of change, a process for curriculum improvement, administrative considerations and procedures, as well as seven cases of actual curriculum improvement programs. Other case approaches in 1960 included Butterweck and Spessart on the unified curriculum; Ewing on primary curriculum in New Zealand; a treatment of the junior high curriculum in London by the National Union of Teachers; and a description of curriculum revision in Japan.

Several other authors of 1960 contemporized topics that had dominated curriculum studies in previous decades: Carlin and Blackman on general education; Anderson on cooperative curriculum improvement; Rudy on liberal arts curriculum; and Ward, Suttle, and Oho on integration. Snyder provided arguments for the self-contained classroom. Although the most prevalent elementary school organizational pattern, this model was under continual fire from those who proposed other grouping strategies. Nancy McCormich Rambusch (1962) sparked renewed interest in the work of Maria Montessori and a network of private schools for young children sprang up in rapid order. Rambusch took on dominant contemporary approaches to early childhood education and demonstrated how Montessori's approach can foster individuality and creative growth.

Thelen's *Education and the Human Quest* (1960), while not explicitly a curriculum book, served as an apology for experientialist education that was compatible with the emphasis on disciplinary knowledge. Education, according to Thelen, is to be the agent for the promotion of reflective inquiry. Deliberation, deviating from Dewey's commitment to unity in consideration of a social problem, is divided into four disciplines: the physical domain, the biological, the social, and the subjective. This last category is a broad field encompassing the concerns of the humanities. Thelen views this last discipline as presenting to the learner "the universal experiences of the human race" (Thelen, 1960, p. 50). Maintained within their proper domains with instruction appropriate to the subject of inquiry, these disciplines provoke maturity, inviting the individual to participate in intelligent living. Skill development is included as a fifth form of inquiry, intended to assist in facilitating the basic forms of inquiry. Thelen's model allowed for the continuation of the structured disciplines of traditional education while incorporating reflective thinking. Thelen illustrated dynamic connections among assumptions, curriculum, instruction, learning environments, and the flow of action. Like Dewey, Thelen argued for a synthesis of inquiry and action in the human quest for growth.

In 1961 the National Education Association contributed to the legacy of national statements on educational purposes by government agencies and professional associations. The kinds of statements produced by these groups exemplified global objectives par excellence. Such objectives were later the brunt of criticism by behavioral objectives advocates. Both groups were usually guilty of lacking serious theoretical justifications. Many seconded the need for serious curriculum theory declared necessary by the 1947 Chicago conference on that topic discussed earlier, although neither did much to contribute to it.

A new kind of book appeared in 1961 that was devoted entirely to curriculum theory. *Curriculum Theory* by George A. Beauchamp was written almost entirely in the vein of systems theory and engineering models that stemmed from the natural sciences. Although criticized by some for oversimplification and lack of specific applicability to educational problems, demand brought new editions in 1968 and 1975. Furthermore, Beauchamp's orientation represented a mode of curriculum theory well suited to the social behaviorist style of curriculum research in the sixties. The emphasis on combining theory with research could be seen in many curriculum books of this period, for example, Haan (1961). The engineering emphasis raised questions about who should be involved in curriculum decisions. Research and theory were frequently viewed as best presented from the top down, relative to organizational charts of schools, within which teachers could be represented in committee structures. Balancing this top-down orientation were treatments of the teachers' roles in curriculum making by Leese, Frasure, and Johnson (1961) and Sowards and Scobey (1961).

A different interpretation of balance was expressed in the Association for Supervision and Curriculum Development Yearbook of 1961, *Balance in the Curriculum*. Its authors questioned the variety of emphases that school experiences brought to students. Variety of experiences was also the concern of Phenix (1961). His approach probed deeply into the fabric of assumptions undergirding curriculum, stressing that any desire to educate implies moral advocacy about conceptions of the common good. Phenix's unique perspective links him to earlier writers on education who thought outside the dominant orientations, providing background for the emergence of reconceptualist thought in the 1970s. Taking the perspective of analytic philosophy, Smith and Ennis produced a book that made clear the need to scrutinize educational and curricular concepts. Old textbooks were interpreted by Nietz in the same year.

School organization and curriculum were a major concern, as evidenced in proposals by Stoddard (1961) and Trump and Baynham (1961). A history of education and curriculum, with special emphasis on the development and decline of progressive education (1876–1957), was brilliantly narrated by Lawrence Cremin in *The Transformation of the School*. Another historical landmark, Raymond Callahan's *Education and the Cult of Efficiency* (1962), criticized the social efficiency image of curriculum and education in general. Similarly, Krug's (1964) historical rendition of the high school is a classic contribution.

The publication of Hilda Taba's *Curriculum Development: Theory and Practice* in 1962 marked a high point among synoptic texts that treated curriculum development generally rather than relative to a particular level of subject area. Her text drew from a variety of disciplines, described forces that influence curriculum, discussed the areas made perennial by Tyler, and added special emphasis on diagnosis and unit construction. The experientialist flavor of John Dewey as well as Tyler, two of her mentors, can be found throughout the text. The work was widely used in curriculum courses, prompting a 1971 reprint.

Parker, Edwards, and Stegeman (1962) provided an elaborate treatment of the state of curriculum in America. In the same year Fraser contributed perspectives on curriculum studies in academic subjects. Harry Passow advanced an array of interpretations of curriculum at the juncture of past and present that merged as proponents of synoptic texts and curriculum projects faced one another. The appearance of the collected papers of Virgil Herrick centralized many of his writings and materials that contributed incisively and insightfully to the development of curriculum thought for many years. Another collection of perceptive essays was made available in 1962 by Northrop Frye and titled *Design for Learning*. Other 1962 citations revealed the following: considerations of sources of curriculum by the ASCD, scholarly interpretations of schooling by the NEA, multidisciplinary approaches by Waetjen, undergraduate curricular flexibility by Cole, and core curriculum by Durham.

While much that had to do with curriculum was highly social behaviorist in nature, the re-emergence of humanized or personalized education was signaled by the popular 1962 ASCD Yearbook entitled *Perceiving, Behaving, Becoming*. This new version of the experientialist position was replete with essays by prominent writers (e.g., Carl Rogers, Abraham Maslow, and Arthur Combs) who added existentialist and phenomenological perspectives to the child-centered, whole person, and interest-based features of experientialist thought.

Developments in the curriculum literature of 1963 illustrate the growing concern for alternative forms of curricular organization. A revised edition of the influential Goodlad and Anderson conceptualization of the nongraded elementary school appeared along with Brown's interpretation of the same topic at the secondary level. *Unit Teaching* by Hanna, Potter, and Hagaman, research on core approaches by Wright, and an emphasis on humanized curriculum by Manning rounded out the newer ideas about curriculum organization. In the years that followed, much literature emerged that profoundly influenced curriculum organization. Readers are encouraged to review literature on such topics as individualized instruction, open education, ability grouping, multigrades, team teaching, departmentalization, differentiated staffing, mini-courses, peer teaching, open space schooling, schools without walls, schools within schools, and alternative schools. Some of these issues were highlighted in the 1963 ASCD Yearbook, *New Insights and the Curriculum*, edited by Frazier.

Still another organizational perspective was aired by the ASCD in *The Unstudied Curriculum*, a publication that presaged by several years the notion of "hidden curriculum," arguing that any intended curriculum has side effects and that these influences, whether unintended or clandestinely designed, can provide profound lessons. Other publications during 1963 continued to present guidelines for curriculum planning in the vein of the synoptic texts; examples are by Davis, Fleming, Fraser, Leese, Shuster and Ploghoft, Thorton and Wright, Wiles, and Wood. Among these, John Goodlad gave special attention to teachers, and Leese emphasized the role of superintendents in curriculum change. A combined effort by the ASCD and the American Association of School Administrators called for action, not just proposals to improve curricula. Kimball Wiles attempted to communicate the impact of changing curricula at the high school level in the same year. This emphasis on curriculum change weighed heavily in the literature of 1964. Alexander dealt with changing content. Anderson noted the need to find new avenues through which changes could meaningfully emerge. Doll combined emphasis on change with the style of the synoptic text in *Curriculum Improvement: Decision-making and Process*, a work that went through revisions for three more decades. John Goodlad reviewed the recent reform movement organized around curriculum projects as it had thus far developed in the United States. Specific contributions to organizational conceptions include Beggs, Blocker and McCabe, Bush and Allen, and Hanson. Elam, and Ford and Pugno, exemplified epistemological organization that facilitated the "structure of the disciplines" orientation of the curriculum projects movement.

Another kind of structuralist position that had vast implications for curriculum organization was articulated at a curriculum conference at Cornell University, namely, the implications of Piagetian research and theory. Krathwohl et al. continued the analytic approach to cognitive levels initiated by Benjamin Bloom and others (1956) by extending a taxonomical structure into the affective domain. Both this work and the earlier taxonomy by Bloom gave organizational structure to curriculum projects and to behavioral objectives. Collections by Rosenbloom and by de Grazia and Sohn surveyed recent curriculum viewpoints, organizational patterns, and technologies for implementing them. Provocative critical appraisals of such movements were provided in collections by Huebner (1964), Passow (1964), and Passow and Leeper (1964). Perhaps an antidote to the pervasive emphasis on structure, Harold Rugg, once aligned with learner-centered experientialism and later with social reconstruction, devoted the remainder of his career to a topic that was not aligned with any of the dominant orientations: a thoroughgoing study of the human imagination and its value in educational endeavor (Rugg, 1963).

Synoptic texts continued to appear in 1964, as exemplified by Beauchamp and also by Crosby at the elementary level, and by the second "University of Illinois" group, Broudy, Smith, and Burnett, at the secondary level. The latter was similar to the Smith, Stanley, and Shores text (1950 and 1957) in that it went far beyond the encyclopedic treatments of usual synoptic texts to build theoretical perspectives from which further curriculum thought could be generated. Thus, *Democracy and Excellence in American Secondary Education* by Broudy, Smith, and Burnett contributed to an integration of classical realist and pragmatic theory vis-à-vis curriculum. Its integration of experientialist thought is not so pronounced, however, as to mark it as squarely within that orientation. Rather, it reminds the reader of another philosophical excursion into curriculum provided by Philip Phenix, who departed markedly from the usual philosophic origins of curriculum writing. His *Realms of Meaning* (1964) explored alternative epistemological bases and their implications for curriculum that fostered general education.

In the historical vein, Elson's *Guardians of Tradition* provided a provocative rendition of text materials and their role in preserving values considered American through the institution of schooling. This is one of the first attempts to analyze functions of schooling by studying the materials that, in fact, become the curriculum in the absence of serious local planning and imagination. Historical remembrances of women educators gave testimony to the value of curricula constructed through life experiences. Rackhorn Holt's (1964) biography of Mary McLeod Bethune gave due attention to the contributions of this pioneer in the education of African American women at the beginning of the century. This work joined other important autobiographical reflections by women educators. Septima Poinsette Clark (1962), an African American teacher and important contributor to the Highlander Center's organizing of citizenship schools, offered a reflection of her life's work; Sylvia Ashton-Warner (1963) provided a stunning alternative to the education of Maori children in New Zealand by detailing the culturally relevant curriculum and instruction she developed as a teacher. The remembrances of Polingaytsi Qoyanayma (1964), an educator of Hopi origins, detailed the struggle of striving to maintain her ethnic identity while living in contemporary New Mexican society.

In 1965, books by Vernon E. Anderson and A. I. Oliver each added to the continued emergence of synoptic texts that were designed to present general overviews and guidelines for curriculum makers. Clark, Klein, and Burks (1965) made similar applications at the secondary level. Two ASCD publications attempted to define roles for professionals involved in supervision and curriculum development. Gladys Unruh and the Ontario Curriculum Institute produced books that continued to emphasize the novelty and rapidity of change in curriculum. Leeper contributed to the curriculum change literature by compiling a fine set of essays in *Strategy for Curriculum Change*. Daniel Tanner called for schools to meet needs of youth, and B. F. Brown advocated "appropriate placement schools," a variation of the nongraded concept. Shack wrote about curriculum from inside teaching in *Armed with a Primer*. The curriculum contributions of Virgil Herrick (mentor of James B. Macdonald, John Goodlad, and Dwayne Huebner, among others) were made even more visible through the editorial efforts of Anderson, Macdonald, and May in their production of *Strategies of Curriculum Development*. Their selection of writings focused on Herrick's conception of the role of organizing centers in curriculum development, interconnections between curriculum and instructional planning and teaching, and other theoretical perspectives on curriculum and teaching. The purpose of assessment in curriculum was moved to the fore by Leeper in his edited work on that matter under the auspices of ASCD. An excellent collection of articles was provided by Hass and Wiles to give a solid overview of curriculum thinking, a publication that would spawn several new editions.

In 1966 Jerome Bruner, author of *The Process of Education* (1960) discussed earlier, expanded on the instructional implications of this earlier work in *Toward a Theory of Instruction*. In the same year the National Education Association, this time through the American Association of School Administrators, produced another statement of focus for educational purposes, urgently labeled as "imperatives." The College Entrance Examination Board, with its continually growing influence, published a work on the challenges presented by curricular change. Two books appeared on the matter of curricular change for which John Goodlad was responsible: *The Changing School Curriculum* (with Von Stoephasius and Klein) and the *Sixty-fifth Yearbook* of the National Society for the Study of Education. Other books on change were authored by Haney, Inlow, Jarvis and Wootton, Leeper, Martin and Pinck, the Ontario Curriculum Institute, the Organization for Economic Cooperation and Development, Sand and Wilson, and Unruh and Leeper.

Goodlad and Richter devised a conceptual system for dealing with curricular and instructional problems, and in *School, Curriculum, and the Individual*, Goodlad wrote about the interwoven nature of these three threads in curriculum fabric: society, institutions, and individuals. These three areas carried considerable influence in the subsequent study of curriculum problems. Several other major issues were raised that provided alternative perspectives on aspects of curriculum thought in 1966. Aceland raised the perennial question about the relationship between curriculum and life. King and Brownell exemplified the need to develop curriculum from a structure of epistemological tenets, thereby contributing a piece of the literature of curriculum theory. Macdonald and Leeper raised issues about language and meaning in educational and curricular discourse and practice, pointing toward expanded notions of curriculum inquiry that emerged in the 1970s and 1980s. Parker and Rubin argued, in an experientialist vein, that process could indeed be the content of curriculum. They challenged curricularists to consider a synthesis of process and content during a time when battles raged between those who demanded strict adherence to content and others who considered process preeminent. Rosenbaum and Toepfer discussed the relationship between curriculum development and school psychology. The need for serious consideration of evaluation was promoted in publications by Lindvall and by Scriven. Additional perspectives on organizational patterns were contributed by the following: the Ontario Association for Curriculum Development on decentralization, Callaway on the core curriculum, and flexible scheduling by Swenson and Keys. In Britain, P. H. Taylor introduced a dual relationship between purpose and structure in curriculum. Meanwhile, 1966, a year of over 40 curriculum books, also found synoptic texts steadily emerging, for example, those by Cay, Koopman, and Jarvis and Wootton, along with new varieties of texts by Saylor and Alexander and by Ragan and Stendler.

As approaches to curriculum rolled off the presses, a tendency prevailed to unknowingly reinvent already discovered curricular "wheels." Thus, the time was ripe for retrospect on earlier events in the curriculum field, for example, the time from just before 1900 to approximately 1940. Such a retrospective was provided by Mary Louis Seguel. In her historical study, she considered the contributions of Frank and Charles McMurry, Dewey, Bobbitt, Charters, Rugg, and Caswell, among others. Moreover, educational practices derived from Dewey's emerging ideas were detailed in Mayhew and Edwards's (1936, reprinted 1966) history of the University of Chicago Laboratory School during the same time period. Dewey founded the school prior to his departure for Columbia University (1896–1903). Dewey's contributions were also insightfully interpreted by Wirth (1966).

Several new initiatives were represented in curriculum literature in 1967. A monograph series under the auspices of the American Educational Research Association was begun in order to stimulate serious consideration of curriculum evaluation. In the first book of the series, Ralph Tyler, Robert Gagne, and Michael Scriven set forth perspectives that, added to Scriven's (1966) treatise on evaluation methodology, were influential for years to come. Although this AERA thrust was geared primarily to broadening the perspectives of scholars, Fred T. Wilhelms spoke to both practitioner leaders as well as scholars on evaluation in the 1967 yearbook of the Association for Supervision and Curriculum Development, advocating the dual role of feedback and guidance in evaluation. Beauchamp and Beauchamp expanded curriculum evaluation's possibilities by introducing aspects of comparative education into the curriculum domain in their analysis of curriculum systems in selected nations. In 1967, works by Burnham, Michaelis, and Gagne helped begin to solidify design language in curriculum writings. Glaser made his concern for adaptive curriculum more visible, thus providing a kind of amalgam of the social behaviorist concern for systematization and that of the experientialist for the person as unique.

In *The Conditions of Learning*, Robert Gagne presented his influential ideas about the hierarchical structure of learning with its progression from the simple and specific to the complex and general as a basis for design. An intelligent diversion from the popular taxonomy of Benjamin Bloom, Gagne asserted that learning is an additive series of capabilities that moves from multiple discriminations to concept learning, to principle learning, to problem solving. In his learning theory he attempted to take into account diverse extant positions on learning, advocating concept analysis, behavioral objectives, systems theory, structuralist approaches, and the research methodologies of empirically oriented social scientists. Another major developmental scheme for curriculum organization, that of Piaget, was critically appraised by Sullivan.

Miscellaneous, yet often significant, contributions to curriculum literature also appeared in 1967. They moved in both novel and previously treated domains. Books by Conner and Ellena and by Neagley and Evans served as synoptic guidebooks for administrators who developed curricula in schools. The budding renewal of humanistic perspectives in curriculum was furthered by Berman and by Leeper. Aceland contributed to the accumulation of works on curricular integration, and Tewksbury expanded notions of non-gradedness. New curricula in Britain were explained conceptually in a work by Kerr, and practical descriptions of projects were provided in a publication of the Great Britain Schools Council. Verduin continued the group process orientation of Miel, Benne, Lawler, and others on cooperative curriculum improvement. Venable reinforced an idea advocated only superficially in many synoptic texts by providing a book-length treatment of the philosophic roots of curriculum. D. K. Wheeler contributed to curriculum literature in the spirit of Hilda Taba, carving out a conception of situation analysis and adding it to traditional categories of curriculum concern in his *Curriculum Process*.

In 1968, Louise Berman continued to explicate her humanistic orientation in *New Priorities in the Curriculum* by showing how such character dimensions as loving, perceiving, and valuing could be integrated into the usual subject areas of language arts, mathematics, science, and social studies. A more radical interpretation of the proposal asserted that these processes could provide an alternative curriculum, replacing the traditional academic subjects. Another realm of experientialist curriculum emerged in England, and was soon deemed worthy of emulation in America, namely, the British primary school. R. F. Dearden synthesized the philosophical tenets of ideals undergirding schools in *The Philosophy of Primary Education*. Works by H. G. Grobman and by R. Karplus broadened the perspectives on curriculum evaluation. H. T. Johnson called for evaluation through consideration of the disciplines that served as the fundamental building blocks of curriculum ideas. Perhaps the most comprehensive and meticulously organized collection of curriculum readings for the decade was provided by Short and Marconnit in 1968.

Major organizational patterns were elaborated in proposals by Trump and Miller and in the work of Alexander, Williams, Compton, Hines, Prescott, and Kealy (1968) on the middle school. Trump argued for flexible organization that combined large group, small group, and independent study, foreshadowing modular and block scheduling in later decades. William Alexander became a founder of the middle school movement, promoting advisories and attention to the full needs of the adolescent. Novelty, with its correlatives innovation and change, were emphasized in the works of the following: Beck, Meadows, Shane, and Galen-Saylor; Cave; Frazier; Keith, Blake, and Tiedt; Kerr; Leeper; Maclure; Sowards and Scobey; Thomas, Sands, and Brubaker; and Unruh and Leeper. Books by Witt and by Bangs and Hillestad illustrated the impact of technology on curriculum development. Revision of a landmark in British curriculum writing, Nisbet's *Purpose in the Curriculum*, came at a time when funding sources made a multiplicity of alternatives possible in the United States. Nisbet's work served as a rational stabilizer for curricularists whose propensity it was to produce innovation *qua* innovation. The analytic sophistication of this work served to demonstrate, by comparison, the paucity of philosophic scrutiny in behavioral objectives and many superficial proposals for change. Of considerable import, Philip Jackson's *Life in Classrooms* began to sensitize curricularists to the powerful impact of the side effects of intended curriculum and the schooling process itself on the actual learning experiences of students. His work did much to stimulate interest in the hidden curriculum and its multiple interpretations.

A barrage of books that offered advice and caution for the future, reviewed past developments, and reemphasized prior thrusts appeared in 1969. Anderson provided guidelines for times of change on the horizon. Frost and Rowland prepared a synoptic text that pointed toward the need to ready ourselves for a new decade. Alterations in the fourth edition of *Curriculum Principles and Social Trends* by Gwynn and Chase did a similar job. Works by H. T. James et al., H. L. Jones, W. G. A. Rudd, and S. S. Symmes accented the need to prepare for the future. Three humanistic thrusts were forwarded by Crary, Frazier, and Hamilton and Saylor. Mager's (1962) instruction on how to write objectives was developed, refined, and extended by, James Popham (Popham & Baker, 1969), thrusting him into a position of prominence with respect to curricular systemization, behavioral outcomes, and the growing push for demonstrating accountability through sound evaluation. Wilson advocated the necessity of giving primary consideration to the subtle pervasiveness of moral education in all curricular domains. H. Grobman contributed again to the curriculum evaluation literature, as did the ASCD in a monograph on assessment that included major statements by Stake, Stufflebeam, and others. A reprint of Tyler's *Basic Principles of Curriculum and Instruction* (1969) testified to the longevity of interest in that work. Another time-honored curriculum style, the core curriculum, was coupled with interdisciplinary and team approaches by Vars.

Springer furthered the idea of comparing curricula, while Bent and Unruh added to the synoptic literature on secondary curriculum.

Also in the final year of the decade some novel explorations were made in curriculum thought. One that is too little known is a fine analysis of the roles of knowledge, experience, and action in effective education by Cassidy. Another book, edited by Guttchen and Bandman, provided a set of philosophical perspectives on curriculum problems. Also influential in the philosophic vein was Meeker's epistemological portrayal of the structure of intellect. Stockmeyer contributed to the philosophical perspectives on curriculum by interpreting Rudolf Steiner's curriculum for Waldorf schools. Bruce Joyce presented curricular implications of alternative models of elementary education. Hass related the idea of continuous progress to curriculum and instruction, an application proposed much more frequently in the instructional literature of the next decade. Schwab and Walton each responded to major societal issues of the sixties by providing curriculum perspectives relative to them; Schwab to student protest and Walton to the civil rights movement.

Two publications, each published under the auspices of a major educational society, captured central features of the state of curriculum thought at the conclusion of the sixties. The first was another of the special reviews of curriculum research prepared by the *Review of Educational Research*. The second, prepared by Louis Rubin under the auspices of the Association for Supervision and Curriculum Development, focused on the kinds of life skills that enable effective living in both school and society.

In conclusion, the quantity of curriculum contributions during the sixties was massive indeed. The amalgamation of the three schools of curriculum thought, manifest in the synoptic texts of the fifties, was perpetuated in the sixties. The response to the space race contributed to the curriculum projects movement, with offshoots that took on the character and rhetoric of business, industry, and technology. This, too, was an amalgam, but tendencies toward the social behaviorists were apparent.

As with previous decades, an "essentialist" intellectual traditionalism dominated policy and practice. Nonetheless, in the midst of maintaining the traditional curriculum, a new experientialist movement began to emerge under several different guises: revivals of the core curriculum, open education, free schools, humanism, and tendencies toward existentialist orientations. One discovery that was ideally suited to the values of the youthful counterculture was A. S. Neill's account of education at *Summerhill* (1960), the alternative school established to provide education without the damaging repression of social control of a young person's interests, including her or his sexuality. The most powerful impetus for the revival of progressive education, however, were the first-person narratives of teachers like John Holt (1964, 1967), Jonathon Kozol (1967), Herbert Kohl (1967, 1969), James Herndon (1969), and George Dennison (1969). Considered by some as unscholarly, anecdotal, and burdened with ideological and personal assumptions, these works became the inspirational reading of a new generation of teachers. They offered something that the so-often dry and theoretical exercises required by colleges of education did not provide: a reason for aspiring to the profession. Although many of these experientialist variations were distant from the main course of curriculum literature in the sixties, they would be emphasized in new ways in the seventies, not wholly unlike the experientialist tradition of the progressive era. By the end of the decade, best-sellers by William Glasser (1969) and Neil Postman and Charles Weingartner (1969) attempted to articulate the assumptions that guided this novel (or perhaps rediscovered) approach to curriculum and instruction. Such persuasions would, however, be overpowered in practice by the continued mobilization of technological and systematic rhetoric and practice of the social behaviorists.

The case was similar with research. The mode of scholarship that dominated curriculum literature and complemented the emergence of curriculum projects, behavioral objectives, and accountability projects, involved methodologies of social science and behaviorist psychology. Increasingly sophisticated quantitative methods began to replace the lists of guidelines that were, presumably, derived from involvement with the schools as the accepted language of curriculum literature. Although quantitative research did not penetrate curriculum scholarship as boldly as it did certain other areas of education, its theoretic propensity to seek generalizations did so quite thoroughly. In the seventies, alternative languages, ones more consonant with the burgeoning philosophy, situationalism, and humanism of the late sixties, would be offered for the development of curriculum scholarship with a new kind of experientialist character. It was an essay by Joseph Schwab in *School Review* (Schwab, 1969) that offered a substantial challenge to curriculum inquiry and its tendency to generalize. He called for practical inquiry that focused on particular situations, investigated by interaction, not detailed induction; sought context-specific insights; and resulted in morally defensible decisions and actions. Moreover, he called for eclectic arts of matching theories and research to situations, tailoring and adopting theory and research to meet contextual needs, and encouraging practitioners to develop experiential repertoires that guide their work. Finally, Schwab suggested that we see curriculum as a dynamic interaction of teachers, learners, subject matter, and milieu or environment. His initial statement was elaborated in key articles, interpreted by those he influenced throughout the 1970s and 1980s. F. Michael Connelly,

Schwab's student at the University of Chicago, founded and edited *Curriculum Theory Network*, which later became the preeminent journal *Curriculum Inquiry*, centered at the Ontario Institute for Studies in Education at the University of Toronto.

BIBLIOGRAPHY OF CURRICULUM BOOKS 1960–1969

1960

American Educational Research Association. (1960, June). Curriculum planning and development. *Review of Educational Research*, (30).

Anderson, R. H. (1960). *Cooperative action program for curriculum improvement*. Washington, DC: Association for Supervision and Curriculum Development.

Beck, R. H., Cook, W. W., & Kearney, N. C. (1960). *Curriculum in the modern elementary school* (second edition). Englewood Cliffs, NJ: Prentice-Hall.

Brown, A. F. (1960). *Curriculum development*. Philadelphia: Saunders.

Bruner, J. S. (1960). *The process of education*. Cambridge: Harvard University Press.

Butterweck, J. S., & Spessart, K. H. (1960). *The unified curriculum; a case study grades 7–8*. New York: Rinehart.

Carlin, E. A., & Blackman, E. B. (Eds.). (1960). *Curriculum building in general education*. Dubuque, IA: W. C. Brown.

Downey, L. W. (1960). *The task of public education: The perceptions of people*. Chicago: Midwest Advisory Center of the University of Chicago.

Ewing, J. L (1960). *Origins of the New Zealand primary school curriculum, 1840–1878*. Wellington, New Zealand: New Zealand Council for Educational Research.

Gwynn, J. M. (1960). *Curriculum principles and social trends*. (third edition). New York: Macmillan.

International Bureau of Education. (1960). *Preparation of secondary school curriculum*. Paris: UNESCO.

Jameson, M. C., & Hicks, W. V. (1960). *Elementary school curriculum: From theory to practice*. New York: American Book Company.

Japan Department of Education. (1960). *Research and Publications Bureau. Revised curriculum in Japan for elementary and lower secondary schools*. Tokyo, Japan: Department of Education.

Krug, E. A. (1960). *The secondary school curriculum*. New York: Harper and Row.

Lee, J. M., & Lee, D. M. (1960). *The child and his curriculum* (third edition). New York: Appleton-Century-Crofts.

McNally, H. J., Passow, A. H., & Associates. (1960). *Improving the quality of public school programs: Approaches to curriculum development.* New York: Bureau of Publications, Teachers College, Columbia University.

Meriam, J. L. (1960). *The traditional and the modern curriculum: An emerging philosophy.* Berkeley, CA: Mechanics and Design.

National Union of Teachers, London. (1960). *The curriculum of the junior school; a report of a consultative committee.* London: Schoolmaster.

Neill, A. S. (1960). *Summerhill: A radical approach to child rearing.* New York: Hart.

Ragan, W., & Stendler, C. B. (1960). *Modern elementary curriculum* (second edition). New York: Holt, Rinehart and Winston.

Rucker, W. (1960). *Curriculum development in the elementary school.* New York: Harper and Row.

Rudy, S. W. (1960). *The evolving liberal arts curriculum; a historical review of basic themes.* New York: Published for the Institute of Higher Education by the Bureau of Publications, Teachers College, Columbia University.

Synder, E. R. (Ed.). (1960). *The self-contained classroom.* Washington, DC: Association for Supervision and Curriculum Development.

Thelen, H. (1960). *Education and the human quest.* New York: Harper and Brothers.

Traxler, A. E. (Ed.). (1960). *Curriculum planning to meet tomorrow's needs.* New York: American Council on Education.

Ward, J. M., Suttle, J. E., & Oho, H. J. (1960). *The curriculum integration concept applied in the elementary school.* Austin: University of Texas.

Wood, H. B. (1960). *Foundations of curriculum planning and development.* Seattle, WA: Cascade-Pacific Books (also 1963).

1961

Association for Supervision and Curriculum Development. (1961). *Balance in the curriculum.* 1961 Yearbook. Washington, DC: Author.

Baughman, M. D. (Ed.). (1961). *Junior high school curriculum.* Danville, IL: Interstate Press.

Beauchamp, G. A. (1961). *Curriculum theory.* Wilmette, IL: The Kagg Press (also 1968 and 1975).

Cremin, L. A. (1961). *The transformation of the school: Progressivism in American education 1876–1957.* New York: Alfred A. Knopf.

Educational Leadership. (1961). *Who should plan the curriculum?* Washington, DC: Association for Supervision and Curriculum Development.

Educational Policies Commission. (1961). *The central purpose of American education.* Washington, DC: National Education Association.

Fliegler, L. A. (1961). *Curriculum planning for the gifted.* Englewood Cliffs, NJ: Prentice-Hall.

Haan, A. E. (1961). *Elementary school curriculum: Theory and research.* Boston: Allyn & Bacon.

Japan. National Commission for UNESCO. (1961). *Development of school curricula in Japan (by Takeo Miyata).* Tokyo, Japan: UNESCO.

Kitzhaber, A. R., Gorrell, R. M., and Roberts, P. (1961). *Education for college: Improving the high school curriculum.* New York: Ronald Press Company.

Lapati, A. D. (1961). *A high school curriculum for leadership.* New Haven, CT: College and University Press.

Leese, J., Frasure, K., & Johnson, M. Jr. (1961). *The teacher in curriculum making.* New York: Harper and Row.

McGrath, E. J. (1961). *Analysis of the curricular offerings in several independent liberal arts colleges; a report to the U.S. Commissioner of Education on contract number 8AE 8193, project number 647, Public Law 531, Eighty-third Congress.* New York: Teachers College, Columbia University.

Nietz, J. A. (1961). *Old textbooks.* Pittsburgh, PA: University of Pittsburgh Press.

Pennsylvania Department of Public Instruction. (1961). *Pennsylvania curriculum improvement series, Number 1.* Harrisburg, PA: Author.

Phenix, P. H. (1961). *Education and the common good: A moral philosophy of the curriculum.* New York: Harper and Brothers.

Smith, B. O., & Ennis, R. H. (Eds). (1961). *Language and concepts in education.* Chicago: Rand McNally.

Sowards, G. W., & Scobey, M. M. (1961). *The changing curriculum and the elementary teacher.* Belmont, CA: Wadsworth.

Stoddard, G. D. (1961). *The dual progress plan: A new philosophy and program in elementary education.* New York: Harper and Row.

Trump, J. L., & Baynham, D. (1961). *Focus on change: Guide to better schools.* Chicago: Rand McNally.

Van Til, W., Vars, G. F., & Lounsbury, J. H. (1961). *Modern education for the junior high school years.* Indianapolis, IN: Bobbs-Merrill.

Willis, M. (1961). *The guinea pigs after twenty years.* Columbus: Ohio State University.

Wright, G. S. (1961). *The core program: One hundred selected references, 1956–1960; with an addendum of some basic references predating 1956.* Washington, DC: U.S. Department of Health, Education, and Welfare, Office of Education.

Wyckoff, D. C. (1961). *Theory and design in Christian education curriculum.* Philadelphia: Westminister Press.

1962

Alberty, H. B., & Alberty, E. J. (1962). *Reorganizing the high school curriculum* (third edition). New York: Macmillan.

Association for Supervision and Curriculum Development. (A.W. Combs, Ed.). (1962a). *Perceiving, behaving, becoming: A new focus in education. 1962 Yearbook.* Washington, DC: Author.

Association for Supervision and Curriculum Development. (R. R. Leeper, Ed.). (1962b). *What are the sources of curriculum? A symposium.* Washington, DC: National Education Association.

Burton, W. H. (1962). *The guidance of learning activities.* (third edition). New York: Appleton-Century-Crofts.

Callahan, R. (1962). *Education and the cult of efficiency.* Chicago: University of Chicago Press.

Clark, S. P. (1962). *Echo in my soul.* New York: E. P. Dutton.

Clift, V. A., Anderson, A. W., & Hullfish, H. G. (Eds.). (1962). *Negro education in America: Its adequacy, problems, and needs.* New York: Harper.

Cole, C. C. (1962). *Flexibility in the undergraduate curriculum.* Washington, DC: U.S. Government Printing Office.

Dottrens, R. (1962). *The primary school curriculum.* Paris: UNESCO.

Durham, J. T. (1962). *An analysis and critique of core policies and programs.* New York: Teachers College.

Fraser, D. M. (Ed.). (1962). *Current curriculum studies in academic subjects.* Washington, DC: National Education Association.

Frye, N. (Ed.). (1962). *Design for learning.* Toronto: University of Toronto Press.

Herrick, V. E. (1962). *Collected papers and source materials on curriculum operations and structure.* Madison, WI: College Printing and Typing Company.

Mager, R. F. (1962). *Preparing instructional objectives.* Palo Alto, CA: Fearon.

National Education Association. (1962). *The scholars look at the schools: A report of the Disciplines Seminar.* Washington, DC: Author.

Parker, J. C., Edwards, T. B., & Stegeman, W. H. (1962). *Curriculum in America.* New York: Thomas Crowell Company.

Passow, A. H. (Ed.). (1962). *Curriculum crossroads.* New York: Teachers College, Columbia University.

Rambusch, N. M. (1962). *Learning how to learn: An American approach to Montessori.* Baltimore: Helicon Press.

Taba, H. (1962). *Curriculum development: Theory and practice.* New York: Harcourt, Brace and World (also British reprint, 1971).

Waetjen, W. B. (Ed.). (1962). *New dimensions in learning: A multidisciplinary approach.* Washington, DC: Association for Supervision and Curriculum Development.

1963

American Association of School Administrators and the Association for Supervision and Curriculum Development. (1963). *Action for curriculum improvement.* Washington, DC: Authors.

American Educational Research Association. (1963, June). *Curriculum planning and development. Review of Educational Research* (33).

Ashton-Warner, S. (1963). *Teacher.* New York: Bantam.

Association for Supervision and Curriculum Development, Commission on Teacher Education. (1963). *Criteria for curriculum decisions in teacher education; a report.* (George W. Denemark, Chair & Ed.). Washington, DC: Author.

Association for Supervision and Curriculum Development Elementary Education Council. (N. V. Overly, Ed.). (1963). *The unstudied curriculum: Its impact on children.* Washington, DC: Association for Supervision and Curriculum Development.

Brown, B. F. (1963). *The nongraded high school.* Englewood Cliffs, NJ: Prentice-Hall.

Chambliss, J. J. (1963). *Boyd H. Bode's philosophy of education.* Columbus: Ohio State University Press.

Colloquium on Curricular Change: Foreign Language. (1963). *Curricular change in the foreign language.* Princeton, NJ: College Entrance Examination Board.

Davis, R. A. (1963). *Planning learning programs in secondary schools.* Nashville, TN: George Peabody College for Teachers.

Fleming, R. S. (Ed.). (1963). *Curriculum for today's boys and girls.* Columbus, OH: C. E. Merrill.

Fraser, D. M. (1963). *Deciding what to teach.* Washington, DC: National Education Association.

Frazier, A. (Ed.). (1963). *New insights and the curriculum. 1963 Yearbook.* Washington, DC: Association for Supervision and Curriculum Development.

Gilchrist, R. S. (1963). *Using current curriculum developments: A report.* Washington, DC: Association for Supervision and Curriculum Development.

Goodlad, J. I. (1963). *Planning and organizing for teaching.* Washington, DC: National Education Association.

Goodlad, J. I., & Anderson, R. H. (1963). *The non-graded elementary school* (revised edition). New York: Harcourt, Brace and World.

Hanna, L. A., Potter, G. L., & Hagaman, N. (1963). *Unit teaching in the elementary school; social sciences and related sciences.* New York: Holt, Rinehart and Winston.

Leese, J. (1963). *The superintendent and curriculum changes.* Albany: State University of New York.

Manning, D. (1963). *The qualitative elementary school: Characteristics of excellent curriculum*. New York: Harper and Row.

National Education Association. (1963). *Schools for the sixties: A report of the Project on Instruction*. New York: McGraw-Hill.

Rugg, H. O. (1963). *Imagination*. New York: Harper and Row.

Shuster, A. H., & Ploghoft, M. E. (1963). *The emerging elementary curriculum: Methods and procedures*. Columbus, OH: Charles E. Merrill.

Sowards, G. W. (Ed.). (1963). *The social studies: Curriculum proposals for the future*. Chicago: Scott Foresman.

Thorton, J. W., Jr., & Wright, J. R. (1963). *Secondary school curriculum*. Columbus, OH: Charles E. Merrill.

Wiles, K. (1963). *The changing curriculum of the American high school*. Englewood Cliffs, NJ: Prentice-Hall.

Wood, H. B. (1963). *Foundations of curriculum planning and development*. Eugene, OR: The American-Nepal Educational Foundation.

Wright, G. (1963). *The core program: Unpublished research 1956–1962*. Washington, DC: U.S. Department of Health, Education and Welfare, Office of Education.

Wright, J. R. (Ed.). (1963). *Secondary school curriculum*. Columbus, OH: Merrill.

1964

Alexander, W. M. (1964). *Changing curriculum content*. Washington, DC: Association for Supervision and Curriculum Development.

Anderson, V. E. (1964). *Man must find new cowpaths*. Portland, OR: Portland State College.

Association for Supervision and Curriculum Development (R. C. Doll, Ed.). (1964). *Individualizing instruction*. 1964 Yearbook. Washington, DC: Author.

Beauchamp, G. A (1964). *The curriculum of the elementary school*. Boston: Allyn & Bacon.

Beggs, D. W. (1964). *Decatur-Lakeview high school: A practical application of the Trump plan*. Englewood Cliffs, NJ: Prentice-Hall.

Blocker, C. E., & McCabe, R. H. (1964). *Relationships between the informal organization and the curriculum in six junior colleges*. Austin: College of Education, University of Texas.

Broudy, H. S., Smith, B. O., & Burnett, J. (1964). *Democracy and excellence in American secondary education: A study in curriculum theory*. Chicago: Rand McNally (Reprinted by Krieger 1978).

Bush, R. N., & Allen, D. W. (1964). *A new design for high school education*. New York: McGraw-Hill.

Centre for Educational Research and Innovation. (1964). *Handbook on curriculum development*. London: OECD, Her Majesty's Stationery Office.

Chasnoff, R. E. (Ed.). (1964). *Elementary curriculum: A book of readings*. New York: Pitman Publishing.

Cornell University & University of California. (1964). *Piaget rediscovered*. Ithaca, NY: Conference on Cognitive Studies and Curriculum Development.

Crosby, M. E. (1964). *Curriculum development for elementary schools in a changing society*. Boston: D. C. Heath.

Curriculum Study Center Conference. (1964). *Curriculum development and evaluation in English and social studies*. Pittsburgh, PA: Carnegie Institute of Technology.

de Grazia, A., & Sohn, D. A. (Eds.). (1964). *Revolution in teaching: New theory technology, and curricula*. New York: Bantam Books.

Doll, R. C. (1964). *Curriculum improvement: Decision-making and process*. Boston: Allyn & Bacon (Also 1970 and 1974).

Douglass, H. R. (Ed.). (1964). *The high school curriculum*. (third edition). New York: Ronald Press.

Elam, S. (Ed.). (1964). *Education and the structure of knowledge*. Chicago: Rand McNally.

Elson, R. M. (1964). *Guardians of tradition*. Lincoln: University of Nebraska Press.

Ether, J. A. (Ed.). (1964). *Current curricular issues: Three dimensions—Technology, morality, aesthetic*. Albany: Center for Curriculum Research and Service, State University of New York at Albany.

Evans, W. G. E. (1964). *Class of '84*. Tenth Winter Conference. Toronto: University of Toronto Press.

Ford, G. W., & Pugno, L. (1964). *The structure of knowledge and the curriculum*. Chicago: Rand McNally.

Fulbright, E. R., & Bolmeier, E. C. (1964). *Courts and the curriculum*. American School Law Series, Cincinnati, OH: W.H. Anderson Company.

Goodlad, J. I. (1964). *School curriculum reform in the United States*. New York: Fund for the Advancement of Education.

Hanson, C. F. (1964). *Four track curriculum for today's high schools*. Englewood Cliffs, NJ: Prentice-Hall.

Heath, R. W. (Ed.). (1964). *New curricula*. New York: Harper and Row.

Holt, J. (1964). *How children fail*. New York: Dell Publishing Co.

Holt, R. (1964). *Mary McLeod Bethune: A biography*. Garden City, NY: Doubleday.

Huebner, D. E. (Ed.). (1964). *A reassessment of the curriculum*. New York: Teachers College, Columbia University.

Krathwohl, D. R., et al. (1964). *Taxonomy of educational objectives, handbook II: Affective domain*. New York: David McKay.

Krug, E. A. (1964). *The shaping of the American high school.* New York: Harper.

Passow, A. H. (Ed.). (1964). *Nurturing individual potential.* Washington, DC: Association for Supervision and Curriculum Development.

Passow, A. H., & Leeper, R. R. (1964). *Intellectual development: Another look.* Papers of Eighth Curriculum Research Institute, Anaheim, CA and Washington, DC. Washington, DC: Association for Supervision and Curriculum Development.

Phenix, P. H. (1964). *Realms of meaning: A philosophy of the curriculum for general education.* New York: McGraw-Hill.

Qoyanayma, P. (1964). *No turning back: A Hopi woman's struggle to live in two worlds.* As told to Vada F. Carlson. Albuquerque: University of New Mexico.

Rosenbloom, P. C. (Ed.). (1964). *Modern viewpoints in the curriculum.* New York: McGraw-Hill.

Schill, W. J. (1964). *Curricular content for technical education.* Urbana: College of Education, University of Illinois.

1965

Anderson, D. W., Macdonald, J. B., & May, F. B. (Eds.). (1965). *Strategies of curriculum development: The works of Virgil E. Herrick.* Columbus, OH: Charles E. Merrill.

Anderson, V. E. (1965). *Principles and procedures of curriculum improvement* (second edition). New York: Ronald Press.

Association for Supervision and Curriculum Development. (1965a). *The humanities and the curriculum.* Washington, DC: Author.

Association for Supervision and Curriculum Development (R. R. Leeper, Ed.). (1965b). *Role of supervisor and curriculum director in a climate of change. 1965 Yearbook.* Washington, DC: Author.

Association for Supervision and Curriculum Development. (1965c). *Toward professional maturity of supervisors and curriculum workers.* Washington, DC: Author.

Brown, B. F. (1965). *The appropriate placement school: A sophisticated non-graded curriculum.* West Nyack, NY: Parker Publishing Company.

California State Department of Education. Patterns for the administration of curriculum development and instructional improvement. (1965). *Proceedings of a conference in Sacramento, California, January 25–26.* Sacramento: Author.

Clark, L. H., Klein, R. L., & Burks, J. B. (1965). *American secondary school curriculum.* New York: Macmillan.

Columbia University Teachers College, Department of Curriculum and Teaching. (1965). *Papers from the seminars on advanced study in curriculum and teaching.* New York: Teachers College, Columbia University.

Cooperative Curriculum Project. (1965). *The church's educational ministry: A curriculum plan.* St. Louis, MO: The Bethany Press.

Hall, G. S. (1965). *Health, growth, and heredity: G. Stanley Hall on natural education.* (C. E. Strickland and C. Burgess, Eds.). New York: Teachers College Press.

Hass, G., & Wiles, K. (Eds.). (1965). *Readings in curriculum.* Boston: Allyn & Bacon.

Leeper, R. R. (Ed.). (1965a). *Assessing and using curriculum content.* Washington, DC: Association for Supervision and Curriculum Development, National Education Association.

Leeper, R. R. (Ed.). (1965b). *Strategy for curriculum change.* Washington, DC: Association for Supervision and Curriculum Development.

Maccia, E. S. (1965). *Methodological considerations in curriculum theory building.* Columbus: Ohio State University.

Macon, R. E., & Haines, P.G. (1965). *Cooperative occupational education and work experience in the curriculum.* New York: Dodd, Mead and Company; Danville, IL: Interstate Printers and Publishers.

Oliver, A. I. (1965). *Curriculum improvement: A guide to problems, principles, and procedures.* New York: Dodd, Mead and Company.

Ontario Curriculum Institute. (1965). *New dynamics in curriculum development.* Toronto: Author.

Shack, S. (1965). *Armed with a primer.* Toronto/Montreal: McClelland and Stewart, Ltd.

Stearns, F. K. (1965). *Knowledge and the school curriculum.* Eugene, OR: University of Oregon (Oregon School Study Council).

Tanner, D. (1965). *Schools for youth—Change and challenge in secondary education.* New York: Macmillan.

Unruh, G. G. (Ed.). (1965). *New curriculum developments.* Washington, DC: Association for Supervision and Curriculum Development.

Wooten, W. (1965). *SMSG, the making of a curriculum.* New Haven, CT: Yale University Press.

1966

Aceland, R. (1966). *Curriculum or Life!* London: Victor Gollancz, Ltd.

American Association of School Administrators. (1966). *Imperatives in education.* Washington, DC: National Education Association.

Bruner, J. S. (1966). *Toward a theory of instruction.* Cambridge, MA: Harvard University Press.

Callaway, R. (Ed.). (1966). *Core curriculum: The why and the what.* Milwaukee, WI: University of Wisconsin–Milwaukee, School of Education.

Cay, D. F. (1966). *Curriculum: Design for learning.* Indianapolis, IN: Bobbs-Merrill.

Coleman, J. S. (1966). *Equality of educational opportunity.* Washington, DC: Government Printing Office.

College Entrance Examination Board. (1966). *The challenge of curricular change.* (Ed. by S. K. Bailey, et al.). New York: Author.

Goodlad, J. I. (Ed.). (1966a). *The changing American school. Sixty-fifth Yearbook of the National Society for the Study of Education, Part II.* Chicago, IL: University of Chicago Press.

Goodlad, J. I. (1966b). *School, curriculum, and the individual.* Waltham, MA.: Blaisdell Publishing Company.

Goodlad, J. I., & Richter, M. M. (1966). *The development of a conceptual system for dealing with problems of curriculum and instruction.* Los Angeles: Institute for Development of Educational Activities, University of California.

Goodlad, J. I., Von Stoephasius, R., & Klein, M. F. (1966). *The changing school curriculum.* New York: Fund for the Advancement of Education.

Halverson, P. M. (Ed.). (1966). *Curriculum innovations in 1966: Trends and issues.* Syracuse, NY: Syracuse University.

Haney, R. E. (1966). *The changing curriculum: Science.* Washington, DC: Association for Supervision and Curriculum Development.

Inlow, G. M. (1966). *The emergent in curriculum.* New York: John Wiley and Sons.

International Curriculum Conference (Second). (1966). *New Dimensions in curriculum development: Proceedings.* Toronto: Ontario Curriculum Institute.

Jarvis, O. T., & Wootton, L. R. (1966). *The transitional elementary school and its curriculum.* Dubuque, IA: William C. Brown.

King, A. R., & Brownell, J. A. (1966). *The curriculum and the disciplines of knowledge: A theory of curriculum practice.* New York: John Wiley and Sons. (Reprinted in 1976)

Koopman, G. R. (1966). *Curriculum development.* New York: The Center for Applied Research in Education.

Leeper, R. R. (Ed.). (1966). *Curriculum change: Direction and process.* Washington, DC: Association for Supervision and Curriculum Development.

Lindvall, C. M. (1966). *The task of evaluation in curriculum development projects: A rationale and case study.* Pittsburgh, PA: Learning Research and Development Center University of Pittsburgh.

Macdonald, J. B., & Leeper, R. R. (Eds.). (1966). *Language and meaning.* Washington, DC: Association for Supervision and Curriculum Development, National Education Association.

Martin, W. T., & Pinck, D. C. (Eds.). (1966). *Curriculum improvement and innovation: A partnership of students, school teachers, and research scholars.* Cambridge, MA: Robert Bently.

Matthew, C. V., & Roam, J. E. (1966). *A curriculum demonstration program for drop-out-prone students.* Edwardsville: Southern Illinois University.

Mayhew, K. C., & Edwards, A. C. (1966). *The Dewey Society: The laboratory school of the University of Chicago, 1896–1903.* New York: Atherton. (originally published 1936).

National Education Association. (1966). *The way teaching is.* Washington, DC: Association for Supervision and Curriculum Development and the Center for the Study of Instruction.

Ontario Association for Curriculum Development. (1966). *Curriculum development in a decentralized educational system (Fifteenth Annual Conference, November).* (R. Luxford, Ed.). Toronto: Author.

Ontario Curriculum Institute. (1966a). *Children, classrooms, curriculum and change; a report of the Committee on the Scope and Organization of the Curriculum.* Toronto: Ontario Curriculum Institute.

Ontario Curriculum Institute. (1966b). *New dimensions in curriculum development (Proceedings of the Second International Conference).* Toronto: Ontario Curriculum Institute.

Organization for Economic Cooperation and Development. (1966). *Curriculum improvement and educational development: Modernizing our schools.* Paris: Author.

Parker, J. C., & Rubin, L. J. (1966). *Process as content: Curriculum design and the application of knowledge.* Chicago: Rand McNally.

Ragan, W. B., & Stendler, C. B. (1966). *Modern elementary curriculum* (third edition). New York: Holt, Rinehart and Winston.

Robison, H. F. (Ed.). (1966). *Precedents and promise in the curriculum field.* New York: Teachers College Press.

Rosenbaum, D. S., & Toepfer, C. F. (1966). *Curriculum planning and school psychology: The coordinated approach.* Buffalo, NY: Hertillon Press.

Sachs, B. M. (1966). *The students, the interviews, and the curriculum.* Boston: Houghton Mifflin.

Sand, O., & Wilson, E. (1966). *Innovation in planning school curricula.* Washington, DC: National Education Association.

Saylor, J. G., & Alexander, W. M. (1966). *Curriculum planning for modern schools.* New York: Holt, Rinehart and Winston.

Scriven, M. (1966). *The methodology of evaluation (Publication 110 of the Social Science Consortium).* Washington, DC: U.S. Department of Health, Education, and Welfare.

Seguel, M. L. (1966). *The curriculum field: Its formative years.* New York: Teachers College, Columbia University Press.

Swenson, G., & Keys, D. (1966). *Providing for flexibility in scheduling and instruction.* Englewood Cliffs, NJ: Prentice-Hall.

Taylor, P. H. (1966). *Purpose and structure in the curriculum (Inaugural address).* Birmingham, England: University of Birmingham.

U.S. National Science Foundation. (1966). *Course and curriculum improvement projects: Mathematics, science, engineering.* Washington, DC: National Science Foundation.

Unruh, G. G., & Leeper, R. R. (1966). *Influences in curriculum change.* Washington, DC: Association for Supervision and Curriculum Development.

Wirth, A. G. (1966). *John Dewey as educator: His design for work in education (1894–1904)*. Melbourne, FL: Krieger Publishing.

1967

Aceland, R. (1967). *A move to the integrated curriculum*. Exeter, England: University of Exeter, Institute of Education.

Alexander, W. M. (Ed.). (1967). *The changing secondary school curriculum: Readings*. New York: Holt, Rinehart and Winston.

Alpren, M. (Ed.). (1967). *The subject curriculum: Grades K–12*. Columbus, OH: Charles E. Merrill.

American Educational Research Association Monograph Series on Curriculum Evaluation, Number 1. (1967). *Perspectives of curriculum evaluation* (by R. W. Tyler, R. M. Gagne , & M. Scriven*)*. Chicago: Rand McNally.

Anderson, W. G. (1967). *What are the subject matter boundaries?* Danville, IL: Interstate Printers and Publishers

Association for Supervision and Curriculum Development. (1967). *Curriculum materials*. Washington, DC: National Education Association.

Beauchamp, G. A., & Beauchamp, K. E. (1967). *Comparative analysis of curriculum systems*. Wilmette, IL: The Kagg Press.

Berman, L. M. (Ed.). (1967). *The humanities and the curriculum*. Washington, DC: Association for Supervision and Curriculum Development.

Bishop, L. J. (1967). *Collective negotiation in curriculum and instruction: Questions and concerns*. Washington, DC: Association for Supervision and Curriculum Development.

Burnham, D. (1967). *New designs for learning: Highlights of the reports of the Ontario Institute 1963–1966*. Toronto: University of Toronto Press.

Conner, F., & Ellena, W. (1967). *Curriculum handbook for school administrators*. Washington, DC: American Association of School Administrators (also 1973).

Cooperative Curriculum Project. (1967). *Tools of curriculum development for the church's educational ministry*. Anderson, IN: Warner Press.

Davis, R. B. (1967). *The changing curriculum: Mathematics*. Washington, DC: Association for Supervision and Curriculum Development.

Fantini, M. D., & Weinstein, G. (1967). *Toward a contact curriculum*. New York: Anti-Defamation League of B'nai B'rith.

Florida State Department of Education. (1967). *Report on strategies for curriculum change*. Tallahassee, FL: Author.

Frymier, J. R. (Ed.). (1967). Curriculum theory development: Work in progress. *Theory into Practice, Volume 6, Number 4* (October), Ohio State University.

Gagne, R. M. M. (1967). *The conditions of learning*. New York: Holt, Rinehart and Winston.

Glaser, R. (1967). *Adapting the elementary school curriculum to individual performance.* Pittsburgh, PA: Learning Research and Development Center, University of Pittsburgh.

Great Britain Schools Council. (1967). *The new curriculum: A presentation of ideas, experiments and practical developments (Selected from Schools Council Publications over the past three years).* London: Her Majesty's Stationery Office.

Holt, J. (1967). *How children learn.* New York: Dell.

Kerr, J. F. (1967). *The problem of curriculum reform.* Leicester, England: Leicester University Press.

Kohl, H. (1967). *36 children.* New York: New American Library.

Kozol, J. (1967). *Death at an early age: The destruction of the hearts and minds of Negro children in the Boston public schools.* Boston: Houghton Mifflin Company.

Leeper, R. R. (Ed.). (1967). *Humanizing education: The person in the process.* Washington, DC: Association for Supervision and Curriculum Development.

Michaelis, J. U., Grossman, R. H., & Scott, L. F. (1967). *New designs for elementary curriculum and instruction.* New York: McGraw-Hill.

Minnesota, University of. (1967). *Working clinic in modern curriculum (Addresses).* Minneapolis: University of Minnesota.

National Education Association, Center for the Study of Instruction. (1967). *Rational planning in curriculum and instruction: Eight essays.* Washington, DC: National Education Association.

Neagley, R. L., & Evans, N. D. (1967). *Handbook for effective curriculum development.* Englewood Cliffs, NJ: Prentice-Hall.

Newfoundland Teachers Association, Curriculum Seminar. (1967). *The curriculum process—A basis for action.* St. John's Newfoundland: Author.

Raths, L. E., Wassermann, S., Jonas, A., & Rothstein, A. (1967). *Teaching for thinking: Theory and application.* Columbus, OH: C. E. Merrill.

School Health Education Study. (1967). *Health education: A conceptual approach to curriculum design: K–12.* St. Paul: Minnesota Mining and Manufacturing Company Education Press.

Schools Council. (1967). *Curriculum development: Teacher's group and centers. Working Paper Number 10.* London: Her Majesty's Stationery Office.

Sullivan, E. V. (1967). *Piaget and the school curriculum: A critical appraisal.* Toronto: Ontario Institute for Studies in Education, Bulletin Number 2.

Tewksbury, J. L. (1967). *Nongrading in the elementary school.* Columbus, OH: Charles E. Merrill.

Theory into Practice. (1967, October). Curriculum theory development: Work in progress (J. Frymier, Ed.). Volume 6, Number 4. Ohio State University.

Van Til, W., Vars, G. F., & Lounsbury, J. H. (1967). *Modern education for the junior high school years*. (second edition). Indianapolis, IN: Bobbs-Merrill.

Venable, T. C. (1967). *Philosophical foundations of the curriculum*. Chicago: Rand McNally.

Verduin, J. R. (1967). *Cooperative curriculum improvement*. Englewood Cliffs, NJ: Prentice-Hall.

Wahle, R. P. (Ed.). (1967). *Toward professional maturity of supervisors and curriculum workers*. Washington, DC: Association for Supervision and Curriculum Development.

Wheeler, D. K. (1967). *Curriculum process*. London: University of London Press (Also 1971 by University of London Press—Unibrooks).

Wilhelms, F. T. (Ed.). (1967). *Evaluation as feedback and guide. 1967 Yearbook*. Washington, DC: Association for Supervision and Curriculum Development.

1968

Alexander, W. M., Williams, E. L., Compton, M., Hines, V. A., Prescott, D., & Kealy, R. (1968). *The emergent middle school*. New York: Holt, Rinehart and Winston.

Allen, E. D. (1968). *The changing curriculum: Modern foreign language*. Washington, DC: Association for Supervision and Curriculum Development.

Bangs, F. K., & Hillestad, M. C. (1968). *Curricular implications of automated data processing for educational institutions*. Boulder, CO: University of Colorado.

Beauchamp, G. A. (1968). *Curriculum theory*. Wilmette, IL: The Kagg Press.

Beck, R. H., Meadows, P. Shane, H. G., & Galen-Saylor, J. (1968). *Curriculum imperative: Survival of self in society*. Lincoln: University of Nebraska, Department of Secondary Education.

Beckner, W., & Cornett, J. D. (1968). *The secondary school curriculum*. Columbus, OH: Charles E. Merrill.

Berman, L. M. (1968). *New priorities in the curriculum*. Columbus, OH: Charles E. Merrill.

Cave, R. G. (1968). *All their future*. Harmondsworth, England: Penguin.

Centre for Curriculum Renewal and Educational Development Overseas. (1968). *Modern curriculum developments in Britain*. London: The Centre.

Dearden, R. F. (1968). *The philosophy of primary education*. London: Routledge and Kegan Paul.

Dreeben, R. (1968). *On what is learned in school*. Reading, MA: Addison-Wesley.

Dressel, P. L. (1968). *College and university curriculum*. Berkeley, CA: McCutchan.

Education Development Center. (1968). *African education programme*. Essex, England: E.T. Heron.

Frazier, A. (1968). *The new elementary school*. Washington, DC: Association for Supervision and Curriculum Development.

Great Britain Schools Council. (1968). *Practical support for curriculum change; the young school leaver*. London: Her Majesty's Stationery Office.

Grobman, H. G. (1968). *Evaluation activities of curriculum projects: A starting point*. Chicago, IL: Rand McNally.

Heller, R. W., & Rosenthal, A. M. (Eds.). (1968). *The child and the articulated curriculum*. New York: Western New York Study Council; Danville, IL: Interstate Printers and Publishers.

Jackson, P. W. (1968). *Life in classrooms*. New York: Holt, Rinehart and Winston.

Jarvis, O. T., & Wootton, L. R. (1968). *The elementary school and its curriculum*. Dubuque, IA: William C. Brown.

Johnson, H. T. (1968). *Foundations of curriculum*. Columbus, OH: Charles E. Merrill.

Karplus, R. (Ed.). (1968). *What is curriculum evaluation? Six answers*. Berkeley, CA: Science Curriculum Improvement Study, University of California.

Keith, L. G., Blake, P., & Tiedt, S. (1968). *Contemporary curriculum in the elementary school*. New York: Harper and Row.

Kerr, J. F. (Ed). (1968). *Changing the curriculum*. London: University of London Press.

Kopp, H. G. (Ed.). (1968). *Curriculum, cognition and content*. Washington, DC: Alexander Graham Bell Association for the Deaf.

Leeper, R. R. (Ed.). (1968). *Curriculum decisions: Social realities*. Washington, DC: Association for Supervision and Curriculum Development.

Maclure, J. S. (1968). *Curriculum innovation in practice. Report of the Third International Curriculum Conference*. London: Her Majesty's Stationery Office.

Martinson, R. A. (1968). *Curriculum enrichment for the gifted in the primary grades*. Englewood Cliffs, NJ: Prentice-Hall.

Nisbet, S. (1968). *Purpose in the curriculum* (second edition). London: University of London Press.

Ontario Association for Curriculum Development. (1968). *Reconciliation of means and ends in education* (R. Luxford and K. Pold, Eds.). Toronto: Ontario Association for Curriculum Development.

Short, E. C., & Marconnit, G. D. (Eds.). (1968). *Contemporary thought in public school curriculum*. Dubuque, IA: William C. Brown.

Sowards, G. W., & Scobey, M. M. (1968). *The changing curriculum and the elementary teacher* (second edition). Belmont, CA: Wadsworth.

Steeves, F. L. (Ed.). (1968). *The subjects in the curriculum: Selected readings*. New York: Odyssey Press.

Thomas, R. M., Sands, L. B., & Brubaker, D. L. (1968). *Strategies for curriculum improvement: Proposal and procedures*. Boston: Allyn & Bacon.

Trump, J. L., & Miller, D. F. (1968). *Secondary school curriculum improvement: Proposals and procedures*. Boston: Allyn & Bacon.

Unruh, G. G., & Leeper, R. R. (Eds). (1968). *Influences in curriculum change*. Washington, DC: Association for Supervision and Curriculum Development.

Witt, P. W. F. (Ed.). (1968). *Technology and the curriculum*. New York: Teachers College Press.

1969

American Educational Research Association. (1969). *Curriculum. Review of Educational Research*, 39, June.

Anderson, V. E. (1969). *Curriculum guidelines in an era of change*. New York: Ronald Press.

Association for Supervision and Curriculum Development (W. H. Beatty, Ed.). (1969). *Improving educational assessment and an inventory of measures of affective behavior*. Washington, DC: Author.

Bar, M. R. (Ed.). (1969). *Curriculum innovation in practice in relation to colleges of education*. Report of the study conference at Edge Hill College of Education: Ormsirk, Lancashire.

Bent, R. K, & Unruh, A. (1969). *Secondary school curriculum*. Lexington, MA: Heath.

Cassidy, H. G. (1969). *Knowledge, experience and action: An essay on education*. New York: Teachers College Press.

Crary, R. W. (1969). *Humanizing the school: Curriculum development and theory*. New York: Random House.

Dennison, G. (1969). *The lives of children*. New York: Random House.

Dragositz, A. (Ed.). (1969). *Curriculum innovations and evaluation. Proceedings of Association for Supervision and Curriculum Development pre-conference seminar, March 1968*. Princeton, NJ: Educational Testing Service.

Ellis, E. V. (1969). *The role of the curriculum laboratory in the preparation of quality teachers*. Tallahassee, FL: Florida A & M University Foundation.

Frazier, A. (Ed.). (1969). *A curriculum for children*. Washington, DC: Association for Supervision and Curriculum Development.

Frost, J. L., & Rowland, G. T. (1969). *Curriculum for the seventies*. New York: Houghton Mifflin.

Glasser, W. (1969). *Schools without failure*. New York: Harper and Row.

Grobman, A. B. (1969). *The changing classroom: The role of the Biological Sciences Curriculum Study, First Edition*. Garden City, NY: Doubleday.

Grobman, H. (1969). *Evaluation activities of curriculum projects*. London: McGraw-Hill.

Guttchen, R. S., & Bandman, B. (Eds.). (1969). *Philosophical essays on curriculum*. Philadelphia: J. B. Lippincott.

Gwynn, J. M., & Chase, J. B. (1969). *Curriculum principles and social trends*. (Fourth Edition). New York: Macmillan.

Hamilton, N. K., & Saylor, J. G. (Eds.). (1969). *Humanizing the secondary curriculum.* Washington, DC: Association for Supervision and Curriculum Development.

Hass, G. (1969). *Curriculum and instruction practices for continuous learner progress.* Clearwater, FL: Clearwater Research and Development Council.

Herndon, J. (1969). *The way it spozed to be.* New York: Bantam.

Hooper, M. (Ed.). (1969). *The curriculum: Context design and development.* Edinburgh, Scotland: Oliver and Boyd.

James, H. T., et al. (1969). *The schools and the challenge of innovation.* Washington, DC: Committee for Economic Development.

Jones, H. L. (Ed.). (1969). *Curriculum development in a changing world.* Syracuse, NY: School of Education, Syracuse University.

Joyce, B. (1969). *Alternative models of elementary education.* Waltham, MA: Blaisdell Publishing Company.

Kohl, H. (1969). *The open classroom.* New York: The New York Review.

Krug, E. A. (1969). *The shaping of the American high school: 1880–1920.* Madison: University of Wisconsin Press.

Larson, M. E. (1969). *Review and synthesis of research: Analysis for curriculum development in vocational education.* Columbus, OH: Center for Vocational and Technical Education.

Meeker, M. N. (1969). *The structure of intellect: Its interpretation and uses.* Columbus, OH: Charles E. Merrill.

Morphet, E. J., & Ryan, C. O. (1969). *Designing education for the future: An eight-state project* (Seven Volumes). New York: Scholastic.

Ohliger, J. (Ed.). (1969). *Project to train teachers in adult basic education curriculum development, July 21–August 8; final report.* Columbus, OH: Center for Adult Education, College of Education, Ohio State University.

Payne, A. (1969). *The study of curriculum plans.* Washington, DC: National Education Association.

Phillips, C. M. (1969). *Changes in subject choice at school and university.* London: Weidenfeld and Nicolson.

Piaget, J., & Inhelder, B. (1969). *The psychology of the child.* New York: Basic Books.

Popham, W. J., & Baker, E. V. (1969). *Establishing instructional goals.* Englewood Cliffs, NJ: Prentice-Hall.

Popham, W. J., Eisner, E. W., Sullivan, H. J., & Tyler, L. L.. (1969). *Instructional objectives* AERA monograph series on curriculum evaluation. Chicago: Rand McNally.

Postman, N., & Weingartner, C. (1969). *Teaching as a subversive activity.* New York: Delacorte.

Rogers, C. (1969). *Freedom to learn.* New York: Bell and Howell.

Rogers, L. R. (1969). *Use of organized knowledge*. Clearwater, FL: Florida Educational Research and Development Council.

Rubin, L. J. (Ed.). (1969). *Life skills in school and society. 1969 Yearbook*. Washington, DC: Association for Supervision and Curriculum Development.

Rudd, W. G. A. (1969). *Curriculum innovation: Regional and local efforts in curriculum practice*. Ormskirk, England: Edge Hill College of Education.

Schwab, J. J. (1969). *College curriculum and student protest*. Chicago: University of Chicago Press.

Skolnick, I. H. (1969). *A guide to curriculum construction for the religious school*. Chicago: Chicago College of Jewish Studies Press.

Springer, U. K. (1969). *Recent curriculum development in France, West Germany and Italy: A study of trends at the middle level of education*. New York: Teachers College, Columbia University Center for Education in Industrial Nations.

Stockmeyer, E. A. K. (1969). *Rudolf Steiner's curriculum for Waldorf schools*. London: Rudolf Steiner Press.

Symmes, S. S. (Ed.). (1969). *Developmental economic education programs: Handbook for curriculum change; guidelines*. New York: Joint Council on Economic Education.

Tyler, R. W. (1969). *Basic principles of curriculum and instruction* (Reprint). Chicago: University of Chicago Press.

Vars, G. F. (Ed.). (1969). *Common learning: Core and interdisciplinary team approaches*. Scranton, PA: International Textbook Company.

Walton, S. F. (1969). *The Black curriculum*. East Palo Alto, CA: Black Liberation Publishers.

Wilson, J. (1969). *Moral education and the curriculum*. Oxford, England: Pergamon Press.

CHAPTER EIGHT

Curriculum Literature aAnd Context
1970–1979

The Vietnam War, its protest movements, troop increases, and rumors of peace, held the attention of U.S. society in the early 1970s. By 1975, the last U.S. forces had been withdrawn, and the South Vietnamese government collapsed. The war had involved the United States for nearly 15 years, claiming over a million Vietnamese and over 55,000 U.S. lives, costing the United States over $140 billion. It had extended armed conflict into Laos and Cambodia and destabilized all of Southeast Asia. The Vietnam War also prompted the 1970 shooting of four student protestors at Kent State University by National Guardsmen.

The seventies was the decade during which the United States celebrated its bicentennial, a cause for festivity. Instead, there was reason for pessimism. The United States had lost an unpopular war. Some had lost more—the lives of dear ones, confidence in their government, and faith in the virtue of their way of life. Veterans returned home with their efforts uncelebrated and motives questioned. Gang violence, centered on the trafficking of illegal drugs sought after by all levels of society, dominated the economies of the inner cities and spread into the suburbs. President Richard Nixon and Vice President Spiro Agnew both resigned their positions because of illegal activities. The affable Gerald Ford problem-solved and muddled through until Jimmy Carter took over as the 39th president. Carter fared little better; undermined by his administration's inability to attend to the myriad political and economic crises that were taking place across the planet, he served only one term. The ability of the U.S. government to exercise its will in global affairs was remembered nightly for an embarrassing duration as ABC's *Nightline* sent people to bed with the anxious stories of 66

American embassy employees who remained hostages of Iranian revolutionaries in Tehran.

The 1970s were besieged by the escalation of a form of political violence that threatened everyone. The first new form of terrorism occurred in the late 1960s with airplane hijackings. The murder of Israeli athletes by Arab extremists at the 1972 Munich Olympics proved that terrorists saw the value of media attention for promoting their causes. Bombings and sabotage plagued Northern Ireland for much of the decade. The Irish Republican Army claimed responsibility for bombing Westminster Hall and Harrods, and for taking the life of Lord Mountbatten and his grandson. One of the more dramatic resolutions of a terrorist kidnapping occurred in 1976 when Israeli commandos raided the Entebbe Airport in Uganda, killing the pro-Palestinian hijacker/kidnappers and freeing 105 hostages. Ugandan President Idi Amin, having assumed power in 1971, apparently provided military support to the hijkackers. A year later, Amin detained 240 U.S. citizens in an act of bravado. The United States was also found to be vulnerable to terrorist attack with bombings in New York placing citizens on guard.

Vietnam captured the headlines, but it was not the only land besieged with violence in the seventies. Industrialized nations from both sides of the Cold War had armed the world under the guise of development aid. The results of this militarization of the Third World were now realized. Bloodshed covered the nation of Cambodia. In the year that South Vietnam fell, Pol Pot directed a program of genocide in this country, renamed Kampuchea. The killings continued until Cambodia was invaded by Vietnam. A coup was narrowly averted in Thailand in 1976.

The nation of Bangladesh was created by Bengalese separatists at the beginning of the decade with much loss of life. The self-proclaimed "Father of Bangladesh," Sheik Mukibur Rahman, held power briefly before being ousted in a coup. Pakistan remained in crisis throughout the decade, culminating a coup against Prime Minister Ali Bhutto led by General Zia ul-Haq. The overthrow of the Shah of Iran by Islamic fundamentalists led by the Ayatollah Khomeini was a dramatic shock to Western nations and precipitated the hostage crisis that plagued Carter's presidency. In 1978, Mohammed Daud was deposed as ruler of Afghanistan. Fearing a militant Moslem nation to their south, the Soviet Union invaded Afghanistan, beginning a war that was to become, in many ways, the USSR's own Vietnam.

Israeli and Egyptian forces continued an ebb and flow of negotiation and conflagration throughout the decade. A new strongman, Muammar al-Gadhafi, consolidated control in Libya and ordered incursions into Egypt's eastern border. Attacks of Katangese rebels plagued Zaire. A coup in Mauritania in 1978 further destabilized the African continent. Tanzania engineered the ousting of Amin from Uganda. In Ethiopia, the half-century rule of Haile Selassie was ended, unsettling the region. Changes in the Somalian government effected the expulsion of Soviet and Cuban advisers. Ethiopia's new leader, Mengistu, engaged in fighting Eritrean secessionists. Civil war in Nigeria left countless Biafrans homeless and starving. Guerrilla warfare challenged white control of Rhodesia, and Angola's civil war engaged the military support of Cuba and the Soviet Union. The struggle against apartheid continued in South Africa.

In 1972, on the other side of the globe, another demagogue, Juan Peron, regained the presidency in Argentina after 17 years in exile. His wife assumed power when Peron died, but a military coup quickly followed. In 1973 Salvadore Allende of Chile, the first elected Marxist president in the Western Hemisphere, was assassinated in a coup d'etat with covert support from the Central Intelligence Agency and International Telephone and Telegraph. Bolivia remained in political upheaval throughout the decade, victim of over 200 coups since its independence from Spain in the nineteenth century. In Central America, armed resistance to the governments of Guatemala, El Salvador, and Nicaragua was monitored carefully by its northern neighbor. When Nicaraguan president Somoza fell to the Sandinistas in 1979, the United States was faced with the reappearance of a socialist regime and political ally to Cuba in the Western Hemisphere.

Europe was also impacted by military violence. In 1974 still another army coup overthrew Portuguese dictator Marcello Caetano. Economic disputes raged over fishing rights in the "cold war" between Iceland and Britain in 1976. In Greece, the people voted against allowing the return of exiled King Constantine II.

Whether or not through peaceful and legal means, the seventies marked transitions for many national leaders. Foremost among these was the unprecedented exit from office of U.S. President Richard Nixon. Nixon had resoundingly defeated George McGovern in the 1972 election. It was realized shortly after the election that a covert operation by Nixon's campaign team was responsible for the break-in at the Democratic National Headquarters in the Watergate Hotel in Washington. The discovery that numerous high officials were directly involved in either authorizing the burglary or directing a cover-up resulted in the collapse of the Nixon administration. Amid the possibility of impeachment during the Watergate scandal in 1974, Nixon resigned, succeeded by Gerald Ford, who immediately granted Nixon immunity from prosecution.

Of at least equal impact on the other side of the world in 1976 were the deaths of Chairman Mao Tse-tung and Premier Chou En-lai, architects of the People's Republic of China and authors of its cultural revolution. In the final years of the decade, China moved into a state of increased acceptance of and by the other powers in the international economy. Elsewhere, world leadership was also in transition: Egypt's Gamal Abdel Nasser died in 1970, succeeded by Anwar Sadat; Kurt Waldheim of Austria succeeded Burma's U Thant as head of the United Nations in 1971; the death of France's President Georges Pompidou and the resignation of Israeli Prime Minister Golda Meir both occurred in 1974. After 11 years in power, Prime Minister Indira Gandhi's Congress Party control of Parliament ended in 1977. The death of Pope Paul VI in 1978 brought about the election of Pope John Paul I. His sudden (and some claim conspired) death approximately a month later was followed by the election of Pope John Paul II, the first non-Italian pope in 500 years.

Energy demands triggered national and international emergencies for these new leaders. The OPEC oil embargo dominated 1973. The price of gasoline escalated as supplies became limited. U.S. automakers, accustomed to producing large gas-guzzling vehicles, lost significant market share to foreign auto companies. At decade's end, Chrysler Corporation asked the U.S. government to underwrite loans to keep the company afloat. The end of cheap fuel contributed to the overall economic malaise of the United States throughout the 1970s. An Amoco tanker, the *Cadiz*, dumped 100,000 gallons of petroleum off the coast of Brittany. Nuclear disaster was narrowly averted at Three Mile Island in 1979, realizing the fears that were fictionalized in the film *The China Syndrome*.

There were other disasters caused by human weakness. Upstate New York's Love Canal became a symbol of environmental poisoning when residents discovered they were living on top of the toxic waste left by Hooker Chemicals. In 1978 came news of the mass suicide by hundreds of religious cult members in Jonestown, Guyana. Disaster and death were by no means due solely to human impingement, however, as evidenced by the following: a 1970 tidal wave that killed 100,000 and left a million homeless in Pakistan; a 1970 earthquake in Peru that killed over 50,000 and left 800,000 homeless; a 1971 tidal wave that killed over 15,000 in India; 1972 earthquakes that killed 5,000 in Iran and 10,000 in Nicaragua; a 1974 hurricane in Honduras that killed 8,000 and left over 300,000 homeless; a 1976 earthquake that killed 665,000 in Tangshan, China, and three more earthquakes that took 22,000 lives in Guatemala City, 8,000 in the Philippines, and 4,000 in Turkey; and a Romanian earthquake in 1977 that killed over 1,000 and left 20,000 homeless. In 1978, Acquired Immune Deficiency Syndrome (AIDS) was first reported as an epidemic. Despite the pervasiveness of these calamities, they do not set the seventies apart from other decades in magnitude of natural disaster. Awareness of these tragedies was heightened through new communications technologies, as satellites provided instantaneous images from around the planet.

There were also successful endeavors to end conflict and to produce policies that made for greater security. Peace talks initiated by U.S. President Carter resulted in a treaty negotiated by Egyptian President Anwar Sadat and Israeli Prime Minister Menachem Begin. The principals were awarded the Nobel Prize in 1978. The People's Republic of China was finally admitted to the United Nations in 1971 as Taiwan withdrew. In 1972 the United States and the USSR reached an agreement to curb the nuclear arms race by placing limits on numbers of nuclear warheads. In the same year President Nixon made visits to Communist China and the USSR. A new era of diplomatic and economic relations with China ensued in the age of détente engineered by Secretary of State Henry Kissinger. By the end of the decade, trade agreements involved various combinations of the major economic powers of the world (e.g., the United States, the USSR, Japan, Germany, Communist China, England, and France). After nearly a century of control, the United States agreed to release the Panama Canal to the government of Panama. Although colonial possessions were becoming relics of a former era, economic colonialism, according to some, was increasing, whether due to official government policy or the growth of multinational corporations that operated largely outside the jurisdiction of any one government. The portent and potential of unprecedented power in a kind of "intercorporationalism" waxed strong as discussion of internationalism waned.

Despite economic woes, activities in the traditional arts of architecture, painting, music, and literature were plentiful. Prominent names of the times in architecture included Kevin Roche, Minoru Yamasaki, Bruce Graham, Welton Becket, Romaldo Giurgola, and Roger Taillibert. Kenzo Tange's space frame at Expo 70 in Osaka, Japan, intimated engineered environments for the near future. It was a decade for the super-skyscraper, with cities and nations competing to build the tallest building. Outdoor art forms and murals enlivened urban life. In sculpture, Armand Vaillancourt, Alexander Calder, and Don Thibodeaux were joined by the minimalist sculpture of Carl Andre and an art form that employed landscaping, exemplified in Robert Smithson's creations in Utah. In music, Shostakovich, Henze, Janacek, Ligeti, Nono, Menotti, and Kirchner vied with the popularity of David Bowie's "glam rock," the monotonous rhythm of disco music, and the stripped-down rock 'n' roll of punk rock — whether outrageously performed by the Sex Pistols or more playfully rendered in the garage band sound of the Ramones. The Beatles disbanded, leaving the Rolling Stones and the Who as patriarchs of British pop music. Modern opera was explored by Robert Wilson and Philip Glass in *Einstein on the Beach*. Opera and the musical met rock 'n' roll in Andrew Lloyd Weber and Tim Rice's major success, *Jesus Christ Superstar*. Jesus was also the subject of a more modest, pop telling of the Gospel of St. Matthew in Steven Schwartz's musical *Godspell*.

In literature, James Baldwin, John Updike, Gore Vidal, Graham Greene, Mary McCarthy, Herman Wouk, Frederick Forsyth, Joseph Heller, Vladimir Nabokov, Saul Bellow, Agatha Christie, Arthur Miller, Harold Pinter, Evelyn Waugh, and James Michener maintained their literary output with novels that depicted the excitement and insight to be found in the ordinary as well as in the sophisticated and renowned. Kurt Vonnegut Jr. and Richard Brautigan were the darlings of the counterculture, along with the rediscovery of Friedrich Nietzsche, science fiction writer Robert Heinlein, and Kahlil Gibran. Alexander Solzhenitzyn, an émigré to the United States, and Jorge Luis Borges were received by an international audience. Thomas Pynchon produced what many consider to be his finest work in *Gravity's Rainbow*. Carlos Fuentes provided insight into Mexican culture and human relationships through his novel *Terre Nostra*. Günter Grass again offered profound personal and social commentary in his writing and in the translation of his work *The Tin Drum* to film.

The popular arts continued to emerge as legitimate expressions of the plights, impediments, ideals, and aspirations of the public, a public for whom nationalism was less important. The arts of advertising, rock music, the comic strip, popular periodicals, television, and the sports world all spoke to everyday interests. Garry Trudeau began satirizing public figures in his *Doonesbury* cartoon. Gloria Steinem founded *Ms* magazine. Elvis Presley was enjoying renewed popularity when he died of a drug overdose in 1977. The seventies solidified an era that Robert Theobald called the communication era, a shift beyond the age of industrialization.[1]

Perhaps even more wholly than the other popular arts was the continued work of film in representing human activity. Some saw a new vulgarity in the popular culture with portrayals of gratuitous sex and violence. Others spoke of the media creating a hyper-reality, a reality accepted by the audience as more real than the real. The variety of societal ills, fantasies, ideals, and individual feelings portrayed in the following films attests that cinema, the popular film as well as the art film, was full-fledged literature: *Patton*, *Women in Love*, *The Prime of Miss Jean Brodie*, *Cabaret*, *One Flew Over the Cuckoo's Nest*, *Network*, and *Rocky*. A creative new director, Steven Spielberg, brought suspense and terror to the screen in the film adaptation of Peter Benchley's best-seller *Jaws*, followed by *Close Encounters of the Third Kind*. George Lucas's *Star Wars*, a high-tech tribute to the science fiction movie serials of his youth, became an international icon. Stanley Kubrick's portrait of an anti-Utopia in *Clockwork Orange* left counterculture advocates gasping. The Vietnam War was interpreted on film in Michael Cimino's *The Deer Hunter*. Francis Ford Coppola, having established his credentials with the direction of *The Godfather*, produced the ambitious allegory *Apocalypse Now*. The work of Martin Scorsese in the 1970s (*Taxi Driver, Raging Bull*) vividly portrayed the dimensions of human violence. Comic Woody Allen's talent as a film producer and director matured in the decade, culminating in *Annie Hall*, a film that captured a slice of U.S. social interaction at the end of the decade. Marvelous imagery and narrative also characterized the films of Bernardo Bertolucci, Akira Kurosawa, Louis Malle, and Nagisa Oshima.

The television sitcom became a venue for political and social commentary with Norman Lear's *All in the Family* and *Maude*. A thinly veiled commentary on the Vietnam War (set safely in an ahistorical Korean War) was offered in the television adaptation of the popular film *M*A*S*H*. The "mini-series" became education with the production of Alex Haley's *Roots*. Public television also had bonafide successes with BBC imports *Upstairs, Downstairs* and *The Duchess of Duke Street*. The emergent sophistication and widespread appeal of the popular arts in the 1970s contributed in their own way to a representation of what the Greeks called "paideia," a source of evidence about the formation of modern character and the ideals it epitomizes.

Sciences and technology, too, corroborated in the progression into the communications era. Computers and cybernetics generally revolutionized the business world and the media. The space race continued and contributed directly and indirectly to the communications revolution. China entered the space race in 1970 with the launching of its first satellite, the same year that communication expertise enabled the United States to recover an explosion-ridden spacecraft, *Apollo 13*, from its orbit around the moon. The Soviet spacecraft *Mars III* successfully landed on Mars, and the U.S. spacecraft *Mariner 9* orbited the same planet in 1971. In that same year Americans saw their astronauts drive a vehicle on the lunar surface; the next trip placed astronomical observatories on the moon. In 1973 dockings were made with the U.S. space station *Skylab*, while Russian scientists sent four unmanned spacecrafts to Mars. *Mariner 10* brought photographs of Mercury to U.S. scientists, and in 1975 *Viking I* transmitted pictures of the Martian surface to Earth. *Voyager I* discovered a thin ring surrounding Jupiter.

Funding was gradually reduced for the exploration of space. Nevertheless, other scientific and technological achievements persisted, with pervasive implications: Artificial tissue was used as a substitute for skin by Japanese scientists in 1973; male birth-control pills were developed by American researchers and the first Apple II computer entered the market in 1977; the Alaskan Pipeline began operation in the same year. David M. Rorvik published a book asserting that a successfully cloned human being had been created, an assertion that was immediately challenged. During the year, however, the birth of a test-tube baby fertilized outside of the body and nurtured in laboratory conditions was clearly documented. Bio-agronomists heralded advances in seed productivity that were predicted to spawn a Green Revolution for developing nations.

Not all scientific discovery pointed directly to human advance. Studies released in 1979 showed with increased assurance that smoking was etiological in varieties of respiratory diseases, cancer, heart disease, and certain types of birth defects. In addition, many studies pointed to the augmented devastation of the environment by human and industrial waste and the exploitation of natural and human resources. The seventies also brought attempts to correct misuses of the biosphere that were amplified by scientific research. Increased attention to the environment resulted in striving to prevent, for example, litter and excess use of gasoline. Massive attempts to correct ecological problems were set in motion by corporations, their foundations, and governmental agencies. Ralph Nader and his associates continued to keep watch over the environment and instigate legislation to promote public health and safety.

The burgeoning inequities of city life in the United States often resulted in economic crises; a federal loan staved off the economic collapse of New York City. Civil rights for African Americans focused more deliberately on economic growth. The inequitable use of the death penalty by states provoked the Supreme Court to declare capital punishment as currently practiced to be a violation of the Constitution's prohibition on cruel and unusual punishment. By 1977, the death penalty was reinstated with the execution of Gary Gilmore by firing squad. Native American Indians voiced their claims for equality through the American Indian Movement. At Wounded Knee, South Dakota, in 1973, 10 hostages were taken to negotiate changes in the federal government's relationship with Native American nations. Equal rights for marginalized peoples became prominent areas of concern, protest, and legislation. During the decade, the rights of women were furthered in social, economic, occupational, and political areas throughout the world due to the hard work of the feminist movement. As early as 1970, the English Parliament ruled that women should receive equal payment for equal work. In the United States, efforts to amend the Constitution to ensure equality made it through the federal government but stalled in state ratification. Movement toward autonomy was pursued by French separatists in Canada at mid-decade. Gay rights, the rights of the elderly, the rights of children, and the rights of the mentally and physically challenged began to be given increased magnification in public consciousness in the United States and in many other parts of the globe. Yet equality was far from adequately defined, much less realized in these domains. By the end of the decade, recession was pounding at the door, the price of gold and other standards of economic value soared, and the heated quest for oil could be felt deeply in the purses of middle- and lower-class people throughout the world.

The seventies moved humankind closer to the stars, closer to an understanding of the intricate makeup of humans themselves, closer to self-reflection through the media of popular arts, and closer to the consciousness that might realign the "haves" with the "have-nots." The decade brought us closer to each other through a transition to communication systems that implode our neurons with information and saturate our ephemeral realms with a dissonance and consonance of impressions and images wrought by increased proximity to one another. With all of this came massive problems of decision and responsibility as to what constitutes just action, as to what constitutes the best of humankind. With these problems—and they continue to be pervasive—came equally massive potential for human growth. There was even a question posed that, according to some scientists, ranks among the most imaginatively provocative of all time. To wit, Professor Gerard O'Neill of the physics department at Princeton University advocated serious consideration of the following: "In the long run is a planetary surface, any planetary surface, really the right place for an expanding technological civilization?"[2] O'Neill urged consideration of the social, political, physical, cultural, ethical, and educational advantages of small communities of human beings traveling in self-sustaining environments through space. Provocative? Most certainly. Imaginative? Without a doubt. Possible? Some scientists indicated that it was! Would not implications for education and curriculum be indeed profound? Are schools, one might ask analogously, the best places for education to occur? Interestingly, in a little-known statement on education in utopia, John Dewey suggested that they are not.[3]

CURRICULUM THOUGHT AND LITERATURE

The late sixties and early seventies were crisis-ridden times. They were also times of immense potential. Scientists, citizens' groups, even politicians, and persons from many avenues of life witnessed and called for changes in policies and practices regarding the environment, technological developments, consumerism, employment practices, women's rights, racial and ethnic rights, corporate power, international relations, and activities of politicians. Much of the widespread critiques that had begun in the counterculture of the sixties were infused into the mainstream consciousness of the seventies. Overt protests were less frequent, but heated demand for equity left few spheres untouched, and many scathed, by demands for accountability.

Education was far from immune from these occurrences. The protest literature of schooling in the sixties, for example, writings by Herb Kohl, George Dennison, Jonathan Kozol, and John Holt, were granted a bit more scholarly recognition after the appearance of Charles Silberman's *Crisis in the Classroom* (1970). Some of the public, practitioners, and academics had little trouble ignoring the counterculture educational writing; a number of classroom teachers, however, were markedly influenced by the reinvention of the experientialist notion that education should provide communities of interested learners with opportunities to explore, create, and construct meaning. The appearance of Silberman's book lent credence to the idea that the schools were educationally bankrupt. After all, Silberman was already a highly regarded sociologist, and his research was not of the first-person variety like so much of the neoprogressive educational literature. Silberman's writing included the kind of knowledge that social behaviorists throughout the world of social science had programmed the public to value with receptivity.

Unlike social behavorist writing, the writing style of counterculture neoprogressive educators was intuitive, usually based on in-depth interaction with small numbers of situations, a long way from the kind of objectivity and generalization that the dominant notion of science taught people to appreciate. This issue will be rejoined in the discussions of curriculum contributions by Schwab, Pinar, Reid, Apple, Greene, and others who utilized alternative orientations to curriculum inquiry. For now, it is sufficient to emphasize that both the counterculture educators and Silberman set precedents for alternatives to conventional writing about curriculum and helped revive interest in the experiential tradition, infused with a critical reconstructionist emphasis on moral purpose as well as social, political, and economic justice.

The "golden days" of educational funding in the 1960s had become a prized relic of the past, victim to an uncertain economy. So had the unquestioned faith in public schools. However, publication and research in the seventies were not dormant. There was a rise in the number of smaller funding agencies, which for a while was combined with federal funding that lingered from the massive programs of the late sixties. There was also the perennial lag from submission of scholarly works to publication. Therefore, it is not surprising that the above factors, combined with the growing number of curricularists and an increased emphasis on publication as a symbol of professional worth, resulted in a total number of curriculum volumes in the seventies that exceeded those of the sixties by over 150 books.

Large-scale empirical studies, such as the federally funded study directed by James Coleman, carried considerable influence. Many curricularists interpreted the Coleman Report (1966) as verifying that school curriculum, instruction, and the like had little impact on scholastic achievement when compared with socio-economic status, home life, and peer culture. The socioeconomic status of the home was consistently upheld as the critical variable in predicting student success in performance on large-scale tests. The International Educational Assessment, a survey of education in approximately 20 nations, arrived at a commonsense conclusion: The best indicator of what students will learn in school is strongly influenced by home environment. Moreover, studies indicated that the duration of exposure (time on task) was important to achievement, leading to a multiplicity of studies on time spent on tasks in the several academic areas. The National Assessment of Educational Progress (with Ralph Tyler assuming a principal role) was the first large-scale assessment to measure the skill and knowledge of American students at specified age intervals. As with standardized achievement tests, the resulting information triggered heated criticism of states that did not top the ranks in performance. It was clear that, with both scholars and the public, empirical studies that portrayed data quanti-tatively were deemed the most defensible kind of contribution.

Other kinds of contributions were, however, beginning to edge their way into educational scholarship. A movement in educational history labeled revi-sionism seemed to stem from increased consciousness of the plight of non-white, non-Anglo, non-Germanic racial and ethnic groups in America's history. No one was immune to the indictments by this inquisition of revisionist educational historians.[4] Even John Dewey, foremost among philosophers who influenced curriculum writers, was among those accused of paving the way to the subjuga-tion of lower socioeconomic classes and those marginalized for reason of gender, ethnicity, or race.

Toward the end of the decade, concern for a branch of sociological and philosophical inquiry that evolved in Britain began to look seriously at the kind of knowledge perpetuated by the dominant social classes in advanced industrial societies. Thomas Kuhn impacted the research community with his *Structure of Scientific Revolutions*,[5] the idea that a paradigm of scholarship in any given era is only one among diverse possibilities that began to surface more fully. Moreover, the epistemological base that pervaded the scholarship of any era could no longer be viewed wholly as a universal and objective language for inquiry, though any system of rules does sustain a sort of objectivity. Instead, the widely accepted social science paradigm was redefined as dominant among alternative possibilities. Dominance in this case depended on a composite of ideological, economic, intellectual, and sociopolitical forces that were too often beyond the scholars' control, if not beyond their consciousness.

It was in this critical vein that the curriculum literature of the seventies began with Joseph Schwab's small but influential book, *The Practical: A Language for Curriculum* (1970), an elaboration of the 1969 article by the same name that concluded our discussion of the 1960s in the previous chapter.[6] Schwab argued that the curriculum field was moribund, dying of adherence to a mode of inquiry that did not suit the task of improving the schools. His critique focused on the assumptive bases of the language or principles of research. Drawing on the Aristotelian distinction between theoretic and practical epistemological bases, Schwab argued that the current theoretic or social science paradigm was largely irrelevant to the task of improving curricular practice in schools. He advocated that scholarly endeavor be changed to the practical paradigm, a mode of inquiry that is consonant with Dewey's epistemology. Whereas the problem source of theoretic research resides in the conceptualizations of researchers, that of practical research is in events and situational conflicts. The method of inquiry of the theoretic paradigm is induction, assuming the possibility of objectivity and the virtual absence of a Heisenberg uncertainty principle. On the contrary, the assumptions of practical inquiry maintain that illuminating insight stems from interaction with problematic arenas rather than from induction upon them. Moreover, the subject matter of theoretic inquiry is universals and its end is the production of publishable knowledge. The practical, on the other hand, takes a subject matter that is unique to situations and acknowledges the need to see an interdependence of causal factors that are not generalizable, but that are necessary knowledge for promoting an end of morally defensible decision and action that rectify specific problems.

In later articles, Schwab called for eclectic arts that matched or tailored theoretic knowledge to situations and generated additional courses of action for application in the myriad of circumstances where theoretic knowledge did not apply.[7] He also bolstered his contextual position by calling for a study of curriculum that was based on nothing less than deliberation that would illuminate the interdependence of four commonplaces of curricular experience: subject matter, learners, teachers, and milieu. Interactions among these factors in problematic classroom encounters create the curricula that actually occur there. Salient writings by Schwab were collected and introduced by Westbury and Wilkof (1978). Schwab's work stimulated increased attention to the nature of curriculum problems and ways in which they could be studied. At the end of the decade, W.A. Reid posed provocative questions and raised arguments about the overarching problem of how to best think about curriculum (1978) and contributed to curricular policy studies by drawing on both rationalist and humanist methodologies.

Schwab's critique and proposal were not wholly unique. Curriculum writers in the seventies loosely gathered under the title of "reconceptualists," a term coined by William Pinar (1975). These scholars shared common ideas but, more importantly, they held the conviction that the dominant model of curriculum scholarship, based on curriculum development for schools, was in decline. Reconceptualists, though surely not of one mind, variously engaged in phenomenological, existential, psychoanalytic, historical, and/or Marxist discourses. The partial similarity between Schwab and the reconceptualists of the late seventies is infrequently noted, and they are seldom recognized as having shared intellectual roots. More will be said later in this chapter about the various reconceptualist positions. It suffices to note here that both Schwab's thought and other novel humanist positions proposed in the early sixties, for example, the *1962 ASCD Yearbook*, and articles by such scholars as James B. Macdonald and Dwayne Huebner, were influential in establishing alternative ways of speaking about curriculum.

While it was evident that these perspectives were growing, those interested in exploring education as a human endeavor were clearly overshadowed by the preponderance of extant theoretic bias in the dominant brand of social behaviorist curriculum thought, which Pinar called "conceptual empiricism." Nevertheless, those of a humanistic persuasion were loosely linked together by assumptions that acknowledged the following: the centrality of situational problems; a necessary interactivity with environments for knowledge creation; a dialectical dialogue among persons for the exchange and growth of knowledge; an emphasis on persons as whole beings in the state of becoming or growing; the need to tie institutionalized learning to larger community functioning; the concomitant priority of interest or a Deweyan psychological organization of subject matter; acceptance of a variety of alternative and defensible ways of knowing; and the importance of acknowledging and fostering individuality. Such assumptions describe the character of a new variation, perhaps a profound one, in curriculum thought. It is respectful of the experientialist tradition but is often also interested in other ways of thinking about education. This listing of assumptions is not intended to be exhaustive; neither is it intended to suggest criteria to which a given author had to adhere to be considered part of this humanistic perspective on curriculum.

The idea that the above group was a loosely knit category should be reemphasized. In practice-focused literature the sources were seldom acknowledged even to be in the curriculum domain. Instead of using "curriculum" in their book titles, most referred to humanistic education or teaching, affective education, confluent education, open education, personalized education, and values clarification. Some curriculum authors, however, can be identified with similar interpretations of experientialist proposals for and reports about practice. Examples include Bremer and Van Moschzisher (1971), Buffie and Jenkins (1971), Featherstone (1971), Kopp and Zufelt (1971), Manning (1971), Dale (1972), Miller (1972), Harmin, Kirschenbaum, and Simon (1973), Silberman (1973), Goodlad (1974), Murphy (1974), Hollaway (1975), UNESCO (1975), Fantini (1976), Frazier (1976), Margolin (1976), Berman and Roderick (1977), Olsen and Clark (1977), Jelinek (1978), and Weston (1978). Quite obviously some of these citations are not directly curricular; however, they are included here as sources of marked influences on or reflections of curriculum thought and practice. Indeed, multifarious in both origins and advocacies, these sources represent important kinds of experiential contributions.

Having considerable impact on curriculum thought and literature, but little influence on schooling, was that group noted earlier as the reconceptualists. This group, whose curricular roots trace to, among others, James Macdonald and Dwayne Huebner, and to their mentor Virgil Herrick, was variously grounded in the humanities, humanistic psychology, contemporary sociology, history, and philosophy. The tenets of their writings were different from but not antithetical to Schwab's practical, Dewey's instrumentalist progressivism, and the practice-focused humanists. Yet their origins were decidedly different. They were first given a conceptual unification in the work of William Pinar through his books published in 1974, 1975, and 1976 (with Grumet); through annual conferences beginning in 1973 at the University of Rochester; and through the inauguration of *The Journal of Curriculum Theorizing* in 1979. Other writers, notably John S. Mann, Michael Apple, Madeleine Grumet, Henry Giroux, Janet Miller, Paul R. Klohr, Alex Molnar, Max van Manen, David C. Williams, and George Willis were linked with this alternative scholarship. The publication of James Macdonald and Esther Zaret's *Schools in Search of Meaning* (1975) by the Association for Supervision and Curriculum Development, *Qualitative Evaluation: Concepts and Cases in Curriculum Criticism* (1978) by George Willis, and *Ideology and Curriculum* (1979) by Michael Apple helped to characterize the several different directions gathered briefly under this umbrella. A similarity of intellectual roots enables clarification of reconceptualist origins. Existential literary sources—Sartre, Camus, Kafka, and others—together with the work of such continental philosophers as Maurice Merleau-Ponty and most notably Jurgen Habermas, constituted a major intellectual base for some reconceptualists. Others relied substantially on the work of Basil Bernstein and other sociologists of knowledge from Britain and the continent. Recommended as early introductions to such sources are Michael F. D. Young's *Knowledge and Control*

(1971) and P. W. Musgrave's *Knowledge, Curriculum, and Change* (1973). Other reconceptualist literature employed the neo-Marxian thought known as critical theory, as explicated by Jurgen Habermas.

Primarily invested in bringing new discourse to curriculum scholarship, reconceptualists did not consider practical application a primary concern. The dramatic exception was the proposal of Paulo Freire in his *Pedagogy of the Oppressed* (1970), a work other reconceptualists accepted as a first important step in understanding how new ways of thinking produce new educational activities. In this work, Freire reflected on the ideas that guided his literacy program with the oppressed peasants of Brazil. He related how he avoided the usual impediments associated with superior and inferior roles in teaching-learning situations by engaging the peasants in dialogue that accented the worth of all involved and by using the opportunity to work together to synthesize strengths and challenge injustice.

In *Toward a Poor Curriculum* (1976), by Pinar and Grumet, practical as well as philosophical application was made of certain central ideas in reconceptualist thought. Poor, as used by these authors, referred to a curriculum that is stripped of distracting accoutrements, a curriculum of inner human feeling that emerges as the course of the learning journey evolves. Experiencing that curriculum was described as follows: regressive, that is, sensitization to one's past self; progressive, that is, projection of one's future self; analytic, that is, sensitization to intricacies of one's present; and a continuously evolving synthesis of the three that accumulates toward self-actualization. A summary and extension of Pinar's position and his interpretation of its relation to other extant positions in the curriculum field may be found in his "State of the Art" address at the 1978 annual conference of the American Educational Research Association, subsequently published in *Educational Researcher*.[8] It should be apparent that there were marked differences among writers who were briefly given the reconceptualist label. Banded together primarily because they differed from the dominant orientation, by the end of the decade the categorization had already begun to outlive its initial utility, especially when applied more rigidly than Pinar and his colleagues intended.

Michael Apple and others contributed to the literature on hidden curriculum, noted earlier as a topic sparked by Philip Jackson in his *Life in Classrooms* (1968). Though not among the reconceptualist authors, Overly, and Snyder each produced works in 1970 that acknowledged the importance of hidden curriculum. Thus, it can be seen that while the curriculum reconceptualists were a significant advance, they are quite different in origin from other curriculum writers of the past three decades, including experientialists. Dewey's version of science was thoroughly practical, pragmatic, and humanistic. It can be argued, however, that it was not principally emancipatory in either the political or epistemological sense advocated by reconceptualists. It is more appropriate to contend that experientialism was influential in the development of the thinking of some reconceptualists, notably those who established the critical reconstructionist orientation (Freire, Apple, Giroux), but their accommodation of discourses that were not previously included in educational scholarship is an important influence.

An example of this kind of new approach to curricular thought is Elliot Eisner's *The Educational Imagination* (1979). It certainly was more compatible with experientialist thought than either social behaviorist or intellectual traditionalist proposals. Yet it stems from different origins. Whereas the ideas of Dewey and his disciples were derived from pragmatic philosophy, Eisner wrote about education from an aesthetic perspective, as an artist, rather than from various other discourses that were beginning to be employed (e.g., continental phenomenology, existentialism, and psychoanalysis). Eisner argued that curricular content that reflects critical perception and alternative modes of representation is central to meaningful education. He offered qualitative modes of evaluation that are analogous to functions of critics and connoisseurs in the arts. In this vein, Eisner shared a tradition with Harry Broudy, another writer on curriculum who stood apart from the dominant orientations.

Before moving to other curriculum orientations of the seventies, it seems pertinent to emphasize that, in comparison with those who were writing about curriculum development for the schools (i.e., social behaviorists or authors of synoptic texts), the reconceptualists were not exceedingly prolific in terms of producing books. Many were at the beginning of their academic careers and expressed their ideas primarily through journals and at professional meetings. Those who wrote about curriculum development for schools maintained what had become a tradition, having worked in essentially the same frame of scholarship for over 20 years. Let us look at several groups within this rather massive category.

Authors of synoptic texts, it should first be recalled, often emerged from the progressive movement, but sought to find a conciliar tone in their presentations. Intending to induct novice curricularists into the field, they produced encyclopedic renditions of curriculum knowledge. Their subtopics for curriculum development were by this decade quite familiar: foundations, purposes, development, design, implementation, evaluation, organization, instruction, materials, planning, and change. Desirous, too, of helping budding curricularists become able to influence practice, they provided guidelines for them, often calling them "principles." Surely they must have known that such formulas would scarcely equip readers to exercise Dewey's concept of practical intelligence, and ironically they cite Dewey more than they do other scholars. What alternative did they have, however, given their limited period of preparation for would-be curricularists? Synoptic text writers wanted to ensure that future curricularists would be aware of recent curriculum innovations and requisite rhetorics.

Thus, one form of synoptic text conveyed the message that future curricularists must be made ready for uncertain futures if they are to fashion the curricular experiences that could either help or hinder children and youth to deal with life. Perhaps they were influenced by the highly popular prognosis of "futurist" Alvin Toffler in *Future Shock*. At a time when rapid technological advance may have been confused with personal instability, many general texts appeared that emphasized innovation and preparation for unknown futures. The synoptic text was modified by the dictum: "We must ready ourselves!" It seemed that such emphasis on the novel aspects of curriculum knowledge helped to legitimize curriculum as an area of study that was almost continuously progressing. It is debatable if this was, in fact, a warranted form of legitimation. The following are examples of curriculum books that promoted novelty; in parentheses are key words taken from their titles that help to characterize this orientation. From 1970: Billett (improving), Burns and Brooks (changing), Doll (improvement), Feyereisen et al. (renewal), Foshay (invention), Frymier and Hawn (improvement), Hicks et al. (new), Shuster and Ploghoft (emerging). From 1971: Alexander and Saylor (tomorrow), and Oliver (improvement). From 1972: Lee and Lee (tomorrow), and the Organization for Economic Cooperation and Development (the eighties and onwards). From 1973: Beck, Cook, and Kearney (modern), Inlow (emergent), and Morley (modern). From 1974: Hass, Bondi, and Wiles (new). From 1977, Oliver (improvement); from 1978, Steeves and English (changing); and from 1979, Trump and Miller (improvement).

More comprehensive synoptic textbooks, though not as dominant a vehicle for sharing novel ideas on the curriculum as the above modernizing efforts, served as introductions or overviews of the general areas of curriculum development and study. Prominent examples include Bell (1971), Cave (1971), Christine and Christine (1971), Nicholls and Nicholls (1972 and 1978), Firth and Kimpston (1973), Owen (1973), Hass, Bondi, and Wiles (1974), Saylor and Alexander (1974), Stenhouse (1975), Tanner and Tanner (1975), Unruh (1975), Barrow (1976), Jenkins and Shipman (1976), Zais (1976), Chandra (1977), Hass (1977), Kelly (1977), McNeil (1977), Gress and Purpel (1978), Lawton et al. (1978), and Taylor and Richards (1979). These texts, with few exceptions, differed in one important way from the synoptic texts of the past. While synoptic texts of the seventies often did attempt to be encyclopedic, at least in the sense of sampling a variety of major issues, they did not contain the massive lists of principles or guidelines that served as prescriptions for practice.

The text by A.V. Kelly, for example, uses Tyler's framework to consider the current options being presented on curriculum planning, objectives, content selection, integration or organization, and evaluation. The social and political process of curriculum development is discussed only after options in rational construction of the curriculum have been discussed. The text concludes with a timely discussion of the possible forms of a national curriculum for schools in Great Britain. Kelly is explicitly conciliar in his writing, contending that his task as a scholar is to empower teachers as agents in curriculum decision making. He dismissed the value of establishing contrasting curriculum theory as being counterproductive to the responsibilities that are facing teachers. He cautioned, "In fact, as is so often the case, the oppositions and polarities exist more in the minds of curriculum theorists than in the realities of curriculum practice" (Kelly, 1977, p. 76). There is no specific, detailed prescription; Kelly provides a con-temporary view on curriculum issues and encourages practitioners to be eclec-tic, choosing paths that appear to be rational, politically astute, and effective.

Texts by Bell, Cave, Firth and Kimpston, Owen, Lawton, Barrow, Jenkins and Shipman, Stenhouse, Taylor and Richards, and Zais tended more toward to incisive analysis than many earlier synoptic texts. In addition, the Zais (1976) text contained an elaborate section on the history of contributions to curriculum thought and action. The text by Daniel and Laurel Tanner (1975) is particularly notable as being grounded in historical scholarship. Fully two-thirds of the text is given over to providing a history of thinking and practice in curriculum for U.S. schools. Even those parts of the text that were not specifically a historical chronicle (e.g., in discussion of general education and technical and vocational education) evidenced the use of historical research methods as a frame for their interpretation. The Tanners recaptured a macroperspective on the curriculum field and reconnected contemporary initiatives and experiments with historical predecessors. Exceptional scholarship and meticulous detail characterize their writing. Their incisive consideration of muddled or self-serving theorizing and/or research was provocative and, at times, contentious. Their own perspec-tive on curriculum is openly indebted to a scholarly, school-centered interpreta-tion of John Dewey and his proposals for twentieth-century education.

Synoptic texts that considered curriculum at separate levels of schooling were also plentiful in the 1970s. Among these were the following treatments: at the secondary school level, Beckner and Cornett (1972), Clark, Klein, and Burks (1972), Trump and Miller (1979); at the elementary level, Lavatelli, Kaltsounis, and Moore (1972), Rodgers (1975), Wiles and Bondi (1979); at the early childhood level, Parker (1972), Cook and Doll (1973), Margolin (1976),

Seefeldt (1976), Jones (1977); and at a level that emphasized the newly evolving middle school and the adolescent years as well as the junior high, Kindred and Wolotkiewicz (1976), Curtis and Bidwell (1977), Lounsbury and Vars (1978).

Another emphasis in the curriculum writing of the seventies that differed from the synoptic type discussed above was concern with novelty. These texts dwelt on the process of change or innovation, and to a frequent extent, on case studies of change. Examples of this kind of contribution include Lawler (1970), Pharis, Robison, and Walden (1970), Skeel and Hagen (1971), Hoyle (1972), Hoyle and Bell (1972), Leithwood and Russell (1972), Mayhew and Ford (1973), Dickson and Saxe (1974), Kingsford (1974), Regan and Leithwood (1974), Wass (1974), Goodlad (1975), Harris, Lawn, and Prescott (1975), Reid and Walker (1975), Roberts (1975), Leithwood, Clipsham, Maynes, Baxter, and McNabb (1976), MacDonald and Walker (1976), and Werner (1979).

Finally, there was still another type of emphasis on the "novel" that dealt with different types of schools and the ways in which the curriculum of schools might be selected and organized. These writings included both proposals and reports, usually taking the form of commentary rather than research. Sources in this domain were quite varied, as illustrated by the following: Turner (1971), on schools that liberated learning; Wilson (1971), on curricula that provided for various avenues to knowledge acquisition; Miller (1972), on a secondary curriculum based on the humanities; Purpel and Belanger (1972), on several kinds of curricula that evolved during the period of the cultural revolution in the sixties; Saylor (1972), on a call for future-oriented schools; Trump and Miller (1972), on organizational plans that influenced modular scheduling; Frymier (1973), on processes for creating schools of tomorrow; Moffett (1973), on student-centered curricula; Silberman (1973), on open education; Talmage (1975), on organization in individualized education systems; Michaelis, Grossman, and Scott (1975), on different conceptions of curriculum and instruction for elementary schooling. Frazier (1976) wrote on strategies for teaching that involved mastery, adventure, and association; Kauffman (1976), on developing programs that are based on teaching about the future; Frymier (1977), on a special style of individualization; Oliver (1977b), on mini-courses; Shane (1977), on futures approaches; Holt (1978), on the common curriculum in comprehensive schools; Bloomer and Shaw (1979), on constraints on innovative curricular organization; and Egan (1979), on a new understanding of development as a key factor in curricular selection and organization that focused on the story form and movement from fantasy to practical deliberation rather than the respected "expanding horizons" curriculum that begins with the immediate and commonplace.

Many of the above variations of emphasizing novelty in curriculum (i.e., the outgrowths of synoptic texts, the procedures and cases, and the proposals for new kinds of curricular organization) combined with the traditional synoptic texts to produce a loose association with a limited but important common agenda. A glance at this combined array of sources seems disparate indeed. However, most of the viewpoints expressed grew out of a long tradition of curricular thought aimed at helping schools. Many of the writers were formerly teachers and administrators, and they perceived their role as practical advocates of ways for schools to overcome problems by replacing old curricular patterns with new ones. Producers of synoptic texts and their descendents who promoted novelty were, as noted earlier, a new tradition. This is not to imply that they were intellectual traditionalists, who were characterized earlier in this book as advocates of liberal arts knowledge of life's great mysteries and ideas and skills that resurfaced during the mental-discipline period and dominated curriculum planning in most elementary and secondary schools throughout the twentieth century. Producers of synoptic texts were part of a tradition of conciliation, one that grew as the curriculum field itself grew in tandem with the rise of universal schooling.

Curriculum knowledge became a specific kind of constructed knowledge as the century progressed and as books called curriculum books were produced in greater numbers. During the thirties, the synoptic text emerged as a catalogue, sometimes as creator of "up-to-date" curriculum knowledge. It became a tradition, a growing compendium of thoughts of an equally growing number of curricularists. The thoughts were sometimes based on research, sometimes on philosophical argument, and ever increasingly they were fashioned from a cacophony of ideas from experientialist, social behaviorist, and intellectual traditionalist thought. Almost invariably, these combinations were intended as prescriptions for schools. For many years the literature distilled the thoughts into "principles" or guidelines to be followed or kept in mind by those who developed curriculum in schools. In the seventies fewer of these guidelines appeared. They were replaced with discussions of issues and the usual presentation of a patchwork of ideas, practices from the recent past, and highlights of other ideas that were considered novel. Thus, the mainstream of curriculum development literature that reached a pinnacle in the synoptic texts of the fifties and sixties had become a "curriculum knowledge tradition" built from the conciliar perspective. The tradition was given form in synoptic texts that usually included a compelling set of questions for continuing discussion advocated by Ralph Tyler and offered a useful construct for curricular knowledge inspired, in part, by Jerome Bruner.

Perhaps the most important contributors to the curriculum knowledge tradition, however, were school people. While sources of this knowledge were rather diverse, the primary focus was the school. The creation of this knowledge seldom took the form of systematic research into schooling; instead, it was acquired through daily laboring in schools. Initially, many curriculum writers were schoolteachers; later perhaps curriculum consultants or administrators in schools. Sooner or later they became associated with colleges and universities and taught school people, consulted with schools, and wrote about schools. Their experiences, their knowledge base, and the ways they spoke about education were from schools instead of from academic discourses. Although they seldom perpetuated the substance of the intellectual traditionalist proposal, they did much to perpetuate the form in which it occurred in the schools.

Let us now look at experientialist and social behaviorist thought as they appeared in the seventies. Experientialists advocated curriculum innovations often consistent with proposals offered by Dewey and his progeny. Nonetheless, tendencies toward the existential, phenomenological, psychoanalytic, and humanistic can also be detected. Examples include the Association for Supervision and Curriculum Development's (1970) emphasis on nurturing humaneness; Nerbovig's (1970) continuation of the unit approach to developing integrated curriculum; Weinstein and Fantini's (1970) integration of humanistic and affective activities within accepted modes of objectives and curriculum activities; Bremer and Van Moschzisher's (1971) description of the dissolving of barriers between school and community in the education of youth; Buffie and Jenkins's (1971) continuance of the idea of nongradedness; Kopp and Zufelt's (1971) advocacy of personally tailored curricula; Manning's (1971) interpretation of humanism; Walton's (1971a) version of integrated curricula in British primary settings; Dale's (1972) interpretation of learning environments; Thelen's (1972) interpenetration of curriculum and instruction with a sense of aims tempered by a union of action and inquiry; Moffett's (1973) student-centered emphasis; Silberman's (1973) presentation of varieties of perspectives on open classrooms; Bowers's (1974) existential perspective on teaching, learning, and policy that can invoke a curriculum of dialogues among teachers and students that is basic to democratic action; Holly's (1974) argument that curricular experiences should go beyond developing basic competencies in skills to inspire such necessities for democracy as self-realization and liberation; Haigh's (1975) interpretation of curriculum integration; Hendricks and Fadiman (1975) on curriculum that engages human beings in encounters through such new modes of communication as meditation, fantasy, altered states of consciousness, and Eastern thought/action; Hollaway's (1975) humanistic orientation to problem solving; UNESCO's (1975) experiential curriculum that involved perception, communication, and action; Timmerman's (1976) version of curriculum integration for teenagers; Berman and Roderick's (1977) process-oriented curriculum that focused on decision-making, communication, and "peopling" for the enhancement of living; Olsen and Clark's (1977) stress on the importance of relating curriculum to life; UNESCO's (1977) case study of integrated curriculum development; Greene's (1978) analysis of landscapes for learning; Reid's (1978) humanistic extrapolation of the practical; and Overly's (1979) call for lifelong learning.

The social behaviorists were, at the same time, by no means idle. Charged with the widespread acceptance of social science methodology that stemmed from involvement of social scientists in curriculum projects during the sixties, curricularists of this persuasion dominated scholarly endeavors. Their propensity to measure stemmed from roots in Thorndike's faith in quantitative and observable facts of human and animal activity. This orientation involved a behavioristic quest for causal relationships, a logical positivist faith in the potential for explanation through pieces of insight in minute but controlled and tested conclusions that had the potential to gradually build the puzzle of any aspect of some realm of knowledge or action.

In short, faith was manifest in the Hobbesian declaration that saw explanation of human behavior as a legitimate object of scientific inquiry. Such faith helped trigger the evolution of modern political science and the diversified social sciences. It should be noted that this conception of scientific methodology was quite distinct from Dewey's proposition. Curriculum development by constructing a skills management system exemplifies this scientific process. It was assumed that atomistic specifications of objectives and competencies could be organized to construct systems of concepts that were technical strategies for schools to apply in their effort to foster human betterment.

The emphasis on combinations of competencies, behavioral objectives, computerization, systematic needs assessments, attempts to combine elements of the humanistic with the behavioristic, and much rhetoric from systems theory, organization development, and management theory pervaded offerings by Ammerman (1970), Bernabei and Leles (1970), Feyereisen (1970), Harnack (1970), Drumheller (1971), Eisele (1971), Kapfer (1971), Utz (1971), Drumheller (1972), Hauenstein (1972), Razik (1972), Vargas (1972), Baker and Popham (1973), Ogletree and Hawkins (1973), Stradley (1973), Gilchrist and Roberts (1974), Beauchamp (1975), English and Kaufman (1975), Hug (1975), Mager (1975), and Casciano-Savignano (1978).

Robert Mager's (1975) work merits special note because of its impact on curriculum technology. His emphasis was derived from his concern for training programs in such areas as business, industry, and the military. His program looked at performance results of prespecified tasks as a curricular end, a call back to the activity analysis of Franklin Bobbitt that was characteristic of social behaviorism in the 1920s. The business ethic was also captured by English (1978) in an emphasis on quality control in curriculum.

A decline of technological emulation in curriculum books can be seen in the second half of the decade. Most of the above works were application-oriented, though they sometimes involved scholarly research. Though writers sought to convince readers, through rhetoric and form that bespeaks a research base, in practice there was a decided absence of curriculum research that convincingly supported their proposals. Moreover, the proponents of social behaviorist applications of curriculum were not alone in the curriculum field. Educational researchers who favored empirical or behaviorist methodologies dominated educational scholarship in the seventies. Many of the journals in the field published positivist empirical studies almost exclusively. The fact that graduate students were increasingly trained in statistical methodologies and research design of greater sophistication speaks to the same point. In this context, all schools of curriculum thought met with criticism for the preponderance of "armchair speculation" and the lack of "scientific" research to support their proposals. It was argued by many who espoused social behaviorist methodologies that little generalized evidence existed to support the efficacy of many means-ends assertions in curriculum literature.

Behind the research efforts of these new social behaviorists was the desire to empirically substantiate facts about learners, the learning process, learning conditions, causal factors in learning acquisition, curricular means and ends, and inputs and outputs. Great numbers of educational research studies and journal articles reflected this social science orientation. Some offered important curriculum implications, but few appeared directly from within conventional curriculum circles. Studies of the behaviorist variety were most frequently found in the area of curriculum evaluation, about which more will be said presently.

Books about curriculum research, however, tended to be more situational, analytic, and interpretative than hypothetical-deductive. They tended more toward the conceptual and/or prescriptive than the empirical and experimental, although some embraced both. Examples of books on curriculum research include Johnston and Burns (1970) on applications of research findings to elementary school curriculum; Lavatelli (1970) on applications of Piagetian research to early childhood curricula; Taylor (1970) on analyses of ways teachers plan courses; Dahllof (1971) on grouping patterns, content validity, and analyses of factors in curriculum process; McClure (1971a) on field studies in curriculum development; Smith and Keith (1971) on their analysis of organizational factors in an innovation; Grobman (1972) on decision aspects of developmental curriculum projects; Harrow (1972) on a continuation of Bloom and Krathwohl's styles of taxonomical objectives into the psychomotor domain; Ulf Lundgren (1972) on research into the curriculum process begun by Dahllof that led to the identification of theoretical constructs, referred to as "frame factors," that govern curriculum. Derr (1973) offered a taxonomical representation of a social domain of educational purposes.

Other perspectives on research, conducted as studies or argument, included Taylor and Walton (1973) on several perspectives on curriculum research, innovation, and change; Shipman, Bolam, and Jenkins (1974) on a case study of curriculum change; Taylor, Reid, and Holley (1974) on a case study of the English "sixth form"; Botel and Botel (1975) on a critical appraisal of taxonomical approaches to the classification of objectives; Eaton (1975) on a survey of uses of curricular terminology; Musgrave (1975) on a presentation of curriculum studies that combined empirical investigation with philosophical and social analysis; Reid and Walker (1975) on case studies in curriculum innovation; Stenhouse (1975) on practice-oriented research perspectives for the curriculum makers; Rudduck and Kelly (1976) on the problem of dissemination; Hamilton et al. (1977) on modes of illuminating curricular phenomena without the usual resource to numbers; Reid (1978) on ways to think about and deal with curricular problems; Willis (1978) on qualitative approaches to curriculum research and evaluation; Apple (1979) on investigation of kinds of knowledge and class relationships perpetuated by curriculum; Schaffarzick and Sykes (1979) on research and experience that wrote value-laden curriculum issues; Goodlad and associates (1979) on the exploration of curriculum practices in schools; and Bremer (1979) on research as a community and personal form of artful growth.

The work of Dahllof and Lundgren on frame factors is a fine example of combining social science methodology and sound theory construction for practical use. Related to time-on-task studies noted earlier, their treatment of frame factors sometimes serves as a theoretical basis for such studies. It can be given practical interpretation since allotment of time, levels of objectives, and teaching methods are frame factors over which teachers can exert control. Such frame factors as student intelligence, student achievement level, class size, length of school year, location of school in community, grouping of students into classes, and curriculum policy requirements are beyond the control of individual teachers yet exert marked impact on the kind and quality of knowledge that students acquire from curricular experience (Dahllof, 1971 Lundgren, 1972).

Curriculum evaluation, closely allied with the social behaviorist mode of research, was an area that often epitomized Schwab's "theoretic" mode of scientific study characterized above more fully than did books on curriculum research in the 1970s. Sometimes a considerable overlap existed between curriculum research and evaluation. Curriculum evaluation books, as noted above, were of considerable variety and were often far removed in style from behaviorist assumptions; case study approaches are prime examples. Variety existed too among major curriculum evaluators. This was evidenced through familiarization with work by Baker, Bloom, Cronhach, Dahllof, Eash, Ebel, Eisner, Gagne, Goodlad, Kallos, Lundgren, Parlett, Popham, Provus, Scriven, Stake, Stenhouse, Stufflebeam, Talmage, Tyler, Walker, Westbury, and Willis. Although not all of these evaluators authored books on curriculum evaluation in the seventies, they wrote articles, headed research agencies, spearheaded notable studies, and/or promoted styles of evaluation used by governmental and private agencies that provided curriculum-related funding.

Examples of books that directly addressed evaluation as a dimension of curriculum development include Lindvall and Cox (1970), Wiseman and Pidgeon (1970), Olson and Richardson (1972), Taylor and Cowley (1972), Weiss (1972), Wiseman and Pidgeon (1972), Great Britain Schools Council (1973a and 1973b), G. G. Greene (1973), Worner (1973), Zenger and Zenger (1973), Shipman, Bolam, and Jenkins (1974), Payne (1974), Case and Lowry (1975), Stenhouse (1975), Hamilton (1976), Mathews (1976), Tyler, Klein, and associates (1976), Bellack and Kliebard (1977), Hamilton et al. (1977), Lewy (1977), Willis (1978), and Eisner (1979).

Among the above, several merit special note. Taylor and Cowley (1972) present a fine sample of writings on curriculum evaluation, while Bellack and Kliebard (1977) provide classic articles that evoke broad perspectives on a more holistic conception of curriculum evaluation. The books by Hamilton et al. (1977), Willis (1978), and Eisner (1979) provide alternatives to social behaviorist interpretations of curriculum evaluation. They offer modes of illumination of curricular phenomena that go beyond what Hamilton and his colleagues called the "numbers game" by examining methods that are naturalistic, literary, and artistic, thus providing what Willis called "qualitative evaluation." The need for such scholars was pointed to by Wilson (1971), who argued that due to their quite limited notion of scientific study, curriculum researchers had overlooked the intellectual growth that took place during the fifties and sixties. Curriculum and evaluation research lagged considerably behind orientations to inquiry in psychology, philosophy, and natural science. Methods employed in such areas acknowledged the value of personal, situational, intuitive, interactive, and emotional avenues to knowing.

Although myopia on what constitutes worthwhile curriculum research was widespread, there were exceptions. Robert Stake, Elliot Eisner, and others argued on numerous occasions for intuitive or artistic human judgment as legitimate knowledge. Both the dominant form of social behaviorist evaluation and the qualitative styles that emerged to counter or complement it were, in part, products of the increased demand for school accountability. Some argued that defensible evaluation is the necessary starting point for curriculum development processes. To know both past and present was deemed by some to be a crucial prerequisite for deciding what should be. Many argued that current modes of evaluation inadequately portrayed extant happenings in perspective. Such arguments were sometimes based on the superficiality of analytic categorization schemes. An even more penetrating criticism was that knowledge of what *is* was assumed to be sufficient for determining what *should* be. Questions of what should be are, of course, ethical or normative at their base. Empirical data may be necessary but are insufficient bases for curricular prescription.

Prescription necessarily builds on the ethical and aesthetic purposiveness. That defensible purposes need to be a paramount curriculum development concern rekindled another focus in curriculum literature. Authors who emphasized purposes frequently tended to use sophisticated theoretical and philosophical tools. Books by William Pinar (1974, 1975, 1976), Macdonald and Zaret (1975), and Maxine Greene (1978) provided phenomenological and existential perspectives on purposes of both educational activity and research. Schwab (see Westbury and Wilkof, 1978) and Reid (1978) offered contributions that called for practical inquiry and action. Armentrout (1971), Krug (1972), and Wilhelms (1972) elaborated on purposes and content geared specifically to America's educational future. Levit (1971), Martin (1970), and Jenkins (1972) produced collections of readings about curriculum drawn from the philosophy of education that represented an array of philosophic styles, especially that of analytic philosophy.

Jenkins's work was part of an ambitious set of related works designed to introduce students to several spheres of curriculum thought, and as such, provided more than the usual magnitude of contextual explanation of the excerpts presented. The nature of objectives and theoretical perspectives in educational literature from 1955 to 1970 was provocatively explored by Morris (1972), whose study has a distinctively British flavor. This relation of philosophy to curriculum was examined by Dixon (1972), and applications of curriculum theory were discussed by Garcia (1973). White (1973) took a serious look at the implications of a compulsory curriculum within a British frame of reference, while Broudy (1974) provided a similar service in America, though both offered a view much broader than nationalistic confines.

The relation of philosophy and theory continued to be explored on a rather large scale. Holly (1974) probed beyond the conventional notions of curriculum to suggest modes of secondary education that contribute to a philosophy of general human growth and well-being. Beauchamp produced a third edition of his *Curriculum Theory* in 1975, continuing his systems-oriented approach, which now included an example of propositions derived from his form of theorizing. In 1977, Mauritz Johnson augmented a combination of his analytic approaches to curriculum theory in the elaborate *Intentionality in Education*. Analytic philosophy applied to curriculum was also provided by P. H. Hirst in a set of papers (1975) that addressed the relation of knowledge and curriculum. Sidney Hook produced another set of papers in the same year that argued in favor of curricula that fostered general education. Barrow (1976) provided a common-sense-based philosophy for liberal education. I. K. Davies (1976) produced a more highly technological treatment of objectives.

A sample of papers presented at a 1976 curriculum theory conference in Milwaukee provided an array of views on curriculum theory that demonstrated purpose, perceptiveness, and disagreement in curriculum theory (Molnar & Zahorik, 1977). In 1978, Brent provided a text called *Philosophical Foundations for the Curriculum*; in it he illustrated at least two points. The first was the growing importance perceived for philosophical analysis as a basis of curriculum, and the second was the concomitant notion that philosophical analysis was one of several bases necessary for curriculum inquiry. In the same year Michael Schiro provided a well-organized treatment of curriculum relative to four ideological bases: scholar academic, social efficiency, child study, and social reconstructionist. His analysis provides the curriculum student or scholar with a good deal of conceptual background for evaluating both the rationale and the implications of each.

The notion was clear that defensible concepts of curriculum needed to grow from a complex context. That curriculum could not derive from philosophical or theoretical discourse alone became clear as educators tried, often in vain, to align it with the conditions of students *en masse*. It could not be done without a broader knowledge base derived from several disciplines and from practical settings. To this end three categories of literature emerged that: (1) discussed curriculum implications of the changing and pluralistic culture; (2) continued the trend of foundational studies in education by embracing curricular dimensions of them; and (3) exposed and analyzed influences of political and ideological factors on curriculum thought and practice.

Books that responded to cultural changes by providing their implications for curriculum include the following: Browne and Ambrosetti (1970 and 1972) on popular culture; Dunfee (1970) on ethnic groups and their values; the Schools Council for Curriculum and Examinations (1971) on early school leavers; Purpel and Belanger (1972) on the cultural revolution and its values; Wootton and Reynolds (1972, 1974, 1977) on a variety of social trends; Ford

(1973) on African American history and culture; Ahlum and Fralley (1974) on the feminist movement and its values; Way (1974) on Spanish-speaking students; Newman (1975) on citizen action; Barnes (1976) on the impact of communications; Newton (1976) on black history and culture; Langenbach and Neskora (1977) on day care situations; Lesser (1977) on television; Robinson and Wilson (1977) on extending economic ideas in the curriculum; the Carnegie Foundation (1978) and Levine (1978), both on increased concern for college curriculum; Hefley (1978) on textbook controversies emphasizing legal perspectives; Jelinek (1978) on curricular responses to several critical social realities; Becker (1979) on curriculum in a global age; Jelinek (1979) on curriculum amid fluctuating educational values and an emerging category of books of curriculum for special education that illustrates the evolving character of that field of education, for example, Sniff (1973), Fredericks (1978), Wechman (1979), and Rumanoff (1979).

Becker (1979) illustrated the growing importance attributed to international cooperation. This orientation toward increased emphasis on pluralism took form in curriculum literature through the appearance of studies that compared curricula from different countries, or proposals for curricula that provided increased international understanding. Miel and Berman (1970) exemplify the latter, while the former was attempted by Beauchamp and Beauchamp (1972) and by Taylor and Johnson (1974). Additional reports on and proposals about curricula in other nations were provided by the following: Achtenhagen and Meyer (1970), Janzen (1970), UNESCO (1971), Hawes (1972), Southeast Asia Ministers of Education Organization (1972), Holmes and Ryba (1973), Netherlands (1973), Centre for Educational Research and Innovation (1975), Kallos (1975), UNESCO (1975), Posner and De Keijzer (1976), UNESCO (1976), Curriculum Development Centre of Malaysia (1978), and Musgrave (1979). Among these, Kallos should be noted for his argument that America is too unaware of research and theory in both highly and less developed cultures. Max van Manen should also be noted here for his attempt to convey work associated with the Utrecht School in the Netherlands to North American scholars. [9]

It is interesting to note that, perhaps due to increased communication technology, the seventies was the first decade in which curriculum books were co-edited by American and British educators. A sizable number of books appeared that included chapters or articles written by authors from different countries. Furthermore, most of these writings were by British, American, Australian, and Canadian authors. As for other countries, the works of Dahllof, Kallos, and Lundgren from Sweden were also visible in the curriculum literature of America. Representation here by curricularists from other countries was indeed lacking. Lack of funds for translating prominent works not written in English provided one major obstacle, but this scholarly isolation was hardly defensible. It should be noted that throughout the history of curriculum literature, aside from a scattering of works from the British Isles, sparse reference was given to curricularists from other nations in American curriculum literature. References to such monumental educational scholars as Herbart, Froebel, Pestalozzi, and Montessori were prevalent, as would be expected, but references to non-English contemporaries other than Piaget were, overall, strikingly absent. By comparison with previous decades, the appearance of a few English translations of non-Anglophone curriculum authors may constitute a positive step for the seventies, albeit a small one.

In addition to literature that sprang from changing and pluralistic culture through treatments of current issues and international perspectives, a second kind of text provided a broadly based context for curriculum study from the foundations of education. Usually, foundations of education referred to an introduction to knowledge derived from such areas as sociology, anthropology, history, philosophy, and/or psychology that served as a basis for the study of education. Curriculum books, particularly those of the synoptic variety, usually contained sections with brief versions of such background. An elaborate example of educational foundations for curriculum development and thought was presented in the first parts of Smith, Stanley, and Shores (1950, 1957). Most texts treated the topic more briefly. In the seventies, entire books came to be published that explored the foundational assumptions of curriculum issues. Examples of such books include Short (1970), Whitfield (1971), Zais (1976), Brent (1978), and Schiro (1978). Though often criticized as ahistorical by their own colleagues, curriculum writers of the seventies did begin to seriously look at their own past.[10] This scrutiny was well exemplified by the following: the History of Education Society's (1971) *The Changing Curriculum*; Elson's (1972) study of textbooks; the ASCD Yearbook at the bicentennial, which was edited by O. L. Davis (1976); and Rudolph's history of undergraduate college curriculum (1978). It was also exemplified by the founding of the Society for the Study of Curriculum History, under the direction of Laurel Tanner, in 1977.[11]

A third way that curriculum writers responded to cultural change provided a perspective that was quite new in curriculum literature. This orientation was concerned with the political and ideological forces that shaped schooling, curriculum studies, and curriculum implementation. Some of the authors on this topic held that action and decision of educators were determined by factors such as social class, race, gender, and values implicit in the ideological contexts in which schools are embedded. Furthermore, they argued that curriculum could not be planned through purely rational activity, that political factors were ever dominant, and that such documents as the "Tyler rationale" were indeed too rational.

Criticism emerging from such standpoints as these can be found in the work of the following authors: Freire (1970) on power in relationships between oppressors and the oppressed, emphasizing the need for dominated peoples to name their worlds to effect emancipation; Young (1971) on the impact of dominant social class ideologies; ASCD (1971) on the influence of bureaucracy and freedom on schooling (with special note given to Herbert Kliebard's essay on curriculum theory); Gracey (1972) on a study of bureaucratic influences on elementary curriculum; Seaman, Esland, and Gosin (1972) on relationships between ideology and innovation; Lawton (1973) on interactivity among educational theory, social change, and curriculum planning; Musgrave (1973) on relations among change, knowledge, and curriculum; the 1974 ASCD Yearbook (Della-Dora & House) on projections about education in an open society; Bowers (1974) on existential problems of freedom and literacy in relation to curriculum, teaching, and social policy; Speiker (1974) on determining reliability of practical community involvement in curriculum planning; Taylor, Reid, Holley, and Exon (1974) on an analysis of purposes, power, and constraint in curriculum planning; Kallos (1975) on comparisons of curriculum research orientations of Americans and Europeans; Lawton (1975) on influences of class and culture on curriculum, with the contention that such influences are minimal; Taylor and Tye (1975) on social determinants of school and curriculum; Cremin (1976) on the need to perceive and deal with an interaction of the many educative forces that actually and potentially guide the public; Pring (1976) on relationships between schooling and knowledge; Reynolds and Skilbeck (1976) on cultural impact on curriculum and classroom life; Comer (1977) on sociological perspectives of curriculum issues; Claydon, Knight, and Rado (1978) on the implications of pluralistic culture and society on curriculum; Nelson (1978) on legal influences on and ramifications of curriculum; Bremer (1979) on curriculum as an outgrowth of community; Apple (1979) on the relationship between school knowledge and ideology; and Schaffarzick and Sykes (1979) on value conflicts and curriculum.

The majority of the books that treated ideological and sociological interpretations of curriculum emphasized the large-scale influence that socioeconomic class has on schooling, curriculum, the kind of knowledge reproduced by schools, and the way it is received. Other noted scholars, for example, Decker Walker, Herbert Kliebard, Michael Kirst, William Pinar, Barry Franklin, Steven Selden, and William Doll have pointed to the importance of political factors in curriculum research, decision, and implementation.

Despite the philosophical debates (i.e., the arguments about the proper kind of research methodologies, the role of ideology in dictating kinds of knowledge provided by schools, and the political forces in curricular decision making), and as laudable as all these concerns were, school administrators and teachers were paid to do their jobs *now*. Although they likely knew well that their decision and action were clouded by political and other influences, students arrived daily, and activities needed to be provided for them. These teachers and administrators needed help, yet they had little time to receive it. Therefore, as in prior decades, curriculum scholars produced books for practitioners on curriculum administration, leadership, supervision, and teaching. They tended to be how-to books about curriculum design, implementation, and materials. Publishers added to this style of literature by reissuing "time honored" texts in second, third, and even more editions, that is, texts that demand by scholars and practitioners alike recalled.

Such books, like the synoptic texts of previous decades, sometimes oversimplified complex matters. Yet some deemed oversimplification to be more productive than no guidance at all. It was unlikely that most practitioners would have the time to pore over complex and lengthy arguments. The prime goal of many authors was to influence those who directly affect children and youth in schools. If teachers didn't have time to be thoroughly entered into the conversation, it was assumed that brief introductions in the text should demonstrate the richness of curriculum considerations. Books of this type appeared on several topics.

Attempts to generate administrative and supervisory influence through the formal organization of schools produced such curriculum books on administration, leadership, and supervision as Lewis and Miel (1972), Olson and Richardson (1972), Conner and Ellena (1973), Ellena (1973), G. G. Greene (1973), Stradley (1973), Worner (1973), Kopp and Zufelt (1974), Tankard (1974), Newfield (1975), Staples (1975), Speiker (1976), Van Geel (1976), Gran (1977), Rubin (1977b), Rubin (1977c), and Speiker (1977). Books on curriculum design were another attempt by scholars to influence practice. They provided means for course developers to systematically consider necessary elements and relationships for building curricula. As can be readily detected, the levels of rigor and practicality vary considerably among these sources: Burns and Brooks (1970), Kemp (1971), Merritt and Harris (1972), Michaelis, Grossman, and Scott (1975), Davies (1976), Gow (1976), McNeil (1976), Sockett (1976), Gower and Scott (1977), Hannah and Michaelis (1977), Johnson (1977), Posner and Rudnitsky (1978). The latter was offered, stemming from a conceptual orientation similar to Johnson (1977), for teachers who wished to carefully design courses. It was analytic and precise, and it acknowledged the importance of teachers in the curriculum development process. Other authors also regarded teachers as central to curriculum making and implementation, as evidenced by the following books: Beechhold (1971), Burdin and McAulay (1971), Christine and Christine (1971), Gracey (1972), Merritt and Harris (1972), Nicholls and Nicholls (1972), P. W. Hughes (1973), Blazier (1974), Murphy (1974), Hendricks and Fadiman (1975), Frymier (1977), Marbach (1977), Joyce (1978), Nicholls and Nicholls (1978), and Postman (1979). Postman's *Teaching as a Conserving Activity* is part sequel, part retraction to his popular *Teaching as a Subversive Activity* (with C. Weingartner, 1969). Both provided educators with a practical philosophy and ideas to create curricula that liberate students from the tyranny of the present.

It seems strange, considering schoolbooks and other teaching materials have been the prime guideposts of much teaching, that curriculum literature would not contain many elaborate treatments and reviews of materials. Books on this topic are indeed scarce; some did appear in the seventies: Seferian and Cole (1970), Elson (1972), Zenger and Zenger (1973), Farguhar (1974), Tyler, Klein, et al. (1976), and Hefley (1978).

In addition to the plethora of new books that focused on change, still others were revised and/or republished in the seventies, signaling that many readers saw in them a high degree of perennial value. Prominent among these were Ragan and Shepherd (1971 and 1977); Miel (1972); Trump and Miller (1972); Doll (1974 and 1978); Anderson and Macdonald, on the works of Virgil Herrick (1975); Beauchamp (1975); Foshay, reprints of his more influential articles (1975); Mager (1975); King and Brownell (1976); and Shuster and Ploghoft (1977). It should also be noted that such publishers as Arno Press, Greenwood Press, AMS, and others produced a large number of reprints of educational classics that were difficult to obtain in the original. Reprints of such authors as Dewey, Rugg, Kilpatrick, Hopkins, Counts, Bobbitt, Charters, and others should be of considerable interest to curriculum scholars. Many of the books that have undergone recent reprints are noted parenthetically in the bibliographical sections of this book.

As can be detected early from the foregoing, the seventies, like the sixties, produced a plethora of curriculum books. The increased modeling of scholarship in education after that in the social and natural sciences resulted in the equating of publication, status, and worthiness in the research community. Hence, the upsurge of new journals and the expansion of old journals. The pressure to contribute to them was intense indeed. This communication barrage was accompanied by the emergence of computerized clearing houses, such as ERIC, in which can be found papers presented at conferences, various other manuscripts, and research reports.

The breadth of curriculum information was too great for any one curriculum scholar to fathom. Thus, as was done in the sixties, but with even greater fervor, curriculum scholars of the seventies took it upon themselves to search out part of the literature, select some of the best writings, and compile books of readings.

A significant variation on the collections of readings emerged in the seventies. Some books of readings were designed to offer contrast and commentary. Contrast was provided by careful categorization of the articles selected, often to represent major lines of curriculum thought and/or activity (e.g., Eisner & Vallance, 1974). Commentary by the editor(s) frequently clarified similarities and differences among selected authors and sharpened problematic areas that needed further study. Further, both the new and traditional collections of readings helped to shape the major concerns of the field by their topical organization. For example, Bellack and Kliebard (1977) organized selections in four major groupings: (1) perspectives on how curriculum problems should be studied, (2) relationships between knowledge and curriculum, (3) perspectives on curriculum evaluation, and (4) relationships between change and curriculum. Other fine collections of curriculum articles include Hass, Wiles, and Bondi (1970), Martin (1970), Eisner (1971), Hillson and Hyman (1971), Hooper (1971), Leeper (1971), Levit (1971), McClure (1971b), Parlardy (1971), Van Til (1971), Alexander (1972), Heidenreich (1972), DeCarlo and Madon (1973), Edward (1974), Hass, Bondi, and Wiles. (1974), Van Til (1974), Curriculum Design and Development Course Team (1975a and 1975b), Taylor and Tye (1975), Petty (1976), Rubin (1977a, 1977b, and 1977c), Willis (1978), Taylor and Reid (1979), and Schaffarzick and Sykes (1979).

While some of these readings provided an overview as a main objective, others focused on particular areas such as elementary education, secondary education, criticism of curriculum, evaluation, and the problem of knowledge. Nevertheless, each provided numerous perspectives within an identified domain. Further, it should be noted that while all of the above were collections, several contain a large proportion of original articles, for example, Willis (1978), Rubin (1977a, 1977b, and 1977c), and McClure (1971b).

Finally, several books went beyond the presentation of selected articles to a considerable extent. George Willis (1978) accomplished this, carving new territory in conceptions of evaluation. In an attempt to identify five conflicting conceptions of curriculum development, Eisner and Vallance (1974) went beyond usual collections. They identified curriculum as: (1) the development of cognitive processes, (2) technology, (3) consummatory experience, (4) a springboard to social reconstruction, and (5) academic rationalism. Orlosky and Smith (1978) coupled elaborate excerpts from influential curriculum writings with a considerable amount of commentary that tied related writings together and provided interpretation, criticism, and analysis at the same time. It is interesting to note that Orlosky and Smith (1978) identified five general topics of concern that were not wholly dissimilar from those of Bellack and Kliebard (1977), noted earlier. These included: (1) an overview of curriculum study, (2) styles of curriculum theory, (3) operational concepts and principles, (4) curriculum change, and (5) evaluation. Under the topic of curriculum theory styles, they presented four: humanistic, disciplinary, technological, and futuristic. A point here is that dissimilarity does not reign omnipotent in curriculum categorization schemes.

Perhaps the most ambitious efforts to catalog, interpret, and criticize major curriculum ideas, proposals, and practices are two sets of books produced in Britain. The first was developed in conjunction with the Open University. Published originally by the Open University Press and later made available in the United States by Harper and Row, the initial version consisted of nine books containing 17 units on curriculum context, design, and development. Both English and U.S. scholars are broadly represented. Excerpts are provided along with substantial interpretation and criticism. The Open University Press also published a set of units in 1976; these are listed together under the authorship of that press in a large citation in the bibliographical section of this chapter.

The other elaborate set of curriculum perspectives is provided in a five-volume set under the general editorship of David Jenkins. It was published in 1976 by Open Books with an overall title of *Curriculum Studies*. The five books are *Curriculum: An Introduction* by Jenkins and Shipman; *Designing the Curriculum* by Sockett; *Changing the Curriculum* by MacDonald and Walker; *Curriculum Evaluation* by Hamilton; *Knowledge and Schooling* by Pring; and *Culture and the Classroom* by Reynolds and Skilbeck. Each book is quite thorough in introducing salient contributions for topics addressed. Each book is concise and copiously referenced. Together they formed a commendable introduction to curriculum thought through the mid-seventies.

In addition to collections and sets of curriculum books, one could become acquainted with curriculum literature by surveying bibliographies in major books, especially those of the synoptic variety. Two books appeared in the seventies that directly treat bibliographical material: Louise Tyler's (1970) annotated guide to selected literature, and Brickman's (1974 and 1976) bibliographical essays on curriculum and instruction. For more brief overviews of curriculum writing in the 1970s, the reader might turn to the "State of the Art" addresses by John McNeil and William Pinar,[12] Decker Walker's review of curriculum writing in the *Review of Research in Education*,[13] and Philip Jackson's 1979 overview and critique of contemporary curriculum research and theory.[14]

Contributions to the seventies were monumental in quantity; at the same time, new quality was witnessed in the curriculum literature. If escalation and variety of contributions are indicators, it would seem that the label of "moribund," placed on the field at the onset of the seventies, had been somewhat overcome.

It is patent that a field's worth cannot be judged by quantity of production alone. We need to seriously reflect on many questions. The defensibility of such reflection is greatly increased if it is rooted in knowledge of former endeavors—scholarly and practical. How do the contextual events and prevailing values of a time period shape the growth of curriculum thought and literature? What is the quality and worth of the accumulated curriculum literature? What aspects of it fit together in meaningful ways? What aspects are independently worthwhile? Does curriculum scholarship offer something of direct benefit to schooling or other educational enterprises? To what extent does the literature contain ideas, proposals, and a record of practices that are inert and should be discarded? Does it contain ideas, proposals, practices, and imaginative projections that can clarify and direct intelligent and effective curriculum activity in the future? Does it educate? As Dewey described education, does it give meaning to experience and help to direct the courses of subsequent experiences in curriculum inquiry and action?[15]

BIBLIOGRAPHY OF CURRICULUM BOOKS 1970–1979

1970

Achtenhagen, F., & Meyer, H. (1970). *Curriculum revision.* Munich, Germany: Kosel.

Ammerman, H. L. (1970). *Systematic approaches for identifying and organizing content for training programs.* Alexandria, VA: Human Resources Research Organization.

Association for Supervision and Curriculum Development (M. M. Scobey & G. Graham, Eds.). (1970). *To nurture humaneness: Commitment for the '70s: Yearbook.* Washington, DC: Author.

Bernabei, R., & Leles, S. (1970). *Behavioral objectives in curriculum and evaluation.* Dubuque, IA: Kendall/Hunt.

Billett, R. O. (1970). *Improving the secondary-school curriculum: A guide to effective curriculum planning.* New York: Atherton Press.

Browne, R. B., & Ambrosetti, R. J. (1970). *Popular culture and curricula.* Bowling Green, OH: Bowling Green University Popular Press.

Burns, R. W., & Brooks, G. D. (Eds.). (1970). *Curriculum design in a changing society.* Englewood Cliffs, NJ: Educational Technology Publishers.

Carr, W. G. (1970). *Values and the curriculum: A report.* Washington, DC: National Education Association, Center for the Study of Instruction.

Cremin, L. A. (1970). *American education: The colonial experience, 1607–1783.* New York: Harper & Row.

Dillon, E. J., Heath, E. J., & Biggs, C. W. (1970). *Comprehensive programming for the success of learning.* Columbus, OH: C. E. Merrill.

Dittman, L. L. (Ed.). (1970). *Curriculum is what happens; planning is the key.* Washington, DC: National Association for the Education of Young Children.

Doll, R. C. (1970). *Curriculum improvement: Decision-making and process* (second edition). Boston: Allyn & Bacon.

Dunfee, M. (1970). *Ethnic modifications of the curriculum.* Washington, DC: National Education Association.

Dunkel, H. B. (1970). *Herbart and Herbartianism: An educational ghost story.* Chicago: University of Chicago Press.

Exeter Curriculum Conference Report. (1970). *Curriculum development.* Exeter, England: University of Exeter.

Feyereisen, K. V., Fiorino, A. J., & Nowak, A. T. (1970). *Supervision and curriculum renewal: A systems approach.* New York: Appleton-Century-Crofts.

Foshay, A. W. (1970). *Curriculum for the seventies: An agenda for invention.* Washington, DC: National Education Association (CSI).

Freire, P. (1970). *Pedagogy of the oppressed.* New York: Continuum.

Frymier, J. R., & Hawn, H. C. (1970). *Curriculum improvement for better schools.* Worthington, OH: Charles A. Jones.

Gattegno, C. (1970). *What we owe children: The subordination of teaching to learning.* New York: Outerbridge and Dienstfrey.

Grobman, H. G. (1970). *Developmental curriculum projects: Decision points and processes.* Itasca, IL: F. E. Peacock.

Harnack, R. S. (1970). *Evaluation of an innovation—Computer based curriculum planning.* Buffalo: State University of New York at Buffalo.

Hass, G., Wiles, K., & Bondi, J. (Eds.). (1970). *Readings in curriculum.* Boston: Allyn & Bacon.

Hicks, W. V., Houston, W. R., Cheney, B. D., & Marquard, R. L. (1970). *The new elementary school curriculum.* New York: Van Nostrand Reinhold Company.

Howson, G. (Ed.). (1970). *Developing a new curriculum.* London: Heinemann.

Janzen, H. (1970). *Curriculum change in a Canadian context*. Toronto: Cage Educational Publications.

Johnston, A. M., & Burns, P. C. (1970). *Research in elementary school curriculum*. Boston: Allyn & Bacon.

Knowles, M. S. (1970). *The modern practice of adult education: Andragogy versus pedagogy*. New York: Association Press. (Revised and reissued as *The modern practice of adult education: From pedagogy to andragony* in 1980, Chicago, Follett.)

Lavatelli, C. S. (1970). *Piaget's theory applied to an early childhood curriculum*. Boston: American Science and Engineering, Inc.

Lawler, M. R. (Ed.). (1970). *Strategies for planned curricular innovation*. New York: Teachers College Press, Columbia University.

Lindvall, C. M., & Cox, R. C. (1970). *Evaluation as a tool in curriculum development*. Chicago: Rand McNally.

Martin, J. R. (Ed.). (1970). *Readings in the philosophy of education: A study of the curriculum*. Boston: Allyn & Bacon.

Miel, A., & Berman, L. M. (1970). *Educating the young people of the world*. Washington, DC: Association of Supervision and Curriculum Development, National Education Association.

Myers, D. A. (1970). *Decision making in curriculum and instruction*. Dayton, OH: Institute for Development of Educational Activities.

Nerbovig, M. (1970). *Unit planning: A model for curriculum development*. Worthington, OH: A. Jones Publishing.

Neufeld, K .A. (Ed.). (1970). *Invitational Conference on Elementary Education, Third, Banff, Alberta, 1969. Individualized curriculum and instruction: Proceedings*. Edmonton: The University of Alberta, Department of Elementary Education.

Overly, N. V. (Ed.). (1970). *The unstudied curriculum: Its impact on children*. Washington, DC: Association for Supervision and Curriculum Development.

Parker, D. H. (1970). *Schooling for what? Sex, money, war, peace*. New York: McGraw-Hill.

Pharis, W. L., Robison, L. E., & Walden, J. C. (1970). *Decision making and schools for the seventies*. Washington, DC: National Education Association.

Pritzkau, P. T. (1970). *On education for the authentic*. Scranton, PA: International Textbook Company.

Schwab, J. J. (1970). *The practical: A language for curriculum*. Washington, DC: National Education Association.

Seferian, A., & Cole, H. P. (1970). *Encounters in thinking: A compendium of curricula for process education*. Buffalo, NY: Creative Education Foundation.

Short, E. C. (Ed.). (1970). *A search for valid content for curriculum courses*. Toledo, OH: College of Education, University of Toledo.

Shuster, A. H., & Ploghoft, M. E. (1970). *The emerging elementary curriculum* (second edition). Columbus, OH: Charles E. Merrill.

Silberman, C. E. (1970). *Crisis in the classroom: The remaking of American education*. New York: Random House.

Snyder, B. R. (1970). *The hidden curriculum*. New York: Knopf.

Taylor, P. H. (1970). *How teachers plan their courses*. London: The National Foundation for Educational Research in England and Wales.

Tyler, L. (1970). *A selected guide to curriculum literature: An annotated bibliography*. Washington, DC: National Education Association.

Weinstein, G., & Fantini, M. D. (1970). *Toward a humanistic education: A curriculum of affect*. New York: Praeger.

Wiseman, S., & Pidgeon, D. (1970). *Curriculum evaluation*. Slough, England: Slough National Foundation for Educational Research in England and Wales.

1971

Alexander, W. M., & Saylor, J. G. (1971). *The high school today and tomorrow*. New York: Holt, Rinehart, and Winston.

Armentrout, W. W. (Ed.). (1971). *What should the purposes of American education be?* Dubuque, IA: Kendall/Hunt.

Association for Supervision and Curriculum Development. (1971). *Freedom, bureaucracy and schooling* 1971 Yearbook. (V.F. Haubrich, Editor). Washington, DC: Author.

Beechhold, H. F. (1971). *The creative classroom*. New York: Charles Scribner's Sons.

Bell, R. (Ed.). (1971). *Thinking about the curriculum*. Bletchley, Bucks, England: The Open University Press.

Bishop, L. K., & Hartley, H. J. (Eds.). (1971). *Individualizing educational systems, the elementary and secondary school: Implications for curriculum, professional staff, and students*. New York: Harper and Row.

Bremer, J., & Van Moschzisher, M. (1971). *The school without walls*. New York: Holt, Rinehart, and Winston.

Buffie, E. G., & Jenkins, J. M. (Eds.). (1971). *Curriculum development in non-graded schools: Bold new venture*. Bloomington: Indiana University Press.

Burdin, J. L., & McAulay, J. D. (1971). *Elementary school curriculum and instruction: The teacher's role*. New York: Wiley.

Cave, R. G. (1971). *An introduction to curriculum development*. London: Ward Lock Educational.

Chai, Hon-Chan. (1971). *Planning education for a plural society*. Paris: UNESCO, International Institute for Education Planning.

Charters, W. W. (1971). *Curriculum construction.* (Reprint of 1923 edition). New York: Arno Press.

Christine, C. T., & Christine, D. W. (1971). *Practical guide to curriculum and instruction.* West Nyack, NY: Parker Publishing Co.

Connelly, F. M., Herbert, J., & Weiss, J. (Eds.). (1971). *Elements of curriculum development.* Toronto: Ontario Institute for Studies in Education.

Dahllof, U. S. (1971). *Ability grouping, content validity and curriculum process analysis.* New York: Teachers College, Columbia University.

Drumheller, S. J. (1971). *Handbook of curriculum design for individualized instruction: A systems approach.* Englewood Cliffs, NJ: Educational Technology Publishers.

Eisele, J. E. (1971). *Computer assisted planning of curriculum and instruction: How to use computer-based resource units to individualize instruction.* Englewood Cliffs, NJ: Educational Technology Publishers.

Eisner, E. W. (Ed.). (1971). *Confronting curriculum reform.* Boston: Little, Brown and Co.

Featherstone, J. (1971). *Schools where children learn.* New York: Liveright Publishing Company.

Ford Foundation. (1971). *A foundation goes to school: The Ford Foundation comprehensive school improvement program 1960–1970.* New York: Ford Foundation.

Green, T. (1971). *The activities of teaching.* New York: McGraw-Hill.

Hathaway, W. E. (1971). *A network-based approach to curriculum development.* Edmonton, Alberta: Author.

Hawkins, E. W. (1971). *Modern languages in the curriculum.* Cambridge, England: Cambridge University Press.

Hillson, M., & Hyman, R. T. (Eds.). (1971). *Changes and innovation in elementary and secondary organization: Selected readings.* New York: Holt, Rinehart and Winston.

History of Education Society. (1971). *The changing curriculum.* London: Methuen Company.

Hooper, R. (Ed.). (1971). *The curriculum: Context, design and development.* Edinburgh, Scotland: Oliver and Boyd.

Hunt, F. J. (1971). *Social science and the school curriculum.* Sydney, Australia: Angus and Robertson.

Kapfer, M. B. (1971). *Behavioral objectives in curriculum development.* Englewood Cliffs, NJ: Educational Technology Publications.

Kemp, J. E. (1971). *Instructional design: A plan for unit and course development.* Belmont, CA: Fearon.

Kopp, O. W., & Zufelt, D. L. (1971). *Personalized curriculum: Method and design.* Columbus, OH: Merrill.

Lawler, M. R. (Ed.). (1971). *Strategies for planned curricular innovation.* New York: Teachers College Press.

Leeper, R. R. (Ed.). (1971). *Curricular concerns in a revolutionary era.* Washington, DC: Association for Supervision and Curriculum Development.

Levit, M. (Ed.). (1971). *Curriculum: Readings in the philosophy of education.* Urbana: University of Illinois Press.

Manning, D. (1971). *A humanistic curriculum.* New York: Harper and Row.

McClure, R. M. (1971a). *Field studies in curriculum development.* Washington, DC: National Education Association.

McClure, R. M. (Ed.). (1971b). *The curriculum: Retrospect and prospect. The Seventieth Yearbook of the National Society for the Study of Education: Part I.* Chicago: University of Chicago Press.

National Education Association Staff Report. (1971). *Schools for the seventies and beyond: A call to action.* Washington, DC: National Education Association.

Oliver, A. (1971). *Curriculum improvement.* New York: Dodd, Mead & Co.

Parlardy, J. M. (Ed.). (1971). *Elementary school curriculum—An anthology of trends and challenges.* New York: Macmillan.

Ragan, W. B., & Shepherd, G. D. (1971). *Modern elementary curriculum* (fourth edition). New York: Holt, Rinehart and Winston.

Richmond, K. W. (1971). *The school curriculum.* London: Methuen and Company.

Schools Council for Curriculum and Examinations. (Eds.). (1971). *Choosing a curriculum for the young school leaver.* Englewood Cliffs, NJ: Scholastic Book Services.

Skeel, D. J., & Hagen, O. A. (1971). *The process of curriculum change.* Pacific Palisades, CA: Goodyear Publishing Company.

Smith, L. M., & Keith, P. M. (1971). *Anatomy of educational innovation: An organizational analysis of an elementary school.* New York: Wiley.

Tanner, D. (1971). *Secondary curriculum: Theory and development.* New York: Macmillan.

Turner, J. (1971). *Making new schools: The liberation of learning.* New York: David McKay Company.

UNESCO. (1971). *Curriculum revision.* Nendeln, Liechtenstein: Kraus Reprint.

Utz, R. T., & Leonard, L. D. (1971). *A competency based curriculum.* Dubuque, IA: Kendall/Hunt Publishing Co.

Van Til, W. (Ed.). (1971). *Curriculum: Quest for relevance.* Boston: Houghton Mifflin.

Walton, J. (1971a). *The integrated day in theory and practice.* London: Ward Lock Educational.

Walton, J. (Ed.). (1971b). *Curriculum: Organisation and design.* London: Ward Lock Educational.

Weikart, D. P., Rogers, L., Adcock, C., & McClelland, D. (1971). *The cognitively oriented curriculum: A framework for preschool teachers.* Urbana: University of Illinois Press.

Whitfield, R. (Ed.). (1971). *Disciplines of the curriculum.* London: McGraw-Hill.

Wilson, L. C. (1971). *The open access curriculum.* New York: Allyn & Bacon.

Wright, B. A., Camp, L. T., Stosberg, W. K., & Fleming, B. L. (1971). *The elementary school curriculum: Better teaching now.* New York: Macmillan.

Young, M. F. D. (Ed.). (1971). *Knowledge and control: New directions for the sociology of education.* London: Collier-Macmillan.

1972

Alexander, W. M. (Ed.). (1972). *Changing secondary school curriculum: Readings* (second edition). New York: Holt, Rinehart and Winston.

Beauchamp, G. A., & Beauchamp, K. E. (1972). *Comparative analysis of curriculum systems* (second edition). Wilmette, IL: The Kagg Press.

Beckner, W., & Cornett, J. D. (1972). *The secondary school curriculum, content and structure.* Scranton, PA: Intext Educational Publishers.

Browne, R. B., & Ambrosetti, R. J. (Eds.). (1972). *Popular culture and curricula.* Bowling Green, OH: Bowling Green University Press.

Clark, L. H., Klein, R. L., & Burks, J. B. (1972). *The American secondary school curriculum* (second edition). New York: Macmillan.

Dale, E. (1972). *Building a learning environment.* Bloomington, IN: Phi Delta Kappa.

Dixon, K. (Ed.). (1972). *Philosophy of education and the curriculum.* Oxford, NY: Pergamon Press.

Drumheller, S. J. (1972). *Teacher's handbook for a functional behavior-based curriculum.* Englewood Cliffs, NJ: Educational Technology Publications.

Eastern Regional Institute for Education. (1972). *How to get new programs into elementary schools.* Englewood Cliffs, NJ: Educational Technology Publications.

Eisenberg, J. A., & MacQueen, G. (1972). *Don't teach us that!* Don Mills, Ontario: Paper Jacks.

Elson, R. M. (1972). *Guardians of tradition.* Lincoln: University of Nebraska Press. (A reprint of 1964 version).

Engle, S., & Longstreet, W. S. (1972). *A design for social education in the open curriculum.* New York: Harper and Row.

Gracey, H. L. (1972). *Curriculum or craftsmanship: Elementary school teachers in a bureaucratic system.* Chicago: University of Chicago Press.

Grobman, H. (1972). *Developmental curriculum projects: Decision points and processes.* Itasca, IL: F.E. Peacock.

Harrow, A. J. (1972). *A taxonomy of the psychomotor domain; A guide for developing behavioral objectives*. New York: David McKay.

Hauenstein, A. D. (1972). *Curriculum planning for behavioral development*. Worthington, OH: Charles A. Jones.

Hawes, H. W. (1972). *Planning the primary school curriculum in developing countries*. Paris: UNESCO.

Heidenreich, R. R. (Ed.). (1972). *Current readings in improvements in curriculum*. Arlington, VA: College Readings.

Hoyle, E. (1972). *Problems of curriculum innovation II*. Bletchley, Bucks, England: The Open University Press.

Hoyle, E., & Bell, R. (1972). *Problems of curriculum innovation I*. Bletchley, Bucks, England: The Open University Press.

Illich, I. (1972). *De-schooling society*. New York: Harper and Row.

Jenkins, D. (Ed.). (1972). *Curriculum philosophy and design*. Bletchley, Bucks, England: The Open University Press.

Joyce, B. R., & Weil, M. (1972). *Models of teaching*. Englewood Cliffs, NJ: Prentice Hall.

Krug, M. M. (Ed.). (1972). *What will be taught: The next decade*. Itasca, IL: F. E. Peacock.

Lavatelli, C. S., Kaltsounis, T., & Moore, W. J. (1972). *Elementary school curriculum*. New York: Holt, Rinehart and Winston.

Lee, J. M., & Lee, D. M. (1972). *Elementary education: Today and tomorrow* (second edition). Boston: Allyn & Bacon.

Leithwood, K. A., & Russell, H. H. (1972). *Planned educational change: Developing an operational model*. Peterborough, Canada: Ontario Institute for Studies in Education, Trent Valley Centre.

Lewis, A. J., & Miel, A. (1972). *Supervision for improved instruction: New challenges and new responses*. Belmont, CA: Wadsworth Publishing Company.

Lundgren, U. P. (1972). *Frame factors and the teaching process: A contribution to curriculum theory and theory on teaching*. Stockholm: Almqvist and Wiksell.

Maclure, S. (1972). *Styles of curriculum development*. Washington, DC: Organization for Economic Cooperation and Development.

Merritt, J., & Harris, A. (1972). *Curriculum design and implementation*. Bletchley, Bucks, England: The Open University Press.

Miel, A., & Associates. (1972). *Cooperative procedures in learning*. Westport, CT: Greenwood. (Reprint of 1952 edition.)

Miller, B. (1972). *The humanities approach to the modern secondary school curriculum*. New York: Center for Applied Research in Education.

Morris, B. (1972). *Objectives and perspectives in education: Studies in educational theory (1955–1970)*. London: Routledge and Kegan Paul.

Nicholls, A., & Nicholls, S. H. (1972). *Developing a curriculum: A practical guide*. London: Allen and Unwin.

Olson, A. V., & Richardson, J. (1972). *Accountability: Curricular applications*. San Francisco, CA: Intext Educational Publishers.

Ontario Association for Curriculum Development. (1972). *Relevance in the curriculum. Twenty-first Annual Conference*. (S. Dubois, Editor). Toronto: Ontario Association for Curriculum Development.

Organization for Economic Cooperation and Development, Center for Educational Research and Innovation. (1972). *The nature of the curriculum for the eighties and onwards*. Paris: Organization of Economic Cooperation and Development.

Parker, R. K. (Ed.). (1972). *The preschool in action: Exploring early childhood programs*. Boston: Allyn & Bacon.

Purpel, D. E., & Belanger, N. (Eds.). (1972). *Curriculum and the cultural revolution*. Berkeley, CA: McCutchan Publishing Company.

Raynor, J., & Grant, N. (1972). *Patterns of curriculum*. Bletchley, Bucks, England: The Open University Press.

Razik, T. A. (1972). *Systems approach to teacher training and curriculum development: The case of developing countries*. Paris: UNESCO, International Institute for Educational Planning.

Reid, W. A. (1972). *The university and the sixth form curriculum*. London: Macmillan.

Rubin, L. J. (1972). *Curriculum and instruction study guide*. Fort Lauderdale, FL: Nova University Press.

Saylor, J. G. (Ed.). (1972). *The school of the future, now*. Washington, DC: Association for Supervision and Curriculum Development.

Seaman, P., Esland, G., & Gosin, B. (1972). *Innovation and ideology*. Bletchley, Bucks, England: The Open University Press.

Segal, R. (1972). *Got no time to fool around: A motivation program for education*. Philadelphia: Westminster Press.

Shipman, M., & Raynor, J. (1972). *Perspectives on the curriculum*. Bletchley, Bucks, England: The Open University Press.

Southeast Asia Ministers of Education Organization. (1972), *Seminar on strategies for curriculum development in Southeast Asia: Final report*. Glugor, Penang, Malaysia: Author.

Tanner, D. (1972). *Secondary education: Perspectives and prospects*. New York: Macmillan.

Taylor, P. A., & Cowley, D. M. (Eds.). (1972). *Readings in curriculum evaluation*. Dubuque, IA: William C. Brown.

Thelen, H. (1972). *Education and the human quest: Four designs for education* (revised edition). Chicago: University of Chicago Press.

Trump, J. L., & Miller, D. F. (1972). *Secondary school curriculum improvement* (second edition). Boston: Allyn & Bacon.

Vance, B. (1972). *Teaching the prekindergarten child: Instructional design and curriculum*. Belmont, CA: Brooke-Cole.

Vargas, J. S. (1972). *Writing worthwhile behavioral objectives*. New York: Harper and Row.

Weiss, J. (1972). *Curriculum evaluation: Potentiality and reality*. Toronto: Ontario Institute for Studies in Education.

Wilhelms, F. (1972). *What should schools teach?* Bloomington, IN: Phi Delta Kappa.

Wiseman, S., & Pidgeon, D. (1972). *Curriculum evaluation*. Briston, England: J. W. Arrowsmith.

Wootton, L. R., & Reynolds, J. C. (Eds.). (1972). *Trends influence curriculum*. New York: MSS Information.

1973

Baker, E. L., & Popham, W. J. (1973). *Expanding dimensions of instructional objectives*. Englewood Cliffs, NJ: Prentice-Hall.

Beck, R. H., Cook, W. W., & Kearney, N. C. (1973). *Curriculum in the modern elementary school*. Englewood Cliffs, NJ: Prentice-Hall.

Center for Educational Research and Innovation. (1973). *Styles of curriculum development*. Paris: Organization for Economic Cooperation and Development.

Conner, F., & Ellena W. (1973). *Curriculum handbook for school administrators* (second edition). Washington, DC: American Association of School Administrators.

Cook, R. C., & Doll, R. C. (1973). *The elementary school curriculum*. Boston: Allyn & Bacon.

DeCarlo, J. E., & Madon, C. A. (Eds.). (1973). *Innovations in education for the seventies: Selected readings*. New York: Behavioral Publications.

Derr, R. L. (1973). *A taxonomy of social purposes of public schools*. New York: David McKay.

Dykhuizen, G. (1973). *The life and mind of John Dewey*. Carbondale, IL: Southern Illinois University Press.

Educational Technology Reviews Series (Twelve Volumes): Various Titles Relating to Curriculum Development. (1973). Englewood Cliffs, NJ: Educational Technology Publications.

Ellena, W. J. (1973). *Curriculum handbook for school executives*. Arlington, VA: American Association of School Administrators.

Firth, G. R., & Kimpston, R. D. (1973). *The curriculum continuum in perspective*. Itasca, IL: F. E. Peacock.

Ford, N. A. (1973). *Black studies: Threat or challenge.* London: Kennikat Press.

Freire, P. (1973). *Education for critical consciousness.* New York: Seabury.

Frymier, J. R. (1973). *A school for tomorrow.* Berkeley, CA: McCutchan Publishing.

Garcia, D. S. (1973). *Curriculum theory and application.* Manila, Philippines: Alemar-Phoenix.

Goodlad, J. I., & Shane, H. G. (Eds.). (1973). *The elementary school in the U.S.: Seventy-second Yearbook of the National Society for the Study of Education: Part II.* Chicago: University of Chicago Press.

Great Britain Schools Council. (1973a). *Evaluation in curriculum development: Twelve case studies.* London: Macmillan.

Great Britain Schools Council. (1973b). *Pattern and variation in curriculum development projects.* Houndmills, Busingstoke, Hampshire, England: Macmillan Education, Ltd.

Greene, G. G. (1973). *Accountability in the elementary school curriculum.* Dubuque, IA: Kendall/Hunt Publishing Company.

Greene, M. (1973). *Teacher as stranger.* Berkeley, CA: Wadsworth.

Harmin, H., Kirschenbaum, H., & Simon, S. (1973). *Clarifying values through subject matter.* Minneapolis, MN: Winston Press.

Hemphill, J. K., & Roseman, F. S. (1973). *Educational development: A new discipline for self-renewal.* Eugene, OR: Center for the Study of Educational Administration.

Holmes, B., & Ryba, R. (Eds.). (1973). *Curriculum development at the second level of education.* Papers read at the fourth general meeting, Prague, Czechoslovakia: Comparative Education Society in Europe.

Hughes, D. (1973). *Social change, educational theory and curriculum.* London: University of London Press.

Hughes, P. W. (Ed.). (1973). *The teacher's role in curriculum.* London: Angus and Robertson.

Hyman, R. T. (Ed.). (1973). *Approaches in curriculum.* Englewood Cliffs, NJ: Prentice-Hall.

Inlow, G. (1973). *The emergent in curriculum* (second edition). New York: John Wiley and Sons.

Lawton, D. (1973). *Social change, educational theory, and curriculum planning.* London: University of London Press.

Lewy, A. (1973). *Using experts' judgments in the process of curriculum evaluation.* Los Angeles: UCLA Graduate School of Education.

Macdonald, J. B., Wolfson, B. J., & Zaret, E. (1973). *Reschooling society: A conceptual model.* Washington, DC: Association for Supervision and Curriculum Development.

Mayhew, L. B., & Ford, P. J. (1973). *Changing the curriculum.* San Francisco: Jossey-Bass.

Moffett, J. (1973). *A student-centered language arts curriculum, grades K–13: A handbook for teachers.* Boston: Houghton-Mifflin.

Morley, F. P. (1973). *A modern guide to effective K–12 curriculum planning*. West Nyack, NY: Parker Publishing.

Musgrave, P. W. (1973). *Knowledge, curriculum, and change*. Carlton, Australia: Melbourne University Press.

Netherlands Workshop on Curriculum Research, Vierhouten, Netherlands. (1973). *Curriculum research and development*. The Hague: Netherlands Foundations for Educational Research.

New Zealand Department of Education. (1973). *Human development and relationships in the school curriculum*. Wellington, New Zealand: Government Printer.

Ogletree, E. J., & Hawkins, M. (1973). *Writing instructional objectives and activities for modern curriculum: A programmed approach*. New York: MSS Information Corporation.

Owen, J. G. (1973). *The management of curriculum development*. Cambridge: Harvard University Press.

Robertson, J. H. (1973). *Courses of study*. Folcroft, PA: Folcroft Library Editions.

Robinson, Y., Bagnal, R. D., & Recchia, M. (1973). *The basis of the curriculum: Curriculum theory and development*. Unpublished doctoral dissertation. Philadelphia: Temple University.

Shane, H. G. (1973). *The educational significance of the future*. Bloomingotn, IN: Phi Delta Kappa Educational Foundation.

Silberman, C. E. (Ed.). (1973). *The open classroom reader*. New York: Vintage Books.

Sniff, W. F. (1973). *A curriculum of the mentally retarded young adult*. Springfield, IL: Charles C. Thomas.

Stradley, W. (1973). *Administrator's guide to an individualized performance results curriculum*. New York: Center for Applied Research in Education.

Taylor, P. H., & Walton, J. (Eds.). (1973). *The curriculum: Research, innovation, and change*. London: Ward Lock Educational.

Trump, J. L., & Miller, D. (1973). *Secondary school curriculum improvement: Challenges, humanism, accountability* (second edition). Boston: Allyn & Bacon.

White, J. P. (1973). *Towards a compulsory curriculum*. London: Routlege and Kegan Paul.

Worner, R. B. (1973). *Designing curriculum for educational accountability: From continuous progress education through PPBS*. New York: Random House.

Zenger, S., & Zenger, W. (1973). *Writing and evaluating curriculum guides*. Belmont, CA: Fearon.

1974

Ahlum, C., & Fralley, J. M. (Eds.). (1974). *Feminist resources for school and colleges: A guide to curriculum materials*. Old Westbury, NY: Feminist Press.

Blazier, W. H. (1974). *Lights! Action! Camera! Learn!* Allison Park, PA: Allison.

Bowers, C. A. (1974). *Cultural literacy for freedom: An existential perspective on teaching, curriculum and school policy.* Eugene, OR: Elan Publishers, Inc.

Brickman, W. W. (1974). *Bibliographical essays on curriculum and instruction.* Folcroft, PA: Folcroft Library Editions. (Reprint of 1948 edition.)

Broudy, H. S. (1974). *General education: The search for a rationale.* Bloomington, IN: Phi Delta Kappa Educational Foundation.

Cawelti, G. (1974). *Vitalizing the high school: A curriculum critique of major reform proposals.* Washington, DC: Association for Supervision and Curriculum Development.

Cohen, D., & Simpson, G. (1974). *Destination debatable: On education objectives.* Sydney, Australia: Ashton Scholastic.

Cross, K. P., Valley, J. R., and Associates. (1974). *Planning non-traditional programs: An analysis of the issues for post-secondary education.* San Francisco: Jossey-Bass.

Della-Dora, D., & House, J. E. (Eds.) (1974). *Education and an open society. 1974 Yearbook.* Washington, DC: Association for Supervision and Curriculum Development.

Dickson, G. E., & Saxe, R. E. (1974). *Patterns for educational reform and renewal.* Berkeley, CA: McCutchan.

Doll, R. C. (1974). *Curriculum improvement: Decision making and process* (third edition). Boston: Allyn & Bacon.

Edward, C. H. (Ed.). (1974). *Readings in curriculum: A process approach.* Champaign, IL: Stipes.

Eisner, E. W., & Vallance, E. (Eds.). (1974). *Conflicting conceptions of curriculum.* Berkeley, CA: McCutchan.

Faculty of Education, British Columbia University. (1974). *Program development in education (monograph).* Vancouver, British Columbia: British Columbia University.

Farguhar, E. E. (1974). *Curriculum materials.* Washington, DC: Association for Supervision and Curriculum Development.

Gilchrist, R. S., & Roberts, B. R. (1974). *Curriculum development: A humanized systems approach.* Belmont, CA: Fearon.

Goodlad, J. I. (1974). *Toward a mankind school: An adventure in humanistic education.* New York: McGraw-Hill.

Hass, G., Bondi, J., & Wiles, J. (Eds.). (1974). *Curriculum planning—A new approach.* Boston: Allyn & Bacon.

Hirst, P. (1974). *Knowledge and the curriculum.* London: Routledge & Kegan Paul.

Holly, D. (1974). *Beyond curriculum: Changing secondary education.* Frogmore, St. Albans, England: Paladin.

Kingsford, R. C. (1974). *Compulsory education and curriculum reconstruction: A brief enquiry into the philosophy and practice of raising the school leaving age.* Exeter, England: University of Exeter School of Education.

Kopp, O. W., & Zufelt, D. L. (1974). *Personalized curriculum through excellence in leadership.* Danville, IL: Interstate Printers and Publishers.

Macintosh, H. G., & Smith, L. A. (1974). *Toward a freer curriculum.* London: University of London Press.

Murphy, R. (1974). *Imaginary worlds: Notes on a new curriculum.* New York: Virgil Books.

Ontario Association for Curriculum Development. (1974). *Action and reaction in the curriculum. Proceeding of the 22nd Annual Conference.* Ottawa, Canada: Author.

Payne, D. A. (Ed.). (1974). *Curriculum evaluation: Commentaries on purpose, process, product.* Lexington, MA: D. C. Heath.

Pinar, W. (Ed.). (1974). *Heightened consciousness, cultural revolution, and curriculum theory.* Berkeley, CA: McCutchan.

Regan, E. M., & Leithwood, K. A. (1974). *Effecting curriculum change: Experiences with the conceptual skills.* Toronto: Institute for Studies in Education.

Rowntree, D. (1974). *Educational technology in curriculum development.* London: Harper and Row.

Saylor, J. G., & Alexander, W. M. (1974). *Planning curriculum for schools.* New York: Holt, Rinehart and Winston.

Schools Council Research Service. (1974a). *Evaluation in curriculum development: Twelve case studies.* New York: APS Publishers. (Also by Macmillan Education, Ltd., London, 1973.)

Schools Council Research Service. (1974b). *Pattern and variation in curriculum development projects.* New York: APS Publishers. (Also by Macmillan Education, Ltd, Hampshire, England, 1973.)

Shipman, M. D., Bolam, D., & Jenkins, D. R. (1974). *Inside a curriculum project: A case study in the process of curriculum change.* Scranton, PA: Barnes and Noble. (Also by Methuen, London, 1974.)

Speiker, C. A. (1974). *A study to determine the reliability of community involvement in curriculum planning.* Minneapolis: University of Minnesota.

Tankard, G. G. (1974). *Curriculum development: An administrator's guide.* West Nyack, NY: Parker.

Taylor, P., Reid, W., & Holley, B. J. (1974). *The English sixth form: A case study in curriculum research.* London: Routledge and Kegan Paul.

Taylor, P. H., & Johnson, M. (Eds.). (1974). *Curriculum development: A comparative study.* Windsor, England: National Foundation for Educational Research.

Taylor, P. H., Reid, W. A., Holley, B. J., & Exon, G. (1974). *Purpose, power, and constraint in the primary school curriculum.* London: Macmillan Education, Ltd.

Van Til, W. (Ed.). (1974). *Curriculum: Quest for relevance* (second edition). Boston: Houghton Mifflin.

Wass, H., et al. (1974). *Humanistic teacher education: An experiment in systematic curriculum innovation.* Fort Collins, CO: Shields Publishing Company.

Way, R. V. (1974). *Adapting the curriculum of an elementary school to serve the language needs of Spanish speaking children.* San Francisco: R & E Research Associates.

Wootton, L. R., & Reynolds, J. C. (Eds.). (1974). *Trends influnce curriculum* (second edition). New York: MSS Information Corporation.

Yarbrough, V. E., Bruce, W. C., & Hubright, R. L. (Eds.). (1974). *Readings in curriculum and supervision.* New York: MSS Information Corporation.

1975

Anderson, D. W., & Macdonald, J. B. (Eds.). (1975). *Strategies in curriculum development: The works of Virgil E. Herrick.* Westport, CT: Greenwood. (Reprint of 1965 edition).

Barnes, J. (Ed.). (1975). *Curriculum innovation in London's E.P.A.s.* London: H.M.S.O.

Beauchamp, G. A. (1975). *Curriculum theory* (third edition). Willmette, IL: The Kagg Press.

Botel, M., & Botel, N. (1975). *A critical analysis of the taxonomy of educational objectives.* Washington, DC: Curriculum Development Associates.

Case, P. N., & Lowry, A. M. (1975). *Evaluation of alternative curricula.* Chicago: American Library Association.

Centre for Educational Research and Innovation. (1975). *Handbook on curriculum development.* Paris: Organization for Economic Cooperation and Development.

Curriculum Design and Development Course Team. (1975). *Curriculum design.* New York: Halsted Press.

Curriculum Design and Development Course Team. (1975). *Curriculum innovation.* New York: Halsted Press.

Eaton, J. M. (1975). *An ABC of the curriculum.* Edinburgh, Scotland: Oliver and Boyd.

English, F. W., & Kaufman, R. A. (1975). *Needs assessment: A focus for curriculum development.* Washington, DC: Association for Supervision and Curriculum Development.

Foshay, A. W. (1975). *Essays on curriculum: Selected papers.* New York: Teachers College, Columbia University.

Glatthorn, A. A. (1975). *Alternatives in education: Schools and programs.* New York: Dodd Mead and Company.

Golby, M., Greenwald, J., & West, R. (Eds.). (1975). *Curriculum design.* London: Croom Helm.

Goodlad, J. I. (1975). *The dynamics of educational change: Toward responsive schools.* New York: McGraw-Hill.

Great Britain Schools Council. (1975). *The whole curriculum. Working Paper 53.* London: Evans/Methuen.

Haigh, G. (1975). *Integrate: Curriculum integration in the school*. New York: Beekman.

Harris, A., Lawn, M., & Prescott, W. (1975). *Curriculum innovation*. New York: John Wiley, A Halsted Press Book.

Hendricks, G., & Fadiman, J. (Eds.). (1975). *Transpersonal education: A curriculum for feeling and being*. Englewood Cliffs, NJ: Prentice-Hall (Spectrum Books).

Hirst, P. H. (1975). *Knowledge and the curriculum: A collection of philosophical papers*. London: Routledge and Kegan Paul.

Hollaway, O. (1975). *Problem solving: Toward a more humanizing curriculum*. Philadelphia: Franklin.

Hook, S. (Ed.). (1975). *The philosophy of the curriculum: The need for general education*. Buffalo, NY: Prometheus Books.

Hug, W. E. (1975). *Instructional design and the media program*. Chicago: American Library Association.

Kallos, D. (1975). *Curriculum and teaching: An unAmerican view*. Lund, Sweden: Institute of Education.

Lawton, D. (1975). *Class, culture and the curriculum*. London: Routledge and Kegan Paul.

Macdonald, J. B., & Zaret, E. (Eds.). (1975). *Schools in search of meaning*. Washington, DC: Association for Supervision and Curriculum Development.

Mager, R. F. (1975). *Preparing instructional objectives* (second edition). Belmont, CA: Fearon.

Martin, J. R. (1975). *Choice, chance, and curriculum (Boyd H. Bode Memorial Lecture Series: Number Three)*. Columbus: Ohio State University Press.

Mayer, W. V. (Ed.). (1975.) *Planning curriculum development (with examples from projects for the mentally retarded)*. Boulder, CO: Biological Sciences Curriculum Study.

Michaelis, J. U., Grossman, R. H., & Scott, L. F. (1975). *New designs for elementary curriculum and instruction* (second edition). New York: McGraw-Hill.

Musgrave, P. W. (Ed.). (1975). *Contemporary studies in the curriculum*. Sydney, Australia: Angus and Robertson.

Newfield, J. W. (1975). *Information demands of curriculum supervisors: Final report, Part I* (NIE Project Number G-74-0056). Washington, DC: National Institute of Education.

Newmann, F. M. (1975). *Education for citizen action: Challenge for the secondary curriculum*. Berkeley, CA: McCutchan.

Pinar, W. (Ed.). (1975). *Curriculum theorizing: The reconceptualists*. Berkeley, CA: McCutchan.

Ponder, G. A., & Davis, O. L. (Eds.). (1975). *Curriculum perspectives*. Austin, TX: Texan House, Incorporated.

Reid, W. A., & Walker, D. F. (Eds.). (1975). *Case studies in curriculum change: Great Britain and the United States*. London: Routledge and Kegan Paul.

Roberts, A. (Ed.). (1975). *Educational innovation: Alternatives in curriculum and instruction.* Boston: Allyn & Bacon.

Rodgers, F. A. (1975). *Curriculum and instruction in the elementary school.* New York: Macmillan.

Rogers, V. R., & Church, B. (1975). *Open education: Critique and assessment.* Washington, DC: Association for Supervision and Curriculum Development.

Schaffarzick, J., & Hampson, D. H. (Eds.). (1975). *Strategies for curriculum development.* Berkeley, CA: McCutchan.

Sharp, R., & Green, A. (1975). *Education and social control: A study in progressive primary education.* London: Routledge and Kegan Paul.

Staples, I. E. (Ed.). (1975). *Impact of decentralization on curriculum: Selected viewpoints.* Washington, DC: Association for Supervision and Curriculum Development.

Stenhouse, L. (1975). *Introduction to curriculum research and development.* New York: Holmes and Meier.

Talmage, H. (Ed.). (1975). *Systems of individualized education.* Berkeley, CA: McCutchan.

Tanner, D., & Tanner, L. (1975). *Curriculum development: Theory into practice.* New York: Macmillan.

Taylor, P. H. (Ed.). (1975). *Aims, influence and change in the primary school curriculum.* Windsor, Berkshire: National Foundation for Educational Research.

Taylor, P. H., & Tye, K. A. (Eds.). (1975). *Curriculum, school and society: An introduction to curriculum studies.* Atlantic Highlands, NJ: Humanities Press.

Thompson, K., & White, J. (1975). *Curriculum development: A dialogue.* London: Pitman.

UNESCO. (1975). *An experience-centered curriculum: Exercises in perception, communication, and action (Educational Studies and Document Set Number Seventeen).* New York: Unipub, Incorporated.

University of London Institute of Education. (1975). *The curriculum. The Doris Lee Lectures delivered at the Institute of Education, University of London.* London: Author.

Unruh, G. G. (1975). *Responsive curriculum development: Theory and action.* Berkeley, CA: McCutchan.

Warwick, D. (1975). *Curriculum structure and design.* Mystic, CT: Lawrence Verry, Incorporated.

Wolsk, D. (1975). *An experience centered curriculum: Exercises in personal and social reality.* Paris: UNESCO.

1976

Barnes, D. (1976). *From communication to curriculum.* New York: Penguin Books, Ltd.

Barrow, R. (1976). *Common sense and the curriculum.* Hamden, CT: Shoe String Press.

Bennis, W., Benne, K., & Chin, R. (1976). *The planning of change.* New York: Holt, Rinehart, and Winston (earlier edition, 1969).

Bowles, S., & Gintis, H. (1976). *Schooling in capitalist America.* New York: Basic Books.

Brickman, W. W. (1976). *Bibliographical essays on curriculum and instruction.* Folcroft, PA: Folcroft.

Bussis, A. M., Chittenden, E. A., & Amarel, M. (1976). *Beyond surface curriculum.* Boulder, CO: Westview Press.

Cremin, L. A. (1976). *Public education.* New York: Basic Books, Inc.

Curriculum Design and Development Course Team. (Open University). (1976). *Curriculum design.* New York: Halsted Press.

Curriculum Design and Development Course Team (Open University). (1976). *Curriculum innovation.* New York: John Wiley and Sons, Inc.

Curriculum for development: Analysis and review of processes, products, and outcomes: Final report sub-regional curriculum workshop, Colombo, Sri Lanka 1–30 October, 1976. Bangkok, Thailand: UNESCO Regional Office for Education in Asia.

Davies, I. K. (1976). *Objectives in curriculum design.* New York: McGraw-Hill.

Davis, O. L. (Ed). (1976). *Perspectives on curriculum development 1776–1976.* 1976 Yearbook. Washington, DC: Association for Supervision and Curriculum Development.

Fantini, M. D. (Ed). (1976). *Alternative education: A source book for parents, teachers, students, and administrators.* Garden City, NY: Doubleday.

Frazier, A. (1976). *Adventuring, mastering, associating—New strategies for teaching children.* Washington, DC: Association for Supervision and Curriculum Development

Fullan, M., & Pomfret, A. (1976). *Review of research on curriculum and instruction implementation.* Toronto: Department of Sociology of Education, Toronto Institute for Studies in Education.

Gow, D. T. (1976). *Design and development of curriculum materials; (Vols. 1-2).* Pittsburgh, PA: University Center for International Studies, University of Pittsburgh.

Great Britain Schools Council. (1976). *Curriculum in the middle school years.* London: Methuen Educational and Evans Brothers.

Hamilton, D. (1976). *Curriculum evaluation.* London: Open Books.

Holland, J. G. (1976). *The analysis of behavior in planning instruction.* Reading, MA: Addison-Wesley Publishing.

Holt, J (1976). *Instead of education.* New York: Delta.

Jenkins, D., & Shipman, M. D. (1976). *Curriculum: An introduction.* London: Open Books.

Kallos, D., & Lundgren, U. P. (1976). *An enquiry concerning curriculum: Foundations for curriculum change.* Molndal, Sweden: Pedagogiske Institutionen, Goteborgs Universitet.

Kallos, D. & Lundgren, U. P. (1976). *Lessons from a comprehensive school system for theory and research on curriculum*. Research Report, Stockholm, Sweden: Department of Educational Research, School of Education.

Kane, J. (Ed.). (1976). *Curriculum development in physical education*. New York: Beekman Publishers.

Kauffman, D. L., Jr. (1976). *Teaching the future: A guide to future-orientated education*. Palm Springs, CA: ETC Publications.

Kindred, L. W., & Wolotkiewicz, R. J., Mickelson, J. M., Coplien, L. E., & Dyson, E. (1976). *The middle school curriculum: A practitioner's handbook*. Boston: Allyn & Bacon.

King, A. R., Jr., & Brownell, J. A. (1976). *Curriculum and the disciplines of knowledge: A theory of curriculum practice*. (Reprint of 1966 edition). Huntington, NY: Krieger.

Leithwood, K. A., Clipsham, J. S., Maynes, F., Baxter, R. P., & McNabb, J. D. (1976). *Planning curriculum change: A model and case study*. Toronto: Ontario Institute for Studies in Education.

MacDonald, B., & Walker, R. (1976). *Changing the curriculum*. London: Open Books.

MacDonald, M., & Roger, D. (1976). *Culture, class, and the curriculum / The politics of curriculum reform*. London: Open University Press.

Margolin, E. (1976). *Young children: Their curriculum and learning processes*. New York: Macmillan.

Mathews, J. (1976). *Examinations: Their use in curriculum evaluation and development*. London: Evans Metheun Educational.

McNeil, J. D. (1976). *Designing curriculum: Self-instructional modules*. Boston: Little, Brown and Company.

Newton, J.E. (1976). *Curriculum evaluation of black studies in relation to student knowledge of Afro-American history and culture*. San Francisco: R & E Research Associates.

Open University Press (England). (1976). *Curriculum design and development; Units 1–2, Scope of curriculum study; Units 3–4, Culture ideology and knowledge; Units 5–8, The child, the school, and society; Case Study 1, Tanzania: Education for self-reliance; Units 9–10, Towards the whole curriculum; Units 11–13, Curriculum organization; Units 14–15, Design issues; Units 16–18, Rationality and artistry; Units 19–21, Curriculum evaluation; Case Study 3, Stantonbury, Campus; Units 22–33, Innovation—problems and possibilities; Case Study 4, A middle school; Unit 24–26, Supporting curriculum development; Case Study 5, Portrait of Countesthorpe College; Case Study 6, Library Guide—using the literature*. London: Open University Press.

Petty, W. T. (Ed.). (1976). *Curriculum for the modern elementary school*. Chicago: Rand McNally and Company.

Pinar, W. F., & Grumet, M. R. (1976). *Toward a poor curriculum: Introduction to the theory and practice of currere*. Dubuque, IA: Kendall/Hunt Publishing Company.

Posner, A., & De Keijzer, A. J. (1976). *China: A resource and curriculum guide* (second edition). Chicago: University of Chicago Press.

Prescott, W., & Bolam, R. (1976). *Supporting curriculum development.* Milton Keynes, Great Britain: Open University Press.

Pring, R. (1976). *Knowledge and schooling.* London: Open Books Publishing, Ltd.

Reynolds, J., & Skilbeck, M. (1976). *Culture and the classroom.* London: Open Books Publishing, Ltd.

Rosenbaum, J. (1976). *Making inequality: The hidden curriculum of high school tracking.* New York: Wiley.

Rudduck, J., & Kelly, P. (1976). *The dissemination of curriculum development.* (J. Wrigley and F. Sparrow, Eds.). Windsor, England: National Foundation for Educational Research.

Seefeldt, C. (Ed.). (1976). *Curriculum for the preschool-primary child: A review of the research (New Edition — Elementary Education Set).* Columbus, OH: Charles Merrill.

Sockett, H. (1976). *Designing the curriculum.* London: Open Books.

Speiker, C. A. (Ed). (1976). *Curriculum leaders: Improving their influence.* Alexandria, VA: Association for Supervision and Curriculum Development.

Spring, J. H. (1976). *The sorting machine: National educational policy since 1945.* New York: David McKay.

Tawney, D. (1976). *Curriculum evaluation today: Trends and implications.* London: Macmillan.

Timmerman, T. (1976). *Finding a way: Integrated curriculum for the pre-teen.* Amherst, MA: Kandala.

Tyler, L. L., Klein, M. F. & Associates, Halperin, M., et al. (1976). *Evaluating and choosing curriculum and instructional materials.* Los Angeles: Educational Resource Associates.

UNESCO. (1976). *Co-operation in curriculum explorations: Report of a high-level personal exchange workshop.* New York: Unipub.

Van Geel, T. (1976). *Authority to control the school program.* Lexington, MA: Lexington Books.

Walton, J., & Welton, J. (Eds.). (1976). *Rational curriculum planning: Four case studies.* London: Ward Lock.

Zais, R. S. (1976). *Curriculum: Principles and foundations.* New York: Thomas Y. Crowell.

1977

Anderson, R. C., Spiro, R. J., & Montague, W. E. (Eds.). (1977). *Schooling and the acquisition of knowledge.* Hillsdale, NJ: Lawrence Erlbaum Associates.

Australian Curriculum Development Center. (1977). *Core curriculum of the Australian schools.* Canberra, Australia: Author.

Bellack, A. A., & Kliebard, H. (Ed). (1977). *Curriculum and evaluation.* New York: McCutchan.

Berman, L. M., & Roderick, J. A. (1977). *Curriculum: Teaching the what, how, and why of living.* Columbus, OH: Charles E. Merrill.

Bernstein, B. (1977). *Class, codes, and control* (Three volumes). London: Routledge and Kegan Paul.

Bourdieu, P., & Passeron, J. C. (1977). *Reproduction in education, society, and culture.* Beverly Hills, CA: Sage.

Bruner, J. (1977). *The process of education* (revised edition). Cambridge, MA: Harvard University Press.

Chandra, A. (1977). *Curriculum development and evaluation in education.* Mystic, CT: Verry.

Comer, J. P. (1977). *Forces affecting curriculum.* Washington, DC: Association for Supervision and Curriculum Development.

Curriculum Design and Development Course Team (The Open University). (1977). *Curriculum design.* New York: John Wiley and Sons, Incorporated.

Curtis, T. E., & Bidwell, W. W. (1977). *Curriculum and instruction for emerging adolescents.* Reading, MA: Addison-Wesley.

Edward, C. H. (Ed.). (1977). *Readings in curriculum: A process approach.* Danville, IL: Stipes.

Eggleston, J. (1977). *The sociology of the school curriculum.* London: Routledge and Kegan Paul.

Frymier, J. (1977). *Annehurst curriculum classification system: A practical way to individualize instruction.* Bloomington, IN: Kappa Delta Pi.

Glatter, R. (1977). *Control over the curriculum.* London: University of London Institute of Education.

Glatthorn, A. A. (1977). *Alternatives in education: Schools and programs.* New York: Harper and Row.

Gower, R. R., & Scott, M. B. (1977). *Five essential dimensions of curriculum design: A handbook for teachers.* Dubuque, IA: Kendall-Hunt.

Gran, E. (1977). *Notes from a board of education: Ways to individualize your basic program.* Amherst, MA: Mandala.

Hamilton, D., MacDonald, B., King, C., Jenkins, D., & Parlett, M. (Eds). (1977). *Beyond the numbers game: A reader in educational evaluation.* Berkeley, CA: McCutchan.

Hannah, L. S., & Michaelis, J. U. (1977). *Comprehensive framework for instructional objectives: A guide to systematic planning and evaluation.* Reading, MA: Addison-Wesley.

Hass, G. (Ed). (1977). *Curriculum planning: A new approach* (second edition). Boston: Allyn & Bacon.

Johnson, M. (1977). *Intentionality in education.* Albany, NY: Center for Curricular Research and Services.

Jones, D. M. (1977). *Curriculum targets in the elementary school.* Englewood Cliffs, NJ: Prentice-Hall.

Kelly, A. V. (1977). *The curriculum: Theory and practice*. New York: Harper and Row.

Kemp, J. E. (1977). *Instructional design: A plan for unit and course development*. Belmont, CA: Fearon.

Klausmeier, H. J. (1977). *Individually guided education in elementary and middle schools: A handbook for implementers and college instructors*. Reading, MA: Addison-Wesley.

Langenbach, M., & Neskora, T. W. (1977). *Day care: Curriculum considerations*. Columbus, OH: Merrill.

Lesser, H. (Ed). (1977). *Television and the preschool child: A psychological theory of instruction and curriculum development*. New York: Academic Press.

Lewy, A. (1977). *Handbook of curriculum evaluation*. New York: Longman, Inc.

Lundgren, U. P. (1977). *Model analysis of pedagogical processes*. Lund, Sweden: Liberlaromedel/ Gleerup.

MacDonald, M. (1977). *Culture, class, and the curriculum*. London: Open University.

MacDonald, M. (1977). *The curriculum and cultural reproduction*. Milton Keynes, England: The Open University Press.

Marbach, E. S. (1977). *Creative curriculum: Kindergarten through grade three*. Provo, UT: Brigham Young University Press.

McNeil, J. D. (1977). *Curriculum: A comprehensive introduction*. Boston: Little, Brown and Company.

Molnar, A., & Zahorik, J. A. (Eds.). (1977). *Curriculum theory*. Washington, DC: Association for Supervision and Curriculum Development.

Oliver, A. I. (1977a). *Curriculum improvement: A guide to problems, principles, and process* (second edition). New York: Harper and Row.

Oliver, A. I. (1977b). *Maximizing minicourses: A curriculum alternative*. New York: Teachers College, Columbia University.

Olsen, E. G., & Clark, P. A. (1977). *Life-centering education*. Midland, MI: Pendell Publishing Company.

Open University Press (England). (1977). *Curriculum design and development: Unit 17–18, Innovation, the school and the teacher; Unit 29–30, Innovation, the school and the teacher, two*. London: Open University Press.

Ragan, W. B., & Shepherd, G. D. (1977). *Modern elementary curriculum* (fifth edition). New York: Holt, Rinehart and Winston.

Richards, C. (Ed.). (1977). *New contexts — for teaching, learning, and curriculum studies*. Horwich: Association for the Study of the Curriculum.

Robinson, K., & Wilson, R. (Eds.). (1977). *Extending economics within the curriculum*. London: Kegan Paul.

Rubin, L. (Ed.). (1977a). *Curriculum handbook: Administration and theory*. Boston: Allyn & Bacon.

Rubin, L. (Ed.). (1977b). *Curriculum handbook: The disciplines, current movements, and instructional methodology*. Boston: Allyn & Bacon.

Rubin, L. (Ed.). (1977c). *Curriculum handbook: The disciplines, current movements, instructional methodology, administration, and theory*. (Abridged edition). Boston: Allyn & Bacon.

Shane, H. G. (1977). *Curriculum change toward the twenty-first century*. Washington, DC: National Education Association.

Shuster, A. H., & Ploghoft, M. E. (1977). *The emerging elementary curriculum* (third edition). Columbus, OH: Merrill.

Speiker, C. (1977). *Standards and guidelines for the evaluation of graduate programs preparing curriculum leaders*. Washington, DC: Association for Supervision and Curriculum Development.

UNESCO. (1977). *Integrated approach to curriculum development in primary education in Sri Lanka*. New York: Unipub.

Willis, P. (1977). *Learning to labor*. Lexington, MA: D. C. Heath.

Wootton, L. R., & Reynolds, J. C. (1977). *Trends and issues affecting curriculum*. Washington, DC: University Press of America.

1978

Becher, T., & Maclure, S. (1978). *The politics of curriculum change*. London: Hutchinson.

Bourne, P., & Eisenberg, J. (1978). *Social issues in the curriculum: Teaching Canadian literature in high school*. Toronto: Ontario Institute for Studies in Education.

Brent, A. (1978). *Philosophical foundations for the curriculum*. Winchester, MA: Allen and Unwin.

Brown, S. J., & Dittman, L. L. (1978). *Curriculum is what happens: Planning is the key*. Washington, DC: National Association for the Education of Young Children.

Carnegie Foundation for the Advancement of Teaching. (1978). *Missions of the college curriculum*. San Francisco: Jossey-Bass.

Casciano Savignano, C. J. (1978). *Systems approach to curriculum and instructional improvement*. Columbus, OH: Merrill.

Claydon, L., Knight, T., & Rado, M. (1978). *Curriculum and culture: Schooling in a pluralist society*. Winchester, MA: Allen & Unwin.

Cohen, D., & Harrison, M. (1978). *Curriculum decision making in Australian schools. Project report no. 4*. Sydney, Australia: Macquarie University.

Conrad, C. F. (1978). *The undergraduate curriculum: A guide to innovation and reform*. Boulder, CO: Westview Press.

Curriculum Design and Development Course Team. (1978). *Curriculum innovation*. New York: Halsted Press.

Curriculum Development Centre of Malaysia. (1978). *Studies of curriculum development centers*. New York: Unipub.

Doll, R. C. (1978). *Curriculum improvement: Decision making and process* (fourth edition). Boston: Allyn & Bacon.

English, F. W. (1978). *Quality control in curriculum development*. Washington, DC: American Association of School Administrators.

Fredericks, H. D. B., & the staff of Teaching Research Infant and Child Center. (1978). *The teaching research curriculum for moderately and severely handicapped: Self-help and cognitive*. Springfield, IL: Charles C. Thomas.

Freire, P. (1978). *Pedagogy in process*. New York: Seabury.

Goodlad, J. I. (1978). *Accountability: An alternative perspective*. The De Garmo Lecture, Society of Professors of Education, February 23, 1978.

Gordon, P., & Lawton, D. (1978). *Curriculum change in the 19th and 20th centuries*. London: Hodder and Stoughton.

Greene, M. (1978). *Landscapes of learning*. New York: Teachers College Press.

Gress, J. R., & Purpel, D. E. (Ed). (1978). *Curriculum: An introduction to the field*. Berkeley, CA: McCutchan.

Harris, A., Lawn, M., & Prescott, W. (Eds.). (1978). *Curriculum innovations*. London: Croom Helm.

Hefley, J. (1978). *Textbooks on trial*. Milford, MI: Mott Media.

Holt, M. (1978). *The common curriculum: Its structure and style in the comprehensive school*. London: Routledge and Kegan Paul.

Jelinek, J. J. (Ed.). (1978). *Improving the human condition: A curricular response to critical realities: 1978 Yearbook*. Washington, DC: Association for Supervision and Curriculum Development.

Joyce, B. (1978). *Selecting learning experiences: Linking theory and practice*. Washington, DC: Association for Supervision and Curriculum Development.

Kapfer, M. B. (Ed.). (1978). *Behavioral objectives: The position of the pendulum*. Englewood Cliffs, NJ: Educational Technology Publications.

Lawton, D., Gordon, P., Ing, M., Gibby, B., Pring, R., & Moore, T. (1978). *Theory and practice of curriculum studies*. London: Routledge and Kegan Paul.

Levine, A. (1978). *Handbook on undergraduate curriculum*. San Francisco: Jossey-Bass.

Lounsbury, J. H., & Vars, G. F. (1978). *A curriculum for the middle school years*. New York: Harper and Row.

Nelson, M. (1978). *Law in the curriculum*. Bloomington, IN: Phi Delta Kappa.

Nicholls, A., & Nicholls, H. (1978). *Developing a curriculum: A practical guide* (second edition). London: Allen and Unwin.

Oliver, A. I. (1978). *Maximizing minicourses: A practical guide to a curriculum innovation.* New York: Teachers College Press.

Orlosky, D. E., & Smith, B. O. (1978). *Curriculum development: Issues and insights.* Chicago: Rand McNally.

Posner, G. J., & Rudnitsky, A. N. (1978). *Course design: A guide to curriculum development for teachers.* New York: Longman. (second edition, 1982; third edition, 1986.)

Raths, L. E., Harmin, M., & Simon, S. B. (1978). *Values and teaching* (second edition). Columbus, OH: Charles E. Merrill.

Reid, W. A. (1978). *Thinking about the curriculum: The nature and treatment of curriculum problems.* London: Routledge and Kegan Paul.

Rudolph, F. (1978). *Curriculum: A history of the American undergraduate course of study since 1636.* San Francisco: Jossey-Bass.

Schiro, M. (1978). *Curriculum for better schools: The great ideological debate.* Englewood Cliffs, NJ: Educational Technology Publications.

Stake, R., & Easley, J. (1978). *Case studies in science education.* Urbana, IL: Center for Instructional Research and Curriculum Evaluation.

Steeves, F. L., & English, F. W. (1978). *Secondary curriculum for a changing world.* Columbus, OH: Charles E. Merrill.

Tanner, L. N. (1978). *Classroom discipline for effective teaching and learning.* New York: Holt, Rinehart, and Winston.

Taylor, P. H. (1978). *The English sixth form: A case study in curriculum research.* Boston: Routledge and Kegan Paul.

Westbury, I., & Wilkof, N. J. (Eds.). (1978). *Science, curriculum, and liberal education: Selected essays, Joseph J. Schwab.* Chicago: University of Chicago Press.

Weston, P. B. (1978). *Framework for the curriculum.* New York: Humanities Press.

Willis, G. (Ed.). (1978). *Qualitative evaluation: Concepts and cases in curriculum criticism.* Berkeley, CA: McCutchan Publishing Company.

1979

Apple, M. W. (1979). *Ideology and curriculum.* London: Routledge and Kegan Paul.

Becker, J. M. (1979). *Schooling for a global age.* New York: McGraw-Hill.

Bloomer, M., & Shaw, K. E. (1979). *Constraint and innovation: The content and organization of schooling.* New York: Pergamon.

Bremer, J. (1979). *Education and community.* Shepparton, Australia: Waterwheel Press.

Crone, R., & Malone, J. (1979). *Continuities in education: The Northern Ireland schools curriculum project.* Windsor, Ontario: NFER; Atlantic Highlands, NJ: distributed by Humanities Press.

Egan, K. (1979). *Educational development.* New York: Oxford University Press.

Eisner, E. (1979). *The educational imagination: On the design and evaluation of school programs.* New York: Macmillan.

Finch, C. R., & Crunkilton, J. R. (1979). *Curriculum development in vocational and technical education: Planning, content, and implementation.* Boston: Allyn & Bacon. (second edition, 1984; third edition, 1989; fourth edition, 1993.)

Goodlad, J. I., and Associates. (1979). *Curriculum inquiry: The study of curriculum practice.* New York: McGraw-Hill.

Harty, S. (1979). *Hucksters in the classroom.* Washington, DC: Center for the Study of Responsive Law.

Hawes, H. W. (1979). *Curriculum and reality in African primary schools.* London: Longman.

Holt, M. (1979). *Regenerating the curriculum.* Boston: Routledge and Kegan Paul.

Hug, W. E. (1979). *40 years of research in curriculum and teaching.* New York: Teachers College, Columbia University.

Jelinek, J .J. (Ed.). (1979). *Education in flux: Implications for curriculum development.* Tempe, AZ: Professors of Curriculum and Arizona State University.

Kallos, D., & Lundgren, U. P. (1979). *Curriculum as a pedagogical problem.* Lund, Sweden: Liber Laromedel/Gleerup.

Lundgren, U. P. (1979). *Organizing the world about us: An introduction to curriculum theory.* Stockholm, Sweden: Liber.

Lundgren, U. P., & Pettersson, S. (Eds.). (1979). *Code, context, and curriculum processes.* Stockholm, Sweden: Stockholm Institute of Education.

Marti, J. (1979). *On education.* (Essays edited by P. S. Foner). New York: Monthly Review Press.

Musgrave, P. W. (1979). *Society and the curriculum in Australia.* Winchester, MA: Allen and Unwin.

Ogletree, E. J. (Ed.). (1979). *Introduction to Waldorf education. Curriculum and methods.* Washington, DC: University Press of America.

Overly, N. V. (Ed.). (1979). *Lifelong learning: 1979 Yearbook.* Washington, DC: Association for Supervision and Curriculum Development.

Postman, N. (1979). *Teaching as a conserving activity.* New York: Delacorte Press.

Richards, C. (1979a). *Curriculum studies: An introductory, annotated bibliography.* Driffield, England: Nafferton Books, Studies in Education printing.

Richards, C. (Ed.). (1979b). *Power and the curriculum: Issues in curriculum studies.* Driffield, England: Nafferton Books, Studies in Education printing.

Richmond, K. W. (1979). *The school curriculum.* London: Methuen.

Rumanoff, L. A. (1979). *A curriculum model for individuals with severe learning and behavior disorders.* Baltimore, MD: University Park.

Schaffarzick, J., & Sykes, G. (Eds). (1979). *Value conflicts and curriculum issues.* Berkeley, CA: McCutchan.

Tamir, P. (Ed.). (1979). *Curriculum implementation and its relationship to curriculum development in science.* Jerusalem, Israel: Israel Science Teaching Center, Hebrew University.

Taylor, P. (Ed.). (1979). *New directions in curriculum studies.* London: Falmer Press.

Taylor, P. H., & Reid, W. A. (Eds.). (1979). *Curriculum, culture, and classroom: Trends in curriculum studies.* New York: Humanities Press.

Taylor, P. H., & Richards, C. M. (1979). *An introduction to curriculum studies.* New York: Humanities Press. (second edition, 1985.)

Tomkins, G. (1979). *The curriculum in Canada in historical perspective: Sixth Yearbook of the Canadian Society for the Study of Education.* Vancouver, British Columbia: Canadian Society for the Study of Education.

Trump, J. L., & Miller, D. F. (1979). *Secondary school curriculum improvement: Meeting challenges of the times* (third edition). Boston: Allyn & Bacon.

Waring, M. (1979). *Social pressures on curriculum innovations: A study of the Nuffield Foundation science teaching project.* London: Methuen.

Wechman, P. H. (1979). *Curriculum design for severely and profoundly handicapped.* New York: Human Sciences Press.

Werner, W. (Ed.). (1979). *Curriculum Canada: Perspectives, practices, prospects.* Vancouver, British Columbia: University of British Columbia Center for the Study of Curriculum and Instruction.

Weston, P. B. (1979). *Negotiating the curriculum: A study in secondary schooling.* Windsor, England: National Foundation for Educational Research.

Wiles, J., & Bondi, J. (1979). *Curriculum development: A guide to practice elementary education.* Columbus, OH: Merrill.

Wise, A. (1979). *Legislated learning.* Berkeley: University of California Press.

CHAPTER NINE

Curriculum Literature and Context
1980–1989

The 1970s was a decade of division and doubt for many U.S. citizens; divisions among people brought on by the Vietnam War, and doubt in integrity of their government caused, in large measure, by the Nixon administration and Watergate. The 1980s were different; the decade of "yuppies," young urban professionals. The youthful protesters of the sixties were replaced by ambitious entrepreneurs; trendy global consumers displaced the hippies in Haight-Ashbury and other major urban areas. Children who had not been alive during the Vietnam War entered high school. In some ways reminiscent of the 1950s, many U.S. citizens paid less attention to social, political, and environmental ills, focusing instead on the business of making a living. While there was no perceptible energy shortage during the 1980s with regard to fossil fuels, some wondered if there was an embargo on human compassion.

The 1980 launch of America's first space shuttle, *Challenger*, a redirecting of the space program to military and corporate usefulness, was a dramatic example of U.S. technological advances. The microcomputer empires emerged from California garages, settling into "Silicon Valley." The "Dream Team" of the 1980 Winter Olympics was the American ice hockey team, when they managed to win gold by defeating first the Finnish and then the Soviet teams. Their triumph symbolized the classic American myth of the underdog overcoming the odds and gave the U.S. people a boost of pride. As we learned in the seventies, Olympic games, far from being immune from international politics, were staged against a backdrop of international rivalries. President Carter chose to boycott the 1980 Summer Olympics in Moscow as a protest of the Soviet invasion of Afghanistan. For eight years the Soviets fought this fruitless and costly war in an attempt to keep their surrogates in power and to halt the spread of Islamic fundamentalism across the border into their predominantly Muslim Eurasian republics. Predictably, the Soviets found reasons to boycott the 1984 Olympic games in Los Angeles. The 1988 games in Seoul, South Korea, was the last Olympic confrontation for the two superpowers.

In the fall of 1980, Jimmy Carter, plagued by a sluggish economy and haunted by the continued captivity of American hostages in Iran, was swept from office by an upbeat Ronald Reagan, who spoke about a renewal of American patriotism and promised to "put Americans back to work." Dubbed "The Great Communicator," former movie actor Reagan championed American rearmament, an aggressive anti-Communist foreign policy, government deregulation, often disengagement, in domestic affairs, and a major tax cut. Reagan's inauguration as the nation's 40th president was a turning point. Coincidentally, the U.S. hostages were released on the day Reagan took the oath of office.

"Supply side" or "trickle-down" economics was designed to benefit the entire U.S. population by providing economic incentives through deregulation of businesses and tax exemptions for the wealthy, thus priming the economy through investment. This theory in practice created opportune times for capitalists and militarists continued misery for workers, the poor, and the disenfranchised, both at home and abroad and resulted in the largest budget deficits in the history of the United States. The president's refusal to rehire the air traffic controllers when they went out on strike set the tone for labor-management relations during a decade in which the average worker's income rose only marginally while corporate profits soared. The United States moved out of recession early in the decade to enjoy the longest period of sustained economic growth since World War II. Middle- and upper-income groups benefited the most. In April 1988, a Census Bureau study reported that the top fifth income group in the country had increased its average salary from $70,260 to $76,300 while the poorest fell from $8,761 to $8,033.

Evidence of America's newfound confidence came in 1987. In October of that year the stock market plunged 508 points, the largest single-day decline since the Great Depression. Despite the drop, an anticipated recession failed to materialize. Within a year the market had regained its losses and the Dow Jones average finished above 2000 points for the first time in its history. The American people enthusiastically decided to hold the course in 1988 when Vice President George Bush easily won the presidential election over Massachusetts governor Michael Dukakis.

The apparent economic boom helped to divert attention from a savings and loan catastrophe that was made possible in part by the federal government's deregulation of those institutions earlier in the decade. Covering bank insurance claims eventually cost taxpayers billions of dollars and ran into the next decade. The national debt grew dramatically, threatening to soak up funds that could be used to promote investment and business expansion. There were also the growing trade imbalances with Japan and other Asian trading partners. While Ronald Reagan was one of the nation's most popular presidents, more individuals were indicted for criminal misconduct in his administration than in any other in the nation's history, including the Watergate conspirators.

Fundamental economic changes were taking place in the 1980s. America turned from an industrial to a postindustrial society. More individuals were employed in the service sector than in manufacturing. The federal government cut back on financial assistance programs to the states and cities; local taxes were raised and revenues were still insufficient to deal with increasingly serious social problems and a neglected and deteriorating infrastructure. Billions of dollars were spent at home and abroad in efforts to halt the trafficking and sale of illegal drugs that, in concert with economic and social stagnation, were at the center of growing urban violence. The admonitions of Ronald Reagan's wife Nancy to "just say no" proved a woefully inadequate strategy. For both the Reagan and Bush administrations, emphasis was placed on foreign rather than domestic affairs. The attention given to education, civil rights, national health care, and the environment was seldom pecuniary and more often oratory.

While some praised Reagan's acting on the strength of his convictions in his foreign policy, others compared him to the gun-toting cowboy he had portrayed when introducing weekly westerns on *Death Valley Days*. He did not hesitate to deploy the U.S. military when he felt it was in the national interest. One of the first of these questionable military excursions resulted in tragedy. In October of 1983, a terrorist attack on the barracks of American Marines sent to Lebanon as part of a United Nations peacekeeping force resulted in 216 deaths. Less than a week later U.S. troops invaded Grenada, a Caribbean island the Reagan administration claimed was about to come under Cuban domination. The pretext for the invasion was a coup in Grenada's government against the elected progressive, Maurice Bishop. The assault was interpreted by many as a warning to Nicaraguan Sandinistas and Fidel Castro's Cuba that the United States would actively oppose the further expansion of Marxism in the hemisphere. Others saw the invasion as a masterful manipulation of the media, deflecting attention away from the debacle in Lebanon.

In April 1986, during his second term, Reagan ordered American jets to attack Libya as punishment for what he called a "reign of terror" that had included, among a half dozen other incidents, an attack on a Berlin discotheque at which over 200 people were injured, including American servicemen. Libyan leader Muammar al-Gadhafi, the intended target, survived the air strike, but his adopted daughter was killed in the attacks.

The Reagan administration's long-standing support of the militaries in El Salvador and in Guatemala was a contributor to the terror of civil war in both of these countries. Economic and military pressure on the Sandinistas in Nicaragua also brought death and suffering. In 1988 Reagan sent troops into Honduras to support that country's anti-Sandinista efforts. Support of the Nicaraguan Contras against the Sandinistas frequently brought Reagan into conflict with the U.S. Congress, which, reflecting on the Vietnam experience, was reluctant to appropriate funds for military assistance or in any other way become directly involved in a Central American civil war. In 1986 the American people learned that their government had illegally sold arms to Iran, and that profits had been used to purchase supplies and equipment for the Contras. Thus began the Iran-Contra scandal, catapulting an unknown Marine colonel, Oliver North, into national prominence as a hero to some and a scoundrel to others. The scandal reached deep into the administration and caused the dismissal of John Poindexter, national security advisor, and William B. Casey, the CIA director. Reagan and Bush claimed no direct knowledge of the affair and, despite the efforts of a special prosecutor, the investigation into Iran-Contra dragged through the remainder of the decade without any major convictions and with dwindling public interest. A Sandinista-Contra cease-fire was arranged in March 1988, but sporadic fighting continued into the next decade until Daniel Ortega and his party were voted from power.

President Bush appeared no less hesitant to use American military force when in 1989 he ordered an invasion of Panama in order to oust dictator and suspected drug trafficker Manuel Noriega. Noriega, a former ally of Reagan and the CIA, was captured and flown to the United States for trial and imprisonment. He was not heard from again.

The People's Republic of China appeared ready to embark on a more moderate economic and social policy during the eighties. Reagan visited China in April 1984, signing cultural, scientific, and business accords. Later in the year, during celebrations of their 35th anniversary under Communism, the Chinese government announced a policy of limited free enterprise. American corporations began to invest in China, and a larger variety of imported Chinese merchandise appeared for sale in the United States. In the same year the British concluded negotiations with the Chinese Communists, agreeing to relinquish Hong Kong to the People's Republic of China in 1997.

There were, however, critical limits on the extent of reform that the Chinese Communist party would abide. The domination of Tibet, for example, was not open for discussion. The growing conflict between Chinese government conservatives and liberals came to a climax in June of 1989 when thousands of students who had gathered in Beijing's Tiananmen Square to demand reform and protest government corruption refused to disperse when ordered. Army troops moved to clear the square by force, resulting in the massacre of over 2,000 people. Despite protests from many human rights activists, no punitive actions were taken against China by the Bush administration.

In the years ahead several images may come to represent more than any others the victories and tragedies of the 1980s. As the decade came to a close, the fall of the Berlin Wall in November of 1989 foreshadowed the collapse of what Ronald Reagan had characterized as the "Evil Empire" of the Soviet Union. Experts had been predicting the collapse of the Soviet Union, but the people of the United States seemed genuinely surprised when it finally came. The USSR had deteriorated under Leonid Brezhnev, but his two immediate successors were in power too short a time to effect change. Leonid Brezhnev died at age 75 in November of 1982 and was replaced by former KGB head Yuri Andropov. Andropov died in February 1984, to be succeeded by Konstantin Chernenko. Chernenko died 13 months later and was replaced by Communist moderate Mikhail Gorbachev, whose refreshing personality made him popular abroad; at home he was considered inept by many in his attempts to solve chronic economic problems. "Glasnost," an openness to criticism and willingness to discuss problems, and "perestroika," a much-needed restructuring of the national bureaucracy, became new buzzwords. The decade ended with Russia's first open elections since 1917. Revolutionaries and noncommunists took their seats in the Great Palace of the People. Inevitably Gobachev will be associated with the fall of the Soviet Union, a result, in part, of policies he inaugurated. By the end of 1989 all six Warsaw Pact members had ousted their Communist governments and Soviet Foreign Minister Eduard Shevardnadze declared, "The Cold War is over."

In time, the image of the Berlin Wall being torn down may come to represent one of the most joyous moments of the decade. But there are also images of great tragedies and suffering that will be forever associated with the eighties. The nuclear accident at Chernobyl in April of 1986 will remind humanity of the very real dangers of nuclear energy. In that same year Americans were horrified and saddened when the *Challenger* space shuttle exploded before millions of television viewers. The crew included Christa McAuliffe, a high school science teacher from Concord, New Hampshire.

There were other tragedies. A Korean airliner (KAL 007), suspected of spying over Soviet territory, was shot down by the USSR in September 1983 with no survivors. Famine gripped Africa in 1984, affecting 150 million people in two dozen nations and provoking an international call for aid. In the same year a typhoon in the Philippines killed over 1,000 people. Mount St. Helens erupted in Washington, killing 57 people. In 1985 a cyclone and tidal wave killed more than 10,000 people in Bangladesh. Also in that year in Colombia a mud slide killed 20,000. The Mexico City earthquake in September 1985 killed thousands. Union Carbide's toxic cloud of methyl isocyanate killed 3,500 and injured 200,000 in Bhopal, India, in 1985, making this the most deadly industrial accident to date in world history. The petroleum industry also contributed to the despoiling of the environment, the most dramatic example being the wreck of the Exxon tanker *Valdez*, spilling tons of oil over Alaska's Prince William Sound. Poisonous gases escaping from a volcano killed 1,500 people, most while they slept, in Cameroon in 1986. In December of 1988 a Pan Am 747 passenger jet was brought down by a terrorist bomb over Lockerbie, Scotland, killing 258 people.

The 1980s saw no respite in assassinations, murders, and assassination attempts, some motivated by political and religious reasons, others by individuals whose motives remain unclear. Former Beatle John Lennon was gunned down by Mark Chapman in December 1980. Three months later President Reagan survived an attempted assassination by John W. Hinckley. In May of 1981 an escaped Turkish convict wounded Pope John Paul II in St. Peter's. Also in that year Nobel Peace Prize recipient and president of Egypt Anwar el-Sadat was killed by Islamic fundamentalist members of his military guard. Benigno Aquino, the major rival to Philippine President Ferdinand E. Marcos, was killed as he stepped off an airliner on his return to his country in August 1983. At age 66, Indira Gandhi was killed by Sikh bodyguards in October 1984. Her son, Rajiv Gandhi, became India's prime minister.

Military and civil struggles motivated by nationalism, militarism, and ethnic differences continued to shape world affairs during the 1980s. These included the military forays by the United States and the Soviet invasion of Afghanistan mentioned previously, as well as the eight-year Iraq-Iran War. In 1982 Israel invaded Lebanon and occupied Beirut, forcing the expulsion of the Palestine Liberation Organization (PLO) from that country and contributing to the massacre of Muslims by Lebanese Christian militia. Great Britain and Argentina went to war in the same year over ownership of the Falkland Islands. A British naval expedition to the South Atlantic succeeded in wresting control of the islands from Argentina. Religious differences plagued India throughout the decade and included the killing of over 600 Muslims in Assam in 1983; the next year the storming of the Sikh Golden Temple in Amristar resulted in the loss of over 400 lives. With covert support from Iran and Syria, Arab terrorists kidnapped and held over a dozen Americans and Europeans in Lebanon. The Irish Republican Army continued sporadic terrorist bombings throughout the decade.

By 1986 international sanctions were imposed on South Africa for its continued apartheid policies. In 1989 F. W. DeKlerk became the new Nationalist leader, and there was evidence that his administration would implement changes in electoral policies. In 1987 Yasser Arafat acknowledged the right of Israel to exist, but it would be another year before the United States agreed to direct talks with the PLO. The decade ended with an ongoing revolt by Palestinians in the occupied Gaza Strip. Differences between Serbs, Croats, and Bosnians threatened the stability of Yugoslavia, and foreign affairs observers wondered how long the country could survive without the strong-arm leadership of Marshal Tito, who had died in 1980.

In 1989 an era came to an end with the death at age 87 of Japanese Emperor Hirohito, the 124th monarch to sit on the Chrysanthemum Throne, the world's oldest dynasty. Forty years after its defeat in World War II, Japan challenged the economic stability of the United States; in response to a wave of Japan bashing, Japanese business leaders became increasingly critical of perceived weaknesses in U.S. business management, labor relations, and work ethic.

The Supreme Court moved to be gender-inclusive in the 1980s when Sandra Day O'Connor was appointed to the bench by Reagan. The court became dominated by conservative justices in the decade but surprisingly did not act on the conservative values platform (e.g., prayer in public school, an end to legalized abortion) that was so much a part of Reagan's election rhetoric. Acknowledging the changing face of America, the federal government first observed Martin Luther King Jr.'s birthday in 1986.

Demonstrating that legislation and public education programs can be successful in effecting social change, the annual prevalence of smoking declined 40% between 1965 and 1990. Per capita annual consumption of cigarrettes, having peaked in 1963 at 4,354, was estimated at 2,136 for 1999. Another serious health problem took center stage: Acquired Immune Deficiency Syndrome (AIDS). Throughout the decade the incidence of AIDS in the United States, Europe, and Africa grew alarmingly. The public learned that AIDS could be transmitted through sexual activity and transfusion of tainted blood. The fear of contracting AIDS was responsible in part for an increasingly conservative attitude about casual sexual encounters. For most of the decade the American people were inclined to consider the disease as an affliction associated with gays and lesbians. This attitude was reinforced by the death of actor Rock Hudson at age 59 in October 1985, followed by the death of popular entertainer Liberace from AIDS-related illness. As the decade came to an end, there was no cure for AIDS, and it appeared that ethnic and low-income groups in the United States and Third World populations were especially vulnerable.

The entertainment industry made elaborate use of new technologies in the 1980s. More viewers began to receive their television via cable, and separate cable networks were established. The success of Ted Turner's CNN demonstrated that there was a 24-hour appetite for news. Millions tuned in to view a storybook romance realized in the royal wedding of Prince Charles and Princess Diana of England in 1981. Personal computers began to find their place in American homes. The compact disc (CD) player replaced the eight-track music cartridge and long-play record. Videotape cassettes allowed people to enjoy films at their convenience.

Attendance at movie theaters, down in the previous decade, grew dramatically. The public was treated to a new breed of escapist special effects films such as *Raiders of the Lost Ark* and *E.T.* American ambivalence about Vietnam was expressed on the one hand by films such as *Rambo: First Blood* and on the other hand by films portraying a more realistic vision of that war, including Oliver Stone's *Platoon* and Stanley Kubrick's *Full Metal Jacket*. As if to underscore the dangers of casual sexual encounters, the male conscience was aroused by *Fatal Attraction*. Large-scale productions such as Sydney Pollack's *Out of Africa*, Richard Attenborough's *Gandhi*, Steven Spielberg's *Empire of the Sun*, and Bernardo Bertolucci's *The Last Emperor* received both critical acclaim and financial success. Onstage, musical hits such as *Cats*, *Phantom of the Opera*, and *Les Miserables* enjoyed tremendous popularity. The plays of August Wilson (*Fences*, *The Piano Lesson*) were recognized by the Pulitzer committee; David Mamet's playcraft provided intelligent, vivid criticism of contemporary U.S. mores

"New wave" emerged as a toned-down version of punk rock, with the Talking Heads providing an esoteric and intellecutal response to the Ramones. Bruce Springsteen, Tina Turner, Phil Collins and Genesis, U-2, Whitney Houston, Prince, Madonna, George Michael, R.E.M., and Michael Jackson dominated pop music. Brooklyn, New York, and the Los Angeles Compton area produced a new musical form that combined prerecorded music in rhythm loops and street poetry. Rap artists such as Run DMC and Public Enemy helped establish a new entertainment industry. Music synthesizers and drum machines augmented electric guitars. Music videos became standard fare on cable channels such as MTV and VH1.

There was also the emergence of a music form based on the repetition of simple themes by solo or small ensemble instrumentalists. Labeled "new age" music, its popularity helped established a new genre and Windham Hill, founded by William Ackerman, provided a venue for the works of George Winston and Mark Isham.

The suspense and horror novels of Stephen King were instant best-sellers, joined by work from other popular authors such as John Grisham, Tom Clancy, and Danielle Steele. Anne Rice's novels on the lives of vampires revived the gothic genre. The literary scene was also graced with notable contributions by Umberto Eco (*The Name of the Rose*), Patrick Suskind (*Perfume*), and Margaret Atwood (*Cat's Eye*). Salman Rushdie, author of *The Satanic Verses*, was compelled to live incognito because of a death sentence placed on him by the ayatollahs of Iran. Other significant international literature was authored by Mario Vargas Llosa, Octavio Paz, Gabriel Garcia Marquez, and Nathalie Sarraute. Naguib Mahfouz was awarded the Nobel Prize in Literature in 1989.

Critics decried that television moguls, in their fight for viewer ratings, had decided to increase airtime portrayals of sex, crime, and violence. Evening soap operas such as *Dallas* and *Dynasty* cluttered the networks. Rupert Murdoch launched the Fox network, a fledging effort to challenge the major networks by coordinating programming on independent stations and filling the slots with mostly banal and tasteless sitcoms and dramas with the exception of the innovative adult cartoon series, *The Simpsons*.

Offended by the media's lack of character, some called for a return to discipline, family values, and Christian ideals. It was a perspective exemplified by Joe Clark, the get-tough principal at Eastside High School in Paterson, New Jersey, portrayed sympathetically in the feature film, *Lean on Me*. Praised by President Reagan, he was also threatened by his school board for insubordination. Clark eventually would run a prison. Some promoters of Christian capitalism and nationalism did not fare well. Television evangelists came under increased scrutiny. Jim Bakker faced trial in 1987 and eventually went to jail; Jimmy Swaggart resigned from the ministry after being caught purchasing the services of a prostitute.

In professional sports, the 1980s were glory years for the National Football League. The industry saw record revenues and captured worldwide attention. The accomplishments of Bill Walsh's San Francisco '49ers, led by Joe Montana and Jerry Rice; Joe Gibbs's Washington Redskins; Mike Ditka's Chicago Bears; and Bill Parcell's New York Giants were reported on and cheered across the globe. Jimmy Johnson's University of Miami teams dominated college football, the NFL's minor league. In tennis, Jimmy Connors topped the sport early in the decade, replaced by Ivan Lendl; Martina Navratilova made a monopoly of the women's game through most of the decade with a young Steffi Graf challenging her domination as the decade closed. In hockey, two teams, the New York Islanders and the Edmonton Oilers, held claim on the Stanley Cup for much of the decade. Wayne Gretzky became an icon of the ice rink. The National Basketball Association also began to come into its own with television audiences enjoying classic duels between the Boston Celtics led by Larry Bird, and the Los Angeles Lakers directed by Magic Johnson and Kareem Abdul-Jabbar.

Julian Schnabel's eclectic approach to painting, borrowing across cultures and mythic structures, had commonalities with the European trans-avant-garde perspective of Bonito Oliva of Italy and Georg Baselitz of Germany. The movement away from ideological and political conviction in art led to a fascination with the revival of "primitivism" in theme and method. In contrast, the art of Georges Mathieu addressed such specific political events as the Soviet attack on the KAL 007 passenger aircraft (*The Massacre of the 269*). The influence of mass culture was evident in the bold and bright art of Robert Combra. Controversy surrounded the artistic contribution of Jean Michel Basquiat, a young graffitti artist whose work was endorsed by Andy Warhol. The market value of his popular works soared when he died of a drug over-dose at 28. Located between the art of popular culture and the art of street protest was the work of Keith Haring, an artist who was comfortable doing both chalk graffitti in New York and studio work for an international market.

In sculpture, the vertical pyramid of automobiles and concrete by Arman posed a disturbing statement on consumerism. Architectural highlights of the eighties included modernist architect Richard Meier's High Museum of Art in Atlanta, first opened in 1983, and postmodernist Jahn Helmut's Agricultural Engineering Building at the Champaign campus of the University of Illinois a year later. In 1988 I. M. Pei's glass pyramid entrance to the Louvre was praised by some, reviled by others, but his critics could not prevent him from winning the design for the Mount Sinai Medical Complex in New York.

During the eighties new superconductive compounds were discovered with applications for ultrafast computers and magnetically levitated trains. Sunspots were found to affect weather; scientists discussed the procedures for human genetic engineering and debated its moral implications. When physi-cists at the Fermi National Accelerator Laboratory in Batavia, Illinois, col-lided subatomic protons into counter-rotating antiprotons, 1.6 trillion electron volts were released. The Fermi accelerator, four miles in diameter, dramati-cally advanced particle smashing and observation.

In 1981 a vaccine for hepatitis was approved by the FDA and the Jarvik artificial heart was implanted in Dr. Barney Clark, who survived 112 days. Plans were made public to build a rail tunnel under the English Channel. The "Chunnel" was completed early in the next decade. In 1985 researchers at the Yerkes Primate Center at Emory University announced the successful transplant of brain cell tissue, resulting in the alleviation of symptoms of Parkinson's Disease.

Environmental problems were both scientific and social. At mid-decade scientists detected a hole in the atmosphere's ozone layer above the Antarctic. The skateboard and rollerblades provided competition for pedestrians on the sidewalks. Drivers worked at guiding their automobiles while holding conversations on their cellular phones, easier to accomplish as urban areas across the globe approached gridlock. The world became concerned about the impact of acid rain on the lakes and forests, and scientists began debating the existence and potential harm of the greenhouse effect. Destruction of the world's rain forests and the release of dangerous chemicals into the atmosphere threatened the climate of the entire planet. Growth in world population challenged the planet's ability to provide humanity with sufficient food and water.

Many people will probably view the end of the Cold War as the single most important event of the decade. But that triumph of representative government and free enterprise presented new challenges. The nations of the world needed to find ways of dealing with the growing fanaticism of religious and ethnic groups, with the inequities in the quality of life between and within advanced and developing nations, and with the environmental threats to planet earth.

CURRICULUM THOUGHT AND LITERATURE

A NATION AT RISK?

The ascendance of Ronald Reagan to the presidency in 1980 appeared to signal a diminished role for education at the federal level. Reagan strongly hinted in his campaign that he would dismantle the Department of Education and hand educational leadership over to the states. Surprisingly, Reagan's secretary of education, William Bennett, a strong proponent for the revival of an intellectual traditionalist perspective in public schooling, brought the Department of Education to high profile by igniting a national debate on curriculum and instruction. The treatise issued in 1983 by the National Commission on Excellence in Education, ominously titled *A Nation at Risk*, posited a relationship between student performance on international tests in math and science with the comparative economic health of industrialized nations. The conclusion: The economic future of the United States was predicated on whether the public schools could be reformed so that young people would be able to compete in the information/technology age. The blame for the "decline" of public schools in the United States was placed on experientialist educators of the late 1960s and 1970s who were alleged to have sacrificed academic rigor for fuzzy humanistic social development. The end result was presented as a national tragedy. The report declared, "If an unfriendly foreign power had attempted to impose on America the mediocre educational performance that exists today, we might well have viewed it as an act of war" (National Commission on Excellence in Education, 1983, p. 1). What is remarkable about *A Nation at Risk*, apart from its imaginative cause-effect relationship and the fanciful rewriting of the history of school practice for the prior 20 years, is that it suggested a remedy that had a limited relationship with the illness that it invented. Courting an alliance with social behaviorists, Secretary Bennett contended that only a return to discipline-centered basics, character education, and high-stakes testing for accountability could improve the intellectual capital of U.S. students. Social behaviorists were welcome to design assessments and refine techniques for instructional effectiveness, but the reform curriculum was to be rooted in the language arts, history, geography, mathematics, the sciences (William T. Harris's *Five Windows to the Soul* revisited), and increased use of technology as a tool fostering intellectual skills and economic efficiency. An opportunity for intellectual traditionalists was thus provided, and various policy groups responded to the invitation to influence public policy.

In the same year that *A Nation at Risk* was published, the Education Commission of the States (ECS) issued *Action for Excellence* (Task Force on Education for Economic Growth, 1983), proposing the establishment of competencies in reading, writing, speaking, listening, reasoning, and economics. Special provision was to be provided for the education of the academically gifted, and college entrance examination standards were to be made more demanding. The ECS would later translate these recommendations into the establishment of discipline-specific content standards and the ratcheting up of student achievement testing. Much of this proposal was seconded by the College Board's recommendations in *Academic Preparation for College* (College Entrance Examination Board, 1983). A third report issued in this landmark year was the Carnegie Foundation for Achievement in Teaching's impressive study on the current state of the high school, directed by Ernest Boyer (Boyer, 1983). The report stressed mastery of language arts, consistent with Boyer's earlier proposal for general education (Boyer & Levine, 1981), but also reaffirmed the design of the comprehensive high school, with greater emphasis on electives, provisions for vocational education, and the requirement for one unit of community service.

The U.S. National Science Board (1983) advocated more rigorous college entrance standards, but rather than join the chorus calling for the renewal of all academic disciplines, the NSB emphsized expanding mathematics and science curriculum for all students and argued that more advanced classes in these subject areas be included in the high school curriculum. The report of the Conference Board of the Mathematical Sciences (1983) shared their emphases: more mathematics for all students and advanced coursework for the academically talented.

Support for A Nation at Risk and the conservative reports that shared its perspective was hardly unanimous. Critics noted the lack of commitment to educational equity, the ungrounded indictment of progressive and neoprogressive education as the source of much that had brought forth the "rising tide of mediocrity," and the proposal of these reports that retention of discipline-specific general education was the appropriate remedy to what ailed public school students. Responses by Passow (1984) and the National Board of Inquiry (1985) are examples of this critical perspective. Gross and Gross (1985) included criticism in the context of offering an overview of the debate. Herb Kohl's (1982) redefining of "basic skills" in a progressive perspective provided an engaging counterpoint. John Holt's restatement of progressive principles through revision of his classic works on the dynamics of learning (J. Holt, 1982; 1983), his support of the option of home schooling (Holt, 1981), and a posthumous collection of Holt's writings (1989) provided an unambiguous alternative conception of worthwhile education. Alexander and Pallas (1983) examined whether the emphasis on "new basics" really translated to better schools. Stanley Aronowitz and Henry Giroux (1985) provided a critical reconstructionist response to the reports. Linda Darling-Hammond (1984) questioned whether the national reports were even addressing the right issue; her argument was that reform policy needed to look more critically at teacher preparation and development. Edmund Short (1984) edited a volume that ably demonstrated that the term "competence" can have a variety of meanings, a precursor to the emerging debate over standards. Arthur Wise (1983) also warned of the growing enchroachment of bureaucracy in curriculum decision making in U.S. schools.

At least one scholarly association had the gumption to criticize this conservative stance in two documents. The American Educational Studies Association (AESA) called for a renewal in the humanities (AESA, 1983), attention to educational foundations (philosophical, historical, social, and cultural bases for education), and teacher preparation with a distinctive progressive (Deweyan) flavor (Raywid, Tesconi, & Warren, 1984).

Several reports issued in the 1980s were not direct considerations of what curriculum was most suitable for the public schools, but their influence on educational thought inevitably shaped thinking about schooling. James Coleman extended his study of the efficacy of schooling to a comparison of public and private schools (Coleman, 1981, and Coleman, Hoffer, & Kilgore, 1982), concluding that private schools outperformed public schools primarily because the investment of the families of private school students in time and interest outweighed limitations on capital resources. This was consistent with Coleman's earlier contention that out-of-school influences are primary determinants of student achievement. The Twentieth Century Fund (1983) issued a report card on the federal initiatives in elementary and secondary education instituted by ESEA legislation. The Carnegie Forum (1986) and the Holmes Group (1986) called for dramatic restructuring of teacher preparation programs, including the extension of preparation time beyond four years, elimination of the education major at the undergraduate level, and expansion of the field experience of preservice teachers (Soltis, 1987).

Contrasted with the tumult raised by *A Nation at Risk*, the substantive findings provided in John Goodlad's Study of Schooling, published in *A Place Called School*, were regarded as good research but were under-reported in public media when it was released in 1984. The report confirmed that an inordinate number of hours are spent in schools with students carrying out institutional procedures or being *talked at* by teachers. To replace current practice, Goodlad recommended an emphasis on language arts, mathematics and science (36% of total instructional time), social studies, the fine and practical arts (up to 30%), and physical education (up to 10%). The balance of school time was given over to electives to allow students to pursue individual interests. A common core was suggested that established disciplinary connections. M. Frances Klein (1989) expanded on the call for reform in elementary education in using the Study of Schooling data to argue for the establishment of a constructivist curriculum that is responsive to the local school.

Another major finding coming out of the Study of Schooling was that tracking or ability grouping influenced teacher expectations on student performance as well as student self-perception, particularly with regard to students who were identified as low in academic achievement. Goodlad's recommendation was to eliminate tracking. Having contributed to the Study of Schooling, Jeannie Oakes's work on the effects of homogenous grouping, *Keeping Track*, published in 1985, reopened a reluctant debate on the long-established tradition of ability grouping (e.g., see Schubert in Rubin, 1977b, pp. 544–555). *Keeping Track* was particularly relevant given the federal government's call to establish a cadre of a young intelligentsia to drive the nation to dominance in the technological marketplace, Oakes's proposal to eliminate tracking in organizing curriculum and instruction was uninvited controversy. In contrast to the conclusions of Oakes's book, academic magnet schools for students with high test scores were established in many cities in the last half of the decade and state-supported math and science residential high schools for the academically gifted were instituted.

An interesting alternative reform proposal that integrated experientialist elements with an intellectual traditionalist foundation was offered in the the first report from *A Study of High Schools*, cosponsored by the National Association of Secondary School Principals and the Commission on Educational Issues of the National Association of Independent Schools. Theodore Sizer, author of the work, used the voice of the fictional Horace Smith, a middle-aged veteran teacher employed by a typical United States public high school, to provide a description of the high school as it was and as it might be. In this report, imaginatively titled *Horace's Compromise*, Sizer (1984) isolated key problems with the contemporary high school and developed a reform platform that emphasized the development of intellectual and moral habits. The Coalition of Essential Schools, the organization established to promote the recommendations of *Horace's Compromise*, centered the curriculum on four areas: a skill base in inquiry and expression, mathematics and science, literature and the arts, and history and philosophy. Assessment of student learning, according to the Coalition of Essential Schools, was to be centered on an extensive exhibition that wove the student's knowledge and skills together in a public demonstration of competence. Education in the high school, it was argued, needed to shift from teacher as deliverer of knowledge to the students as intellectual workers. Instruction was based on universal goals, delivered to address personal student needs.

Over the next four years, the Reagan administration's Department of Education produced curriculum proposals that explained its thinking on educational reform, making full use of the "bully pulpit" provided by the Government Printing Office and the national media. Documents were produced on the best high school curriculum (Bennett, 1987), traditional school practices that were defended by quantitative research findings to be "what works" (United States Department of Education, 1986), and a report card on the success of the conservative reform movement (Bennett, 1988).

Having learned the value of providing political interpretations of standardized national and international assessments, the release of the results of the National Report on the Second International Mathematics Study

(McKnight et al., 1987), wherein U.S. students finished last among industrialized nations, furthered the case that reform was critical. The title of the report, *The Underachieving Curriculum*, provided what they contended was the likely cause for this poor performance. Travers and Westbury (1988) conducted a detailed curriculum analysis based on the results of this assessment. The National Council of Teachers of Mathematics issued its statement of content standards for the reform of mathematics the following year, heralding significant changes in the topics included in mathematics education (National Council of Teachers of Mathematics, 1989). Ravitch and Finn produced a volume based on the findings of the first national assessment in the social studies (1987) calling for renewed emphasis on the specific disciplines of history and geography to remedy what they interpreted as the lamentable performance of ninth-grade students. The assessment findings were used to give urgency to their earlier call for renewal in the humanities (Finn, Ravitch, & Fancher, 1984).

A number of important perspective pieces and proposals came forward to build on this renascence of intellectual traditionalism. Allan Bloom's *The Closing of the American Mind* (1987) was reminiscent of the attack by Arthur Bestor (1953, 1955) a generation earlier. An intelligent, curmudgeonly assault on the lack of intellectual preparation that current undergraduate students brought to the college classroom, Bloom's work argued for a revival of foundational disciplinary studies and renewal of family life. Another University of Chicago icon, Mortimer Adler, produced a trilogy that detailed "paideia" education, a curriculum that commenced with the acquisition of foundational knowledge and skills, guided young people in the development of intellectual habits, and culminated in the exercise and expansion of this intellectual repertoire in the dynamics of contemporary living (Adler, 1982, 1983, 1984).

The public acceptance of proposals for discipline-specific traditional education was also confirmed by the spectacular success of E. D. Hirsch's *Cultural Literacy* (1987). Although his curriculum proposal had similarities to Adler, Hirsch advocated a socially relative and practical understanding of the intellectual disciplines. With two colleagues at the University of Virginia, Hirsch undertook to determine what every American would need to acquire as basic knowledge in order to be an effective reader, listener, and discussant in the humanities, history, and the sciences. Their final list of 5,000 essential names, phrases, dates, and concepts attracted national attention and elevated Hirsch as a standard-bearer for the revival of basic education. What is important to note, however, is that Hirsch's methodology for determining a curriculum has stronger similarities to W. W. Charters than it does to Adler or Bloom. Whereas Adler and Bloom were translators of a perennial educational philosophy, preparing students to participate in the "great conversation," Hirsch proposed imparting a common core of history, legend, myth, and literature to all students. Having recourse to this essential knowledge, students are able to function effectively in contemporary society. As society evolves, the list is reconstructed to address the new cultural essentials. To effect this reform, Hirsch suggested that influences be extended over school textbooks and achievement tests. In several ways, Hirsch's cultural literacy marks a marriage of intellectual traditionalism to social behaviorism, a design envisioned by the framers of *A Nation at Risk*. The concepts of "general education" and "cultural literacy" gave rise to dialogue in works by G. Miller (1988) and the 1988 NSSE Yearbook (Westbury & Purves, 1988). For a contrasting perspective, the notion of "multicultural literacy" was articulated in essays by James Baldwin, Carlos Fuentes, and others (Simonson & Walker, 1988), demonstrating the richness that can result from openness to understanding cultural differences.

PROPOSALS FOR CURRICULUM INTEGRATION

Although the Department of Education curriculum proposal tacitly accepted that student learning should be maintained in traditional academic disciplines, a variety of writers suggested a central focus to which academic subjects were subordinate. Absent from the proposals were new interpretations of John Dewey's "way out of educational confusion" (John Dewey, 1931), by integrating the school curriculum around the genuine interests and concerns of learners. There were suggestions for curriculum coordination around preparing for the future, the use of technology, the expansion of democracy or global citizenship, or at least mapping connections among the standard academic disciplines to enhance their relevance or instructional effectiveness.

Reminiscent of the life-adjustment curricula proposals of the late 1940s, McGuire and Priestley (1981) and Wilcox, Dunn, Lavercombe, and Burn (1984) suggested that school curricula be constructed from the practical concerns of living in contemporary society. Cumming (1988) connected curriculum to contemporary vocational opportunities. Other writers recognized that the present was in rapid transition and the school curriculum should effectively prepare young people for their future. A number of authors forecast the kind of world that young people would inherit in the next millennium. Tonkin and Edwards (1981) emphasized the global interdependence that would characterize the next century; White (1987) reflected on the curriculum for the postindustrial "information age." Other works that promoted curriculum reform for a future world were authored by Haas (1980) and Fisher (1980).

A number of writers gave attention to the advancing role of technology and argued for its expanded influence in the school curriculum. The publication of Pappert's *Mindstorms* (1980) generated excitement on the possible creative uses of computers in education. Scholarship was conventionally interested, however, in the institutional use of electronic intelligence. At one level, numerous authors wrote about the use of computers and other electronic media as a component in planning for curriculum (e.g., Eraut, Connors, & Hewton, 1981; Gillespie, 1980; Kelly, 1984; Mamidi & Ravishankar, 1984; Potter, 1984; Rowntree, 1982, 1985; Schostak, 1988; Tucker, 1986); other authors considered how technology will transform instructional delivery (e.g., Collis, 1988; Crompton, 1989; Grady & Gawronski, 1983; Kepner, 1982; O'Shea & Self, 1983; O'Neil, 1981; Pappert, 1980). The most dramatic proposals, however, questioned the overall costs and benefits to the human community for embracing technology as a partner in learning and living. Sloan (1985) offered critical assessment of the possibilities that the computer brings to education; Bullough, Goldstein, and Holt (1984) provided an ethical/social evaluation of curriculum and technology in light of the needs of the human community.

A perspective that gained increased support in curriculum literature through the 1980s was the promotion of democracy as the coordinating focus for the public school curriculum. Treatises from venerable educators such as R. Freeman Butts (1980, 1988), Herbert Thelen (1981), and Harry Broudy (1981), as well as books from an emerging group of critical reconstructists (e.g., Peter McLaren and Ira Shor, discussed below), maintained that a curriculum for public schools in the United States should honor, foster, and expand democratic life. Democracy was the compelling focus for a relevant curriculum. Works by Campbell (1980), Reid and Filby (1982), and Gutmann (1987) sought to articulate the difference that schooling in a democratic society can make. Gutmann, for example, argued that democratic education is the sharing of socially validated goals and practices founded on the requirements that all education be nonrepressive and nondiscriminatory. Gutmann recommended that teacher education and professional development foster this approach to education.

Other authors articulated practical methods for democratic education. Eliot Wigginton's (1985) reflection on the *Foxfire* curriculum demonstrated a grassroots approach to education founded on the sharing of community voices and leadership. Mayberry (1980) encouraged the study of the city as a living curriculum. Thelen (1981) promoted the incorporation of democratic practices into the operation of the classroom society. Stewart (1985) offered practical suggestions on involving students in decision making at the classroom level; Bricker (1989) reflected on how classroom activity translated into civics education. The conflict between democratic values and competitive structures that are an extension of motivation in and surrounding education was examined by Nicholls (1989). Gordon (1986) provided a case study on how participation in decision making was expanded across the school community. Boomer (1982) edited a volume exploring the inclusion of students directly in curriculum construction. Kemmis, Cole, and Suggett (1983) viewed the democratic school as the place where social criticism was learned. Engle and Ochoa (1988) explored the relationship between the social sciences curriculum and democratic citizenship. This notion was consonant with ideas being put forward by critical reconstructionists. Carnoy and Levin's examination of schooling for labor (1985), Ira Shor's work on critical teaching (1980), and Peter McLaren's application of critical theory to the study of both pedagogy and the educational foundations (1989) provided new direction for the relationship between democracy and education.

Other authors contended that a reconstructed sense of moral purpose was needed to orient curriculum construction. Although some works were limited to an exploration of the place of values in the school (Frazier, 1980; Tomlinson & Quinton, 1986; Yates, 1981), ethics in the college curriculum (Rosen & Caplan, 1980), or the relationship between denominational religious belief and education (Cully, 1983; Rose, 1988), new perspectives on the ethical grounding of education were provided by David Purpel, both in his overview of contemporary thinking on moral education (Giroux and Purpel, 1983) and in his call for the reconstruction of the curriculum around a renewed understanding of spirituality and morality (Purpel, 1988). Gabriel Moran (1981) reflected on the relationship of education to religious expression understood in an unconventional, nondenominational sense. Nel Noddings oriented the curriculum around the ethic of caring, an integrating concept supported by research on the moral development and priorities of women (Noddings, 1984), a proposal that Noddings developed more fully in the 1990s.

Other writers maintained the need to establish a moral integration of the curriculum, but presented their views from the perspective of global citizenship and the responsibilities that attend to this role. Hicks and Townley (1982) edited a volume that served as an introduction to global perspectives in the curriculum. Louise Berman and Alice Miel (1983) and Elise Boulding (1988) were forthright in their call for education that advocated for global interdependence and cooperation. The contribution of the Council for Education in World Citizenship was discussed by Heater (1984). Finally, the works of Betty Reardon were a passionate call for education to be an agent of peacemaking. In her volume on sexism and the war system, she examined the relationship between gender identities and moral development, and how this translates into perspectives on violence. The transition from violent confrontation to global responsibility and the promotion of a just world order become the integrating focus of the curriculum, an educational model that emphasized virtue and prudence (Reardon, 1988a, 1988b).

Conciliarist proposals, the practical intertwining of experiential, intellectual traditionalist, and social behaviorist ideas and instructional designs, encouraged the making of connections among the academic disciplines to make learning more relevant, more effective, and more interesting for young people. Maurer (1981, 1985) proposed interdisciplinary approaches for middle schools and high schools. Driscoll (1986) suggested a curriculum that made use of the intellectual traditionalist notion of the humanities as an integrating focus. Among approaches that relied on experientialist insights, Katz and Chard (1989) kept the project method alive and Heidi Hayes Jacobs's work in the design and implementation of a thematic interdisciplinary curriculum (1989) gained the extensive support of ASCD.

Another conciliar approach located a common emphasis across the academic disciplines. The most frequent proposal was to address language arts across content areas. Moffett (1981), Spencer (1983), Myers (1984), and McLeod (1988) provided guidance on how to use writing as a tool for understanding across the disciplines. Chilver and Gould (1982) included oral discourse in language expression; Thaiss (1986) addressed language in various disciplines at the elementary school level; Robertson wrote on language development across the curriculum (1980). Other orientations emphasized creativity (Poole, 1980) and drama (Nixon, 1982).

The above approaches sought to fuse or find commonalities, but none challenged schools to direct curriculum away from disciplinary knowledge to an alternative construct. In contrast McPeck (1981) suggested that the standard disciplinary curriculum should be subordinate to the facilitating of critical thinking. Hyde and Bizar (1989) emphasized the teaching of cognitive processes as a primary for all academic disciplines in the curriculum. Robert Marzano and his associates (Marzano, 1985; Marzano et al., 1988) argued for the conceptual reframing of the curriculum around key thinking skills and learning strategies. This proposal challenged the long-standing popularity of Bloom's taxonomy (Bloom, 1956) by having educators build learning experiences around core thinking skills: focusing, gathering information, remembering, organizing, analyzing, generating new ideas, integrating and summarizing knowledge. Unlike Bloom, Marzano and his colleagues contended that these cognitive skills were not hierarchical and that within each skill there could be low-level or high-level cognitive engagement. This proposal was endorsed by the Association for Supervision and Curriculum Development and was disseminated through professional development venues.

A PROLIFERATION OF CURRICULUM THEORIES

In contrast to proposals to integrate the curriculum, much of the writing in curriculum theory in the 1980s was characterized by expanding "discourses," that is, perspectives on or ways of looking at and talking about how curricula are experienced. The highly influential anthology of Giroux, Penna, and Pinar (1981) on contemporary writers on curriculum suggested three dominant inquiry perspectives on curriculum research and writing. Borrowed from Habermas's work on social knowledge, the perspectives are the "traditional," the "conceptual empiricist," and the "reconceptualist." These categories opened debate on how to characterize contemporary discourses (e.g., Is "reconceptual" too encompassing a classification? Did it capture a new richness and diversity of the field? Were these perspectives presented in a manner that was self-promotional to reconceptualists?). Nevertheless, the categorization was widely employed as an organizational design for understanding the proliferating approaches to thinking about curriculum. Noting the significant differences in the discourses used within each of these three categories, the anthology demonstrated that a variety of inquiry postures were being employed in curriculum theory, from a narrow technical/analytic focus on institutionalized schooling (the conceptual empiricist) to a concern for practical development and implementation of the curriculum (the traditionalist) to placing the curriculum in the context of a larger personal or social theory (the reconceptualist).

In looking at how these three inquiry postures translated into writing books about the curriculum, it must be conceded, contrary to the implication of Giroux, Penna, and Pinar (1981), that the traditional perspective, centered on curriculum development for schools, continued to hold dominance in book publishing. Conceptual empiricists, relative to curriculum theory, became a relatively small category with regard to books produced in the 1980s, although they were somewhat more represented in scholarly and research journals. The wide range of scholars grouped under reconceptual inquiry, although in ascendance in the 1980s, remained a diverse and multifaceted minority perspective. The transition from curriculum theories largely based in traditional educational philosophy, practical politics, and study of the learner to works that examined the larger questions of what curriculum is for was verified by the texts produced in curriculum theory in the decade. Stoughton's edited volume on curriculum issues (1981), and the considerations by Barnes (1982), Barrow (1981, 1984), and Dearden (1984) are examples of the established and conventional approach to theorizing about curriculum. Louis Rubin's (1984) imaginative study of and reflection on artistry in teaching was an indication of how inquiry could be refashioned away from control and prediction to consider atheistic quality and understanding. In contrast, Lawn and Barton's volume on curriculum studies (1981), Feinberg's (1985) extended essay that employed the insights of the Jewish existentialist Martin Buber, and Bernstein's essay on postmodern thought (1983) indicated new directions for curriculum theory. In *Contemporary Curriculum Discourses*, William Pinar (1988) identified a variety of "discourses" or ways of looking at and talking about the curriculum that emerged in the decade: the historical, political, aesthetic, phenomenological, and feminist. William Reynolds produced an important work in curriculum theory from a postmodern perspective in 1989; in the same year Oliver and Gershman offered a process theory of teaching and learning that was responsive to postmodern thought, helping to establish yet another discourse.

A NEW ORIENTATION EMERGES: CRITICAL RECONSTRUCTION

One prominent reconceptual discourse, influenced by critical theory, provided an important new conversation about curriculum in the 1980s. Its importance came not only from what it contributed to the understanding of and conversation about curriculum, it was also provocative of insightful criticism pertaining to equity and justice vis-à-vis underrepresented or oppressed groups. The shared premise of a critical reconstructionist perspective was that curriculum in the United States' public schools already held an integrating focus, a focus established by capitalist interests. Scholars dedicated reflection and research to determining how this ideology translated to school practices in all forms of the curriculum (overt, hidden, and null). The conclusion that the U.S. public schools were among the least democratic social institutions in the nation was put forward by a prolific and scholarly group of curriculum writers. In doing so, they established a distinct orientation to the curriculum founded on critical reconstruction, calling for the democratic reconstruction of both education and of society at large. Critical reconstructionists share concerns as well as proposals with social reconstructionist variations within what we have called experientialist writers of the 1930s, such as George Counts and Carter G. Woodson, as well as the social reconstruction proposal of Theodore Brameld from 1945 through the 1960s. This does not, however, imply continuity or direct lineage. Rather, the concept that public schooling should be analyzed in light of its participation in economic and political structures provided an interesting advance from the hidden curriculum studies of the late 1960s and 1970s.

This line of inquiry moved from a neo-Marxist structural correspondence theory at the beginning of the decade, with reliance on social and historical revisionist scholarship, to scholarly inquiry into the dynamics of the school institution in lived experience. Michael Apple and Henry Giroux were dominant voices in this line of inquiry. Giroux's *Ideology, Culture, and the Process of Schooling* (1981) and Apple's *Cultural and Economic Reproduction in Education* (1982) and *Education and Power* (1982) are powerful arguments that public schools in the United States are designed to perpetuate social stratification and economic inequalities in the design and enactment of the curriculum, an argument that Apple (1979) had begun to fashion in the previous decade. These works articulated a social hegemony that was being reproduced in school teaching. Hegemony is the process whereby a society or power dominant culture reproduces patterns of inequity. Each institution of the society, schools being prominent, passes along the hierarchical structure of society. Students of a given race, social class, or gender, for instance, are given messages, through the overt, hidden, and null curriculum that reinforce social inequalities. This is not to contend that teachers are in a conscious conspiracy with the ruling classes to plan and implement a program of reproduction. Instead, hegemonic understandings are tacitly accepted as social reality; teachers work out of this reality in forming relationships with students. Michael Apple's foundational arguments (1982a, 1982b) attracted a worldwide audience with publications in many languages. His writing invited a research agenda to determine the specific ways in which social hegemony is supported through the school curriculum. Lois Weis collaborated with Apple in editing a volume on ideology and school practices (Apple and Weis, 1983) that documented practices that supported the critical reconstructionist contentions.

The "correspondence" theory, that institutional propaganda reproduces the economic and political order of the society, was explored by both Giroux and Apple. Giroux indicated in *Theory and Resistance in Education* (1983) that although school curricula are designed to perpetuate the interests of owners of capital, students find methods for resisting hegemonic reproduction. Giroux's interests expanded beyond school curriculum in two directions in this decade. One interest was in the role that popular culture has assumed in the education of young people (1989). The other was an attempt to establish a model of education that is compatible with critical theory, an approach that came to be labeled "critical pedagogy" (1988b). Peter McLaren, a writer who had produced his own unique analysis of schooling (1986), used constructs that went beyond critical theory, and he joined with Giroux in a reflection on the political possibilities of critical pedagogy (Giroux & McLaren, 1989).

Other writers engaged in critical analysis of how ideology was translated to curriculum and school practice. Sharp (1980) offered an analysis of schooling in neo-Marxist scholarship. Barton and Walker (1981), Barton, Meighan, and Walker (1981), and Gilbert (1984) examined the relationship between ideology and the curriculum of the public schools.

A primary artifact of education, the school textbook, became a focus for critical analysis. Fitzgerald's study of history textbooks and historical revision (1980) critically examined both what was being asserted and what was left silent in student textbooks. Sewall's criticism of American history textbooks (1987) was compatible with Tyson-Bernstein's analysis of contemporary textbooks (1988). Both castigated publishers for trying to produce texts that are all things to all peoples and sacrificing scholarship in the process. Michael Apple turned his attention to the publishing industry and the political control of school textbooks in his important *Teachers and Texts* (1986), providing a critical reconstructionist's perspective on the issue of cultural representation and academic quality. Decastell, Luke, and Luke (1989) also contributed to the discussion on the school textbook using the evolving tools of postmodern thought.

Paulo Freire, repatriated to Brazil, allied with U.S. and global educators to develop a model of education that advocated social reconstruction through the expansion of democracy in a curriculum relevant to schools in the United States. Freire authored or coauthored a number of works that expanded his vision of a pedagogy for liberation extending beyond the Third World (Freire, 1985; Freire & Macedo 1987; Freire & Faundez, 1989). Ira Shor won a popular audience for critical reconstructionist analysis with the publication of *Culture Wars* (Shor, 1986), a stinging assessment of educational policy and practice in the previous two decades. Shor produced a work with Freire on the possibilities of establishing educational practices that promote human liberation (Shor & Freire, 1986). Shor also edited a volume (1987) translating Freire's ideas for classroom practices in the United States.

CRITICS AND DISTINCT VOICES

Critical reconstructionists provoked immediate criticism for their acceptance of structural Marxism. One of the most compelling of these critics was C. A. Bowers. In his own statement on how political theory can inform thinking on the curriculum (Bowers, 1984), Bowers identified three liberal approaches to change in education: the technocratic, the romantic free school advocates, and neo-Marxists. He argued that these seemingly disparate perspectives share a common mythology regarding individualism, self-direction, and change through structural modifications. In contrast, Bowers suggested that a curriculum for "communicative competence" would serve as an alternative understanding of a curriculum more likely to invite reflective thought. Bowers posited five propositions indicating a poststructural and postmodern reading of curriculum. He asked educators to consider the following questions to challenge tacit socialization:

❖ Does the curriculum reflect what the student already experiences as taken for granted?

❖ Is the content of the curriculum presented as reified reality?

❖ What are the areas of audible silence in the curriculum?

❖ Is the curriculum characterized by a limited or a complex language code?

❖ Does socialization involve using the legitimation process to make students feel powerless?

❖ Does the curriculum contribute to social stratification and inequalities of opportunities?

❖ What is the influence of the purposive-rational system of thought in the liberalizing potential of school knowledge? (Paraphrased from Bowers, 1984, pp. 57–69)

The new directions provided by postmodern and poststructural thinking in both research and reflection on the curriculum were organized by Cleo Cherryholmes (1988). *Power and Criticism: Poststructural Investigations in Education* provided a context for criticism of traditional and conceptual empiricist practical theories of the past (e.g., Tyler, Bloom, and Schwab) as well as the writings of critical theorists produced earlier in the decade. Lynch's examination of the legitimacy of a theory of cultural reproduction provided another challenge to critical theorist analysis (1989).

Joining Bowers in criticism of the experientialist contention that education should move from the immediate to the distant was Kieran Egan. Egan presented a challenge to classical developmental theory's notion that the most engaging and psychologically sound curriculum is that which moves from the immediate, concrete, and local to the abstract, general, and theoretical. Egan contended that the "expanding horizons" curriculum prevalent in elementary school practice (since Hollis Caswell and others helped revise the Virginia curriculum in the 1920s) provided information on the mundane and parochial at a time in the lives of students when they are most captivated by the fantastic and the possible limits of the known (Egan, 1986a, 1988a). The everyday environment holds limited interest; it is in the fantastic that a more compelling and meaningful curriculum can be established. Drawing from sources in literature, archeology, and philosophy, Egan posited stages of development that are dramatically different from Piaget and Dewey. Egan suggested movement from the mythic to the romantic, the philosophic, and the ironic. He urged curriculum developers to heed the power that stories have as influences on people's attention and outlook and suggested the adoption of the *story form* for curriculum design and teaching (Egan, 1986b, 1988b). His call for the revival of narrative as a key aspect of the curriculum established a new curriclum theory influenced by but not derived from intellectual traditionalists.

THE INDIVIDUAL AND THE CURRICULUM

A dramatic shift in thinking about the individual's relationship with curriculum also occurred in the 1980s. The prior understanding of the individual as a defined set of characteristics that could be identified and placed against an appropriate curriculum was replaced with a perspective influenced by existential, phenomenological, and postmodern thought of the individual as a unique and undetermined agent who can only speak for him or herself in partial and autobiographical sharing. A sense of the earlier view is offered in *The 82nd Yearbook of the NSSE*, edited by Fenstermacher and Goodlad (1984). The contrast is Madeleine Grumet's autobiographical inquiries into the "currerre" and how a curriculum speaks to an individual (Grumet, 1988).

One of the major forces for effecting the change in thinking about how students and teachers create an individual curriculum from the events and relationships of life was the work of Ted Aoki and his colleagues and students at the University of Alberta. Terry Carson (1988) and Max van Manen (1986), influenced by the phenomenological thought of Martin Heidegger, M. J. Langeveld, M. Merleau-Ponty, and others, invoked the need to be mindful and attentive to singular educational acts in order to uncover their meaning for the student or for the teacher. Works by Chamberlin (1981) and Aoki, Carson, Favaro, and Berman (1984) contributed to the revised appreciation for students as individuals reading and finding meaning in lived experience. In a different way, the contribution of Beane and Lipka (1986), employing self-concept and self-esteem as lenses for reading curriculum, further redefined the "individualized curriculum." Noddings and Shore produced a work that explored the seldom studied realm of intuition in education (1984).

The identity of women in the school curriculum was not a widely articulated discourse in curriculum books until mid-decade. Aside from Abrams's work on women's studies for middle school (1981) and Parker's reflection on nonsexist curriculum development (1984), the National Association of Independent Schools published a resource book on the influence of gender on education (Chapman, 1988). These works, however, could not be classed as evoking a feminist understanding. It was Jane Roland Martin's *Reclaiming a Conversation* (1985) that marked an important advance in rethinking the traditional understanding of the educated woman. In this same year, Schuster and Van Dyne (1985) wrote on the feminization of the liberal arts curriculum, and Portuges and Culley edited a collection that was groundbreaking in the consideration of feminist teaching. By 1988, this discourse was better established. Works were produced on feminist thinking on the curriculum edited by Aiken, Anderson, Dinnerstein, Lensink, and MacCorquodale (1988), Belenky, Clinchy, Goldberg, and Tarule (1988), and Weiler (1988). Madeleine Grumet's *Bitter Milk* (1988) wove a personal tapestry about teaching and curriculum from the weft and warp of autobiographical and feminist studies. Nel Noddings assumed a variant posture on women's consciousness, consistent with her understanding of feminine morality. This was expressed in her 1989 volume on *Women and Evil*.

Understanding how gender influences the individual's reading of curriculum was accompanied by increased attention to culture and its impact on curriculum choices by schools and teachers, how culture shapes instruction, and how curriculum is read by students. Interest in influencing the school curriculum so that it addresses cultural diversity grew dramatically in the 1980s. Whereas earlier writing on the issues of race, ethnicity, and what is taught in public schools focused on issues of equal access to a common curriculum (e.g., Kirp, 1982), consideration of the kind of curriculum that is appropriate for the contemporary social order established a new direction. The work of James Banks is particularly noted as responsible for calling attention to this area of curriculum study and development. The proposal for a curriculum that is attentive to the many different cultures that constitute contemporary U.S. society was articulated first in his work on multiethnic education (1981) and was expanded to attend to issues of instruction in his 1987 work, *Teaching Strategies for Ethnic Studies*. Titles were also produced on this theme to address British (Lynch, 1983) and Australian (Bullivant, 1981) societies.

Two other significant voices in this aspect of curriculum thought were Christine Sleeter and Carl Grant (Sleeter & Grant, 1988). They established a framework for understanding options for enacting multicultural education in schools, ranging from providing compensatory education to assist students with entry into dominant culture, to a human relations approach to multicultural diversity, to their proposal that multicultural education be engaged as a curriculum for social reconstruction.

An alternative proposal argued that the development of positive cultural identity requires that the curriculum address the heritage of ethnic populations directly and positively. This idea was placed into practice in schools where the population was exclusively African American. Asante (1987) called for education that enabled pluralism without the hierarchy imposed by the dominating Anglo-Eurocentric curriculum. The idea of an Afrocentric curriculum drew attention and criticism in the popular media and was often misinterpreted. Other works that related to this conversation were books of readings edited by Craft and Bardell (1984) and by Weis (1988) on class, race, and gender.

As the ideas of the individual's relationship to curriculum took on new definitions in the 1980s, so did the notion of the teacher as a key agent of curriculum creation. A variety of works examined the influential role teachers assume in fashioning a curriculum. One aspect of how teachers relate to a curriculum is the study of what teachers do. Lieberman and Miller (1984) and Connell (1985) focused on the work of teachers and how it shaped curriculum; Davis examined teachers as curriculum evaluators (1980). Powell offered a reflection on teacher craft (1985), while Alan Tom's book on teaching as a moral craft (1984) provided a persuasive argument that teaching brings forward ethical qualities, decisions, and ultimately, responsibilities.

Teacher education and professional development were promoted as vehicles for implementing curriculum reform. The potential of preservice education was explored by Beyer, Feinberg, Pagano, and Whitson (1989). A volume edited by Nissen (1981) argued that how teachers were certified could be an instrument for educational change. Readings edited by Wideen and Andrews (1987) looked at staff development that focuses on the identity of the teacher.

In writing on the curriculum in the 1980s, there was growing acceptance of the notions that curriculum (1) is not limited to a school or a formal listing of academic content, (2) is individually expressed by teachers and students, and (3) is individually "read" or interpreted by teachers and students. Enthusiasm for "reflective practice" was inspired by two compatible approaches, both influenced by the deliberative process detailed by Dewey (1910). The emphasis on the practical by Joseph Schwab (1970) was extended in the research of F. Michael Connelly and Jean Clandinin (Connelly and Clandinin, 1988) and in Clandinin's (1986) examination of teacher self-image and its translation in practice. Their seminal work emphasized teachers' personal practical knowledge in problem solving. Elbaz (1983), another of Connelly's students, offered a study of how teachers solve problems and make professional decisions. Whereas the notion of reflection considered by Connelly, Clandinin, and Elbaz was structured with deliberation flowing into reform of practice, Donald Schön (1983) examined the ability of the reflective practitioner to think and act concurrently. Knowledge-in-action, the intelligent exercise of craft, is dynamic, situational, and not easily codified or reduced to recipe. Schön contended that the best approach to develop this ability to reflect on craft, to frame problems, consider solutions, act deliberately, and evaluate effect is to provide the novice with simulated and authentic teaching experiences (Schön, 1987). In a related contribution, Ashton and Webb (1986) posited a relationship between teacher self-perception of efficacy and student achievement. Schubert and Lopez Schubert (1982) edited a volume on curriculum knowledge as conceptualized by teachers and students, a precursor to later interests in "teacher lore" and "student lore." Teaching and teacher identity were also considered in the *88th Yearbook of the NSSE*, edited by Jackson and Haroutunian (1989). Part 1 of the *84th Yearbook of the NSSE* (Fantini & Sinclair, 1985) provided a look at education in non-school settings. Squires (1987) also examined curricula beyond the confines of schooling.

THE EXPANSION OF CURRICULUM RESEARCH

Establishing new discourses for thinking about the curriculum influenced research and evaluation. Leithwood's studies in curriculum decision making (1982), Barr and Dreeben's study of the dynamics of schooling (1983), and the case studies of Klausmeier, Serlin, and Zindler (1983) on how high school personnel used research for program improvement were consistent with curriculum research designed to improve existing practice. A volume edited by Philip Jackson (1988) provided an overview on the impact of current research on educational change. The growing support for qualitative research and for research that was focused on the dynamics of school practices gave rise to renewed interest in the work of Lawrence Stenhouse. An edited volume of Stenhouse's writings by Rudduck and Hopkins (1985) provided background on the dynamics of practical research. Carr and Kemmis (1986) argued for the value of critical action research. Milburn, Goodson, and Clark (1989) edited a volume that indicated the growing redirection of curriculum research, from assisting in the refining of practice to gaining critical and social understanding of curriculum.

The adoption of research models used in sociology provided another avenue for new kinds of inquiry on curricula. Hammersley and Hargreaves (1983) edited a volume of sociological case studies on curriculum practice. Another major sociological voice was Philip Wexler, with a work on the critical analysis of education (1987). Roth, Anderson, and Smith provided case studies in science teaching that employed a sociological framework (1986). Whitty (1985) furthered the argument for use of the tools of critical sociology for better understanding the curriculum.

Landon Beyer's study of curriculum research as influenced by critical theory and postmodern thought (1988), employing critical ethnography as an instrument of inquiry, provided a useful interpretation of these new directions in curriculum studies in the 1980s. Dalton's comparison of curriculum ideologies in two schools (1981) and of the relationship of ideology to curriculum innovation (1988) were among the first works to employ critical theory in curriculum research. Popkewitz, Tabachnick, and Wehlage (1982) contributed a study of educational reform; Everhart used the lens of critical reconstruction to examine junior high students and resistance (1983). Lois Weis (1985) and Linda McNeil (1986) provided two highly regarded research studies that employed critical reconstructionist perspectives. Such studies reveal much of the reality of contentions of critical theory.

The case study was also revised with an emphasis on artistry. Sarah Lightfoot established a research model that she labeled "portraiture." The book produced using this method, *The Good High School: Portraits of Character and Culture* (1983), was among the most widely read education books of the decade.

Research in curriculum history in the 1980s was of various kinds. A number of impressive large-scale studies of education and the curriculum in historical eras were produced. An emerging class of studies, promoted in particular by Ivor Goodson, focused on detailed descriptive analysis of particular institutions or academic subjects. There were a number of biographies, retrospectives, and papers collected from the meetings of learned societies.

Perhaps the two most ambitious efforts in historical scholarship on education in the decade were William Connell's *A History of Education in the Twentieth-Century World* (1980) and Lawrence Cremin's trilogy on *American Education* (*The Colonial Experience*) [1970]; *The National Experience* [1980]; *The Metropolitan Experience* [1988]). Connell presented a history that was more global in perspective than any work previously written, providing information and insight on education's evolutions. Cremin put American education in a broader context of educative institutions and relationship than schooling alone. *The National Experience* was awarded the Pulitzer Prize for history. The Cremin and Connell volumes are major resources for curriculum scholars in the 1980s and onward. Another important work was Larry Cuban's *How Teachers Taught* (1984), portraits of teaching throughout the century that evidenced the maintenance of standard academic subjects taught through recitation despite various efforts to reform curriculum and instruction. Cuban (1986) also contributed a related study on the use of technology by teachers in the classroom since the 1920s. Fraley's (1981) history of the limited impact of innovation on the dynamics of schooling was placed in contrast to the many bold institutional reforms offered throughout the century.

Three other works examined the formation of ideas about the curriculum for public schools in the United States in the twentieth century. Herbert Kliebard's *Struggle for the American Curriculum* (1986) established four major curriculum perspectives that have directed thought and action on curriculum in the United States in the twentieth century: humanist, social efficiency, developmental, and social meliorism. Barry Franklin (1986) offered an alternative framework for understanding thinking and writing on the curriculum, using contrasting notions of social control as his basis for categorization. A third categorization of curriculum thought in this century was provided by William Schubert and Ann Lopez Schubert in the first edition of *Curriculum Books* (1980), which identified three orientations to curriculum thought: intellectual traditionalist, social behaviorist, and experientialist.

There was marked growth in historical case study research of the curriculum of local institutions or specific subject matter. Ivor Goodson was especially prolific in creating works related to this type of curriculum history. He produced a volume on school subjects (Goodson, 1983), edited and shared editorship for volumes on the history of school subjects (Goodson, 1985; Goodson & Ball, 1984), edited a collection on international perspectives (Goodson, 1988a), and collected essays that argued for and demonstrated this form of scholarly research (Goodson, 1988b). A related work on the formation of school subjects was edited by Tom Popkewitz (1987).

Biographies of luminaries who influenced curriculum thought expanded historical understanding. Robert Bullough examined the life and ideas of Boyd Bode (1981), L. J. Dennis produced a critical study of the shared ideas and efforts of George Counts and Charles Beard (1989), and William Van Til's autobiographical reflection provided personal insight into the scholarly discussion that has taken place on curriculum for much of the twentieth century (1983). A collection of the writings of Ralph Tyler was edited by Madaus and

Stufflebeam (1989). There were also personal reflections on innovations in individual schools (Grant, 1988; Puckett, 1989; Lloyd, 1987).

The meetings of the Society for the Study of Curriculum History, founded in 1977 under the leadership of Laurel Tanner and with valuable support from Lawrence Cremin, O. L. Davis, Arthur Foshay, Arno Bellack, Hollis Caswell, Daniel Tanner, and others and first convened in Toronto a year later, extended historical scholarship and research agendas. Papers presented at these meetings were published throughout the decade (e.g., Tanner, 1981; Nelson, 1983; Jorgenson, Schubert, & Seguel, 1985; and Kridel, 1989). Histories of organizations that have been influential in providing forums for dialogues on the curriculum were published, specifically, Louise Berman's history of the early years of the World Council for Curriculum and Instruction (1982) and William Van Til's retrospective on the Association for Supervision and Curriculum Development (1986). Short, Willis, and Schubert (1985) produced a specialized history of the American Educational Research Association's Special Interest Group (SIG) on Creation and Utilization of Curriculum Knowledge.

A variety of topical histories complete this form of curriculum research: Wagner's discussion of the liberal arts in the middle ages (1983), Albisetti's examination of secondary school reform in imperial Germany (1983), and Monaghan's analysis of the influence of Webster's Blue-Back Speller (1983). Carl Kaestle's *Pillars of the Republic* (1983) is a scholarly overview of the growth of the common school in the United States. Travers's (1983) history of the impact of scholarly research on curriculum, instruction, and assessment in U.S. schools in the previous century was decidedly social behaviorist in its orientation.

Particular studies were contributed on aspects of twentieth-century education in the United States. Romberg looked at Wisconsin's individualized education (IGE) experiment (1985), Valentine analyzed the impact of the College Board on the school curriculum (1987), and Woolnough produced a history of physics teaching (1987). Other works were produced on Sunday schools (Boylan, 1988), the Welsh county intermediate school (Davies, 1989) and curriculum change in primary schools in the United States (Cunningham, 1988).

BUSINESS AS USUAL: CURRICULUM DEVELOPMENT

Despite the growing influence of critical reconstructionists and other writers who brought forth new languages in speaking about curriculum, works on curriculum development produced in the 1980s either as texts for university classrooms, as guides for school leaders, or as critical overviews of current options continued as the most widely published form for curriculum books. The incredibly large number of works produced relative to curriculum development requires further divisions. Books that provided an overview of curriculum development are distinguished from those that dealt specifically with issues of instruction or evaluation. Other books responded to the perceived needs of school practitioners, considering curriculum by ability groups, by age groups, or by academic discipline. Much of the scholarship on curriculum in other nations was influenced by the movement to national standards; this literature is reviewed. Finally, a separate consideration is given to synoptic texts that were produced in this decade.

Works on the planning, design, and implementation of a curriculum program are plentiful in the decade, either in new editions of standard works or in first entries. New editions of works by Posner and Rudnitsky, (1982, 1986), Print (1988), Unruh and Unruh (1984), and Brady (1983, 1987) were joined by a host of new entries (e.g., Allman, Kopp, & Zufelt, 1980; Armstrong, 1989; Bagnall, Recchia, & Robinson, 1980; Bellon & Handler, 1982; Brubaker, 1982; Cohen & Fraser, 1987; Ellis, Makey, & Glenn, 1987; Frey, 1982; Garnet, 1980, Glatthorn, 1980a, 1987b; Hass, 1980, 1983, 1987; Hunkins, 1980; Kelly, 1986; Pratt, 1980; Robinson and Hedges, 1982; Robinson, Ross, & White, 1985; Romiszowski, 1981; Skilbeck, 1984b; Wulf & Schave, 1984; Zenger & Zenger, 1983, 1986). There were also a number of collected essays that considered curriculum development, edited by Brandt (1988), Lawton (1986), Lee and Zeldin (1982), Leithwood (1986), Simkin and Simkin (1984), Skilbeck (1984c), and Soliman (1981).

Connelly, Dukacz, and Quinlan (1980) produced a work on curriculum planning at the classroom level, a topic that was also considered by Funkhouser, Beach, Ryan, and Fifer (1981), Rowntree (1981), and Carkhuff (1984). Specific dimensions of curriculum development were considered by Ron Brandt on curriculum implementation (1980), Wilcox and Eustace on the curriculum review process (1983), Anderson and Tomkins on how selection of materials influences curriculum development (1981), and Gall on the evaluation and selection of curriculum materials (1981). Rowntree (1985) reflected on the impact that educational technology has on the dynamics of curriculum development.

Instructional delivery as a component of curriculum development remained a popular topic. Madeline Hunter became the patron of effective instructional planning for many school administrators (Hunter, 1982). Another approach to instructional planning that retained its value in both teacher preparation and staff development was the models of teaching identified by

Joyce and Weil (1986), a scholarly classification of models of teaching as options for instruction. Related classifications of instruction were provided by Melton (1982) and Reigeluth (1983). Works were produced that served to guide educators in establishing an instructional system, including the revision of the volume by Gagne, Wager, and Briggs (1988) and new works by Dick and Carey (1985) and Romiszowski (1989). The construction of unit plans continued to be a mainstay of preservice teacher education. Books assisted aspiring educators in the writing of instructional objectives (Kibler, 1981; Pope, 1983) and designing the unit plan (Ogletree, 1983). Earl (1987) detailed the specifics of course design.

Evaluation of educational programs was undergoing the same transformation in the 1980s that educational research was experiencing, with growing acceptance of the value of qualitative inquiry methods as sources of knowledge and insight (e.g., Guba and Lincoln, 1981). Standard approaches to program evaluation described by Cronbach (1982) and Cronbach and associates (1980) were now joined with innovative models of evaluation (House, 1986). Elliot Eisner (1985b) introduced the dimension of "connoisseurship" to educational evaluation, redefining the case study as an examination of quality rooted in aesthetic criticism as well as in social inquiry.

A number of works examined contemporary options for curriculum evaluation (e.g., Boruch, Wortman, & Cordray, 1981; Fraser, 1981; Kemmis & Stake, 1988; McCormick & James, 1983; Norris & Sanger, 1984; Russell, Hughes, & McConachy, 1982). Books that served as collections of current thinking on curriculum evaluation were edited by Brandt (1981), Skilbeck (1984a), and Tamir (1984). Fraser collected a series of case studies in curriculum evaluation (1985). A related interest was in how student assessment could be more closely aligned to the curriculum to provide information on effectiveness (e.g., Bagnato, 1981; Hargis, 1987; Idol, 1986; Pelgrum, 1989). An elaborate annotated bibliography on curriculum evaluation assembled by Fraser and Houghton (1982) provided an overview of practices and theories in use at the outset of the decade. Davis (1980) localized the practice of curriculum evaluation, describing the teacher's role in this process.

Conventional school practices also perpetuated the structure of dividing students by ability and academic achievement. A variety of works were produced that offered guidance on curriculum planning for students with identified physical, cognitive, or behavioral challenges (e.g., Adams, 1980; Crawford, 1980; Ruxanoff, 1980; Teaching Research Infant and Child Center, 1980; Goldstein, 1981; Hinson & Hughes, 1981; Kissinger & Stewart, 1981; Popovich & Laham, 1981; Radabaugh & Yukish, 1982; Brennan, 1985; Ferguson, 1987; Solity & Bull 1987; Ford, Schnorr, Meyer, Davern, Black, &

Dempsey, 1989; and Center, 1989). Students identified as gifted were also given attention, with works by Maker (1982), Clendening and Davies (1983), Tuttle, Becker, and Sousa (1988), and Van Tassell-Baska, Feldhusen, Johnson, Seeley, and Silverman (1988). Jeter (1980) maintained the notion that all students have exceptionality and that the educational program must be individualized. The study of Cookson and Persell (1985) on the social and political influence of private boarding schools gave another meaning to a gifted curriculum as a preparation for elitism and privilege.

Curriculum development also gave attention to the commonplace division of children by age groups. A number of works were produced on early childhood curriculum design, organization, and assessment (e.g., Brown, 1982; Curtis, 1986; Day & Drake, 1983; Eliason & Jenkins, 1981, 1986; Fowler, 1980; Hendrick, 1980; Lombardo, 1983; Robison & Schwartz, 1982); Seefeldt edited a volume reviewing current research on the early childhood curriculum (1987). The curriculum of the kindergarten was given consideration with works by Regan and Harris (1980) and an edited volume by Spodek (1986) on the kindergarten curriculum.

Consideration of the curriculum for primary education was principally in the form of college texts for introductory methods classes (e.g., Blenkin, 1981; Blenkin and Kelly, 1987; Lemlech, 1984) or considerations of the primary curriculum in Great Britain (Blyth, 1984; Boyd, 1984; Campbell, 1985). Richards and Lofthouse (1985) conducted a book-length study of primary education.

The growth of the middle school as the preferred institution for young adolescents was responded to with several texts on curriculum design and implementation (e.g., Kindred, Wolotkiewicz, Michelson, & Coplein, 1981; Wiles & Bondi, 1981; Lounsbury, 1984). Derricott edited a volume on establishing curriculum atriculation between primary and secondary schools (1985).

Aside from Price's (1986) work on the secondary school curriculum in Great Britain, titles on secondary school curriculum produced in the decade were critical evaluations of the conventional high school in the United States. *The Shopping Mall High School* by Powell, Farrer, and Cohen (1985) contended that high schools were structured to serve only the most talented and most challenged students, leaving the remaining students with little by way of academic content or rigor. Their proposal for reform was consistent with the ideas promoted by Theodore Sizer and noted earlier. Other reform proposals were forwarded by Brown (1984) and Sedlak, Wheeler, Pullin, and Cusick (1986), with special emphasis on how high schools sell students short. Cusick (1983) also contributed a study on educational equity and the high school.

Texts on the college curriculum were also predominantly reform proposals. Aside from Miller's (1987) guide for course design; Bergquist, Gould, and Greenberg on the undergraduate curriculum (1981); and Levine's handbook on the undergraduate curriculum (1981), works included Dressel (1981) on the improvement of the college curriculum, Keller's description of curricular reform at Harvard (1982), and a volume edited by Hall and Kelvels on alternatives to the core curriculum (1981). Adult education or andragogy was given increased attention, with several works on curriculum development for this population (e.g., Griffin, 1983; Knowles, 1980; Knowles & Associates, 1984; Knox, 1986; and Langenbach, 1988).

Academic content standards for a national curriculum were already in place in other English-speaking nations. National curriculum development was established in the 1980s in Great Britain, Canada, Northern Ireland, and Australia. Responding to these national curricula was an important topic for curriculum writers in these countries. In England, works produced by academics, government agencies, committees, and councils detailed and suggested implementation strategies for the school curriculum, from form 5 through form 18 (Brockington, White, & Pring, 1983, 1985; Department of Education and Science, 1981; Northumberland Education Committee, 1982; Plunkett, 1983; Pring, 1987; Schools Councils, 1981). Other scholarship examined curriculum change in the 1970s (Galton, 1980) and school-based curriculum development (Eggleston, 1980; Saber, Rudduck, & Reid, 1987). Scholars researched the dynamics of the primary classroom in England (Galton, Simon, & Croll, 1980), or reflected on the core curriculum (Skilbeck, 1982). The national curriculum reform was also subject to evaluation studies (Kushner & Logan, 1984; Lawton, 1989).

In Canada, books were produced by Fullan and Park (1981) on curriculum implementation, by Anderson and Tompkins on the role of materials in curriculum development (1981), and by Robinson, White, and Ross (1983) on curriculum analysis. Babin provided historical context with a reflection on curriculum issues in Canada in the 1970s (1981), and a volume was edited by Milburn and Enns (1985) on the Canadian national curriculum.

Works by curriculum scholars in Australia were produced in the 1980s that were responsive to dimensions of governmental curriculum policies. Texts were published on the Australian core curriculum (ACDC, 1980), the core curriculum and values education (Yates, 1981), curriculum development specific to Australian schools (Cohen & Harrison, 1980; Marsh & Stafford, 1984; Rawlinson, 1982; Soliman, 1981), curriculum materials for social studies and mathematics (Marsh, Willis, Newby, Deschamp, & Davis, 1981), curriculum evaluation (Fraser, 1986; Russell et al., 1982), and curriculum development and evaluation relative to the Australian Science Education Project (Fraser & Cohen, 1987). Caldwell and Spinks (1986) produced a work that responded to the Tasmanian school curriculum. In Ireland and Northern Ireland, Mulcahy (1981) and Sutherland (1981; Sutherland, O'Shea, & McCartney, 1983) offered perspectives on primary and post-primary education. Kirk (1982) provided an overview of Scottish secondary schools.

Although the scope of this work is on curriculum books written in English, there are works that considered the curricula of non-English-speaking countries. The core curriculum was discussed as national policy in the Netherlands; contributions by Jozefzoon (1986), Jozefzoon and Gorter (1985), Gorter (1986), and van Bruggen (1985) examined policies and practices. Salia-Bao (1989) produced a book on the relationship between curriculum development and African culture; Onwuka (1981) edited a work on curriculum development for African nations; and Hunter, Ashley, and Millar produced a work on South African curriculum (1983).

The responsibilities of school administrators in managing the curriculum for school districts and the topics related to this task remained a viable category for curriculum books. Fenwick English was perhaps the most recognized author relative to curriculum management and alignment, producing texts for use in educational adminstration courses and guides for practitioners (English, 1980, 1983, 1987, 1988). Another popular title for use in teaching curriculum to educational leaders was Alan Glatthorn's overview of curriculum leadership (1987a). Other works on curriculum management were produced by Bradley (1985), Pajak (1989), and Preedy (1989). Westmeyer (1981) produced a guide for curriculum planning at the school or district level. Musgrave (1985), Print (1986), and Walker (1987) offered perspectives on the administration of the curriculum from an Australian perspective. Other titles of related interest to administrators responsible for curriculum development and management were the NASSP volume on curriculum reduction (1982), an NASSP Curriculum Council report on the role of the principal in curriculum improvement (Tanner & Keefe, 1988), Butterworth's report on staffing and curriculum needs for English schools (1983), Weinstein's guide to the techniques of curriculum mapping (1986), and a volume edited by Martin, Glatthorn, Winters, and Saif on curriculum leadership (1989).

Synoptic curriculum texts remained a popular forum for summarizing contemporary trends, issues, and thinking. In addition to revisions of existing texts, new volumes and edited anthologies of readings provide further evidence that the traditional or institutional (see Pinar, Reynolds, Slattery, & Taubman, 1995) view of curriculum study remained in full strength in the decade. New editions were produced of curiculum texts by Tanner and Tanner (1980), with continued emphasis on curriculum history and other issues in social foundations set in an issue context. The final edition of Saylor, Alexander, and Lewis (1981) was published. In contrast to Tanner and Tanner, Saylor, Alexander, and Lewis limit their focus on history and contemporary issues and emphasize development; the work employed Tyler's design but maintained currency with scholarship in the field and integrated this through guidelines for curriculum practice.

Another final entry in a long-enduring synoptic title was Shepherd and Ragan's *Modern Elementary Curriculum* (1982). Consideration was given to the variables that construct the existing school institution. These included environments (children, the organizational patterns of the school, curriculum settings, deliveries, and strategies) and a consideration of each of the subject areas and foundational perspectives (history, sociology, and current and future trends). Doll's *Curriculum Improvement: Decision Making and Process* was revised twice (1982, 1986) in its fifth and sixth editions. The volume begins with an extensive consideration of options within the elements of curriculum development outlined by Tyler; the second half of the book details a process for curriculum change.

J. D. McNeil's original 1977 text was revised and updated in 1981 and again in 1985, organizing curriculum orientations into categories compatible with Eisner's orientations: humanist, social reconstructionist, technology, and academic subjects. The second part of McNeil's book centered on dimensions of curriculum development: learning opportunities; management; implementation; evaluation; and politics, theory, and research (McNeil, 1981, 1985).

A number of new synoptic treatments of the curriculum were produced in the 1980s. Some served primarily as handbooks for curriculum development but included an overview of current curriculum thought. Peter Oliva's (1982, 1988) *Developing the Curriculum* was designed to respond to the professional needs of school administrators with curricular responsibilities. The structure of the work is itself a model of social behaviorist curriculum construction; each chapter opens with stated cognitive objectives and there is an appendix of exit competencies. The book is divided into four parts. The introduction to the field is directed to practice, with a consideration of theory that settles into a practical, institutional understanding of the field and defines the roles of personnel in curriculum development. The second part of the work considers the political dimensions of curriculum development and how the various stakeholders in the school interact in the planning of a curriculum. The model for curriculum development provided by Oliva is set in comparison with other contemporary designs (Tyler, Taba, Saylor, and Alexander). Oliva adapts various aspects of these designs in proposing a 12-step process of development divided into a planning phase (steps 1–4 and 6–9 in his design), a planning and operational phase to indicate that the development is concurrent with and informed by implementation (step 5), and an operational phase (steps 10–12). The balance of Part 3 of the text explains this model in detail. The planning phase consists of (1) a statement of aims and philosophy, (2) a needs assessment of students, the community, and subject matter, (3) the specifying of curriculum goals, which are then (4) translated to specific curriculum objectives for a group of students, (6) further refined to instructional goals, and (7) instructional objectives for individual student achievement. (8) Instructional strategies are selected to achieve the objective and outcomes and (9) the evaluation system is sketched out. The final components are (10) the implementation of the selected strategies and (11–12) conducting the evaluation of student and group achievement. The text concludes with a look at continuing and current problems that curriculum developers will face, and common artifacts used in planning.

Allan Glatthorn's *Curriculum Leadership* (1987a) is as much a work to guide the practice of a school administrator responsible for curriculum as it is a synoptic view of the field. Nonetheless, the consideration of the foundational issues at the beginning of the text have a synoptic character, with the balance of the text given over to curriculum development, administration issues, and contemporary trends.

Beane, Toepfer, and Alessi (1986) focused principally on curriculum planning and development, using the institutional structure of U.S. schools to present a framework for curriculum planning. However, a large portion of the text is devoted to providing an understanding of curriculum foundations. Similarly, *The School Curriculum* by Arthur Ellis, James Mackey, and Allen Glenn (1988) was oriented primarily toward social and political issues that impact on curriculum and instructional planning rather than curriculum development. The authors argued that curriculum is an important dimension of public policy determined by three competing social values: efficiency (students as acceptable social product), equality of opportunity, and freedom of choice. Contemporary issues that reflect the tension over values provide a real-life approach to thinking about the curriculum. The teacher is portrayed as the central character in this social drama. The text walks the reader through lesson planning and concludes with a look at emerging educational concerns.

Works by David Pratt (1980) from Queen's College in Ontario and Murray Print (1986, 1988) from Western Australia also maintained this practical orientation responsive to the institutional demands of their home countries. Pratt's approach, while providing historical perspective and an awareness of contemporary conversations in curriculum theory, relies on a social behaviorist model to guide practitioners in the design of a school curriculum. Defending the need for systematic procedure as a necessary component of artistry, Pratt details a specific process in curriculum, a curriculum based on client identification to meet their present and projected needs. These needs are recognized by application of Abraham Maslow's needs hierarchy (self-actualization, meaning, social needs, aesthetic needs, and survival needs) and by specific needs assessment of stakeholders in the education of the specified learners. Pratt instructs the reader on how to organize personnel and resources to conduct the development of a curriculum. With this background information in place, the construction of the curriculum takes place with the identification of aims and objectives, the specification of criteria of successful performance, and identification of the tests that will be employed to determine student achievement of objectives. Instruction begins with diagnosis of the knowledge and skill level of students as a determinant of approaches. Pratt contends that instruction is not a central concern of the curriculum developer; it being the responsibility of the teacher to find methods best suited to attain the stated objectives. To implement the curriculum, Pratt suggests a cycle of piloting and field testing using multiple data sources to gain information for adaptation and refinement of the curriculum plan.

Print's work is also primarily a guide for curriculum development. A brief explanation of contemporary options in curriculum development is explained as being rational (Tyler and Taba), cyclical (Nicholls), or dynamic (Walker and Skilbeck). Print contends that he has developed an eclectic approach that combines elements of all these. He employs the basic structure of the Tyler rationale with an expansion of deliberation on purpose and the setting of the process in the context of curriculum "presage," or self-study, of the dispositions in place in the construction of the curriculum and notions on extending evaluation to provide feedback for modification.

Colin Marsh's contribution (1986) includes details of particular interest to Australian school people, but his skill in interpreting curriculum development models and contemporary curriculum theory made this work of international significance. Marsh approached curriculum as including planning, implementation, and evaluation. He provided four alternative orientations to curriculum (social interaction, personal development, information processing, and behavior modification) and promoted an eclectic conciliation among these alternatives. In looking at models of development, Marsh described Tyler's construct, Goodlad's emphasis on values at different levels of planning, Stenhouse's alternative teacher-centered approach to planning, and Huberman's descriptive model. Marsh also detailed the specific step-by-step approaches, labeled as "curriculum algorithms," of Decker Walker, Malcolm Skilbeck, and George Posner. Marsh writes at length on curriculum implementation with specific examples of curriculum reform and change models and strategies. Proposals for curriculum evaluation by Ralph Tyler and Robert Stake are joined by the contributions of Parlett, Hamilton, and Eisner. The concluding chapters are interesting scholarly interpretations of historical developments in curriculum and curriculum theorizing in the twentieth century.

Included among the works that focused primarily on providing an understanding of contemporary thinking on curriculum was John Miller's *The Educational Spectrum: Orientations to Curriculum* (1983). Miller categorized thinking on the curriculum into approaches that were behavioral, subject discipline, social, developmental, cognitive-process, humanistic, and transpersonal. Miller and Seller's *Curriculum, Perspectives and Practice* (1985) expanded on these orientations to the curriculum, classifying them according to their intent for transmission, transaction, or transformation of the individual. Miller and Seller then applied the perspective options to specific curriculum scholars, indicating how the goals of education are affected by their orientation.

Wiles and Bondi (1984) produced one of several books in the decade that elected to use words beginning with "p" to describe the organization of their text (Apple and Beyer, 1988; Brady, 1983; Schubert, 1986). The first section of the work, *perspectives*, reflected on defining the field, historical foundations, and the contribution of educational philosophy. The *procedures* section was an elaboration on components of the Tyler rationale. *Practices* were divided by the levels of U.S. schools. *Prospectives* considered politics, policies, and alternatives for the future.

Ornstein and Hunkins (1987) produced a general introduction to curriculum thought that was organized around curriculum foundations (philosophy, history, psychology, and sociology) and included an extended discussion of approaches within the Tyler rationale in the second part of the text.

A number of edited books of readings were also published that provided a synoptic view of the field. Gress and Purpel (1988) updated their 1978 volume with an edition that provided an effective overview of scholarship relative to the curriculum in the 1980s. Essays are organized around the topics of defining the field, alternative frameworks for organizing the curriculum, the planning and design of the formal school curriculum, the dimensions of the hidden curriculum, curriculum implementation, evaluation and curriculum change, and theory and research orientations. Landon Beyer and Michael Apple's *The Curriculum: Problems, Politics, and Possibilities* (1988) was a collection of essays produced specifically for this volume that considered contemporary topics relevant to curriculum study. The orientation of the editors to social change and critical analysis of the school is evident in the topics and the invited authorship. Consideration is given to curriculum history, present school practices, curriculum planning, the selection of knowledge, the role of the teacher in curriculum planning, technology's impact on curriculum, and evaluation.

Glen Hass produced three versions of a book of readings on curriculum thought (1980, 1983, 1987). The readings are introduced with substantial contextual passages that establish a synoptic context of comparison. The topics include a consideration of alternative orientations for establishing a curriculum in values, social needs, the dynamics of learning, and child development, and then the book translates this foundation to the various institutional age groupings of students.

Since the second decade of the twenieth century, each chapter's review of the curriculum literature has concluded with a look at a work that proved very influential in directing the future of curriculum literature and educational study at large. In Chapter Three, the *Cardinal Principles* were offered as an expanded vision of secondary education as well as a reconciliation of the competing curriculum orientations developed over the preceding 20 years (intellectual traditionalist, social behaviorist, and experientialist). In the 1920s, *Part II of the Twenty-sixth Yearbook of the National Society for the Study of Education* chronicled the unsuccessful effort to find a common direction for curriculum studies. Hollis Caswell and Doak Campbell's *Curriculum Development* (1935), the first synoptic text, invented a new way of writing about the curriculum field and of preparing curriculum specialists. The decade of World War II and reconstruction was closed with a discussion of Ralph Tyler's (1949) enduring questions in the developing of curriculum and instruction. The response to the Cold War and *Sputnik* provided in James Bryant Conant's *The American High School Today* (1959) blueprinted the kinds of high schools the "baby boomers" would live and learn in. A decade of change was symbolized in the close of the reflection on the 1960s by celebrating the variety of first-person reflections on the personal construction of curriculum with learners, in the neoprogressive accounts of Ashton-Warner, Dennison, Glasser, Herdon, Holt, Kohl, Postman and Weingartner, and others, along with Joseph Schwab's invitation to reorient curriculum study to the practical. The final reflection of the 1970s was the variety of directions that the synoptic texts and curriculum readers were taking in the decade. It was becoming evident as the first edition of this work was produced that the curriculum field was finding it more difficult to locate a single work or genre that offered direction for curriculum in the 1980s. This led some to the perception that curriculum studies were "balkanizing" into conflicting camps.

While it is a temptation to look to the work of any of the various new and important voices in curriculum thought (e.g., Michael Apple, Henry Giroux, William Pinar, Max van Manen, Madeleine Grumet) as setting a direction for the 1990s, it would be a historical distortion to offer any single work as a culmination of the decade. Instead, three works are commended to the reader that, while all offering a conceptualization of curriculum scholarship in the decade, are different in style and content. All three texts were cited by the professors of curriculum as being among the 10 most influential of contemporary textbooks in curriculum (see Behar, 1994). By placing them against each other, one gains an appreciation for what occurred in this decade of transitions in scholarship, for each represents a striving to capture salient essences of the state of curriculum studies. Each attempted to be synoptic.

Elliot Eisner's revision of *The Educational Imagination* (1985c) posited a contemporary understanding of the curriculum field placed in a historical context and restated five orientations to curriculum: as cognitive processes, academic rationalism, personal relevance, social adaptation and reconstruction, and curriculum as technology. Eisner's revision of *The Educational Imagination* provided an insight into how scholarship was opening to new identities and directions while working within the recognizable school framework established in the previous decade. William Pinar's *Contemporary Curriculum Discourses* (1988) challenged the reader to consider the many new ways that curriculum was being "read" by employing discourses adopted and adapted from various social and scholarly communities. The text includes scholarly essays written on the theory/practice/experience hermeneutics in curriculum as well as from the language forms of historical inquiry, political analysis, aesthetic criticism, phenomenology, and feminist consciousness and scholarship.

William Schubert's *Curriculum: Perspective, Paradigm, and Possibility* (1986) was an effort to construct an interpretive portrait of curriculum scholarship in the decade. In Behar's study, Schubert's book was noted as a book of contemporary influence by 25.5% of the professors of curriculum surveyed (Tanner and Tanner's *Curriculum Development* was second in frequency at 17.8%). Providing an overview of where curriculum thought had been, analysis of current alternatives for curriculum inquiry and a consideration of future directions, *Curriculum: Perspective, Paradigm, and Possibility* expanded on the curriculum orientations Schubert had established in *Curriculum Books* (Schubert & Lopez Schubert, 1980): the intellectual traditionalist, the social behaviorist, and the experientialist. Employing these perspectives as discussants throughout his text, Schubert provided a view of how the contemporary field was developed from history, philosophy, and policy; described three paradigms of contemporary curriculum inquiry (empirical analytic, hermeneutic/practical, and critical praxis); and reflected on curriculum issues, trends, and applications to professional development. According to Pinar et al. (1995), *Curriculum: Perspective, Paradigm, and Possibility* is the first synoptic text to fully integrate into conversations about curriculum purpose, organization, instruction, assessment, and inquiry the contributions of critical reconstructionists and other writers who were thinking outside the conventions of curriculum development for schools, including those sometimes placed under the reconceptualist umbrella.

Professors of education and their graduate students were reading these and myriad other works, creating, responding to, or in some cases, renouncing the new directions indicated in the texts by Eisner, Pinar, and Schubert. This novel scholarship did not, however, supplant the long-standing practical labors of curriculum development that had been ongoing from the previous generation. While there was a national debate that was closely watched by the public, it was about how big the stakes should be for large-scale assessment and what content standards should look like. Intellectual traditionalists had moved comfortably into deliberation on disciplinary standards, and social behaviorists drifted out of curriculum development into assessment development. Experientialists assumed their traditional role as policy and practice critics; the debate within the field about the countenance of curriculum study was overshadowed in many school-based circles. That is to say that the debate over what constitutes meaningful curriculum study was provocative, profound, and productive, but this debate had limited influence on school practices in the next decade.

BIBLIOGRAPHY OF CURRICULUM BOOKS 1980–1989

1980

Abbs, P. (1980). *Reclamations: Essays on mass culture and the curriculum*. Exeter, NH: Heinemann Educational Books. (Previous edition: 1979 by Heinemann, London).

Adams, J. L. (1980). *An education curriculum for the moderately, severely, and profoundly mentally handicapped pupil*. Springfield, IL: Charles C. Thomas.

Al-Afendi, M. H., & Baloch, N. A. (1980). *Curriculum and teacher education*. Islamic Education Series. London: Hodder and Stoughton.

Allman, S. A., Kopp. O. W., & Zufelt, D. L. (1980). *Curriculum development: A reflection of programmatic trends*. Boston: American Press.

Annarino, A. A., Cowell, C. C., & Hazelton, H. W. (1980). *Curriculum theory and design in physical education*. St. Louis, MO: Mosby.

Aoki, T. T. (1980). *Toward a curriculum inquiry in a new key*. Edmonton, Alberta: Department of Secondary Education, University of Alberta.

Australian Curriculum Development Centre (ACDC). (1980). *Core curriculum for Australian schools*. Canberra, Australia: Author.

Bagnall, R. D., Recchia, M. A., & Robinson, Y. (1980). *The basis of the curriculum: Theory and development*. Lake Grove, NY: Distributed by CurrDelCo.

Bantock, G. H. (1980). *Dilemmas of the curriculum*. London: Halstead Press.

Biological Science Curriculum Study (BSCS). (1980). *Biological science: An inquiry into life*, (fourth edition). New York: Harcourt Brace Jovanovich.

Brandt, R. S. (Ed.). (1980). *Curriculum implementation*. Washington, DC: Association for Supervision and Curriculum Development.

Butts, R. F. (1980). *The revival of civic learning: A rationale for citizenship education in American schools*. Bloomington, IN: Phi Delta Kappa.

Campbell, D. E. (1980). *Education for a democratic society: Curriculum ideas for teachers*. Cambridge, MA: Schenkman Publishing Company.

Cohen, D., & Harrison, M. (Eds.). (1980). *Curriculum developments in Australia: Descriptive profiles*. Canberra, Australia: Curriculum Development Centre. (Second printing 1985).

Comer, J. P. (1980). *School power: Implications of an intervention project*. New York: The Free Press.

Connell, W. F. (1980). *A history of education in the twentieth-century world*. New York: Teachers College Press and the Curriculum Development Centre of Australia.

Connelly, F. M., Dukacz, A. S., & Quinlan, F. (Eds.). (1980). *Curriculum planning for the classroom*. Toronto: Ontario Institute for Studies in Education.

Courtney, R. (1980). *The dramatic curriculum*. New York: Drama Book Specialists; Toronto: The Ontario Institute for Studies in Education.

Crawford, N. B. (1980). *Curriculum planning for the educationally subnormal child: Workshop proceedings*. Kidderminster, Worcshester, England: British Institute of Mental Handicap.

Cremin, L. (1980). *American education: The national experience, 1783–1876*. New York: Harper and Row.

Cronbach, L. J., & Associates. (1980). *Toward reform of program evaluation: Aims, methods and institutional arrangements*. San Francisco: Jossey-Bass.

Curriculum Development Centre of Australia. (1980). *Core curriculum for Australian schools*. Canberra, Australia: Author.

Davis, E. (1980). *Teachers as curriculum evaluators*. Sydney, Australia: Allen & Unwin.

Dove, L. A. (1980). *Curriculum reform in secondary schools: A Commonwealth survey*. London: Commonwealth Secretariat.

Dressel, P. L. (1980). *Improving degree programs: A guide to curriculum development, administration, and review*. San Francisco: Jossey-Bass.

Dukacz, A. S., & Quinlan, F. (Eds.). (1980). *Curriculum planning for the classroom*. Toronto: Ontario Institute for Studies in Education.

Eggleston, J. (Ed.). (1980). *School-based curriculum development in Britain: A collection of case studies*. London; Boston: Routledge and Kegan Paul.

English, F. W. (1980). *Improving curriculum management in the schools*. Washington, DC: Council for Basic Education.

Fisher, S., in collaboration with F. Magee & J. Wetz. (Ed.). (1980). *"Ideas into action": Curriculum for a changing world*. London: One World Trust.

Fitzgerald, F. (1980). *America revised: History schoolbooks in the twentieth century*. New York: Random House.

Foshay, A. W. (Ed.). (1980a). *Considered action for curriculum improvement*. Alexandria, VA: Association for Supervision and Curriculum Development.

Foshay, A. W. (Ed.). (1980b). *Curriculum development: A guide to effective practice*. Alexandria, VA: Association for Supervision and Curriculum Development.

Fowler, W. (1980). *Curriculum and assessment guides for infant and child care*. Boston: Allyn & Bacon.

Frazier, A. (1980). *Values, curriculum, and the elementary school*. Boston: Houghton Mifflin.

Galton, M. (Ed.). (1980). *Curriculum change: The lessons of a decade*. Leicester, England: Leicester University Press.

Galton, M., Simon, B., & Croll, P. (1980). *Inside the primary classroom*. London: Routledge and Kegan Paul.

Garnet, A. E. (1980). *Curriculum for better schools*. Dubuque, IA: Kendall/Hunt.

Gillespie, J. (1980). *Media resources in curriculum development*. Glasgow, Scotland: Scottish Council for Educational Technology.

Giroux, H., Penna, A., & Pinar, W. (Eds.) (1980). *Introduction to curriculum*. Berkeley, CA: McCutchan.

Glatthorn, A. A. (1980a). *Curriculum development and reform: A practical resource*. Urbana, IL: National Council of Teachers of English.

Glatthorn, A. A. (1980b). *A guide for developing an English curriculum for the eighties*. Urbana, IL: National Council of Teachers of English.

Great Britain Department of Education and Science. (1980). *A view of the curriculum*. HMI Series: Matters for Discussion No. 11, HMSO.

Haas, J. D. (1980). *Future studies in the K–12 curriculum.* Boulder, CO: Social Science Education Consortium, Inc.

Hass, G. (1980). *Curriculum planning: A new approach* (third edition). Boston: Allyn & Bacon.

Hendrick, J. (1980). *Total learning for the whole child: Holistic curriculum for children ages 2–5.* St. Louis, MO: Mosby.

Holt, M. (1980). *The common curriculum: Its structure and style in the comprehensive school.* London: Routledge and Kegan Paul.

Holt, M. (1980). *Schools and curriculum change.* New York: McGraw-Hill.

Hunkins, F. P. (1980). *Curriculum development: Program improvement.* Columbus, OH: Charles E. Merrill.

Jeter, J. (Ed.). (1980). *Approaches to individualized education.* Alexandria, VA: Association for Supervision and Curriculum Development.

Joint Committee on Standards for Educational Evaluation (Daniel L. Stufflebeam, Director). (1980). *Standards for evaluation of educational programs, policies, and materials.* Hightstown, NJ: McGraw-Hill.

Joyce, B., & Weil, M. (1980). *Models of teaching* (second edition). Englewood Cliffs, NJ: Prentice-Hall. (Previous edition, 1972).

Kelly, A. V. (Ed). (1980). *Curriculum context.* London: Harper and Row.

Knowles, M. S. (1980). *The modern practice of adult education: From pedagogy to andragogy.* New York: Follett.

Lawton, D. (1980). *The politics of the school curriculum.* London: Routledge and Kegan Paul.

Mandel, B. J. (1980). *Three language-arts curriculum models: Pre-kindergarten through college.* Urbana, IL: National Council of Teachers of English.

Marsh, C. J. (1980). *Curriculum process in the primary school.* Sydney, Australia: Ian Novak Publishing Co.

Mayberry, C. (Ed.). (1980). *Urban education: The city as a living curriculum.* Washington, DC: Association for Supervision and Curriculum Development.

Munby, H., Orpwood, G., & Russell, T. (Eds.). (1980). *Seeing curriculum in a new light: Essays from science education.* Toronto: Ontario Institute for Studies in Education.

Ogilvie, E. (1980). *The Schools Council curriculum enrichment project.* London: Schools Council.

Ogletree, E. J., Gebauer, P., & Ujlaki, V. E. (1980). *The unit plan: A plan for curriculum organizing and teaching.* Lanham, MD: University Press of America.

Pain, L., & Tollifson, J. (Eds.). (1980). *What's an art curriculum for, anyway?* Columbus, OH: Department of Education.

Pappert, S. (1980). *Mindstorms: Children, computers, and powerful ideas.* New York: Basic Books, Inc.

Pinar, W. F. (1980). Life history and educational experience. *The Journal of Curriculum Theorizing*, 2(2), 159–212.

Poole, M. (1980). *Creativity across the curriculum*. Sydney, Australia: Allen & Unwin.

Pratt, D. (1980). *Curriculum design and development*. New York: Harcourt, Brace, Jovanovich.

Regan, E., & Harris, M. (1980). *To learn/to think: Curriculum materials for the kindergarten*. Toronto: The Ontario Institute for Studies in Education.

Robertson, I. (1980). *Language across the curriculum: Four case studies*. Schools Council Working Paper 78. New York: Methuen Education.

Rosen, B., & Caplan, A. L. (1980). *Ethics in the undergraduate curriculum*. New York: The Hastings Center.

Ruxanoff, L. A. (1980). *A curriculum model for individuals with severe learning and behavior disorders*. Baltimore: University Park Press.

Schubert, W. H., & Lopez Schubert, A. L. (1980). *Curriculum books: The first eighty years*. Lanham, MD: University Press of America.

Sharp, R. (1980). *Knowledge, ideology and the politics of schooling: Towards a Marxist analysis of education*. London: Routledge.

Shor, I. (1980). *Critical teaching and everyday life*. Boston: South End Press.

Stenhouse, L. (Ed.). (1980). *Curriculum research and development in action*. London: Heinemann.

Tanner, D., & Tanner, L. N. (1980). *Curriculum develoment: Theory into practice*. New York: Macmillan. (Previous edition: 1975).

Teaching Research Infant and Child Center. (1980). *The teaching research curriculum for moderately and severely handicapped: Gross and fine motor*. Springfield, IL: Charles Thomas.

Tronick, E., & Greenfield, P. M. (1980). *Infant curriculum: The Broomley Heath guide to the care of infants in groups* (Revised edition). Santa Monica, CA: Goodyear Publishing Company.

Tuttle, F. B., & Becker, L. A. (1980). *Program design and development for gifted and talented students*. Washington, DC: National Education Association.

Verduin, J. R., Jr. (1980). *Curriculum building for adult learning*. Carbondale: Southern Illinois Press.

Westbury, I., & Wilkof, N. J. (Eds.). (1980). *Science, curriculum and liberal education: Selected essays Joseph J. Schwab*. Chicago: University of Chicago Press.

Woodbury, M. (1980). *Selecting materials for instruction* (in three volumes): *Issues and policies, Media and the curriculum*; and *Subject matter areas and implementation*. Littleton, CO: Libraries Unlimited, Inc.

Wootton, L. R., Reynolds, J. C., Jr., & Gifford, C. S. (Eds.). (1980). *Trends and issues affecting curriculum: Programs and practices*. Lanham, MD: University Press of America.

1981

Abrams, E. (1981). *A curriculum guide to women's studies for the middle school: Grades 5–9*. Old Westbury, NY: Feminist Press.

Anderson, D. C. (1981). *Evaluating curriculum proposals: A critical guide*. London: Croom Helm.

Anderson, R., & Tompkins, G. (Eds.). (1981). *Understanding materials: The role of materials in curriculum development*. Vancouver, British Columbia: Center for the Study of Curriculum and Instruction.

Association for Supervision and Curriculum Development. (1981). *Staff development: Organization development* (B. Dillon-Peterson, Editor). 1981 Yearbook. Washington, DC: Author.

Babin, P. (1981). *Canadian curriculum issues in perspective (1970–1980)*. Ottawa, Ontario: University of Ottawa Press.

Bagnato, S. J. (1981). *Linking developmental assessment and curricula*. Rockville, MD: Aspen Systems Corporation.

Bank, A., Henderson, M., & Eu, L. (1981). *A practical guide to program planning: A teaching models approach*. New York: Teachers College Press.

Banks, J. (1981). *Multiethnic education: Theory and practice*. Boston: Allyn & Bacon.

Barrow, R. (1981). *Educational and curriculum theory*. Vancouver, British Columbia, Canada: University of British Columbia.

Barton, L., Meighan, R., & Walker, S. (Eds.). (1981). *Schooling, ideology and the curriculum*. London: Falmer Press.

Barton, L., & Walker, S. (Eds.). (1981). *Schools, teachers, and teaching*. London, England: Falmer.

Beauchamp, G. A. (1981). *Curriculum theory* (fourth edition). Itasca, IL: F. E. Peacock Publishers. (Previous editions: 1975, 1968, 1961 by Kagg Press, Wilmette, IL)

Beckett, L. (1981). *Maintaining choice in the secondary curricula: Report of an investigation into the problems caused by falling rolls*. London: Center for Educational Technology.

Bergquist, W. H., Gould, R. A. & Greenberg, E. M. (1981). *Designing undergraduate education: A systematic guide*. San Francisco: Jossey-Bass.

Berlak, A., & Berlak, H. (1981). *Dilemmas of schooling: Teaching and social change*. London: Methuen.

Blenkin, G. M. (1981). *The primary curriculum*. New York: Harper and Row.

Bloom, B. S. (1981). *All our children learning: A primer for parents, teachers, and other educators*. New York: McGraw-Hill.

Boruch, R. F., Wortman, P. M., & Cordray, D. S. (1981). *Reanalyzing program evaluation*. San Francisco: Jossey-Bass.

Boyer, E. L., & Levine, A. (1981). *A quest for common learning: The aims of general education*. Washington, DC: Carnegie Foundation for the Advancement of Teaching.

Boyle, P. G. (1981). *Planning better programs*. New York: McGraw-Hill.

Brandt, R. S. (Ed.). (1981). *Applied strategies for curriculum evaluation*. Alexandria, VA: Association for Supervision and Curriculum Development.

Broudy, H. S. (1981). *Truth and credibility: The citizen's dilemma*. New York: Longman.

Bullivant, B. (1981). *Race, ethnicity and curriculum*. Melbourne, Australia: Macmillan.

Bullough, R. V. (1981). *Democracy in education: Boyd H. Bode*. Bayside, NY: General Hall.

Bullough, R. V., Goldstein, S., & Holt, L. (1981). *Human interests in the curriculum: Teaching and learning in a technological society*. New York: Teachers College Press.

Chamberlin, J. G. (1981). *The education act: A phenomenological view*. Lanham, MD: University Press of America.

Christensen, J. E. (1981). *Curriculum, education, and educology*. Sydney, Australia: Educology Research Associates.

Clark, C. M., & Elmore, J. L. (1981). *Transforming curriculum in mathematics, science, and writing: A case-study of teacher yearly planning*. East Lansing: Michigan State University Institute for Research on Teaching.

Coleman, J. S. (1981). *Public and private schools*. Washington, DC: National Center for Educational Statistics.

Colson, H. P., & Rigdon, R. M. (1981). *Understanding your church's curriculum*. (Revised edition). Nashville, TN: Broadman Press.

Dalton, T. (1981). *The challenge of curriculum change: A study of curriculum ideologies and practice in two secondary schools*. London: Falmer Press.

Davis, E. (1981). *Teachers as curriculum evaluators*. (Classroom and Curriculum in Australia Series, No. 4). London: Allen and Unwin.

Department of Education and Science. (1981). *Curriculum 11-16: A review of progress*. London: HMSO.

Dressel, P. (1981). *Guide to curriculum development: "Improving Degree Programmes."* San Francisco: Jossey-Bass.

Edinger, L. V., Houts, P. L., & Meyer, D. V. (Eds.). (1981). *Education in the 80s: Curricular challenges*. Washington, DC: National Education Association.

Eliason, C. F., & Jenkins, L. R. (1981). *A practical guide to early childhood curriculum* (second edition). St. Louis, MO: C. V. Mosby.

Eraut, M., Connors, B., & Hewton, E. (1981). *Training in curriculum development and educational technology*. Windsor, England: NFER-Nelson.

Fraley, A. E. (1981). *Schooling and innovation: The rhetoric and the reality.* New York: Tyler Gibson.

Fraser, B. J. (1981). *Learning environment in curriculum evaluation: A review. Evaluation in Education Series.* London: Pergamon.

Fullan, M., & Park, P. (1981). *Curriculum implementation: A resource booklet.* Toronto: Ontario Ministry of Education Publication.

Funkhouser, C. W., Beach, D. M., Ryan, G. T., & Fifer, F. L. (1981). *Classroom applications of the curriculum: A systems approach.* Dubuque, IA: Kendall-Hunt.

Gall, M. D. (1981). *Handbook for evaluating and selecting curriculum materials.* Boston; Allyn & Bacon.

Giles, H. H., & McCutchen, S. P. (1981). *Exploring the curriculum.* Norwood, PA: Telegraph Books. (Reprint of 1942 Edition).

Giroux, H. A. (1981). *Ideology, culture, and the process of schooling.* Philadelphia: Temple University Press.

Giroux, H. A., Penna, A. N., & Pinar, W. F. (Eds.). (1981). *Curriculum and instruction: Alternatives in education.* Berkeley, CA: McCutchan.

Goldstein, H. (Ed). (1981). *Curriculum development for exceptional children.* San Francisco: Jossey-Bass.

Gordon, P. (Ed.). (1981). *The study of the curriculum.* London: Batsford Academic and Educational Ltd.

Gowin, D. B. (1981). *Educating.* Ithaca, NY: Cornell University Press.

Guba, E. G., & Lincoln, Y. S. (1981). *Effective evaluation: Improving the usefulness of evaluation results through responsive and naturalistic approaches.* San Francisco: Jossey-Bass.

Hall, J. W., & Kelvels, B. L. (Eds.). (1981). *In opposition to core curriculum: Alternative models for undergraduate education.* Westport, CT: Greenwood.

Hawkins, E. W. (1981). *Modern languages in the curriculum.* New York: Cambridge Unviersity Press.

Hinson, M., & Hughes, M. (Eds.). (1981). *Planning effective progress: Planning and implementing the curriculum for children with learning difficulties.* Amersham, England: Hulton Educational and The National Association for Remedial Education.

Holt, J. (1981). *Teach your own.* New York: Dell.

Howson, A. G., Kilpatrick, J., & Keitel, C. (1981). *Curriculum development in mathematics.* Cambridge, England: Cambridge University Press.

Kibler, R. J. (1981). *Objectives for instruction and evaluation* (second edition). Boston: Allyn & Bacon.

Kindred, L.W., Wolotkiewicz, R. J., Michelson, J. M., & Coplein, L. (1981). *The middle school curriculum: A practioner's handbook* (Second edition). Boston: Allyn & Bacon. (Previous Edition, 1976).

Kissinger, E. M., & Stewart, J. (1981). *A sequential curriculum for the severely and profoundly mentally retarded multi-handicapped.* Springfield, IL: Charles C. Thomas.

Kissock, C. (1981). *Curriculum planning for social studies and teaching cultural approach.* New York: John Wiley.

Lawn, M., & Barton, L. (Eds.). (1981). *Rethinking curriculum studies: A radical approach.* London: Croom Helm.

Levine, A. (1981). *Handbook on undergraduate curriculum.* San Francisco: Jossey-Bass.

Marsh, C., Willis, S., Newby, J. H., Deschamp, P., & Davis, B. P. (1981). *Selection, distribution and use of social studies and mathematics curriculum materials in government primary schools of Western Australia* (Co-operative Research Series Report No. 5). Crawley, Australia: Education Department of Western Australia.

Mason, R. E., Haines, P. G., & Furtado, L. T. (1981). *Cooperative occupational education and work experience in the curriculum* (third edition). Danville, IL: Interstate Printers and Publishers.

Maurer, R. E. (1981). *Designing interdisciplinary curriculum in middle, junior high, and high schools.* Dubuque, IA: Kendall-Hunt. (second edition published, 1985; third edition published, 1995, Champaign, IL: Human Kinetics).

McGuire, J., & Priestley, P. (1981). *Life after school: A social skills curriculum.* Oxford, England: Pergamon Press.

McNeil, J. D. (1981). *Curriculum: A comprehensive introduction* (second edition). Boston: Little, Brown and Company.

McPeck, J. (1981). *Critical thinking and education.* New York: St. Martin's Press.

Meiklejohn, A. (1981). *The experimental college* (Edited and abridged by J. W. Powell from 1932 edition by Harper and Brothers). Washington, DC: Seven Locks Press.

Moffett, J. (1981). *Active voice: A writing program across the curriculum.* Montclair, NJ: Boynton/Cook.

Moran, G. (1981). *Interplay: A theory of religion and education.* Winona, MN: St. Mary's Press.

Mulcahy, D. G. (1981). *Curriculum and policy in Irish post-primary education.* Dublin: Institute of Public Administration.

Nissen, G. (Ed.). (1981). *Curriculum change through qualification and requalification of teachers.* London: Swets Publishing Service.

O'Neil, H. F., Jr. (Ed.). (1981). *Computer-based instruction: A state-of-the-art assessment.* New York: Academic Press.

Onwuka, U. (Ed.). (1981). *Curriculum development for Africa*. Onitsha, Nigeria: Africana-FEP Publishers.

Open University Courses. (1981). *Curriculum evaluation and assessment in educational institutions. Case study 4 and Units 3, 4, 5*. Buckingham, England: Open University Press.

Pinar, W. F. (1981). Life history and educational experience: Part two. *The Journal of Curriculum Theorizing*, 3(1), 259–286.

Popovich, D., & Laham, S. L. (Eds.). (1981). *The adaptive behavior curriculum (ABC): Prescriptive behavior analyses for moderately, severely, and profoundly handicapped persons*. Baltimore: P. H. Brookes.

Romiszowski, A. J. (1981). *Designing instructional systems: Decision making in course planning and curriculum design*. New York: Nichols. (Second edition, 1984 as *Producing instructional systems*).

Rowntree, D. (1981). *Developing courses for students*. New York: McGraw-Hill.

Saylor, J. G., Alexander, W. M., & Lewis, A. J. (1981). *Curriculum planning for better teaching and learning* (fourth edition). New York: Holt, Rinehart, and Winston. (Previous editions by Saylor and Alexander, 1974, 1966, and 1954 under similar titles.)

Schools Council. (1981). *The practical curriculum: Schools Council working paper 70*. London: Methuen Educational.

Shane, H. G., & Tabler, M. B. (1981). *Educating for a new millennium: Views of 132 international scholars*. Bloomington, IN: Phi Delta Kappa.

Soliman, I. (Ed.). (1981). *A model for school-based curriculum planning*. Canberra, Australia: Curriculum Development Centre.

Stieglitz, M. N. (1981). *Self-concept curriculum (K–8)*. Albertson, NY: Research and Training Institute, National Center on Employment of the Handicapped at Human Resources Center.

Stoughton, C. R. (Ed.). (1981). *Issues in curriculum theory*. Lanham, MD: University Press of America.

Sutherland, A. E. (1981). *Curriculum projects in Northern Ireland primary schools: An investigation of project adoption and implementation in 185 Northern Ireland schools*. Belfast: Northern Ireland Council for Educational Research.

Tanner, L. N. (Ed.). (1981). *Papers of the Society for the Study of Curriculum History*. University Park: Pennsylvania State University.

Thelen, H. A. (1981). *The classroom society: The construction of educational experience*. New York: John Wiley.

Thomason, N. W. (Ed.). (1981). *The library media specialist in curriculum development*. Metuchen, NJ: Scarecrow Press.

Tonkin, H., & Edwards, J. (1981). *The world in the curriculum: Curricular strategies for the 21st century*. New Rochelle, NY: Change Magazine Press.

UNESCO. (1981). *Curricula and lifelong education*. London: HMSO.

Westmeyer, P. (1981). *Curriculum planning on the local, school, or district level: A guide for committees or individuals*. Springfield, IL: Charles C. Thomas.

Wiles, J., & Bondi, J. (1981). *The essential middle school*. Columbus, OH: Charles E. Merrill Publishing Company.

Winter, D. G., McClelland, D. C., & Stewart, A. J. (1981). *A new case for the liberal arts: Assessing institutional goals and student development*. San Francisco: Jossey-Bass.

Yates, C. (1981). *Core curriculum and values education: A literature review*. Canberra, Australia: Curriculum Development Centre.

1982

Abbs, P. (1982). *English within the arts: A radical alternative for English and the arts in the curriculum*. Sevenoaks, UK: Hodder and Stoughton Educational.

ACO/DSE Review Conference and Study Tour. (1982). *Curriculum development in Africa*. Bonn, Germany: German Foundation for International Development.

Adler, M. J. (1982). *The paideia proposal: An educational manifesto*. New York: Macmillan.

Apple, M. W. (Ed.). (1982a). *Cultural and economic reproduction in education*. London: Routledge and Kegan Paul.

Apple, M. W. (1982b). *Education and power*. Boston: Routledge and Kegan Paul.

Barnes, D. (1982). *Practical curriculum study*. London: Routledge and Kegan Paul.

Bellon, J., & Handler, J. R. (1982). *Curriculum development and evaluation: A design for improvement*. Dubuque, IA: Kendall-Hunt.

Berman, L. (1982). *The world council for curriculum and instruction: The story of its early years*. Bloomington, IN: World Council for Curriculum and Instruction.

Bevis, E. O. (1982). *Curriculum planning in nursing* (third edition). St. Louis, MO: C. V. Mosby.

Boomer, G. (Ed.). (1982). *Negotiating the curriculum: A teacher-student partnership*. Gosford, New South Wales, Australia: Teachers Assistant Trust, Ashton Scholastic.

Brown, J. R. (Ed.). (1982). *Curriculum planning for young children*. Washington, DC: National Association for the Education of Young Children.

Brubaker, D. L. (1982). *Curriculum planning: The dynamics of theory and practice*. Glenview, IL: Scott, Foresman.

Butt, R. L., & Olson, J. K. (Eds.). (1982). *Insiders realities, outsiders dreams: Prospects for curriculum change (Curriculum Canada IV)*. Vancouver: Centre for the Study of Curriculum and Instruction, University of British Columbia.

Chapman, L. (1982). *Instant art, instant culture: The unspoken policy for American schools*. New York: Teachers College Press.

Chilver, P., & Gould, G. (1982). *Learning and language in the classroom: Discursive talking and writing across the curriculum.* Oxford, England: Pergamon Press.

Clark, A. S. (1982). *Managing curriculum materials in the academic library.* Metuchen, NJ: Scarecrow Press.

Cohen, B. (1982). *Means and ends in education.* Winchester, MA: Allen and Unwin, Inc.

Cohen, D., & Harrison, M. (1982). *Curriculum action project: A report of curriculum decision-making in Australian secondary schools.* Sydney, Australia: Macquarie University.

Coleman, J. S., Hoffer, T., & Kilgore, S. (1982). *High school achievement: Public, Catholic, and private schools compared.* New York: Basic Books.

Connell, R. F., Ashenden, D. J., Kessler, S., & Dowsett, G. W. (1982). *Making the difference: Schools, families and social division.* Sydney, Australia: Allen and Unwin.

Cronbach, L. J. (1982). *Designing evaluation of educational and social programs.* San Francisco: Jossey-Bass.

Doll, R. C. (1982). *Curriculum improvement: Decision making and process* (fifth edition). Boston: Allyn & Bacon. (Previous editions: 1978, 1974, 1970, and 1964.)

Dow, G. (1982). *Teacher learning.* London: Routledge and Kegan Paul.

Eisner, E. W. (1982). *Cognition and curriculum: A basis for deciding what to teach.* New York: Longman.

Fraser, B. J., & Houghton, K. (1982). *Annotated bibliography of curriculum evaluation literature.* Israel Curriculum Center, Tel Aviv: Ministry of Education and Culture.

Frey, K. (1982). *Curriculum-conference: An approach for curriculum development in groups.* Kiel, Germany: Institute for Science Education.

Fullan, M. (1982). *The new meaning of educational change.* New York: Teachers College Press.

Hargreaves, D. H. (1982). *The challenge for the comprehensive school: Culture, curriculum, and community.* London: Routledge and Kegan Paul.

Hewitson, M. (1982). *The hidden curriculum.* St. Lucia, Queensland, Australia: Author.

Hicks, D., & Townley, C. (Eds.). (1982). *Teaching world studies: An introduction to global perspectives in the curriculum.* London: Longman.

Hillocks, G., Jr. (Ed.). (1982). *The English curriculum under fire: What are the real basics?* Urbana, IL: National Council of Teachers of English.

Holt, J. (1982). *How children fail.* (Revised edition). New York: Delacorte Press, Seymour Lawrence.

Hook, S., Kurtz, P., & Todorovich, M. (Eds.). (1982). *The philosophy of the curriculum.* Buffalo, NY: Prometheus Books.

Horton, T., & Raggatt, P. (Eds.). (1982). *Challenge and change in the curriculum.* London: Hodder and Stoughton.

Howson, A. G., Keitel, C., & Kilpatrick, J. (1982). *Curriculum development in mathematics.* New York: Cambridge University Press.

Hunter, M. (1982). *Mastery teaching.* El Segundo, CA: TIP Publications.

Keller, P. (1982). *Getting at the core: Curricular reform at Harvard.* Cambridge, MA: Harvard University Press.

Kelly, A. V. (1982). *Curriculum: Theory and practice.* New York: Harper and Row.

Kepner, H. S., Jr. (Ed.). (1982). *Computers in the classroom.* Washington, DC: National Education Association.

Kirk, G. (1982). *Curriculum and assessment in the Scottish secondary school: A study of the Munn and Dunning report.* London: Ward Lock Educatoinal.

Kirp, D. L. (1982). *Just schools: The idea of racial equality in American education.* Berkeley: University of California Press.

Kirst, M. W. (1982). *Policy implications of individual differences and the common curriculum.* Stanford, CA: Institute for Research on Educational Finance and Governance, Stanford University.

Kohl, H. (1982). *Basic skills: A plan for your child, a program for all children.* Boston: Little, Brown.

Kristo, J. V., & Heath, P. A. (Eds.). (1982). *Today's curriculum: An integrative approach. The Ohio State University at Lima.* Washington, DC: University of America Press.

Lee, V., & Zeldin, D. (Eds.). (1982). *Planning in the curriculum.* London: Hodder and Stoughton.

Leithwood, K. A. (Ed.). (1982). *Studies in curriculum decision-making.* Toronto: Ontario Institute for Studies in Education Press.

List, L. K. (1982). *Music, art, and drama experience for the elementary curriculum.* New York: Teachers College Press.

Maker, J. C. (1982). *Curriculum development for the gifted.* Rockville, MD: Aspen Systems Corporation.

McCutcheon, G. (Guest Ed.). (1982). Curriculum Theory (Special theme issue). *Theory Into Practice, 21*(1).

Melton, R. F. (1982). *Instructional models for course design and development.* Englewood Cliffs, NJ: Educational Technology Publishers, Inc.

National Association of Secondary School Principals. (1982). *Reducing the curriculum: A process model.* Reston, VA: Author.

Nixon, J. (Ed.). (1982). *Drama and the whole curriculum.* London: Hutchinson.

Northumberland Education Committee. (1982). *The school curriculum 5–16: A statement of policy.* Northumberland, England: Northumberland Education Committee.

Oliva, P. F. (1982). *Developing the curriculum*. Boston: Little, Brown. (second edition, 1988, third edition, 1992, New York: Harper Collins, fourth edition, 1997, New York: Longman).

Olson, J. K. (Ed.). (1982). *Innovation in the science curriculum*. New York: Nichols.

Open University Courses. (1982). *Curriculum evaluation and assessment in educational institutions. Case studies 1, 2, 3, 5, and Units 1, 2, 6*. London: Open University Press.

Polakow, V. S. (1982). *The erosion of childhood*. Chicago: University of Chicago Press.

Popkewitz, T. S., Tabachnick, B. R., & Wehlage, G. (1982). *The myth of educational reform: A study of school responses to a program of change*. Madison: University of Wisconsin Press.

Posner, G. J., & Rudnitsky, A. N. (1982). *Course design: A guide to curriculum development for teachers*. New York: Longman. (Previous edition 1978).

Radabaugh, M. T., & Yukish, J. F. (1982). *Curriculum and methods for the mildly handicapped*. Boston: Allyn & Bacon.

Rawlinson, R. (1982). *Curriculum development styles and structures for Australian needs*. Canberra, Australia: Curriculum Development Centre.

Reid, W., & Filby, J. (1982). *The sixth: An essay in education and democracy*. London: Falmer Press.

Robinson, F., & Hedges, H. G. (1982). *Curriculum design for improved learning: A systematic approach*. St. Catherine's, Ontario: Ontario Institute for Studies in Education.

Robison, H. F., & Schwartz, S. L. (1982). *Designing curriculum for early childhood*. Boston: Allyn & Bacon.

Rowntree, D. (1982). *Educational technology in curriculum development* (second edition). New York: Harper and Row.

Rubber and Plastics Industry Training Board, Fourth Report of the study group on the education/training of young people. (1982). *The way forward: A practical proposal for introducing change in school curricula*. Middlesex, UK: Brent.

Russell, N., Hughes, P., & McConachy, D. (Eds.). (1982). *Curriculum evaluation: Selected readings*. Canberra, Australia: Curriculum Development Centre of Australia.

Sarason, S. B. (1982). *The culture of the school and the problem of change* (second edition). Boston: Allyn & Bacon.

Saylor, J. G. (1982). *Who planned the curriculum*? West Lafayette, IN: Kappa Delta Pi.

Schubert, W. H., & Lopez Schubert, A. (Eds.). (1982). *Conceptions of curriculum knowledge: Focus on students and teachers*. College Station: College of Education, The Pennsylvania State University.

Schwartz, S. L., & Robison, H. F. (1982). *Designing curriculum for early childhood*. Boston: Allyn & Bacon.

Seidel, R. J., Hunter, B., & Anderson, R. E. (Eds.). (1982). *Computer literacy: Issues and directions for 1985*. New York: Academic Press.

Shaftel, F. R., & Shaftel, G. (1982). *Role playing in the curriculum* (second edition). Englewood Cliffs, NJ: Prentice-Hall.

Shepherd, G. D., & Ragan, W. B. (1982). *Modern elementary curriculum*. New York: Holt, Rinehart and Winston. (Previous editions by Ragan & Shepherd, 1977, 1971; Ragan & Stendler, 1966, 1960; Ragan, 1953).

Skilbeck, M. (1982). *Core curriculum for the common school: Inaugural lecture*. London: University of London, Institute of Education.

United States Department of Education. (1982). *High school and beyond*. Washington, DC: Center for Education Statistics.

White, J. (1982). *The aims of education restated*. Boston: Routledge and Kegan Paul.

1983

Adler, M. J. (1983). *Paideia problems and possibilities*. New York: Macmillan.

Albisetti, J. C. (1983). *Secondary school reform in imperial Germany*. Princeton, NJ: Princeton University Press.

Alexander, K. L., & Pallas, A. M. (1983). *Curriculum reform and school performance: An evaluation of the "new basics."* Baltimore: Center for Social Organization of Schools, Johns Hopkins University.

American Educational Studies Association. (1983). *The humanities in education: Rebirth or burial in the 1980's*. Ann Arbor, MI: Prakken.

Apple, M. W., & Weis, L. (Eds.). (1983). *Ideology and practice in schooling*. Philadelphia: Temple University Press.

Arons, S. (1983). *Compelling belief: The culture of American schooling*. New York: McGraw-Hill.

Barr, R., & Dreeben, R. (1983). *How schools work*. Chicago: University of Chicago Press.

Berman, L. M., & Miel, A. (1983). *Education for world cooperation*. West Lafayette, IN: Kappa Delta Pi.

Bernstein, R. (1983). *Beyond objectivism and relativism: Science, hermeneutics, and praxis*. Philadelphia: Univerisity of Pennsylvania Press.

Blenkin, G., & Kelly, A. V. (Eds.). (1983). *The primary curriculum in action*. London: Harper and Row.

Boyer, E. L., for the Carnegie Foundation for the Advancement of Teaching. (1983). *High school: A report on secondary education in America*. New York: Harper and Row.

Brady, L. (1983). *Curriculum development in Australia: Presage, process, product*. Sydney, Australia: Prentice-Hall of Australia.

Brockington, D., White, R., & Pring, R. (1983). *Implementing the 14-18 curriculum: New approaches.* London: Schools Council.

Brumbaugh, R. S. (1983). *Whitehead, process philosophy, and education.* Albany: State University of New York Press.

Butterworth, I. (1983). *Staffing for curriculum needs: Teacher shortages and surpluses in comprehensive schools.* Windsor, England: NFER-Nelson.

Carr, W., & Kemmis, S. (1983). *Becoming critical: Knowing through action research.* Waurn Ponds, Victoria, Australia: Deakin University Press. (Revised, 1986).

Clendening, C. P., & Davies, R. A. (1983). *Challenging the gifted: Curriculum enrichment and acceleration models.* New York: Bowker.

College Entrance Examination Board. (1983). *Academic preparation for college: What students need to know and be able to do.* New York: Author.

Conference Board of the Mathematical Sciences. (1983). *The mathematical sciences curriculum K–12: What is still fundamental and what is not?* Washington, DC: Author.

Cully, I. V. (1983). *Planning and selecting curriculum for Christian education.* Valley Forge, PA: Judson Press.

Cusick, P. A. (1983). *The egalitarian ideal and the American high school.* New York: Longman.

Day, B. D., & Drake, K. N. (1983). *Early childhood education: Curriculum organization and classroom management.* Alexandria, VA: Association for Supervision and Curriculum Development.

Eggleston, J. (1983). *Work experience in secondary schools.* Boston: Routledge and Kegan Paul.

Elbaz, F. (1983). *Teacher thinking: A study of practical knowledge.* New York: Nichols.

English, F. W. (Ed.). (1983). *Fundamental curriculum decisions.* ASCD Yearbook. Washington, DC: Association for Supervision and Curriculum Development.

Everhart, R. B. (1983.) *Reading, writing, and resistance: Adolescence and labor in a junior high school.* Boston: Routledge and Kegan Paul.

Feinberg, W. (1983). *Understanding education: Toward a reconstruction of educational inquiry.* Cambridge, England: Cambridge University Press.

Fielding, A. J., & Cavanagh, D. M. (Eds.). (1983). *Curriculum priorities in Australian higher education.* Canberra, Australia: Croom Helm.

Galton, M., & Moon, B. (Eds.). (1983). *Changing schools...changing curriculum.* London: Harper and Row.

Giroux, H. A. (1983). *Theory and resistance in education: A pedagogy for the opposition.* South Hadley, MA: Bergin and Garvey.

Giroux, H. A., & Purpel, D. (Eds.). (1983). *The hidden curriculum and moral education: Deception or discovery?* Berkeley, CA: McCutchan.

Goodson, I. F. (1983). *School subjects and curriculum change: Case studies in curriculum history.* London: Croom Helm.

Grady, M. T., & Gawronski, J. D. (1983). *Computers in curriculum and instruction.* Alexandria, VA: Association for Supervision and Curriculum Development.

Great Britain Department of Education and Science. (1983). *Curriculum 11–16: Towards a statement of entitlement — Curricular reappraisal in action.* London: HMSO.

Griffin, C. (1983). *Curriculum theory in adult education.* Beckenham, England: Croom Helm.

Hammersley, M., & Hargreaves, A. (Eds.). (1983). *Curriculum practice: Some sociological case studies.* London: Falmer Press.

Hass, G. (Ed.). (1983). *Curriculum planning: A new approach* (fourth edition). Boston: Allyn & Bacon.

Holt, J. (1983). *How children learn* (Revised edition). New York: Delta/Seymour Lawrence.

Holt, M. (1983). *Curriculum workshop: An introduction to whole curriculum planning.* Boston: Routledge and Kegan Paul.

Hunter, A. P., Ashley, M. J., & Millar, C. J. (Eds.). (1983). *Education, curriculum and development. Papers presented at conferences at the University of Cape Town and the University of Witwatersrand.* Cape Town and Johannesburg, South Africa: Universities of Cape Town and Witwatersrand.

Joyce, B., McKibbin, M., & Hersh, R. H. (1983). *The structure of school improvement.* New York: Longman.

Kaestle, C. F. (1983). *Pillars of the republic: Common schools and American society, 1780–1860.* New York: Hill and Wang.

Kemmis, S., Cole, P., & Suggett, D. (1983). *Orientations to curriculum and transition: Toward the socially critical school.* Victoria, Australia: Victorian Institute of Secondary Education.

Klausmeier, H. J., Serlin, R. C., & Zindler, M. C. (1983). *Improvement of secondary education through research: Five longitudinal case studies.* Madison, WI: Wisconsin Center for Education Research.

Kristo, J. V., & Heath, P. A. (Eds.). (1983). *Today's curriculum: An integrative approach.* Lanham, MD: University Press of America.

Lawton, D. (1983). *Curriculum studies and educational planning.* London: Hodder and Stoughton.

Lightfoot, S. L. (1983). *The good high school: Portraits of character and culture.* New York: Basic Books.

Lombardo, V. S. (1983). *Developing and administering early childhood programs.* Springfield, IL: Charles C. Thomas.

Lundgren, U. P. (1983). *Between hope and happening: Text and context in curriculum.* Geelong, Victoria, Australia: Deakin University Press.

Lynch, J. (1983). *The multicultural curriculum.* London: Batsford.

McCormick, R., & James, M. (1983). *Curriculum evaluation in schools.* London: Croom Helm. (second edition, 1988).

Miller, J. P. (1983). *The educational spectrum: Orientations to curriculum.* New York: Longman.

Minogue, W. J. (Ed.). (1983). *Adventures in curriculum.* Sydney, Australia: Allen and Unwin.

Moffett, J., & Wagner, B. (1983). *A student-centered language arts curriculum, K–13: A handbook for teachers.* Boston: Houghton Mifflin.

Monaghan, E. J. (1983). *A common heritage: Noah Webster's blue-back speller.* Hamden, CT: Archon Books.

National Commission on Excellence in Education. (1983). *A nation at risk: An imperative for educational reform.* Washington, DC: U.S. Government Printing Office.

Nelson, M. R. (Ed.). (1983). *Papers of the society for the study of curriculum history.* DeKalb, IL: The Society.

Noddings, N. (Guest Ed.). (1983). Curriculum change: Promise and practice. *Theory into Practice, 22*(3).

Nunan, T. (1983). *Countering educational design.* New York: Nichols; London: Croom Helm.

Ogletree, E. J. (1983). *A plan for curriculum organizing and teaching: "Unit plan."* Lanham, MD: University Press of America.

Okazu, M. (1983). *The encyclopedia of curriculum.* Tokyo: Shogakkan.

Organization for Economic Cooperation and Development. (1983). *Educational planning: A reappraisal.* Paris: Author.

O'Shea, T., & Self, J. (1983). *Learning and teaching with computers.* Englewood Cliffs, NJ: Prentice-Hall.

Pitman Learning. (1983). *The curriculum development library.* Belmont, CA: Author.

Plunkett, D. (Ed.). (1983). *Curriculum matters: 14–19.* Southhampton, England: University of Southhampton.

Pope, D. (1983). *Objectives model of curriculum planning and evaluation.* London: Council for Educational Technology.

Reigeluth, C. M. (1983). *Instructional design theories and models: An overview of their current status.* Mahwah, NJ: Lawrence Erlbaum Associates.

Richards, C., & Holford, D. (Eds.). (1983). *The teaching of primary science: Policy and practice.* London: Falmer Press.

Robinson, F. G., White, F., & Ross, J. (1983). *Curriculum analysis for effective instruction.* Toronto: Ontario Institute for Studies in Education.

Rogers, C. R. (1983). *Freedom to learn for the 80's.* Columbus, OH: Charles E. Merrill. (Previous edition, 1969 by Bell & Howell).

Rohlen, T. (1983). *Japan's high schools.* Berkeley: University of California Press.

Schön, D. A. (1983). *The reflective practitioner.* New York: Basic Books.

Schools Council. (1983). *Primary practice: A sequel to the practical curriculum.* Schools Council Working Paper 75. London: Schools Council.

Shulman, L., & Sykes, G. (Eds.). (1983). *Handbook of teaching and policy.* New York: Longman.

Spencer, E. (1983). *Writing matters across the curriculum.* Sevenoaks, Scotland: Hodder and Stoughton for the Scottish Council for Research in Education.

Stenhouse, L. (1983). *Authority, education, and emancipation.* London: Heinemann Educational Books.

Sutherland, A., O'Shea, A., & McCartney, R. (1983). *Curriculum projects in post-primary schools.* Belfast: Northern Ireland Council for Educational Research.

Task Force on Education for Economic Growth. (1983). *Action for excellence: A comprehensive plan to improve our nation's schools.* Denver, CO: Education Commission of the States.

Travers, R. M. W. (1983). *How research has changed American schools: A history from 1884 to the present.* Kalamazoo, MI: Mythos Press.

Twentieth Century Fund. (1983). *Report of the Twentieth Century Fund task force on federal elementary and secondary education policy.* New York: Author.

Underwood, G. (1983). *The physical education curriculum in the secondary school: Planning and implementation.* London: Falmer Press.

United States National Science Board. (1983). *Educating Americans for the 21st century.* Washington, DC: National Science Foundation.

Van Til, W. (1983). *My way of looking at it: An autobiography.* Terre Haute, IN: Lake Lure Press.

Wagner, D. L. (Ed.). (1983). *The seven liberal arts in the middle ages.* Bloomington: Indiana University Press.

Wilcox, B., & Eustace, P. (1983). *Tooling up for curriculum review.* Windsor, England: NFER-Nelson.

Wirth, A. G. (1983). *Productive work in industry and schools: Becoming persons again.* Lanham, MD: University Press of America.

Wise, A. E. (1983). *Legislated learning: The bureaucratization of the American classroom.* Berkeley: University of California Press.

Wootton, L. (Ed.). (1983). *Trends and practices.* Lanham, MD: University Press of America.

Zenger, S. K., & Zenger, W. (1983). *Curriculum planning: A ten-step process*. Palo Alto, CA: R & E Research Assoc.

1984

Adler, M. J. (1984). *The paideia program: An educational syllabus*. New York: Macmillan.

Aoki, T. T., Carson, T. R., Favaro, B. J., & Berman, L. M. (1984). *Understanding situational meanings of in-service curriculum acts: Implementing, consulting, inservicing*. Monograph No. 9. Alberta, Canada: Department of Secondary Education, Faculty of Education, University of Alberta.

Australia Minister of Education. (1984). *Curriculum development and planning in Victoria*. Melbourne, Australia: Government Printer.

Bailey, C. H. (1984). *Beyond the present and the particular: A theory of liberal education*. Boston: Routledge and Kegan Paul.

Barrow, R. (1984). *Giving teaching back to teachers: A critical introduction to curriculum theory*. London, Ontario: The Althouse Press.

Beane, J. A., & Lipka, R. P. (1984). *Self-concept, self-esteem, and the curriculum*. Boston: Allyn & Bacon.

Blyth, W. A. L. (1984). *Development, experience and curriculum in primary education*. London: Croom Helm.

Bowers, C. A. (1984). *The promise of theory: Education and the politics of cultural change*. New York: Longman.

Boyd, J. (1984). *Understanding the primary curriculum*. London: Hutchinson.

Brown, B. R. (1984). *Crisis in secondary education: Rebuilding America's high schools*. Englewood Cliffs, NJ: Prentice-Hall.

Bullough, R. V., Jr., Goldstein, S. L., & Holt, L. (1984). *Human interests in the curriculum: Teaching and learning in a technological society*. New York: Teachers College Press.

Carkhuff, R. R. (1984). *The productive teacher 1: An introduction to curriculum development*. Amherst, MA: Human Resource Development Press.

Caswell, H. L., & Campbell, D. S. (1984). *Readings in curriculum development*. (Reprint of 1937 Edition). Darby, PA: Darby Books.

Craft, A., & Bardell, G. (Eds.). (1984). *Curriculum opportunities in a multicultural society*. New York: Harper and Row.

Cuban, L. (1984). *How teachers taught: Constancy and change in American classrooms 1890–1980*. White Plains, NY: Longman. (second edition, 1993).

Darling-Hammond, L. (1984). *Beyond the commission reports: The coming crisis in teaching*. Washington, DC: Rand Corporation.

Dearden, R. F. (1984). *Theory and practice in education*. Henley-on-Thames, England: Routledge and Kegan Paul.

Dow, I. I., Whitehead, R. Y., & Wright, R. L. (1984). *Curriculum implementation: A framework for action*. Toronto, Ontario: Ontario Public School Teachers' Federation.

Dublin Curriculum Development Unit. (1984). *Integrated science curriculum innovation project*. Dublin, Ireland: O'Brien Educational.

Dunkel, H. B. (1984). *Writ in water: The epitaph of educational innovation*. Unpublished book manuscript at the University of Chicago.

Edwards, T. A. (1984). *The youth training scheme: A new curriculum, Episode 1*. London and Philadelphia: Falmer Press.

Fenstermacher, G. D., & Goodlad, J. I. (Eds.). (1984). *Individual differences and the common curriculum: Eighty-second yearbook of the National Society for the Study of Education, Part I*, Vol. 24. Chicago: University of Chicago Press.

Finch, C. R., & Crunkilton, J. R. (1984). *Curriculum development in vocational and technical education: Planning content and implementation*. (second edition). Boston: Allyn & Bacon.

Finn, C. E., Jr., Ravitch, D., & Fancher, R. T. (Eds.). (1984). *Against mediocrity: The humanities in America's high schools*. New York: Holmes and Meier.

Gilbert, R. (1984). *The impotent image: Reflections of ideology in the secondary curriculum*. Philadelphia: Taylor and Francis.

Goodlad, J. I. (1984). *A place called school. Prospects for the future*. Hightstown, NJ: McGraw-Hill.

Goodson, I., & Ball, S. (Eds.). (1984). *Defining the curriculum: Histories and ethnographies of school subjects*. London: Falmer Press.

Heater, D. (1984). *Peace through education: The contribution of the Council for Education in World Citizenship*. London: Falmer Press.

Hess, R. D., & Walker, D. F. (Eds.). (1984). *Instructional software: Principles and perspectives for design and use*. Belmont, CA: Wadsworth.

Heywood, J. (1984). *Considering the curriculum during student teaching*. New York: Nichols.

Hopkins, D., & Wideen, M. (1984). *Alternative perspectives on school improvement*. London and New York: Falmer.

Hosford, P. L. (Ed.). (1984). *Using what we know about teaching*. ASCD Yearbook. Alexandria, VA: Association for Supervision and Curriculum Development.

Inner London Education Authority (ILEA). (1984). *Improving secondary schools*. London: Hargreaves.

Johnson, D. W., Johnson, R. T., Holubec, E. J., & Roy, P. (1984). *Circles of learning: Cooperation in the classroom*. Alexandria, VA: Association for Supervision and Curriculum Development.

Kelly, A. V. (Ed.). (1984). *Microcomputers and the curriculum*. New York: Harper and Row.

Knowles, M. S., & Associates (1984). *Andragogy in action: Applying modern principles of adult learning.* San Francisco: Jossey-Bass.

Kushner, S., & Logan, T. (1984). *Made in England: An evaluation of curriculum in transition.* (Care Occasional Publications No. 14). Norwich, England: CARE, University of East Anglia.

Lemlech, J. K. (1984). *Curriculum and instructional methods for the elementary school.* New York: Collier Macmillan.

Lieberman, A., & Miller, L. (1984). *Teachers, their world and their work.* Washington, DC: Association for Supervision and Curriculum Development.

Lounsbury, J. H. (Ed.). (1984). *Perspectives: Middle school education 1964–1984.* Columbus, OH: National Middle School Association.

Mamidi, M. R., & Ravishankar, S. (Eds.). (1984). *Curriculum development and educational technology.* New Delhi, India: Sterling.

Marsh, C., & Stafford, K. (1984). *Curriculum: Australian practices and issues.* Sydney, Australia: McGraw-Hill.

Microelectronics Education Programme. (1984). *Computers in the primary curriculum.* DES/MEP 1984 Conference Report. Winchester, England: Author.

Milburn, G., & Enns, R. (Eds.). (1984). *Curriculum Canada VI: Alternative research perspectives — The secondary school curriculum.* Vancouver: University of British Columbia.

Miller, J. (Ed.). (1984). *Eccentric propositions: Literature and the curriculum.* Boston: Routledge and Kegan Paul.

Munby, H., Orpwood, G., & Russell, T. (Eds.). (1984). *Seeing curriculum in a new light: Essays from science education.* Lanham, MD: University Press of America.

Myers, J. W. (1984). *Writing to learn across the curriculum.* Bloomington, IN: Phi Delta Kappa.

Noddings, N. (1984). *Caring: A feminine approach to ethics of moral education.* Berkeley, CA: University of California Press.

Noddings, N., & Shore, P. J. (1984). *Awakening the inner eye: Intuition in education.* New York: Teachers College Press.

Norris, N., & Sanger, J. (1984). *Inside information: Evaluating curriculum innovation.* Norwich, England: Center for Applied Research in Education, University of East Anglia.

Open University Courses. (1984). *Purpose and planning in the curriculum. Units 1–7, 9–15, 17–20, 23, 25–30 and case studies.* London: Open University Press.

Parker, B. (1984). *Nonsexist curriculum development: Theory into practice.* Boulder, CO: University of Colorado.

Passow, A. H. (1984). *Reforming schools in the 1980's: A critical review of the national reports*. New York: Institute for Urban and Minority Education, Teachers College, Columbia University.

Potter, R. L. (1984). *Using television in the curriculum*. Bloomington, IN: Phi Delta Kappa.

Pring, R. (1984). *Personal and social education in the curriculum*. London: Hodder and Stoughton.

Raywid, M. A., Tesconi, C. A., & Warren, D. A. (1984). *Pride and promise: Schools of excellence for all the people*. Westbury, NY: America Educational Studies Association.

Richards, C. (1984). *Curriculum studies. An introductory annotated bibliography* (second edition, enlarged from the 1979 edition). London: Falmer Press.

Richards, C., Clayfield, R., & Lofthouse, B. (Eds.). (1984). *The study of primary education: A source book, Volume 1*. Lewes, East Sussex, England: Falmer Press.

Roberts, A. D., & Cawelti, G. (1984). *Redefining general education in the American high school*. Alexandria, VA: Association for Supervision and Curriculum Development.

Rowland, S. (1984). *The enquiring classroom: An approach to understanding children's learning*. London: Falmer Press.

Rubin, L. J. (1984). *Artistry in teaching*. New York: Random House.

Schools Council, SSCR Project Report. (1984). *Secondary school curriculum review: Toward the specification of minimum entitlement*. London: Schools Council.

Seffrin, J. R., & Torabi, M. R. (1984). *Education in healthy lifestyles: Curriculum implications*. Bloomington, IN: Phi Delta Kappa.

Short, E. C. (Ed.). (1984). *Competence: Inquiries into its meaning and acquisition in educational setting*. Lanham, MD: University Press of America.

Simkin, D., & Simkin, J. (Eds.). (1984). *Curriculum development in action*. Brighton, England: Tressell Publications.

Sizer, T. R. for the National Association of Secondary School Principals and the National Association of Independent Schools. (1984). *Horace's compromise: The dilemma of the American high school*. Boston: Houghton Mifflin.

Skilbeck, M. (Ed.). (1984a). *Evaluating the curriculum in the eighties*. London: Hodder and Stoughton.

Skilbeck, M. (1984b). *School-based curriculum development*. London: Harper and Row.

Skilbeck, M. (Ed.). (1984c). *Readings in school-based curriculum development*. London: Harper & Row.

Spanier, B., Bloom, A., & Boroviak, D. (Eds.). (1984). *Toward a balanced curriculum*. Cambridge, MA: Schenkman Books.

Spodek, B. (1984). *Mainstreaming young children*. Belmont, CA: Wadsworth Publishing Co.

Tamir, P. (Ed.). (1984). *The role of evaluators in curriculum development*. Kent, England: Croom Helm.

Taylor, P. H., & Richards, C. M. (1984). *An introduction to curriculum studies*. London: NFER-Nelson Publishing Co.

Tom, A. R. (1984). *Teaching as a moral craft*. New York: Longman.

Unruh, G., & Unruh, A. (1984). *Curriculum development: Problems, processes, and progress*. Berkeley, CA: McCutchan Publishing Corporation.

Weston, P. B. (1984). *Framework for the curriculum*. Windsor, England: NFER-Nelson.

Wilcox, B., Dunn, J., Lavercombe, S., & Burn, L. (1984). *The preparation for life curriculum*. Dover, NH: Longwood.

Wiles, J., & Bondi, J. C. (1984). *Curriculum development: A guide to practice*. (second edition). Columbus, OH: Charles E. Merrill.

Wulf, K. M., & Schave, B. (1984). *Curriculum design: A handbook for educators*. Glenview, IL: Scott Foresman and Company.

1985

Aronowitz, S., & Giroux, H. A. (1985). *Education under siege: The conservative, liberal and radical debate over schooling*. South Hadley, MA: Bergin and Garvey.

Bradley, L. H. (1985). *Curriculum leadership and development handbook*. Englewood Cliffs, NJ: Prentice Hall.

Brennan, W. K. (1985). *Curriculum for special needs*. Philadelphia: Open University Press.

Brockington, D., White, R., & Pring, R. (1985). *The 14–18 curriculum: New approaches*. London: School Curriculum Development Committee.

Campbell, R. J. (1985). *Developing the primary school curriculum*. Philadelphia: Taylor and Francis.

Carnoy, M., & Levin, H. (1985). *Schooling and work in the democratic state*. Stanford, CA: Stanford University Press.

Cohen, D., & Maxwell, T. (Eds.). (1985). *Blocked at the entrance: Context, cases, and commentary on curriculum change*. Armidale, New South Wales, Australia: Entrance Publications.

Committee on Research in Mathematics, Science and Technology Education. (1985). *Mathematics, science, and technology education: A research agenda*. Washington, DC: National Academy Press.

Connell, R. W. (1985). *Teacher's work*. Sydney, Australia: Allen and Unwin.

Cookson, P. W., & Persell, C. H. (1985). *Preparing for power*. New York: Basic Books.

Cooper, B. (1985). *Renegotiating secondary school mathematics: A study of curriculum change and stability*. London: Falmer Press.

Cuff, E. C., & Payne, G. C. (Eds.). (1985). *Crisis in the curriculum.* London and Dover, NH: Croom Helm.

Derricott, R. (Ed.). (1985). *Curriculum continuity: Primary to secondary.* Philadelphia: Taylor and Francis.

Dick, W., & Carey, L. (1985). *The systematic design of instruction* (second edition). Glenview, IL: Scott Foresman. (first edition, 1978).

Edel, A. (1985). *Interpreting education: Science, ideology, and values, volume 3.* New Brunswick, NJ: Transaction/Rutgers.

Eisner, E. W. (Ed.). (1985a). *Learning and teaching the ways of knowing. Eighty-fourth Yearbook of the National Society for the Study of Education, Part 2.* Chicago: University of Chicago Press.

Eisner, E. W. (1985b). *The art of educational evaluation: A personal view.* London: Falmer Press.

Eisner, E. W. (1985c). *The educational imagination: On the design and evaluation of school programs* (second edition). New York: Macmillan. (first edition, 1979; third edition, 1994).

Elias, M. (1985). *Formative and summative evaluation of the improving social awareness–social problem-solving primary prevention curriculum program.* New Brunswick, NJ: Rutgers University.

Fantini, M., & Sinclair, R. (Eds.). (1985). *Education in school and nonschool settings. Eighty-fourth Yearbook of the National Society for the Study of Education, Part I.* Chicago: University of Chicago Press.

Feinberg, P. R. (1985). "Four curriculum theorists: A critique in light of Martin Buber's philosophy of education." Book length article in *The Journal of Curriculum Theorizing.* 6(1), 5–164.

Fraser, B. J. (1985). *Case studies in curriculum evaluation.* Bentley, Western Australia: Social Science Education Consortium.

Freire, P. (1985). *The politics of education: Culture, power and liberation.* South Hadley, MA: Bergin and Garvey.

Glatthorn, A. A. (1985). *Curriculum reform and at-risk youth.* Philadelphia: Research for Better Schools.

Goodson, I. F. (Ed.). (1985). *Social histories of the secondary curriculum: Subjects for study.* London and Philadelphia: Falmer Press.

Goodson, I., & McGivney, V. (1985). *European dimensions and the secondary school curriculum.* London: Falmer Press.

Gross, B., & Gross, R. (Eds.). (1985). *The great school debate: Which way for American education.* New York: Simon and Schuster.

Hannan, W. (1985). *Democratic curriculum.* Sydney & London: Allen and Unwin.

Husén, T., & Postlethwaite, N. (Eds.). (1985). *The international encyclopedia of education* (ten volumes). London: Pergamon.

Inglis, F. (1985). *The management of ignorance: A political theory of the curriculum.* Oxford and New York: Basil Blackwell.

Inner London Education Authority (ILEA). (1985). *Improving primary schools.* London: Author.

Jewett, A. E., & Bain, L. L. (1985). *The curriculum process in physical education.* Dubuque, IA: Wm. C. Brown.

Jorgenson, G., Schubert, W. H., & Seguel, M. L. (Eds.). (1985). *Papers of the Society for the Study of Curriculum History.* Cleveland, OH: The Society.

Jozefzoon, E. O. I., & Gorter, R. J. (Eds.). (1985). *Core curriculum: A comparative analysis.* Enschede, Netherlands: National Institute for Curriculum Development.

Kemp, J. E. (1985). *Instructional design: A plan for unit and course development* (second edition). New York: Harper and Row.

Lazerson, M., McLaughlin, J. B., McPherson, B., & Bailey, S. K. (1985). *An education of value: The purpose and practices of schools.* Cambridge: Cambridge University Press.

Lengrand, P. (Ed). (1985). *Areas of learning basic to lifelong education.* Hamburg, Germany: Pergamon Press and the UNESCO Institute of Education.

Lewis, M. H. (1985). *An adventure with children.* Lanham, MD: University Press of America.

Martin, J. R. (1985). *Reclaiming a conversation: The ideal of an educated woman.* New Haven, CT: Yale University Press.

Marzano, R. J. (1985). *Integrated instruction in thinking skills, learning strategies, traditional content, and basic beliefs: A necessary unity.* Denver, CO: Mid-Continent Regional Educational Laboratory.

Maurer, R. E. (1985). *Designing interdisciplinary curriculum in middle, junior high, and high schools* (second edition). Dubuque, IA: Kendall-Hunt.

McLaughlin, J. (1985). *An education of value.* New York: Cambridge University Press.

McNeil, J. D. (1985). *Curriculum: A comprehensive introduction* (third edition). Boston: Little, Brown and Company.

Milburn, G., & Enns, R. (Eds.). (1985). *Curriculum Canada IV.* Norwood, NJ: ABLEX Publishing Co.

Miller, J. P., & Seller, W. (1985). *Curriculum, perspectives and practice.* New York: Longman.

Molnar, A. (Ed.). (1985). *Current thought on curriculum.* ASCD Yearbook. Alexandria, VA: Association for Supervision and Curriculum Development.

Musgrave, P. (1985). *Curricular decisions in their administrative context.* Victoria, Australia: Deakin University Press.

National Board of Inquiry. (1985). *Barriers to excellence: Our children at risk*. Boston: The National Coalition of Advocates for Students.

Oakes, J. (1985). *Keeping track: How high schools structure inequality*. New Haven, CT: Yale University Press.

Plaskow, M. (Ed.). (1985). *Life and death of the schools council*. London: Falmer Press.

Portuges, C., & Culley, M. (Eds.). (1985). *Gendered subjects: The dynamics of feminist teaching*. Boston: Routledge and Kegan Paul.

Powell, A. G., Farrer, E., & Cohen, D. K. (1985). *The shopping mall high school: Winners and losers in the educational marketplace*. Boston: Houghton Mifflin.

Powell, J. (1985). *The teacher's craft*. Buffalo, NY: Ontario Institute for Studies in Education.

Raggatt, P. C. M., & Weiner, G. (1985). *The struggle for the curriculum*. Oxford, England: Pergamon Press.

Raggatt, P. C. M., & Weiner, G. (1985). *Curriculum and assessment*. New York: Pergamon Press in association with The Open University.

Raven, J., Hohnstone, J., & Varley, T. (1985). *In the primary classroom*. Edinburgh, Scotland: Scottish Council for Research in Education.

Ravitch, D. (1985). *The schools we deserve*. New York: Basic Books, Inc.

Reardon, B. (1985). *Sexism and the war system*. New York: Teachers College Press.

Richards, C., & Lofthouse, B. (1985). *The study of primary education: A source book, Volume 2, The curriculum*. Philadelphia: Taylor and Francis.

Robinson, F., Ross, F., & White, F. (1985). *Curriculum development for effective instruction*. Toronto: Ontario Institute for Studies in Education.

Romberg, T. A. (1985). *Toward effective schooling: The IGE experience*. Lanham, MD: University Press of America.

Rosales-Dordelly, C. L., & Short, E. C. (1985). *Curriculum professors' specialized knowledge*. Lanham, MD: University Press of America.

Rowntree, D. (1985). *Educational technology in curriculum development* (third edition). New York: Teachers College Press.

Rudduck, J., & Hopkins, D. (Eds.). (1985). *Research as a basis for teaching: Readings from the work of Lawrence Stenhouse*. London and Philadelphia: Falmer Press.

Schug, M. C. (1985). *Economics in the school curriculum K–12*. New York and Washington, DC: NEA and The Joint Council on Economic Education.

Schuster, M., & van Dyne, S. (1985). *Women's place in the academy: Transforming the liberal arts curriculum*. Totowa, NJ: Rowan & Allanheld.

Sheikh, A. A., & Sheikh, K. S. (1985). *Imagery in education: Imagery in the educational process*. Farmingdale, NY: Baywood Publishing.

Short, E. C., Willis, G. H., & Schubert, W. H. (1985). *Toward excellence in curriculum inquiry: The story of the AERA Special Interest Group on Creation and Utilization of Curriculum Knowledge: 1970–1984.* State College, PA: Nittany Press.

Sloan, D. (Ed.). (1985). *The computer in education: A critical perspective.* New York: Teachers College Press.

Stewart, W. (1985). *How to involve the student in classroom decision making.* Saratoga, CA: R & E Publishers.

Tuttle, F. B. (Ed.). (1985). *Fine arts in the curriculum.* Washington, DC: National Education Association.

van Bruggen, J. C. (1985). *Establishing a modern core curriculum: A tricky business or a political art?* Enshede, Netherlands: SLO.

Weiner, G., & Raggatt, P. C. M. (Eds.). (1985). *Curriculum and assessment: some policy issues: A reader.* Oxford, England and New York: Pergamon Press in association with Open University Press.

Weis, L. (1985). *Between two worlds.* Boston: Routledge and Kegan Paul.

Whitty, G. (1985). *Sociology and school knowledge: Curriculum theory, research, and politics.* London: Methuen.

Wigginton, E. (1985). *Sometimes a shining moment: The Foxfire experience.* Garden City, NY: Anchor Press/Doubleday.

1986

Apple, M. W. (1986). *Teachers and texts: A political economy of class and gender relations in education.* London and New York: Routledge and Kegan Paul.

Ashton, P. T., & Webb, R. B. (1986). *Making a difference: Teachers' sense of efficacy and student achievement.* New York: Longman.

Beane, J. A., & Lipka, R. P. (1986). *Self-concept, self-esteem, and the curriculum.* New York: Teachers College Press.

Beane, J. A., Toepfer, C. F., & Alessi, S. J. (1986). *Curriculum planning and development.* Boston: Allyn & Bacon.

Bruner, J. (1986). *Actual minds, possible worlds.* Cambridge, MA: Harvard University Press.

Caldwell, B., & Spinks, J. (1986). *Policy making and planning for school.* Hobart: Education Department of Tasmania.

Carnegie Forum's Task Force on Teaching as a Profession. (1986). *A nation prepared: Teachers for the 21st century.* New York: Carnegie Corp.

Carr, W., & Kemmis, S. (1986). *Becoming critical: Education, knowledge, and action research.* London: Falmer Press.

Chittenden, P., & Kiniry, M. (Eds.). (1986). *Making connections across the curriculum.* New York: St. Martin's Press.

Clandinin, D. J. (1986). *Classroom practice: Teacher images in action.* London: Falmer Press.

Cuban, L. (1986). *Teachers and machines: The classroom use of technology since 1920.* New York: Teachers College Press.

Curtis, A. (1986). *A curriculum for the pre-school child: Learning to learn.* Philadelphia: NFER-Nelson. (second edition, 1998).

Doll, R. C. (1986). *Curriculum improvement: Decision-making and process* (sixth edition). Boston: Allyn & Bacon. (Previous editions 1982, 1978, 1974, 1970, 1964).

Driscoll, K. J. (1986). *Humanities curriculum guidelines for the middle and secondary years.* London and Philadelphia: Falmer Press.

Egan, K. (1986a). *Individual development and the curriculum.* London, Ontario: Hutchinson.

Egan, K. (1986b). *Teaching as story telling: An alternative approach to teaching and curriculum in the elementary school.* London, Ontario: The Althouse Press (also Routledge and Kegan Paul, and University of Chicago Press).

Eliason, C., & Jenkins, L. (1986). *A practical guide to early childhood curriculum.* (third edition). New York: Merrill.

Englund, T. (1986). *Curriculum as a political problem: Changing education conceptions with reference to citizen education.* (Uppsala Studies in Education). Lund, Sweden: Studentlitteratur.

Fantini, M. D. (1986). *Regaining excellence in education.* Columbus, OH: Merrill Publishing Co.

Franklin, B. M. (1986). *Building the American community: The school community and the search for psocial control.* London: Falmer Press.

Fraser, B. J. (1986). *Classroom environment.* Kent, England: Croom Helm.

Gibson, R. (1986). *Critical theory and education.* London: Hodder and Stroughton.

Ginzberg, E. (1986). *The nation's children.* New Brunswick, NJ: Transaction/Rutgers.

Goodson, I. (Ed.). (1986). *International perspectives in curriculum history.* Wolfboro, NH: Croom Helm.

Goodson, I. (1986). *School subject and curriculum change: Studies in curriculum history.* London: Falmer.

Gordon, T. (1986). *Democracy in one school: Progressive education and restructuring.* London: Falmer Press.

Gorter, R. J. (Ed.). (1986). *Views on core curriculum: Contributions to an international seminar.* Enschade, Netherlands: National Institute for Curriculum Development.

Gorwood, B. T. (1986). *School transfer and curriculum continuity.* London: Croom Helm.

Grant, C., & Sleeter, C. (1986). *After the school bell rings.* Philadelphia: Falmer.

Hameyer, U., Frey, K., Haft, H., & Kuebart, F. (Eds.). (1986). *Curriculum research in Europe.* Strasbourg, France: The Council of Europe: Kiel, Germany: Institute for Science Education: Lisse, Natherlands: Swets and Zeitlinger.

Hampel, R. L. (1986). *The last little citadel: American high schools since 1940.* Boston: Houghton Mifflin.

Hill, J. C. (1986). *Curriculum evaluation for school improvement.* Springfield, IL: Charles C. Thomas.

Holmes Group. (1986). *Tomorrow's teachers.* East Lansing, MI: Author.

House, E. R. (Ed.). (1986). *New directions in educational evaluation.* London and Philadelphia: Falmer Press.

Idol, L., with Nevin, A., & Paolucci-Whitcomb, P. (1986). *Models of curriculum-based assessment.* Rockville, MD: Aspen Publishers.

Jackson, P. W. (1986). *The practice of teaching.* New York: Teachers College Press.

Joyce, B. R. (1986). *Improving America's schools.* White Plains, NY: Longman, Inc.

Joyce, B. R., & Weil, M. (1986). *Models of teaching* (third edition). Englewood Cliffs, NJ: Prentice-Hall. (previous editions, 1980, 1972).

Jozefzoon, E. O. I. (Ed.). (1986). *Coordinating curriculum policy and practice.* Enschade, Netherlands: National Institute for Curriculum Development.

Kealey, R. J. (1986). *Curriculum in the Catholic school.* Washington, DC: National Catholic Education Association.

Kelly, A. V. (1986). *Knowledge and curriculum planning.* London: Harper and Row.

Kemmis, S., with Fitzclarence, L. (1986). *Curriculum theorising: Beyond reproduction theory.* Victoria, Australia: Deakin University.

Kirk, G. (1986). *The core curriculum.* Princeton, NJ: Princeton Book Company for Hodder and Stoughton Educational.

Klein, M. F. (Guest Ed.). (1986). Beyond the measured curriculum. In *Theory into Practice, 25*(1).

Kliebard, H. M. (1986). *The struggle for the American curriculum: 1893–1958.* London and Boston: Routledge and Kegan Paul.

Knox, A. B. (1986). *Helping adults learn: A guide to planning, implementing, and conducting programs.* San Francisco: Jossey-Bass, Inc.

Lawton, D. (Ed.). (1986). *School curriculum planning.* Princeton, NJ: Princeton Book Company for Hodder and Stoughton Educational.

Leithwood, K. A. (Ed.). (1986). *Planned educational change: A manual of curriculum review, development, and implementation: Concepts and procedures.* Buffalo, NY: Ontario Institute for Studies in Education.

Marsh, C. (1986). *Curriculum: An analytic introduction*. Sydney, Australia: Ian Novak.

McLaren, P. L. (1986). *Schooling as ritual performance*. New York: Routledge.

McNeil, L. M. (1986). *Contradictions of control: School structures and school knowledge*. New York: Routledge and Kegan Paul.

Moon, B. (1986). *The "new maths" curriculum controversy: An international story*. London: Falmer Press.

Posner, G. J., & Rudnitsky, A. N. (1986). *Course design: A guide to curriculum development for teachers* (third edition). New York: Longman. (previous editions 1981, 1978).

Price, M. H. (Ed.). (1986). *The development of the secondary curriculum*. London: Croom Helm.

Print, M. (1986). *Curriculum planning and management*. Perth, Australia: WACAE Monograph.

Raths, L. E., Wassermann, S., Jonas, A., & Rothstein, A. (1986). *Teaching for thinking: Theory, strategies, and activities for the classroom* (second edition). New York: Teachers College Press.

Roth, K., Anderson, C., & Smith, E. (1986). *Curriculum materials, teacher talk, and student learning: Case studies in fifth-grade science teaching*. East Lansing: Michigan State University, Institute for Research on Teaching.

Rowntree, D. (1986). *Teaching through self-instruction: A practical handbook for course developers*. New York: Nichols.

Schubert, W. H. (1986). *Curriculum: Perspective, paradigm, and possibility*. New York: Macmillan.

Schweinhart, L. J., Weikart D. P., & Larner, M. B. (1986). *Consequences of three preschool curriculum models through age 15*. Ypsilanti, MI: High/Scope Educational Research Foundation.

Sedlak, M. W., Wheeler, C. W., Pullin, D. C., & Cusick, P. A. (1986). *Selling students short: Classroom bargains and academic reform in the American high school*. New York: Teachers College Press.

Shor, I. (1986). *Culture wars: School and society in the conservative restoration, 1969–1984*. Boston: Routledge and Kegan Paul. (Revised, 1992).

Shor, I., & Freire, P. (1986). *A pedagogy for liberation: Dialogues on transforming education*. Westport, CT: Bergin & Garvey.

Smith, F. (1986). *Insult to intelligence: The bureaucratic invasion of our classrooms*. Portsmouth, NH: Heinemann.

Smith, L. M., Kleine, P. F., Prunty, J. P., & Dwyer, D. C. (1986). *Educational innovators: Then and now*. London: Falmer Press.

Spodek, B. (Ed.). (1986). *Today's kindergarten: Exploring the knowledge base, expanding the curriculum*. New York: Teachers College Press.

Strickland, K. (Guest Ed.). (1986). Ralph W. Tyler. A special edition of *The Journal of Thought*, 21(1), Spring.

Taylor, P. H. (Ed.). (1986). *Recent developments in curriculum studies*. London: Taylor and Francis.

Thaiss, C. (1986). *Language across the curriculum in the elementary grades*. Champaign-Urbana, IL: Education Resources Information Center Clearinghouse.

Tomkins, G. S. (1986). *A common countenance: Stability and change in the Canadian curriculum*. Scarborough, Ontario: Prentice-Hall Canada, Inc.

Tomlinson, P., & Quinton, M. (Eds.). (1986). *Values across the curriculum*. London: Falmer.

Tomlinson, T. M., & Walberg, H. J. (Eds.). (1986). *Academic work and educational excellence*. Berkeley, CA: McCutchan.

Tucker, R. N. (1986). *Integration of media into the curriculum*. New York: Nichols.

United States Department of Education. (1986). *What works: Research about teaching and learning*. Washington, DC: Author.

van Manen, M. (1986). *The tone of teaching*. London: Heinemann.

Van Til, W. (1986). *ASCD in retrospect*. Alexandria, VA: Association for Supervision and Curriculum Development.

Walberg, H. J., & Keefe, J. W. (Eds.). (1986). *Rethinking reform: The principal's dilemma. A special report of the NASSP curriculum council*. Reston, VA: National Association of Secondary School Principals.

Walker, D. F., & Soltis, J. F. (1986). *Curriculum and aims*. New York: Teachers College Press.

Weinstein, D. F. (1986). *Administrator's guide to curriculum mapping: A step-by-step manual*. Englewood Cliffs, NJ: Prentice-Hall.

Wiles, J., & Bondi, J. (1986). *The essential middle school*. Tampa, FL: Wiles, Bondi, and Associates, Inc.

Wittrock, M. (Ed.). (1986). *The handbook of research on teaching* (third edition). New York: Macmillan.

Zenger, W. F., & Zenger, S. K. (1986). *Curriculum development (accountability): At the local level*. Saratoga, CA: R & E Publishers.

1987

Altbach, P. G. (1987). *The knowledge context: Comparative perspectives on the distribution of knowledge*. Albany: State University of New York Press.

Anther, J. (1987). *Lucy Sprague Mitchell: The making of a modern woman*. New Haven, CT: Yale University Press.

Asante, M. (1987). *The Afrocentric idea*. Philadelphia: Temple University Press.

Banks, J. (1987). *Teaching strategies for ethnic studies*. Boston: Allyn & Bacon.

Benne, K. D., & Tozer, S. (1987). *Society as educator in an age of transition. Eighty-sixth Yearbook of the Society for the Study of Education, Part II*. Chicago: University of Chicago Press.

Bennett, W. (1987). *James Madison high school: A curriculum for American students*. Washington, DC: U.S. Department of Education.

Blenkin, G. M., & Kelly, A. V. (1987). *The primary curriculum: A process approach to curriculum planning* (second edition). London: Harper and Row.

Bloom, A. (1987). *The closing of the American mind: How higher education has failed democracy and impoverished the souls of today's students*. Chicago: University of Chicago Press.

Booth, T., & Coulby, D. (Eds.). (1987). *Producing and reducing disaffection: Curricula for all*. Philadelphia: Open University Press.

Bowers, C. A. (1987). *Elements of a post-liberal theory of education*. New York: Teachers College Press.

Brady, L. (1987). *Curriculum development* (second edition). Sydney, Australia: Prentice-Hall.

Chambliss, J. J. (1987). *Education theory as theory of conduct: From Aristotle to Dewey*. Albany: State University of New York Press.

Champagne, A., & Horning, L. (1987). *The science curriculum: This year in school science: 1986*. Washington, DC: American Association for the Advancement of Science.

Cheney, L. V. (1987). *American memory: A report on the humanities in the nation's public schools*. Washington, DC: National Endowment of the Humanities.

Choate, J. S., Enright, B., Miller, L., Potest, J., & Rakes, T. (1987). *Assessing and programming basic curriculum skills*. Boston: Allyn & Bacon.

Clark, J. L. (1987). *Curriculum renewal in school foreign language learning*. Oxford: Oxford University Press.

Cohen, D., & Fraser, B. J. (1987). *The processes of curriculum development and evaluation*. Woden, Australia: The Curriculum Development Centre.

Dubin, F., & Olshtain, E. (1987). *Course design: Developing programs and materials for language learning*. New York: Cambridge University Press.

Duckworth, E. R. (1987). *"The having of wonderful ideas" and other essays on teaching and learning*. New York: Teachers College Press.

Earl, R. (1987). *The art and craft of course design*. New York: Nichols.

Edwards, D., & Mercer, W. (1987). *Common knowledge: The development of understanding in the classroom*. New York: Routledge. London: Methuen.

Ellis, A. K., Makey, J. A., & Glenn, A. E. (1987). *The school curriculum*. Boston: Allyn & Bacon.

English, F. W. (1987). *Curriculum management for schools, colleges, business*. Springfield, IL: Charles C. Thomas.

Ferguson, D. L. (1987). *Curriculum decision making for students with severe handicaps*. New York: Teachers College Press.

Fraser, B., & Cohen, D. (1987). *The processes of curriculum development and evaluation: A retrospective account of the processes of the Australian Science Education Project*. Canberra, Australia: Curriculum Development Centre.

Freire, P., & Macedo, D. (1987). *Literacy: Reading the word and the world*. South Hadley, MA: Bergin & Garvey.

Glatthorn, A. A. (1987a). *Curriculum leadership*. Glenview, IL: Scott Foresman and Company.

Glatthorn, A. A. (1987b). *Curriculum renewal*. Alexandria, VA: Association for Supervision and Curriculum Development.

Goodlad, J. I. (Ed.). (1987). *The ecology of school renewal. Eighty-sixth Yearbook of the Society for the Study of Education, Part I*. Chicago: University of Chicago Press.

Goodlad, J. I., & Anderson, R. H. (1987). *The nongraded elementary school* (Revised edition). New York: Teachers College Press.

Goodson, I. (1987). *School subjects and curriculum change* (second edition). Philadelphia: Falmer Press.

Gothard, W. P., & Goodhew, E. (1987). *Guidance and the changing curriculum*. New York: Routledge & Kegan Paul.

Grundy, S. (1987). *Curriculum: Product or praxis?* London: Falmer Press.

Gutmann, A. (1987). *Democratic education*. Princeton, NJ: Princeton University Press.

Hargis, C. H. (1987). *Curriculum-based assessment: A primer*. Springfield, IL: Charles C. Thomas. (Second edition, 1995).

Hass, G. (1987). *Curriculum planning: A new approach* (fifth edition). Boston: Allyn & Bacon.

Hirsch, E. D. (1987). *Cultural literacy: What every American needs to know*. Boston: Houghton Mifflin.

Hoffman, C. M. (1987). *Curriculum gone astray: When push came to shove*. Lancaster, PA: Technomic.

Huff, J. (1987). *The contemporary writing curriculum*. New York: Teachers College Press.

International Association for the Evaluation of Educational Achievement. (1987). *The underachieving curriculum: A national report on the second international mathematics study*. Champaign, IL: Stipes Publishing.

Jones, B. F., Palinscar, A. S., Ogle, D. S., & Carr, E. G. (1987). *Strategic teaching and learning: Cognitive instruction in the content areas.* Alexandria, VA: Association for Supervision and Curriculum Development.

Katz, M. (1987). *Reconstructing American education.* Cambridge, MA: Harvard University Press.

LePage, A. (1987). *Transforming education: The new 3 R's.* Oakland, CA: Oakmore House.

Lloyd, S. M. (1987). *The Putney School: A progressive experiment.* New Haven, CT: Yale University Press.

McKnight, C., Crosswhite, F., Dossey, J., Kifer, E., Swafford, J., Travers, K. & Cooney, T. (1987). *The underachieving curriculum: Assessing U.S. mathematics from an international perspective.* Champaign, IL: Stipes.

Miller, A. H. (1987). *Course design for university lecturers.* New York: Nichols.

Mobley, M. (1987). *Former schools council programme 2: Helping individual teachers to become more effective.* Layerthorpe, York, England: Longman.

Molnar, A. (Ed.). (1987). *Social issues and education: Challenge and responsibility.* Alexandria, VA: Association for Supervision and Curriculum Development.

Murphy, R., & Torrance, H. (Eds.) (1987). *Evaluating education: Issues and methods.* London: Harper and Row.

Ornstein, A. C., & Hunkins, F. P. (1987). *Curriculum: Foundations, principles, and issues.* Englewood Cliffs, NJ: Prentice-Hall.

Parsons, C. (1987). *The curriculum change game.* London: Falmer Press.

Popkewitz, T. S. (Ed.). (1987). *The formation of school subjects: The struggle for creating an American institution.* Philadelphia: Falmer Press.

Portal, C. (Ed.). (1987). *The history curriculum for teachers.* London: Falmer Press.

Presseinsen, B. Z. (1987). *Thinking skills throughout the curriculum: A conceptual design.* Bloomington, IN: Phi Lambda Theta.

Pring, R. (1987). *The emerging 14–18 curriculum.* Princeton, NJ: Princeton Book Company for London: Hodder and Stoughton Educational.

Ravitch, D., & Finn, C. E. (1987). *What do our 17-year olds know? A report on the first national assessment of history and literature.* New York: Harper and Row.

Resnick, L. B. (1987). *Education and learning to think.* Washington, DC: National Academic Press.

Saber, N., Rudduck, J., & Reid, W. (1987). *Partnership and autonomy in school-based curriculum development.* Sheffield, UK: University of Sheffield, Division of Education.

Schön, D. A. (1987). *Educating the reflective practitioner: Toward a new design for teaching and learning in the professions.* San Francisco: Jossey-Bass.

Seefeldt, C. (Ed.). (1987). *The early childhood curriculum: A review of current research.* New York: Teachers College Press.

Sewall, G. (1987). *American history textbooks: An assessment of quality.* New York: Education Excellence Network.

Shor, I. (Ed.). (1987). *Freire for the classroom: A sourcebook for liberatory teaching.* Portsmouth, NH: Boynton/Cook.

Sinclair, R. L., & Ghory, W. J. (1987). *Reaching marginal students: A primary concern for school renewal.* Berkeley, CA: McCutchan Publishing.

Solity, J., & Bull, S. (1987). *Special needs: Bridging the curriculum gap.* Philadelphia: Open University Press.

Soltis, J. F. (Ed.). (1987). *Reforming teacher education: The impact of the Holmes Group report.* New York: Teachers College Press.

Squires, G. (1987). *The curriculum beyond school.* Princeton, NJ: Princeton Book Company for Hodder and Stoughton Educational.

Valentine, J. A. (1987). *College board and the school curriculum: A history of the college board's influence on the substance and standards of American education, 1900–1980.* New York: College Entrance Examination Board.

Walker, J. C. (1987). *Educative leadership for curriculum development.* Canberra, Australia: ACT Schools Authority.

Warne, M. M., & Waite, W. W. (1987). *Assessment-based vocational curriculum manual: The bridge between school and community.* Lanham, MD: University Press of America.

Wexler, P. (1987). *Social analysis of education: After the new sociology.* Boston: Routledge & Kegan Paul.

White, M. (1987). *The Japanese educational challenge: A commitment to children.* New York: The Free Press.

White, M. A. (Ed.). (1987). *What curriculum for the information age?* Hillside, NJ: Lawrence Erlbaum Associates.

Wideen, M. F., & Andrews, I. (Eds.). (1987). *Staff development for school improvement: A focus on the teacher.* London and Philadelphia: Falmer Press.

Wilcock, R. (1987). *RE-readings: RE in the school curriculum.* London: Falmer Press.

Woolnough, B. E. (1987). *Of people, policy, and power: The shaping of the curriculum, physics teaching in schools, 1960–1985.* London and Philadelphia: Falmer Press.

1988

Aiken, S. H., Anderson, K., Dinnerstein, M., Lensink, J. N., & MacCorquodale, P. (Eds.). (1988). *Changing our minds: Feminist transformations of knowledge.* Albany: State University of New York Press.

Arnold, P. J. (1988). *Education, movement and the curriculum: A philosophic enquiry.* London: Falmer Press.

Bates, I., Manthorpe, C., & Layton, D. (1988). *The changing curriculum.* London: Croom Helm.

Belenky, M., Clinchy, B., Goldberg, N., & Tarule, J. (1988). *Women's ways of knowing: The development of self, voice and mind.* New York: Basic Books.

Bennett, W. J. (1988). *American education: Making it work.* Washington, DC: U.S. Government Printing Office.

Beyer, L. E. (1988). *Knowing and acting: Inquiry, ideology and educational studies.* London: Falmer Press.

Beyer, L. E., & Apple, M. W. (Eds.). (1988). *The curriculum: Problems, politics, and possibilities.* Albany: State University of New York Press.

Blenkin, G. M., & Kelly, A. V. (Eds.). (1988). *Assessment in early childhood education.* London: Paul Chapman.

Boulding, E. (1988). *Building a global civic culture: Education for an interdependent world.* New York: Teachers College Press.

Bowers, C. A. (1988). *The cultural dimensions of educational computing.* New York: Teachers College Press.

Boylan, A. M. (1988). *Sunday school: The formation of an American institution, 1790–1880.* New Haven, CT: Yale University Press.

Brandt, R. S. (Ed.). (1988). *Content of the curriculum.* Alexandria, VA: Association for Supervision and Curriculum Development.

Broudy, H. S. (1988). *The uses of schooling.* New York: Routledge & Kegan Paul.

Bullough, R., Jr. (1988). *The forgotten dream of American public education.* Ames: Iowa State University Press.

Butts, R. F. (1988). *The morality of democratic citizenship.* Calavasas, CA: Center for Civic Education.

Carson, T. R. (Ed.). (1988). *Toward a renaissance of humanity: Rethinking and reorienting curriculum and instruction.* Edmonton, Alberta: World Council for Curriculum and Instruction and University of Alberta.

Cazden, C. B. (1988). *Classroom discourse: The language of teaching and learning.* Portsmouth, NH: Heinemann.

Chapman, A. (1988). *The difference it makes: A resource book on gender for educators.* Boston: National Association of Independent Schools.

Cherryholmes, C. H. (1988). *Power and criticism: Post-structural investigations in education.* New York: Teachers College Press.

Collis, B. (1988). *Computers, curriculum, and whole-class instruction*. Belmont, CA: Wadsworth Publishers.

Connelly, F. M., & Clandinin, D. J. (1988). *Teachers as curriculum planners: Narratives of experience*. New York: Teachers College Press.

Cremin, L. (1988). *American education: The metropolitan experience, 1876–1980*. New York: Harper and Row.

Cumming, J. (1988). *Curriculum and work: A joint enterprise*. Canberra, Australia: Curriculum Development Centre.

Cunningham, P. (1988). *Curriculum change in the primary school since 1945: Dissemination of the ideal*. New York: Falmer Press.

Dalton, T. H. (1988). *The challenge of curriculum innovation: A study of ideology and practice*. Bristol, PA: Falmer Press.

Egan, K. (1988a). *Primary understanding: Education in early childhood*. London: Routledge.

Egan, K. (1988b). *Teaching as storytelling: An alternative approach to teaching and the curriculum*. London: Routledge.

Elias, M., & Clabby, J. (1988). *Social skills and social decision making skills for the elementary grades: A curriculum guide for educators*. Rockville, MD: Aspen.

Ellis, A. K., Mackey, J. A., & Glenn, A. D. (1988). *The school curriculum*. Boston: Allyn & Bacon.

Engle, S. H., & Ochoa, A. S. (1988). *Education for democratic citizenship: Decision-making in the social sciences*. New York: Teachers College Press.

English, F. W. (1988). *Curriculum auditing*. Lancaster, PA: Technomic Publishing.

Gagne, R. M., Wager, W. W., & Briggs, L. L. (1988). *Principles of instructional design* (third edition). New York: Holt, Rinehart, and Winston. (Previous editions 1979, 1974)

Giroux, H. A. (1988a). *Schooling and the struggle for public life*. Minneapolis: University of Minnesota Press.

Giroux, H. A. (1988b). *Teachers as intellectuals: Toward a critical pedagogy of learning*. Granby, MA: Bergin & Garvey.

Goodson, I. F. (Ed.). (1988). *International perspectives in curriculum history*. London: Routledge.

Goodson, I. F. (1988) *The making of curriculum: Collected essays*. London: Falmer Press.

Grant, G. (1988). *The world we created at Hamilton high*. Cambridge, MA: Harvard University Press.

Greene, M. (1988). *The dialectic of freedom*. New York: Teachers College Press.

Gress, J. R., & Purpel, D. E. (Eds.). (1988). *Curriculum: An introduction to the field* (second edition). Berkeley, CA: McCutchan. (Previous edition 1978).

Grumet, M. (1988). *Bitter milk: Women and teaching.* Amherst: University of Massachusetts Press.

Jackson, P. W. (Ed.). (1988). *Contributing to educational change: Perspectives on research and practice.* Berkeley, CA: McCutchan.

Jervis, K., & Tobier, A. (Eds.). (1988). *Education for democracy. Proceedings from the Cambridge School Conference on Progressive Education,* October 1987. Weston, MA: The Cambridge School.

Johnston, B., & Dowdy, S. (1988). *Work required: Teaching and assessing in a negotiated curriculum.* Cammeray, New South Wales, Australia: Martin Educational.

Kemmis, S., & Stake, R. (1988). *Evaluating curriculum.* Victoria, Australia: Deakin University Press.

Kirk, D. (1988). *Physical education and curriculum study: A critical introduction.* London: Croom Helm.

Langenbach, M. (1988). *Curriculum models in adult education.* Malabar, FL: Krieger.

Lindsey, C. W. (1988). *Teaching students to teach themselves.* New York: Nichols.

Lopez, D. D. (1988). *Teaching children: A curriculum guide to what children need to know at each level through sixth grade.* Westchester, IL: Crossway Books.

Marsh, C., & Stafford, K. (1988). *Curriculum: Australia practice and issues* (Second edition). Sydney, Australia: McGraw-Hill.

Marzano, R. J., Brandt, R. S., Hughes, C. S., Jones, B. E., Presseinsen, B. Z., Rankin, S. C., & Suhor, C. (1988). *Dimensions of thinking: A framework for curriculum and instruction.* Alexandria, VA: Association for Supervision and Curriculum Development.

McLeod, S. H. (Ed.). (1988). *Strengthening programs for writing across the curriculum.* San Francisco: Jossey-Bass.

Menges, R. J., & Mathis, B. C. (1988). *Key resources on teaching, learning, curriculum, and faculty development.* San Francisco: Jossey-Bass.

Miller, G. E. (1988). *The meaning of general education: The emergence of a curriculum paradigm.* New York: Teachers College Press.

Miller, J. P. (1988). *The holistic curriculum.* Toronto: Ontario Institute for Studies in Education Press. (Revised and expanded 1993 and 1996).

Moon, B. (Ed.). (1988). *Modular curriculum.* London: Paul Chapman Publishing.

Muckle, J. Y. (1988). *A guide to the Soviet curriculum: What the Russian child is taught in school.* London: Croom Helm.

Oliva, P. F. (1988). *Developing the curriculum.* (second edition). Glenview, IL: Scott Foresman. (Previous edition 1982).

Ornstein, A. C., & Hunkins, F. P. (1988). *Curriculum: Foundations, principles, and issues.* Englewood Cliffs, NJ: Prentice-Hall.

Pinar, W. F. (Ed.). (1988). *Contemporary curriculum discourses*. Scottsdale, AZ: Gorsuch Scarisbrick.

Print, M. (1988). *Curriculum development and design*. St. Leonards, New South Wales, Australia: Allen & Unwin.

Purpel, D. E. (1988). *The moral and spiritual crisis in education: A curriculum for justice and compassion in education*. Westport, CT: Greenwood Publishing Group.

Reardon, B. A. (1988). *Comprehensive peace education: Educating for global responsibility*. New York: Teachers College Press.

Reardon, B. A. (Ed.). (1988). *Educating for global responsibility: Teacher designed curricula for peace education, K–12*. New York: Teachers College Press.

Rose, S. (1988). *Keeping them out of the hands of satan: Evangelical schooling in America*. New York: Routledge.

Scheirer, E. A., & Hunter, R. (1988). *The organic curriculum*. London: Falmer Press.

Schostak, J. (Ed.). (1988). *Breaking into the curriculum: The impact of information technology on schooling*. London: Methuen.

Sharpes, D. K. (1988). *Curriculum traditions and practices*. New York: St. Martin's Press.

Simonson, R., & Walker, S. (Eds.). (1988). *The Graywolf annual five: Multi-cultural literacy*. St. Paul, MN: Graywolf Press.

Sinclair, R., & Nieto, S. (1988). *Renewing school curriculum*. Amherst, MA: Coalition for School Improvement.

Sleeter, C., & Grant, C. (1988). *Making choices for multicultural education: Five approaches to race, class, and gender*. Columbus, OH: Merrill.

Smith, F. (1988). *Joining the literacy club: Further essays into education*. Portsmouth, NH: Heinemann.

Stodolsky, S. S. (1988). *The subject matters: Classroom activity in math and social studies*. Chicago: University of Chicago Press.

Swartz, E. (1988). *Multicultural curriculum development*. Rochester, NY: Rochester City School District.

Tanner, D., & Keefe, J. W. (Eds.). (1988). *Improving the curriculum: The principal's challenge*. (A report of the NASSP Curriculum Council). Reston, VA: National Association of Secondary School Principals.

Tanner, L. N. (Ed.). (1988). *Critical issues in curriculum. The Eighty-Seventh Yearbook of the National Society for the Study of Education*. (Part I). Chicago: University of Chicago Press.

Travers, K. J., & Westbury, I. (1988). *The second international mathematics study: Curriculum analysis*. New York: Pergamon.

Tuttle, F. B., Becker, L. A., & Sousa, J. A. (1988). *Program design and development for gifted and talented students*. Washington, DC: National Education Association.

Tyson-Bernstein, H. (1988). *A conspiracy of good intentions: America's textbook fiasco*. Washington, DC: Council for Basic Education.

Van Tassel-Baska, J., Feldhusen, J., Johnson, D., Seeley, K., & Silverman, L. (1988). *Comprehensive curriculum for gifted learners*. Boston: Allyn & Bacon. (second edition, 1994).

Weiler, K. (1988). *Women teaching for change: Gender, class and power*. South Hadley, MA: Bergin and Garvey.

Weis, L. (Ed.). (1988). *Class, race, and gender in American education*. Albany: State University of New York Press.

Westbury, I., & Purves, A. C. (Eds.). (1988). *Cultural literacy and the idea of general education. The Eighty-Seventh Yearbook of the National Society for the Study of Education*. (Part II). Chicago: University of Chicago Press.

Wisconsin Department of Public Instruction. (1988). *A guide to curriculum planning in technology education*. Madison: Wisconsin Dept. of Public Instruction.

Wunungmurra, W. (1988). *Dhawurrpunaramirra: Finding the common ground for a new Yolngu curriculum*. Northern Territory, Australia: Yirrkala Community School.

1989

Armstrong, D. G. (1989). *Developing and documenting the curriculum*. Boston: Allyn & Bacon.

Bazalgette, C. (Ed.). (1989). *Primary media education: A curriculum statement*. London: British Film Institute.

Beyer, L. E., Feinberg, W., Pagano, J. A., & Whitson, J. A. (1989). *Preparing teachers as professionals: The role of educational studies and other liberal disciplines*. New York: Teachers College Press.

Brady, M. (1989). *What's worth teaching?: Selecting, organizing and integrating knowledge*. Albany: State University of New York Press.

Bricker, D. C. (1989). *Classroom life as civic education: Individual achievement and student cooperation in schools*. New York: Teachers College Press.

Center, D. (1989). *Curriculum and teaching strategies for students with behavioral disorders*. Englewood Cliffs, NJ: Prentice-Hall.

Crompton, R. (Ed.). (1989). *Computers and the primary curriculum 3–13*. London: Falmer Press.

Davies, W. (1989). *The curriculum and organization of the county intermediate school, 1880–1926*. Cardiff, Wales: University of Wales Press.

Decastell, S., Luke, A., & Luke, C. (1989). *Language, authority, criticism: Readings on the school textbook*. Bristol, PA: Falmer Press.

Dennis, L. J. (Ed.). (1989). *George S. Counts and Charles A. Beard: Collaborators for change*. Albany: State University of New York Press.

Diamond, R. M. (1989). *Designing and improving courses and curricula in higher education.* San Francisco: Jossey-Bass.

Doll, R. C. (1989). *Curriculum improvement: Decision making and process* (seventh edition). Boston: Allyn & Bacon. (Previous editions 1986, 1982, 1978, 1974, 1970, 1964).

Early Year Curriculum Group. (1989). *Early childhood education: The early years curriculum and the national curriculum.* Stoke on Trent, England: Trentham Books.

Emihovich, C. (Ed.). (1989). *Locating learning across the curriculum: Ethnographic perspectives on classroom research.* Norwood, NJ: Ablex Publishing.

Finch, C., & Crunkilton, J. (1989). *Curriculum development in vocational and technical education: Planning, content, and implementation* (third edition). Boston: Allyn & Bacon.

Ford, A., Schnorr, R., Meyer, L., Davern, L., Black, J., & Dempsey, P. (Eds.). (1989). *The Syracuse community-referenced curriculum guide for students with moderate and severe disabilities.* Baltimore, MD: Paul H. Brookes.

Freire, P., & Faundez, A. (1989). *Learning to question: A pedagogy of liberation.* New York: Continuum Publishing.

Giroux, H., & McLaren, P. L. (1989). *Critical pedagogy, the state, and cultural struggle.* Albany: State University of New York.

Giroux, H. A., Simon, R. I., & Contributors. (1989). *Popular culture: Schooling and everyday life.* New York: Bergin and Garvey.

Hamilton, D. (1989) *Toward a theory of schooling.* London: Falmer Press.

Hargreaves, A. (1989). *Curriculum and assessment reform.* Bristol, PA: Open University Press c/o Taylor & Francis.

Holmes, B., & McLean, M. (1989). *The curriculum: A comparative perspective.* Boston: Unwin Hyman.

Holt, J. (1989). *Learning all the time.* New York: Addison-Wesley.

Hyde, A., & Bizar, M. (1989). *Thinking in context: Teaching cognitive processes across the elementary school curriculum.* New York: Longman.

Jackson, P. W., & Haroutunian, G. S. (Eds.). (1989). *From Socrates to software: The teacher as text and the text as teacher. The Eighty-Eighth Yearbook of the National Society for the Study of Education* (Part I). Chicago: University of Chicago Press.

Jacobs, H. H. (Ed.). (1989). *Interdisciplinary curriculum: Design and implementation.* Alexandria, VA: Association for Supervision and Curriculum Development.

Katz, L. G., & Chard, S. C. (1989). *Engaging children's minds: The project approach.* Norwood, NJ: Ablex Publishing.

Klein, M. F. (1989). *Curriculum reform in the elementary school: Creating your own agenda.* New York: Teachers College Press.

Kridel, C. (Ed.). (1989). *Curriculum history: Conference presentations from the Society for the Study of Curriculum History*. Lanham, MD: University Press of America and The Society for the Study of Curriculum History.

Lawton, D. (1989). *Education, culture, and the national curriculum*. London: Hodder and Stoughton.

Luke, C. (1989). *Pedagogy, printing, and protestantism: The discourse on childhood*. Albany, NY: State University of New York Press.

Lynch, K. (1989). *The hidden curriculum: Reproduction in education, a re-appraisal*. Bristol, PA: Falmer Press c/o Taylor & Francis.

Madaus, G. F., & Stufflebeam, D. L. (Eds.). (1989). *Educational evaluation: Classic works of Ralph W. Tyler*. Boston: Kluwer Academic Publishers.

Martin, D. S., Glatthorn, A., Winters, M., & Saif, P. (1989). *Curriculum leadership: Case studies for program practitioners*. Alexandria, VA: Association for Supervision and Curriculum Development.

McLaren, P. L. (1989). *Life in schools: An introduction to critical pedagogy in the foundations of education*. New York: Longman.

Milburn, G., Goodson, G., & Clark, R. (Eds.). (1989). *Reinterpreting curriculum research: Images and arguments*. Bristol, PA: Falmer Press c/o Taylor & Francis.

National Council of Teachers of Mathematics. (1989). *Curriculum and evaluation standards for school mathematics*. Reston, VA: Author.

Nicholls, J. G. (1989). *The competitive ethos and democratic education*. Cambridge, MA: Harvard University Press.

Noddings, N. (1989). *Women and evil*. Berkeley: University of California Press.

Oliver, D. W., & Gershman, K. W. (1989). *Education, modernity, and fractured meaning: Toward a process theory of teaching and learning*. Albany: State University of New York Press.

Pajak, E. (1989). *The central office supervisor of curriculum and instruction*. Boston: Allyn & Bacon.

Pelgrum, W. J. (1989). *Educational assessment: Monitoring, evaluation, and the curriculum*. DeLier, Netherlands: Academisch Boeken Centrum.

Preedy, M. (Ed.). (1989). *Approaches to curriculum management*. Bristol, PA: Open University Press c/o Taylor & Francis.

Pring, R. (1989). *The new curriculum*. London: Cassell.

Puckett, J. L. (1989). *Foxfire reconsidered: A twenty year experiment in progressive education*. Urbana: University of Illinois Press.

Purpel, D. E. (1989). *The moral and spiritual crisis in education: A curriculum for justice and compassion in education*. Granby, MA: Bergin and Garvey.

Purves, A. C. (Ed.). (1989). *International comparisons of educational reform*. Alexandria, VA: Association for Supervision and Curriculum Development.

Resnick, L. B., & Klopfer, L. E. (1989). *Toward the thinking curriculum: Current cognitive research. Yearbook of the Association for Supervision and Curriculum Development*. Alexandria, VA: Association for Supervision and Curriculum Development.

Reynolds, W. M. (1989). *Reading curriculum theory: The development of a new hermeneutic*. New York: Peter Lang.

Romiszowski, A. J. (1989). *Designing instructional systems: Decision-making in course planning and curriculum design*. East Brunswick, NJ: Nichols/GP.

Rose, M. (1989). *Lives on the boundary: The struggles and achievements of America's underprepared*. New York: The Free Press of Macmillan.

Rosenholtz, S. J. (1989). *Teachers' workplace: The social organization of schools*. White Plains, NY: Longman.

Salia-Bao, K. (1989). *Curriculum development and African culture*. New York: Edward Arnold.

Sears, J. T., & Marshall, J. D. (Eds.). (1989). *Teaching and thinking about curriculum*. New York: Teachers College Press.

Spring, J. (1989). *The sorting machine revisited*. New York: Longman.

Walker, D. F. (1989). *Fundamentals of curriculum*. San Diego, CA: Harcourt, Brace & Jovanovich.

Whitson, J. A. (1989). *Constitution and curriculum: Hermeneutical semiotics of cases and controversies in education, law, and social science*. London: Falmer Press.

Wiegand, P., and Rayner, M. (Eds.). (1989). *Curriculum progress 5–16: School subjects and the national curriculum debate*. Bristol, PA: Falmer Press c/o Taylor & Francis.

CHAPTER TEN

Curriculum Literature and Context
1990–2000

Just as we bemoaned the hazards of attempting to capture the *zeitgeist* of the 1970s in the first edition of this work without the advantage of perspective that time provides, we are now faced with a similar predicament as we reflect on the historical significance of the 1990s. Events that impress us as profound, unique, or progressive may ultimately prove trivial as the years pass. We risk committing such errors in judgment in regard to the 1990s when we offer the opinion that America reached a turning point of sorts during this decade. It was the first decade in over 40 years when the United States was not involved in a military struggle with another superpower. The growing global influence of the People's Republic of China is unmistakable. China possesses the world's largest standing army and an economy that is likely to supersede that of the United States within a generation. Nonetheless, the United States was the world's preeminent military superpower, spending more than five times in defense than the nearest national power.

It was a decade of growth, consolidation, and possibility. The unprecedented economic growth during the decade offered the American people a variety of options, including lowering taxes, paying off the national debt, and/or assuring the continued fiscal health of social security and/or the possibility of expanding the availability of health care. By decade's end it was clear that Europe was moving closer to economic integration, as demonstrated by the appearance of a single currency, the euro. China was firmly committed to the adoption of new economic policies that held the potential for extraordinary economic growth fueled by those foreign investors who were not dissuaded by an often criticized civil rights record. Leaders of North and South Korea appeared to be moving toward a rapprochement of sorts and a growing number of U.S. citizens came to believe with the rest of the world that it was time to relax the trade embargo and travel restrictions against Cuba. Did citizens of the United States understand that this situation offered opportunities to think about and perhaps re-conceptualize the relationship they desired between themselves and their government?

The presidential election victory by Democrat William Jefferson Clinton was not a signal that the nation was willing to embark on major social service programs or in other ways permit expansion of the federal government. President George Bush's inability to formulate or communicate a vision for the post–Cold War era may have played at least as important a role in his failure to win a second term as did his inability to keep his promise of "no new taxes." There was talk about a "peace dividend" that would accrue with the financial savings from a diminished military, but the increase in national debt was viewed as a threat to the viability of the country's economic future. Any savings would have to be, in part, applied to reducing the national debt. The Pentagon cautioned citizens that while the United States had triumphed in the Cold War, vigilance was still needed. In the end, there was no "peace dividend"; military spending in the first Clinton administration averaged $280 billion. In 1997, $255 billion was spent by the federal government on the military, pursuing a preparedness plan that would enable the United States to fight two major wars simultaneously without the assistance of allies. In this same year, the federal government spent $27 billion on education.

Republicans took control of Congress in an electoral landslide in 1994. Their claim of a mandate of approval for their "Contract with America" was overstated, but it was obvious that many Americans were disenchanted with big government and politicians, fed up with governmental overregulation, and impatient with the corruption that seemed to accompany each new administration into office. Under aggressive leadership by Newt Gingrich in the House and Robert Dole in the Senate, Republicans announced their intentions to cut the federal spending deficit in seven years, provide the president with a line item veto, overhaul welfare and taxes, reduce the incursion by the federal government into the lives of its citizens, return money and power to the states, and seek amendments to the Constitution limiting congressional terms of office and requiring a balanced federal budget. The conservative agenda also included legalization of prayer in the public schools, the outlawing of abortion, and imprisonment of those who desecrated the flag, combined with the repeal of a variety of laws upholding affirmative action, environmental protection, and a ban on assault weapons.

By mid-decade, it was clear that the majority of Americans did not fully support this conservative social agenda. In any case, it was difficult to find either Democrats or Republicans who did not favor tax reduction, a downsizing of the federal government, welfare reform, limitations on the use of American military forces abroad, or initiatives to restore traditional moral principles and civic pride. The call to family values was applauded by policymakers even before the sexual escapades and evasive testimony of President Clinton became public knowledge. The entertainment media came in for particular criticism for its excessive portrayal of sex and violence: from the Democrats, through an effort spearheaded by Tipper Gore, wife of the vice president, to post parental advisory statements on compact discs; and from the Republicans with Robert Dole attacking liberal Hollywood in his presidential campaign stumping. In the schools, educators were encouraged to adopt character or moral education programs.

The conflicting perspectives on the role of government between the Clinton administration and Newt Gingrich's Republican Congress climaxed in a government shutdown when a budget impasse stalled a funding allocation. This stalemate became a symbol of partisan gridlock and helped to shift popular opinion toward Clinton's less ideological approach to government. When Robert Dole attempted to overcome the popularity Bill Clinton enjoyed as result of a fired-up economy, he proved to have little to offer that was new. With the economy a non-issue and the Contract with America proposals too closely tied to the abrasive, unpopular rhetoric of Newt Gingrich, Dole, the standard-bearer of traditional Republican power, had little to bring to the fight. The ineffective third party effort of Ross Perot indicated that this moment in the sun had perhaps moved to twilight. Clinton won reelection by a comfortable margin.

Perhaps the most memorable characteristic of the 1990s was the resurgent U.S. economy. The stock market became a dynamic engine of growth while interest rates, inflation, and unemployment remained low. With the exception of a brief downturn in 1996, the 1990s were a time of prosperity for those in the United States who had capital to invest. The Dow Jones industrial average skyrocketed over 6,000 points from 1990 through 1998, topping 10,000 before the end of the decade; the NASDAQ index for technology stocks ascended to dizzying heights. The shift from a manufacturing base to an information and management base effected dramatic growth in wealth, symbolized by the multibillionaire Bill Gates, head of Microsoft and guru of the techno-economy. Concerns for the expanding power of Microsoft over the industry led to federal and state antitrust lawsuits to curb its dominance in technology.

A hidden story of the decade was that real wages for workers in the United States in this decade declined. The poverty rate in the United States in 1997 was 13.5%, higher than in 1989 despite record employment. The working poor lost ground with average weekly earnings for American workers dropping from $315 in 1973 to $256 in 1996 in constant dollars. CEO salaries rose to 115 times the average worker's wage in 1997.

Corporate consolidation was another dimension of neoliberal capitalism, with large companies merging to form gigantic global powers that rivaled nations in influence and control. The reinvention of Standard Oil, target of federal trustbusters at the beginning of the century, through the merger of Texaco and Exxon, was but one sign. Time Warner and Turner Broadcasting merged and Westinghouse purchased CBS for $5 billion, joining General Electric, another of the giants in the military-industrial complex, in controlling major access to the American airwaves. AT&T joined with TCI communications in a bid to control the transmission of electronic media. *Time* magazine and Warner Brothers assumed control of Ted Turner's cable empire. In another critical industry, bank deregulation led the way to large-scale mergers, which, it was predicted, would reduce the number of banks in the United States to less than 1,000 within the first decade of the new millennium. In 1998, over $1.6 trillion was involved in eight major mergers.

While expanding in capital influence, corporations also eliminated jobs, particularly in salaried positions. "Downsizing," despite the healthy economy, was instrumental in shifting the economic profile of the American people. A dramatic example was the decision of AT&T to cut 40,000 jobs in 1995. According to the National Priorities Project, 74% of jobs in categories with the most growth paid less than a livable wage for a family of four.

The Clinton administration expended great effort in the beginning of the first term of office in establishing a national health care program, but failed to find congressional support for this proposal. Clinton did gain some satisfaction with the establishment of Americorp, a national service program for young Americans. There was also the adoption of a new welfare program, placing a five-year limit on benefits for recipients and cutting welfare spending by $69 billion. The final legislation was a leaner and, some contended, meaner approach to providing assistance to the country's poorest citizens.

While both Democrats and Republicans took credit for welfare reform and Republicans castigated Democrats for their failure to advance legislation on abortion and other family values, two issues that were conspicuous in their absence in the national debate were gun control and capital punishment. Despite token action by the federal government to limit the import of assault weapons (an interesting strategy given that the United States is now the world's leading exporter of arms) and the passing of the Brady Bill in 1993, the United States continued to develop a "weapons" culture in the number of people buying and using guns. Even the shooting of students and teachers in public schools throughout the United States in 1997, 1998, and 1999 awakened new appeals to curb appetites for weaponry but no meaningful legislative action. Given that the Southern Poverty Law Center reported the existence of over 500 active hate groups (Ku Klux Klan, Neo-Nazi, Skinhead, Black Separatist, and others) in the United States in 1999, armed, organized violence from within became ever more likely.

Despite the renewal of awareness regarding the use of the death penalty promoted through books and films such as *Dead Man Walking*, *The Green Mile*, and *A Lesson Before Dying*, the United States remained the only postindustrial nation to continue the use of capital punishment, one of five nations to have executed children for crimes since 1990. As the century came to a close, state governments had executed over 500 people since the Supreme Court reinstated the death penalty in 1976. Prison building remained a major revenue source for contractors, with the rate of incarceration for the U.S. people at 461 per 100,000 people, up from 292 per 100,000 people in 1990. One in every 113 men in the United States was a sentenced prisoner in 1998.

The United Nations entered its fifth decade of existence actively involved in efforts to resolve military conflicts across the globe. In 1992 Boutros Boutros-Ghali began a five-year term as Secretary-General of the United Nations, succeeded in 1997 by Kofi Annan, and UN peacekeeping forces entered El Salvador in 1992 following the signing of peace accords. This, along with United Nations' action in East Timor, were relatively peaceful interventions. In Kuwait, in Somalia, in Haiti, in Liberia, and in Bosnia, UN involvement was directed by the U.S. military, with U.S. or NATO forces taking prominent positions in the confrontations.

Aside from being in office to witness the collapse of the Soviet Union, the highlight of the Bush administration was the successful military and media management of Operation Desert Storm. In 1990 Saddam Hussein ordered Iraqi troops to invade the oil-rich kingdom of Kuwait, announcing that it was a legal province of Iraq. A United Nations coalition organized by the United States constituted well over a half million troops. In February 1991, UN forces entered Kuwait and quickly drove out the Iraqis, following them into southern Iraq. The attack was terminated when Hussein accepted 12 UN resolutions, including unconditional withdrawal. A rebellion by Kurds against Saddam Hussein in the aftermath of the Persian Gulf War failed to effect his overthrow, with the international community providing initial encouragement but no sustained support for this insurgency. The relationship with Hussein remained tense as UN sanctions on economic trade with Iraq crippled the life of the Iraqi people. Relief organizations estimated that the imposition of sanctions resulted in the deaths of from 300,000 to 1.2 million Iraqis due to inadequate health care and access to common necessities.

Rumblings of war surfaced in 1997 and 1998 when Hussein refused to allow UN weapons monitors to carry out scheduled inspections for weapons. Concerns that Hussein had stockpiled biological and chemical weapons brought the United States into an open declaration that military action would be taken if inspections were halted. Operation Desert Fox, four days of strategic bombing of Iraqi military and infrastructure sites, was conducted in December 1998. This attack that had a surreal context since the decision to bomb delayed House of Representatives deliberations on the impeachment of Clinton and led some members of Congress to contend that Clinton's decision to bomb was predicated on his desire to divert attention from the impeachment. Life closely imitated art as elements of the drama closely paralleled a satirical film popular at the time, *Wag the Dog*. In any case Hussein's reign as Iraqi head of state appeared at century's end to outlast Clinton's term in office.

Bill Clinton inherited the commitment by the Bush administration to use U.S. troops as part of a UN mission to assist in famine relief in Somalia. While succeeding in averting further tragedy from hunger, U.S. troops were less successful in disarming the country's warlords and establishing a democratic government. Unclear about their ultimate objectives and suspicious of UN policy, U.S. troops departed from Somalia in 1993.

United Nations peacekeeping forces, comprised principally of British and French troops, were sent into Bosnia-Herzegovina to help provide civilians with much-needed food and medical supplies. The United States also became involved in the effort to establish various "safe haven" zones in which civilians would be protected from the fighting between Serbs, Muslims, and Croats, and to encourage the factions to find a peaceful solution to their differences.

The inability of the UN forces to gain the cooperation of the antagonists prompted many by mid-decade to call for a pullout of peacekeeping forces from Bosnia. President Clinton brought the antagonists to a peace conference in Dayton, Ohio, and then committed 20,000 American ground forces in addition to the American naval and air support already being provided as part of an international peacekeeping force under NATO command. The international community was resolute in its condemnation of Bosnian Serb leadership and its genocidal campaign of ethnic cleansing. The International Criminal Tribunal for the former Yugoslavia indicted Radovan Karadzic and Ratko Mladic for war crimes. The Hague Tribunal condemned Serbian atrocities at Srebrenica, where 8,000 people were killed. The combatants finally agreed to a peace plan after Serbs suffered losses in the Krajini region and were subject to persistent NATO bombing attacks.

Factional fighting in the Balkans resumed in 1998 with ethnic Albanians in Kosovo pressing Yugoslavia for independence. A liberation army appeared in Kosovo, fueled by the collapse of the military regime in Albania, a situation that made weaponry readily available. Yugoslavian Serbs moved into Kosovo to quell the ethnic Albanians, and numerous atrocities were committed. Attempts to bring the Serbs to accept the autonomy of Kosovo failed and Slobodan Milosevic, president of Yugoslavia, was placed under a deadline to withdraw troops from Kosovo or face NATO air attacks. In March 1999, the assault began on Yugoslavian and Kosovar targets. The Serbs responded by moving into Kosovo and forcing ethnic Albanians to flee. The end result was the creation of a refugee population of over half a million people to neighboring states and countries in less than a month. By early summer, after extensive bombing by NATO air forces, Serbia agreed to withdrawal of troops and a NATO peacekeeping force entered Kosovo to clean up the aftermath and prevent reprisals against the minority Serbs.

Numerous other conflicts in the first half of the decade resulted in new directions for several nations. In 1994, aided by the United States at the outset and then through the presence of United Nations peacekeeping forces, Jean-Bertrand Aristide was restored to power in Haiti. As the century came to a close, power had been transferred to President Rene Preval, but UN troops remained a presence through "Operation Uphold Democracy" in Port-au-Prince and throughout Haiti. A revolution in Ethiopia toppled the Mengistu government in 1991. Civil war in the former Soviet Republic of Georgia was brought to a conclusion in 1992 when former Soviet foreign minister Eduard Shevardnadze took the reigns of the government in Tiblisi. Shevardnadze survived an attempt on his life three years later.

The bloody attempt by Russian troops to quell rebellion in the breakaway state of Chechnya in 1994 was unresolved. The Chechnyan rebels reemerged in 1995, taking control of a hospital and holding 2,000 people hostage. The rebels demanded that Russia draw back from its offensive. When forays to retake the hospital failed, negotiations resulted in peace talks. This in turn prompted a no-confidence vote in the Russian Duma for the government of Boris Yeltsin. A truce was signed in 1995. When a final reemergence of rebel activity occurred in 1996, the Russians attacked the rebel convoys while they were in retreat in an attempt to decisively end this uprising, but intensity of fighting would escalate into the new century under a new Russian president, Vladimir Putin.

Contesting factions in Northern Ireland moved closer to peace as Bill Clinton realized his best hope of establishing a legacy for his administration by bringing resolution to this conflict. Clinton met with all sides beginning in 1995, including a controversial meeting with Sinn Fein leader Gerry Adams. A settlement was brokered between most of the principals in the conflict, and a referendum was passed by the people of Northern Ireland in 1998. A quarter century of violence resulted in 3,200 people killed and more than 32,000 injured.

The Israeli-Palestinian conflict also appeared closer to resolution by mid-decade, with new accords reached that freed 900 Palestinians and an agreement to pull Israeli settlements from the West Bank. In recognition of this progress, the 1994 Nobel Peace Prize was shared by the unlikely trio of Shimon Perez, Yitzhak Rabin, and Palestinian leader Yasser Arafat. The assasination of Rabin by Yigal Amir, an opponent to the peace settlement, began to unravel progress toward resolution of the Palestinian-Israeli dispute. Rabin's tragic death cast a pallor over the optimism of the first part of the decade. Benjamin Netanyahu, leader of the Likud party, was named prime minister of Israel following elections in 1996. This retrenchment left the Middle East in tension despite negotiations between Palestinians and Israelis in 1998. The shift to a new conciliatory Israeli prime minister, Ehud Barak, gave rise to optimism that Israel will finally realize mutual relations with its Arab neighbors and Palestinians.

Other conflicts remained unresolved through the decade. Fighting continued between Christians and Muslims in Armenia and Azerbaijan. A revolt by a coalition of indigenous peoples who called themselves "Zapatistas" in the southern Mexican province of Chiapas alerted the world to the Mexican government's oppression of native peoples. In Algeria, the approval of a new constitution in 1989 stirred hopes that the decades-long hold of the National Liberation Front (FLN) would finally come to an end. When the election results of 1992 showed support for the Islamic Salvation Front (FIS), the Algerian government cancelled the election results and ordered that all nonreligious activities at mosques be suspended. The FIS responded with a bloody street uprising. President Mohammed Boudiaf was assassinated. The FIS boycotted the elections of 1995, and outbreaks of violence throughout the decade resulted in 100,000 people dead and 20,000 people disappeared. Political violence in Rwanda between Hutu and Tutsi resulted in over 80,000 Tutsi and moderate Hutu dead at the hands of militant Hutu and their collaborators in a 100-day bloodbath between April and June of 1994. In Burundi, conflict claimed 200,000 lives and left thousands of people living in inhuman conditions in government camps. This conflict set off a chain reaction in the Congo civil conflict, with Laurent Kabila gaining tenuous control of the government in 1997. In contrast to Rwanda, a Tutsi-dominated Burundi government and military have oppressed the Hutu majority. Unrest also characterized the politics of Sierra Leone, Angola, and Eritrea. There was renewed strife in Liberia upon the arrest of faction leader D. Roosevelt Johnson in 1996. Over 150,000 lives had been claimed since 1989 in civil strife. Clinton responded to this crisis by committing 5,000 Marines in a United Nations peacekeeping initiative. Tensions between Pakistan and India accelerated with India's decision to detonate three nuclear explosives in underground testing. The long-standing dispute over the province of Kashmir continued to be a flashpoint that the global community watched with anxiety.

Transition in international leadership also occurred through peaceful means. In 1990 John Major replaced Prime Minister Margaret Thatcher of Great Britain as leader of the Conservatives. Major failed to capture the confidence of the British people and the Labour party regained power, with Tony Blair named as prime minister in 1997. Germany was reunified under Helmut Kohl. In 1991 Boris Yeltsin was elected president of the Russian Republic, then survived a coup attempt by communists in the Congress of People's Deputies. Despite chronic health and political setbacks, Yeltsin maintained control of Russia for the balance of the decade, resigning his position to Vladimir Putin on New Year's Eve 1999. Latvia, Lithuania, and Estonia declared independence from Russia. Czechoslovakia split peacefully into the Czech and Slovakian Republics. Lech Walesa was elected president of Poland at the beginning of the decade but his failure to ignite the economy of Poland brought about his loss in a bid for reelection. Iran emerged from its two decades of control by the conservative ayatollahs and President Mohammed Khatami promised reforms.

Nelson Mandela, a political prisoner for 27 years, was elected president of South Africa in that nation's first multiracial election in 1994. Mandela, awarded the Nobel Peace Prize with Frederik de Klerk in 1993, distinguished himself as a statesman and a peacemaker and was given accolades by supporters and by his former jailers when he left office in 1999.

Violeta Barrios de Chamorro succeeded Sandinista leader Daniel Ortega as president in Nicaragua. In elections at mid-decade, the Sandinistas saw their base of support erode further. Patricio Aylwin took the office of president in Chile after 16 years of military dictatorship. Augusto Pinochet remained as head of the military until his resignation in 1998. Although Fidel Castro remained in power in Cuba, the visit of Pope John Paul II in 1998 signaled a new approach to international relations by the last socialist revolutionary still in power in the Western Hemisphere.

In 1994 Ernesto Zedillo Ponce de Leon succeeded Carlos Salinas de Gortari as president of Mexico. Within a year Leon had to arrest Gortari's brother on charges involving the assassination of Jose Massieu during the election campaign. Leon was then confronted with a major economic crisis that shocked Mexico and caused the value of the peso to plummet. Leon announced a severe austerity program and sought financial assistance from foreign sources. In Canada, the movement for secession of the Quebec province from Canada threatened to bring about the collapse of the national government. With a referendum for independence barely failing to gain approval, a reorganized configuration of provinces remained very possible.

South America remained a continent of political experiments. Contrast Hugo Chavez of Venezuela's social agenda (a commitment to basic housing, health care, and education for all) with the stark disparity of wealth in Brazil where, according to the Inter-American Development Bank, 10% of the population controls 47% of the income. The stranglehold that the drug lords held on Colombia was loosened somewhat with the arrest of Gilberto Rodriguez Orejuela, alleged leader of the Cali drug cartel. It was alleged that this cartel was responsible for 80% of the cocaine smuggled into the United States. Six other drug leaders were rounded up later in 1995. Socialist rebels continued to maintain control of half of the country in a decade-long civil war. Arguing that it was fighting a war on drugs, the United States committed a dramatic increase in aid to a Colombian military that was renowned for its brutality. Guatemala appeared to be on the road to healing after a 36-year civil war that took an estimated 140,000 lives. The brutal killing of Bishop Juan Gerardi Conedera, a high-profile defender of human rights, in 1998 cast uncertainty on the fragile peace.

Prince Norodom Sihanouk was returned to power in Cambodia. Former president Jimmy Carter helped diffuse a crisis with North Korea involving that nation's apparent desire to join the nuclear weapons club. South Korea closed a chapter in recent history with the 1996 conviction of former president Chun Doo Hwan for his part in a coup. The economic crisis in the Pacific Rim contributed to the end of the autocratic regime of Suharto in Indonesia in 1998. Protest led by students prompted the decision by Suharto to hand over the presidency to B. J. Habibie with the promise of elections before the end of the decade. The limits of Habibie's power were tested in 1999 when he agreed to honor a referendum by the people of East Timor on their independence. When 78% of the voters called for independence from Indonesia, paramilitary supporters of the Indonesian army and armed troops attacked the promoters of independence. UN peacekeepers were called to enter East Timor only after international pressure was brought to bear on Habibie. Hong Kong was turned over to control of the People's Republic of China in 1998, uniting a center of Asian capitalistic commerce with communist politics.

The voices of peace continued to be heard despite opposition. Daw Aung San Sui Kyi of Myanmar, recipient of the 1991 Nobel Peace Prize, was released after five years of house arrest. In the same year, Harry Wu, an activist for democratic reform who had spent 19 years in Chinese labor camps, was expelled from China. Wu had entered China illegally and was convicted of spying. The People's Republic of China, while seeking new economic markets, continued to exert totalitarian control over dissidents, oppressing competing ideological perspectives. The Falun Gong sect was subjected to a crackdown by Chinese authorities, and the Dalai Lama continued his exile from Tibet, campaigning for release of his nation from Chinese control. In 1995, the government of Nigeria hanged nine dissenters, including Ken Saro-Wiwa, advocate for minority population and environmental rights and critic of Royal Dutch Shell's control of Nigerian oil resources.

The leader of the Nation of Islam, Louis Farrakhan, was a principal agent in assembling the Million Man March on Washington, D.C., in 1995. It is estimated that up to 837,000 men participated in this public display of commitment by African American men for personal accountability for their families and their people.

The nuclear abolition movement was not nearly as prominent in the 1990s as a result of the Soviet Union's collapse, but it rose up in 1995 to contest nuclear testing by France. New concerns about the aging nuclear arsenals of the former Soviet nations brought forth calls for dismantling the nuclear arsenals, but the prestige of owning nuclear warheads precluded national leaders from taking any actions toward changing the status quo.

During the 1990s, terrorism expanded beyond its historical theater of operations in Europe and the Middle East. In 1993, the New York World Trade Center was the bomb target of extremists led by Ramzi Ahmed Yousef. The group was apprehended before other selected sites in the city could be bombed. In 1995 poison gas attacks occurred in the subway systems of several Japanese cities, the work of members of a secret religious cult. Besides the loss of life and injury to thousands of people, the Japanese were shocked by such violent acts in their normally tranquil society. A total of 169 people were killed and 400 injured in April 1995, including many children in a day care center, when a truck filled with explosives blew away a third of the federal office building in Oklahoma City. The bombing was carried out by Timothy McVeigh, with the assistance of Terry Nichols and the complicity of Michael Fortier. These domestic terrorists sought revenge for the storming by federal agents of the headquarters of the Branch Davidians and the ultimate death of most of its religious cult's members in Waco, Texas.

Theodore Kaczynski, identifed as the infamous Unibomber, was apprehended in 1996, ending 17 years of terrorist activity that killed 3 people and injured 23 others. Kaczynski was captured on a lead from his brother, who recognized the writing style of his sibling. Kaczynski demanded that a manifesto be printed in national newspapers to allay a bombing attack. The accomplishments of athletes at the twentieth Summer Olympics in Atlanta shared headlines with news of a pipe bomb explosion that killed one person.

A suicide bomber representing the Liberation Tigers of Tamil Eelam killed 86 people and injured 1,400 when the explosion rocked the Central Bank in Colombo, Sri Lanka, in 1996, and terrorism continued to plague the Middle East with suicide bombers striking Gaza in 1995. An attack was leveled at President Hosni Mubarak of Egypt by advocates for an Islamic-controlled government. Seventeen Greek tourists were killed in Egypt, with Gamara al Islamirya claiming responsibility. President Kiro Gilgorov of Macedonia was seriously wounded by an assassin in 1995. That same year, a bomb on a Paris underground commuter train injured 29 people. The Irish Republican Army put fragile peace negotiations in jeopardy when a bomb exploded in an elevated rail station in London, killing 2 and injuring 100. In 1998 attacks on U.S. embassies in the African nations of Kenya and Tanzania resulted in U.S. air attacks on sites in Sudan and Afghanistan.

The most severe natural disasters included Hurricane Andrew, America's most costly hurricane, with damage exceeding $20 billion; the high winds and rain cut a path from east to west across southern Florida in 1992. The North American Midwest experienced the floods of the century from the Mississippi and Red Rivers in 1993. Massive and deadly earthquakes hit Los Angeles; Kobe, Japan; and Turkey in 1994. Hurricane Mitch, the deadliest Atlantic storm in 200 years, cut a path of destruction across Guatemala, Honduras, and Nicaragua in the fall of 1998, with torrential rain causing mudslides and raging rivers. More than 11,000 people were killed.

Not all disasters were natural. A dramatic example was the 1996 Valujet plane crash in the Florida Everglades, which killed 110 and brought forth calls of concern for public safety in low cost air carriers. Of over 1,000 passengers, only 141 survived the sinking of the automobile and passenger ferry *Estonia* in 1994. When TWA Flight 800 outbound from New York for Paris exploded and crashed into the Atlantic in 1996 without survivors, faulty wiring in fuel storage tanks was suspected but no definitive cause was given.

While the attention of George Bush's administration was often devoted to the unfolding drama of international events, there were still several significant and interesting political developments in the early nineties. One involved the controversy over the appointment of Clarence Thomas in 1991 to replace Supreme Court Justice Thurgood Marshall. Thomas was accused of sexual harassment by a former employee, Anita Hill. Despite these charges, Thomas was confirmed to the high court. In a holdover from the Iran-Contra affair, federal charges against Oliver North stemming from the sale of weapons to Iran were dropped. North later ran unsuccessfully for the U.S. Senate for Virginia.

Bill Clinton had yet to take the oath of office before he was forced to confront accusations of financial and sexual misconduct. The financial inquiry stemmed from land speculation along the Whitewater River in Arkansas when he was governor of the state. A former State of Arkansas employee, Paula Jones, charged Clinton with sexual harassment, a charge that was later dismissed by the court as without merit. Other sensational allegations of sexual encounters arose throughout 1998, but Bill Clinton appeared to have the same "teflon" persona as Ronald Reagan and his approval ratings continued to be highly favorable. Clinton was never formally indicted although the investigation by independent counsel Kenneth Starr cost taxpayers over $40 million. Clinton's denial of sexual relations with Monica Lewinsky, a White House intern, in the Paula Jones deposition and to the grand jury, was center point of Starr's report to Congress. Under the direction of Representative Henry Hyde, the Republican-led House Judiciary Committee recommended that the House of Representatives consider impeachment of Clinton. The House considered the four broadly stated charges and determined there were two impeachable offenses related to perjury and obstruction of justice. A Senate trial determined that the charges did not warrant dismissal from office.

Members of Bill Clinton's cabinet were also charged with illegalities. Most notable was the investigation of Secretary of Commerce Ron Brown for personal financial dealings and Secretary of Agriculture Michael Espy. The investigation of Brown became moot when he died with 34 others while flying over Croatia; Espy was exonerated from legal wrongdoing in his federal trial.

There was a tragic reminder that civil rights demand continual vigilance. In 1992 an amateur videotaped Los Angeles police savagely beating an African American, Rodney King, in a parking lot late in the evening. Support for King was heavily divided along racial lines. Four Los Angeles police officers were subsequently found innocent of brutality in the first trial, but were found guilty of violating King's civil rights in a second federal trial. In response to the first verdict, a public uprising in South Los Angeles resulted in the loss of over 50 lives and millions of dollars in property damage.

The scientific community was notably disappointed when it was discovered after launch into orbit in 1990 that the mirror in the Hubble Space Telescope was flawed. A subsequent shuttle mission was successful in improving the telescope's efficiency. The space shuttle *Atlantis* also made history in the summer of 1995 when it docked with the Russian space station, *Mir*, signaling a new era of cooperation in space exploration. Celebration faded, however, when the support systems on *Mir* placed the lives of the astronauts in jeopardy. Fearing funding cutbacks, NASA mounted a successful public relations effort by putting Senator John Glenn back into space on a shuttle mission, reinvigorating media interest in the program. In 1998 work began on assembly of an international space station.

The world was treated to a spectacular astronomical show when the Shoemaker-Levy 9 comet smashed into Jupiter in 1994, creating 2,000-mile-high fireballs in that planet's atmosphere. Also in that year astronomers confirmed discovery of a solar system composed of three planets orbiting a small star that had previously exploded. At the other end of the physical spectrum, scientists at Fermilab in Batavia, Illinois, announced that its physicists had identified six types of quarks that are thought to be the building blocks of all atomic nuclei particles.

By the end of the decade it was confirmed by British and American scientists that, indeed, the earth was getting warmer. Data supported reports that since 1861 global surface temperature had increased 1.03 degrees Fahrenheit and that the 1990s was the warmest decade of the millennium.

Advances in health continued for industrialized nations. Magnetic Resonance Imaging (MRI) became a commonplace exploratory tool for diagnosis. Scopic technology transformed the techniques of surgery. The U.S. Food and Drug Administration mandated more accurate and literate labeling of food under the watchdog leadership of Ralph Nader. Viagra, a drug for sexual impotence introduced in 1998, quickly became a staple of stand-up comedians. This best-seller could be easily obtained from Internet sources.

Genetic engineering was the hot topic for medicine, the stock market, consumer advocates, and ethicists. Researchers were able to link breast cancer and obesity to specific genes. It was announced in 2000 that the genetic code for human beings had been substantively mapped. A sheep named Dolly caused a scientific furor in 1996 and awakened ethical issues as well: Researchers at the Roslin Institute in Scotland, starting from a cell taken from the udder of an adult ewe, had produced a genetic duplicate of a living mammal. Questions regarding the application of genetic engineering to the reproduction of human beings led to legislators calling for a ban on human cloning.

As a result of advances in the field, biotechnology companies became glamour stocks for a time.

Chemical pesticide companies such as Monsanto quickly employed the technology to ensure a sustained market for their product by altering seed DNA so that the crop yielded sterile seed. Genetically engineered food came on the market to a mixed response. The European Union rejected genetically engineered corn products; Japan demanded that products that use genetically engineerg food be labeled.

The spread of diseases in Africa highlighted the relationship between medical care, access to science, and public policy. The reappearance of the Ebola virus in Zaire in 1995 caused alarm. The virus had last been identified in 1976 in Zaire and Sudan. Sleeping sickness reemerged in Sudan and Angola. Nearly 70% of the world's carriers of HIV lived in Africa. According to the World Health Organization, 20 of 33 new and unexpected epidemics from 1994 to the end of the decade occurred in Africa. At the same time, foreign aid to African nations shrunk in the post-Cold War geopolitical environment, and socialized health care was abandoned for privatization at the insistence of the International Monetary Fund and the World Bank.

In "Contextual Reminders" from earlier decades, sports were given only cursory treatment. By century's end, sports had become a major leisure time preoccupation, whether through direct participation or vicariously through school or professional venues. ESPN, the cable sports network, expanded to multiple television channels, the Internet, printed media, and high-tech sports bars, and the public appetite for sports entertainment was not assuaged.

The Winter Olympics in Albertville, France, and the Summer Olympics in Barcelona, Spain, held in 1992 were the last to be scheduled in the same year. The International Olympic Committee decided that henceforth each competition would be held in separate four-year blocks. Highlights of these games included victories in speed skating by "America's sweetheart" Bonnie Blair, who won her third gold in the 500 meters and her second gold in the 1,000 meters; and Jackie Joyner-Kersee, who won her second Olympic gold in the heptathlon. Michael Jordon led the Chicago Bulls to an unprecedented third consecutive NBA championship in 1993, then left to play minor league baseball before returning to the NBA in 1995. When he retired again in 1999, Jordon had led the Bulls to three more NBA championships and at $35 million a year, became the highest paid athlete in the world. Basketball ascended over football and baseball as the premier American sport, accelerated in part by the Olympic "dream teams" and the global recognition of Michael Jordan. Baseball entered into a combined strike/lockout in 1994 that resulted in the cancellation of the World Series. This confrontation alienated fans, and attendance and interest in the sport declined. It took a home run derby hosted by Mark McGwire and the charismatic Sammy Sosa to help to revive interest in the game. McGwire set a new single-season home run record of 70 in 1998.

The National Football League saw the revival of the Dallas Cowboys as "America's team." Professional hockey crowned Scotty Bowman's Pittsburgh Penguins, led by Mario Lemiuex, at the beginning of the decade, and the Detroit Red Wings came to prominence at the end of the decade. In tennis, Steffi Graf was the number one seed through much of the decade, with Monica Seles grunting her way to victories; the men's game belonged to Pete Sampras, Andre Agassi, and Patrick Rafter. Meanwhile, golfer Tiger Woods became the premier figure in sports following the retirement of Michael Jordan.

Television in the early nineties featured a plethora of situation comedies, sea and sand melodramas, and action adventures. Documentary filmmaker Ken Burns attracted an impressive audience to public television with his lengthy treatment of *The Civil War* and *Baseball*. The television networks continued to lose viewers to the cable channels. "Infomercials" and "shopping channels" clogged the video lanes. The trial of O. J. Simpson for murder of his wife was available on CNN on a daily basis with twists and turns and periods of high drama that could never have been matched by a fiction writer. Quality television programming was found on Discovery, Arts and Entertainment, Bravo, and the History Channel. Trash television, symbolized by *The Jerry Springer Show* and numerous yellow journalism news magazine shows, profoundly affected the quality of all news broadcasting. For some people the demise of the marriage of Prince Charles and Princess Diana of England became as important a national event as the violence in Bosnia. The death of Diana, "The English Rose," in a car accident in 1997 became an unprecedented news event, superseding virtually all national and international events for several weeks.

Witold Lutoslawski was praised posthumously for his *Fourth Symphony* in a major release of his compositions by Sony, with Esa-Pekka Salonen conducting the Los Angeles Philharmonic. John Eliot Gardner and the Orchestre Revolutionnaire et Romantique found wide approval for their period renditions of Beethoven's nine symphonies. Henryk Gorecki was hailed by many critics as the "Bruckner of our day," while Alfred Schnitke shared with American audiences somber but passionate expressions of Slavic culture in his orchestral compositions. Under the leadership of director Christoph von Dohnanyi, the Cleveland Orchestra was cited by some critics as perhaps the best in the nation, challenging the dominance of the Chicago Symphony under Daniel Barenboim.

Popular music had shifted into a variety of specific market-responsive categories, including "new age," "smooth jazz," "classic rock," and "adult contemporary" for the older set and "grunge," "alternative," "hip hop," "gangsta rap," and "headbanger" for younger listeners. This left the pop charts open for mainstream performers like Mariah Carey and flavor-of-the-month male harmony groups (from BOYZ II MEN to 'N Sync).

Lucien Freud, at age 71, received recognition as arguably the best realist painter alive during his exhibition at the Metropolitan Museum of Art in 1995. The rediscovery of the life work of Frida Kahlo served as inspiration for feminist artists. The everyday scenes of Scottish life were brushed on canvas by Calum Frazer. Miquel Barcelo approached the organic and mineral while striving for a phenomenological expression of the essence of a subject. Gerhard Richter's eclecticism in medium and subject made his art a continuing adventure. In contrast, the voluptuous, portly, and emotionally complex figures of Bolivian artist Fernando Botero were instantly recognized even as Botero shifted his craft to three-dimensional productions. Works by César expressed the issues of being human in the medium of ironwork. Tony Cragg brought his scientific knowledge of plastics to art in pieces that are studies in organic relationship and geometry. Daniel Buren redefined space through color and shape in his performance art. In architecture I. M. Pei reaffirmed his creative talent with the construction of the 70-story Bank of China in Hong Kong. Japanese architect Tadao Ando was awarded the Pritzker Prize for his minimalist approach to traditional Japanese building forms (e.g, the Chikatsu Asuka Museum of Art).

Devotees of fine literature were not disappointed during this last decade of the century. In 1990 Thomas Pynchon published his novel *Vineland* to high acclaim, and John Updike completed the fourth and last of his series of Rabbit novels with *Rabbit at Rest*. The next year Norman Mailer published his 1,300-page *Harlot's Ghost*. In 1993 Richard Reeves provided new insights into the personality of John Kennedy in his biography *President Kennedy*. Also an insightful best-seller was David Remnick's *Lenin's Tomb: Last Days of the Soviet Empire*. John Updike scored another success in 1994 with *The Afterlife*, which joined Tim O'Brien's *In the Lake of the Woods* on the best-seller list. Wally Lamb was recognized as a promising novelist with *She's Come Undone*. Louise Erdrich, Barbara Kingsolver, Anne Tyler, Jamaica Kincaid, Kenzaburo Oe, Carol Shields, and E. Annie Proulx rendered outstanding new works in fiction. Octavio Paz of Mexico, Nadine Gordimer of South Africa, and Toni Morrison were recognized by the Nobel committee for their literary artistry. Jane Kenyon and Wendell Berry offered poetic insight into living in relationship with the earth. Other important poets of the decade include Yusef Komunyakaa, Jorie Graham, Mona van Duyn, and Charles Wright.

Audiences attending live theater praised *Kiss of the Spider Woman* (regarded as much superior to the film); Terrence McNally's *Love, Valour, Compassion*; and Edward Albee's *Three Tall Women*. Lee Blessing's *Two Room* considered a Beirut hostage and his wife separated in space but united in fantasy; and *Keely and Du* brought the difficult and emotional arguments between pro-choice and right-to-life advocates to the stage. Horton Foote's portrayal of the South in the twentieth century continued to win audiences, with *The Young Man from Atlanta* also gaining him the 1995 Pulitzer prize for drama. Musicals included the revivals of *Tommy* and *Showboat* and the introduction of another Andrew Lloyd Weber hit, *Sunset Boulevard*. The musical *Rent* promoted itself as the first alternative rock entry to the genre and attracted a popular and cult following and a 1996 Pulitzer. E. L. Doctorow's novel *Ragtime* was transformed into a successful musical and was nominated for 12 Tony Awards in 1998.

Outstanding feature films of the early 1990s included *Dancing with Wolves* and *Driving Miss Daisy*, for which Jessica Tandy won an Academy Award (1990); and the film adaptation of Thomas Harris's chilling *The Silence of the Lambs*, which starred Anthony Hopkins and Jodie Foster (1991). The western as a film genre was revived with the gritty *Unforgiven*, starring Gene Hackman and Clint Eastwood, who also directed the Oscar winner (1992). The story of one man's efforts to save hundreds of Jews during the Nazi Holocaust, Steven Spielberg's *Schindler's List* was cited by many critics as one of the most important films of the century. Harrison Ford maintained his box office supremacy with a big-screen adaptation of the television series *The Fugitive* (1993). Disney scored consecutive animated hits in the decade including *Alladin*, using a formula approach and some first-rate musical scores. *Forrest Gump* starred Tom Hanks in the quirky story of a slow-witted but kindhearted individual who succeeded in becoming an accomplished athlete, medal of honor winner, and millionaire (1994). Hanks's popularity carried over to the successful Ron Howard film *Apollo 13* and Steven Spielberg's acclaimed *Saving Private Ryan* (1998). Stanley Kubrick closed out a distinguished cinematic career with *Eyes Wide Shut* (1999). Claude Berri's moving *Germinal* commanded the largest budget ever spent on a French film. The filmmaking of Zhang Yimou (*Raise the Red Lantern, The Story of Qui Jui*) and Akira Kurosawa (*Dreams*), the human insight of Iranian filmmaker Abbas Kiarostami (*Taste of Cherries*), the rich sentimentality and humor of Roberto Benigni (*Life Is Beautiful*), and the liberatory perspective of Jane Campion (*The Piano*) broadened the cinematic landscape beyond Hollywood. Independent producers found a mainstream audience with the success of Quentin Tarantino's *Pulp Fiction*, *Fargo* by the

Coen brothers, *The Blair Witch Project*, and Academy Award nominee *The Full Monty*.

By the end of the decade, one wonders if the public's fascination with a historical catastrophe from the beginning of the century, the sinking of the *Titanic*, was merely a coincidence. In book (*Raise the Titanic*), film, and Broadway musical, the story of a large expensive ship, the apogee in technological achievement, loaded with the excessively rich and the desperately poor, churning the cold ocean waters with assured arrogance only to end in disaster and romantic fictions, was enthusiastically received by audiences throughout the world. To what extent could this serve as a terrifying metaphor for a century's journey? On the contrary, the remarkable popular acclaim for the film adaptation of Laura Esquival's *Like Water for Chocolate* provided contrasting metaphors for achievement, consolidation, and growth.

CURRICULUM THOUGHT AND LITERATURE

NATIONAL SOP (STANDARD OPERATING PROCEDURES)

in the United States... The final decade of the twentieth century witnessed the realization, in part, of that which could only have been aspired to by the Committee of Ten and the Committee of Fifteen a century before: a detailed blueprint for a national curriculum. The development of national standards was transparently more political than it was rational. Responding to the call for higher academic standards in select subject areas in *A Nation at Risk* and prodded to completion by financial backing with the *Goals 2000: Educate America Act*, voluntary national standards were drafted in an astounding 13 different disciplines (Kendall & Marzano, 1997). The process was sometimes contentious; the language arts standards drafted by the International Reading Association and the National Council of Teachers of English (National Council of Teachers of English, 1996) and the national standards for history (National Council for the Social Studies, 1994) found it particularly rough going. The content standards were heralded by policymakers, government officials, and even the national teachers' unions as a new day for U.S. public schools. Generally following a template set down by the National Council of Teachers of Mathematics (NCTM, 1989), the content standards were statements of what students should know and be able to do at benchmark years in their school careers and consequently what teachers should teach. Related to the move toward national content standards was the promotion of state achievement testing of students to ensure that they had attained the content standards based on elaborate state goals set forth in nearly every state. The piece in the middle, between stating what students should be learning and testing them to determine if the students did learn, was the province for the technical exercise of the craft of school personnel. Textbook publishers, however, conveniently filled this void, providing student texts and support materials that directly employed the national standards. This left Michael Apple and others to argue that the policymakers and publishers had done all they could to "teacher proof" the curriculum (Apple & Christian-Smith, 1991).

Accompanying the production of the national content standards came a variety of resources to assist school personnel with the work of aligning their district curriculum and their assessment systems with these stated learning goals. The Association for Supervision and Curriculum Development provided support in the dissemination of standards with publication of works by Marzano and Kendall (1996; Kendall & Marzano, 1997) that listed content knowledge from the various disciplines and guided curriculum design for local educational agencies. A volume by Harris and Carr suggested how to implement standards at the classroom level (1996). Foriska (1998) and Solomon (1998) also produced works on how to align school practices with national standards. Curry and Temple (1992) coauthored an ASCD book on how to use curriculum frameworks to initiate curriculum reform. Although the intent of the standards as described in these books is to inform and counsel curriculum development, the "reification" of standards at the state level too often led to control and dictation. The interest in promoting standards was applied to student assessment as well as to the design of curriculum. Marc Tucker and Judy Codding (1998) argued that measurement is an integral part of effective implementation of standards. Grant Wiggins became a popular in-service speaker on how to develop performance-based assessments that measured educational standards through complex authentic student activities (Wiggins, 1998; Wiggins & McTigue, 1998). Exemplars of how performance assessment related to content standards were produced by Mitchell, Willis, and Chicago Teachers' Union Quest Center (1995). John Kordalewski (2000) examined how standards are negotiated and transformed in classroom practices by teachers and students.

Challenges to the national standards project were also published. Ron Miller (1995) edited a volume of criticism; Ohanian's *One Size Fits Few* (1999) analyzed the contention that content standards can encompass the diversity of cultures and learners that constitute contemporary U.S. society. M. Frances Klein (1991) and Sandra Stotsky (2000) edited volumes that looked at the political issues that emerge in centralizing the curriculum. Linda McNeils (2000) considered the negative impact that teaching to improve scores on standardized tests can have on efforts to develop a curriculum and instruction that is responsive to student needs.

...And in the U.K. The policymakers' delight in standards and a national curriculum was not unique to the United States. Other English-speaking countries had already established national curricula that were more directive than the advisory content standards implemented in the United States. The kinds of books produced in response to the national curricula are perhaps instructive of how scholarship reacts to policy initiative. The revision of the national curriculum in Great Britian provoked scholarly works that explained the curriculum's origins or elements, facilitated implementation, or contended that the project was contrary to meaningful education. A volume by Harnett, Carr, and Naish (1993), a historical overview by Thomas (1990), a review of the establishment of the recent curriculum by Graham and Tytler (1993), an examination of international themes in the national curriculum by Andrews (1993), and edited volumes by Proctor (1990) and Hall (1992) provided an explanation of policy developments, themes, dimensions, and standards of the British national curriculum. Anning (1995) edited a work on early childhood education and its relationship to the national curriculum. Cox and Sanders (1994) considered the impact of the curriculum on the lives of 5-year-old children. Ahier and Ross (1995) edited an examination of the social subjects in the national curriculum. Daughtery (1995) examined national curriculum assessment policies.

General works on implementation of the primary core national curriculum were provided by the National Union of Teachers (1990) and in an edited volume by Coulby and Ward (1990, revised 1997). Considerations of the national curriculum for post-16 students were offered by Higham, Sharp, and Yeomans (1996) and Bloomer (1997). Helsby and McCullough (1997) edited a work on teachers and their relationship to the national curriculum. Treatment of specific key stages was provided by Lever (1990). Davies edited a work on the development of subject area leadership in "key stage 1" curriculum (1995). Edgington, Fisher, Morgan, Pound, and Scott provided an interpretation of the curriculum at "key stage 1" (1998).

Tabor examined curriculum continuity in English and its relationship to the national curriculum (1991); Protherough and King (1995) edited a volume on English and the national curriculum (1995). O'Hear and White (1993) edited a book on assessment of the national curriculum. Attention was given to the problem of relating a national curriculum to students with special needs and challenges (Ashdown, Bovair, & Carpenter, 1991; Lewis, 1991 and 1995).

Great Britain's national curriculum was also criticized. Dowling and Nass (1990) challenged the curriculum's approach to mathematics. The title of Ted Wragg's critical statement, *Mad Curriculum Disease* (1991), provides a clear sense of his perspective on the national curriculum initiative. Barber and Graham (1993) offer a mixed review of the national curriculum's impact. Lawton argued that teacher professionalization and development demanded national resources if the national curriculum was to have any lasting impact (1997). The movement toward national curricula also occupied the attention of scholars in Scotland (Hartley & Roger, 1990) and Australia (Brady, 1992; Hughes, 1990; and Print, 1990).

RESTRUCTURING SCHOOLING

In the United States, the topic of school reform dominated much of the writing on education for the general public in the 1990s, having pervasive curriculum implications. Conservative reports issued in the early part of the 1980s presented public schools as vessels adrift, pushed about by the whimsical breezes of progressive educators. In contrast, the educational systems of other industrial nations were portrayed in popular media as institutions with direction and purpose. Nonetheless, conservative policymakers rejected the Clinton administration's advocacy of national curriculum or national testing as manifestations of excessive federal control. That a national curriculum and assessments already existed to some extent in the form of advanced placement course curricula, nationally published textbooks, or ACT and SAT tests seldom entered the conversation.

In the 1990s sound critical discussion of the contention that U.S. public schools were without focus and produced an inferior product created a very different profile (e.g., Berliner & Biddle, 1995; Schrag, 1995; Sowell, 1993). Scholars counseled that the first step in reform was meaningful public conversation on education (Garrison & Rud, 1995; Kincheloe & Steinberg, 1993). Having spent the better part of a decade thinking through and attempting changes in the schools, most writers about reform directed their attention to improving practice rather than illuminating public discourse and policymaking. Perspective pieces in the 1990s decided for the most part that reform of the present was best effected by projecting the future rather than lamenting the past. Their authors were convinced that what may have been broken most certainly could be fixed with the proper agenda. The popularity of the Bracey reports in the *Kappan* (Bracey, 1997a, 1997b) on U.S. schools is an indicator that the people who work in schools were ready to defend their recent successes. Berliner and Biddle (1995) offered a critique of the conservative reform movement in U.S. education to provide a forum for surpressed research on international comparative testing, research that indicated that public schools in the United States performed much better than the popular press indicated.

The popularity of the topic of reform is reflected in the attention given to the work of Michael Fullan. Fullan, who began his work in curriculum studies, became an international resource on how change is effected and what administrators and teachers can do to promote reform in their districts and schools (Fullan, 1991, 1992, 1993, 1999). A more pessimistic perspective was offered by Seymour Sarason (1990, 1995, 1996) on how "school culture" is resistant to change. With knowledge of the dynamics of reform, school personnel had no lack of options—whether to implement established programs from the previous decade, revive historical models, or act on new conceptions of teaching and learning.

A number of the reform proposals of the 1980s continued to undergo development and evolution in the 1990s. E. D. Hirsch continued to campaign for cultural literacy and a standard national knowledge base (the list of essential facts and concepts presented in *Cultural Literacy* was revised and much expanded in Hirsch, Kett, & Trefil, 1993). His proposal transformed into a publishing industry, with Hirsch and his associates providing guidance on what knowledge is essential from kindergarten through the elementary grades (Hirsch, 1992, 1993a, 1993b, 1993c, 1993d, 1994, 1995a, 1995b, 1996; Hirsch & Holdren, 1997). In *The Schools We Need and Why We Don't Have Them*, Hirsch (1996) continued to support the standardization of knowledge by grade level and renewed his charge that colleges of education, Teachers College at Columbia in particular, were responsible for the collapse of public education.[1] He also shared his perspective on standards-based/accountability initiatives. The need for a common literacy was given further support in a work by Powell (1999) and a core application by Mackley (1999).

A number of proposals for education in the 1980s retained vitality in the 1990s as alternatives within the structures of conventional schooling. The Paideia school movement of the 1980s continued as an intellectual traditionalist option maintaining the Adler/Hutchins emphasis on disciplined knowledge, skill development, and reasoning (Roberts et al., 1998). As a progressive antidote, Theodore Sizer's Coalition of Essential Schools maintained limited but healthy membership, with advocates in both public and private schools (Sizer, 1992). A qualitative study of eight charter member schools of the coalition was produced by Donna Muncey and Patrick McQuillan (1996), considering the impact of the reform movement on the lives of participants. Application of the principles and practices of the essential schools movement

to work readiness was effected in a work by Adria Steinberg, Kathleen Cushman, and Robert Riordan (2000). Two school administrators, Dennis Litky
and Deborah Meier (1997), gained national attention for their successes in
transforming their high schools employing elements of the essential schools
model (Sizer, 1996). Robert Fried translated the principles of the essential
schools into suggestions for teacher renewal (Fried, 1996).

Other structured approaches to school reform, notably the "Success for
All" model promoted by Robert Slavin (Slavin, Madden, Dolan, & Wasik,
1998), Henry Levin's accelerated schools approach (Eidson & Hillhouse,
1998; Hopfenberg, Levin, & Associates, 1993), and the innovations of James
Comer (1993, 1995, 1997; Comer, Haynes, Joyner, & Ben-Avie, 1996), remained influential in discussion of institutional reform and in schools that
aligned themselves with these national movements. The "Best Practices"
approach advocated by Steve Zemelman, Harvey Daniels, and Arthur Hyde
(1993) dovetailed with the political popularity of charter schools and school
choice advocates (Nathan, 1996), resulting in the establishment of a best
practices school in Chicago. Science-Technology-Society (STS), a project-
centered approach to science education based on situations that children
encounter in their daily lives, enjoyed international attention as a reform
program (Solomon & Aikenhead, 1994). Finally, the variety of small school
initiatives (e.g., Ayers, Klonsky, & Lyon, 2000) epitomized in the Small
Schools Workshop in Chicago ascended in popularity and funding attention
by the end of the century.

John Goodlad further clarified his proposal for school reform, with an
emphasis on equality of opportunity, equity in resources, and enhancing the
quality of the teaching profession (Goodlad, 1994a; Goodlad & Keating,
1990). Goodlad's contributions to educational thought over the past four
decades and his consistent voice for reform were recognized in a volume of
congratulatory essays (Sirotnik & Soder, 1999). The elimination of tracking, a
prominent reform initiative for Goodlad and Jeanne Oakes in the 1980s,
sustained some momentum with Reba Page's (1991) study of lower track
classrooms and the suggestions by Anne Wheelock (1992) and Pool and Page
(1995) on how to "untrack" U.S. schools. Oakes also collaborated in developing a proposal for "virtuous" school reform (Oakes, Quartz, Ryan, & Lipton, 1999).

John White's vision of a future (1997), related to Jeremy Rifkin's prediction on the "end of work"[2] where technology reconfigures labor, demands that
one attempt to predict the kinds of societies that will be fashioned in the
coming century. Lois Weis (1990) looked at the educational opportunities and
possible futures of working-class youth in a deindustrialized economy. Jane

Roland Martin (1992) conceptualized the "schoolhome" as the kind of educational institution responsive to the diverse realities of contemporary U.S. families. Charles Reid (2000) retained optimism that technology combined with a willingness to think outside institutional parameters can effect truly individualized instruction.

James Coleman and his associates called for "school restructuring" (Coleman, et al., 1997), a popular notion in corporate boardrooms whereby leadership configures an organization to respond most effectively to context and purposes. Reform proposals contended that curriculum innovation could effect restructuring (Williams, 1993) and that restructuring could be brought into the classroom (Elmore, Peterson, & McCarthy, 1996). The Chicago Public School redesign of the late 1980s was offered as a portrait of school restructuring (Hess, 1991). The detailed proposal of Linda Darling-Hammond (1997) called for comprehensive reconstruction of both the teaching profession and the institutions in which teachers labor. Madeline Hunter's (1992) final reform suggestion was for movement to a nongraded school; multiage grouping was also supported, with guidelines for implementation in a manual produced by Bachrach, Hassley, and Anderson (1995).

Reform proposals designed to ready schools and students for the twenty-first century ranged from the politically conservative and neoliberal (Allen, 1992; Schlechty, 1997) to the progressive and radical (e.g., McDonald, 1996; O'Sullivan, 1999; Perkins, 1990). Stephen Ball (1994) considered the kind of reform suggested from a critical and poststructural perspective. This plethora of recommendations for change included the suggestion by Simpson and Jackson (1997) that John Dewey's ideas could inspire educational transformation.

In addition to these many authors, those interested in school reform can also refer to a mulitiplicity of provocative and influential recommendations such as those by Ron Brandt (1998), Michael Fullan and Andy Hargreaves (Fullan & Hargreaves, 1992; Hargreaves, 1997; Hargreaves & Fullan, 1998), Elliot Eisner (1998), and Carl Glickman (1993, 1997).

Other authors influenced understanding of reform even though they advanced no specific agenda or set of recommendations on curriculum reform. Books by such diverse voices as Jacques Barzun (1991), William Glasser (1990), Donald Graves (1996), Herbert Kohl (1998), and Frank Smith (1995, 1998) while not directly considering curriculum, were influential to conversations about the reform of the curriculum. Jonathon Kozol's examination of educational equity (1991) and the lives of children of the poor in the United States (Kozol, 1995) drew attention from the popular media and revived calls for changes in states' funding of education to provide curricular choice. Herbert Kohl (1998), Thomas Gregory (1993), Michael Rose (1989, 1995), and James Nehring (1997) provided progressive perspectives on change based on personal labors and observations in schools. It is notable that in this wealth of scholarship on the dynamics of reform and the varieties of proposals for change, only two works were explicitly titled as addressing change through the curriculum, *Change and the Curriculum* (Blenkin, Edwards, & Kelly, 1992) and *Restructuring Through Curriculum Innovation* (Williams, 1993).

POSSIBILITIES IN CRITICAL RECONSTRUCTION

While writings for general readership called for school reforms, writers who shared a critical reconstructionist perspective argued persuasively against the repressive social function of schooling and advocated for justice in education. Relative to the development of curriculum theory, the contributions of the critical reconstructionist perspective in the 1990s were rivaled only by the expanding conversations of scholars who thoroughly embraced postmodern discourses. Arguing that schooling in the United States perpetuates economic and class inequities in service to the dominant power elite, critical reconstructionists contended that authentic education can and should be emancipating. In this way, education assists in transforming society by nurturing young people to promote democratic deliberation and global justice (Gordon, 1999). Introductions to and overviews of this field of curriculum scholarship were provided by Kanpol (1994, 1997a), Hinchey (1998), and Darder and Torres (2000).

Options in critical reconstructionist thought were exemplified by the works of three highly influential advocates. Each voice maintained a distinctive foundation for criticism of contemporary society, engaged in different research interests, and had a proposal on how to theorize reform. Whether following the approach to critical reconstruction using characteristics in the writing of Michael Apple, Paulo Freire, or Henry Giroux, each held in common a respect for Deweyesque experientialist thought in reconceptualizing the dynamics of democracy, an appreciation for efforts by radical progressives to engage education as a tool for promoting social change, an openness to the promise offered by postmodern theorizing, and a passion to see the world transformed to be a place of greater tolerance, peace making, and justice in all dimensions of human interaction.

In the late 1970s and the 1980s, Michael Apple opened up new languages of inquiry into the ideological ramifications of curriculum in schools (1979, revised 1990). Employing the theoretical construct of neo-Marxist scholars such as Antonio Gramsci, Apple's early writings reflected an economic-political lens, focusing on the hegemonic domination of U.S. public schooling. His later inquiries opened into a broader sphere of the interplay of education and power in schools (1982) and to the political economy of texts (1986; Apple & Christian-Smith, 1991). In the 1990s, Apple saw the problem of ideological domination as even more pervasive and dealt with matters of official knowledge (1993, 1999a) and cultural politics (1996) that actually create or subvert democratic education. Despite these obstacles, Apple was able to identify schools and teachers who embraced and practiced democracy in their schools and classrooms (Apple & Beane, 1995). Apple was consistent in employing an economic and political construct for understanding the power relationships of public schools and control of knowledge. In his writing, Apple maintained focus on the institution of the American public school or one of its primary curricular artifacts, the commercial textbook (Apple, 1999b). His scholarship was a critical examination of the ideological constructs of public schooling through much of the 1980s.

In the 1990s, Apple explored the possibilities of what democratic public schooling means (Carlson & Apple, 1998) and what it can look like in practice (Apple & Beane, 1999). Apple has expressed appreciation for progressive efforts at schooling, taken largely out of the experientialist orientation in advancing ideas on critical pedagogy. He has been open to the contributions made by postmodern thought and how gender and racial difference can provide complementary understandings of power relationships.

A variety of works have been produced in the 1990s that share Apple's theoretical lens in criticizing school curriculum and practice, his research into how textbooks and other elements of the public school curriculum act as vehicles for social control, and his interests in promoting democratic schooling. Avis, Bloomer, Esland, Gleeson, and Hodkinson (1996) adopted a compatible economic/political construct in their study of nationhood and control of knowledge. The use of the textbook as a vehicle for social control was the subject of a work edited by Altbach, Kelly, Petrie, and Weis (1991); the politics of the high school history text were examined by Liston, Nagai, and Rothman (1995). The textbook was also considered by scholars who did not employ a critical reconstructionist frame. Jane Delfattore (1992) considered the phenomena of textbook censorship in the United States directed by the Gabler Institute in Texas and other powerful conservative interest groups in states with rigid textbook adoption control procedures. Elliott and Woodward (1990) edited an NSSE yearbook on the topic of textbooks and schools in the United States.

A number of scholars who studied with Apple took the lead in the discussion of the elements of critical pedagogy and democratic schooling. It is important to note that many of Apple's former students have employed postmodern theorizing in the development of their proposals, extending the frame of understanding provided in economic/political analysis. Landon Beyer, co-editor with Apple of a book on contemporary perspectives on curriculum (Beyer & Apple, 1998), discussed how theory and practice can come together in the creation of democratic schools (Beyer, 1996). Beyer also coauthored a work with Dan Liston, another scholar who studied with Apple, on efforts at progressive school reform (Beyer & Liston, 1996). Jesse Goodman has been an influential voice in describing critical democratic practices in elementary schools (Goodman, 1991). Linda McNeil (1998) offered suggestions on how democratic teaching can be realized in public schooling.

Another variation of critical reconstructionist thinking that gained attention in the 1990s was the expansion of thought from the work of Paulo Freire. The release of a number of new works by Freire prior to his death in 1997 were personal reflections on his work and convictions. There was a consistency in Freire's thought from the 1970s throughout the remainder of his career that allows a reader to look at any of his works, from the revision of the classic *Pedagogy of the Oppressed* (1993b) to *Education for Critical Consciousness* (Freire, 1990) to works produced in the late 1990s (Freire, 1996, 1997, 1998a, 1998b) and find core themes maintained and developed. Although Freire has been identified as Marxist or post-Marxist, a careful reading of his proposal reveals an alliance with experientialist thought, informed by Marxist theory but perhaps most directly shaped by his own life work and relationships. The intellectual kinship that Freire found with Myles Horton, principal educator at the Highlander Center in Tennessee (whose own story is told in *The Long Haul*, [Horton, 1990]), is captured in a volume of conversations on education and social change that Horton and Freire engaged in during the late 1980s (Bell, Gaventa, & Peters, 1990). In this conversation, personal recollection and aspirations for social renewal are prominent, not the advancement of formal ideological constructs. To read Freire's work is both intimidating and rewarding on many levels because he does not hesitate to share his personal language and experiences in the efforts to use education as a force for social transformation for justice and the expansion of love.

Freire gained a number of important interpreters of his thought, placing his contribution in new contexts. Among the works produced that expanded understanding of Freirian thought were an edited volume of his writings (McLaren & Leonard, 1993), an intellectual biography by Gadotti (1994), a work Freire coauthored with Macedo (1998), as well as dialogues on mentoring for critical consciousness (Freire with Fraser, Macedo, McKinnon, & Stokes, 1997) and on higher education (Escobar, Fernandez, & Guevara-

Niebla, 1994). Gadotti provided a structured philosophical statement based on Freirian principles (Gadotti, 1996). Macedo provided a work on the silences in the U.S. curriculum that is based on Freire's ideas (1994). Ira Shor and Caroline Pari edited a tribute describing classroom practices influenced by Freire (Shor & Pari, 1999). Antonia Darder produced a reflection on Freire's life work and beliefs (1999).

Freire's liberatory model of education was viewed by his proponents as trans-social, cross-cultural, and international. Freire's approach was the most pedagogically specific of these three approaches to critical reconstruction. Democratic educators (e.g., Apple and Beane) relied principally on revised experientialist practice, and Giroux provided suggestions for critical cultural literacy. The Freirian process of facilitating critical consciousness has been applied by practitioners in various global settings. It was the recollection and reflection on these lived experiences that also formed a research agenda. Freire's research agenda was true to his concept of "praxis" (Gadotti, 1996): Understanding comes through the dialectic of action and reflection.

A most prolific group of contributors to critical reconstructionist thought were the scholars affiliated with Henry Giroux: Stanley Aronowitz, Peter McLaren, Joe Kincheloe, and Shirley Steinberg. Giroux's work has its origins in the experientialist tradition. A student of Edwin Fenton at Carnegie Mellon, Giroux's work in the late 1970s and early 1980s examined the hidden curriculum of schools (1981; Giroux & Purpel, 1983) and how students contest its impositions (1983). With a self-acknowledged debt to Freire's contributions (Freire collaborated with Giroux, McLaren, and others aligned with this stream of critical reconstruction [e.g., Castells, Flecha, Freire, Giroux, Macedo, & Willis, 1999]), Giroux also enthusiastically assimilated postmodern and feminist theory into his own thought and writings in the late 1980s and 1990s (e.g., Aronowitz & Giroux, 1991; Giroux, 1990; Giroux, 1991a). As his thinking evolved and expanded, Giroux advocated both a research agenda that analyzes broadcast or micro-cast cultural expression and a proposal for educational reform that has been labeled "critical pedagogy" (Giroux, 1997b). Nonetheless, Giroux has remained rooted in the critical reconstructionist aspirations that a more just social and world order can emerge by exposing the "lessons" of those who dominate and by empowering those who have been denied voice (e.g., Aronowitz & Giroux, 1993). In curriculum research his interests have expanded into the educational venues of identity and culture, for example, work (1991b), difference (1994b), popular media (1994a), social representations of youth, race, and violence (1996, 1997a), and cultural studies (Giroux & Shannon, 1997). In recent works, he has also challenged the social constructions promoted by the global influence of the Disney entertainment empire (Giroux, 1998 and 1999).

Critical pedagogy, a proposal for educational reform espoused by Giroux, has its origins in the recognition that hegemonic domination of youth does not automatically translate into ideological transmission. There are possibilities afforded in the resistances and contestations that those designated as learners employ to challenge conformity. If teachers are willing to stand in solidarity with those who are politically, economically, and culturally marginalized by critically analyzing the dominant social order and creating opportunities for the voices of the marginalized to be heard (Simon, 1992), education can be an agent for social transformation. Peter McLaren (1994a) developed a proposal for critical pedagogy consistent with Giroux's interests in social analysis of dominant political and economic cultural forces (e.g, Giroux & McLaren, 1993). Whereas Giroux's research agenda translated curriculum into the broadest possible definition of what social power brokers promote as worth knowing and being, Peter McLaren remained closer to the dynamics of U.S. public schooling (1994b and 1998), offering both a critique of the performances of the school in a political/economic frame and a proposal for educating for social revolution. His ideas on the reform of education and the elements of critical pedagogy were strongly influenced by the contribution of Freire (e.g, McLaren & Lankshear, 1994) and other social reformers of emerging nations (McLaren, 1999). Dimensions of critical pedagogy expanded on the literacy empowerment approach of Freire. Recognizing that literacy is an ever-developing skill, critical pedagogy focuses on helping students to critically read the world (Lankshear & McLaren, 1993; McLaren, Hammer, Sholle, & Reilly, 1995). The emphasis on expanding literacy to participate critically in multiple discourses and engage in cultural and electronic forms of symbolic expression fostered the concept of media literacy or media knowledge (e.g., Morgan, 1997; Schwoch, White, & Reilly, 1991; Semali & Pailliotet, 1998; see also Spring, 1992).

Critical pedagogues encouraged proclaiming the counternarratives of socially marginalized peoples (Giroux, Lankshear, McLaren, & Peters, 1996) and the promotion of social dissent against the oppression of the economically or politically powerless (McLaren, 1997). A multicultural curriculum, to be authentic, is critical and confrontational, giving attention to the relationship between power and cultural expression (e.g., Kanpol & McLaren, 1995). Like Giroux, McLaren has commented on the research agenda for critical theorists (McLaren & Giarelli, 1995) and the politics of culture (McLaren, 1995). He has also revised his text for use in educational foundations coursework for preservice educators (McLaren, 1998).

OTHER CONTRIBUTORS TO CRITICAL RECONSTRUCTION

This comparison of three approaches to critical reconstruction, based in large part on the influence of Apple, Freire, and Giroux, their collaborators, and others they influenced, is not intended to exclude the many other reconstructionist contributors in the decade. Various explanatory frameworks provide an interpretation of critical theory's relevance to education (e.g., Carr, 1995; Young, 1990), reflecting openness to the insights of poststructural and postmodern thought (e.g., Peters, 1996; Shannon, 1998). Joe Kincheloe and Shirley Steinberg (1998b) edited a volume on the application of critical thinking methods to educational settings interpreted in the broadest sense. Kincheloe (1998) took particular interest in vocational education and worker training. Steinberg and Kincheloe also edited a volume that considered capitalist interests in popular culture that constitutes much of early childhood education (1997).

Various works were produced that employed a critical theory methodology in the analysis of educational activities. Macro-analytic studies (e.g., Fuller, 1991; Gatto, 1991) and case studies (e.g. Fine, 1991) were conducted. Scholars considered the possibilities and barriers created by school politics (e.g., Leistyna, 1998), whether relative to school choice (Fuller & Elmore, 1996), the professional lives of teachers (Popkewitz, 1991), or the formal uniting of schools with commerce (Molnar, 1996). Jean Anyon (1997) brought political/economic analysis to the policies and practices of urban school reform. Roman and Eyre (1997) examined the tensions between difference and equality in education. Block (1997) offered the disturbing argument that public schooling by its structure is institutionalized violence against children.

The expansion of curriculum research beyond the conventional limits of schooling has provided understanding of the dynamics of how knowledge and skills are shaped by ideological assumptions. Two scholars who studied with Michael Apple, Kenneth Teitelbaum (1995) and Linda Christian-Smith (1991), have convincingly posed the need to bring ideological curriculum critique to non-school venues. Other authors expanded on the development of critical pedagogy (e.g, Kreisberg, 1992) and the relationship of critical pedagogy to liberation theology and its expression in Catholic schools (Oldenski, 1997).

Leistyna, Woodrum, and Sherblom (1996) edited a work that served as both introduction and apologia for critical pedagogy. The movement for democratic, multicultural curricula was chronicled in collected pieces from the alternative periodical *Rethinking Schools* (Levine, Lowe, Peterson, & Tenorio,

1995). Confronting controversial social topics in the fabric of a meaningful curriculum is another aspect of the critical reconstructionist program (Williams, 1994). Marciano (1997) addressed the need to deal with the civic illiteracy of youth in the United States. Knapp (1995) contended that a focus on meaning would establish relevance for the children of the poor. The need to reshape teacher education and professional development to advocate for change was addressed by Barry Kanpol (1997b).

The relationship of critical reconstruction to gender and race perspectives on curriculum prompted conversation among scholars who participated in these discourses. Carmen Luke and Jennifer Gore (Gore, 1992; Luke & Gore, 1992) explored the possibilities of critical and feminist pedagogies working in concert with a revised critical reconstructionist program. Ng, Staton, and Scane (1995) edited a volume that surveyed how anti-racism and feminist proposals could be allied with critical approaches to education. Gallas (1997) explored the exercises of power and gender in a primary school classroom. Weis and Fine (1993) examined the silences created by class, race, and gender. Zou and Trueba (1998) wrote on political action in schools. Although bell hooks is often characterized as writing from racial/ethnic discourse (hooks, 1994), it is also possible to interpret her work in the context of revolutionary pedagogy (e.g., Florence, 1998).

With the expansion of critical reconstruction, scholarly criticism of the theory and practices from this perspective began to emerge. James (1995) edited a volume of essays that provide historical perspective with a particular emphasis on the experientialist influences on the development of critical reconstruction. Peter Hlebowitsh (1993) offered integrative and historical analysis of critical reconstruction. William Stanley (1992) traced the lineage of reconstructionist thought from Counts and Rugg through to present-day advocates and critics. Stanley suggested a theoretical structure that incorporates poststructuralism and critical pragmatism using the Aristotelian concept of "phronesis" or practical judgment as a basis of action in a reconstructed critical pedagogy. Stanley called his approach a "post-structural counter-hegemonic praxis."

There was criticism that critical reconstructionists relied too heavily on structural explanations of the processes of social conduct. Postmodernist thought posed a challenge to simple causal constructions, demanding that inquiry be specific and employ a variety of discourse models to successfully provide understanding of social phemomena. Relying exclusively on political/economic structures to analyze social relationships, cultural patterns, and identity development produced conclusions, but observation is often made to fit set patterns (e.g., Morrow & Torres, 1995; Shapiro, 1990). Elizabeth

Ellsworth (Ellsworth & Whatley, 1990) offered insightful analysis of critical reconstruction, noting that education that sustains patriarchal relationships and maintains the dominant role of the teacher cannot be upheld as liberating. Critical reconstructionists were also criticized for their inability to effect a program for school reform that meaningfully influences school practices. Wink (1997) offered a reflection on translating critical pedagogy into contemporary public school practice.

THE FLOURISHING OF DIFFERENCE

The compelling variety of curriculum studies in the 1980s that were neither aligned nor derived from social behaviorist, intellectual traditionalist, experientialist, or critical reconstructionist perspectives came to maturity in the 1990s. Engaging in phenomenological, postmodern, feminist, racial, aesthetic, literary, theological, and psychoanalytic discourses to more fully understand curricular meaning, their contributions combined with critical reconstructionists to realize Pinar's "reconceptualizing" of the curriculum field. This proliferation of distinct curriculum voices gave rise to renewed interest in authors who had previously worked without alignment with the major curricular orientations. A collection of the essays of Dwayne Huebner (edited by Hillis, 1999) and the publishing of key essays of James Macdonald (1995) provided important resources for historical context and an opportunity for new scholars to discover these important theorists. Testimony was also offered in the 1990s to the influence of Maxine Greene on the many educators who found different ways of looking at life and education. Books that considered the contribution of Maxine Greene in both reflecting on and experiencing curriculum were edited by Bill Ayers and Janet Miller (1997) and by William Pinar (1998b). Greene continued to offer personal insight and wisdom to conversations on education, with a collection of essays that considered education, the arts, and the possibilities of social change (Greene, 1995).

William Pinar is a prominent example of a curriculum theorist who employed languages outside of the major curriculum orientations of the century. Pinar was a contributor to discourses on the curriculum in psychoanalysis, sexual identity, and autobiography (Pinar, 1994) as well as an analyst and critic of contemporary curriculum scholarship (Pinar, 1998a). Pinar served as co-editor for works that consider curriculum understanding as phenomenological and deconstructed text (Pinar & Reynolds, 1992), social psychoanalysis (Kincheloe & Pinar, 1991), and he offered commentary on the various perspectives that were published in the 20-year history of *JCT* (Pinar, 1999). His shared contribution to a significant new form of synoptic curriculum text, considered later in this chapter, and his advocacy of new discourses to better understand curricula established his claim as a powerful influence on the identity of curriculum theory and research at century's end (Pinar, Reynolds, Slattery, & Taubman, 1995).

Ted Aoki at the University of Alberta fostered conceptions of curriculum and pedagogy predicated on mindful observation and expression (Aoki, 1991). His student and colleague at the University of Alberta, Max van Manen (1991; van Manen & Levering, 1996), espoused the presence of "tact" as a critical characteristic of worthwhile teaching, encouraging a fuller understanding of and sensitivity to the lives of learners and teachers. Consistent with his perspective, van Manen promoted a phenomenological research model that translated lived experience to narrative expression (van Manen, 1990). Stephen Smith (1998) also considered the personal relationship of teacher to children and the risks of encounter. Other authors listened with care to the perspectives of children and discovered the character of their curriculum (Adan, 1991; Pollard, Filer, & Theissen, 1996).

C.A. Bowers's post-liberal alternative to curriculum scholarship was distinct from both the major curriculum perspectives and from other postmodern theorists. He amplified important curricular issues that he had first addressed in the previous decades: generating awareness of dominant cultural assumptions or "modern orthodoxies" (Bowers, 1995); challenging these assumptions with new educational approaches that empower learners; and setting the curriculum in action to address the ecological crisis (Bowers, 1992, 1993, 1997; Bowers & Flinders, 1990). The ecological imperative became a hopeful focus for curriculum integration (e.g., Laura & Cotton, 1998), with books that structured learning on awareness of ecological limits (Smith, 1992) or renewal (Hutchison, 1998), emphasized the compatibility of postmodern thought with ecology education (Orr, 1991; Callicott & da Rocha, 1996), or offered suggestions for the classroom (Palmer, 1998; Smith & Williams, 1998).

Postmodern thought also provided new frameworks for researching and writing about curricular meaning. Working from a perspective that multiple discourses are needed to understand experience and that difference is the outcome of engaging in explanatory discourses, educators participated in and responded to postmodern conversations (Esteva & Prakash, 1998; Peters, 1998; Sidorkin, 1999). A major impact of the addressing of the postmodern in curriculum thought was the delineation of discourse communities within education, scholars who write out of the context of difference. Considering how difference reconstructs the experience of curriculum, new presentations of curriculum theory as integral to hermeneutics rather than an aspect of curriculum development were provided (e.g., Gallagher, 1992; Jardine, 1998).

Works explored the relationship of contemporary postmodern philosophers such as Michel Foucault (Ball, 1991; Popkewitz & Brennan, 1998), Hans-Georg Gadamer (Misgeld & Nicholson, 1991), and Richard Rorty (Arcilla, 1995) to curriculum theory. William Doll (1993), writing from a postmodern perspective, argued for the usefulness of the thought of Dewey, Whitehead, and Bruner to reorient curriculum thought away from Ralph Tyler's principles of curriculum and instruction (Tyler, 1949) and toward the consideration of "four r's": richness (uncovering the depth and multidimensionality of experience and reflection), recursion (the transaction of the self with others, culture, environment), relations (making connections among experiences), and rigor (to engage in critical interpretation while open to revision). Cleo Cherryholmes, whose foundational work (Cherryholmes, 1988) first introduced many educators to postmodern thought, gave attention to the viability of pragmatism viewed through postmodern lenses (Cherryholmes, 1999). The acceptance of postmodern theorizing and inquiry was exemplified in the expansion of writing focused on particularity in perspective and the abandonment of metanarrative, generalizations, and structural explanations.

The remarkable diversity in theoretical models for curriculum reflection and in research approaches bears witness to the postmodern contention that there is no superordinate discourse or mode of inquiry to which meaningful scholarship must be compliant. Books offered story and descriptive analysis on how curriculum interplays with cultural difference, racial difference, and difference based on gender and sexual expression. As demonstrated in the postmodern landscape presented by Usher and Edwards (1995) and in the discussion of how curriculum cultures are fashioned into practice from diverse belief systems by Pamela Bolotin Joseph and her coauthors (Joseph, Bravmann, Windschit, Mikel, & Green, 1999), the dedicated and diligent curriculum scholar was required to have an awareness of the scholarly conversations in philosophy, literary criticism, the social sciences, statistical methods, and psychoanalysis, as well as contemporary social discourses emerging from differences in race/ethnicity, gender and sexual expression, and physical/cognitive functioning. Although there continued to be authors who wrote within the traditional frame of the public school and existent political, social, and economic options (e.g., Reid, 1994), curriculum theorists also wrote reflections that required in-depth participation in the humanities (e.g, B. Miller, 1993), social sciences (e.g., Peters, 1995; Popkewitz & Fendler, 1999), or multiple discourses (e.g., D. Smith, 1998).

Curriculum inquiry or research was also a complex affair, as demonstrated in Edmund Short's (1991) categorization of options and Nelson Haggerson's (2000) discussion of the use of multiple research approaches. William

Carr advocated critical educational inquiry (1995) as a promising approach to effect change. Andrew Gitlin (1994) linked educational research with political activism, suggesting that advocacy is a part of inquiry itself. Elliot Eisner's (1991) aesthetic orientation to research and evaluation provided another compelling alternative to curriculum research as educational criticism or connoisseurship.

Research studies demonstrated this diversity. There were studies that examined characteristics of schools and argued for generalized conclusions (e.g., Bryk, Lee, & Holland, 1993; Newmann, 1992), studies that sought to provide understanding through particularized description (LeCompte & Dworkin, 1991; Metz, 1992), and volumes that employed eclectic inquiry methods and arguments (e.g., Donmoyer & Kos, 1993; Morris, 1991).

Postmodern sociologists such as Basil Bernstein (1990) continued to influence the re-defining of curriculum scholarship. A number of authors who worked principally in educational sociology offered insight into curriculum experiences and theories (e.g., Torres & Mitchell, 1998). The insistence that curriculum be understood within context as social practices assisted in both understanding the exercise of a curriculum (e.g, Levinson, Foley, & Holland, 1996) and fostering new theories on learning (e.g., Young, 1998). Works employed social analysis in providing interpretation of school culture (e.g., Henry, 1993; Wyner, 1991). The dynamics of social cartography were applied to educational settings (Paulston, 1996). Philip Wexler (1990) explained the new social research methodology rooted in the contributions of Bourdieu (Grenfell & James, 1998) and its application to the study of education. He gave attention to the interaction of the individual in a social and political context (Wexler, 1992; Smith & Wexler, 1995) and offered an ambitious proposal, influenced by Martin Buber's writing, for redirecting educational theory to the consideration of mysticism as a value base (Wexler, 1996).

REVISING CURRICULUM HISTORY

A revival of interest in the historical study of curriculum thought and school practice, which began in the 1980s, grew substantially in the 1990s. Historical methodology had undergone significant revision in the 1970s with the acceptance that the great person/great event histories of the past often served only to perpetuate mythic and ideological interests of socially dominant groups. Historical writing expanded with particular studies that addressed events in the lives of specific educators, learners, and institutions. Ivor Goodson was a leading scholar in this form of historical writing, arguing persuasively that the study of how official curricula are constructed by social structures and groups can be instructive in finding ways of effecting influence on contemporary curriculum (Goodson, 1994). Goodson and his associates have given detailed consideration to the historical evolution of school subjects (Goodson, 1992; Goodson & Marsh, 1996; Goodson & Medway, 1990; Goodson with Anstead & Morgan, 1997) and the lives of educators (Goodson & Walker, 1990). Goodson contended that curriculum proposals cannot be effective until plans of action informed by historical study are developed (Goodson, 1994, 1995). His interest in the historical study of the evolution of school subjects was shared by other scholars, although their contributions were not uniform to Goodson's suggested methodology. As examples, Saxe (1991) and Lybarger (1998) examined social studies as a school subject; DeBoer (1991) chronicled the development of ideas in science education.

The contributions of historians of education deepened understanding of the work of schooling in the United States in the twentieth century. Historians were often intentional in relating their historical study to contemporary problems. For example, David Tyack collaborated with Larry Cuban on an interpretation of public school reform in the United States in the twentieth century (Tyack & Cuban, 1995), suggesting that the additive approach that schools employed to cope with reform efforts continues in current practice. Tyack also collaborated with Elisabeth Hansot on a history of coeducation in American schools (Tyack & Hansot, 1990). Progressive education retained the interest of historians as the preeminent reform proposal for public schools in the United States in the twentieth century (e.g., Berube, 1994; Zilversmit, 1993). Diane Ravitch (2000) offered a century retrospective on school reform, castigating how various experientialist movements continually cluttered the efforts of schoolpeople to accomplish their essential function: the promotion of literacy and the transmission of culture.

Other historical studies of reform reflected on the contemporary relevance of progressive education (Semel & Sadovnik, 1998), and what past reform efforts can teach us about implementing change (Ravitch & Vinovskis, 1995). The Eight Year Study was reexamined to highlight its contemporary relevance for middle school practitioners (Lipka, Lounsbury, et al., 1998). Larry Cuban (1999) provided an interpretation on the dynamics of university curriculum, teaching, and research in this century. Herbert Kliebard (1992) offered a collection of essays on curriculum history and theory relative to the American curriculum, a study on vocationalism and its influence on the U.S. curriculum from 1876 to 1946 (Kliebard, 1999) and revised his influential history of curriculum thought in the United States from the Committee of Ten to *Sputnik* (Kliebard, 1995). David Labaree (1997) offered important social criticism in the context of historical consideration of schooling for credentialing status. Daniel and Laurel Tanner more fully developed a historical focus thorough their *History of the School Curriculum* (1990). Laurel Tanner (1997) also penned a historical portrait of the Chicago Laboratory School under the direction of John Dewey as a consideration of the contemporary significance of this educational experiment. Mary Novello's (1998) historical and philosophical analysis argued that state education is an institution tied to bankrupt notions of human fulfullment. The history of the U.S. high school was interpreted by David Angus and Jeffrey Mirel (1999) as an institution that did not fulfill its promise of opportunity and equity; William Reese (1995) analyzed the social and political forces that developed the U.S. high school in the nineteenth century. The ignoble social proposal for eugenics, which captured the interest and support of a number of prominent educational leaders, was chronicled by Selden (1999).

The instructional value of history was also emphasized in historical studies that were less expansive in time or place. Richard Gibboney's *The Stone Trumpet* (1994) examined the dynamics of school reform from 1960 to 1990. The role of public schooling in the politics of Southern Reconstruction was examined by McAfee (1998); Payne (1996) provided a view of education in the context of the civil rights struggle in the 1960s.

Professional societies were a subject of historical study and an impetus for production of historical scholarship. Daniel Tanner (1991) chronicled the history of the John Dewey Society, while Gordon Cawelti (1993) edited a volume that considered the influence of ASCD on education after a half century of activity. The Society for the Study of Curriculum History (SSCH) continued the tradition of publishing the proceedings of its annual meetings, evidencing the vitality of this field of research (Burlbaw, 1994, 1998; SSCH, 1992, 1993).

A biography of William Heard Kilpatrick (Beineke, 1998) detailed the contributions of this influential educator. The historical contribution of women educators was included in Peltzman's (1998) bio-bibliography of early childhood educators and was prominent in the volume by Crocco, Munro, and Weiler (1999) on women educator activists.

To exemplify the emergence of different approaches to writing about curriculum history in this decade, one can compare two projects that William Schubert contributed to in this decade. A selection of excerpts from historical documents that have been influential in the development of curriculum thought and practice in the United States was edited by Willis, Schubert, Bullough, Kridel, and Holton (1992). This collection is composed largely of high-profile and influential institutional policy statements. In contrast, *Turning Points in Curriculum: A Contemporary American Memoir*, authored by Dan Marshall, James Sears, and William Schubert (2000), employs personal reflection and historical metaphor to interpret and better understand proposals, experiments, and theories on curriculum in the last half of the twentieth century.

THE TEACHER, THE SELF AS CURRICULUM

Autobiography and biography were research models that responded to the postmodern emphasis on deconstructed analysis and narrative as a resource for finding significance in a curriculum. The use of autobiography as an instructional tool was considered early in the decade by Graham (1991). Craig Kridel's (1998) consideration on the art/research of writing educational biography offered guidance on this challenging effort at inquiry and narrative. The authoring of a personal narrative gained acceptance as a source for meaningful inquiry and was understood as a vehicle for educational change, giving voice to those who were socially marginalized (e.g., Hutchinson, 1999; McLaughlin and Tierney, 1994). An autobiographical narrative could take the form of a personal vision offered to speak to the life experience of others (Doll, 1995) or to examine social and power relationships in the context of education (Torres, 1997).

The identity of the teacher revealed through narrative took on new importance in a postmodern context. The recognition that the teacher is, with her or his students, often the final arbiter of curriculum as a vehicle for self-expression, evoked scholarship that ranged from the descriptive to the prescriptive. There were works that examined the specifics of how the curriculum was shaped by the identities of teachers. Others offered guidance on how the teacher can be a resource for curricular change. The teacher's identity was portrayed from diverse perspectives. Whether the descriptive concept was that of an "uncertain craft" (McDonald, 1992), a "vocation" (Aoki & Shamsher, 1993; Hansen, 1995), a "sublime vocation" (Inchausti, 1993), "rough magic" (Lindley, 1993), or a "search for immortality" (Blacker, 1997), a consistent theme was that a teacher is more than an instructional conduit and that fashioning the curriculum is an important part of the teacher's life work. In personal recollection (e.g., Ayers, 1993; Tompkins, 1997) and in listening to the voices of other teachers (e.g., Westheimer, 1998), it is consistently affirmed that remarkable teachers have a passion for direction of the curriculum. The exercise of this artistry begins with a skilled teacher's recognition that s/he attends to the voices of students and can respond meaningfully to their needs and emerging selves (Ayers, 1995). A living examplar of this commitment to teaching that promotes active learning and inquiry was offered in the collection of essays written by the remarkable educator Lillian Weber

(1997). Weber's work in the open classroom movement in the 1970s and the innovative City College Workshop Center is translated into guiding ideas on the critical roles of teachers and parents in developing learning experiences that awaken student creative investigation and production. Responsiveness to (Woods & Jeffrey, 1996) and responsibility for the community of learners is what constitutes teaching as a moral activity (Goodlad, Sirotnik, & Soder, 1993). For worthy teachers, this demand for a voice in the exercise of craft can conflict politically with stakeholders who would like to limit the influence of the teacher over the experiences that take place in the classroom (see Ginsburg, 1995; Newman, 1998; Popkewitz, 1998).

The recognition that teachers are critical negotiators of the classroom curriculum led to scholarship on how they effect this influence. The practices of teachers were studied by Hawthorne (1992) and Paris (1993) to determine the various ways that teachers co-create or re-create a curriculum with their students. Woods (1996) examined how professional practices in language teaching were shaped by the beliefs and decision-making models of the teachers. Miriam Ben-Peretz (1990) considered how teachers liberate themselves from the controlling influence of the academic subject textbook to foster experiences relevant to learners. The narratives of teachers who successfully took control of their classrooms were included in a book by Wasley (1994). The primary voices in curriculum development become the teacher and her or his students (See Ayers & Ford, 1996; Fisher, 1995)

With the pretense challenged that a curriculum is developed for teachers and not by teachers and certainly not with students, qualitative research into what teachers have to say about how they do what they do took on new importance. Cohn and Kottkamp (1992) reminded scholars and policymakers that teachers were a powerful voice in the classroom but were relatively unheard outside of this familiar environment. A number of works were dedicated to teachers speaking and writing about their craft (Bell, 1994; Thomas, 1995). George Willis and William Schubert (1991) edited a volume that asked noted educators to reflect on artistic/literary experiences that shaped their personal theories on and professional design of curriculum. The implication was that accomplished curriculum scholars and works of art that influenced them were worthwhile resources for educators at many levels, that is, valuable sources of personal theory. Schubert and William Ayers (1992) edited a volume of "teacher lore" that explored these personal theories in the lives of teachers and implications for curriculum construction. Miriam Ben-Peretz (1995) offered teachers' self-recollections on the elements of their craft. A consistency that was emphasized in this research was that remarkable teachers facilitated the curriculum with, not merely for, students (see Berman, Hultgren, Lee, Rivkin, & Roderick, 1991; Duckworth, 1996; Nicholls & Hazzard, 1993). The impetus was not simply to describe how teachers shape a curriculum, but to share their understandings and methods with new teachers (Jalongo & Isenberg, 1995) or to use teacher lore as professional development (Schwarz & Alberts, 1998). As an altnernative to conventional professional development, John Adams (2000) described how teacher networks assisted in implementation of a new math curriculum.

Postmodern Reflections on Practice. Action research retained popularity as a model for teacher engagement in reflection. McTaggert (1990) provided a history of the research model and described the various international expressions of action research (McTaggart, 1997). McKernan (1991) authored a handbook on methods and resources to conduct action research, one of various textbooks produced to assist the novice teacher in trying out alternative modes of local inquiry (Altrichter, Posch, & Somekh, 1994; McNiff, 1994).

If remarkable teachers engage in personal theorizing and facilitate the construction of a curriculum that is responsive to their students, is it possible to do more than inform new teachers that this is what they must aspire to? Is it possible to teach professional reflection on craft? The scholarship on reflective practice established in the 1980s had evolved to include efforts to empower teachers to engage in meaningful personal problem solving and theory construction. Jean Clandinin and Michael Connelly offered insight into the professional knowledge landscapes of teachers (Clandinin & Connelly, 1995) as studies of how teachers build on and engage this knowledge base (Connelly & Clandinin, 1999). Ross, Cornett, and McCutcheon (1992) edited a volume that demonstrated how teachers connect theory and research to professional practice. Donald Schön (1991), promoting an interpretation of Deweyan deliberation, offered case studies from various applications on educational practice. There were also course textbooks produced (Clark, 1995; Henderson, 1996; Zeichner & Liston, 1996) to guide preservice teachers in the dynamics of reflective practice, with suggested techniques that teachers and others could employ to foster reflection on curriculum and instruction. Lieberman and Miller (1999) argued that a restructured teacher's workplace should provide time to reflect and collaborate. Janet Miller (1990) concurred that finding opportunities for teachers to collaborate in development of their professional craft was essential for empowerment.

New directions in the fashioning of curriculum out of the lived experience of teachers included an emphasis on dialogue and conversation as integral to curricular and personal growth (Applebee, 1996; Burbules, 1993; Duckworth & the Experienced Teachers Group, 1997). Curriculum deliberation was considered in works on teacher decision making (Brubacher & Simon, 1993; Burbules & Hansen, 1997). There were also proposals for teachers to encounter postmodern theorizing in fashioning a model for reflective practice (Kincheloe, 1993; Parker, 1997) and creating an environment for reconstructing the profession (Hargreaves, 1994). The use of literary works as a basis for renewal of craft and the sparking of the imagination was investigated by Rummel and Quintero (1997) and Atwell-Vasey (1998). James Bradbeer (1998) offered a new translation of Schwab's practical inquiry through the lens of James Macdonald's mytho-poetic method and Madeleine Grumet's "looking within." Through interviews with male teachers in a school in suburban Melbourne, Bradbeer offered episodes on "imaginal" reflection, "access to the inner process of responding to intangible experience—to subtle change in the image world of the mind, or, one might say, of the heart" (Bradbeer, 1998, p. 4). Parker Palmer (1998) suggested that rather than build a model of teacher reflection on problem solving, the starting point is the remembrance of passion for the craft and confrontation of fears. With Palmer, Craig Kridel, Bob Bullough, and Paul Shaker (1996) contended that there is value in recollecting those teachers who have shaped your craft, not to find lessons in techniques, but to renew enthusiasm and purpose.

Shaping Curriculum by Shaping Teachers. The importance of teacher identity in the creation of a curriculum gave relevance to the relationship between curriculum thought and teacher education. Proposals and studies offered perspective on the development of the teacher through professional preparation and development. Sears, Otis-Wilson, and Marshall (1994) presented the results of their study on teacher recruitment and educational reform. Clandinin, Davies, Hogan, and Kennard (1993) provided stories of collaboration in the conduct of teacher education. Deborah Britzman (1991) looked at the experiences of the novice teacher. Liston and Zeichner contributed an analysis of teacher education and its relationship with the social conditions of schooling (1996).

Books were produced for use in teacher preparation programs to provide structure for the preservice educator's experience. Dillard and Maguire (1997) edited a consideration of the issues that confront a new teacher in secondary education. Bullough, Knowles, and Crow (1991) offered a structure for understanding the various problems that confront the new teacher. Knowles also produced a work with Cole and Presswood (1994) on processing field experiences through narrative and inquiry. George Posner offered methods for fostering reflective teaching in preservice field experiences. Reflective teacher education was also the subject of a volume edited by Valli (1992).

THE VARIETIES OF DIFFERENCE

A postmodern reading of curriculum also recognizes there are significant differences that establish the identity of the learner—the narratives of cultural, race, gender, and sexual expression being among those most often considered in inquiry and in consideration of meaningful practice. This is not to contend that these identifying discourses necessarily define the person; the integrity of the person provides the opportunity to engage in the languages, dis-engage, provoke language conflict, or transport into new personal landscapes. The importance of each of these differences in the life of the learner has encouraged scholarship on how curriculum must attend to the diverse narratives that constitute the self.

Culture as Difference. Energized in part by the political urgency for many school districts in the United States to serve diverse ethnic populations and in part by the increased attention of scholars, writing about cultural diversity as it impacts on the curriculum dramatically expanded in the 1990s. Multicultural education as a discourse was described in course textbooks (e.g., Manning & Baruth, 1996) and in an international overview of contemporary scholarship (Mitchell & Salsbury, 1996). "Pioneers" in the field—James Banks, Christine Sleeter, and Carl Grant—were joined by several new voices. Multicultural education was described, categorized, subjected to research, and translated into practice.

James Banks's work was a vanguard in considering the relationship of cultural difference to education. He continued to author and edit works that demonstrated the growth of scholarship in multicultural education in the 1990s. Banks coauthored a handbook on research in multicultural education (1995), an overview on historical and contemporary perspectives (1996), course textbooks on multicultural education (1994; Banks & Banks, 1997), and a perspective piece on how cultural diversity redefines citizenship (Banks, 1997) and he revised his classic contribution, *Multiethnic Education: Theory and Practice* (Banks, 1993).

Christine Sleeter advocated understanding multicultural education in the broadest terms, including difference in race, class, and gender (Sleeter & Grant, 1994, 1999). Her categorization of options for multicultural education remained a viable interpretation of proposals (see Timm, 1996, for a variant categorization). Sleeter also advanced the relationship of multicultural education and the critical reconstructionist agenda (Sleeter, 1990, 1996; Sleeter & McLaren, 1995).

Other writers who came to prominence for their contributions to the understanding of cultural pluralism were Lisa Delpit, Sonia Nieto, Etta Hollins, and

Antonia Darder. Delpit's *Other People's Children* (1995) employed personal experience as a reference point for understanding cultural interaction in schooling. Nieto's *Affirming Diversity* (1996), issued in a revised edition, examined the impact of language as well as cultural difference on how what is taught is interpreted by the learner. In *The Light in Their Eyes* (1999), Nieto offered recommendations and reflections by teachers for fostering a learning community that embraces diversity. Hollins understood cultural difference as foundational if the educator is to be intentional in his/her teaching. Her perspective is offered in *Culture in School Learning* (1996a) and is included in an anthology on schooling for diverse populations (Hollins, King, & Hayman, 1994) and essays on restructuring the curriculum for cultural pluralism (Hollins, 1996b). Antonia Darder contended that bicultural education should be interpreted as an agenda for social, economic, and political reconstruction in her writing about the exercise of culture and power in the classroom (Darder, 1991, 1995).

The criticial reconstructionist's interest in both giving voice to cultural difference and expanding democracy and justice for marginalized peoples resulted in a number of works that supported multicultural education as an agent in social change (e.g., Adams, Bell, & Griffin, 1997; Kincheloe & Steinberg, 1997; May, 1998; Noya, Geismar, & Nicoleau, 1997; Renyi, 1993; Weil, 1998). Walter Feinberg (1998) discussed a proposal for public schooling that addressed principled liberal education in the context of cultural diversity.

How recognition of cultural diversity impacts on what is worth knowing and sharing was an important discussion in the 1990s and several authors considered the characteristics of a multicultural curriculum (Booth, Swann, Masterson, & Potts, 1991; Butler & Walter, 1991; Edgerton, 1996). There was also no lack of books that provided specific guidance on the implementation of multicultural education. Boyer and Baptiste (1996) authored a "practitioner's handbook" on curriculum reform; Stock (1995) offered an approach to teaching and learning in a multicultural society that was "dialogic," suggesting that teachers and learners share their cultural differences. Lutzker (1995) authored a work offering strategies and resources for college faculty in addressing cultural diversity. Instructive case studies describing successes in educating the culturally different were produced by Lipka, Mohatt, and the Cuilistet Group (1998) on the education of Yupik Eskimos and by Cornelius (1999) on Iroquois education. Fraser and Perry (1993) edited a popular anthology of ideas and resources. Davidman and Davidman (1997) revised a practical guide on multicultural education for use as a course text. Other recommended practices were explained by Ramsey (1998), Roberts and colleagues (1994), and Tierney (1993). The widespread recognition of the need to address cultural difference is reflected in the NEA's publication of a perspective piece on multicultural education (Diaz, 1992). Dunn and Griggs (1995) examined the research on cultural difference and learning styles and offered recommendations for both teachers and counselors.

Race as Difference. Attention to racial difference was due in part to the evolution of attention to educational equality for peoples of color (e.g., Beauboeuf-Lafontant & Augustine, 1990) and in part to the desire to confront racist practices in education (Derman-Sparks & Phillips, 1997). The concept of race exists as a construct to socially define classes of peoples (black, yellow, red, or brown) as physically and therefore humanly distinct from a dominant social group (white). Whereas culture and ethnicity are largely produced within a self-determined community, race exists by virtue of perceived physical differences employed for economic, political, and social purposes. Although the racial construct has been most often examined in terms of the dichotomy of white and black, the expansion of the notion of race has meanings for a variety of non-white groups (e.g., Fine, Powell, Weis, & Mun Wong, 1996; Searle, 1998). The identification of race as a text for understanding curriculum is reflected in the essays on identity and difference edited by Castenell and Pinar (1993). Cameron McCarthy provided a narrative for understanding the relationship of race and curriculum as it is reflected in research on schooling (McCarthy, 1990). McCarthy also co-edited a volume with Crichlow (1993) providing an overview of contemporary scholarship on race and the curriculum, and he explored the complexities of cultural assignment in understanding relevant educational practice (McCarthy, 1997).

A number of works examined dimensions of African American education. Lomotey (1990) edited a volume on the African American experience of schooling. Willie, Garibaldi, and Reed edited a retrospective on public schools and African Americans since *Brown v. Board of Education* (1991). The response of African American youth to the public school experience was the subject of works by Solomon (1991) and Gentry (1994). Gloria Ladson-Billings (1994) authored an inspirational description of the actions of successful teachers of African American children. Taylor (1997) proposed social skills intervention through the curiculum to empower African American males. Theresa Perry (1995) authored a piece on racial identity, popular culture, and literacy and joined with Lisa Delpit in considering the power issues at work when widespread media attention was given to the acceptance of "ebonics" as a primary language for some African American children (Perry & Delpit, 1998).

The race text was also pondered beyond the black-white identity (e.g., Sellar & Weis, 1997). Teachers working in multiracial schools (see Howard, 1999) were coming to an awareness that curriculum must attend to the diverse ethnic and racial experiences of their learners. Scholarship focused on Latinos and education (Darder, Torres, & Gutierrez, 1998; Padilla, 1997) and the personal and political educational experience of Mexican-American students (Chawla-Duggan & Carger, 1996; Valenzuela, 1999). Scholarship also offered insight into the Asian-American educational experience (Nakanishi & Nishida, 1995).

Gender and Sexual Orientation as Difference. The discourse on how gender informs both personal and school curricula was a major conversation in the 1990s. When compared with the limited attention given to this discourse just a decade before, the new voices that emerged to speak to the relationship of gender to what is taught and what is learned is remarkable. Jane Roland Martin's contention that feminist thought was "changing the educational landscape" (Martin, 1994) was realized at least in terms of scholarship on how gender, and feminine identity in particular, shapes the curricular experience. Anthologies on the feminist text in understanding curriculum and reforming education (e.g., Stone, 1994; Woysner & Gelfond, 1998) and introductory texts to the feminine discourse (Weiner, 1994) evidenced the rapid development of this area of study (e.g., Bilken & Pollard, 1993). The dominant mode of inquiry at the beginning of the decade concerned feminist identity as it related to curriculum, as encountered in institutions and in the construction of alternatives. This inquiry into the relationship of gender identity expanded in the 1990s to include studies on how sexual expression impacts on the construction of meaning relative to curricula.

The important work of researching the lessons learned from a feminist consciousness in an encounter with a patriarchical curriculum (e.g., Lather, 1991) was joined with efforts to establish a feminist curriculum that expresses the identities of women (e.g., Mayberry & Rose, 1999). Gaskell and Willinsky (1995) edited a volume that examined how consideration of gender can impact on curricular choice and sharing. Janice Jipson and her colleagues (1995) argued that the examination of the feminist perspective relative to education can bring about a platform for social transformation. J. Brady (1995) examined how the education of young children can be constructed around feminist liberatory learning.

Examination of women's identities in the conventional U.S. school and confrontation of institutional curricula that silenced women was a significant curriculum inquiry in the 1990s. Middleton and Weller (1998) edited a volume of historical narratives on the education of women. Streitmatter (1994) and Clark and Millard (1998) focused on gender equity in school practice. Raissiguier (1994) chronicled the forming of a woman worker identity in

French vocational schools. The consideration of gender gained complexity as challenges to male identities were also the subject of scholarship (Diller, Houston, Morgan, & Ayim, 1996; Kleinfield, & Yeria, 1995; Epstein, Elwood, Hey, & Maw, 1998).

Authors explored how women construct a curriculum from experiences both in school (Blake, 1997) and beyond school (Christian-Smith & Kellor, 1998; Luke, 1996; Proweller, 1998) and make declarations of meaning from this curriculum (Neumann & Peterson, 1997). Reflections were offered on the intrapersonal (Wear, 1993) and the spiritual (Carmody, 1991) dimensions of the feminine consciousness.

In 1990 Joanne Pagano wrote on the identity of the woman teacher/educator in institutions that are developed to promote a patriarchal understanding of the world. By decade's end, the life experiences of women teachers, voices that were too seldom publicly acknowledged (Lewis, 1994), were revealed in historical narrative (Munro, 1998), postmodern analysis (Ellsworth, 1997; Ropers-Huilman, 1998), social inquiry (Acker, 1994; Biklen, 1995), and ethnographic research (Henry, 1998). The insights of the feminist teacher (e.g., Cohee et al., 1998) were argued to be a necessary influence in the reshaping of teacher education (McWilliams, 1994). Works also spoke to the elements of approaching the teacher's craft from a feminist perspective in early childhood education (Goldstein, 1997) and in science education (Barton, 1998).

The influence of gender on public action and policy relative to the school curriculum (Riddell, 1992) and public schooling (Hernandez, 1997) was another dimension of scholarship that employed gender as a discourse for understanding. Brine (1998) offered a global perspective on how women's educations maintain systems of gender inequality.

Although the discourse on gender tended toward consideration of the feminist realization of curricula, a growing body of scholarship was considering sexual expression identity as an important text for self-understanding. The literature addressed questions such as: How does schooling contribute to sexual identity (Epstein & Johnson, 1998; Mac An Ghaill, 1994)? How are school curricula developed to address sexual identity (Sears, 1992)? How does postmodern philosophy inform educating to a sexual identity (e.g., Middleton, 1997)? How can schools accommodate the voices of gay and lesbian students in the curriculum and community life (Letts & Sears, 1999; Lipkin, 1997; Pinar, 1998c; Unks, 1995)? Are students encouraged to address the personal and public tragedy of Acquired Immune Deficiency Syndrome (AIDS) (Lather & Smithies, 1997; Silin, 1995; Tonks, 1995)?

Crossing Over Differences. The interrelationship of race, class, and sexual identity was also recognized as an important context for curriculum study. Etter-Lewis and Foster (1995) used the personal narratives of women to examine the relationship of race and gender as related and unrelated points of self-understanding. Other works that examined the interaction of racial and sexual identity relative to schooling were produced by Connolly (1998) in a study of young children, Davidson (1996), Fiol-Matta and Chamberlain (1994) on women of color and the college curriculum, Tsolidis (1998), and Woods and Hammersley (1993).

Developing a "Centered" Curriculum

Among the most creative proposals for writing of school curricula were those that either offered a point of integration for the school curriculum or pushed the conventional envelope by giving attention to dimensions of the human experience that are not addressed by standard school subjects. While the disciplinary structure of the national standards appeared to dismiss such efforts, scholars continued to attest to the need for curriculum reform that maintained a center point, a hub, to use Theodore Brameld's image (1956), from which subject areas could find relevance. Scholars also pointed to dimensions of human life that provided insight and interest. Dimensions that gained scholarly attention in the 1990s included the affective, spiritual, and ethical concerns of being human; a commitment to democracy as social process and/or ideal; and responding to the structures of cognitive processing.

Centered on virtue and care. A significant concern for writers on curriculum in the 1990s was with what has been described as the affective or value domains of human thought and interaction. A number of voices responded to the call by David Purpel (1989) to give consideration to the moral and spiritual crisis in public education. Purpel continued to insist eloquently that discussion of curricular purpose should be relocated from conceptions of excellence and liberation to considerations of virtue. For scholars working from either an experientialist or intellectual traditionalist orientation, the notion of a separate field for the study of the affective missed the mark, since all deliberation has value considerations. Jackson, Boostrom, and Hansen (1993) reminded readers that teaching and the activities of the school carry inevitable moral loadings. Being aware of these ethical dimensions, they suggested, empowers educators to be responsible in their craft. A volume edited by Goodlad, Sirotnik, and Soder (1993) offered a scholarly consideration of the value dimensions of teaching. This investigation into the morally implicit in the labors of school people, an extension of Jackson's "hidden curriculum" (1990), was conducted by Blumberg and Blumberg (1994). Stephenson, Ling, Burman, and Cooper (1997) edited a volume on the role of values in education.

A number of works provided perspective and reflection on value dimensions of education. Philip W. Jackson contributed a work on the "untaught lessons" of contemporary schooling (1992b). Marion Wright Edelman offered a personal appeal to attend to the needs of contemporary youth (Edelman, 1992). A book by Fine (1995) considered the value dimensions of school reform proposals. An NSSE yearbook (Molnar, 1997) examined various approaches to character education.

Other authors moved to prescription of how values can appropriately be infused into the school curriculum. James Beane (1990b) promoted a cross-disciplinary approach that emphasized values anchored in democracy, tolerance, and justice. Lisman (1996) explained how ethics could be integrated into the curriculum. Barrow (1990) argued for attention to the practical skills of thinking, feeling, and caring. Thomas Sergiovanni (1994), recognized for his contribution to scholarship on educational administration, turned his attention to the task of community building in the schools.

An alternative approach to educating for values was to attend to the insights of child development as a basis for constructing a curriculum that addresses values. Garrod (1992) edited a volume on moral education theory and practice that examined contemporary perspectives on how moral values are, in conflicting perspectives, acquired, instilled, or evoked. A work by Berman (1997; Berman & LaFarge 1993) examined methods for teaching children social responsibility in accord with developmental growth. DeVries and Zan (1994) proposed the use of constructivist practices to foster moral growth in younger children. Cohen (1999) produced a work that described the social emotional learning process for young adolescents. The highly influential and best-selling ASCD book from 1962, a foundational call to redirect curriculum to issues of affective development, was revisited in a book of essays (Freiberg, 1999).

Nel Noddings's work on caring, first articulated in the previous decade, had its origins in Deweyan thought but also incorporated the insights of women's scholarship in moral development. In *The Challenge to Care in Schools* (1992), Noddings provided a model for reconstruction of the school curriculum around expanding considerations of care for self, people, ideas, and the planet. Noddings's perspective avoided both dogmatic allegiance as well as relativism; she employed an experientialist rationale in arguing for a curriculum centered on caring for others. Erickson (1995) also produced a work that reworked curriculum and instruction to incorporate moral and spiritual dimensions. Whereas Erickson's model reformed current practice, Noddings's proposal advocated reconstruction of conventional structures. In addition to Noddings, other scholars began to consider how schools can engage students in values deliberations in a postmodern perspective that is informed by, but not derived from, Deweyan experientialism (e.g., Eaker-Rich & Van Galen, 1996; Katz, Noddings, & Strike, 1999; Lasley, 1994). Works also examined a particular moral issue as it related to education, whether the overcoming of violence (e.g., Betty Reardon [1993] offered a feminist perspective on global confrontation, also Reardon & Nordland, 1994; Hutchinson, 1996) or developing ecological awareness (Milbrath, 1996).

Attention was given to the dynamics of classroom management as they related to the development of a sense of values in human action. Jones and Jones (1992) offered a volume on how the curriculum can be a focal point for the fostering of responsible behavior in young people. Alfie Kohn (1998, 1999), a popular speaker at conferences and conventions, addressed the impact that competition and reward structures have on the social values of young people. He also offered common-sense criticism of the administrative use of standardized testing to measure student learning and direct the curriculum (Kohn, 2000).

An approach more accommodating to social behaviorist and practical intellectual traditionalist perspectives was the revival of character education programs, a popular movement of the 1920s and 1930s. Attaining widespread popularity was use of homeroom and advisory periods to consider principles of conduct that were socially sanctioned and uncontroversial. With slight adjustments to the standard disciplinary curriculum (enhancement activities in the language arts were typical), school personnel could advance the principles of trust, honesty, courage, and tolerance. An examplar of this approach was Edward Wynne and Kevin Ryan's 1993 text, *Reclaiming Our Schools*. Ryan and Karen Bohlin (1999) followed with a practical guide on implementing a curriculum for character education. Former Secretary of Education William J. Bennett (1993) revived the design of most nineteenth-century readers to promote moral virtues through instructive literature. Eyre and Eyre (1994) authored a work on teaching responsibility. DeRoche and Williams (1998) produced a character education program for practitioners. Heath (1994) outlined an approach that addressed both the character and intellect of the student. Mary Ann Conroy (1999) offered practical lesson plans organized around nurturing personal development by revisiting activities popular in the era of values clarification, but constructed around guiding principles.

An initiative that gained support from school practitioners in the 1990s was the institution of community service as a lived experience designed to provide the student with a sense of charitable action and to appreciate the quality of life for those with economic or physical limitations. Kinsley and McPherson (1995) edited a book advocating inclusion of service learning as a component of the curriculum. An NSSE yearbook was dedicated to the topic of service learning (Schine, 1997). Related works on translating moral or character education into action were authored by Oliner and Oliner (1995) and Brown (1998).

The relationship of religious belief to education gained renewed attention in the decade. Works discussed religion and public education in the United States (Nash, 1998; Nord & Haynes, 1998; Sears & Carper, 1998). Pumfrey and Verma (1993) edited a volume on religious education in the English primary schools. A facet of the relationship between religion and education that gained increased interest was the spiritual dimensions of teaching and learning. Parker Palmer was recognized as a leading voice in understanding how a spiritually grounded approach to education impacts on curricular choices (Palmer, 1993). Works by Paul Theobald (1997), John Miller (1999), and an anthology of writings on the topic by Glazer (1999) opened up conversation on a provocative focus for education.

Centered on Democracy. The fostering, cultivating, or instilling of democratic values through the agency of the schools was certainly not an aspiration exclusive to critical reconstructionists. Promoting democratic convictions through education was often upheld as a core value by intellectual traditionalists (e.g., Mortimer Adler); democratic practices were integral to the experientialist proposal for education as well. Scholars continued to devote attention to the contributions of John Dewey to democratic thought, practice, and reform (Boisvert, 1997; Jackson, 1998; Levine, 1996; Paringer, 1990; Ryan, 1995; Westbrook, 1991) and to the craft of educators (Cuffaro, 1995; Fishman & McCarthy, 1998; Garrison, 1997; Simpson & Jackson, 1997). The dedication to education as a democratic process remained a core tenet of Dewey's and experientialists' understanding of life, ethics, and education. A variety of authors examined what it meant to be educated in a democratic society, how schools dedicated to democratic values practice their craft, and the dynamics of democratic classroom activities.

The conversation on democratic education begins with a defining of the meaning of democracy. Joel Spring, a noted scholar of American schooling and social policy (Spring, 1998), argued that an education for human rights that transcended relative allegiance to a democratic process was a defensible curriculum that promoted social and personal liberation (Spring, 1999). Spring (2000b) promoted a model of education based on an interpretation of the United Nations Statement on Human Rights. Human rights as a focus for education was also advocated in a work by Vandenberg (1990). Quicke (1999) resonated with the Jeffersonian aspiration that an educated populace could rule itself wisely and that the curriculum of the schools should meet this challenge. Contributing authors to the journal *Democracy and Education* shared the conviction that democratic education is authenticated when it promotes social justice in curriculum, instruction, and school culture (Ayers, Hunt, & Quinn, 1998).

Other authors interpreted democracy to mean the political process of social determination of policy (e.g., Carr & Hartnett, 1996; Parker, 1995; Sehr, 1997; Soder, 1995). The College Entrance Examination Board published a collection of essays that revisited the debate between experientialists and intellectual traditionalists on the role of collegiate liberal education in fostering a democratic society (Orrin, 1994). Warehime (1993) examined the dynamics of cultural conflict and its potential for resolution through creative democracy. A variety of topics related to the social reconstruction of schools through democratic action were related in a collection of articles from *Rethinking Schools*, the grass-roots periodical on school reform (Bigelow, Christenson, Karp, Miner, and Peterson, 1994).

James Fraser (1997), whose earlier work provided insights into the practice of multicultural education, proposed that democratic living be the process and the goal of schooling in a democratic society. Influenced by critical reconstructionists Paulo Freire and Henry Giroux, Fraser contended that democracy be understood as the full participation of all citizens in establishing policies and social action, ensuring that all people share in the benefits of the society, and creating a more just, participatory economic and political order. The work discusses contemporary educational issues such as cultural diversity, attention to the needs of the child, the role of technology in education, and teacher preparation. Fraser renewed George Counts's (1932) foundational challenge to educators in a democratic society, *Dare the School Build a New Social Order?*, suggesting how school curriculum, structures, resources, and teacher preparation can creatively accept this challenge.

George Wood (1992) provided portraits of several high-profile schools that support democratic principles and practices. His involvement in the practices of a school directed by democratic vision led him to return to school-based practices as the principal of a high school in Ohio, an experience he described and reflected on in *A Time to Learn* (Wood, 1998). Central Park East (CPE) High School was heralded by critical reconstructionists (see Apple & Beane, 1995) as well as proponents of Sizer's Essential Schools coalition as a model for educational reform. Perspectives on CPE were provided by Fliegel (1993), Bensman (2000), and Deborah Meier (1997), the administrator of

CPE. Another chronicle of the life of a school was that of the Albany Free School told by Mercogliano (1998).

More traditional approaches to addressing democracy in classroom practice focused on the development of citizenship through the curriculum (e.g., Burstyn, 1996; Edwards & Fogelman, 1993; Isaac, 1992; Mosher, Kenny, & Garrod, 1994; Reeher & Cammarano, 1997; White, 1996). Other authors promoted having students share in the development of the curriculum, from advising on content (Passe, 1996) to models that advocated for teacher-student collaboration. Short and Burke (1991) produced a practitioner's approach to collaborative curriculum construction, which was also the subject of a volume edited by Nicholls and Thorkildsen (1995). Gross (1997) explained the process of "joint curriculum design" for high school classrooms. Levy (1996) offered a personal case study on collaborative development of the classroom curriculum. Ostrow (1995) extended collaborative construction of the curriculum from first- through third-grade classrooms. Oyler (1996) and Shor (1996) wrote on the need to share authority with students. Cynthia McDermott (1998) edited a volume that investigated the dimensions of the democratic classroom. Areglado, Bradley, and Lane (1996) offered ideas on establishing a classroom that promotes self-directed learning. Wolk (1998) advised on the essentials of the democratic classroom.

Mara Sapon-Shevin (1999) offered guidance on the creation of a cooperative, inclusive classroom. The use of the case method as a model for democratic instructional method was advocated in a book edited by McNergney, Ducharme, and Ducharme (1999). Allen (1999) moved democratic deliberation into action for social justice by elementary and middle school students. Henkin (1998) explained how literacy can facilitate equity and social justice. John Dewey's ideas on classroom practice, still perhaps the most ambitious proposal for democracy as education, were the focus of reflection in a volume by Fishman and McCarthy (1998).

Centered on the Brain and Cognition. An integrating center for curriculum development that emerged in the 1990s employed research into the functioning of the brain to more effectively determine the appropriate sequencing of curriculum content and the forms of instruction that are responsive to how the brain receives, processes, and retains different kinds of information and skills. The forging of a relationship between cognitive processes and curriculum was an established interest of Elliot Eisner (1994a) in his *Cognition and Curriculum Reconsidered*, but the new direction informed curriculum planning with neurological research findings.

The Association for Supervision and Curriculum Development led a major effort to foster educator use of recent conclusions in brain functioning and development. The writings of Caine and Caine (1997a, 1997b) spearheaded the effort to inform and reform educational practice in light of cognitive research. Art Costa edited a two-volume work on the development of the mind and implications for education (Costa, 1991). Costa's interest in the reconceiving of thinking skills was also promoted in works he authored and coedited with Liebmann (Costa & Liebmann, 1996; 1997a, 1997b). Works by Sylwester (1995) and Jensen (1998), also published by ASCD, provided practitioners with an introduction to recent brain research. The implications of cognitive research on the designing of instruction were considered by West, Farmer, and Wolff (1991) and were translated into school practice by Sternberg and Williams (1998). Hedley, Baratta, and Houtz (1990) edited a volume that considered the relationship between cognitive processing and literacy acquisition.

There were hints of revolution in the field of cognitive development as it related to determining appropriate curricular content. Constructivism (Fosnot, 1996), an amorphous amalgam of Dewey, Vgotsky (Lipman, 1996), Piaget, and Gardner, remained the dominant conceptual frame for educational psychology, shaping the dynamics of teaching skill development and instructional practice. The long-standing relationship of Piaget's developmental scheme to constructivist theories of human learning, however, came under criticism. A interesting alternative was provided by Kieran Egan. Egan's inventive revival of a social recapitulation theory (1997) argued that children's cognitive development was shaped by their use of cognitive tools. The initial somatic stage involves the use of the body as an instrument for meaning construction and expression. This stage is superseded sequentially by the acquisition of oral language, by basic literacy, by the use of symbolic analysis, and by the ability to apprehend and construct theories. A final stage is the "ironic," in which the agent is able to integrate these cognitive tools and evaluate the value of the information and meaning that is afforded by them. With the acquisition of each of these cognitive tools, the kind of content that the learner seeks responds to the dynamics of the cognitive tool. The implication is that Piaget's notion that children begin with the concrete and move to the abstract is challenged by Egan's argument that the young child is most engaged with fantasy rather than immediate objects because the fantastic best resonates with the cognitive development of the young learner. Important activities for learning involve the use of narrative (e.g., McEwan & Egan, 1995) and the exercise of the imagination (Egan, 1992, 1999). Lauritzen and

Jaeger (1996) built on this conception of cognitive development with a "narrative curriculum," integrating storytelling into various traditional disciplines.

Howard Gardner's theory of multiple intelligences, the popularly received challenge to the concept of an intelligence quotient, blossomed into a movement for educational reform, with professional development opportunities, videos, and how-to books (e.g., Carreiro, 1998) broadening educators' notions on intelligence. Gardner edited a book on translating the theory of multiple intelligences to practice (1993b), revised the important *Unschooled Mind* (1993c), produced an argument for reform based on his research, and expanded on the original categorization of intelligences in *Intelligence Reframed* (1999a). Gardner offered perhaps his most personal statement on curriculum and educational reform in *The Disciplined Mind* (1999b). The proposal is in many ways an insightful contribution to the intellectual traditionalist orientation, even though Gardner's theory has most often been translated into practices that have experientialist conceptions of curriculum. Thomas Armstrong (1994, 1998) was a popular translator of Gardner's theory in volumes produced for ASCD. Books were published that examined the implications of intelligences neglected by conventional schooling (e.g., Moody [1990] on artistic intelligences).

Centered on Interests and Needs. Locating an integrating center to the curriculum whereby learning becomes engaging and personally relevant to the learners continued to be of interest to curriculum writers (e.g., Clark, 1997). In contrast to the academic disciplines that structure national and state content standards, those advocating constructivist learning, whether experientialist or conciliatory in their orientation, argued for the need to find a center of relevance across the disciplines. For example, James Beane (1995) edited a volume for ASCD that, while looking at the contributions made by each of the academic disciplines, argued for a "coherence" in curriculum construction (see also Pate, Homestead, & McGinnis, 1997). Beane placed democratic practice as the integrating focus of his proposal (Beane, 1997). As Beane recognized, the term "integration," as defined by L. Thomas Hopkins (1954), had unfortunately lost its precise meaning as locating a center in the developmental needs and interests of the learners. Many writers in the 1990s used the term to denote any interdisciplinary approach (e.g., Drake, 1998; Jacobs, 1997; Rothlein, Fredericks, & Meinbach, 1996).

Some authors promoted an integrating framework, a conceptual framework of what is needed to educate young people for contemporary life. Robert Marzano continued to develop the "Dimensions of Thinking" construct on skills, content knowledge, and dispositions introduced in the 1980s with works on how this model impacts on curriculum and instruction (Marzano, 1992) and assessment (Marzano, Pickering, & McTighe, 1993). Jones and Idol (1990) edited a volume that argued for the Dimensions of Thinking construct as an integrating center for curriculum development. Ron Miller established his own publishing house to promote the concept of "holistic learning" where the emotional, intellectual, and spiritual needs of the learner are addressed through integrated studies (Miller, Cassie, & Drake, 1990; Flake, 1993). Siraj-Blatchford and Siraj-Blatchford (1995) identified cross-curricular skills, themes, and dimensions for integration. Benson, Glasberg, and Griffith (1998) edited a volume that considered the unity and integration inherent in knowledge. Workplace relevance was proposed as the integrating center in works by Marshall and Tucker (1993) and Resnick and Wirt (1995), as well as in a two-volume work edited by Grubb (1995). Nagel (1996) called attention to real-world problem solving. Villani (1998) offered a synthesized curriculum focused on the needs of citizens in the next century centered on the possibilities of technology and the lessons learned from an international perspective on curriculum. An imaginative proposal was to have the play of children be the organizing center of the curriculum in early childhood education (Van Hoorn, Monighan Nourot, Scales, and Alward, 1993, 1999).

Linked without a Center. There were titles that promoted the need for connections among the disciplines but with no overriding theoretical construct. The value of interdisciplinary connections for these authors was rooted in the contention that they would be more engaging and more relevant to the lives of students and thus provide greater educational effect (e.g., Drake, 1998; Post, Ellis, Humphreys, & Bugget, 1997; Sharpe & Lee, 1998). Heidi Hayes Jacobs (1997) shifted her interest in interdisciplinary connections to a program where the existing curriculum of a school is "mapped" to locate points of connection among disciplines. Clark and Wawrytko edited a volume arguing for the need to establish integration in the college curriculum (1990). Jenkins and Tanner (1991) as well as Clarke and Agne (1997) suggested interdisciplinary connections at the high school level. Maurer (1994, 1995) produced course texts on designing interdisciplinary curriculum for middle schools and high schools. Interdisciplinary inquiry was promoted by Martinello and Cook (1994); Manning, Manning, and Long (1994) explained an inquiry-based curriculum for elementary and middle schools. Other works on interdisciplinary connections for elementary and middle schools were produced by Five and Dionisio (1995), Short and colleagues (1996), and Wood (1997). Charbonneau and Reider (1995) suggested a developmental model for curriculum integration in the elementary schools. Roberts and Kellough (1996, 2000) offered a detailed guide for the development of an interdisciplinary thematic unit.

There was no lack of support for the need to maintain emphasis on cognitive skills such as reading, writing, or numeracy across the academic disciplines. Hedley, Feldman, and Antonacci (1992) edited a volume emphasizing literacy across the disciplines. Tchudi (1993; Tchudi & Levy, 1996) argued that language arts could establish integration of science and the humanities. Purves, Rogers, and Soter (1990) advocated a literature-connected curriculum. Drake (1993; Drake et al., 1993) presented a story model as the focus for integration. Bearne (1998, 1999) advocated language skill development across the curriculum. House and Coxford demonstrated how mathematics could be cross-disciplinary (1995); Schiro explained how children's literature and mathematics could be integrated (1997).

Centered on Technology? Technology remained a subject of interest to curriculum writers, but the enthusiasm exhibited in the 1980s for making electronic information gathering, processing, and communicating the center of a new curriculum was dampened by social critics representing diverse perspectives (e.g., Postman, 1992; Bromley & Apple, 1998). Channel One, portrayed in the 1980s variously as an exciting or disturbing new advance in school/media/corporate relationships, proved a non-event in many classrooms, with students busy catching up on homework or social events to the drone of fast food sales pitches (DeVaney, 1994). The use of computers in education, an established practice in many schools for over a decade, was subject to historical review (Fischer, 1996). Although there remained interest in the social and political implication of integrating use of computers in the curriculum (e.g., Muffoletto & Knupfer, 1993; Provenzo, Brett, & McCloskey, 1998), the majority of titles offered advice on how to bring technology on board as an instructional tool that needs to be considered when developing a curriculum. Examples of course texts include Bullough and Beatty (1991), Geisert and Futrell (1995), Edwards, Roblyer, and Havriluk (1996), and Robyler (1999). Titles were published in England in response to the "delivery" of technology in the national curriculum (e.g., Beyner & MacKay, 1992; Eggleston, 1990, 1996; Kimball, Stables, and Green, 1996; Warren, 1992). Other works provided understanding of how technology has and can impact on classroom practice (e.g., Gooden, 1996; Harris, 1998; Hayemore Sandholtz, Ringstaff, and Dwyer, 1997; Raizen, Sellwood, Todd, & Vickers, 1995; Zimmerman and Hayes, 1998).

SPECIAL NEEDS, ONE CURRICULUM

Although education of the mentally or physically challenged expanded dramatically in resources and as a field of research, there were few books produced that addressed curriculum development for special needs learners. This can be attributed to two advances in the education of children with identified special needs. Growth of scholarship in addressing the educational needs of identified mental or physical challenges resulted in the establishing of a distinct area of research and pedagogy with limited cross-referencing to authors in curriculum theory, research, or development. In addition, the 1990s saw expansion of inclusion as the preferred approach to educating the student with special needs. This approach meant that students who formerly were provided with "special education" were now included in the mainstream classroom with accommodations and modifications of the curriculum replacing an alternative curriculum (Goodlad & Lovitt, 1993; Stainback & Stainback, 1996). Inclusion meant, however, that curriculum reform needed to be attentive to how changes in the curriculum will affect students with special needs as well as those students not requiring accommodation or ancillary resources (Pugach & Warger, 1996). Inclusion also carried the responsibility to educate students on positive relationships with those possessing mental or physical challenges (e.g., Quicke, Beasley, & Morrison, 1990).

Those students identified as gifted also attracted continued attention, with advocates for these students demonstrating little enthusiasm for the concept of inclusion. Again, scholarship in gifted education tended toward maintaining a conversation within the parameters of serving the needs of those students identified as gifted and developing a curriculum that is responsive to this population (e.g., VanTassel-Baska, 1992). Given the attention to de-tracking and to inclusion, gifted education was open to criticism as elitist and classist (Sapon-Shevin, 1994).

CURRICULUM DEVELOPMENT: ANACHRONISTIC OR REFORMED?

From the perspective of both curriculum theorists who explored new ways of thinking, inquiring, and writing about the curriculum and practitioner-scholars busy translating national standards and administering and interpreting norm-referenced testing tied to these standards, continued efforts to develop formal school curricula were formulaic, perhaps even manipulative on the one hand, or redundant, perhaps anachronistic on the other hand. In either case, could it be defended as a worthwhile endeavor for contemporary educators? The answer, at least when considering the publication of books on curriculum, was an emphatic "Yes!" Guidance and directives on how to develop a curriculum for the schools continued to be a major interest of writers about curriculum. Several books were produced by long-standing contributors to curriculum development, whether in revised works (e.g., Doll, 1996; English & Larsen, 1996; Glatthorn, 1996; Hass & Parkay, 1993; Lemlech, 1994; Lorber & Pierce, 1996; Oliva, 1992, Posner & Rudnitsky, 1994, 1997; Wiles & Bondi, 1993a, 1998) or new titles (e.g., Glatthorn, 1994, McNeil, 1995; Posner, 1992; Wiles, 1999). The use of instructional objectives, long advanced by Norman Gronlund (1995) as a means of organizing the classroom curriculum, continued to receive attention, particularly given the compatibility of this approach with the standards-based movement. Hauenstein (1998) proposed a reworking of the instructional taxonomies of Bloom, and Anderson and Sosniak (1994) edited an NSSE yearbook dedicated to a retrospect on Bloom's taxonomy.

The continued responsibilities of curriculum specialists to the district, the school, and the classroom provided a market for texts for graduate courses (e.g., Blair & Fischer, 1995; Henson, 1995; Pratt, 1994; Ross, 1998) or specific guidance on how to construct a curriculum (e.g., Carr & Harris, 1993; Mueller, 1992; Nelson, 1990). The Association for Supervision and Curriculum Development maintained a resource manual for curriculum specialists with publication of the *ASCD Curriculum Handbook* (1995). ASCD (1998) also produced a CD-ROM that reviewed curriculum software for the decade. The Kraus Curriculum Development Library (1998) provided specialists with a P-12 "curriculum finder." There were also books that explained specific techniques for curriculum development programs. Mulder (1992) offered an evaluation of the "curriculum conference" designed to justify curriculum content. Gail McCutcheon (1995) explained the process of deliberation in curriculum development. Logan (1997) provided detailed instruction on how to conduct a curriculum management audit.

Other works in curriculum development showed the influence of curriculum theory in their proposals. Reid (1998) produced a volume of essays that were self-identified as consistent with the deliberative tradition. Marsh, Day, Hannay, and McCutcheon (1990) offered one of the first efforts at reconceptualizing curriculum development at the school level in light of contemporary curriculum scholarship. Patrick Slattery (1995) considered the development of curriculum informed by postmodern thought. Joseph, Bravmann, Windschitl, Mikel, and Green (1999) provided an imaginative lens for examining the belief systems and classroom practices of six curricular orientations in contemporary U.S. schools. The popularity of curriculum reform (see Skilbeck [1990] for an overview of options available at the beginning of the decade) resulted in works that were aligned with the standards movement (e.g., Curry & Temple, 1992), outcome-based education (Desmond, 1996), or classroom innovation (R. C. White, 1997). Clem and Wilson (1991) and Ozar (1994) offered perspectives on curriculum renewal for private schools and schools that have religious affiliation, with Ozar (1994) advancing outcomes-based curriculum.

Academic Subjects and Curriculum Development. The development of content standards by academic disciplines emphasized the value of curriculum books that considered the dynamics of learning by specific subject areas (e.g., Siskin, 1994; Siskin & Little, 1995) or to subject area curriculum reform (O'Neill & Willis, 1998). The discussion of specific academic disciplines, however, could also assume a critical or postmodern perspective in reflecting on and/or offering guidance in the subject area. Art educators, for example, who were looking for a practical guide on curriculum development in art education would be challenged, perhaps even startled, by new voices. Some art educators continued to argue for the value of art as a necessary academic subject for personal and intellectual growth (e.g., Andrews & Taylor, 1993; Greer, 1997; B. Miller, 1993). Suggestions were also posited, however, for the value of teaching art as a postmodern project (e.g., jagodzinski, 1997a, 1997b; Walling, 1997) or even as a foray into experiencing and declaring self beyond postmodern discourses (Neperud, 1995). Comparative perspectives on art education in different cultures were provided in a volume edited by Freedman and Hernandez (1998).

In other subject areas the same intriguing dynamic was at work; volumes that offered practical guidance in developing a school curriculum shared shelf space with works that considered new conceptions of the teaching of the academic subjects. Professional guidance was provided in drama (Hornbrook, 1991; Somers, 1993); physical education (Hellison & Templin, 1991); language arts (Tchudi, 1991); social studies (Freeland, 1991; Martorella, 1991; Parker, 1991; Parker and Jarolimek, 1997; Ross, 1997); vocational education (Duenk & Smith, 1993; Finch & Crunkilton, 1993); science (Gott & Duggan, 1994); and mathematics (Black & Atkin, 1996). Some authors offered alternative renderings on the academic subjects, including the consideration of the physical education curriculum in a critical cultural context (Kirk & Tinning, 1990), the relationship between language arts and cultural learning (Swiderski, 1993), or the reconceptualizing of literacies in adolescents' lives (Alvermann, Hinchman, Moore, Phelps, & Waff, 1998). Mathematics education was considered in light of educational discourse and popular culture (Applebaum,

1995). Science education was presented as a social and personal act (Bybee, 1993), as a curriculum built from children's curiosity and inquiries (Gallas, 1995; Shapiro, 1994) or as procedures of power, employing a frame for analysis provided by Foucault (Blades, 1997). Joe Kincheloe (1995) and Penn and Williams (1997) offered alternative proposals for the restructuring of vocational education. Roberts and Ostman (1998) edited a volume reflecting on problems of meaning in the science curriculum; Hurd (1997) offered a perspective on science education for the twenty-first century. Peter Martorella's (1991) historical discussion of alternative perspectives and scope and sequence patterns in the social studies illustrated the competing views of intellectual traditionalists, social behaviorists, and experientialists since the issuing of the Report of the Committee on the Social Studies in 1916.

Curriculum Development by Institutional Levels. Curriculum literature was responsive to the developmental levels of the learners as defined by the social institutions designed to serve them. The burgeoning field of early childhood education was prompted by an expanded childcare industry. This in turn resulted in an increase in publication of textbooks for preparation of teachers for early childhood education centers. In addition to revision of textbooks on early childhood curriculum by Eliason and Jenkins (1990 and 1994), Hendrick (1990 and 1998), and Taylor (1991 and 1999), new texts were offered by Curtis (1997), Fortson and Reiff (1995), Heritage (1993), Krogh (1990, 1995), and Rosser (1993, 1998), as well as a book of readings by Schickedanz, Pergantis, Kanosky, Blaney, and Ottinger (1997). The proliferation of approaches to the early childhood curriculum was represented in the overview provided by McAdoo and Schweinhart (1996).

In addition to textbooks written for the classroom, writings reflected theorizing about and research on early childhood education. Yearbooks edited by Spodek and Saracho (1991 and 1996) as well as a research review edited by Seefeldt (1992) served as useful overviews of scholarship in early childhood education. There was also the introduction of critical reconstructionist and postmodern influences in writing about early childhood education (e.g., Cannella, 1997; Kessler & Swadener, 1992; Weis, Altbach, Kelly, & Petrie, 1991). Authors centered on children's need for creative expression and play (Isenberg & Jalongo, 1993, 1997; Van Hoorn et al., 1993, 1999; Wood & Attfield, 1996), the integration of content and activity in the curriculum (Hart, Burts, & Charlesworth, 1997; Lawler-Prince, Altieri, & Cramer, 1995), and the need to establish an assessment system coordinated with curricular aims and instruction (Genishi, 1992; Wortham, 1996).

As the number of families who chose early childhood institutions to provide care and education for their young learners increased, there was a call to expand public education to include this opportunity and to reform institutions and practices to meet this social demand (Rust, 1993). The value of these programs was given testimony with studies and personal observations on practice. Washington and Bailey (1994) offered both retrospective and future proposals for the Head Start program. Cadwell (1997) described the Reggio Emilia innovation, which redesigned early childhood education in this Italian city and generated considerable interest in English-speaking nations (Gandini & Edwards, 2000). Mitchell and David (1992) edited a curriculum guide developed from the experiences of early childhood educators at the Bank Street College of Education.

There was considerable attention given to curriculum development in the elementary school, with most books specifically designed for the teacher education market. Textbooks by Morrison (1993), Queen (1999), Passe (1995), Reinhartz and Beach (1997), Ross, Bondy, and Kyle (1993), and Wishon, Crabtree, and Jones (1998) joined revisions of Lemlech (1990, 1998) and the classic text by Ragan, revised by Shepherd (Shepherd & Ragan, 1992). Books for curriculum specialists advised on curriculum development (Merrion & Rubin, 1996; Nias, Southworth, & Campbell, 1992), curriculum management (O'Neill & Kitson, 1996), and curriculum coordination and integration (Campbell, 1993; Wolfinger & Stockard, 1997). Ashcroft and Palacio (1997) provided teachers with direction on curriculum implementation.

The emergent middle school, a structure for adolescent education that was aligned with experientialist ideas on curriculum and instruction, continued to ascend in popularity with the corresponding demise of its early-twentieth-century predecessor, the junior high school. James Beane provided theoretical and practical advice on the development of the middle school curriculum with a variety of works. In addition to a synoptic primer that examined alternative proposals for educating adolescents and offered a proposal for curriculum integration (Beane, 1990a, 1993), Beane's retrospective on curriculum integration as democratic practice (1997) and the 1995 ASCD yearbook that he edited on curriculum coherence have particular relevance to middle school curriculum design. Coherence and integration were key emphases of curriculum theory for the middle school (e.g., Brazee & Capelluti, 1995; Pate, Homestead, & McGinnis, 1997; Stevenson & Carr, 1993). Dickinson (1993) provided an overview of current conversation on middle school curriculum with a volume of readings. Instructional planning emphasized thematic units (e.g., Forte & Schurr, 1994; Schurr, Lewis, LeMorter, & Shewey, 1996; Springer, 1994), interdisciplinary teaching (Lounsbury, 1993; Vars, 1993), and inquiry-based curriculum (e.g., Burkhardt, 1994; Compton & Hawn, 1993). Other works explained how the middle school model could be effectively implemented (Alexander, 1995; Hargreaves, Earl, & Ryan, 1996; Messick & Reynolds, 1992).

High schools received scant attention in curriculum development. Apparently practitioners were content with national and state efforts to have schools attend to the content standards, divided rather conveniently as though they were departments in the conventional comprehensive high school. High school personnel found it simple to remain relatively unchanged in their curriculum approach while simultaneously engaging in the most recent reform initiative (e.g., Wilson & Rossman, 1993). A revised edition of Lorber and Pierce's (1996) textbook on the high school is the sole entry for high school on curriculum development.

The structure of the undergraduate collegiate curriculum was subject to study, interpretation, and prescription. Conrad and Haworth examined recent changes in undergraduate study (1990). Stark and Lattuca (1997) offered an overview of academic plans in operation in U.S. colleges and universities. Bartolome (1998) brought attention to the contemporary politics of language in the teaching of the academic discourses. Gaff and Ratcliff (1997) edited a handbook on the development of the undergraduate curriculum. How cultural diversity has impacted college curriculum was the subject of several writers (Lutzker, 1995; Morey & Kintano, 1997; Schmitz, 1992); Geismar and Nicoleau (1993) edited a volume that examined issues of difference relative to the college classroom. Friedman Kolmar, Flint, and Rothenberg (1996) offered a volume that provided suggestions for the creation of an inclusive college curriculum. Feagin, Vera, and Imani (1996) examined the lived experience of African American students at a predominantly white institution. As a method of expanding cultural awareness, the integration of foreign study into the undergraduate liberal arts curriculum was studied in a book edited by Burn (1991). The education of adults in literacy was considered by Soifer and colleagues (1990).

Instruction. The expanded discussions of curricularists were influencing and being influenced by the content and organization of older and newer teaching methods texts, albeit not as dramatically as some would have liked. The more narrowly focused methods texts for use in teacher education programs demonstrated amazing abilities to synthesize old and new befitting the eclectic perspectives represented by teacher educators. Lacking the scope of the typical synoptic text and open to criticism that they failed to provide a proper historical or theoretical foundation for curriculum development, these texts illustrated that the authors were usually sensitive to the more esoteric discussions of curriculum theorists and referenced this literature as they felt appropriate for neophytes in relevant discussions, activities, and applications (e.g., Ornstein, 1990). *Instruction: A Models Approach* (Gunter, Estes, & Schwab, 1990, 1995) included discussions about describing educational goals using concepts similar to those in Tyler's model, the domains of learning and the importance of measurable objectives, and teaching models that reflect traditional approaches and newer developments in constructivist psychology as well as concern for resolution of conflict and development of ethical and social values. The sixth edition of *Models of Teaching* by Bruce Joyce and Marsha Weil (2000) emphasized creating communities of learners and presented teaching models organized into four families, including social, information-processing, personal, and behavioral systems. Gender and ethnicity issues are among the topics included for consideration. In a chapter on "Creating Curricula" the authors explain the influence of Robert Gagné on their efforts to craft multiple-models curricula.

Textbooks for students engaged in graduate work in instructional design included a variety of constructs for understanding options in teaching methods. Texts that provided practical guidance on the design of instruction were provided by Kemp, Morrison, and Ross (1994 and 1998) and Reiser and Walker (1996). Shambaugh and Magliaro (1997) offered a process approach to instructional design. Seels and Glasgow (1998) counseled decision making relative to instruction.

Hillocks (1999) and Tomlinson (1999) emphasized the necessary relationship between learning styles and instructional choices, advocating the need to differentiate instruction to address individual students. Dijkstra and Tennyson (1997) offered a description of various instructional models as they related to theory and research on learning. Adams and Hamm focused on more recent instructional designs (1994). Zemelman, Daniels, and Hyde (1998) revised their volume on "best practices," reflecting on their work with a charter school and a network of best practices schools.

Works were also produced that reflected on the dynamics of effective instruction. Joyce and Calhoun (1996) emphasized the need for theory and research in creating learning experiences, establishing the link between how students learn and how they should be taught (Joyce, Calhoun, & Hopkins, 1997). Cawelti (1995) edited a "handbook" on research into improving student achievement built on the several extant handbooks in different subject areas. Gibboney and Webb (1998) offered a reflection on what practical principles are offered by teachers who have been recognized for the quality of their instruction.

Significant instructional designs established in the 1970s and 1980s retained their popularity. Detailed explanation was available on mastery learning (Guskey, 1997). The emphasis on constructivist practices (Brooks & Brooks, 1993; Davis, Hawley, McMullen, & Spilka, 1997) and the learner-centered classroom (e.g., McCombs & Whisler, 1997) promoted the conciliarists' notion that instructional practice can be student centered even when the curriculum is not determined with the learners' counsel. Cooperative learning remained a popular instructional method, with detail on the methods provided by its principal proponents, David and Roger Johnson (1994; Johnson, Johnson, & Holubec, 1994a, 1994b), Robert Slavin (1995), and other advocates (Davidson & Worsham, 1992; Jacob, 1999). Problem-based learning gained in popularity in the decade as a complex and open-ended investigation of real-life problems (e.g., Delisle, 1997; Evenson & Hmelo, 2000; Glasgow, 1997; Torp & Sage, 1998).

Other long-standing instructional designs and tools were also considered. Lubienski-Wentworth (1999) served as a contemporary apologist for instructional designs promoted by Maria Montessori at the beginning of the century. The value of museums as learning environments was discussed by Hein (1998). LaSpina (1998) chronicled the aesthetic changes that have taken place in the publication of school textbooks.

Leadership in Curriculum Development. School administrators were encouraged to provide leadership in curriculum development. The most optimistic view was that curriculum leadership could spearhead school reform (Bernhardt, Hedley, Cattaro, & Svolopoulos, 1997). James Henderson expanded his promotion of reflective, collaborative, and democratic educational practice to consider curriculum leadership in a text coauthored with Hawthorne (1995) and a volume of essays coauthored with Kathleen Kesson (Henderson & Kesson, 1999). Curriculum leaders were encouraged to be creative (Brubaker, 1994) and effective (Kitson & O'Neill, 1996) but also provide stability for school institutions in the politically contentious decade (Gross, 1998). Collections of essays examined the dynamics of curriculum governance (Elmore and Fuhrman, 1994) and curriculum policy (Moore & Ozga, 1991). Robert Donmoyer (1995) edited a volume that advocated a knowledge base on educational administration, attending to the roles of curriculum management and leadership. Textbooks useful for graduate course work in educational administration were produced by Day, Hall, Gammage, and Coles (1993), Glatthorn (1997), and Markee (1997).

THE SYNOPTIC TEXT AT CENTURY'S END

The 1990s was a decade in which production of the synoptic text became an ominous undertaking. The burgeoning scholarship classed as considerations of curriculum placed extraordinary demands on authors determined to capture a portrait of the field. There were, in fact, more revisions of existing synoptic texts than there were new titles. In addition to the ninth edition of R. C. Doll's text, Peter Oliva (1997) published a fourth edition, Daniel Tanner and Laurel Tanner (1995) produced their third edition, and Elliot Eisner (1994b) offered his third revision of *The Educational Imagination*. Ornstein and Hunkins (1993, 1998) continued revision of their text, and Print (1993) produced a revision of *Curriculum Development and Design*. John McNeil issued a fifth edition of *Curriculum: A Comptehensive Introduction* (1996) and also produced an interesting work on curriculum practice called *Curriculum: The Teacher's Initiative* (1995). This work is difficult to classify as a text on curriculum development. While the text looks at dimensions of the Tyler rationale (purposes, methods, organization), McNeil accepts the commonplace culture of most schools, recognizing that everyday curriculum development is, for many practitioners, more about political and consumer choices than rational planning. McNeil invites teachers to consider constructivist practice, address the personal development of the learner, and entertain the possibilities of social change through curricular choices. McNeil also offers a consumer's guide on textbook selection, choosing curriculum materials, and creating unit plans that match the inclinations and needs of the classroom teacher.

Just as it is hard to categorize McNeil's practical approach to curriculum, it is difficult to classify the brief volume on curriculum aims by Decker Walker and Jonah Soltis (1992, 1997) as either a synoptic text or a work on curriculum development. The authors intended the work to be used in foundations courses to introduce the topic of curriculum theory to students. As such, it provided an introduction to important historical and contemporary writers on curriculum. The specific focus on possible purposes for curriculum development, however, limited the scope of this work. Fortunately, Decker Walker (1990) provided a comprehensive statement on curriculum in 1990, an evolution of the grassroots construct of Hilda Taba. Substantial history and theory sections introduced the curriculum field to the reader. Curriculum considerations were examined in a variety of ever-widening contexts (e.g., the classroom, the school, and national perspectives) and implementing change in curriculum policy and practice from grounded theory and reasoned deliberation was explained and advocated. The work is consistent with Walker's earlier naturalistic design[3] but places this design in the context of contemporary scholarly writing on curriculum.

George Posner's *Analyzing the Curriculum* (1992) was intended to serve as a textbook for a foundational graduate course in curriculum, recognizing that most teachers and administrators will never create a curriculum. Instead, they need the skill to analytically evaluate a curriculum that they have selected, adopted, or inherited. Posner promoted "reflective" in contrast to "garbage can" eclecticism. Analysis provides a critical process to determine the suitability of a formal curriculum document. Posner lists a series of questions, based on the Tyler rationale and Mauritz Johnson's process for curriculum development, that the educator should ask in analyzing a proposed curriculum:

❖ How is the curriclum documented?

❖ What social/historical situation resulted in the development of this curriculum? What perspectives does the curriculum represent?

❖ What are the purposes and content of the curriculum? How is the curriculum organized?

❖ How should the curriculum be implemented? What can be learned from an evaluation of the curriculum?

❖ What are the curriculum's strengths and limitations? (Posner, 1992, p. 24)

The text is structured to facilitate options in addressing each of these questions taken from current and historical perspectives on curriculum. Posner presents five theoretical perspectives on the curriculum with representative scholars: traditional (W. T. Harris, E. D. Hirsch), structure of the disciplines (Bruner), cognitive (Piaget), behavioral (Bobbitt, Mager), and experiential (Dewey). There is acknowledgment but no development of the contributions of critical reconstructionists. The work also provides the reader with concise background information on some of the high-profile curriculum efforts of the past half century.

Kenneth Henson's (1995) text on curriculum development is practitioner-oriented and centered on institutional reform through the use of a conciliar model of curriculum construction and the effective use of reform strategies to translate a curriculum plan into effective instruction. Acknowledging his proposal for development to be structured on Taba's inverted model, Henson incorporated the Tyler rationale with insights from Macdonald, Zais, and Oliva. Numerous case studies and contemporary curriculum plans and products illustrate the components of development. Henson was adamant that research be a guide to curriculum development. The text provided an introduction to some of the major theorists in curriculum in the past half century, but the contributions of critical reconstructionists and the various postmodern interpretations of curriculum were conspicuously absent.

David Pratt's *Curriculum Planning* (1994) was a practitioner's handbook on curriculum development, but he was amenable to sharing the contributions of critical reconstructionists and other contemporary curriculum theorists (e.g., feminist perspectives). Pratt maintained the direction he established in his text *Curriculum Design and Development* (1980), but he also provided an understanding of his relationship to other curriculum scholarship. Pratt's facility for the use of quotation, including Nobel laureates, was creatively displayed throughout the text. He placed his proposal of a curriculum for well-being and happiness in contrast to perspectives advocating social transmission, social transformation, individual fulfillment, and feminist pedagogy, arguing for the value of curriculum planning to both the present and future lives of the learners. The body of the text offered a detailed approach to curriculum development, from the self-reflection of curriculum planners through needs assessment and a statement of aims and objectives. Pratt contended that student assessments should be established prior to instructional design and that evaluation of the curriculum be much broader than interpretation of student performance on these assessments.

Evelyn Sowell's introductory text to curriculum development (1996, 2000) is also a text principally designed for use by those seeking a graduate degree in school administration, where an introduction to curriculum development is required. The work shared a discussion of curriculum design with strategies for implementing the redesign of school curriculum. The approach was labeled by Sowell as "integrative," a reference to the combining of what she called "technical" and "non-technical" approaches to curriculum. The technical approach employs a Tylerian design (from aims through to evaluation) and results in statements of formal objectives for learning in academic disciplines. The technical approach to a curriculum considers educational purposes. Sowell suggested five alternative purposes: promoting the cumulative tradition of organized knowledge, advancing social reconstruction, self-actualization of the learner, developing cognitive processes, and a technological delivery of social purposes. The content statements are informed by knowledge forms and structures, social demands (literacies, socioeconomic structures, cultural institutions, the demographic background of the learners) and the psychological development of the learners. Content statements are then translated to learning objectives. Non-technical approaches are derived from the interaction of students with teachers in the classrooms and recognize environmental and resource dimensions that shape educational experiences.

Sowell emphasized that these two different ways of making a curriculum do not need to be exclusive, that teachers must be involved in either process, and she contended that school-based curriculum decision making was the most efficacious. The text was replete with examples of how the process results in actual curriculum plans and classroom activities. Sowell also guided the reader through the challenges of the change process. The text concluded with an overview on curriculum evaluation.

Jon Wiles's *Curriculum Essentials* (1999) contained more information about the historical, philosophical, and theoretical background of curriculum development than other works that focus on the practice of curriculum development, but in a handbook format. Rather than discuss the historical influences on curriculum development, Wiles provided a one-chapter synopsis of foundations by offering lists of names and books to know. His discussion of educational philosophy and its relationship to curriculum was also brief and consistent with recognized categorization of current philosophic orientations. He provided the reader with a quick reference to school models that have been implemented in U.S. schools in the nineteenth and twentieth centuries and important developmental theories that have influenced scope and sequence decisions. The third chapter, the centerpiece of the book, introduced a process Wiles labeled "deductive curriculum development." Wiles's process of development is conciliar, with an anchoring in intellectual traditionalism. He is comfortable staying within academic disciplines but also promotes curriculum alignment and the weaving of subject areas to address broad educational goals. A chapter on implementation with attention to change processes and a discussion of how to accommodate the curriculum plan to meet the needs of exceptional learners completed this concise overview.

Curriculum for a New Millennium, by Wilma Longstreet and Harold Shane (1993), centered on curriculum development from the perspective of the future rather than the present, an interest Shane had reflected on for over a quarter century (e.g., Shane, 1973, 1977; Shane & Tabler, 1981). Longstreet and Shane argued that curriculum development is not effective if there is no projection of possible futures that learners will confront. The book promoted curriculum development that considered political realities, philosophic orientations, theories of learning, and evaluation options. There was an efficient historical orientation to curricular thought combined with references to curriculum designs through the 1980s. The discussion of future studies as an integral part of curriculum development was a major section of the text, followed by an overview of curriculum policy in each of the major academic disciplines, elective subjects, and co-curricular studies. The text concluded with an outline for curriculum design. Absent from this future-oriented work were references to the emergent postmodern curriculum scholarship and the expansion of the conceptualization of curriculum study beyond institutional development.

An approach to the synoptic text that effectively bridged the practitioner orientation of Henson, Sowell, Wiles, and Pratt in curriculum development and the analytic consideration of current discussions about curriculum was Colin Marsh and George Willis's *Curriculum: Alternative Approaches, Ongoing Issues* (1995). Marsh and Willis's text spoke directly to people who work in schools, providing a sense of current scholarship in curriculum while including practical guidance on curriculum planning by carefully outlining alternatives. The reader was given a description of Tyler's, Walker's, and Eisner's approaches to curriculum planning without being directed to a preferred model. To provide context, attention was given to curriculum history and to a brief overview of current curriculum theorizing, using William Reid's categories. This presentation of curriculum thought, with attention to representative contributors and subcategories, efficiently introduced the reader to conversations and retained a perspective toward schooling.

In the second part of the text, Marsh and Willis examined curriculum development by describing the major stakeholders in development, the possibilities for interaction, and change processes. Curriculum planning was differentiated as meeting one of three purposes: policy, program, and the classroom. The involvement of parents and students in the planning process was a particularly democratic feature of their description of planning in action. The third movement in development was implementation, with suggestions on how research can provide insight on enacting a curriculum. The final part of development was evaluation, again providing options for techniques and interpretation. The text examined contemporary political activity in control of the curriculum, reintroducing various stakeholders competing for control of the curriculum and how curriculum theorists are writing about the contest for the school curriculum. The text concluded by considering major contemporary issues in curriculum development and theorizing. The responsive approach to thinking about curriculum development in a social/political context and curriculum theory as a fluid set of conversations has warranted a second edition of the text (Marsh & Willis, 1999).

Anthologies of curriculum studies provided students with an efficient view of scholarship, but the emphasis of the editors made for very different portraits. The anthologies by Glen Hass (with Forrest Parkay, 1993; Parkay & Hass, 2000) are an example of this literature genre. First published in 1974, this book of readings was constructed to provide scholarly reflection on what are referred to as the four bases of curriculum: values and goals (philosophy);

social forces; the psychological development of the learners and their learning styles; and the structure of knowledge and cognition. The editors rely for the most part on historical perspectives and the comprehensive viewpoint of synoptic authors, leaving aside much of the conversations and discourses that emerged in the 1980s. In the second part of the text, there is a specific treatment of curriculum issues that are relevant to different student age groups.

The Curriculum Studies Reader, edited by David Flinders and Stephen J. Thornton (1997), was an anthology that provided historical perspective (e.g., Dewey, Counts, Bobbitt, Schwab), background to contemporary curriculum theorizing (e.g., Huebner, Greene, Pinar, and Freire) and discussion of enduring issues and conversations in curriculum (Jardine on ecology, Oakes on tracking, Eisner on standards, Sleeter and Grant on multicultural education). The anthology looked both backward and forward, introducing the novice scholar to deliberations and debates in curriculum scholarship.

There are two anthologies that relate strongly to the synoptic texts produced by the authors and again indicate the contrast in perspectives on what constituted significant curriculum scholarship. Alan Ornstein's book of readings, coedited with Behar-Horenstein (1994 and 1998), considers alternative historical and contemporary approaches to philosophy, teaching, learning, instruction, supervision, and policy, coordinated with the structure of his curriculum text. William Pinar (1998a) edited a volume focused exclusively on possible future directions in curriculum scholarship.

A number of books offered critical perspective on current curriculum scholarship, expanding the direction established with the 1988 first edition of Landon Beyer and Michael Apple's (revised, 1998) book of readings (e.g., Erdman & Herdson, 1991; Martusewicz & Reynolds, 1994; Sears & Marshall, 1990). No single anthology was able to definitively capture the remarkable explosion of diversity in curriculum scholarship that characterized the end of the twentieth century.

Given that curriculum studies were far-ranging, inclusive of a plethora of discourses, efforts to portray contemporary scholarship were exceptionally challenging. At the beginning of the decade, a scholarly compilation on the field that crossed national preoccupations was *The International Encyclopedia of Curriculum* (Lewy, 1991). This volume was constructed from articles included in *The International Encyclopedia of Education.* The text is organized to consider conceptual frameworks (e.g., what is curriculum, what are its components, and what factors affect the curriculum); approaches to the curriculum; curriculum development; innovation, participation, and implementation; curriculum evaluation; and consideration of the curriculum of academic disciplines.

Philip Jackson's important essay on curriculum thought in historical perspective introduces *The Handbook of Research on Curriculum*, another perspective on the state of the field produced under the auspices of AERA (Jackson, 1992a). Jackson outlined a two-path mapping of contemporary alternatives in curriculum thought, one road leading to practice in school and the other to theory in university scholarship. Although William Pinar and his colleagues (1995) argued that the road to the schools was effectively under reconstruction, Jackson elected to emphasize a more school-based path of time-honored curriculum topics in the selection of issues in the *Handbook*.

The sheer scope of *Understanding Curriculum: An Introduction to the Study of Historical and Contemporary Curriculum Discourses* by William Pinar, William Reynolds, Patrick Slattery, and Peter Taubman (1995) merits recognition as exceptionally thorough and significant scholarship. The bibliography alone of 166 pages combines with more than 100 pages of index to make an indispensable reference for curriculum scholars. The narrative line of the work presented scholarship in curriculum from 1975 to 1995 as having been transformed or "reconceptualized" by new approaches to theory and inquiry. The practitioner who picked up *Understanding Curriculum* was likely to be confounded if she or he hoped to find a model for curriculum development placed in the context of historical and contemporary alternatives. The authors contended that the discourse of institutionalized, school-oriented curriculum development, the main focus of curriculum thought from 1918 until 1969, was no longer the principal language of scholarly writing about curriculum. Rather, the work of curriculum thinking had shifted to understanding curriculum by adopting and developing scholarship from other discourse communities. Thus, no one discourse dominates, either in the field or in this volume. There are instead multiple "texts" or coherent and emergent bodies of literature based on diverse discourses. Pinar and his colleagues organized their work by providing detailed descriptions of historical, political, racial, gender, phenomenological, postmodern, autobiographical/biographical, aesthetic, theological, institutional, and international discourses. In their introduction, the authors assert that *Understanding Curriculum* represents the next generation in synoptic texts, superseding the "Tyler rationale" and the variants most synoptic texts presented in the preceding 30 years. Curriculum development, they argued, was an activity that held little promise as scholarly activity, since the practices of school had "slipped further into the hands of the business community, politicians, bureaucrats and the social engineers" (Pinar et al., 1995, p. 236). Pinar and his colleagues argued that theorizing and researching for understanding was the most worthwhile activity field participants could engage in. The proposal offered in the book was to continue the labors of scholarly understanding and language development, awaiting the opportunity when impact on schools is possible. Pinar and coauthors suggested that the next movements in curriculum scholarship were in three directions. One direction is the production of ethnographic studies of schools from a theory-informed base. Another movement is the coordination of the various voices to establish "thematic continuity," indicating that John Dewey's emphasis on shared deliberation can be a possible ally in this effort. This will create a new language for curriculum theorizing. A third movement in time is back to the schools for authentic reform.

Those who did not have the resource of time or background to explore the various discourse alternatives detailed by Pinar, Reynolds, Slattery, and Taubman but wanted to capture a sense of the diversity in contemporary scholarship can read Patrick Slattery's *Curriculum Development in the Postmodern Era* (1995). Slattery placed particular emphasis on the theological and post-modern discourses, conversations in which he is an active participant, but also provided the reader with an introduction to the other significant ways of talking and writing about curriculum.

In the 1980s, the reflection closed without a central text to represent future influence; a statement on what we contended was an accurate representation of the field in transition. In choosing *Understanding Curriculum* to conclude this chapter, we are not prognosticating that the text will have enduring influence on educational policy and practice. We do assert that no other single work provides the reader with a better overview of the remarkable diversity of voices and texts that constituted scholarship in the decade. *Understanding Curriculum* was a new creation in the history of the synoptic curriculum text. A thoroughly postmodern synoptic view of the curriculum field, it captured the diversity of approaches to curriculum that had emerged during the past quarter century, leaving one to wonder what dimension of educating, thinking, and living did not translate into some form of curriculum theorizing or inquiry.

BIBLIOGRAPHY OF CURRICULUM BOOKS 1990–2000

1990

Amano, I. (1990). *Education and examinations in modern Japan.* Tokyo: University of Tokyo Press.

Apple, M. W. (1990). *Ideology and curriculum* (second edition). New York: Routledge & Kegan Paul.

Barrow, R. (1990). *Understanding skills: Thinking, feeling and caring.* London, Ontario, Canada: The Althouse Press, University of Western Ontario, Faculty of Education.

Beane, J. A. (1990a). *A middle school curriculum: From rhetoric to reality.* Columbus, OH: National Middle School Association.

Beane, J. A. (1990b). *Affect in the curriculum: Toward democracy, dignity, and diversity.* New York: Teachers College Press.

Beauboeuf-Lafontant, T., & Augustine, D. Smith. (1990). *Facing racism in education.* Cambridge, MA: Harvard Educational Review. (second edition, 1996).

Bell, B., Gaventa, J., & Peters, J. (Eds.). (1990). *We make the road by walking: Conversations on education and social change [by] Myles Horton and Paulo Freire.* Philadelphia: Temple University Press.

Ben-Peretz, M. (1990). *The teacher-curriculum encounter: Freeing teachers from the tyranny of texts.* Albany: State University of New York Press.

Bernstein, B. (1990). *The structuring of pedagogic discourse: Class, codes, and control.* New York: Routledge.

Bowers, C. A., & Flinders, D. J. (1990). *An ecological approach to classroom patterns of language, culture, and thought.* New York: Teachers College Press.

Boyer, E. L. (1990). *Scholarship reconsidered: Priorities of the professoriate.* San Francisco: The Carnegie Foundation for the Advancement of Teaching.

Bruner, J. (1990). *Acts of meaning.* Cambridge, MA: Harvard University Press.

Clark, M. E., & Wawrytko, A. (Eds.). (1990). *Rethinking the curriculum: Toward an integrated, interdisciplinary college education.* New York: Greenwood Press.

Conrad, C. F., & Haworth, J. G. (1990). *Curriculum in transition: Perspectives on the undergraduate experience.* Needham Heights, MA: Ginn Press.

Cornbleth, C. (1990). *Curriculum in context.* New York: Falmer Press.

Coulby, D., & Ward, S. (Eds.). (1990). *The primary core national curriculum: Policy into practice.* London: Cassell.

Dewey, J. (1990). *The school and society* and *The child and curriculum* (Expanded edition). Chicago: University of Chicago Press.

Dowling, P., & Nass, R. (Eds.). (1990). *Mathematics versus the national curriculum.* London: Falmer Press.

Dufour, B. (Ed.). (1990). *The new social curriculum: A guide to cross-curricular issues.* New York: Cambridge University Press.

Eggleston, J. (Ed). (1990). *Delivering the technology curriculum: Six case studies in primary and secondary schools.* Stoke on Trent, England: Trentham Books.

Eliason, C. F., & Jenkins, L. T. (1990). *A practical guide to early childhood curriculum* (fourth edition). Columbus, OH: Merrill.

Elliott, D., & Woodward, A. (Eds.). (1990). *Textbooks and schooling in the United States*: eighty-ninth yearbook of the National Society for the Study of Education, Part 1. Chicago: University of Chicago Press.

Ellsworth, E., & Whatley, M. H. (Eds.). (1990). *The ideology of images in educational media: Hidden curriculums in the classroom.* New York: Teachers College Press.

Freire, P. (1990). *Education for critical consciousness.* New York: Continuum Publishing.

Giroux, H. A. (1990). *Curriculum discourse as postmodernist critical practice.* Geelong, Australia: Deakin University Press.

Glasser, W. (1990). *The quality school.* New York: Harper and Row.

Goodlad, J. I., & Keating, P. (Eds.). (1990). *Access to knowledge: Agenda to our nation's schools.* New York: College Entrance Examination Board.

Goodson, I., & Medway, P. (1990). *Bringing English to order: The history and politics of a school subject.* London: Falmer.

Goodson, I., & Walker, R. (1990). *Biography, identity and schooling: Episodes in educational research.* New York: Falmer.

Gunter, M. A., Estes. T. H., & Schwab, J. H. (1990). *Instruction: A models approach.* Boston: Allyn & Bacon. (second edition, 1995; third edition, 1999).

Haft, H., & Hopmann, S. (Eds.). (1990). *Class studies in curriculum administration history.* London: Falmer.

Hamilton, D. (1990a). *Curriculum history.* Geelong, Australia: Deakin University Press.

Hamilton, D. (1990b). *Learning about education: An unfinished curriculum.* Philadelphia: Open University Press.

Hartley, D., & Roger, A. (Eds.). (1990). *Curriculum and assessment in Scotland: A policy for the 90s.* Edinburgh, Scotland: Scottish Academic Press.

Hedley, C., Baratta, A. N., & Houtz, J. (Eds.). (1990). *Cognition, curriculum, and literacy.* Norwood, NJ: Ablex.

Hendrick, J. (1990). *Total learning: Developmental curriculum for the young child* (third edition). Columbus, OH: Merrill.

Horton, M. (1990). *The long haul: An autobiography of Myles Horton.* New York: Doubleday Press (with Herbert Kohl and Judith Kohl). (Reprinted by Teachers College Press, 1998).

Hughes, P. (1990). *A national curriculum: Promise or warning.* Canberra: Australian College of Education.

Jackson, P. W. (1990). *Life in classrooms* (second edition). New York: Teachers College Press.

Jones, B. F., & Idol, L. (Eds.). (1990). *Dimensions of thinking and cognitive instruction.* Mahwah, NJ: Lawrence Erlbaum Associates.

Kirk, D., & Tinning, R. (Eds.). (1990). *Physical education, curriculum, and culture: Critical issues in contemporary crisis.* London: Falmer.

Krogh, S. (1990). *The integrated early childhood curriculum.* New York: McGraw-Hill. (second edition, 1995).

Lemlech, J. K. (1990). *Curriculum and instructional methods for the elementary school* (second edition). New York: Macmillan.

Lever, C. (1990). *National curriculum design technology key stages 1–3.* Stoke on Trent, England: Trentham Books.

Lomotey, K. (Ed.). (1990). *Going to school: The African-American experience.* Albany: State University of New York Press.

Lorber, M. A., & Pierce, W. D. (1990). *Objectives, methods, and evaluation for secondary teaching* (third edition). Boston: Allyn & Bacon.

Marsh, C., Day, C., Hannay, L., & McCutcheon, G. (1990). *Reconceptualizing school-based curriculum development.* Bristol, PA: Falmer Press.

McCarthy, C. (1990). *Race and curriculum: Social inequality and theories and politics of difference in contemporary research on schooling.* Bristol, PA: Falmer.

McTaggart, R. (1990). *Action research: A short modern history.* Geelong, Victoria, Australia: Deakin University Press.

Miller, J. L. (1990). *Creating spaces and finding voices: Teachers collaborating for empowerment.* Albany: State University of New York Press.

Miller, J. P., Cassie, J. R. B., & Drake, S. M. (1990). *Holistic learning: A teacher's guide to integrated studies.* Toronto, Ontario: OISE Press.

Moody, W. (Ed.). (1990). *Artistic intelligences: Implications for education.* New York: Teachers College Press.

National Union of Teachers. (1990). *A strategy for the curriculum.* London: Author.

Nelson, A. (1990). *Curriculum design techniques.* Dubuque, IA: Wm. C. Brown.

Ornstein, A. C. (1990). *Strategies for effective teaching.* Chicago: Harper Collins. (second edition, 1995, Chicago: Brown & Benchmark).

Pagano, J. (1990). *Exiles and communities: Teaching in the patriarchal wilderness.* Albany: State University of New York Press.

Page, R., & Valli, L. (Eds.). (1990). *Curriculum differentiation: Interpretive studies in the U.S. secondary schools.* Albany: State University of New York Press.

Paringer, W. A. (1990). *John Dewey and the paradox of liberal reform.* Albany: State University of New York Press.

Perkins, D. (1990). *Smart schools: Better thinking and learning for every child*. New York: The Free Press.

Print, M. (1990). *Curriculum review of social studies and social sciences*. Perth, Australia: Westerm Australia Ministry of Education.

Proctor, N. (Ed.). (1990). *Aims of primary education and the national curriculum*. London: Falmer.

Purves, A., Rogers, T., & Soter, A. (1990). *How porcupines make love II: Teaching a literature-connected curriculum*. New York: Longman.

Quicke, J., Beasley, K., & Morrison, C. (1990). *Challenging prejudice through education: The story of a mental handicap awareness project*. London: Falmer.

Salvia, J., & Hughes, C. (1990). *Curriculum-based assessment: Testing what is taught*. New York: Macmillan.

Sarason, S. (1990). *The predictable failure of educational reform*. San Francisco: Jossey-Bass.

Sears, J. T., & Marshall, J. D. (Eds.). (1990). *Teaching and thinking about curriculum: Critical inquiries*. New York: Teachers College Press.

Shapiro, H. (1990). *The end of radical hope? Postmodernism and the challenge to radical pedagogy*. Greensboro: University of North Carolina at Greensboro, School of Education.

Skilbeck, M. (1990). *Curriculum reform: An overview of trends*. Paris: OCED, Center for Educational Research in Education.

Sleeter, C. E. (Ed.). (1990). *Empowerment through multicultural education*. Albany: State University of New York Press.

Soifer, R., Irwin, M. E., Crumrine, B. M., Honzaki, E., Simmons, B. K., & Young, D. L. (1990). *The complete theory-to-practice handbook of adult literacy: Curriculum design and teaching approaches*. New York: Teachers College Press.

Tanner, D., & Tanner, L. (1990). *History of the school curriculum*. New York: Macmillan.

Thomas, N. (1990). *Primary education from Plowden to the 1990s*. London: Falmer.

Tyack, D., & Hansot, E. (1990). *Learning together: A history of coeducation in American schools*. New Haven, CT: Yale University Press.

Tye, K. A. (Ed.). (1990). *Global education: School-based strategies*. Orange, CA: Interdependence Press.

Vandenberg, D. (1990). *Education as a human right: A theory of curriculum and pedagogy*. New York: Teachers College Press.

van Manen, M. (1990). *Researching lived experience: Human science for an action sensitive pedagogy*. Albany: State University of New York Press.

Walker, D. F. (1990). *Fundamentals of curriculum*. San Diego, CA: Harcourt, Brace, Jovanovich.

Weis, L. (1990). *Working class without work: High school students in a de-industrialized economy.* New York: Routledge.

Weis, L., et al. (1990). *Curriculum for tomorrow's schools.* Buffalo, NY: Buffalo Research Institute on Education for Teaching.

Wexler, P. (1990). *Social analysis of education: After the new sociology.* New York: Routledge.

Wolf, R. M. (1990). *Evaluation in America: Foundations of competency assessment and program review.* (Third edition). New York: Praeger.

Young, R. E. (1990). *A critical theory of education.* New York: Teachers College Press.

1991

Adan, J. (1991). *The children in our lives: Knowing and teaching them.* New York: Teachers College Press.

Aers, L., & Wheale, N. (Eds.). (1991). *Shakespeare in the changing curriculum.* New York: Routledge.

Altbach, P. G., Kelly, G. P., Petrie, H. G., & Weis, L. (Eds.). (1991). *Textbooks in American society: Politics, policy and pedagogy.* New York: Teachers College Press.

Aoki, T. T. (1991). *Inspiring curriculum and pedagogy: Talks to teachers.* Edmonton, Alberta, Canada: Department of Secondary Education, University of Alberta.

Apple, M. W., & Christian-Smith, L. K. (Eds.). (1991). *The politics of the textbook.* New York: Routledge.

Aronowitz, S., & Giroux, H. (1991). *Postmodern education: Politics, culture, and social criticism.* Minneapolis, MN: University of Minnesota Press.

Ashdown, R., Bovair, K., & Carpenter, B. (Eds.). (1991). *The curriculum challenge: Pupils with severe learning difficulties and the national curriculum.* London: Falmer.

Ball, S. J. (Ed.). (1991). *Foucault and education: Disciplines and knowledge.* New York: Routledge.

Barzun, J. (1991). *Begin here: The forgotten conditions of teaching and learning.* Chicago: University of Chicago Press.

Berman, L. M., Hultgren, F., Lee, D., Rivkin, M. S., & Roderick, J. A. (1991). *Toward curriculum for being: Voices of educators.* Albany: State University of New York Press.

Booth, D., & Thornley-Hall, C. (1991). *Talk curriculum.* Portsmouth, NH: Heinemann.

Booth, T., Swann, W., Masterson, M., & Potts, P. (1991). *Curriculum for diversity in education.* New York: Routledge.

Bowers, C. A., & Flinders, D. J. (1991). *Culturally responsive teaching and supervision: A handbook for staff development.* New York: Teachers College Press.

Bowker, J. (Ed.). (1991). *Secondary media education: A curriculum statement.* London: British Film Institute.

Britzman, D. P. (1991). *Practice makes practice: A critical study of learning to teach*. Albany: State University of New York Press.

Bullough, R. V., & Beatty, L. F. (1991). *Classroom applications of microcomputers* (second edition). Columbus, OH: Merrill.

Bullough, R. V., Jr., Knowles, J. G., & Crow, N. (1991). *Emerging as a teacher*. New York: Routledge.

Burn, B. B. (Ed.). (1991). *Integrating study abroad into the undergraduate liberal arts curriculum: Eight international case studies*. Westport, CT: Greenwood Press.

Butler, J. E., & Walter, J. C. (Eds.). (1991). *Transforming the curriculum: Ethnic studies and women's studies*. Albany: State University of New York Press.

Carmody, D. (1991). *The good alliance: Feminism, religion, and education*. Lanham, MD: University Press of America.

Carpenter, B. O. (1991). *Curriculum handbook for parents and teachers: What we ought to find happening in the public school classrooms of America*. Springfield, IL: Charles C. Thomas.

Christian-Smith, L. K. (1991). *Becoming a woman through romance*. New York: Routledge.

Clem, S. C., & Wilson, Z. V. (1991). *Paths to a new curriculum*. Boston: National Association of Independent Schools.

Common, D. L. (1991). *Curriculum design and teaching for understanding*. Toronto: Kagan & Woo Ltd.

Costa, A. (Ed.). (1991). *Developing minds*. 2 volumes. Alexandria, VA: Association for Supervision and Curriculum Development.

Darder, A. (1991). *Culture and power in the classroom: A critical foundation for bicultural education*. Westport, CT: Bergin & Garvey.

DeBoer, G. E. (1991). *A history of ideas in science education: Implications for practice*. New York: Teachers College Press.

Eggleston, J. (Ed.). (1991). *Delivering the technology curriculum No. 2*. Stoke on Trent, England: Trentham Books.

Eisner, E. (1991). *The enlightened eye: Qualitative inquiry and the enhancement of educational practice*. New York: Macmillan.

Erdman, J., & Herdson, J. (Eds.). (1991). *Critical discourse on current curriculum issues*. Chicago: Midwest Center for Curriculum Studies.

Fine, M. (1991). *Framing dropouts: Notes on the politics of an urban high school*. Albany: State University of New York Press.

Freeland, J. K. (1991). *Managing the social studies curriculum*. Lancaster, PA: Technomic.

Fuhrman, S. H., & Malen, B. (1991). *The politics of curriculum and testing: The 1990 yearbook of the Politics of Education Association*. New York: Falmer.

Fullan, M., with Stiegelbauer, S. M. (1991). *The new meaning of educational change*. New York: Teachers College Press.

Fuller, B. (1991). *Growing up modern: The western state builds third world schools*. New York: Routledge.

Gatto, J. T. (1991). *Dumbing us down: The hidden curriculum of compulsory schooling*. Philadelphia: New Society Publishers.

Giroux, H. (Ed.). (1991a). *Postmodernism, feminism, and cultural politics: Redrawing educational boundaries*. Albany: State University of New York Press.

Giroux, H. (1991b). *Border crossings: Cultural workers and the politics of education*. New York: Routledge.

Goodman, J. (1991). *Elementary schooling for critical democracy*. Albany: State University of New York Press.

Graham, R. (1991). *Reading and writing the self: Autobiography in education and the curriculum*. New York: Teachers College Press.

Green, B. (Ed.). (1991). *The insistence of the letter: Literacy studies and curriculum theorizing*. Bristol, PA: Falmer Press.

Haroutunian, G. S. (1991). *Turning the soul: Teaching through conversation in the high school*. Chicago: University of Chicago Press.

Hellison, D. R., & Templin, T. J. (1991). *A reflective approach to teaching physical education*. Champaign, IL: Human Kinetics.

Hess, G. A., Jr. (1991). *School restructuring, Chicago style*. Newbury Park, CA: Corwin.

Hornbrook, D. (1991). *Education in drama: Casting the dramatic curriculum*. London: Falmer.

Jenkins, J. M., & Tanner, D. (Eds.). (1991). *Restructuring for an interdisciplinary curriculum*. Reston, VA: National Association of Secondary School Principals.

Kennedy, M. M. (Ed.). (1991). *Teaching academic subjects to diverse learners: What teachers need to know*. New York: Teachers College Press.

Kincheloe, J., & Pinar, W. F. (Eds.). (1991). *Curriculum as social psychoanalysis: The significance of place*. Albany: State University of New York Press.

Klein, M. F. (Ed.). (1991). *Politics of curriculum decision making: Issues in centralizing the curriculum*. Albany: State University of New York Press.

Kozol, J. (1991). *Savage inequalities: Children in America's schools*. New York: Crown.

Lather, P. (1991). *Getting smart: Feminist research and pedagogy with/in the postmodern*. London: Routledge.

LeCompte, M. D., & Dworkin, A. G. (1991). *Giving up on school: Student dropouts and teacher burnouts*. Newbury Park, CA: Corwin.

Lewis, A. (1991). *Primary special needs and the national curriculum*. New York: Routledge.

Lewy, A. (Ed.). (1991). *The international encyclopedia of curriculum*. London: Pergamon.

Liston, D. P., & Zeichner, K. M. (1991). *Teacher education and the social conditions of schooling*. New York: Routledge.

Lovat, T. J., & Smith, D. L. (1991). *Curriculum: Action on reflection* (revised edition). Wentworth Fall, New South Wales, Australia: Social Science Press.

Marsh, C. J. (1991). *Key concepts for understanding curriculum*. Bristol, PA: Falmer. (Second edition, 1997).

Marsh, C., & Morris, P. (Eds.). (1991). *Curriculum development in East Asia*. Bristol, PA: Falmer Press c/o Taylor & Francis.

Martorella, P. H. (1991). *Teaching social studies in the middle and secondary schools*. Columbus, OH: Merrill. (Second edition, 1996).

McKernan, J. (1991). *Curriculum action research: A handbook of methods and resources for the reflective practitioner*. New York: St. Martin's Press.

Misgeld, D., & Nicholson, G. (1991). *Hans-Georg Gadamer on education, poetry and history: Applied hermeneutics*. Albany: State University of New York Press.

Moore, R., & Ozga, J. (Eds.). (1991). *Curriculum policy: A reader*. Oxford, England: Pergamon Press.

Morris, R. C. (Ed.). (1991). *Youth at-risk*. Lancaster, PA: Technomic.

Nixon, J. (1991). *Evaluating the whole curriculum*. Bristol, PA: Open University Press c/o Taylor & Francis.

Orr, D. W. (1991). *Ecological literacy: Education and the transition to a postmodern world*. Albany: State University of New York Press.

Page, R. N. (1991). *Lower-track classrooms: A curricular and cultural perspective*. New York: Teachers College Press.

Parker, W. C. (1991). *Renewing the social studies curriculum*. Alexandria, VA: Association for Supervision and Curriculum Development.

Perrone, V. (1991). *A letter to teachers: Reflections on schooling and the art of teaching*. San Francisco: Jossey-Bass.

Popkewitz, T. (1991). *A political sociology of educational reform: Power/knowledge in teaching, teacher education and research*. New York: Teachers College Press.

Saxe, D. W. (1991). *Social studies in schools: A history of the early years*. Albany: State University of New York Press.

Schön, D. (Ed.). (1991). *The reflective turn: Case studies in and on educational practice*. New York: Teachers College Press.

Schwoch, J., White, M., & Reilly, S. (1991). *Media knowledge: Readings in popular culture, pedagogy, and critical citizenship*. Albany: State University of New York Press.

Short, E. C. (Ed.). (1991). *Forms of curriculum inquiry.* Albany: State University of New York Press.

Short, K. G., & Burke, C. (1991). *Creating curriculum: Teachers and students as a community of learners.* Portsmouth, NH: Heinemann.

Solomon, R. P. (1991). *Black resistance in high school: Forging a separatist culture.* Albany: State University of New York Press.

Spiecker, B., & Straughan, R. (Eds.). (1991). *Freedom and indoctrination in education: International perspectives.* New York: Cassell.

Spodek, B., & Saracho, O. N. (Eds.). (1991). *Issues in early childhood curriculum. Yearbook in early childhood education, volume 2.* New York: Teachers College Press.

Tabor, D. (1991). *Curriculum continuity in English and the national curriculum: Working together at transition.* Bristol, PA: Falmer Press.

Tanner, D. (1991). *Crusade for democracy: Progressive education at the crossroads.* Albany: State University of New York Press.

Taylor, B. J. (1991). *A child goes forth: A curriculum guide for preschool children* (seventh edition). New York: Macmillan.

Tchudi, S. (1991). *Planning and assessing the curriculum in English language arts.* Alexandria, VA: Association for Supervision and Curriculum Development.

Tye, K. A. (Ed.). (1991). *Global education: From thought to action. (1991 yearbook of ASCD).* Alexandria, VA: Association for Supervision and Curriculum Development.

van Manen, M. (1991). *The tact of teaching: The meaning of pedagogical thoughtfulness.* Albany: State University of New York Press.

Weaver, F. S. (1991). *Liberal education: Critical essays on professions, pedagogy, and structure.* New York: Teachers College Press.

Weis, L., Altbach, P. G., Kelly, G. P., & Petrie, H. G. (Eds.). (1991). *Critical perspectives on early childhood education.* Albany: State University of New York Press.

West, C., Farmer, J. A., & Wolff, P. M. (1991). *Instructional design: Implications from cognitive science.* Englewood Cliffs, NJ: Prentice-Hall.

Westbrook, R. B. (1991). *John Dewey and American democracy.* Ithaca, NY: Cornell University Press.

White, J. (1991). *Education and the good life: Autonomy, altruism, and the national curriculum.* New York: Teachers College Press.

Whitson, J. A. (1991). *Constitution and curriculum.* London: Falmer.

Willie, C., Garibaldi, A., & Reed, W. (1991). *The education of African Americans.* New York: Auburn House.

Willis, G. H., & Schubert, W. H. (1991). *Reflections from the heart of educational inquiry.* Albany: State University of New York Press. (Republished by Educator's International Press, Troy, NY, 2000).

Wragg, T. (1991). *Mad curriculum disease*. Stoke on Trent, England: Trentham Books.

Wyner, N. (Ed.). (1991). *Current perspectives on the culture of schools*. Boston: Brookline Books.

1992

Allen, D. W. (1992). *Schools for a new century: A conservative approach to radical school reform*. New York: Praeger.

Beyner, J., & MacKay, H. (Eds.). (1992). *Technological literacy and the curriculum*. London: Falmer Press.

Blenkin, G. M., Edwards, G., & Kelly, A. V. (1992). *Change and the curriculum*. London: Paul Chapman.

Boomer, G., Lester, N., Onore, C., & Cook, J. (1992). *Negotiating the curriculum: Educating for the 21st century*. London: Falmer Press.

Bowers, C. A. (1992). *Education, cultural myths and the ecological crisis: Toward deep changes*. Albany: State University of New York Press.

Brady, L. (1992). *Curriculum development in Australia* (fourth edition). Sydney, Australia: Prentice-Hall.

Carlson, D. (1992). *Teachers and crisis: Urban school reform and teachers' work culture*. New York: Routledge.

Cohn, M. M., & Kottkamp, R. B. (1992). *Teachers: The missing voice in education*. Albany: State University of New York Press.

Curry, B., & Temple, T. (1992). *Using curriculum frameworks for systemic reform*. Washington, DC: Association for Supervision and Curriculum Development.

Davidson, N., & Worsham, T. (Eds.). (1992). *Enhancing thinking through cooperative learning*. New York: Teachers College Press.

DelFattore, J. (1992). *What Johnny shouldn't read: Textbook censorship in America*. New Haven, CT: Yale University Press.

Diaz, C. (Ed.). (1992). *Multicultural education for the 21st century*. Washington, DC: National Education Association.

Doll, R. C. (1992). *Curriculum improvement: Decision making and process* (eighth edition). Needham Heights, MA: Allyn & Bacon.

Duschl, R. A., & Hamilton, R. J. (Eds.). (1992). *Philosophy of science, cognitive psychology, and educational theory and practice*. Albany: State University of New York Press.

Edelman, M. W. (1992). *The measure of our success: A letter to my children and yours*. New York: Beacon.

Egan, K. (1992). *Imagination in teaching and learning: The middle school years*. Chicago: University of Chicago Press.

English, F. W. (1992). *Deciding what to teach and test: Developing, aligning, and auditing the curriculum.* Thousand Oaks, CA: Corwin Press.

Fullan, M. (1992). *Successful school improvement: The implementation perspective and beyond.* Buckingham, England: Open University Press.

Fullan, M., & Hargreaves, A. (1992). *What's worth fighting for in your school? Working together for improvement.* Bristol, PA: Open University Press.

Gallagher, S. (1992). *Hermeneutics and education.* Albany: State University of New York Press.

Garrod, A. (Ed.). (1992). *Learning for life: Moral education theory and practice.* Westport, CT: Praeger.

Genishi, C. (1992). *Ways of assessing children and curriculum: Stories of early childhood practice.* New York: Teachers College Press.

George, P. (1992). *How to untrack your school.* Alexandria, VA: Association for Supervision and Curriculum Development.

Goodson, I. (1992). *School subjects and curriculum change* (third edition). London: Falmer.

Gore, J. M. (1992). *The struggle for pedagogies: Critical and feminist discourses as regimes of truth.* New York: Routledge.

Graff, G. (1992). *Beyond the culture wars: How teaching the conflicts can revitalize American education.* New York: W. W. Norton.

Hall, G. (Ed.). (1992). *Themes and dimensions of the national curriculum.* Dover, NH: Kogan Page.

Hawthorne, R. K. (1992). *Curriculum in the making: Teacher choice and classroom experience.* New York: Teachers College Press.

Hedley, C., Feldman, D., & Antonacci, P. (Eds.). (1992). *Literacy across the curriculum.* Norwood, NJ: Ablex.

Hirsch, E. D. (Ed.). (1992). *What your third grader needs to know: Fundamentals of a good third grade education.* New York: Delta Tradebooks.

Hunter, M. (1992). *How to change to a non-graded school.* Alexandria, VA: Association for Supervision and Curriculum Development.

Isaac, K. (with R. Nader). (1992). *Civics for democracy: A journey for teachers and students.* Washington, DC: Essential Books.

Jackson, P. W. (Ed.). (1992a). *Handbook of research on curriculum.* New York: Macmillan.

Jackson, P. W. (1992b). *Untaught lessons.* New York: Teachers College Press.

Jones, E. B., & Jones, N. (1992). *Learning to behave: Curriculum and whole school management approaches to discipline.* London: Kogan Page.

Joyce, B., & Weil, M. (1992). *Models of teaching.* (Fourth edition). Englewood Cliffs, NJ: Prentice-Hall.

Kessler, S. A., & Swadener, B. B. (Eds.). (1992). *Reconceptualizing the early childhood curriculum: Beginning the dialogue.* New York: Teachers College Press.

Kliebard, H. M. (1992). *Forging the American curriculum: Essays in curriculum history and theory.* New York: Routledge.

Kreisberg, S. (1992). *Transforming power: Domination, empowerment, and education.* Albany: State University of New York Press.

Luke, C., & Gore, J. (1992). *Feminisms and critical pedagogy.* New York: Routledge.

Martin, J. R. (1992). *The schoolhome: Rethinking schools for changing families.* Cambridge, MA: Harvard University Press.

Marzano, R. J. (1992). *A different kind of classroom: Teaching with dimensions of learning.* Alexandria, VA: Association for Supervision and Curriculum Development.

McDonald, J. (1992). *Teaching: Making sense of an uncertain craft.* New York: Teachers College Press.

Messick, R. G., & Reynolds, K. E. (1992). *Middle level curriculum in action.* New York: Longman.

Metz, M. H. (1992). *Different by design: The context and character of three magnet schools.* New York: Routledge.

Meyer, J., Kamens, D., & Benavot, A. (1992). *School knowledge for the masses: World models and national primary curricular categories in the twentieth century.* Bristol, PA: Falmer Press.

Mitchell, A., & David, J. (Eds.). (1992). *Explorations with young children: A curriculum guide from the Bank Street College of Education.* Mt. Rainer, MD: Gryphon House.

Mueller, D. (1992). *A guide for curriculum writers.* Lanham, MD: University Press of America.

Mulder, M. (1992). *The curriculum conference: Evaluation of a tool for curriculum content justification.* The Hague, Netherlands: CIP Gegevens Koninklojke Biblioteek.

Newmann, F. M. (Ed.). (1992). *Student engagement and achievement in American secondary schools.* New York: Teachers College Press.

Nias, J., Southworth, G., & Campbell, P. (1992). *Whole school curriculum development in the primary school.* London and Washington, DC: Falmer Press.

Noddings, N. (1992). *The challenge to care in schools: An alternative approach to education.* New York: Teachers College Press.

Oliva, P. F. (1992). *Developing the curriculum* (fourth edition). New York: Harper Collins.

Pinar, W., & Reynolds, W. (Eds.). (1992). *Understanding curriculum as phenomenological and deconstructed text.* New York: Teachers College Press.

Posner, G. (1992). *Analyzing the curriculum.* New York: McGraw-Hill.

Poster, C., & Zimmer, J. (1992). *Community and education in the third world.* New York: Routledge, Chapman & Hall.

Postman, N. (1992). *Technopoly: The surrender of culture to technology*. New York: Vintage.

Riddell, S. I. (1992). *Gender and the politics of the curriculum*. New York: Routledge.

Ross, E. W., Cornett, J., & McCutcheon, G. (Eds.). (1992). *Teacher personal theorizing: Connecting curriculum practice, theory, and research*. Albany: State University of New York Press.

Sanders, J. R. (1992). *Evaluating school programs: An educator's guide*. Thousand Oaks, CA: Corwin.

Schmitz, B. (1992). *Core curriculum and cultural pluralism: A guide to campus planners*. Washington, DC: Association of American Colleges.

Schubert, W. H., & Ayers, W. C. (Eds.). (1992). *Teacher lore: Learning from our own experience*. New York: Longman. (Republished by Educator's International Press, Troy, NY, 2000).

Sears, J. (1992). *Sexuality and the curriculum: The politics and practices of sexuality education*. New York: Teachers College Press.

Seefeldt, C. (Ed.). (1992). *The early childhood curriculum: A review of current research*. New York: Teachers College Press.

Shepherd, G. D., & Ragan, W. B. (1992). *Modern elementary curriculum* (seventh edition). New York: Harcourt Brace & Jovanovich.

Shiundo, J. S. (1992). *Curriculum: Theory and practice in Kenya*. Nairobi, Kenya: Oxford University Press.

Shor, I. (1992). *Empowering education: Critical teaching for social change*. Chicago: University of Chicago Press.

Simon, R. (1992). *Teaching against the grain*. South Hadley, MA: Bergin & Garvey.

Sizer, T. (1992). *Horace's school: Redesigning the American high school*. Boston: Houghton Mifflin.

Smith, G. A. (1992). *Education and the environment: Learning to live with limits*. Albany: State University of New York Press.

Society for the Study of Curriculum History. (1992). *Proceedings: Annual meeting of the Society for the Study of Curriculum History*. College Station, TX: Author.

Spring, J. (1992). *Images of American life: A history of ideological management in schools, movies, radio, and television*. Albany: State University of New York Press.

Stainback, S., & Stainback, W. (Eds.). (1992). *Curriculum considerations in inclusive classrooms: Facilitating learning for all students*. Baltimore: P. H. Brooks Publishing Company.

Stanley, W. B. (1992). *Curriculum for utopia: Social reconstructionism and critical pedagogy in the postmodern era*. Albany: State University of New York Press.

Taylor, C. (1992). *Multiculturalism and the politics of recognition*. Princeton, NJ: Princeton University Press.

Trend, D. (1992). *Cultural pedagogy: Art/education/politics*. Westport, CT: Bergin & Garvey.

Valli, L. (Ed.). (1992). *Reflective teacher education: Cases and critiques*. Albany: State University of New York Press.

VanTassel-Baska, J. (1992). *Planning effective curriculum for gifted learners*. Denver, CO: Love.

Walker, D., & Soltis, J. (1992). *Curriculum and aims* (second edition.). New York: Teachers College Press.

Warren, G. (Ed.). (1992). *Delivering the technology curriculum No. 3*. Stoke on Trent, England: Trentham Books.

Weiler, K., & Mitchell, C. (1992). *What schools can do: Critical pedagogy and practice*. Albany: State University of New York Press.

Wexler, P. (1992). *Becoming somebody: Toward a social psychology of school*. London: Falmer.

Wheelock, A. (1992). *Crossing the tracks: How "untracking" can save America's schools*. New York: Teachers College Press.

Willis, G., Schubert, W. H., Bullough, R. V., Jr., Kridel, C., & Holton, J. T. (Eds.). (1992). *The American curriculum: A documentary history*. Westport, CT: Greenwood Press.

Wirth, A. G. (1992). *Education and work for the year 2000*. San Francisco: Jossey-Bass.

Wood, G. A. (1992). *Schools that work: America's most innovative public education programs*. New York: Dutton.

1993

Andrews, G., & Taylor, R. (1993). *The arts in the primary school*. London: Falmer Press.

Andrews, R. (1993). *International dimensions to the national curriculum*. Stoke on Trent, England: Trentham Books.

Aoki, T., & Shamsher, M. (Eds.). (1993). *The call of teaching*. Vancouver, British Columbia, Canada: British Columbia Teachers' Federation.

Apple, M. W. (1993). *Official knowledge: Democratic education in a conservative age*. New York: Routledge.

Aronowitz, S., & Giroux, H. A. (1993). *Education still under siege* (second edition). Westport, CT: Bergin & Garvey.

Ayers, W. (1993). *To teach: The journey of a teacher*. New York: Teachers College Press.

Banks, J. A. (1993). *Multiethnic education: Theory and practice* (third edition). Needham Heights, MA: Allyn & Bacon.

Barber, M., & Graham, D. (1993). *Sense, nonsense and the national curriculum*. London: Falmer.

Beane, J. A. (1993). *A middle school curriculum: From rhetoric to reality* (second edition). Columbus, OH: National Middle School Association.

Bennett, W. J. (Ed.). (1993). *A book of virtues: A treasury of great moral stories.* New York: Simon and Schuster.

Berman, S., & LaFarge, P. (Eds.). (1993). *Promising practices in teaching social responsibility.* Albany: State University of New York Press.

Biklen, S., & Pollard, D. (Eds.) (1993). *Gender and education.* Chicago: National Society for the Study of Education.

Bowers, C. A. (1993). *Against the grain: Critical essays on education, modernity, and the recovery of the ecological imperative.* New York: Teachers College Press.

Brooks, J. G., & Brooks, M. G. (1993). *In search of understanding: The case for constructivist classrooms.* Alexandria, VA: Association for Supervision and Curriculum Development.

Brown, S., & McIntyre, D. (1993). *Making sense of teaching.* Bristol, PA: Open University Press.

Brubaker, D. L., & Simon, L. H. (1993). *Teacher as decision maker: Real-life cases to hone your people skills.* Thousand Oaks, CA: Corwin.

Bryk, A. S., Lee, V., & Holland, P. B. (1993). *Catholic schools and the common good.* Cambridge, MA: Harvard University Press.

Burbules, N. C. (1993). *Dialogue in teaching: Theory and practice.* New York: Teachers College Press.

Bybee, R. W. (1993). *Reforming science education: Social perspectives and personal reflections.* New York: Teachers College Press.

Campbell, R. J. (Ed.). (1993). *Breadth and balance in the primary curriculum.* London: Falmer Press.

Carnochan, W. B. (1993). *The battleground of the curriculum: Liberal education and American experience.* Stanford, CA: Stanford University Press.

Carr, J. F., & Harris, D. E. (1993). *Getting it together: A process workbook for K–12 curriculum development, implementation, and assessment.* Boston: Allyn & Bacon.

Casey, K. (1993). *I answer with my life: Life histories of women teachers working for social change.* New York: Routledge.

Castenell, L., Jr., & Pinar, W. F. (Eds.). (1993). *Understanding curriculum as racial text: Representations of identity and difference in education.* Albany: State University of New York Press.

Cawelti, G. (Ed.). (1993). *Challenges and achievements of American education. Fiftieth anniversary yearbook of ASCD.* Alexandria, VA: Association for Supervision and Curriculum Development.

Clandinin, J., Davies, A., Hogan, P., & Kennard, B. (Eds). (1993). *Learning to teach, teaching to learn: Stories of collaboration in teacher education.* New York: Teachers College Press.

Comer, J. P. (1993). *School power: Implications of an intervention project.* New York: The Free Press.

Compton, M. F., & Hawn, H. C. (1993). *Exploration: The total curriculum.* Columbus, OH: National Middle School Association.

Cuban, L. (1993). *How teachers taught: Constancy and change in American classrooms, 1890–1990* (second edition). New York: Teachers College Press.

Day, C., Hall, C., Gammage, P., & Coles, P. (1993). *Leadership and curriculum in the primary school: The roles of senior and middle management.* London: Paul Chapman.

Dickinson, T. (Ed.). (1993). *Readings in middle school curriculum: A continuing conversation.* Columbus, OH: National Middle School Association

Doll, W. E. (1993). *A postmodern perspective on curriculum.* New York: Teachers College Press.

Donmoyer, R., & Kos, R. (Eds.). (1993). *At risk students: Portraits, policies, programs, and practices.* Albany: State University of New York Press.

Drake, S., Bebbington, J., Laksman, S., Mackie, P., Maynes, N., & Wayne, L. (1993). *Developing an integrated curriculum using the story model.* Toronto, Ontario: Ontario Institute for Studies in Education.

Drake, S. M. (1993). *Planning integrated curriculum: The call to adventure.* Alexandria, VA: Association for Supervision and Curriculum Development.

Duenk, L. G., & Smith, H. (Eds.). (1993). *Improving vocational curriculum.* South Holland, IL: Goodheart-Willcox.

Edwards, J., & Fogelman, K. (Eds). (1993). *Developing citizenship in the curriculum.* London: D. Fulton.

Finch, C. R., & Crunkilton, J. R. (1993). *Curriculum development in vocational and technical education: Planning, content and implementation* (fourth edition). Boston: Allyn & Bacon.

Flake, C. L. (1993). *Holistic education: Principles, perspectives, practices: A book of readings based on Education 2000.* Brandton, VT: Holistic Education Press.

Fliegel, S., with MacGuire, J. (1993). *Miracle in East Harlem: The fight for choice in public education.* New York: Random House.

Fraser, J., & Perry, T. (Eds.). (1993). *Freedom's plow: Teaching in the multicultural classroom.* New York: Routledge.

Freire, P. (1993a). *Pedagogy of the city.* New York: Continuum.

Freire, P. (1993b). *Pedagogy of the oppressed* (revised edition). New York: Continuum Press.

Fullan, M. (1993). *Change forces: Probing the depths of educational reform.* Levittown, PA: Falmer.

Gardner, H. (1993a). *Frames of mind: The theory of multiple intelligences* (revised edition). Boulder, CO: Basic Books.

Gardner, H. (1993b). *Multiple intelligences: The theory in practice.* New York: Basic Books.

Gardner, H. (1993c). *The unschooled mind.* New York: Basic Books.

Geismar, K., & Nicoleau, G. (Eds.). (1993). *Teaching for change: Addressing issues of difference in the college classroom.* Cambridge, MA: Harvard Educational Review.

Giroux, H. A., & McLaren, P. (Eds.). (1993). *Between borders: Pedagogy and the politics of cultural studies.* New York: Routledge.

Glickman, C. D. (1993). *Renewing America's schools: A guide for school-based action.* San Francisco: Jossey-Bass.

Goodlad, J. I., & Lovitt, T. C. (Eds.). (1993). *Integrating general and special education.* New York: Merrill.

Goodlad, J. I., Sirotnik, R., & Soder, K. A. (Eds.). (1993). *The moral dimensions of teaching.* San Francisco: Jossey-Bass.

Goodson, I. (1993). *School subjects and curriculum change—10 year anniversary* (third edition). New York: Falmer Press.

Graham, D., & Tytler, D. (1993). *A lesson for us all: The making of the national curriculum.* New York: Routledge.

Gregory, T. (1993). *Making high school work: Lessons from the open school.* New York: Teachers College Press.

Gutek, G. L. (1993). *American education in a global society: Internationalizing teacher education.* White Plains, NY: Longman.

Harnett, A., Carr, W., & Naish, M. (1993). *Understanding the national curriculum.* New York: Cassell.

Hass, G., & Parkay, F. (Eds.). (1993). *Curriculum planning: A new approach* (sixth edition). Boston: Allyn & Bacon.

Henry, M. E. (1993). *School cultures: Universes of meaning in private schools.* Greenwich, CT: Ablex.

Heritage, M. (1993). *The curriculum in the early years.* New York: Cassell.

Hirsch, E. D. (Ed.). (1993a). *What your fifth grader needs to know: Fundamentals of a good fifth grade education.* New York: Delta Tradebooks.

Hirsch, E. D. (Ed.). (1993b). *What your first grader needs to know: Fundamentals of a good first grade education.* New York: Delta Tradebooks.

Hirsch, E. D. (Ed.). (1993c). *What your second grader needs to know: Fundamentals of a good second-grade education.* New York: Delta Tradebooks.

Hirsch, E. D. (Ed.). (1993d). *What your sixth grader needs to know: Fundamentals of a good sixth grade education.* New York: Delta Tradebooks.

Hirsch, E. D., Kett, J. F., & Trefil, J. (Eds.). (1993). *The dictionary of cultural literacy: What every American needs to know* (second edition). Boston: Houghton Mifflin.

Hlebowitsh, P. S. (1993). *Radical curriculum theory: A historical approach*. New York: Teachers College Press.

Hopfenberg, W. S., Levin, H. M., & Associates. (1993). *The accelerated schools resource guide*. San Francisco: Jossey-Bass.

Howell, K. W., Fox, S. L., & Moorehead, M. K. (1993). *Curriculum-based evaluation: Teaching and decision-making*. Pacific Grove, CA: Brooks/Cole.

Inchausti, R. (1993). *Spitwad sutras: Classroom teaching as sublime vocation*. Westport, CT: Bergin & Garvey.

Isenberg, J. P., & Jalongo, M. R. (1993). *Creative expression and play in the early childhood curriculum*. New York: Merrill.

Jackson, P., Boostrom, R. E., & Hansen, D.T. (1993). *The moral life of schools*. San Francisco: Jossey-Bass.

Joostens, T. H., Heijnen, G. W. H., & Heevel, A. J. (Eds.). (1993). *Doability of curricula*. Berwyn, PA: Swets & Zeitlinger.

Kincheloe, J. L. (1993). *Toward a critical politics of teacher thinking: Mapping the postmodern*. Westport, CT: Bergin & Garvey.

Kincheloe, J. L., & Steinberg, S. R. (1993). *Thirteen questions: Reforming education's conversation*. New York: Peter Lang Publishing.

Lankshear, C., & McLaren, P. (1993). *Critical literacy: Politics, praxis, and the postmodern*. Albany: State University of New York Press.

Lindley, D. A. (1993). *This rough magic*. Westport, CT: Bergin & Garvey.

Longstreet, W. S., & Shane, H. G. (1993). *Curriculum for a new millennium*. Boston: Allyn & Bacon.

Lounsbury, J. H. (Ed.). (1993). *Connecting the curriculum through interdisciplinary instruction*. Columbus, OH: National Middle School Association.

Mangan, J. A. (Ed.). (1993). *The imperial curriculum: Racial images and education in the British colonial experience*. New York: Routledge.

Marshall, R., & Tucker, M. (1993). *Thinking for a living*. New York: Basic Books.

Marzano, R. J., Pickering, D., & McTighe, J. (1993). *Assessing student outcomes: Performance assessment using the dimensions of learning model*. Alexandria, VA: Assocation for Supervision and Curriculum Development.

McCarthy, C., & Crichlow, W. (Eds.) (1993). *Race, identity, and representation in education*. New York: Routledge.

McLaren, P. (1993). *Schooling as a ritual performance: Towards a political economy of educational symbols and gestures* (second edition). New York: Routledge.

McLaren, P., & Leonard, P. (Eds.) (1993). *Paulo Freire: A critical encounter*. New York: Routledge.

Miller, B. (1993). *The arts as the basis of education.* Lanham, MD: University Press of America.

Miller, R. (Ed.). (1993). *The renewal of meaning in education: Responses to the cultural and ecological crisis of our times.* Brandon, VT: Holistic Education Press.

Morrison, G. S. (1993). *The contemporary curriculum: K–8.* Boston: Allyn & Bacon.

Muffoletto, R., & Knupfer, N. N. (Eds.). (1993). *Computers in education: Social, political, and historical perspectives.* Cresskill, NJ: Hampton Press.

Nicholls, J. G., & Hazzard, S. (1993). *Lessons from second graders: Education as adventure.* New York: Teachers College Press.

Nisbet, J. D. (Ed.). (1993). *Curriculum reform: Assessment in question / La reforme des programmes scolaires: L'evaluation en question.* Paris: Organisation for Educational Cooperation and Development.

Noddings, N. (1993). *Education for intelligent belief or unbelief.* New York: Teachers College Press.

O'Hear, P., & White, J. (Eds.). (1993). *Assessing the national curriculum.* London: Paul Chapman.

Ornstein, A., & Hunkins, F. P. (1993). *Curriculum: Foundations, principles and issues* (second edition). Boston: Allyn & Bacon.

Palmer, P. J. (1993). *To know as we are known: Education as a spiritual journey* (revised edition). San Francisco: Harper.

Paris, C. (1993). *Teacher agency and curriculum-making in classrooms.* New York: Teachers College Press.

Phelan, P., & Davidson, A. L. (Eds.). (1993). *Renegotiating cultural diversity in American schools.* New York: Teachers College Press.

Pigden, K., & Woolley, M. (Eds.). (1993). *The big picture: Integrating children's learning.* Portsmouth, NH: Heinemann.

Pring, R. (1993). *The new curriculum* (second edition). New York: Cassell.

Print, M. (1993). *Curriculum development and design* (second edition). St. Leonard, New South Wales, Australia: Allen & Unwin.

Pumfrey, P., & Verma, G. (Eds.). (1993). *The foundation subjects and religious education in primary schools.* London: Falmer Press.

Reardon, B. A. (1993). *Women and peace: Feminist visions of global security.* Albany: State University of New York Press.

Reid, W. A. (1993). *The pursuit of curriculum: Schooling and the public interest.* Norwood, NJ: Ablex.

Renyi, J. (1993). *Going public: Schooling for a diverse democracy.* New York: New Press.

Ross, A., & Olsen, K. (1993). *The way we were, the way we can be: A vision for the middle school through integrated thematic instruction* (second edition). Kent, WA: Books for Educators.

Ross, D. D., Bondy, E., & Kyle, D. W. (1993). *Reflective teaching for student empowerment: Elementary curriculum and methods.* New York: Macmillan.

Rosser, C. P. (1993). *Planning activities for child care: A curriculum guide for early childhood education.* South Holland, IL: Goodheart-Willcox. (second edition, 1998).

Runnymede Trust. (1993). *Equality assurance in the school curriculum.* Stoke on Trent, England: Trentham Books and Runnymede Trust.

Rust, F. O'C. (1993). *Changing teaching, changing schools. Bringing early childhood practice into public education.* New York: Teachers College Press.

Smith, D. L. (Ed.). (1993). *Australian curriculum reform: Action and reaction.* Belconnen, Australian Capital Territory: Australian Curriculum Studies Association in association with Social Science Press.

Society for the Study of Curriculum History. (1993). *Proceedings: Annual meeting of the Society for the Study of Curriculum History.* College Station, TX: Author.

Somers, J. (1993). *Drama and the national curriculum.* New York: Cassell.

Sowell, T. (1993). *Inside American education: The decline, the deception, the dogmas.* New York: The Free Press.

Steiner, M. (Ed.). (1993). *World studies in curriculum.* Stoke on Trent, England: Trentham Books.

Stevens, L. R. (Ed.). (1993). *The core and the canon: A national debate.* Denton, TX: University of North Texas Press.

Stevenson, C., & Carr, J. (Eds.). (1993). *Integrated studies in the middle grades: "Dancing through walls."* New York: Teachers College Press.

Swiderski, R. (1993). *Teaching language, learning culture.* Greenwood, CT: Bergin & Harvey.

Tchudi, S. (1993). *The astonishing curriculum: Integrating science and humanities through language.* Urbana, IL: National Council of Teachers of English.

Tierney, W. (1993). *Building communities of difference: Higher education in the twenty-first century.* Westport, CT: Bergin & Garvey.

Van Hoorn, J., Monighan Nourot, P., Scales, B. J., & Alward, K. R. (1993). *Play at the center of the curriculum.* Columbus, OH: Merrill.

Vars, G. (1993). *Interdisciplinarty teaching in the middle grades: Why and how.* Columbus, OH: Natonal Middle School Association.

Warehime, N. (1993). *To be one of us: Cultural conflict, creative democracy, and education.* Albany: State University of New York Press.

Wear, D. (Ed.). (1993). *The center of the web: Women and solitude.* Albany: State University of New York Press.

Weis, L., & Fine, M. (1993). *Beyond silenced voices: Class, race, and gender in American education*. Albany: State University of New York Press.

Wiggins, G. P. (1993). *Assessing student performance: Exploring the purpose and limits of testing*. San Francisco: Jossey-Bass.

Wiles, J., & Bondi, J. (1993). *Curriculum development: A guide to practice* (fourth edition). New York: Macmillan.

Wiles, J., & Bondi, J. (1993). *The essential middle school* (second edition). Columbus, OH: Merrill.

Williams, S. A. (Ed.). (1993). *Restructuring through curriculum innovation*. Bloomington, IN: Phi Delta Kappa.

Wilson, B., & Rossman, G. (1993). *Mandating academic excellence: High school responses to state curriculum reform*. New York: Teachers College Press.

Woods,. P., & Hammersley, M. (Eds.). (1993). *Gender and ethnicity in schools: Ethnographic accounts*. New York: Routledge.

Wynne, E., & Ryan, R. (1993). *Reclaiming our schools: A handbook on teaching, character, academics, and discipline*. New York: Merrill.

Zemelman, S., Daniels, H., & Hyde, A. (1993). *Best practice: New standards for teaching and learning in America's schools*. Portsmouth, NH: Heinemann.

Zilversmit, A. (1993). *Changing schools: Progressive education theory and practice, 1930–1960*. Chicago: University of Chicago Press.

1994

Acker, S. (1994). *Gendered education: Sociological reflections on women, teaching, and feminism*. Bristol, PA: Open University Press.

Adams, D., & Hamm, M. (1994). *New designs for teaching and learning*. San Francisco: Jossey-Bass.

Altrichter, H., Posch, P., & Somekh, B. (1994). *Teachers investigate their work: An introduction to the methods of action research*. London: Routledge.

Anderson, C. C., with Nicklas, S. K., & Crawford, A. R. (1994). *Global understandings: A framework for teaching and learning*. Alexandria, VA: Association for Supervision and Curriculum Development.

Anderson, L. W., & Sosniak, L. A. (Eds.). (1994). *Bloom's taxonomy: A forty-year retrospective*. Ninety-third yearbook of the National Society for the Study of Education, Part 2. Chicago: University of Chicago Press.

Armstrong, T. (1994). *Multiple intelligences in the classroom*. Alexandria, VA: Association for Supervision and Curriculum Development.

Ball, S. J. (1994). *Education reform: A critical and post-structural approach*. Bristol, PA: Open University Press.

Banks, J. A. (1994). *An introduction to multicultural education*. Needham Heights, MA: Allyn & Bacon.

Beare, H., & Slaughter, R. (1994). *Education for the 21st century*. New York: Routledge.

Behar, L. S. (1994). *The knowledge base of curriculum: An empirical analysis*. Lanham, MD: University Press of America.

Bell, J. (1994). *Teachers talk about teaching: Coping with change in turbulent times*. Bristol, PA: Open University Press.

Berube, M. R. (1994). *American school reform: Progressive equity and excellence movements, 1883–1993*. Westport, CT: Praeger.

Bigelow, B., Christenson, L., Karp, S., Miner, B., & Peterson, B. (1994). *Rethinking our classrooms: Teaching for equity and justice*. Milwaukee, WI: Rethinking Schools.

Blumberg, A., & Blumberg, P. (1994). *The unwritten curriculum: Things learned but not taught in schools*. Thousand Oaks, CA: Corwin.

Borman, K. M., & Greenman, N. P. (Eds.). (1994). *Changing American education: Recapturing the past or inventing the future?* Albany: State University of New York Press.

Brubaker, D. L. (1994). *Creative curriculum leadership*. Thousand Oaks, CA: Corwin.

Burkhardt, R. (1994). *The inquiry process: Student-centered learning*. Columbus, OH: National Middle School Assocation.

Burlbaw, L. M. (Ed.). (1994). *Curriculum history*. College Station, TX: Society for the Study of Curriculum History.

Chase, P., & Doan, J. (1994). *Full circle: A new look at multiage education*. Portsmouth, NH: Heinemann.

Cox, T., & Sanders, S. (1994). *The impact of the national curriculum on the teaching of 5-year-olds*. London: Falmer.

DeVaney, A. (1994). *Watching channel one: The convergence of students, technology and private business*. Albany: State University of New York Press.

DeVries, R., & Zan, B. S. (1994). *Moral classrooms, moral children: Creating a constructivist atmosphere in early education*. New York: Teachers College Press.

Dillon, J. T. (Ed.). (1994). *Deliberation in education and society*. Norwood, NJ: Ablex.

Eisner, E. W. (1994a). *Cognition and curriculum reconsidered* (second edition). New York: Teachers College Press.

Eisner, E. W. (1994b). *The educational imagination: On the design and evaluation of school programs* (third edition). New York: Macmillan.

Eliason, C., & Jenkins, L. (1994). *A practical guide to early childhood curriculum* (fifth edition). New York: Merrill.

Elmore, R. F., & Fuhrman, S. H. (Eds.). (1994). *The governance of curriculum* (ASCD yearbook). Alexandria, VA: Association for Supervision and Curriculum Development.

Escobar, M., Fernandez, A. L., & Guevara-Niebla, G. (1994). *Paulo Freire on higher education: A dialogue at the National University of Mexico.* Albany: State University of New York Press.

Eyre, L., & Eyre, R. (1994). *Teaching your children responsibility.* New York: Fireside/Simon and Schuster.

Fine, M. (Ed.). (1994). *Chartering urban school reform: Reflections on public high schools in the midst of change.* New York: Teachers College Press.

Fiol-Matta, L., & Chamberlain, M. K. (Eds.). (1994). *Women of color and the multicultural curriculum: Transforming the college classroom.* New York: The Feminist Press.

Fonte, J., & Ryerson, A. (1994). *Education for America's role in world affairs.* Lanham, MD: University Press of America.

Forte, I., & Schurr, S. (1994). *Interdisciplinary units and projects for thematic instruction.* Columbus, OH: National Middle School Association.

Freire, P. (1994). *Pedagogy of hope.* New York: Continuum.

Gadotti, M. (1994). *Reading Paulo Freire: His life and work.* Albany: State University of New York Press.

Garber, L. (Ed.). (1994). *Tilting the tower: Lesbians/teaching/queer subjects.* New York: Routledge.

Gentry, A., with Peelle, C. C. (1994). *Learning to survive: Black youth look for education and hope.* Westport, CT: Auburn House.

Gibboney, R. A. (1994). *The stone trumpet: A story of practical school reform, 1960–1990.* New York: Teachers College Press.

Giroux, H. A. (1994a). *Disturbing pleasures: Learning popular culture.* New York: Routledge.

Giroux, H. A. (1994b). *Living dangerously: Multiculturalism and the politics of difference.* New York: Peter Lang Publishing.

Gitlin, A. (Ed.). (1994). *Power and method: Political activism and educational research.* New York: Routledge.

Glatthorn, A. (1994). *Developing a quality curriculum.* Alexandria, VA: Association for Supervision and Curriculum Development.

Goodlad, J. I. (1994a). *Educational renewal: Better teachers, better schools.* San Francisco: Jossey-Bass.

Goodlad, J. I. (1994b). *What schools are for* (second edition). Bloomington, IN: Phi Delta Kappa.

Goodson, I. F. (1994). *Studying curriculum: Cases and methods*. New York: Teachers College Press.

Gott, R., & Duggan, S. (1994). *Investigative work in the science curriculum*. Philadelphia: Open University Press.

Hargreaves, A. (1994). *Changing teachers, changing times: Teachers' work and culture in the postmodern age*. New York: Teachers College Press.

Hawkins, M. L., & Graham, M. D. (1994). *Curriculum architecture: Creating a place of our own*. Columbus, OH: National Middle School Association.

Heath, D. H. (1994). *Schools of hope: Developing mind and character in today's youth*. San Francisco: Jossey-Bass.

Hendrick, J. (1994). *Total learning: Developmental curriculum for the young child* (fourth edition). New York: Merrill.

Hirsch, E. D. (Ed.). (1994a). *What your fourth grader needs to know: Fundamentals of a good fourth grade education*. New York: Delta Tradebooks.

Hirsch, E. D. (Ed.). (1994b). *What your third grader needs to know: Fundamentals of a good third grade education*. New York: Delta Tradebooks.

Hollins, E. T., King, J. E., & Hayman, W. C. (Eds.). (1994). *Teaching diverse populations: Formulating a knowledge base*. Albany: State University of New York Press.

hooks, b. (1994). *Teaching to transgress: Education as the practice of freedom*. New York: Routledge.

Hunter, M. (1994). *Enhancing teaching*. Columbus, OH: Merrill.

Husén, T., Postlethwaite, N., Clark, B. R., & Neave, G. (Eds.). (1994). *The international encyclopedia of education* in 16 volumes (second edition). New York: Pergamon. (CD-ROM produced in 1998).

Johnson, D. W., & Johnson, R. T. (1994). *Learning together and alone: Cooperative, competitive, and individualistic learning* (fourth edition). Needham Heights, MA: Allyn & Bacon.

Johnson, D. W., Johnson, R. T., & Holubec, E. J. (1994a). *Cooperative learning in the classroom*. Alexandria, VA: Association for Supervision and Curriculum Development.

Johnson, D. W., Johnson, R. T., & Holubec, E. J. (1994b). *The new circles of learning: Cooperation in the school and classroom*. Alexandria, VA: Association for Supervision and Curriculum Development.

Kanpol, B. (1994). *Critical pedagogy: An introduction*. Westport, CT: Bergin & Garvey.

Kemp, J. E., Morrison, G., & Ross, S. M. (1994). *Designing effective instruction*. Upper Saddle River, NJ: Merrill. (Second edition, 1998).

Knowles, J. G., Cole, A. L., & Presswood, C. S. (1994). *Through preservice teachers' eyes: Exploring field experience through narrative and inquiry*. Columbus, OH: Merrill and Prentice-Hall.

Kohl, H. (1994). *"I won' t learn from you" and other thoughts on creative maladjustment*. New York: New Press.

LaBelle, T. J., & Ward, C. R. (1994). *Multiculturalism and education: Diversity and its impact on schools and society*. Albany: State University of New York Press.

Ladson-Billings, G. (1994). *The dreamkeepers: Successful teachers of African American children*. San Francisco: Jossey-Bass.

Lasley, T. J. (1994). *Teaching peace: Toward cultural selflessness*. Westport, CT: Bergin & Garvey.

Lemlech, J. K. (1994). *Curriculum and instructional methods for the elementary and middle school* (third edition). New York: Macmillan.

Lewis, M. G. (1994). *Without a word: Teaching beyond women's silence*. New York: Routledge.

Mac An Ghaill, M. (1994). *The making of men: Masculinities, sexualities, and schooling*. Bristol, PA: Open University Press.

Macedo, D. (1994). *Literacies of power: What Americans are not allowed to know*. Boulder, CO: Westview Press.

Manning, M. L. (1994). *Celebrating diversity: Multicultural education in middle level schools*. Westerville, OH: National Middle School Association.

Manning, M., Manning, G., & Long, R. (1994). *Theme immersion: Inquiry based curriculum in elementary and middle schools*. Portsmouth, NH: Heinemann.

Martin, J. R. (1994). *Changing the educational landscape: Philosophy, women, and curriculum*. New York: Routledge.

Martinello, M. L., & Cook, G. E. (1994). *Interdisciplinary inquiry in teaching and learning*. New York: Merrill.

Martusewicz, R., & Reynolds, W. (Eds.) (1994). *Inside/Out: Contemporary critical perspectives in education*. New York: St. Martin's Press.

Maurer, R. E. (1994). *Designing interdisciplinary curriculum in middle, junior high, and high schools*. Needham Heights, MA: Allyn & Bacon.

McLaren, P. (1994). *Life in schools: An introduction to critical pedagogy in the foundations of education* (second edition). New York: Longman.

McLaren, P., & Lankshear, C. (Eds.). (1994). *Politics of liberation: Paths from Freire*. New York: Routledge.

McLaughlin, D., & Tierney, W. G. (1994). *Naming silenced lives: Personal narratives and the process of educational change*. New York: Routledge.

McNiff, J. (1994). *Teaching as learning: An action research approach*. New York: Routledge.

McWilliams, E. (1994). *In broken images: Feminist tales for a different teacher education*. New York: Teachers College Press.

Moffett, J. (1994). *The universal schoolhouse: Spiritual awakening through education.* San Francisco: Jossey-Bass.

Mosher, R., Kenny, R. A., & Garrod, A. (1994). *Preparing for citizenship: Teaching youth to live democratically.* Westport, CT: Praeger.

National Council for the Social Studies. (1994). *Curriculum standards for social studies.* Washington, DC: Author.

Novak, J. M. (Ed.). (1994). *Democratic teacher education: Programs, processes, problems and prospects.* Albany: State University of New York Press.

Ornstein, A. C., & Behar, L. S. (Eds.). (1994). *Contemporary issues in curriculum.* Boston: Allyn & Bacon.

Orrin, R. (Ed.). (1994). *Education and democracy: Reimagining liberal learning in America.* New York: College Entrance Examination Board.

Ozar, L. A. (1994). *Creating a curriculum that works: A guide to outcomes-centered curriculum decision-making.* Washington, DC: National Catholic Education Association.

Pinar, W. F. (1994). *Autobiography, politics, and sexuality.* New York: Peter Lang.

Posner, G. J., & Rudnitsky, A. N. (1994). *Course design: A guide to curriculum development for teachers* (fourth edition). New York: Longman.

Pratt, D. (1994). *Curriculum planning: A handbook for professionals.* Fort Worth, TX: Harcourt Brace.

Quint, S. (1994). *Schooling homeless children: A working model for America's public schools.* New York: Teachers College Press.

Radnor, H. A. (1994). *Across the curriculum.* New York: Cassell.

Raissiguier, C. (1994). *Becoming women/becoming workers: Identity formation in a French vocational school.* Albany: State University of New York Press.

Reardon, B., & Nordland, E. (1994). *Learning peace: The promise of ecological and cooperative education.* Albany: State University of New York Press.

Reid, W. A. (1994). *The pursuit of curriculum: Schooling and the public interest.* Norwood, NJ: Ablex.

Roberts, H. R., Gonzales, J. C., Harris, O. D., Huff, D., Johns, A. M., Lou, R., & Scott, O. (1994). *Teaching from a multicultural perspective.* Thousand Oaks, CA: Sage.

Sapon-Shevin, M. (1994). *Playing favorites: Gifted education and the disruption of community.* Albany: State University of New York Press.

Sears, J. T., Otis-Wilson, A., & Marshall, J. D. (1994). *When best doesn't equal good: Educational reform and teacher recruitment. A longitudinal study.* New York: Teachers College Press.

Sergiovanni, T. (1994). *Building community in schools.* San Francisco: Jossey-Bass.

Shapiro, B. (1994). *What children bring to light: A constructivist perspective on children's learning in science*. New York: Teachers College Press.

Siskin, L. S. (1994). *Realms of knowledge: Academic departments in secondary schools*. Washington, DC: Falmer Press.

Sleeter, C., & Grant, C. (1994). *Making choices for multicultural education: Five approaches to race, class, and gender* (second edition). Columbus, OH: Merrill.

Smith, G. A. (1994). *Public schools that work: Creating community*. New York: Routledge.

Solomon, J., & Aikenhead, G. (1994). *STS education: International perspectives on reform*. New York: Teachers College Press.

Somers, J. (1994). *Drama and the curriculum*. Herndon, VA: Cassell.

Spring, J. (1994a). *Deculturalization and the struggle for equality: A brief history of the education of dominated cultures in the United States*. New York: McGraw-Hill.

Spring, J. (1994b). *Wheels in the head: Educational philosophies of authority, freedom, and culure from Socrates to human rights*. Boston: McGraw-Hill.

Springer, M. (1994). *Watershed: A successful voyage into integrative learning*. Columbus, OH: National Middle School Association.

Steiner, D. M. (1994). *Rethinking democratic education: The politics of reform*. Baltimore: Johns Hopkins University Press.

Stone, L. (Ed.). (1994). *The education feminism reader*. New York: Routledge.

Stopsky, F., & Lee, S. (1994). *Social studies in a global society*. Albany, NY: Delmar Publishers.

Streitmatter, J. (1994). *Toward gender equity in the classroom: Everyday teachers' beliefs and practices*. Albany: State University of New York Press.

Torrance, H. (Ed.). *Evaluating authentic assessment: Problems and possibilities in new approaches to assessment*. Bristol, PA: Open University Press.

Tripp, D. (1994). *Critical incidents in teaching*. New York: Routledge.

Van Tassel-Baska, J., Feldhusen, J., Johnson, D., Seeley, K., & Silverman, L. (1994). *Comprehensive curriculum for gifted learners* (second edition). Boston: Allyn & Bacon.

Washington, V., & Bailey, V. (1994). *Project Head Start: Models and strategies for the twenty-first century*. Hamden, CT: Garland Publishing.

Wasley, P. A. (1994). *Stirring the chalkdust: Tales of teachers changing classroom practice*. New York: Teachers College Press.

Weiner, G. (1994). *Feminisms in education: An introduction*. Bristol, PA: Open University Press.

Williams, J. A. (1994). *Classroom in conflict: Teaching controversial subjects in a diverse society*. Albany: State University of New York Press.

Willis, G., Schubert, W. H., Bullough, R., Jr., Kridel, C., & Holton, J. T. (Eds.). (1994). *The American curriculum: A documentary history.* Westport, CT: Praeger.

Wilson, K. G., & Daviss, B. (1994). *Redesigning education: A Nobel Prize winner reveals what must be done to reform American education.* New York: Teachers College Press.

Witmer, J., & Anderson, C. S. (1994). *How to establish a high school service learning program.* Alexandria, VA: Association for Supervision and Curriculum Development.

Wraga, W. G. (1994). *Democracy's high school: The comprehensive high school and educational reform in the United States.* Lanham, MD: University Press of America.

1995

Ahier, J., & Ross, A. (Eds.). (1995). *The social subjects within the curriculum: Children's social learning in the national curriculum.* London: Falmer.

Alexander, W., with Carr, D., & McAvoy, K. (1995). *Student-oriented curriculum: Asking the right question.* Westerville, OH: National Middle School Association.

Anning, A. (Ed.). (1995). *The national curriculum for the early years.* Bristol, PA: Open University Press.

Apple, M. W. (1995). *Education and power* (second edition). New York: Routledge.

Apple, M. W., & Beane, J. A. (Eds.). (1995). *Democratic schools.* Alexandria, VA: Association for Supervision and Curriculum Development.

Applebaum, P. M. (1995). *Popular culture, educational discourse, and mathematics.* New York: Teachers College Press.

Arcilla, R. V. (1995). *For the love of perfection: Richard Rorty and liberal education.* New York: Routledge.

Association for Supervision and Curriculum Development. (1995). *ASCD Curriculum Handbook.* Alexandria, VA: Education and Technology Resources Center, Association for Supervision and Curriculum Development.

Ayers, W. (Ed.). (1995). *To become a teacher: Making a difference in children's lives.* New York: Teachers College Press.

Bachrach, N., Hassley, R. C., & Anderson, J. (1995). *Learning together: A manual for multiage grouping.* Thousand Oaks, CA: Corwin.

Banks, J. A., & Banks, C. M. (1995). *Handbook of research on multicultural education.* New York: Macmillan.

Beane, J. A. (Ed.). (1995). *Toward a coherent curriculum.* Alexandria, VA: Association for Supervision and Curriculum Development.

Beatty, B. (1995). *Preschool education in America: The culture of young children from the colonial era to the present.* New Haven, CT: Yale University Press.

Bell, J. (Ed.). (1995). *Teachers talk about teaching: Coping with change in turbulent times*. Bristol, PA: Open University Press.

Bennett, C. (1995). *Comprehensive multicultural education: Theory and practice* (third edition). Needham Heights, MA: Allyn & Bacon.

Ben-Peretz, M. (1995). *Learning from experience: Memory and the teacher's account of teaching*. Albany: State University of New York Press.

Berliner, D. C., & Biddle, B. J. (1995). *The manufactured crisis: Myths, fraud, and the attack on America's public schools*. New York: Longman.

Biklen, S. K. (1995). *School work: Gender and the cultural construction of teaching*. New York: Teachers College Press.

Blair, B. G., & Fischer, C. F. (1995). *Curriculum: The strategic key to schooling* (second edition). Dubuque, IA: Kendall/Hunt.

Block, A. A. (1995). *Occupied reading: Critical foundations for an ecological theory*. Hamden, CT: Garland.

Bowers, C. A. (1995). *Educating for an ecologically sustainable culture: Rethinking moral education, creativity, intelligence, and other modern orthodoxies*. Albany: State University of New York Press.

Brady, J. (1995). *Schooling young children: A feminist pedagogy for liberatory learning*. Albany: State University of New York Press.

Brady, L. (1995). *Curriculum development* (fifth edition). Melbourne, Australia: Prentice-Hall.

Brazee, E., & Capelluti, J. (1995). *Dissolving boundaries: Toward an integrative curriculum*. Westerville, OH: National Middle School Association.

Burke, J. (Ed.). (1995). *Outcomes, learning, and the curriculum*. Washington, DC: Falmer.

Carr, W. (1995). *For education: Towards critical educational inquiry*. Bristol, PA: Open University Press.

Cawelti, G. (Ed.). (1995). *Handbook of research on improving student achievement*. Arlington, VA: Education Research Service.

Charbonneau, M. P., & Reider, B. E. (1995). *The integrated elementary classroom: A developmental model of education for the 21st century*. Needham Heights, MA: Allyn & Bacon.

Choate, J. S., Enright, B., Miller, L., Potest, J., & Rakes, T. (1995). *Curriculum-based assessment and programming* (third edition). Boston: Allyn & Bacon.

Clandinin, D. J., & Connelly, F. M. (1995). *Teachers' professional knowledge landscapes*. New York: Teachers College Press.

Clark, C. M. (1995). *Thoughtful teaching*. New York: Teachers College Press.

Clark, S. N., & Clark, D. C. (1995). *The middle level principal's role in interdisciplinary curriculum*. Columbus, OH: National Middle School Association.

Cole, D. J., Ryan, C. W., & Kick, F. (1995). *Portfolios across the curriculum and beyond*. Thousand Oaks, CA: Corwin.

Comer, J. P. (1995). *School power: Implications of an intervention project* (revised edition). New York: The Free Press.

Cordeiro, P. (Ed.). (1995). *Endless possibilities: Generating curriculum in social studies and literacy*. Portsmouth, NH: Heinemann.

Cornbleth, C., & Waugh, D. (1995). *The great speckled bird: Multicultural politics and educational policymaking*. New York: St. Martin's Press.

Cuffaro, H. K. (1995). *Experimenting with the world: John Dewey and the early childhood classroom*. New York: Teachers College Press.

Cullinan, B. E., Scala, M. C., & Schroder, V. C. (1995). *Three voices: An invitation to poetry across the curriculum*. York, ME: Stenhouse.

Darder, A. (Ed.). (1995). *Culture and difference: Critical perspectives on the bicultural experience in the United States*. Westport, CT: Bergin & Garvey.

Darling-Hammond, L., Ancess, J., & Falk, B. (1995). *Authentic assessment in action: Studies of schools and students at work*. New York: Teachers College Press.

Daughtery, R. (1995). *National curriculum assessment: A review of policy 1987–1994*. London: Falmer.

Davies, J. (Ed.). (1995). *Developing leadership role in key stage 1 curriculum*. London: Falmer.

Delpit, L. (1995). *Other people's children: Cultural conflict in the classroom*. New York: New Press.

Doll, M. A. (1995). *To the lighthouse and back: Writings on teaching and living*. New York: Peter Lang.

Donmoyer, R. (Ed.). (1995). *The knowledge base in educational administration*. Albany: State University of New York Press.

Dunn, R. & Griggs, S. A. (1995). *Multiculturalism and learning style: Teaching and counseling adolescents*. Westport, CT: Praeger.

Erickson, H. L. (1995). *Stirring the head, heart, and soul: Redefining curriculum and instruction*. Thousand Oaks, CA: Corwin.

Etter-Lewis, G., & Foster, M. (1995). *Unrelated kin: Race and gender in women's personal narratives*. New York: Routledge.

Fine, M. (1995). *Habits of mind: Struggling over values in America's classrooms*. San Francisco: Jossey-Bass.

Fisher, B. (1995). *Thinking and learning together: Curriculum and community in a primary classroom*. Portsmouth, NH: Heinemann.

Five, C. L., & Dionisio, M. (1995). *Bridging the gap: Integrating curriculum in upper elementary and middle schools*. Portsmouth, NH: Heinemann.

438 ■CHAPTER TEN■

Fortson, L. R., & Reiff, J. C. (1995). *Early childhood curriculum: Open structures for integrative learning*. Boston: Allyn & Bacon.

Frase, L. E., English, F. W., & Posten, W. K. (Eds.). (1995). *The curriculum management audit: Improving school quality*. Lancaster, PA: Technomics.

Gallas, K. (1995). *Talking their way into science: Hearing children's questions and theories, responding with curricula*. New York: Teachers College Press.

Garrison, J. W., & Rud, A. G. (1995). *The educational conversation: Closing the gap*. Albany: State University of New York Press.

Gaskell, J., & Willinsky, J. (Eds.). (1995). *Gender in/forms curriculum: From enrichment to transformation*. New York: Teachers College Press.

Geisert, P. G., & Futrell, M. K. (1995). *Teachers, computers, and curriculum: Microcomputers in the classroom* (second edition). Needham Heights, MA: Allyn & Bacon.

Ginsburg, M. B. (Ed.). (1995). *The politics of educators' work and lives*. Hamden, CT: Garland.

Goodman, R. F. & Fisher, W. R. (Eds.). (1995). *Rethinking knowledge: Reflections across disciplines*. Albany: State University of New York Press.

Goodson, I. (1995). *The making of curriculum* (second edition). Bristol, PA: Falmer.

Greene, M. (1995). *Releasing the imagination: Essays on education, the arts, and social change*. San Francisco: Jossey-Bass.

Gronlund, N. E. (1995). *How to write and use instructional objectives* (fifth edition). Columbus, OH: Merrill.

Grubb, W. N. (Ed.). (1995). *Education through occupations in American high schools. Volume 1: Approaches to integrating academic and vocational education. Volume 2: The challenges of implementing curriculum integration*. New York: Teachers College Press.

Gunter, M. A., Estes. T. H. & Schwab, J. H. (1995). *Instruction: A models approach* (second edition). Boston: Allyn & Bacon.

Hansen, D. T. (1995). *The call to teach*. New York: Teachers College Press.

Harris, D. A. (Ed.). (1995). *Multiculturalism from the margins: Non-dominant voices on difference and diversity*. Westport, CT: Bergin & Garvey.

Henderson, J., & Hawthorne, R. (1995). *Transformative curriculum leadership: Paradigm, process, reflective inquiry*. Columbus, OH: Merrill.

Henson, K. T. (1995). *Curriculum development for educational reform*. New York: Longman.

Hirsch, E. D. (Ed.). (1995a). *What your fifth grader needs to know: Fundamentals of a good fifth grade education*. New York: Delta Tradebooks.

Hirsch, E. D. (Ed.). (1995b). *What your sixth grader needs to know: Fundamentals of a good sixth grade education*. New York: Delta Tradebooks.

Horwood, B. (Ed.). (1995). *Experience and the curriculum*. Dubuque, IA: Kendall/Hunt.

House, P. A., & Coxford, A. F. (1995). *Connecting mathematics across the curriculum*. Reston, VA: National Council of Teachers of Mathematics.

Jackson, S., & Solis, J. (Ed.). (1995). *Beyond comfort zones in multiculturalism*. Westport, CT: Bergin & Garvey.

Jalongo, M. R., & Isenberg, J. P. (1995). *Teachers' stories: From personal narrative to professional insight*. San Francisco: Jossey-Bass.

James, M. E. (Ed.). (1995). *Social reconstruction through education: The philosophy, history, and curricula of a radical idea*. Greenwich, CT: Ablex.

Jipson, J., Munro, P., Victor, S., Jones, K. F., & Freed-Rowland, G. (1995). *Repositioning feminism & education: Perspectives on educating for social change*. Westport, CT: Bergin & Garvey.

Kanpol, B., & McLaren, P. (Eds.). (1995). *Critical multiculturalism: Uncommon voices in a common struggle*. Westport, CT: Bergin & Garvey.

Kincheloe, J. L. (1995). *Toil and trouble: Good work, smart workers, and the integration of academic and vocational education*. New York: Peter Lang.

Kincheloe, J. L., & Steinberg, S. R. (Eds.). (1995). *Thirteen questions: Reframing education's conversation* (second edition). New York: Peter Lang.

Kinsley, C. W., & McPherson, K. (Eds.). (1995). *Enriching the curriculum through service learning*. Alexandria, VA: Association for Supervision and Curriculum Development.

Kleinfield, J. S., & Yeria, S. (Eds.). (1995). *Gender tales: Tensions in the schools*. Mahwah, NJ: Lawrence Erlbaum Associates.

Kliebard, H. M. (1995). *The struggle for the American curriculum, 1893–1958* (second edition). New York: Routledge.

Knapp, M. (1995). *Teaching for meaning in high poverty classrooms*. New York: Teachers College Press.

Kozol, J. (1995). *Amazing grace: The lives of children and the conscience of a nation*. New York: Crown.

Krogh, S. (1995). *The integrated early childhood curriculum* (second edition). New York: McGraw-Hill.

Kucer, S. B., Silvia, C., & Delgado-Larocco, E. L. (1995). *Curricular conversations: Themes in multilingual and monolingual classrooms*. York, ME: Stenhouse Publications.

Larkin, J. M., & Sleeter, C. E. (Eds.). (1995). *Developing multicultural teacher education curricula*. Albany: State University of New York Press.

Lawler-Prince, D., Altieri, J. L., & Cramer, M. K. (1995). *Moving toward an integrated curriculum in early childhood education*. Washington, DC: National Education Association.

Levine, D., Lowe, R., Peterson, B., & Tenorio, R. (1995). *Rethinking schools: An agenda for change* (based on the education newspaper, *Rethinking Schools*). New York: New Press.

Lewis, A. (1995). *Primary special needs in the national curriculum* (second edition). New York: Routledge.

Liston, R., Nagai, A. K., & Rothman, S. (1995). *Molding the good citizen: The politics of high school history textbooks*. Westport, CT: Praeger.

Loewen, J. W. (1995). *Lies my teacher told me*. New York: Simon and Schuster.

Lutzker, M. (1995). *Multiculturalism in the college curriculum: A handbook of strategies and resources for faculty*. Westport, CT: Greenwood.

Macdonald, J. B. (B. J. Macdonald, Ed.). (1995). *Theory as a prayerful act: The collected essays of James B. Macdonald*. New York: Peter Lang.

Maker, C. J., & Nielson, A. B. (1995). *Curriculum development in education of the gifted*. Austin, TX: Pro-Ed.

Marsh, C., & Willis, G. (1995). *Curriculum: Alternative approaches, ongoing issues*. Columbus, OH: Merrill.

Maurer, R. E. (1995). *Designing interdisciplinary curriculum in middle, junior high, and high schools* (third edition). Champaign, IL: Human Kinetics

McCutcheon, G. (1995). *Developing the curriculum: Solo and group deliberation*. New York: Longman.

McEwan, H., & Egan, K. (Eds.). (1995). *Narrative in teaching, learning, and research*. New York: Teachers College Press.

McLaren, P. (1995). *Critical pedagogy and predatory culture: Oppositional politics in a postmodern era*. New York: Routledge.

McLaren, P. L., & Giarelli, J. M. (Eds.). (1995). *Critical theory and educational research*. Albany: State University of New York Press.

McLaren, P., Hammer, R., Sholle, D., & Reilly, S. (1995). *Rethinking media literacy: A critical pedagogy of representation*. New York: Peter Lang.

McNeil, J. D. (1995). *Curriculum: The teacher's initiative*. Columbus, OH: Merrill.

Meier, D. (1995). *The power of their ideas: Lessons for America from a small school in Harlem*. New York: Beacon Press.

Miller, R. (Ed.). (1995). *Educational freedom for a democratic society: A critique of national educational goals, standards, and curriculum*. Brandon, VT: Holistic Education Press.

Mitchell, R., Willis, M., & The Chicago Teachers' Union Quest Center. (1995). *Learning in overdrive: Designing curriculum, instruction, and assessment from standards. A manual for teachers*. Golden, CO: North American Press.

Morrow, R. A., & Torres, C. A. (1995). *Social theory and education: A critique of theories of social and cultural reproduction*. Albany: State University of New York Press.

Murphy, P., Sellinger, M., Bourne, J., & Briggs, M. (1995). *Subject learning in the primary curriculum*. New York: Routledge.

Myrsiades, K., & McGuire, J. (Eds.). (1995). *Order and partialities: Theory, pedagogy, and the "postcolonial."* Albany: State University of New York Press.

Nakanishi, D. T., & Nishida, T. Y. (1995). *The Asian American educational experience: A sourcebook for teachers and students.* New York: Routledge.

Neperud, R. W. (1995). *Context, content, and community in art education: Beyond postmodernism.* New York: Teachers College Press.

Ng, R., Staton, P., & Scane, J. (Eds.). (1995). *Anti-racism, feminism, and critical approaches to education.* Westport, CT: Bergin & Garvey.

Nicholls, J. G., & Thorkildsen, T. A. (Eds.). (1995). *Reasons for learning: Expanding the conversation on student-teacher collaboration.* New York: Teachers College Press.

Noddings, N. (1995). *Philosophy of education.* Boulder, CO: Westview.

Oliner, P. M., & Oliner, S. P. (1995). *Toward a caring society: Ideas into action.* Westport, CT: Praeger.

Ostrow, J. (1995). *A room with a different view: First through third graders build community and create curriculum.* York, ME: Stenhouse Publications.

Paley, N. (1995). *Finding art's place: Experiments in contemporary education and culture.* New York: Routledge.

Parker, W. C. (Ed.). (1995). *Educating the democratic mind.* Albany: State University of New York Press.

Passe, J. (1995). *Elementary school curriculum.* Madison, WI: Brown & Benchmark.

Perry, T. (1995). *Teaching Malcolm X: Popular culture and literacy.* New York: Routledge.

Peters, M. (Ed.). (1995). *Education and the postmodern condition.* Westport, CT: Bergin & Garvey.

Pinar, W. F., Reynolds, W. M., Slattery, P., & Taubman, P. M. (1995). *Understanding curriculum: An introduction to the study of historical and contemporary curriculum discourses.* New York: Peter Lang.

Pool, H., & Page, J. A. (Eds.). (1995). *Beyond tracking: Finding success in inclusive schools.* Bloomington, IN: Phi Delta Kappa.

Posner, G. (1995). *Analyzing the curriculum* (second edition). New York: McGraw-Hill.

Protherough, R., & King, P. (Eds.). (1995). *The challenge of English in the national curriculum.* London: Routledge.

Purpel, D. E., & Shapiro, S. (1995). *Beyond liberation and excellence: Reconstructing the public discourse on education.* Westport, CT: Bergin & Garvey.

Raizen, S. A., Sellwood, P., Todd, R. D., & Vickers, M. (1995). *Technology education in the classroom: Understanding the designed world.* San Francisco: Jossey-Bass.

Ravitch, D., & Vinovskis, M. A. (Eds.). (1995). *Learning from the past: What history teaches us about school reform.* Baltimore: Johns Hopkins University Press.

Reese, W. J. (1995). *The origins of the American high school*. New Haven, CT: Yale University Press.

Resnick, L. B., & Wirt, J. (Eds.). (1995). *Linking school and work: Roles for standards and assessment*. San Francisco: Jossey-Bass.

Rose, M. (1995). *Possible lives: The promise of public education in America*. New York: Penguin Putnam.

Ryan, A. (1995). *John Dewey and the high tide of American liberalism*. New York: W.W. Norton.

Sarason, S. B. (1995). *School change: The personal development of a point of view*. New York: Teachers College Press.

Schrag, F. (1995). *Back to basics: Fundamental educational questions reexamined*. San Franscisco, CA: Jossey-Bass.

Senese, G., with Page, R. (1995). *Simulation, spectacle, and the ironies of education reform*. Westport, CT: Bergin & Garvey.

Shannon, P. (1995). *Texts, lies, & videotape: Stories about life, literacy, and learning*. Portsmouth, NH: Heinemann.

Shapiro, A. S., Benjamin, W. F., & Hunt, J. J. (1995). *Curriculum and schooling: A practitioner's guide*. Palm Springs, CA: ETC Publications.

Silin, J. G. (1995). *Sex, death, and the education of children: Our passion for ignorance in the age of AIDS*. New York: Teachers College Press.

Siraj-Blatchford, J., & Siraj-Blatchford, I. (Eds.). (1995). *Educating the whole child: Cross curricular skills, themes, and dimensions*. Bristol, PA: Open University Press.

Siskin, L. S., & Little, J. W. (Eds.). (1995). *The subjects in question: Departmental organization and the high school*. New York: Teachers College Press.

Slattery, P. (1995). *Curriculum development in the postmodern era*. New York: Garland.

Slavin, R. E. (1995). *Cooperative learning: Theory, research, and practice* (second edition). Needham Heights, MA: Allyn & Bacon.

Sleeter, C. E., & McLaren, P. (Eds.). (1995). *Multicultural education, critical pedagogy, and the politics of difference*. Albany: State University of New York Press.

Smith, D. L., & Lovat, T. J. (1995). *Curriculum: Action on reflection revisited* (third edition). Wentworth Falls, New South Wales, Australia: Social Science Press.

Smith, F. (1995). *Between hope and havoc: Essays into human learning and education*. Portsmouth, NH: Heinemann.

Smith, R., & Wexler, P. (1995). *After postmodernism: Education, politics, and identity*. Hamden, CT: Falmer.

Soder, R. (Ed.). (1995). *Democracy, education, and the schools*. San Francisco: Jossey-Bass.

Stephens, S. (Ed.). (1995). *Children and the politics of culture*. Princeton, NJ: Princeton University Press.

Stock, P. L. (1995). *The dialogic curriculum: Teaching and learning in a multicultural society.* Portsmouth, NH: Boyton/Cook.

Stones, E. (1995). *Quality teaching: A sample of classes.* New York: Routledge.

Sylwester, R. (1995). *A celebration of neurons: An educator's guide to the human brain.* Alexandria, VA: Association for Supervision and Curriculum Development.

Tanner, D., & Tanner, L. (1995). *Curriculum development: Theory into practice* (third edition). Columbus, OH: Merrill.

Teitelbaum, K. (1995). *Schooling for "good rebels": Socialism, American education, and the search for radical curriculum.* New York: Teachers College Press.

Thomas, D. (Ed.). (1995). *Teachers' stories.* Bristol, PA: Open University Press.

Tonks, D. (1995). *Teaching AIDS.* New York: Routledge.

Tyack, D., & Cuban, L. (1995). *Tinkering toward utopia: A century of public school reform.* Cambridge, MA: Harvard University Press.

Unks, G. (Ed.). (1995). *The gay teen: Educational practice and theory for lesbian, gay, and bisexual adolescents.* New York: Routledge.

Usher, R., & Edwards, R. (1995). *Postmodernism and education: Different voices, different worlds.* New York: Routledge.

Wien, C. A. (1995). *Developmentally appropriate practice in "real life."* New York: Teachers College Press.

1996

Appiah, K. A., & Gates, H. L., Jr. (Eds.). (1996). *The dictionary of global culture.* New York: Knopf.

Apple, M. W. (1996). *Cultural politics and education.* New York: Teachers College Press.

Applebee, A. N. (1996). *Curriculum as conversation: Transforming traditions of teaching and learning.* Chicago: University of Chicago Press.

Areglado, R. J., Bradley, R. C., & Lane, P. S. (1996). *Learning for life: Creating classrooms for self-directed learning.* Thousand Oaks, CA: Corwin.

Avis, J., Bloomer, M., Esland, G., Gleeson, D., & Hodkinson, P. (1996). *Knowledge and nationhood: Education, politics, and work.* Herndon, VA: Cassell.

Ayers, W., & Ford, P. (Eds.). (1996). *City kids, city teachers.* New York: The New Press.

Banks, J. (Ed.). (1996). *Multicultural education, transformative knowledge and action: Historical and contemporary perspectives.* New York: Teachers College Press.

Beauboeuf-Lafontant, T., & Augustine, D. Smith. (1990). *Facing racism in education* (second edition). Cambridge, MA: Harvard Educational Review.

Becker, T. L., & Couto, R. A. (1996). *Teaching democracy by being democratic.* Westport, CT: Praeger.

Beyer, L. E. (Ed.). (1996). *Creating democratic classrooms: The struggle to integrate theory and practice.* New York: Teachers College Press.

Beyer, L. E., & Liston, D. P. (1996). *Curriculum in conflict: Social visions, educational agendas, and progressive school reform.* New York: Teachers College Press.

Black, P., & Atkin, J. M. (1996). *Changing the subject: Innovations in science, mathematics, and technology.* New York: Routledge.

Boyer, J. B., & Baptiste, H. P. (1996). *Transforming the curriculum for multicultural understandings: A practitioner's handbook.* San Francisco: Caddo Gap Press.

Burstyn, J. N. (Ed.). (1996). *Educating tomorrow's valuable citizen.* Albany: State University of New York Press.

Burz, H. L., & Marshall, K. (1996–8). *Performance-based curriculum: From knowing to showing series. Performance-based curriculum for mathematics (1996); Performance-based curriculum for science (1997); Performance-based curriculum for U.S. language arts (1997); Performance-based curriculum for social studies (1998).* Thousand Oaks, CA: Corwin.

Callicott, J. B., & da Rocha, F. J. R. (Eds.). (1996). *Earth summit ethics: Toward a reconstructive postmodern philosophy of environmental education.* Albany: State University of New York Press.

Carey-Webb, A., & Benz, S. (Eds.). (1996). *Teaching and testimony: Rigoberta Menchu and the North American classroom.* Albany: State University of New York Press.

Carger, C. L. (1996). *Of borders and dreams: A Mexican American experience of urban education.* New York: Teachers College Press.

Carr, W., & Hartnett, A. (1996). *Education and the struggle for democracy: The politics of educational ideas.* Bristol, PA: Open University Press.

Chawla-Duggan, R., & Carger, C. L. (1996). *Of borders and dreams: A Mexican-American experience of urban education.* New York: Teachers College Press.

Christenson, M. (Ed.). (1996). *Reclaiming at-risk youth for the 21st century workplace.* Alexandria, VA: Association for Supervision and Curriculum Development.

Comer, J. P., Haynes, N. M., Joyner, E. T., & Ben-Avie, M. (1996). *Rallying the whole village: The Comer process for reforming education.* New York: Teachers College Press.

Costa, A. L., & Liebmann, R. M. (Eds.). (1996). *Envisioning process as content: Toward a renaissance curriculum.* Thousand Oaks, CA: Corwin.

Danielson, C. (1996). *Enhancing professional practice: A framework for teaching.* Alexandria, VA: Association for Supervision and Curriculum Development.

Davidson, A. L. (1996). *Making and molding identity in schools: Student narratives on race, gender and academic engagement.* Albany: State University of New York Press.

Desmond, C. T. (1996). *The rise of outcome-based education.* Albany: State University of New York Press.

Diller, A., Houston, B., Morgan, K. P., & Ayim, M. (1996). *The gender question in education: Theory, pedagogy, and politics*. Boulder, CO: Westview.

Doll, R. C. (1996). *Curriculum improvement: Decision making and process* (ninth edition). Boston: Allyn & Bacon.

Duckworth, E. (1996). *"The having of wonderful ideas" and other essays on teaching and learning.* New York: Teachers College Press.

Eaker-Rich, D., & VanGalen, J. A. (Eds.). (1996). *Caring in an unjust world: Negotiating borders and barriers in schools*. Albany: State University of New York Press.

Edgerton, S. (1996). *Translating the curriculum: Multiculturalism into cultural studies*. New York: Routledge.

Edwards, J., Roblyer, M. D., & Havriluk, M. A. (1996). *Integrating educational technology into teaching*. Upper Saddle River, NJ: Prentice-Hall.

Eggleston, J. (1996). *Teaching design and technology*. Bristol, PA: Open University Press.

Elmore, R. F., Peterson, P. L., & McCarthy, S. J. (1996). *Restructuring in the classroom: Teaching, learning, and school organization*. San Francisco: Jossey-Bass.

English, F. W., & Larsen, R. L. (1996). *Curriculum management for educational and social service organizations*. Springfield, IL: Charles C. Thomas. (Revised edition of *Curriculum management for schools, colleges, and businesses*, 1987).

Epstein, A. S., McAdoo, L., & Schweinhart, L. J. (1996). *Models of early childhood curriculum*. Ypsilanti, MI: High/Scope Press.

Farnham, N. H., & Yarmolinsky, A. (Eds.). (1996). *Rethinking liberal education*. New York: Oxford University Press.

Feagin, J. R., Vera, H., & Imani, N. (1996). *The agony of education: Black students at a white university*. New York: Routledge.

Fine, M., Powell, L. C., Weis, L., & Mun Wong, L. (Eds.). (1996). *Off white: Readings on race, power, and society*. New York: Routledge.

Fischer, C. (Ed.). (1996). *Education and technology: Reflections on a decade of experience in the classroom*. San Francisco: Jossey-Bass.

Forrest, M. (1996). *Modernising the classics: A study in curriculum development*. Exeter, England: University of Exeter Press.

Fosnot, C. T. (Ed.). (1996). *Constructivism: Theory, perspectives, and practice*. New York: Teachers College Press.

Freire, P. (1996). *Letters to Cristina: Reflections on my life and work*. New York: Routledge.

Fried, R. L. (1996). *The passionate teacher: A practical guide*. Boston: Beacon.

Friedman, E. G., Kolmar, W. K., Flint, C. B., & Rothenberg, P. (Eds). (1996). *Creating an inclusive college curriculum*. New York: Teachers College Press.

Fullan, M., & Hargreaves, A. (1996). *What's worth fighting for in your school?* New York: Teachers College Press.

Fuller, B., & Elmore, R. F., with Orfield, G. (1996). *Who chooses? Who loses? Culture, institutions, and the unequal effects of school choice.* New York: Teachers College Press.

Gadotti, M. (1996). *Pedagogy of praxis: A dialectical philosophy of education.* Albany: State University of New York Press.

Giroux, H. A. (1996). *Fugitive cultures: Race, violence, and youth.* New York: Routledge.

Giroux, H. A., Lankshear, C., McLaren, P., & Peters, M. (1996). *Counter narratives: Cultural studies and critical pedagogies in postmodern spaces.* New York: Routledge.

Glatthorn, A. A. (Ed.). (1996). *Content of the curriculum* (second edition). Alexandria, VA: Association for Supervision and Curriculum Development.

Gooden, A. R. (1996). *Computers in the classroom.* San Francisco: Jossey-Bass.

Goodson, I. F., & Haragreaves, A. (Eds.). (1996). *Teachers' professional lives.* London: Falmer Press.

Goodson, I. F., & Marsh, C. (1996). *Studying school subjects.* Washington, DC: Falmer.

Graves, D. H. (1996). *Hidden literacies: Children learning at home and at school.* Portsmouth, NH: Heinemann.

Hargreaves, A., Earl, L., & Ryan, J. (1996). *Schooling for change: Reinventing education for early adolescents.* London: Falmer.

Harris, D., & Carr, J. F. (1996). *How to use standards in the classroom.* Alexandria, VA: Association for Supervision and Curriculum Development.

Hart, S. (Ed.). (1996). *Differentiation and the secondary curriculum.* New York: Routledge.

Hauenstein, A. D. (1996). *A conceptual framework for educational objectives: A holistic approach to traditional taxonomies.* Lanham, MD: University Press of America.

Henderson, J. (1996). *Reflective teaching: The study of your constructivist practices* (second edition). Columbus, OH: Merrill.

Hern, M. (Ed.). (1996). *Deschooling our lives.* Philadelphia: New Society Publishers.

Higham, J., Sharp, P., & Yeomans, D. (1996). *The emerging 16–19 curriculum: Policy and provision.* London: David Fulton.

Hirsch, E. D. (1996). *The schools we need and why we don't have them.* New York: Doubleday.

Hirsch, E. D., & Holdren, J. (Eds.). (1996). *What your kindergartner needs to know: Preparing your child for a lifetime of learning.* New York: Delta Tradebooks.

Hollins, E. R. (1996a). *Culture in school learning: Revealing the deep meaning.* Mahwah, NJ: Lawrence Erlbaum Associates.

Hollins, E. R. (Ed.). (1996b). *Transforming curriculum for a culturally diverse society.* Mahwah, NJ: Lawrence Erlbaum Associates.

Hutchinson, F. (1996). *Educating beyond violent futures*. New York: Routledge.

Jones, B. L., & Maloy, R. W. (1996). *Schools for an information age: Reconstructing foundations for learning and teaching*. Westport, CT: Praeger.

Joyce, B., & Calhoun, E. (1996). *Creating learning experiences: The role of instructional theory and research*. Alexandria, VA: Association for Supervision and Curriculum Development.

Joyce, B., & Weil, M. (1996). *Models of teaching* (fifth edition). Needham Heights, MA: Allyn & Bacon.

Kimball, R., Stables, K., & Green, R. (1996). *Understanding practice in design and technology*. Bristol, PA: Open University Press.

Kitson, N., & O'Neill, J. (Eds.). (1996). *Effective curriculum management: Coordinating learning in the primary school*. New York: Routledge.

Kridel, C., Bullough, R.V., Jr., & Shaker, P. (Eds.). (1996). *Teachers and mentors: Profiles of distinguished twentieth-century professors of education*. Hamden, CT: Garland Publishing.

Lauritzen, C., & Jaeger, M. (1996). *Integrating learning through story: The narrative curriculum*. Albany, NY: Delmar Publishers.

Leistyna, P., Woodrum, A., & Sherblom, S. (Eds.). (1996). *Breaking free: The transformative power of critical pedagogy*. Cambridge, MA: Harvard Educational Review.

Levine, B. (Ed.). (1996). *Works about John Dewey, 1886–1995*. Carbondale and Edwardsville, IL: Southern Illinois University Press.

Levinson, B. A., Foley, D. E., & Holland, D. C. (Eds.). (1996). *The cultural production of the educated person: Cultural ethnographies of schooling and local practice*. Albany: State University of New York Press.

Levy, S. (1996). *Starting from scratch: One classroom builds its own curriculum*. Portsmouth, NH: Heinemann.

Lieberman, A. (Ed.). (1996). *The work of restructuring schools: Building from the ground up*. New York: Teachers College Press.

Lipman, M. (1996). *Natasha: Vygotskian dialogues*. New York: Teachers College Press.

Lisman, C. D. (1996). *The curricular integration of ethics*. Westport, CT: Praeger.

Liston, D. P., & Zeichner, K. M. (1996). *Culture and teaching*. Mahwah, NJ: Lawrence Erlbaum Associates.

Liu, X. (1996). *Mathematics and science curriculum change in the People's Republic of China*. Lewiston, NY: Edwin Mellen Press.

Lorber, M. A., & Pierce, W. D. (1996). *Objectives, methods, and evaluation for secondary teaching* (fourth edition). Needham Heights, MA: Allyn & Bacon.

Luke, C. (Ed.). (1996). *Feminisms and pedagogies of everyday life*. Albany: State University of New York Press.

Manning, M. L., & Baruth, L. G. (1996). *Multicultural education of children and adolescents* (second edition). Needham Heights, MA: Allyn & Bacon.

Marzano, R. J., & Kendall, J. S. (1996). *A comprehensive guide to designing standards-based districts, schools, and classrooms.* Alexandria, VA: Association for Supervision and Curriculum Development.

Maurer, R. E. (1996). *Designing alternative assessments for interdisciplinary curriculum in middle and secondary schools.* Boston: Allyn & Bacon.

McAdoo, L., & Schweinhart, L. J. (1996). *Models of early childhood curriculum.* Ypsilanti, MI: High/Scope Press.

McDonald, J. P. (1996). *Redesigning school: Lessons for the 21st century.* San Francisco: Jossey-Bass.

McKernan, J. (1991). *Curriculum action research: A handbook of methods and resources for the reflective practitioner* (second edition). London: Kogan Page.

McLaren, P. (1996). *Critical pedagogy and predatory culture.* New York: Routledge.

McNeil, J. (1996). *Curriculum: A comprehensive introduction* (fifth edition). New York: Harper Collins.

Merrion, M., & Rubin, J. E. (1996). *Creative approaches to elementary curriculum.* Portsmouth, NH: Heinemann.

Milbrath, L. W. (1996). *Learning to think environmentally while there is still time.* Albany: State University of New York Press.

Miletta, M. Mc. (1996). *A multiage classroom: Choice and possibility.* Portsmouth, NH: Heinemann.

Miller, J. P. (1996). *The holistic curriculum.* Toronto, Ontario: OISE Press.

Mitchell, B. M., & Salsbury, R. E. (1996). *Multicultural education: An international guide to research, policies and programs.* Westport, CT: Greenwood.

Molnar, A. (1996). *Giving kids the business: The commercialization of America's schools.* Boulder, CO: Westview Press.

Muncey, D. E., & McQuillan, P. J. (1996). *Reform and resistance in schools and classrooms: An ethnographic view of the Coalition of Essential Schools.* New Haven, CT: Yale University Press.

Nagel, N. G. (1996). *Learning through real-world problem solving: The power of integrative teaching.* Thousand Oaks, CA: Corwin.

Nathan, J. (1996). *Charter schools: Creating hope and opportunity for American education.* San Francisco: Jossey-Bass.

National Council of Teachers of English & The International Reading Association. (1996). *Standards for the English language arts.* Urbana, IL: National Council of Teachers of English.

Newmann, F. M., & Associates. (1996). *Authentic achievement: Restructuring schools for intellectual quality*. San Francisco: Jossey-Bass.

Nieto, S. (1996). *Affirming diversity* (second edition). New York: Longman.

Oliva, P. F. (1996). *Developing the curriculum* (fourth edition). New York: Longman.

Olser, A. (Ed.). (1996). *Development education: Global perspectives in the curriculum*. Herndon, VA: Cassell Academic.

O'Neill, J., & Kitson, N. (Eds.). (1996). *Effective curriculum management: Coordinating learning in the primary school*. New York: Routledge.

Oyler, C. (1996). *Making room for students: Sharing authority in room 104*. New York: Teachers College Press.

Passe, J. (1996). *When students choose content: A guide to increasing motivation, autonomy, and achievement*. Thousand Oaks, CA: Corwin Press.

Paulston, R. G. (Ed.). (1996). *Social cartography: Mapping the ways of seeing social and educational change*. Hamden, CT: Garland.

Payne, C. (1996). *I've got the light of freedom*. Berkeley, CA: University of California Press.

Peters, M. (1996). *Poststructuralism, politics, and education*. Westport, CT: Bergin & Garvey.

Pollard, A., Filer, A., & Theissen, D. (1996). *Children and their curriculum: The perspectives of primary and elementary school children*. Bristol, PA: Falmer.

Posner, G. J. (1996). *Field experience: A guide to reflective teaching*. New York: Longman.

Pugach, M. C., & Warger, C. L. (1996). *Curriculum trends, special education and reform: Refocusing the conversation*. New York: Teachers College Press.

Reiser, R. A., & Walker, D. (1996). *Instructional planning: A guide for teachers*. Boston: Allyn & Bacon.

Roberts, P. L., & Kellough, R. D. (1996). *A guide for developing an interdisciplinary thematic unit*. Columbus, OH: Merrill.

Robinson, R. E., & Beswick, B. A. (1996). *Success oriented schools: An educator's handbook for the 21st century*. Lanham, MD: University Press of America.

Rothlein, L., Fredericks, A. D., & Meinbach, A. M. (1996). *More thematic units for creating the integrated curriculum*. Norwood, MA: Christopher-Gordon Publishers.

Sarason, S. B. (1996). *Revisiting "The culture of the school and the problem of change."* New York: Teachers College Press.

Schmidt, P. A. (1996). *Beginning in retrospect*. New York: Teachers College Press.

Schurr, S., Lewis, S., LeMorte, K., & Shewey, K. (1996). *Signalling student success: Thematic learning stations and integrated units*. Columbus, OH: National Middle School Association.

Shor, I. (1996). *When students have power: Negotiating authority in a critical democracy.* Chicago: University of Chicago Press.

Short, K. G., Schroeder, J., Laird, J., Kaufman, G., Ferguson, M. J., & Crawford, K. M. (1996). *Learning together through inquiry: From Columbus to integrated curriculum.* York, ME: Stenhouse Publishers.

Sizer, T. R. (1996). *Horace's Hope: What works for the American school.* Boston: Houghton-Mifflin.

Sleeter, C. E. (1996). *Multicultural education as social activism.* Albany: State University of New York Press.

Sowell, E. J. (1996). *Curriculum: An integrative introduction.* Columbus, OH: Merrill.

Spodek, B., & Saracho, O. N. (Eds.). (1996). *Issues in early childhood educational assessment and evaluation: Yearbook in early childhood education.* New York: Teachers College Press.

Stainback, S., & Stainback, W. (Eds.). (1996). *Curriculum considerations in inclusive classrooms: Facilitating learning for all students.* Baltimore: P. H. Brookes.

Tchudi, S., & Levy, S. (1996). *The interdisciplinary teacher's handbook: Integrating teaching across the curriculum.* Portsmouth, NH: Boynton-Cook.

Timm, J. T. (1996). *Four perspectives in multicultural education.* Florence, KY: Wadsworth.

Uchida, D., with Cetron, M., & McKenzie, F. (1996). *Preparing students for the 21st century.* Arlington, VA: American Association of School Administrators.

van Manen, M., & Levering, B. (1996). *Childhood's secrets: Intimacy, privacy, and the self reconsidered.* New York: Teachers College Press.

Van Til, W. (1996). *My way of looking at it* (expanded second edition). San Francisco: Caddo Gap Press.

Walsh, C. E. (Ed.). (1996). *Education reform and social change.* Mahwah, NJ: Lawrence Erlbaum Associates.

Wexler, P. (1996). *Holy sparks: Social theory, education and religion.* New York: St. Martin's Press.

White, P. (1996). *Civic virtues and public schooling: Educating citizens for a democratic society.* New York: Teachers College Press.

Wood, E., & Attfield, J. (1996). *Play, learning, and the early childhood curriculum.* London: Paul Chapman.

Woods, D. (1996). *Teacher cognition in language teaching: Beliefs, decision-making, and classroom practice.* New York: Cambridge University Press.

Woods, P., & Jeffrey, B. (1996). *Teachable moments: The art of teaching in primary schools.* Bristol, PA: Open University Press.

Wortham, S. C. (1996). *The integrated classroom: The assessment-curriculum link in early childhood education.* Englewood Cliffs, NJ: Merrill.

Zeichner, K. M., & Liston, D. P. (1996). *Reflective teaching: An introduction*. Mahwah, NJ: Lawrence Erlbaum Associates.

1997

Adams, M., Bell, L., & Griffin, P. (1997). *Teaching for diversity and social justice: A sourcebook*. New York: Routledge.

American Educational Research Association. (Ed.) (1997). *The hidden consequences of a national curriculum*. Washington, D.C.: AERA.

Anyon, J. (1997). *Ghetto schooling: A political economy of urban educational reform*. New York: Teachers College Press.

Ashcroft, K., & Palacio, D. (Eds.). (1997). *Implementing the primary curriculum: A teacher's guide*. Bristol, PA: Falmer.

Ayers, W. (1997). *A kind and just parent: The children of juvenile court*. New York: Beacon Press.

Ayers, W., & Miller, J. L. (Eds.). (1997). *A light in dark times: Maxine Greene and the unfinished conversation*. New York: Teachers College Press.

Banks, J. A. (1997). *Educating citizens in a multicultural society*. New York: Teachers College Press.

Banks, J. A., & Banks, C. A. M. (1997). *Multicultural education: Issues and perspectives* (third edition). Needham Heights, MA: Allyn & Bacon.

Barreca, R., & Morse, D. D. (Eds.). (1997). *The erotics of instruction*. Hanover, NH: University of New England Press.

Beane, J. (1997). *Curriculum integration: Designing a core of democratic education*. New York: Teachers College Press.

Bennett, N., Wood, L., & Rogers, S. (1997). *Teaching through play: Teacher's thinking and classroom practice*. Philadelphia: Open University Press.

Berman, S. (1997). *Children's social consciousness and the development of social responsibility*. Albany: State University of New York Press.

Bernhardt, R., Hedley, C. N., Cattaro, G., & Svolopoulos, V. (1997). *Curriculum leadership: Rethinking schools for the 21st century*. Cresskill, NJ: Hampton Press.

Blacker, D. J. (1997). *Dying to teach: The educator's search for immortality*. New York: Teachers College Press.

Blades, D. W. (1997). *Procedures of power and curriculum change: Foucault and the quest for possibilities in science education*. New York: Peter Lang.

Blake, B. E. (1997). *She say, he say: Urban girls write their lives*. Albany: State University of New York Press.

Block, A. A. (1997). *I'm only bleeding: Education as the practice of social violence against children*. New York: Peter Lang.

Bloomer, M. (1997). *Curriculum making in post 16 education: The social conditions of studentship.* New York: Routledge.

Boisvert, R. D. (1997). *John Dewey: Rethinking our time.* Albany: State University of New York Press.

Bowers, C. A. (1997). *The culture of denial: Why the environmental movement needs a strategy for reforming universities and public schools.* Albany: State University of New York Press.

Boyer, E. (1997). *Selected speeches 1979–1995.* San Francisco: Jossey-Bass.

Bracey, G. (1997a). *Setting the record straight: Responses to misconceptions about public education in the United States.* Alexandria, VA: Association for Supervision and Curriculum Development.

Bracey, G. W. (1997b). *The truth about America's schools: The Bracey reports: 1991–1997.* Bloomington, IN: Phi Delta Kappa.

Burbules, N. C., & Hansen, D. T. (Eds.). (1997). *Teaching and its predicaments.* Boulder, CO: Westview Press.

Burden, R., & Williams, M. (Eds.). (1997). *Thinking through the curriculum.* New York: Routledge.

Burz, H. L., & Marshall, K. (1997). *Performance-based curriculum for language arts: From knowing to showing.* Thousand Oaks, CA: Corwin.

Cadwell, L. B. (1997). *Bringing Reggio Emilia home: An innovative approach to early childhood education.* New York: Teachers College Press.

Caine, R. N., & Caine, G. (1997a). *Education on the edge of possibility.* Alexandria, VA: Association for Supervision and Curriculum Development.

Caine, R. N., & Caine, G. (1997b). *Unleashing the power of perceptual change: The potential of brain based teaching.* Alexandria, VA: Association for Supervision and Curriculum Development.

Canaan, J. E., & Epstein, D. (Eds.). (1997). *A question of discipline: Pedagogy, power, and the teaching of cultural studies.* Boulder, CO: Westview.

Cannella, G. S. (1997). *Deconstructing early childhood education: Social justice and revolution.* New York: Peter Lang.

Carlson, D. (1997). *Making progress: Education and culture in new times.* New York: Teachers College Press.

Clark, E. T., Jr. (1997). *Designing and implementing an integrated curriculum: A student-centered approach.* New York: Beacon.

Clarke, J. H., & Agne, R. M. (1997). *Interdisciplinary high school teaching: Strategies for integrated learning.* Needham Heights, MA: Allyn & Bacon.

Cohen, E. G., & Lotan, R. A. (1997). *Working for equity in heterogeneous classrooms: Sociological theory in practice.* New York: Teachers College Press.

Coleman, J. S., Schneider, B., Plank, S., Shiller, K. S., Shouse, R., Wang, H., & Lee, S. (1997). *Redesigning American education*. Boulder, CO: Westview.

Comer. J. P. (1997). *Waiting for a miracle: Why schools can't solve our problems—and how we can*. New York: Dutton.

Costa, A. L., & Liebmann, R. M. (Eds.). (1997a). *The process-centered school: Sustaining a renaissance community*. New York: Corwin.

Costa, A. L., & Liebmann, R. M. (Eds.). (1997b). *Supporting the spirit of learning: When process is content*. Thousand Oaks, CA: Corwin.

Coulby, D., & Ward, S. (1997). *The primary core national curriculum* (second edition). Herndon, VA: Cassell.

Courts, P. L. (1997). *Multicultural literacies: Dialect, discourse, and diversity*. New York: Peter Lang.

Crompton, R., & Mann, P. (Eds.). (1997). *IT across the primary curriculum*. Herndon, VA: Cassell.

Cummins, J., & Sayers, D. (1997). *Brave new schools: Challenging cultural illiteracy through global learning networks*. New York: St. Martin's Press.

Curtis, A. (1997). *A curriculum for the pre-school child*. New York: Routledge.

Darling-Hammond, L. (1997). *The right to learn: A blueprint for school reform*. San Francisco: Jossey-Bass.

Davidman, L., & Davidman, P. T. (1997). *Teaching with a multicultural perspective: A practical guide* (second edition). New York: Longman.

Davis, M., Hawley, P., McMullan, B., & Spilka, G. (1997). *Design as a catalyst for learning*. Alexandria, VA: Association for Supervision and Curriculum Development.

De Castell, S., & Bryson, M. (Eds.). (1997). *Radical in(ter)ventions: Identity, politics, and differences in educational praxis*. Albany: State University of New York Press.

Delisle, R. (1997). *How to use problem based learning in the classroom*. Alexandria, VA: Association for Supervision and Curriculum Development.

Derman-Sparks, L., & Phillips, C. B. (1997). *Teaching/learning anti-racism: A developmental approach*. New York: Teachers College Press.

Diamond, R. M. (1997). *Designing and assessing courses and curricula: A practical guide* (revised edition). San Francisco, CA: Jossey-Bass.

Dijkstra, S., & Tennyson, R. D. (1997). *Instructional design: Theory, research, and models, Vol. 1*. Mahwah, NJ: Lawrence Erlbaum Associates.

Dillard, J., & Maguire, M. (Eds). (1997). *Becoming a teacher: Issues in secondary teaching*. Philadelphia: Open University Press.

Doyle, D. P., & Pimentel, S. (1997). *Raising the standard: An eight-step action guide for school and communities*. Thousand Oaks, CA: Corwin.

Duckworth, E., and the Experienced Teachers Group. (1997). *Teacher to teacher: Learning from each other*. New York: Teachers College Press.

Egan, K. (1997). *The educated mind: How cognitive tools shape our understanding*. Chicago: University of Chicago Press.

Elias, M. J., et al. (1997). *Promoting social and emotional learning: Guidelines for educators*. Alexandria, VA: Association for Supervision and Curriculum Development.

Elliott, J. (1997). *The curriculum experiment: Meeting the challenge of social change*. Philadelphia: Open University Press.

Ellsworth, E. (1997). *Teaching positions: Difference, pedagogy, and the power of address*. New York: Teachers College Press.

Fine, M., Weis, L., Powell, L. C., & Mun Wong, L. (Eds.). (1997). *Off white: Readings on race, power, and society*. New York: Routledge.

Flinders, D. J., & Thornton, S. J. (Eds.). (1997). *The curriculum studies reader*. New York: Routledge.

Fraser, J. (1997). *Reading, writing and justice: School reform as if democracy mattered*. Albany: State University of New York Press.

Freire, P. (1997). *Teachers as cultural workers: Letters to those who dare teach*. Boulder, CO: Westview Press.

Freire, P., with Fraser, J. W., Macedo, D., McKinnon, T., & Stokes, W. T. (Eds.). (1997). *Mentoring the mentor: A critical dialogue with Paulo Freire*. New York: Peter Lang.

Gaff, J. G., & Ratcliff, J. L. (Eds.). (1997). *Handbook of the undergraduate curriculum: A comprehensive guide to purposes, structures, practices, and change*. San Francisco: Jossey-Bass.

Gallas, K. (1997). *"Sometimes I can be anything": Power, gender and identity in a primary classroom*. New York: Teachers College Press.

Garrison, J. (1997). *Dewey and eros: Wisdom and desire in the art of teaching*. New York: Teachers College Press.

Giroux, H. A. (1997a). *Channel surfing: Racism, the media, and the destruction of today's youth*. New York: St. Martin's Press.

Giroux, H. A. (1997b). *Pedagogy and the politics of hope: Theory, culture, and schooling*. Boulder, CO: Westview Press.

Giroux, H. A., with Shannon, P. (Eds.). (1997). *Education and cultural studies: Toward a performative practice*. New York: Rotuledge.

Glasgow, N. A. (1997). *New curriculum for new times: A guide to student-centered, problem-based learning*. Thousand Oaks, CA: Corwin.

Glatthorn, A. A. (1997). *The principal as curriculum leader: Shaping what is taught and tested*. Thousand Oaks, CA: Corwin.

Glickman, C. (1997). *Revolutionizing America's schools*. San Francisco: Jossey-Bass.

Goldstein, L. S. (1997). *Teaching with love: A feminist approach to early childhood education*. New York: Peter Lang.

Goodlad, J. I. (1997). *In praise of education*. New York: Teachers College Press.

Goodlad, J. I., & McMannon, T. J. (Eds.). (1997). *The public purpose of education and schooling*. San Francisco: Jossey-Bass.

Goodson, I. (1997). *The changing curriculum: Studies in social construction*. New York: Peter Lang.

Goodson, I., with Anstead, C., & Morgan, J. M. (1997). *Subject knowledge: Readings for the study of school subjects*. Hamden, CT: Falmer.

Greer, W. D. (1997). *Art as a basic: The reformation in art education*. Bloomington, IN: Phi Delta Kappa.

Griffiths, M., & Tennyson, C. (1997). *The extended curriculum: Meeting the needs of young people*. London: D. Fulton.

Gross, P. (1997). *Joint curriculum design: Facilitating learner ownership and active participation in secondary classrooms*. Mahwah, NJ: Lawrence Erlbaum Associates.

Guskey, T. R. (1997). *Implementing mastery learning* (second edition). Florence, KY: Wadsworth.

Halpern, D. F. (1997). *Critical thinking across the curriculum: A brief edition of thought and knowledge*. Mahwah, NJ: Lawrence Erlbaum Associates.

Hargreaves, A. (Ed.). (1997). *Rethinking educational change with heart and mind*. Alexandria, VA: Association for Supervision and Curriculum Development.

Hart, C. H., Burts, D. C., & Charlesworth, R. (Eds.). (1997). *Integrated curriculum and developmentally appropriate practice: Birth to age eight*. Albany: State University of New York Press.

Hayemore-Sandholtz, J., Ringstaff, C., & Dwyer, D. C. (1997). *Teaching with technology: Creating student centered classrooms*. New York: Teachers College Press.

Helsby, G., & McCullough, G. (Eds.). (1997). *Teachers and the national curriculum*. Herndon, VA: Cassell.

Hendrick, J. (Ed.). (1997). *First steps toward teaching the Reggio way*. Upper Saddle River, NJ: Merrill.

Hernandez, A. (1997). *Pedagogy, democracy, and feminism: Rethinking the public sphere*. Albany: State University of New York Press.

Hirsch, E. D., & Holdren, J. (Eds.). (1997). *What your first grader needs to know: Fundamentals of a good first grade education* (revised). New York: Delta Tradebooks.

Holzman, L. (1997). *Schools for growth: Radical alternatives to current educational models*. Mahwah, NJ: Lawrence Erlbaum Associates.

Hurd,. P. D. (1997). *Inventing science education for the new millennium.* New York: Teachers College Press.

Isenberg, J. P., & Jalongo, M. R. (1997). *Creative expression and play in the early childhood curriculum* (second edition) Upper Saddle River, NJ: Merrill.

Jacobs, H. H. (1997). *Mapping the big picture: Integrating curriculum and assessment K–12.* Alexandria, VA: Association for Supervision and Curriculum Development.

jagodzinski, j. (1997a). *Pun(k) deconstruction: Experifigural writings in art and art education.* Mahwah, NJ: Lawrence Erlbaum Associates.

jagodzinski, j. (1997b) *Outrageous essays in art and art education.* Mahwah, NJ: Lawrence Erlbaum Associates.

Joyce, B., Calhoun, E., & Hopkins, D. (1997). *Models of learning — Tools for teaching.* Buckingham, UK: Open University Press.

Kanpol, B. (1997a). *Issues and trends in critical pedagogy.* Cresskill, NJ: Hampton Press.

Kanpol, B. (1997b). *Teachers talking back and breaking bread.* Cresskill, NJ: Hampton Press.

Kelly, U. A. (1997). *Schooling desire: Literacy, cultural politics, and pedagogy.* New York: Routledge.

Kendall, J. S., & Marzano, R. J. (1997). *Content knowledge: A compendium of standards and benchmarks for K–12 education* (second edition). Alexandria, VA: Association for Supervision and Curriculum Development.

Kimbell, R. (1997). *Assessing technology: International trends in curriculum and assessment UK — USA — Germany — Taiwan — Australia.* Bristol, PA: Open University Press.

Kincheloe, J. L., & Steinberg, S. R. (1997). *Changing multiculturalism: New times, new curriculum.* Bristol, PA: Open University Press.

King, J. E., Hollins, E. R., & Hayman, W. C. (Eds.). (1997). *Preparing teachers for cultural diversity.* New York: Teachers College Press.

Labaree, D. F. (1997). *How to succeed in school without really learning: The credentials race in American education.* New Haven, CT: Yale University Press.

Lankshear, C. (1997). *Changing literacies.* Bristol, PA: Open University Press.

Lather, P., & Smithies, C. (1997). *Troubling the angels: Women living with HIV/AIDS.* Boulder, CO: Westview. (Earlier edition self-published in Columbus, OH: Greyden Press, 1995).

Lawton, D. (1997). *Beyond the national curriculum: Teacher professionalism and empowerment.* London: Hodder and Stoughton.

Lipkin, A. (1997). *Homosexuality and schools: Staff curriculum and student development.* Boulder, CO: Westview.

Logan, K. M. (1997). *Getting the schools you want: A step-by-step guide to conducting your own curriculum management audit.* Thousand Oaks, CA: Corwin.

Marciano, J. (1997). *Civic illiteracy and education: The battle for the hearts and minds of American youth*. New York: Peter Lang.

Markee, N. (1997). *Managing curriculum innovation*. New York: Cambridge University Press.

Marsh, C. J. (1997a). *Perspectives: Key concepts for understanding curriculum, Vol 1*. New York: Falmer Press.

Marsh, C. J. (1997b). *Planning, management, and ideology: Key concepts for understanding curriculum, Vol. 2* (revised and extended). London: Falmer Press.

Marton, F., & Booth, S. (1997). *Learning and awareness*. Mahwah, NJ: Lawrence Erlbaum Associates.

McCarthy, C. (1997). *The uses of culture: Education and the limits of ethnic affiliation*. New York: Routledge.

McCombs, B. L., & Whisler, J. S. (1997). *The learner-centered classroom and school: Strategies for increasing student motivation and achievement*. San Francisco: Jossey-Bass.

McLaren, P. (1997). *Revolutionary multiculturalism: Pedagogies of dissent for the new millennium*. Boulder, CO: Westview Press.

McTaggart, R. (Ed.). (1997). *Participatory action research: International contexts and consequences*. Albany: State University of New York Press.

Mee, C. (1997). *2,000 Voices: Young adolescents' perceptions and curriculum implications*. Columbus, OH: National Middle School Association.

Meier, D. (1997). *Learning in small moments: Life in an urban classroom*. New York: Teachers College Press.

Middleton, S. (1997). *Disciplining sexuality: Foucault, life histories, and education*. New York: Teachers College Press.

Molnar, A. (Ed.). (1997). *The construction of children's character. The ninety-sixth yearbook of the National Society for the Study of Education, part 2*. Chicago: University of Chicago Press.

Morey, A. I., & Kintano, M. (Eds.). (1997). *Multicultural course transformation in higher education: A broader truth*. Boston MA: Allyn & Bacon.

Morgan, W. (1997). *Critical literacy in the classroom: The art of the possible*. New York: Routledge.

Nehring, J. (1997). *The school within us: The creation of an innovative public school*. Albany: State University of New York Press.

Neumann, A., & Peterson, P. L. (Eds.). (1997). *Learning from our lives: Women, research, and autobiography in education*. New York: Teachers College Press.

Newman, F., & Holzman, L. (1997). *The end of knowing: A new developmental way of learning*. New York: Routledge.

Noya, G. C., Geismar, K., & Nicoleau, G. (Eds.). (1997). *Shifting histories: Transforming schools for social change.* Cambridge, MA: Harvard Educational Review.

Oldenski, T. (1997). *Liberation theology and critical pedagogy in today's Catholic schools.* Hamden, CT: Garland.

Oliva, P. F. (1997). *Developing the curriculum* (fourth edition). New York: Longman.

Padilla, F. M. (1997). *The struggle of latino/latina university students.* New York: Routledge.

Parker, S. (1997). *Reflective teaching in the postmodern world. A manifesto for education in postmodernity.* Bristol, PA: Open University Press.

Parker, W. C., & Jarolimek, J. (1997). *Social studies in elementary education.* Columbus, OH: Merrill.

Pate, E. P., Homestead, E. R., & McGinnis, K. L. (1997). *Making integrated curriculum work: Teachers, students and the quest for coherent curriculum.* New York: Teachers College Press.

Penn, A., & Williams, D. (1997). *Integrating academic and vocational education: A model for secondary schools.* Alexandria, VA: Association for Supervision and Curriculum Development.

Posner, G. J., & Rudnitsky, A. N. (1997). *Course design: A guide to curriculum development for teachers* (fifth edition). New York: Longman.

Post, T. R., Ellis, A. K., Humphreys, A. F., & Bugget, L. J. (1997). *Interdisciplinary approaches to curriculum: Themes of teaching.* Columbus, OH: Merrill.

Reeher, G., & Cammarano, J. (Eds.). (1997). *Education for citizenship: Ideas and innovations in political learning.* Lanham, MD: Rowman and Littlefield.

Reinhartz, J., & Beach, D. M. (1997). *Teaching and learning in the elementary school: Focus on curriculum.* Columbus, OH: Prentice-Hall.

Roman, L. G., & Eyre, L. (1997). *Dangerous territories: Struggles for difference and equality in education.* New York: Routledge.

Ross, E. W. (1997). *The social studies curriculum: Purposes, problems and possibilities.* Albany: State University of New York Press.

Rummel, M. K., & Quintero, E. P. (1997). *Teachers' reading/Teachers' lives.* Albany: State University of New York Press.

Sandholtz, J. H., Ringstaff, C., & Dwyer, D. C. (1997). *Teaching with technology: Creating student-centered classrooms.* New York: Teachers College Press.

Schickedanz, J. A., Pergantis, M. L., Kanosky, J., Blaney, A., & Ottinger, J. (1997). *Curriculum in early education: A resource guide for preschool and kindergarten teachers.* Needham Heights, MA: Allyn & Bacon.

Schine, J. (Ed.). (1997). *Service learning. Ninety-sixth yearbook of the National Society for the Study of Education, Part I.* Chicago: University of Chicago Press.

Schiro, M. (1997). *Integrating children's literature and mathematics in the classroom.* New York: Teachers College Press.

Schlechty, P. C. (1997). *Inventing better schools: An active plan for educational reform.* San Francisco: Jossey-Bass.

Schmidt, W. H. (Ed.). (1997). *Many visions, many aims.* Boston: Kluwer.

Schutz, R. (1997). *Interpreting teacher practice: Two continuing stories.* New York: Teachers College Press.

Sehr, D. T. (1997). *Education for public democracy.* Albany: State University of New York Press.

Sellar, M., & Weis, L. (Eds.). (1997). *Beyond black and white.* Albany: State University of New York Press.

Shambaugh, R. N., & Magliaro, S. G. (1997). *Mastering the possibilities: A process approach to instructional design.* Boston: Allyn & Bacon.

Simpson, D., & Jackson, M. J. B. (1997). *Educational reform: A Deweyan perspective.* Hamden, CT: Garland.

Stark, J. S., & Lattuca, L. R. (1997). *Shaping the college curriculum: Academic plans in action.* Boston: Allyn & Bacon.

Steinberg, S. R., & Kincheloe, J. L. (Eds.). (1997). *Kinderculture: The corporate construction of childhood.* Boulder, CO: Westview Press.

Stephenson, J., Ling, L., Burman, E., & Cooper, M. (Eds.). (1997). *Values in education.* New York: Routledge.

Tanner, L. N. (1997). *Dewey's laboratory school: Lessons for today.* New York: Teachers College Press.

Taylor, G. R. (1997). *Curriculum strategies: Social skills intervention for young African-American males.* Westport, CT: Praeger.

Theobald, P. (1997). *Teaching the commons: Place, pride, and the renewal of community.* Boulder, CO: Westview.

Todd, S. (Ed.). (1997). *Learning desire: Perspectives on pedagogy, culture, and the unsaid.* New York: Routledge.

Tom, A. (1997). *Redesigning teacher education.* Albany: State University of New York Press.

Tompkins, J. (1997). *A life in school: What the teacher learned.* Boulder, CO: Perseus.

Torres, C. A. (1997). *Education, power, and personal biography: Dialogues with personal educators.* New York: Routledge.

Torres, C. A., & Puiggros, A. (Eds.). (1997). *Latin American education: Comparative perspectives.* Boulder, CO: Westview.

Trend, D. (1997). *Cultural democracy: Politics, media, new technology.* Albany: State University of New York Press.

Walberg, H. J., Reyes, O., & Weissberg, R. P. (Eds.). (1997). *Children and youth: Interdisciplinary perspectives.* Thousand Oaks, CA: Sage.

Walker, D. F., & Soltis, J. F. (1997). *Curriculum and aims* (third edition). New York: Teachers College Press.

Walling, D. R. (Ed.). (1997). *Under construction: The role of the arts and humanities in postmodern schooling.* Bloomington, IN: Phi Delta Kappa.

Wasley, P. A., Hampel, R. L., & Clark, R.W. (1997). *Kids and school reform.* San Francisco: Jossey-Bass.

Weber, L. (1997). *Looking back and thinking forward: Reexaminations of teaching and schooling.* (Beth Alberty, Ed.). New York: Teachers College Press.

Webster, Y. O. (1997). *Against the multicultural agenda: A critical thinking alternative.* Westport, CT: Greenwood.

White, J. (1997). *Education and the end of work.* Herndon, VA: Cassell.

White, R. C. (1997). *Curriculum innovation: A celebration of classroom practice.* Bristol, PA: Open University Press.

Wink, J. (1997). *Critical pedagogy: Notes from the real world.* New York: Longman.

Wolfinger, D. M., & Stockard, J. W. (1997). *Elementary methods: An integrated curriculum.* New York: Longman.

Wood, K. E. (1997). *Interdisciplinary instruction: A practical guide for elementary and middle school teachers.* Columbus, OH: Merrill.

Wragg, T. (1997a). *Assessment and learning.* New York: Routledge.

Wragg, T. (1997b). *The cubic curriculum.* New York: Routledge.

Wynne, E., & Ryan, R. (1997). *Reclaiming our schools: A handbook on teaching, character, academics, and discipline* (second edition). Columbus, OH: Merrill.

1998

Adams, N. G, Shea, C. M., Liston, D., & Deever, B. (1998). *Learning to teach: A critical approach to field experiences.* Mahwah, NJ: Lawrence Erlbaum Associates.

Allen, D. (1998). *Assessing student learning: From grading to understanding.* New York: Teachers College Press.

Alvermann, D. E., Hinchman, K. A., Moore, D. W., Phelps, S. F., & Waff, D. R. (Eds.). (1998). *Reconceptualizing the literacies in adolescents' lives.* Mahwah, NJ: Lawrence Erlbaum Associates.

Armstrong, T. (1998). *Awakening genius in the classroom.* Alexandria, VA: Association for Supervision and Curriculum Development.

Association for Supervision and Curriculum Development. (1998). *Curriculum software: Only the best, 1998–99.* Alexandria, VA: Author.

Atwell, N. (1998). *In the middle: New understandings about writing, reading, and learning* (second edition). Westport, CT: Boynton & Cook.

Atwell-Vasey, W. (1998). *Nourishing words: Bridging private reading and public teaching.* Albany: State University of New York Press.

Ayers, W., Hunt, J. A. & Quinn, T. (Eds.). (1998). *Teaching for social justice: A democracy and education reader.* New York: Teachers College Press.

Bartolomé, L. I. (1998). *The misteaching of academic discourses: The politics of language in the classroom.* Boulder, CO: Westview.

Barton, A. B. (1998). *Feminist science education.* New York: Teachers College Press.

Bearne, E. (1998). *Use of language across the primary curriculum.* New York: Routledge.

Beineke, J. A. (1998). *And there were giants in the land: The life of William Heard Kilpatrick.* New York: Peter Lang.

Benson, G., Glasberg, R., & Griffith, B. (Eds.). (1998). *Perspectives on the unity and integration of knowledge.* New York: Peter Lang.

Beyer, L. E., & Apple, M. W. (Eds.). (1998). *The curriculum: Problems, politics, and possibilities* (second edition). Albany: State University of New York Press.

Blake, N., Smeyers, P., Smith, R., & Standish, P. (1998). *Thinking again: Education after postmodernism.* Westport, CT: Bergin & Garvey.

Books, S. (Ed.). (1998). *Invisible children in the society and its schools.* Mahwah, NJ: Lawrence Erlbaum Associates.

Bradbeer, J. (1998). *Imagining curriculum: Practical intelligence in teaching.* New York: Teachers College Press.

Brandt, R. (1998). *Powerful learning.* Alexandria, VA: Association for Supervision and Curriculum Development.

Briggs, D. (1998). *A class of their own: When children teach children.* Westport, CT: Bergin & Garvey.

Brine, J. (1998). *(Under)educating women: Globalizing inequality.* Bristol, PA: Open University Press.

Britzman, D. P. (1998). *Lost subjects, contested objects: Toward a pschoanalytic inquiry of learning.* Albany: State University of New York Press.

Bromley, H., & Apple, M. (Eds.). (1998). *Education/technology/power: Educational computing as a social practice.* Albany: State University of New York Press.

Brown, D. (1998). *Schools with heart: Voluntarism and public education.* Boulder, CO: Westview.

Burlbaw, L. M. (Ed.). (1998). *Curriculum history 1998.* College Station, TX: Society for the Study of Curriculum History.

Carlson, D., & Apple, M. (Eds.). (1998). *Power/knowledge/pedagogy: The meaning of democratic education in unsettling times*. Boulder, CO: Westview.

Carreiro, P. (1998). *Tales of thinking: Multiple intelligences in the classroom*. York, ME: Stenhouse Publishers.

Cary, R. (1998). *Critical art pedagogy: Foundations for postmodern art education*. Levittown, PA: Falmer.

Chavez Chavez, R., & O'Donnell, J. (Eds.). (1998). *Speaking the unpleasant: The politics of (non)engagement in the multicultural education terrain*. Albany: State University of New York Press.

Christian-Smith, L., & Kellor, K. (1998). *Everyday knowledge and uncommon truths: Life writings and women's experiences in and outside the academy*. Boulder, CO: Westview.

Clark, A., & Millard, E. (Eds.). (1998). *Gender in the secondary curriculum: Balancing the books*. New York: Routledge.

Cohee, G. E., Daumer, E., Kemp, T. D., Krebs, P. M., Lafky, S., & Runzo, S. (Eds.). (1998). *The feminist teacher anthology*. NewYork: Teachers College Press.

Cohen, A. M. (1998). *The shaping of American higher education: Emergence and growth of the contemporary system*. San Francisco: Jossey-Bass.

Connolly, P. (1998). *Racism, gender identities, and young children*. New York: Routledge.

Darder, A., Torres, R. D., & Gutierrez, H. (Eds.). (1998). *Latinos and education: A critical reader*. New York: Routledge.

Daspit, T., & Weaver, J. A. (Eds.). (1998). *Popular culture and critical pedagogy: Reading, constructing, connecting*. New York: Falmer.

DeRoche, E. F., & Williams, M. M. (1998). *Educating hearts and minds: A comprehensive character education framework*. Thousand Oaks, CA: Corwin.

Dore, R. P., & Sako, M. (1998). *How the Japanese learn to work* (second edition). New York: Routledge.

Drake, S. M. (1998). *Creating integrated curriculum: Proven ways to increase student learning*. Thousand Oaks, CA: Corwin.

Edgington, M., Fisher, J., Morgan, M., Pound, L., & Scott, W. (1998). *Interpreting the national curriculum at key stage 1: A developmental approach*. Buckingham, England: Open University Press.

Eidson, C. B., & Hillhouse, E. D. (1998). *The accelerated high school: A step by step guide for administrators and teachers*. Thousand Oaks, CA: Corwin.

Eisner, E. W. (1998). *The kind of schools we need: Personal essays*. Westport, CT: Heinemann.

Elliott, J. (1998). *The curriculum experiment: Meeting the challenge of social change*. Bristol, PA: Open University Press.

Ellis, A. K., & Stuen, C. J. (1998). *The interdisciplinary curriculum*. Larchmont, NY: Eye on Education.

Epstein, D., Elwood, J., Hey, V., & Maw, J. (Eds.). (1998). *Failing boys? Issues in gender and achievement*. Bristol, PA: Open University Press.

Epstein, D., & Johnson, R. (1998). *Schooling sexualities*. Bristol, PA: Open University Press.

Erickson, H. L. (1998). *Concept based curriculum and instruction*. Thousand Oaks, CA: Corwin.

Esteva, G., & Prakash, M. (1998). *Grassroots postmodernism: Remaking the soil of cultures*. New York: ZED Books, distributed by St. Martin's Press.

Feinberg, W. (1998). *Common schools/Uncommon identities*. New Haven, CT: Yale University Press.

Fishman, S. M., & McCarthy, L. (1998). *John Dewey and the challenge of classroom practice*. New York: Teachers College Press.

Florence, N. (1998). *bell hooks' engaged pedagogy: A transgressive education for critical consciousness*. Westport, CT: Bergin & Garvey.

Fogarty, R., & Bellanca, J. (1998). *Multiple intelligences: A collection*. Needham Heights, MA: Allyn & Bacon.

Foriska, T. J. (1998). *Restructuring around standards: A practitioner's guide to design and implementation*. Thousand Oaks, CA: Corwin.

Franklin, B. M. (1998). *When children don't learn: Student failure and the culture of teaching*. New York: Teachers College Press.

Freedman, K., & Hernandez, F. (Eds.). (1998). *Curriculum, culture, and art education: Comparative perspectives*. Albany: State University of New York Press.

Freeland, K., & Hammons, K. (1998). *Curriculum for integrated learning: A lesson-based approach*. Albany, NY: Delmar.

Freire, A. M. A., & Macedo, D. (Eds.). (1998). *The Paulo Freire reader*. New York: Continuum.

Freire, P. (1998a). *Pedagogy of freedom: Ethics, democracy, and civic courage*. Lanham, MD: Rowman and Littlefield.

Freire, P. (1998b). *Pedagogy of the heart*. New York: Continuum.

Freire, P., & Macedo, D. (1998). *Ideology matters*. Lanham, MD: Rowman and Littlefield.

George, P. S., Lawrence, G. D., & Bushnell, D. L. (1998). *Handbook of middle school teaching* (second edition). New York: Longman.

Gibboney, R. A., & Webb, C. D. (1998). *What every great teacher knows: Practical principles for effective teaching*. Brandon, VT: Holistic Education Press.

Giroux, H. A. (1998). *Learning with Disney: Youth, commerce, and the construction of culture*. Lanham, MD: Rowman and Littlefield.

Glickman, C. (1998). *Supervision of instruction* (fourth edition). San Francisco: Jossey-Bass.

Goodman, K. S. (1998). (Ed.). *In defense of good teaching: What teachers need to know about the "reading wars."* York, ME: Stenhouse Publishers.

Graves, K. (1998). *Girl's schooling during the progressive era: From female scholar to domesticated citizen.* New York: Falmer.

Grenfell, M., & James, D. (1998). *Bourdieu and education: Acts of practical theory.* New York: Falmer.

Gross, S. J. (1998). *Staying centered: Curriculum leadership in a turbulent era.* Alexandria, VA: Association for Supervision and Curriculum Development.

Gundem, B. B., & Hopmann, S. (Eds.). (1998). *Didaktik and/or curriculum.* New York: Peter Lang.

Hargreaves, A., & Fullan, M. (1998). *What's worth fighting for out there?* New York: Teachers College Press.

Harris, J. (1998). *Design tools for the internet-supported classroom.* Alexandria VA: Association for Supervision and Curriculum Development.

Hauenstein, A. D. (1998). *A conceptual framework for educational objectives: A holistic approach to traditional taxonomies.* Lanham, MD: University Press of America.

Haw, K. (1998). *Educating Muslim girls: Shifting discourses.* Bristol, PA: Open University Press.

Hein, G. E. (1998). *Learning in the museum.* New York: Routledge.

Hendrick, J. (1998). *Total learning: Developmental curriculum for the young child* (fifth edition). Upper Saddle River, NJ: Merrill.

Henkin, R. (1998). *Who's invited to share? Using literacy to teach for equity and social justice.* New York: St. Martin's Press.

Henry, A. (1998). *Taking back control: African Canadian women, teachers' lives and practice.* Albany: State University of New York Press.

Hinchley, P. H. (1998). *Finding freedom in the classroom: A practical introduction to critical theory.* New York: Peter Lang.

Hutchison, D. (1998). *Growing up green: Education for ecological renewal.* New York: Teachers College Press.

Jackson, P. W. (1998). *John Dewey and the lessons of art.* New Haven, CT: Yale University Press.

Jardine, D. W. (1998). *To dwell with a boundless heart: Essays in curriculum theory, hermeneutics, and the ecological imagination.* New York: Peter Lang.

Jensen, E. (1998). *Teaching with the brain in mind.* Alexandria, VA: Association for Supervision and Curriculum Development.

Kemp, J. E., Morrison, G., & Ross, S. M. (1998). *Designing effective instruction* (second edition). Upper Saddle River, NJ: Merrill.

Kenway, J., Blackmore, J., Willis, S., & Rennie, L. (1998). *Answering back*. New York: Routledge.

Kincheloe, J. (1998). *How do we tell the workers? The socioeconomic foundations of work and vocational education*. Boulder, CO: Westview.

Kincheloe, J., & Steinberg, S. (Eds.). (1998a). *Cutting class: Social class and education*. Lanham, MD: Rowman and Littlefield.

Kincheloe, J., & Steinberg, S. (Eds.). (1998b). *Unauthorized methods: Strategies for critical thinking*. New York: Routledge.

Kincheloe, J., Steinberg, S., Rodriguez, N. M., & Chennault, R. E. (1998). *White reign: Deploying whiteness in America*. New York: St. Martin's Press.

Kohl, H. (1998). *The discipline of hope: Learning from a lifetime of teaching*. New York: Simon and Schuster.

Kohn, A. (1998). *What to look for in a classroom...and other essays*. San Francisco: Jossey-Bass.

Kraus Curriculum Development Library. (1998). *Curriculum finder: KCDL's annotated guide for grades P through 12*. Lanham, MD: Bernan Associates.

Kridel, C. (1998). *Writing educational biography: Explorations in qualitative research*. Levittown, PA: Garland.

LaSpina, J. A. (1998). *The visual turn and the transformation of the textbook*. Mahwah, NJ: Lawrence Erlbaum Asscociates.

Laura, R. S., & Cotton, M. C. (1998). *New foundations for an environmental education: An ecological approach*. Hamden, CT: Falmer Press.

Leistyna, P. (1998). *Presence of mind: Education and the politics of deception*. Boulder, CO: Westview.

Lemlech, J. K. (1998). *Curriculum and instructional methods for the elementary school* (fourth edition). Columbus, OH: Merrill.

Lewin, L., & Shoemaker, B. J. (1998). *Great performances: Creating classroom-based assessment tasks*. Alexandria, VA: Association for Supervision and Curriculum Development.

Lipka, J., Mohatt, G. V., & The Cuilistet Group. (1998). *Transforming the culture of schools: Yupik Eskimo examples*. Mahwah, NJ: Lawrence Erlbaum Associates.

Lipka, R., Lounsbury, J., Toepfer, C., Vars, G., Allessi, S., & Kridel, C. (1998). *The eight year study revisited: Lessons from the past for the present*. Columbus, OH: National Middle School Association.

Lockwood, A. T. (1998). *Standards: From policy to practice*. Thousand Oaks, CA: Corwin.

Lybarger, M. B. (1998). *Origins of the social studies curriculum: An essay in archeology of ideas*. New York: Peter Lang.

May, S. (Ed.). (1998). *Towards critical multiculturalism*. Hamden, CT: Falmer.

McAfee, W. M. (1998). *Religion, race, and reconstruction: The public school in the politics of the 1870s*. Albany: State University of New York Press.

McDermott, J. C. (Ed.). (1998). *Beyond the silence: Listening for democracy*. Westport, CT: Heinemann.

McLaren, P. (1998). *Life in schools: An introduction to critical pedagogy in the foundations of education* (third edition). New York: Longman.

McNeil, L. (1998). *Missing a voice: Critical pedagogy and the possibilities of democratic teaching*. Boulder, CO: Westview.

Mercogliano, C. (1998). *Making it up as we go along: The story of the Albany free school*. Westport, CT: Heinemann.

Middleton, S., & Weller, K. (Eds.). (1998). *Telling women's lives: Narrative inquiries in the history of women's education*. Bristol, PA: Open University Press.

Moyles, J. R., & Hargreaves, L. (Eds.). (1998). *The primary curriculum: Learning from international perspectives*. New York: Routledge.

Munro, P. (1998). *Subject to fiction: Women teachers' life history narratives and the cultural politics of resistance*. Bristol, PA: Open University Press.

Nash, R. J. (1998). *Faith, hype, and clarity: Teaching about religion in American schools and colleges*. New York: Teachers College Press.

Newman, J. M. (1998). *Tensions of teaching*. New York: Teachers College Press.

Nord, W. A., & Haynes, C. C. (1998). *Taking religion seriously across the curriculum*. Alexandria, VA: Association for Supervision and Curriculum Development.

Novello, M. K. (1998). *All the wrong reasons: The story behind government schools*. Lanham, MD: University Press of America.

O'Cadiz, P., Wong, P. L., & Torres, C. A. (1998). *Education and democracy: Paulo Freire, social movements, and educational reform in Sao Paulo*. Boulder, CO: Westview.

O'Neill, J., & Willis, S. (Eds.). (1998). *Revitalizing the disciplines: The best of ASCD's curriculum update*. Alexandria, VA: Association for Supervision and Curriculum Development.

Ornstein, A. C., & Hunkins, F. P. (1998). *Curriculum: Foundations, principles, and issues* (third edition). Boston: Allyn & Bacon.

Palmer, J. (1998). *Environmental education in the 21st century: Theory, practice, progress, and promise*. New York: Routledge.

Palmer, P. (1998). *The courage to teach: Exploring the inner landscape of a teacher's life*. San Francisco: Jossey-Bass.

Peltzman, B. R. (1998). *Pioneers of early childhood education: A bio-bibliographical guide*. Westport, CT: Greenwood.

Perry, T., & Delpit, L. (1998). *The real ebonics debate: Power, language and the education of African-American children*. New York: Ballantine.

Peters, M. (1998). *Naming the multiple: Poststructuralism and education*. Westport, CT: Bergin & Garvey.

Pinar, W. (Ed.). (1998a). *Curriculum: Toward new identities*. Levittown, PA: Garland.

Pinar, W. (Ed.). (1998b). *The passionate mind of Maxine Greene: "I am...not yet."* Hamden, CT: Falmer.

Pinar, W. (Ed.) (1998c). *Queer theory in education*. Mahwah, NJ: Lawrence Erlbaum Associates.

Popkewitz, T. S. (1998). *Struggling for the soul: The politics of schooling and the construction of the teacher*. New York: Teachers College Press.

Popkewitz, T. S., & Brennan, M. (Eds.). (1998). *Foucault's challenge: Discourse, knowledge, and power in education*. New York: Teachers College Press.

Provenzo, E. F., Brett, A., & McCloskey, G. N. (1998). *Computers, curriculum, and cultural change: An introduction for teachers*. Mahwah, NJ: Lawrence Erlbaum Associates.

Proweller, A. (1998). *Constructing female identities: Meaning making in an upper middle class youth culture*. Albany: State University of New York Press.

Ramsey, P. G. (1998). *Teaching and learning in a diverse world: Multicultural education for young children*. New York: Teachers College Press.

Reid, W. A. (1998). *Curriculum as institution and practice: Essays in the deliberative tradition*. Mahwah, NJ: Lawrence Erlbaum Associates.

Roberts, D. A., & Ostman, L. (Eds.). (1998). *Problems of meaning in science curriculum*. New York: Teachers College Press.

Roberts, T., & The staff of the National Paideia Center. (1998). *The power of the paideia schools: Defining lives through learning*. Alexandria, VA: Association for Supervision and Curriculum Development.

Rohlen, T., & Bjork, C. (1998). *Education and training in Japan* (Three volumes). New York: Routledge.

Ropers-Huilman, B. (1998). *Feminist teaching in theory and practice: Situating power and knowledge in post-structural classrooms*. New York: Teachers College Press.

Ross, A. (1998). *Curriculum construction and critique*. Bristol, PA: Falmer.

Rosser, C. P. (1993). *Planning activities for child care: A curriculum guide for early childhood education* (second edition). South Holland, IL: Goodheart-Willcox.

Schwarz, G., & Alberts, J. (1998). *Teacher lore and professional development for school reform*. Westport, CT: Bergin & Garvey.

Searle, C. (1998). *None but our words: Critical literacy in classroom and community*. Bristol, PA: Open University Press.

Sears, J. T., & Carper, J. C. (Eds.). (1998). *Curriculum, religion, and public education: Conversations for an enlarging public square.* New York: Teachers College Press.

Seels, B., & Glasgow, Z. (1998). *Making instructional design,* (second edition). Upper Saddle River, NJ: Merrill.

Seller, M., & Weis, L. (1998). *Beyond black and white: New faces and voices in U.S. schools.* Albany: State University of New York Press.

Semali, L., & Pailliotet, A. W. (Eds.). (1998). *Intermediality: Teaching critical media literacy.* Boulder, CO: Westview.

Semel, S. F., & Sadovnik, A. R. (1998). *"Schools of tomorrow," schools of today: What happened to progressive education.* New York: Peter Lang.

Shannon, P. (1998). *Reading poverty.* Westport, CT: Heinemann.

Shapiro, H. S., & Purpel, D. E. (1998). *Critical social issues in American education* (second edition). Mahwah, NJ: Lawrence Erlbaum Associates.

Shapiro, S. (1998). *Pedagogy and the politics of the body.* New York: Routledge Falmer.

Sharpe, R., & Lee, J. (Eds.). (1998). *Learning and teaching the core curriculum.* Hamden, CT: Falmer.

Slavin, R. E., Madden, N. A., Dolan, L. J., & Wasik, B. A. (1998). *Every child, every school, success for all.* Thousand Oaks, CA: Corwin.

Smith, D. G. (1998). *Pedagon: Interdisciplinary essays in the human sciences, pedagogy, and culture.* New York: Peter Lang.

Smith, F. (1998). *The book of learning and forgetting.* New York: Teachers College Press.

Smith, G. A., & Williams, D. R. (Eds.). (1998). *Ecological education in action: On weaving education, culure, and the environment.* Albany: State University of New York Press.

Smith, S. (1998). *Risk and our pedagogical relation to children.* Albany: State University of New York Press.

Solomon, P. G. (1998). *The curriculum bridge: From standards to actual classroom practice.* Thousand Oaks, CA: Corwin.

Spring, J. (1998a). *American education* (eighth edition). Boston: McGraw-Hill.

Spring, J. (1998b). *Education and the rise of the global economy.* Mahwah, NJ: Lawrence Erlbaum Associates.

Sternberg, R. J., & Williams, W. (1998). *Intelligence, instruction, and assessment: Theory into practice.* Mahwah, NJ: Lawrence Erlbaum.

Theobald, P. (1998). *Teaching the commons: Place, pride, and the renewal of community.* Boulder, CO: Westview.

Torp, L., & Sage, S. (1998). *Problems as possibilities: Problem-based learning for K–12 education.* Alexandria, VA: Association for Supervision and Curriculum Development.

Torres, C. A., & Mitchell, T. R. (Eds.). (1998). *Sociology of education: Emerging perspectives*. Albany: State University of New York Press.

Tsolidis, G. (1998). *Feminist pedagogies of difference: Gender, ethnicity and schooling*. Bristol, PA: Open University Press.

Tucker, M., & Codding, J. (1998). *Standards for our schools: How to set them, measure them and reach them*. San Francisco: Jossey-Bass.

Urban, W. (Ed.). (1998). *Essays in twentieth-century Southern education: Exceptionalism and its limits*. New York: Falmer/Garland.

Villani, C. J. (1998). *A synthesized curriculum for the 21st century*. Lanham, MD: University Press of America.

Weil, D. (1998). *Towards a critical multicultural literacy: Theory and practice for education for liberation*. New York: Peter Lang.

Westheimer, J. (1998). *Among schoolteachers: Community, autonomy, and ideology in teachers' work*. New York: Teachers College Press.

Wiggins, G. P. (1998). *Educative assessment: Designing assessments to inform and improve student performance*. San Francisco: Jossey-Bass.

Wiggins, G. P., & McTighe, J. (1998). *Understanding by design*. Alexandria, VA: Association for Supervision and Curriculum Development.

Wiles, J., & Bondi, J. (1998) *Curriculum development: A guide to practice* (fifth edition). Upper Saddle River, NJ: Merrill.

Willinsky, J. (1998). *Learning to divide the world: Education at empire's end*. Minneapolis, MN: University of Minnesota Press.

Wishon, P., Crabtree, K., & Jones, M. (1998). *Curriculum for the primary years*. Upper Saddle River, NJ: Merrill.

Wolk, S. (1998). *A democratic classroom*. Westport, CT: Heinemann.

Wood, G. H. (1998). *A time to learn: The story of one high school's remarkable transformation and the people who made it happen*. New York: Dutton.

Woysner, C. A., & Gelfond, H. (Eds.). (1998). *Minding women: Reshaping the educational realm*. Cambridge, MA: Harvard Educational Review.

Young, M. F. D. (1998). *The curriculum of the future: From the new sociology of education to a critical theory of learning*. Hamden, CT: Falmer.

Zemelman, S., Daniels, H., & Hyde, A. (1998). *Best practice: New standards for teaching and learning in America's schools* (second edition). Westport, CT: Heinemann.

Zimmerman, I. K., & Hayes, M. F. (1998). *Beyond technology: Learning with the wired curriculum*. Alexandria, VA: Association for Supervision and Curriculum Development.

Zou, Y., & Trueba, E. T. (1998). *Ethnic identity and power: Cultural contexts of political action in school and society*. New York: Teachers College Press.

1999

Allen, J. (1999). *Class actions: Teaching for social justice in elementary and middle schools.* New York: Teachers College Press.

Angus, D. L., & Mirel, J. E. (1999). *The failed promise of the American high school, 1890–1995.* New York: Teachers College Press.

Apple, M. W. (1999a). *Official knowledge: Democratic education in a conservative age* (second edition). New York: Routledge.

Apple, M. W. (1999b). *Power, meaning, and identity: Essays in critical educational studies.* New York: Peter Lang.

Apple, M. W., & Beane, J. A. (Eds.). (1999). *Democractic schools: Lessons from the chalkface.* Philadelphia: Open University Press.

Arnove, R. F., & Torres, C. A. (Eds.). (1999). *Comparitive education: The dialectic of the global and the local.* Lanham, MD: Rowman and Littlefield.

Banks, J. A. (1999). *An introduction to multicultural education* (second edition). Needham Heights, MA: Allyn & Bacon.

Bass, C. (1999). *Education in Tibet: Policy and practice since 1950.* New York: St. Martin's Press.

Bearne, E. (Ed.). (1999). *Use of language across the secondary curriculum.* New York: Routledge.

Belle, D. (1999). *The after school lives of children: Alone and with others.* Mahwah, NJ: Lawrence Erlbaum Associates.

Bennett, C. I. (1999). *Comprehensive multicutural education: Theory and practice* (fourth edition). Needham Heights, MA: Allyn & Bacon.

Boler, M. (1999). *Feeling power: Emotions and education.* New York: Routledge.

Campbell, L., Campbell, B., & Dickson, D. (1999). *Teaching and learning through multiple intelligences* (second edition). Needham Heights, MA: Allyn & Bacon.

Castells, M., Flecha, R., Freire, P., Giroux, H. A., Macedo, D., & Willis, P. (1999). *Critical education in the new information age.* Lanham, MD: Rowman & Littlefield.

Chatton, B., & Collins, N. L. D. (1999). *Blurring the edges: Integrated curriculum through writing and children's literature.* Westport, CT: Heinemann.

Cherryholmes, C. (1999). *Reading pragmatism.* New York: Teachers College Press.

Churma, M. (1999). *A guide to integrating technology standards into the curriculum.* Columbus, OH: Merrill.

Clandinin, D. J., & Connelly, F. M. (1999). *Narrative inquiry: Experience and story in qualitative research.* San Francisco: Jossey-Bass.

Clinchy, E. (1999). *Reforming American education from the bottom to the top*. Westport, CT: Heinemann.

Cohen, J. (1999). *Educating minds and hearts: Social emotional learning and the passage into adolescence*. New York: Teachers College Press.

Cole, D. J., Ryan, C. W., Kick, F., & Mathies, B. (1999). *Portfolios across the curriculum and beyond* (second edition). Thousand Oaks, CA: Corwin.

Cole, R. A. (Ed.). (1999). *Issues in web-based pedagogy*. Westport, CT: Greenwood.

Comer, J. P., Ben-Avie, M., Haynes, N. M., & Joyner, E. T. (1999). *Child by child: The Comer process for change in education*. New York: Teachers College Press.

Connelly, F. M., & Clandinin, D. J. (1999). *Shaping a professional identity: Stories of educational practice*. New York: Teachers College Press.

Conroy, M. A. (1999). *101 ways to integrate personal development into core curriculum*. Lanham, MD: University Press of America.

Cornelius, C. (1999). *Iroquois corn in a culture-based curriculum: A framework for respectfully teaching about cultures*. Albany: State University of New York Press.

Crocco, M. S., Munro, P., & Weiler, K. (1999). *Pedagogies of resistance: Women educator activists, 1880–1960*. New York: Teachers College Press.

Cuban, L. (1999). *How scholars trumped teachers: Change without reform in university curriculum, teaching, and research, 1890–1990*. New York: Teachers College Press.

Cushner, K. H. (1999). *Human diversity in action: Developing multicultural competencies for the classroom*. New York: McGraw-Hill.

Dalton, M. M. (1999). *The Hollywood curriculum: Teachers and teaching in the movies*. New York: Peter Lang.

Darder, A. (1999). *Living a pedagogy of love: Paulo Freire in practice*. Boulder, CO: Westview.

Dilg, M. (1999). *Race and culture in the classroom: Teaching and learning through multicultural education*. New York: Teachers College Press.

Egan, K. (1999). *Children's minds, talking rabbits, and clockwork oranges: Essays on education*. New York: Teachers College Press.

English, F. (1999). *Deciding what to teach and test, millennium edition*. Thousand Oaks, CA: Corwin.

Eyler, J., & Giles, D. E. (1999). *Where's the learning in service learning?* San Francisco: Jossey-Bass.

Finch, C. R., & Crunkilton, J. R. (1999). *Curriculum development in vocational and technical education: Planning, content, and implementation* (fifth edition). Boston: Allyn & Bacon.

Ford, D. Y., & Harris, J., III. (1999). *Multicultural gifted education*. New York: Teachers College Press.

Ford, T. (1999). *Becoming multicultural: Personal and social construction through critical teaching.* New York: Falmer.

Freiberg, H. J. (Ed.). (1999). *Perceiving, behaving, becoming: Lessons learned.* Alexandria, VA: Association of Supervision and Curriculum Development.

Fullan, M. (1999). *Change forces: The sequel.* Levittown, PA: Falmer.

Gabbard, D. A. (1999). *Knowledge and power in the global economy: Politics and the rhetoric of school reform.* Mahwah, NJ: Lawrence Erlbaum Associates.

Gardner, H. (1999a). *Intelligence reframed: Multiple intelligences for the 21st century.* New York: Basic Books.

Gardner, H. (1999b). *The disciplined mind: What all students should understand.* New York: Simon and Schuster.

Giroux, H. A. (1999). *The mouse that roared: Disney and the end of innocence.* Lanham, MD: Rowman and Littlefield.

Glazer, S. (Ed.). (1999). *The heart of learning: Spirituality in education.* New York: Penguin Putnam.

Gordon, E. W. (1999). *Education & justice: A view from the back of the bus.* New York: Teachers College Press.

Graves, D. H. (1999). *Bring life into learning.* Westport, CT: Heinemann.

Gunter, M. A., Estes. T. H., & Schwab, J. H. (1999). *Instruction: A models approach* (third edition). Boston: Allyn & Bacon.

Henderson, J. G., & Kesson, K. R. (1999). *Understanding democratic curriculum leadership.* New York: Teachers College Press.

Hess, F. M. (1999). *Spinning wheels: The politics of urban school reform.* Washington, DC: Brookings Institute.

Hicks, D. V. (1999). *Norms and nobility: A treatise on education.* Lanham, MD: University Press of America.

Hillocks, G. (1999). *Ways of thinking, ways of teaching.* New York: Teachers College Press.

Howard, G. R. (1999). *We can't teach what we don't know: White teachers, multiracial schools.* New York: Teachers College Press.

Huebner, D. (V. Hillis, Ed.). (1999). *The lure of the transcendent: Collected essays.* Mahwah, NJ: Lawrence Erlbaum Associates.

Hutchinson, J. N. (1999). *Students on the margins: Education, stories, dignity.* Albany: State University of New York Press.

Jacob, E. (1999). *Cooperative learning in context: An educational innovation in everyday classrooms.* Albany: State University of New York Press.

Jonassen, D. H., Tessmer, M., & Hannum, W. H. (1999). *Task analysis method for instructional design.* Mahwah, NJ: Lawrence Erlbaum Associates.

Joseph, P. B., Bravmann, S. L., Windschitl, M. A., Mikel, E. R., & Green, N. S. (1999). *Cultures of curriculum*. Mahwah, NJ: Lawrence Erlbaum Associates.

Kanpol, B. (1999). *Critical pedagogy: An introduction* (second edition). Westport, CT: Bergin & Garvey.

Katz, M. S., Noddings, N., & Strike, K. A. (1999). *Justice and caring: The search for common ground in education*. New York: Teachers College Press.

Kelly, A. V. (1999). *The curriculum* (fourth edition). Thousand Oaks, CA: Corwin.

Kincheloe, J. L., Steinberg, S. R., & Hinchley, P. (Eds.). (1999). *The post-formal reader: Cognition and education*. New York: Falmer.

Kincheloe, J. L., Steinberg, S. R., & Villaverde, L. (Eds.). (1999). *Rethinking intelligence: Confronting psychological assumptions about teaching and learning*. New York: Routledge.

Kliebard, H. M. (1999). *Schooled to work: Vocationalism and the American curriculum, 1876–1946*. New York: Teachers College Press.

Kohn, A. (1999). *The schools our children deserve: Moving beyond traditional classrooms and tougher standards*. Boston: Houghton Mifflin.

Kohn, D. (1999). *Practical pedagogy for the Jewish classroom: Classroom management, instruction, and curriculum development*. Westport, CT: Greenwood.

Lee, S., & Speight, A. (1999). *Tradition and innovation: Selected plenary and panel papers from the third annual conference of the Assocation for Core Texts and Courses*. Lanham, MD: University Press of America.

Letts, W. J., IV, & Sears, J. T. (Eds.). (1999). *Queering elementary education: Advancing the dialogue about sexualities and schooling*. Lanham, MD: Rowman and Littlefield.

Lieberman, A., & Miller, L. (1999). *Teachers: Transforming their world and their work*. New York: Teachers College Press.

Lipka, R. P., & Brinthaupt, T. M. (Eds.). (1999). *The role of self in teacher development*. Albany: State University of New York Press.

Lubienski-Wentworth, R. A. (1999). *Montessori for the new millennium: Practical guidelines on the teaching and education of children of all ages*. Mahwah, NJ: Lawrence Erlbaum Associates.

Luykx, A. (1999). *The citizen factory: Schooling and cultural production in Bolivia*. Albany: State University of New York Press.

Mackley, T. A. (1999). *Uncommon sense: Core knowledge in the classroom*. Alexandria, VA: Association for Supervision and Curriculum Development.

Marsh, C. J., & Willis, G. (1999). *Curriculum: Alternative approaches, ongoing issues* (second edition). Columbus, OH: Merrill.

Marsh, D. D. (Ed.). (1999). *Preparing our schools for the 21st century*. The 1999 ASCD yearbook. Alexandria, VA: Association for Supervision and Curriculum Development.

Mayo, P. (1999). *Gramsci, Freire, and adult education: Possibilities for transformative action.* New York: St. Martin's Press.

McLaren, P. (1999). *Schooling as a ritual performance: Towards a political economy of educational symbols and gestures* (third edition). Lanham, MD: Rowman and Littlefield.

McNeil, J. D. (1999). *Curriculum: The teacher's initiative* (second edition). Columbus, OH: Merrill.

McNeil, L. M. (1999). *Missing a voice: Critical pedagogy and the possibilities of democratic teaching.* Boulder, CO: Westview.

McNergney, R. F., Ducharme, E. R., & Ducharme, M. K. (Eds.). (1999). *Educating for democracy: Case method teaching and learning.* Mahwah, NJ: Lawrence Erlbaum Associates.

Michie, G. (1999). *Holler if you hear me: The education of a teacher and his students.* New York: Teachers College Press.

Mills, K. (1999). *Something better for my children: How Head Start has changed the lives of millions of children.* New York: Plume.

Moon, B., & Murphy, P. (1999). *Curriculum in context.* Thousand Oaks, CA: Corwin.

Neilsen, A. R. (1999). *Daily meaning: Counternarratives of teacher's work.* Point Robert, WA: Bendall Books.

Nesin, G., & Lounsbury, J. (1999). *Curriculum integration: Twenty questions—with answers.* Westerville, OH: National Middle School Association.

Nieto, S. (1999). *The light in their eyes: Creating multiracial learning communities.* New York: Teachers College Press.

Nitza Hidalgo Westfield State College & Bowman, B. (1999). *Multicultural thematic teaching.* New York: Routledge.

Oakes, J., Quartz, K. H., Ryan, S., & Lipton, M. (1999). *Becoming good American schools.* San Francisco: Jossey-Bass.

Ohanian, S. (1999). *One size fits few: The folly of educational standards.* Westport, CT: Heinemann.

Ornstein, A. C., & Behar-Horenstein, L. S. (Eds.). (1999). *Contemporary issues in curriculum* (second edition). Needham Heights, MA: Allyn & Bacon.

O'Sullivan, E. (1999). *Transformative learning: Educational visions for the 21st century.* New York: St. Martin's Press.

Peters, M. (Ed.). (1999). *After the disciplines: The emergence of cultural studies.* Westport, CT: Bergin & Garvey.

Pinar, W. F. (Ed.). (1999). *Contemporary curriculum discourses: Twenty years of JCT.* New York: Peter Lang.

Popkewitz, T., & Fendler, L. (Eds.). (1999). *Critical theories in education: Changing terrains of knowledge and politics*. New York: Routledge.

Powell, R. (1999). *Literacy as a moral imperative: Facing the challenges of a pluralistic society*. Lanham, MD: Rowman and Littlefield.

Provenzo, E. F., Brett, A., & McCloskey, G. N. (1999). *Computers, curriculum, and cultural change*. Mahwah, NJ: Lawrence Erlbaum Associates.

Purpel, D. (1999). *Moral outrage in education*. New York: Peter Lang.

Queen, J. A. (1999). *Curriculum practice in the elementary and middle school*. Columbus, OH: Merrill.

Quicke, J. (1999). *A curriculum for life: Schools for a democratic learning society*. Philadelphia: Open University Press.

Reid, W. A. (1999). *Curriculum as institution and practice: Essays in the deliberative tradition*. Mahwah, NJ: Lawrence Erlbaum.

Reigeluth, C. (Ed.). (1999). *Instructional design theories and models. Volume II: A new paradigm of instructional theory*. Mahwah, NJ: Lawrence Erlbaum Associates.

Roberts, T., with Billings, L. (1999). *The Paideia classroom: Teaching for understanding*. Larchmont, NY: Eye on Education.

Roblyer, M. D. (1999). *Integrating technology across the curriculum: A database of strategies and lesson plans*. Columbus, OH: Merrill.

Rose, E. C., & Mayberry, M. (Eds.). (1999). *Meeting the challenge: Innovative feminist pedagogies in action*. New York: Routledge.

Ryan, K., & Bohlin, K. E. (1999). *Building character in schools: Practical ways to bring moral instruction to life*. San Francisco: Jossey-Bass.

Sapon-Shevin, M. (1999). *Because we can change the world: A practical guide for building cooperative, inclusive classroom communities*. Des Moines, IA: Allyn & Bacon/Longwood.

Sarason, S. (1999). *Teaching as a performing art*. New York: Teachers College Press.

Searle, C. (1999). *Dimensions of exclusion: Race, class and rejection in British schools*. Philadelphia: Open University Press.

Selden, S. (1999). *Inheriting shame: The story of eugenics and racism in America*. New York: Teachers College Press.

Shor, I. (1999). *Critical literacy in action: A tribute to the teachings of Paulo Freire*. Westport, CT: Heinemann.

Shor, I., & Pari, C. (Eds.). (1999). *Education is politics: Critical teaching across differences*. Westport, CT: Heinemann.

Sidorkin, A. M. (1999). *Beyond discourse: Education, the self, and dialogue*. Albany: State University of New York Press.

Sirotnik, K. A., & Soder, R. (Eds.). (1999). *The beat of a different drummer: Essays in honor of John I. Goodlad*. New York: Peter Lang.

Sleeter, C., & Grant, C. (1999). *Making choices for multicultural education: Five approaches to race, class, and gender* (third edition). Columbus, OH: Merrill.

Smith, D. J. (1999). *Stepping inside the classroom through personal narratives*. Lanham, MD: University Press of America.

Smith, P. L., & Ragan, T. J. (1999). *Instructional design* (second edition). New York: John Wiley and Sons.

Spring, J. (1999). *Wheels in the head: Educational philosophies of authority, freedom, and culture from Socrates to human rights* (second edition). Boston: McGraw-Hill.

Stanton, T. K., Giles, D. E., & Cruz, N. I. (1999). *Service-learning: A movement's pioneers reflect on its origins, practice, and future*. San Francisco: Jossey-Bass.

Steiner, S. S., Krank, H. M., McLaren, P., & Bahruth, R. E. (1999). *The Paulo Freire collection*. New York: Falmer.

Stotsky, S. (1999). *Losing our language: How multicultural classroom instruction is undermining our children's ability to read, write, and reason*. New York: Free Press.

Taylor, B. J. (1999). *A child goes forth: A curriculum guide for preschool children* (eighth edition). Columbus, OH: Prentice-Hall.

Tomlinson, C. A. (1999). *The differentiated classroom: Responding to the needs of all learners*. Alexandria, VA: Association for Supervision and Curriculum Development.

Torres, C. A. (1999). *Democracy, education, and multiculturalism*. Lanham, MD: Rowman and Littlefield.

Valenzuela, A. (1999). *Subtractive schooling: U.S.-Mexican youth and politics of schooling*. Albany: State University of New York Press.

Van Hoorn, J., Monighan Nourot, P., Scales, B. J., & Alward, K. R. (1999). *Play at the center of the curriculum* (second edition). Upper Saddle River, NJ: Prentice-Hall.

Westbury, I., Hopmann, S., & Riquartz, K. (Eds.) (1999). *Teaching as reflective practice: The German didaktic condition*. Mahwah, NJ: Lawrence Erlbaum Associates.

Whitehead, B. (Ed.). (1999). *Women's education in early modern Europe: A history, 1500–1800*. New York: Falmer.

Wiles, J. W. (1999). *Curriculum essentials: A resource for educators*. Needham Heights, MA: Allyn & Bacon.

Yagelski, R. P. (1999). *Literacy matters: Writing and reading the social self*. New York: Teachers College Press.

Yonehama, S. (1999). *The Japanese high school: Silence and resistance*. New York: Routledge.

Zemelman, S., Daniels, H., & Bizar, M. (1999). *Rethinking high school: Best practice in action*. Westport, CT: Heinemann.

2000

Adams, J. (2000). *Taking charge of curriculum: Teacher networks and curriculum implementation.* New York: Teachers College Press.

Armstrong, T. (2000). *Multiple intelligences in the classroom* (second edition). Alexandria, VA: Association for Supervision and Curriculum Development.

Ayers, W., Klonsky, M., & Lyon, G. H. (Eds.). (2000). *A simple justice: The challenge of small schools.* New York: Teachers College Press.

Ball, S., Maguire, M., & Macrae, S. (2000). *Choice, pathways, and transitions: Post 16.* New York: Routledge Falmer.

Barone, T. (2000). *Aesthetics, politics, and educational inquiry: Essays and examples.* New York: Peter Lang.

Bensman, D. (2000). *Central Park East and its graduates: "Learning by heart."* New York: Teachers College Press.

Brandt, R. (Ed.). (2000). *Education in a new age.* Alexandria, VA: Association for Supervision and Curriculum Development.

Brown, S. G. (2000). *Words in the wilderness: Critical literacy in the borderlands.* Albany: State University of New York Press.

Burbules, N., & Callister, T., Jr. (2000). *Watch it: The risks and promises of information technologies in education.* Boulder, CO: Westview.

Burbules, N. C., & Torres, C. A. (Eds.). (2000). *Globalization and education: Critical perspectives.* New York: Routledge.

Cornbleth, C. (Ed.). (2000). *Curriculum, politics, policy, practice: Cases in comparative conflict.* Albany: State University of New York Press.

Costa, A. L., & Kallick, B. (Eds.). (2000). *Discovering and exploring habits of the mind.* Alexandria, VA: Association for Supervision and Curriculum Development.

Coulby, D. (2000). *Beyond the national curriculum: Curricular considerations and cultural diversity in Europe and the USA.* New York: Routledge Falmer.

Darder, A., & Torres, A. (Eds.). (2000). *The critical pedagogy reader.* New York: Routledge.

Doll, M. A. (2000). *Like letters in running water: A mythopoetics of curriculum.* Mahwah, NJ: Lawrence Erlbaum Associates.

Edwards, R. (Robin Usher, Ed.). (2000). *Globalization and pedagogy: Space, place, and identity.* New York: Routledge.

Evenson, D. H., & Hmelo, C. E. (Eds.). (2000). *Problem-based learning: A research perspective on learning interactions.* Mahwah, NJ: Lawrence Erlbaum Associates.

Falk, B. (2000). *The heart of the matter: Using standards and assessment to learn.* Westport, CT: Heinemann.

Finnan, C., & Swanson, J. D. (2000). *Accelerating the learning of all students.* Boulder, CO: Westview.

Fletcher, S. (2000). *Education and emancipation: Theory and practice in a new constellation.* New York: Teachers College Press.

Foshay, A. W. (2000). *The curriculum: Purpose, substance, practice.* New York: Teachers College Press.

Franklin, B. (Ed.). (2000). *Curriculum and consequences: Herbert M. Kliebard and the promise of schooling.* New York: Teachers College Press.

Gandini, L., & Edwards, C. P. (Eds.). (2000). *Bambini: The Italian approach to infant/toddler care.* New York: Teachers College Press.

Gay, G. (2000). *Culturally responsive teaching: Theory, practice and research.* New York: Teachers College Press.

Giroux, H. A. (2000). *Impure acts: The practical politics of cultural studies.* New York: Routledge.

Glanz, J., & Behar-Horenstein, L. S. (2000). *Paradigm debates in curriculum and supervision: Modern and postmodern perspectives.* Westport, CT: Bergin & Garvey.

Glatthorn, A. A. (2000). *The principal as curriculum leader: Shaping what is taught and tested* (second edition). Thousand Oaks, CA: Corwin.

Goldstein, H. (2000). *Educational standards.* New York: Routledge.

Good, T. L. (Ed.). (2000). *American education: Yesterday, today, and tomorrow. Ninety-ninth yearbook of the National Society for the Study of Education, Part 2.* Chicago: University of Chicago Press.

Groate, J. E. (2000). *Paideia agonistes: The lost soul of modern education.* Lanham, MD: University Press of America.

Haggerson, N. (2000). *Expanding curriculum research and understanding: A mytho-poetic perspective.* New York: Peter Lang.

Henderson, J. G., & Hawthorne, R. D. (2000). *Transformative curriculum leadership* (second edition). Columbus, OH: Merrill.

Hoerr, T. R. (2000). *Becoming a multiple intelligences school.* Alexandria, VA: Association for Supervision and Curriculum Development.

Howell, K. W., Fox, S. L., & Moorehead, M. K. (2000). *Curriculum-based evaluation: Teaching and decision-making* (third edition). Pacific Grove, CA: Brooks/Cole.

Jensen, E. (2000). *Brain-based learning.* San Diego, CA: The Brain Store, Inc.

Jossey-Bass. (2000). *The Jossey-Bass reader on school reform.* San Francisco: Author.

Joyce, B. R., & Weil, M., with Calhoun, E. (2000). *Models of teaching* (sixth edition). Needham Heights, MA: Allyn & Bacon.

Kohn, A. (2000). *The case against standardized testing: Raising the scores, ruining the schools.* Westport, CT: Boynton/Cook.

Kordalewski, J. (2000). *Standards in the classroom: How teachers and students negotiate learning.* New York: Teachers College Press.

Kridel, C. (Ed.). (2000). *Books of the century catalog.* Columbia: The University of South Carolina Museum of Education.

Lankshear, C., de Alba, A., Gonzalez-Guadiano, E., & Peters, M. (Eds.). (2000). *Curriculum in the postmodern tradition.* New York: Peter Lang.

Lockledge, A., & Hayn, J. (2000). *Using portfolios across the curriculum.* Westerville, OH: National Middle School Association.

Madden, S. J. (2000). *Service learning across the curriculum: Case applications in higher education.* Lanham, MD: University Press of America.

Mahalingham, R., & McCarthy, C. (Eds.). (2000). *Multicultural education: New directions for social theory, practice, and policy.* New York: Routledge.

Marshall, J. D., Sears, J. T., & Schubert, W. H. (2000). *Turning points in curriculum: A contemporary American memoir.* Columbus, OH: Prentice-Hall.

Martinello, M. L., & Cook, G. E. (2000). *Interdisciplinary inquiry in teaching and learning* (second edition). Columbus, OH: Merrill.

Marzano, R. J. (2000). *Designing a new taxonomy of educational objectives.* Thousand Oaks, CA: Corwin.

McKay, A. (2000). *Sexual ideology and schooling: Towards democratic sexuality education.* Albany: State University of New York Press.

McLaren, P. (2000). *Che Guevara, Paulo Freire, and the pedagogy of revolution.* Lanham, MD: Rowman & Littlefield.

McNeil, L. (2000). *Contradictions of school reform: Educational costs of standardized testing.* New York: Routledge.

Meier, D. (2000). *Will standards save public education?* Boston: Beacon.

Miller, J. P. (2000). *Education and the soul: Toward a spiritual curriculum.* Albany: State University of New York Press.

Nager, N., & Shapiro, E. K. (2000). *Revisiting a progressive pedagogy: The developmental-interaction approach.* Albany: State University of New York Press.

Nieto, S. (2000). *Affirming diversity: The sociopolitical context of multicultural education* (second edition). New York: Longman.

Nolet, V., & McLaughlin, M. J. (2000). *Accessing the general curriculum: Making it happen for students with disabilities.* Thousand Oaks, CA: Corwin.

Pappas, C. C., & Zecker, L. B. (Eds.). (2000). *Transforming literacy curriculum genres: Working with teacher researchers in urban classrooms.* Mahwah, NJ: Lawrence Erlbaum Associates.

Parkay, F. W., & Hass, G. (Eds.). (2000). *Curriculum planning: A contemporary approach* (seventh edition). Needham Heights, MA: Allyn & Bacon.

Perry, M. (2000). *Walking the color line: The art and practice of anti-racist teaching.* New York: Teachers College Press.

Peters, M., Marshall, J., & Smeyers, P. (Eds.). (2000). *Nietzsche's legacy for education: Past and present values.* Westport, CT: Bergin & Garvey.

Phillips, D. C. (Ed.). (2000). *Constructivism in education: Opinions and second opinions on controversial issues. Ninety-ninth yearbook of the National Society for the Study of Education, part 1.* Chicago: University of Chicago Press.

Ravitch, D. (2000). *Left back: A century of failed school reforms.* New York: Simon and Schuster.

Reid, C. R. (2000). *Education and evolution: School instruction and the human future.* Lanham, MD: University Press of America.

Ritchie, J. S., & Wilson, D. E. (2000). *Teacher narrative as critical inquiry: Rewriting the script.* New York: Teachers College Press.

Roberts, P. (2000). *Education, literacy, and humanization: Exploring the work of Paulo Freire.* Westport, CT: Bergin & Garvey.

Roberts, P. L., & Kellough, R. D. (2000). *A guide for developing interdisciplinary thematic units.* Columbus, OH: Merrill.

Shearer, C. B. (2000). *The MIDAS handbook of multiple intelligences in the classroom.* Thousand Oaks, CA: Corwin.

Simon, R. I., Rosenberg, S., & Eppert, C. (Eds.). (2000). *Between hope and despair: Pedagogy and the remembrance of historical trauma.* Lanham, MD: Rowman and Littlefield.

Slavin, R. E., & Madden, N. A. (2000). *One million children: Success for all, roots and wings.* Thousand Oaks, CA: Corwin.

Smith, G. A., & Williams, D. R. (2000). *Ecological education in action: On weaving education, culture, and the environment.* Albany: State University of New York Press.

Sowell, E. J. (2000). *Curriculum: An integrated introduction* (second edition). Columbus, OH: Merrill.

Spring, J. (2000). *The intersection of cultures: Multicultural education in the United States and the global economy* (second edition). New York: McGraw-Hill.

Spring, J. (2000). *The universal right to education: Justification, definition, and guidelines.* Mahwah, NJ: Lawrence Erlbaum Associates.

Stambach, A. (2000). *Lessons from Mount Kilimanjaro: Schooling, community, and gender in east Africa*. New York: Routledge Falmer.

Steinberg, A., Cushman, K., & Riordan, R. (2000). *Schooling for the real world: The essential guide to rigorous and relevant learning*. San Francisco: Jossey-Bass.

Stotsky, S. (Ed.). (2000). *What's at stake in the K–12 standards war*. New York: Peter Lang.

Thayer-Bacon, B. J. (2000). *Transforming critical thinking: Thinking constructively*. New York: Teachers College Press.

Trifonas, P. (Ed.). (2000). *Revolutionary pedagogies: Cultural politics, education, and discourse of theory*. New York: Routledge.

Weiler, J. D. (2000). *Codes and contradictions: Race, gender identity, and schooling*. Albany: State University of New York Press.

Wineberg, S., & Grossman, P. (Eds.). (2000). *Interdisciplinary curriculum: Challenges to implementation*. New York: Teachers College Press.

Yon, D. A. (2000). *Elusive culture: Schooling, race, and identity in global times*. Albany: State University of New York Press.

CHAPTER ELEVEN

Curriculum Literature and Its Authors

Profile, Observations, and Recommendations
(Conclusion from First Edition)

As I reflect on the foregoing chapters and on the accumulation of work that each citation symbolizes, I am struck by the richness of curriculum study. This richness cannot be captured wholly by categorization. There is always a sense in which each book on the same general topic remains unique. Thus, my categorization schemes are not offered with great rigidity. A large number of books fall into more than one category. This fact is not intended as an inconsistency. Categorization serves great value in pointing to tendencies; yet any intent to do so must be recognized as superficial. If categorization were deemed easy and clear, the study that derives from it would be simplistic. From my perspective, this is certainly not the case with curriculum books.

Though arguments and classifications presented in some books may be criticized as simplistic, the field as a whole is clearly robust. The lack of agreement, definitional and the like, may indeed be attributed to the seriousness with which curriculum scholars take their work rather than to a lack of seriousness. Agreement is difficult when issues are treated with much scrutiny, and when profound consequences are attributed to matters studied. Many scholars acknowledge, for example, the importance to the process of inducting the young into social and cultural life. I argue that it is in this mission that the glory of curriculum inquiry and its applications resides. That curriculum scholars center their concern for this mission almost entirely on schools may be a distinct limitation. Relative costs and benefits of this mission are discussed in the paragraphs that follow. The emergence of curriculum studies as a specialized area of inquiry is, quite obviously, a result of its existence in a particular cultural context. My conviction that this is the case is reflected in each chapter's section entitled *Contextual Reminders*.

In some instances the connection between social developments and curriculum thought is obvious, for example, the growth of science and technology; the existence or lack of prosperity; the perils of war; the priorities of politics; the ebb and flow of economics; and the ideals and propensities of artistic expression. These are reflected in each decade treated. They contributed to the existence, orientation, and evolution of schools, and to the curriculum scholars and practitioners who emerged to serve them. Indeed, they contributed, in fact, to the very emergence of scholars and practitioners to serve schools. (This is, of course, not to deny the role of unique insight by perceptive individuals in the growth of curriculum inquiry.)

More social, political, economic, scientific, intellectual, and artistic information is provided in the *Contextual Reminders* than is directly connected with curriculum literature of the same time periods. The hope here is to encourage others to look more deeply within the fabric of social forces for the major threads of influence that have contributed to curriculum thought, literature, and practice. More often than not, the influence of such forces is more subtle, diffuse, and pervasive than reveals itself.[1] One major purpose of juxtaposing the curriculum literature with contextual information is to ease and encourage further inquiry.

The research done for this book encouraged me to pursue further study as well. It led me to couple a focus on curriculum literature with focus on the professoriates that produced it.[2] It led to inquiry into interconnections among curriculum scholars, that is, mentor-student relationships.[3] Findings for these studies are integrated with ideas drawn from work on earlier chapters of this book.

To this end the conclusion is divided into three sections. The first section reviews highlights of the literature and those who created it. In it I attempt to profile the shape of curriculum knowledge—its frames, boundaries, and scope—as it evolved in the literature during the first eight decades of the twentieth century. The second section consists of several observations and possibilities that emerged as I pursued the work leading to this book and the related studies mentioned above. In the third section, I describe recommendations that I suggest for the creators of further developments in curriculum scholarship. Such suggestions are offered with a good deal of humility. They are, however, derived from my perception of gaps and omissions in the literature that I have surveyed.

REVIEW AND PROFILE

Each decade brought new form and substance and strengthened curriculum as an area of study. The date 1918 is a frequently acknowledged starting point for curriculum studies. It is the date of both Bobbitt's *The Curriculum* and the *Cardinal Principles of Secondary Education*. This was indeed the period of emergence for curriculum as a separate area differentiated within the field of education. Nonetheless, it is a bit unfair to begin at 1918. Direct roots of the curriculum professoriate can be traced to earlier times. As readers will readily recall, over 30 curriculum books were published between 1900 and 1918. Let us consider the developments of the final years of the previous century.

In these years we find a combination of events that included the ever-rising tide of universal schooling, the academic pronouncements of the Committees of Ten and Fifteen, and the existence of several fertile coteries of scholarship. Universal schooling heightened the necessity for experts whose sole attention could be devoted to the production of defensible substance for the children and the youth who were recipients of that schooling. The Committees of Ten and Fifteen encouraged universal schooling to continue the perpetuation of mental disciplines or intellectual traditions, a subject-oriented curriculum heavily influenced by faculty psychology. I have referred to the proponents of this view as *intellectual traditionalists*.

Influential professors at certain American universities, for example, John Dewey, G. S. Hall, and Charles and Frank McMurry, were uneasy about the possibilities for intellectual traditionalist futures for curriculum in the American experiment of universal schooling. These professors cannot formally be called curriculum professors, since curriculum had not yet developed as a professional area of study. Yet they shared a concern for the form and substance of education. The students whom they influenced became the founders of curriculum study. They originated the curriculum professoriate.

Let us look at a few of the coteries of professors and students who were identifying the occupational characteristics of the curriculum professoriate near the turn of the century. Let us look, again, at the kinds of books that they produced. Both the scholars and their books fall roughly into two camps. The two camps have many variations, but they both offer alternatives to the intellectual traditionalist domination of educational practice. One is oriented to quantitative measurement, behavioristic psychology, and a Hobbesian faith in the science of education. For the convenience of labeling, I have referred to them as *social behaviorists*. The other group has its roots in philosophy, and is oriented toward a situational and contextual interaction of art and science as it applies to education. I called this group *experientialists*.

The origins of the social behaviorist position trace to Wilhelm Wundt at Leipzig, Germany. E. L. Thorndike's mentor, J. McKeen Cattell, studied with Wundt, as did G. Stanley Hall and Charles H. Judd. Although Thorndike, Hall, and Judd were not primarily curriculum scholars, their leadership created many such scholars. Hall influenced Bobbitt, who received his doctorate in 1909 from Clark University. From there Bobbitt went to the University of Chicago where Judd had just assumed leadership, altering the orientation considerably from the time that Dewey directed the university's Laboratory School. George D. Strayer completed his doctorate under Thorndike's direction in 1905. Strayer influenced his students at Columbia Teachers College for nearly 40 years. Hollis Caswell and Paul Hanna were among his prominent students, whose influence on the curriculum professoriate is unquestioned. They, in turn, influenced many who moved throughout the country.

Experientialist roots can be traced to John Dewey and Charles De Garmo. At the turn of the century, when Dewey was at Chicago, Ella Flagg Young and W. W. Charters studied with him. Later at Columbia, Kilpatrick not only studied with Dewey, he became a kind of self-appointed interpreter and popularlizer of his educational views. De Garmo, who studied with K. V. Stoy in Germany, brought Herbartian interpretations to America, as did Frank and Charles McMurry. Boyd H. Bode and William C. Bagley received doctorates in 1900 at Cornell University, where De Garmo was professor of art and science of education. They studied with Edward Titchener and Charles Tyler. Books such as Dewey's *The Child and the Curriculum* (1902a) and McMurry's two-volume *Course of Study in the Eight Grades* (1906) illustrate experientialist commitments to child study, the primacy of interest in curricular organization, and an interdependence between living and schooling in the educative process.

Books by Bagley, Strayer, Judd, and others often focused on school surveys. This kind of focus helped to gear the emergent area of curriculum study toward schools. This was the case with the mental discipline interpretation of the intellectual traditionalist approach as well; it was furthered by the work of national committees that were mentioned earlier, and perpetuated by the Commission on the Reorganization of Secondary Education (1918). Despite Dewey's holistic treatment of curriculum matters in *Democracy and Education* (1916) and despite its widespread citation in curriculum books, curriculum writers increasingly geared their writing to schools.

By the mid-1920s the "descendants" of Thorndike and Judd, of Dewey and the Herbartians, of Horne and Bagley and of the commissions; each formed fairly distinct groupings of curriculum scholars: social behaviorists, experientialists, and intellectual traditionalists. Curriculum was indeed an identifiable subdivision of educational inquiry. Bobbitt (1915, 1918, 1922, 1924, 1926), Charters (1923), and Snedden (1921, 1927) led the social behaviorists. Dewey (1900, 1902a, 1902b, 1916), Kilpatrick (1918, 1926a, 1926b), Counts (1926), McMurry (1923), and Rugg (1928) led the experientialists.

Both social behaviorists and experientialists tried to apply interpretations of science to curriculum construction, a process deemed by some as riddled by unsystematic selection governed by expedience, tradition, and politics. Social behaviorists used a mechanistic, atomistic, measurement style of science. They analyzed activities, translated the findings to curriculum, and sought generalized knowledge. On the contrary, experientialists sought a situational application of science. The educator's job was to read the character of problematic circumstances, project possible courses of action and their probable consequences, and act in such ways that led to growth. Though vague in many respects, professors who wrote in this persuasion tried to describe a complex application of scientific methodology that accounted for uniqueness in situations as well as commonalities among them. Even the more practice-oriented books in this group, such as Rugg and Shumaker (1928), tended to be philosophical.

Another kind of curriculum book outnumbered both of these in the twenties and early thirties. This was the highly school-oriented text that focused on curriculum in the secondary, elementary, junior high school, etc. Examples include Koos (1920) and Bonser (1920). Others of a similar type dealt with general curriculum procedures and problems, for example, Meriam (1920), Monroe (1925), Briggs (1926), Harap (1928), Williams (1928), Hopkins (1929), and Lide (1933). Thus, the alternative to social behaviorist and experientialist literature became not so much the old version of intellectual tradition, but a new school-oriented text that borrowed elements from these orientations, a *conciliar* approach. The point was to provide guidelines, often called "principles," for school people. The curriculum professoriate was grappling with the issue of how to present knowledge about a complex process in *one book*. Practitioners would be likely to have only one or two courses in curriculum. Somehow the necessary procedures needed to be conveyed in that scope.

By the mid-1930s many members of the professoriate had apparently internalized the guideline approach. Texts contained list after list of "how tos" and "when tos." Many continued to use this recipe-orientation into the fifties and sixties. This was the case despite the admonitions of writers such as Bode (1927), Rugg-NSSE (1927), and Hopkins (1929) to engage in serious and complex discourse about the assumptions that undergird alternative positions on major curriculum questions.

The schools of curriculum thought became less distinct and more conflated with one another. At the same time curriculum study began to embrace more areas: organization, administration, students, teachers, instruction. In a sense, curriculum had returned to its state before it was differentiated from education. That is to say, curriculum study expanded to treat almost as many aspects of schooling as did the study of education itself. This expansion of boundaries relative to schooling and the amalgamation of schools of thought are both reflected in the books of "principles" for practitioners.

To this end a new kind of text was produced that was encyclopedic or synoptic in character. Early in this book it was labeled the *synoptic text*. Through the synoptic text, authors attempted to provide procedures for curriculum development as well as distillations of background information on a host of related topics. First examples of these texts were *Curriculum Development* (1935) by Caswell and Campbell and *Foundations of Curriculum Building* (1936) by Norton and Norton.

The synoptic text dominated curriculum writing for more than three decades. It is interesting to note that each text seemed to be designed as a "one-shot" professional training course in curriculum. Each tried to cover, or sample, the territory. That there is little gradation in level of these texts supports the assumption that just one exposure to curriculum was the usual expectation. Examples include Spears (1940), Gwynn (1943), Burton (1944), Leonard (1946), Stratemeyer et al. (1947), Tyler (1949), Smith, Stanley, and Shores (1950), Ragan (1953), Saylor and Alexander (1954), Lee and Lee (1960), and Taba (1962).

With *Readings in Curriculum Development* (1937) Caswell and Campbell also innovated another kind of curriculum book; from that date to the present, books of readings served as a major means of conveying curriculum knowledge. Usually they included articles that had already achieved prominence in journals. Sometimes they included new articles that were especially prepared for their publications.

Synoptic texts and books of readings were the major type of curriculum books from the forties throughout the sixties. Added to these were monographs and yearbooks of such organizations as the Association for Supervision and Curriculum Development and the National Society for the Study of Education.

In the sixties the emphasis on the structure of disciplines and curriculum projects became manifested in the synoptic and readings texts. Alternative curricula of humanistic education emerged and were reminiscent of the earlier experientialists. Behavioral objectives, competency-based curricula, systems rhetoric, and technological approaches evidenced a resurgence of social behaviorism. Of similar genre, a major alteration that reached fruition in the sixties was the increased use of social science and behavioristic methodologies that are labeled "conceptual-empiricist" by Pinar (1975), the "theoretic" research mode that Schwab (1970) called "moribund."

The seventies brought increased diversification of the types of curriculum books and a resultant decline in the production of new synoptic texts. More attention also was given in America to British, German, Scandinavian, Australian, and Canadian sources. Schwab and others emerged to advocate practical epistemologies and qualitative methodologies that evolved in the mid-seventies, causing a revival of philosophic scrutiny and speculation that had once characterized a style of study led by Dewey and the Herbartians. Yet the literature, especially the journals, remained dominated by conceptual analysis and empirical research. The sophistication of conceptual and statistical analysis soared. To some this represented progress, or at least its potential. To others, a group loosely classed for a time as "reconceptualists," it symbolized slavery to one epistemological orientation and ignorance that others existed.

OBSERVATIONS AND POSSIBILITIES

Reflection on the curriculum books and their authors has led to several observations about the characteristics of the curriculum professoriate. The characteristics are presented here both chronologically and cumulatively, according to the following observations: (1) the curriculum professoriate evolved as an inheritor; (2) it created and delimited a future course of inquiry; (3) it grew as a purveyor of schooling; (4) it became preoccupied with the determination of the content of *school* learning; (5) it professed knowledge; (6) it generated knowledge; and (7) it sought freedom from the boundary of that knowledge. Let us consider each of these in a bit more detail.

INHERITORS OF A JOURNEY

Probing the roots of curriculum reveals that concern for curriculum is perennial. The etymological origins of curriculum as a chariot race course can be applied metaphorically to the journey of inducting humans into society. The basic human concern for induction of new members into adult-oriented society marks a basis of legitimization for curriculum as a professional domain. The concern is supported in several modes of representation.

To trace the roots of prominent curriculum scholars to the educators of the latter nineteenth century is only a beginning. For example, a chain exists from Madeleine Grumet to William Pinar, Paul Klohr, Harold Alberty, Boyd H. Bode, to association with Charles De Garmo, who can be traced to K. V. Stoy and Herbart. Herbart, in turn, can be traced in a mentor-student network to Pestalozzi and Fitche, Lessing, Kant, Martin Knutzen, Christian Wolff, Leibnitz, and more indirectly to Descartes and to Rousseau, and to the

French Jesuits. All of these wrote covertly, if not overtly, about education, and concomitantly about curriculum.

These writers represent a concern shared by philosophers since antiquity. Philosophical grand schemes almost invariably treat problems associated with introducing the young to the structure, resources, and functioning of social groups. Whether proposals or social criticisms, these writings deal not only with curriculum in a formal educational setting, but with education as one of many aspects in any context of social forces. The treatment of curriculum within such a context is part of a tradition of social philosophical writing.

Similarly, one can surely turn to novels, poetry, plays, biographies, diaries, and other literary portrayals for curriculum insights. They illuminate journeys that educate persons. They portray experiences that enhance and retard human growth. They deal with growth holistically, not in cognitive, affective, or psychomotor segmentations. The point, perhaps an obvious one, is that a heritage of curriculum literature runs deeper than the overt occupational characteristics of the curriculum professoriate. It interpenetrates literature from Homer to Plutarch, to Shakespeare, to Dickens, to Tolstoy, to Dostoyevski and Joyce, Hesse and Kafka, Vonnegut and Borges. Moreover, curriculum has permeated human concern since it was decided that the young needed induction into human society. Whether such induction pertained to schooling institutions or whether it pertained to a child following an adult through daily routine, curriculum was being done.

Thus, those who emerged to be known as a curriculum professoriate early in the twentieth century were the inheritors of a basic human concern. The informal provision of activities to induct the young into adult-oriented life is a perennial parental concern. With the growth of complex social groups, this induction became more formalized in school institutions. The substance of education and schooling was represented in the arts, discussed in philosophy, and criticized in both. In all of these it was integrated with and contingent on living itself. Education was treated as part and parcel of the journey of living. The emergence of the educational professoriate brought more specialized study. Increased specialization, and change of residence from life at large to universities, evolved with the emergence of the curriculum inquiry and development as occupations.

DELIMITERS OF THE JOURNEY

The specialization implicit in a curriculum professoriate magnified the focus on a concern that had heretofore been subsidiary. What had begun as a concern for the induction of the young into adult-oriented living, a concern expressed within broad cultural, artistic, and intellectual contexts, became a preoccupation with schooling as the means of induction that pushed contextual concerns to the periphery. Books on curriculum, especially the synoptic texts, almost invariably treated the larger contextual forces as mere influences on curriculum, rather than presenting school experiences as one thread in a fabric of forces that all influence the induction of the young into adult life. Specialization was, in no small measure, dictated by increased pressure for universal schooling. Specialized inquiry into curriculum was considered legitimate so long as it appeared to contribute to the learning substance to be conveyed by universal schooling. It is ironic that the curriculum professoriate, a group commissioned to prepare the young to effectively engage in life as a whole, is the same group that turned its attention from induction as a function of life in a holistic sense to schooling. Put another way, the historical journey of those concerned with inducting the young into life was, in this century, placed in the hands of curriculum specialists commissioned to introduce the young to effective living with those institutions known as schools.

PURVEYORS OF SCHOOLING

The curriculum professoriate emerged in response to universal schooling. In short, if the form was there it needed substance. When the conveyor belts were set in motion, something had to be conveyed. It seemed clear that it would be the quasi-classical subject matter that dominated schooling unless alternatives were offered. If nothing definite was available to convey, caprice would dictate substance. If caprice governed, the message would be the medium itself. Universal schooling would convey the universal need to be schooled. Would this perpetuate a land of students, persons who would be prepared not to be directors of their own curriculum, but to have the curriculum of their learning directed by others? Would the curriculum of schooling become schooling itself? Is this not symbolized by the attention given to "hidden curriculum" in the 1970s and 1980s?

At the turn of the century too few educators could devote full-time consideration to the content of universal schooling. Some educational scholars centered their concern on the substance of education generally. Such concern had grown from focus on private schooling or informal learning experiences rather than mass schooling. As mentioned earlier, alternatives to intellectual traditionalist interpretations were found in the theory and practice of Herbartians and Dewey, and in the measurement and behaviorism of Thorndike, Judd, and Cattell. Both alternatives were fueled by public sentiments. The social behaviorists derived their validity from the growing faith in science and technology, and the experientialists sprang from the faith in individualism, democracy, and reflective science and ethics.

It is clear that the curriculum professoriate was legitimated by the need to create or perpetuate learning substance for universal schooling. Educational scholars (e.g., De Garmo, Dewey, Hall, Judd, and Thorndike) offered alternative orientations to the piecemeal intellectual traditionalist curriculum that had dominated schooling.

DEVELOPERS OF CURRICULUM

It was a kind of occupational commission that the curriculum professoriate would develop curriculum. What else could be the purpose of curriculum inquiry than to discover or invent curricula? Curriculum scholars did, on occasion, develop curriculum; they prepared curriculum materials, proposed examples of programs, and surveyed or assessed extant curriculum implementation. It seems, however, that curricularists soon realized that general programs could not be formulated to meet specific needs of unique situations. Therefore their discussion was elevated to a meta-level, and it addressed the issue of *how* a curriculum is developed instead of *what* knowledge and skills were important for young people to acquire or develop.

The scholars decentralized the decision about what learning substance should constitute the curriculum of schools. Instead of using their expertise to advocate, they placed advocacy in state and local hands. They attempted to provide "principles" to guide curriculum development to be done by planners in schools. This was often defended as compliant to the democratic ideal of self-determination. Perhaps, too, it was a response to the realization that curriculum development is primarily a practical task. In any event, the curriculum professoriate became known largely as scholars concerned with problems and procedures of pointing the way to sound curriculum development. They were less frequently developers of extant local curricula.

PROFESSORS OF CURRICULUM KNOWLEDGE

Service to schools was an initial concern of the curriculum professoriate. The widespread existence of normal schools for teacher training set a precedent for service to schools. As certain prominent philosophers, psychologists, and educators turned their attention and that of their students to curriculum matters, curriculum became associated with universities as well.

The role of curriculum workers was altered by the virtue or vice of the professoriate's emergent residence in the universities. The faction of curriculum workers known as professors had much of their role directed by the system of rewards and expectations that is incumbent upon university faculty members. A professoriate professes by publication as well as by consulting and teaching. Books became a major symbol of legitimation. Books facilitated teaching and consulting, but even more, they provided evidence of scholarly productivity.

As professors of specialized knowledge, curriculum professors began by publishing an amalgam of prescriptions and descriptions drawn from teaching teachers and administrators with eclectically selected positions from the three growing orientations: social behaviorist, experientialist, and intellectual traditionalist. As latecomers to the university scene, it was undoubtedly difficult for curriculum professors to find a body of lore to use as a basis for subsequent writing. Thus, they chose from a host of sources that sometimes held only remote resemblance to their own practical pursuits.

Understandably, a lag persisted between curriculum and the more established areas or disciplines of study. The lag in both methodology and substance was blatantly evident. Methodologically, curricularists, like other educational researchers, emulated social scientists who, in turn, emulated successes of natural sciences. When natural scientists moved from heavy reliance on statistics to the formulation of theory, social scientists gave prime concern to statistics and educationalists upgraded statistics requirements for their students. When natural scientists moved from theory to situational analysis, social scientists began to develop theories, and curricularists expressed a need (Herrick & Tyler, 1950) for theory and speculated about what it might entail.

Substantively, the case for lag is similar. Existential psychology and philosophy were the central philosophical and literary concerns of Sartre, Camus, Jaspers, Heidegger, Kafka, and others by the 1930s. Yet, it was not until the 1970s that existential perspectives were significantly represented in curriculum scholarship.

A point similar to that asked by Harry S. Broudy[4] is highly relevant. Broudy asked, "What do professors of education profess?" The academic community at large has, justifiably or not, asked similar questions of educational scholars throughout this century. The same is true, of course, for those who claimed to be curriculum scholars. Moreover, they asked themselves this question, as well, as they produced a body of literature. It was clear that the curriculum professoriate had to profess to live. Thus, curriculum scholars needed to develop knowledge. As they did so, the development of curriculum itself ironically took a backseat to scholarly publications.

GENERATORS OF KNOWLEDGE

If the job of curriculum professors was to profess knowledge, it was necessary for them to create a steady flow of it. Furthermore, this knowledge had to conform to that deemed acceptable in academia. It had to conform to the epistemology of the day, or at least to one of a recent yesterday.

The problem of what kind of knowledge should be produced plagued curriculum scholars. As creators of scholarly research, the curriculum professoriate had to produce empirically warranted descriptions of school phenomena. They had to conform to the theoretic (Schwab, 1970) or conceptual empiricist (Pinar, 1975) epistemologies of the day.[5] Simultaneously, as a professional area of study, curriculum needed to prescribe services to practitioners in schools. Throughout its 80-year history, the curriculum professoriate has come under fire for doing too much and too little in both its research and school-based roles. Generally, it has been strong on prescription and weak on description. Authors produced books that reflected this proportion. By attempting to simultaneously satisfy the demands of scholarly description and those of practical prescription, they provided books that were amalgams of both. Books for practitioners often turned out to be more theoretic and conceptual empiricist; thus, they did not meet the needs of specific practical problems. Conversely, books for scholars often lacked the rigor, detachment, and generalizability that merit praise by the scholarly community. The domain of curriculum inquiry clearly embraced a set of problems that too few understood and even fewer devoted energies to understand. As a consequence, the books were often criticized by scholars for being superficial, and by practitioners for not relating to specific practical concerns.

Despite the criticism, books were a source of legitimation and their production grew steadily as the decades passed. The proliferation of books was indeed great. The growth of the field was cumulative, and more than a bit haphazard. At first, curriculum was acknowledged as a domain important enough to be treated as an educational subdivision deserving attention in its own right. Many early curriculum scholars no doubt relied on traditions embodied in the mental disciplines position that empowered the existence of curriculum workers. Hence, a number of books appeared in the first three decades that quite wholly reflected the intellectual traditionalist orientation. Others relied more on their immediate scholarly ancestors in education, philosophy, and psychology: Thorndike, Strayer, Wundt, Herbart, De Garmo, Dewey, Peirce, James, etc. These scholars were not curricularists, though they markedly influenced the existence of social behaviorist and experientialist curriculum thought.

As the decades progressed, more specialized dimensions of curriculum knowledge emerged. At first, these segments included elementary, secondary, and junior-high levels of education. Some treated the subject areas separately. A few probed for assumptions behind these prescriptions and descriptions. Others advocated processes or procedures for developing curricula. Still others treated curriculum administration, implementation, materials, and a host of miscellaneous ideas often called "problems" or "issues." Some books provided data, usually of the informal case study or survey variety. A few probed implications for teaching that might be drawn from these prescriptions and descriptions.

By 1950, curriculum knowledge appeared in so many different shapes and styles that it was becoming impossible for anyone but a full-time curriculum scholar to grasp it as a whole. This was the knowledge that was used to prepare administrators, supervisors, and teachers, not just other scholars. Most administrators, supervisors, and teachers would take only one or two curriculum courses. Thus, synoptic texts were created to provide one-shot orientations, that is, everything practitioners needed to know about curriculum.

By the sixties such literature was criticized ferociously as armchair speculation. Even though much was derived from direct involvement in schools, it was not derived in ways deemed defensible through the epistemological lenses that had come to dominate educational inquiry. Defensible knowledge needed to take the form of conceptual analysis sanctioned by analytic philosophers, and/or empirical studies sanctioned by social scientists and psychologists. A plethora of studies from both vantage points dominated curriculum writing from the early 1960s to 1980.

A CLAMOR FOR FREEDOM

Finally, in the seventies, the epistemological powers that dominated curriculum inquiry were castigated. Schwab's critique of the theoretic research paradigm is well known. Other prominent curriculum scholars call vehemently for inquiry that embraces phenomenological, dialectical, existential, literary, psychoanalytic, practical and/or aesthetic sources: Michael Apple, Dwayne Huebner, J. S. Mann, James B. Macdonald, Maxine Greene, Robert Stake, Elliot Eisner, William Pinar, George Willis, C. A. Bowers, Lawrence Stenhouse, William Reid, Max van Manen, Ted Aoki, and others. Although their orientations may differ considerably from one another in many respects, they share an argument for freedom from the chains of domination by one epistemological base. This criticism pertains broadly to several dimensions of curriculum study: scholarly curriculum inquiry, curriculum development, the content of school curriculum, and the overarching quality of school experience and its relation to living outside of classrooms.

RECOMMENDATIONS

The purpose of studying curriculum history should be to provide insight to guide the curricular present and future. Knowledge about occupational characteristics of the curriculum professoriate in the past enables the development of directions that it might take in the future. Though the connection between the work of curriculum scholars and its influence on curriculum implementation by teachers and acquisition by students is not entirely clear, I submit that scholarly work should be conducted with the intent of ultimately providing more worthwhile experiences for teachers and students. Therefore, I will share five recommendations, though they are rudimentary, that I offer to the attention of those who create curriculum literature.

THE SEARCH FOR ORIGINS

The search for origins of the curriculum professoriate has begun. Several contributions have appeared in the sixties and seventies that provide steps toward preventing ahistoricism. This book is an attempt to portray the books produced by curriculum scholars in the twentieth century. It is also an attempt to interpret and discuss salient contributions. Further, it provides highlights of the sociocultural context in which curriculum literature evolved. Finally, in this concluding chapter, I attempt to connect fragments of knowledge about the curriculum professoriate and the literature that symbolizes its work.

The origins, however, run much deeper than the beginning of books with *curriculum* in the title. The roots of curriculum study are portrayed in history, philosophy, and the arts of antiquity. Their archetypes can be traced to ordinary family life, social evolution, and the arts of high culture. Together, these illuminate perennial interest in the content of the journey of children and youth as they are inducted into the culture perpetuated by adults. Literary, artistic, historical, and philosophical sources interpret, evaluate, and criticize that journey. They sometimes propose its reform. It is imperative that those who wish to study curriculum today learn more of the saga of human concern which, in part, gave birth to curriculum as a specialized area of study in our world of specialization.

THE EMULATION OF ORIGINS

The search for roots in many fields today discredits the long-held notion that the growth of knowledge always ferrets out inert ideas and preserves productive ones. Even natural scientists revive documents previously believed to be archaic. Viewed with new perspectives, such documents often reveal method and substance that illuminate current problems.

Curricularists have had similar experiences. Some have begun to realize that while increased curriculum specialization magnified schooling, it clouded a holistic vision of childhood's curriculum to adulthood. Such a vision is portrayed in novels, poetry, film, painting, music, and the performing arts. It is analyzed in psychology, philosophy, anthropology, and history. These and other sources reflect an array of epistemological bases: intuition, empiricism, experience, revelation, reason, authority, utility. The science of behaviorism does not monopolize the route to curricular wisdom. The richness of perspectives that contributed to curricular insight before the advent of specialization needs to be revitalized. The variety of methodologies in such perspectives should not be ignored.

Speculative endeavor, though today in demise, ignited the contributions made by the recent ancestors of the curriculum professoriate. Fodor describes it well in reference to psychology, noting ancestors who are common to those of the curriculum professoriate.

> There used to a discipline called speculative psychology. It wasn't quite philosophy because it was concerned with empirical theory construction. It wasn't quite psychology because it wasn't an experimental science. But it used the methods of both philosophy and psychology because it was dedicated to the notion that scientific theories should be both conceptually disciplined and empirically constrained. What speculative psychologists did was this: They thought about such data as were available about mental processes, and they thought about such first-order psychological theories as had been proposed to account for the data. They then tried to elucidate the general conception of the mind that was implicit in the data and the theories. Speculative psychology was, by and large, quite a good thing: William James and John Dewey were speculative psychologists and so, in certain of his moods, was Clark Hull. But it's commonly said that there aren't any speculative psychologists any more.[6]

I suggest that the curriculum professoriate repel pressures to expunge its tendency to engage in speculation. It needs to resist the force to increase specialization that limits attention to schooling alone. I suggest that curriculum scholars advance the emergent tendency to perceive curriculum broadly, as a function of culture, not merely of schooling. As a prerequisite to doing this, at least in the process of doing so, curriculum scholars need to expose the limits and impositions of the epistemological assumptions that undergird the several social and behavioral sciences that direct the course of educational inquiry today. In 1979, Schwab called for a moratorium on the prostitution of educators after academic respectability, that is, to blind adherence to values implicit in dominant social science methodology.[7] At the same conference, Michael Scriven challenged educational researchers to develop research methodologies that are based on epistemological assumptions worthy of emulation by social scientists themselves. [8]

Applied to curriculum inquiry, I suggest that the above necessitates the orchestration of many methodologies. Relevant modes of inquiry and expression would not be wholly unlike the rich precedent of illumination of human situations that is available in the literature of philosophy, the humanities, the arts, religion, technologies, and the professions, as well as the social and natural sciences. The striving to understand curricular problems should be taken with no less seriousness than seeking the good, the beautiful, and the true. It should be utmost seriousness because the induction of children into society and the attempt to reflectively and imaginatively guide their journey toward greater meaning, goodness, and wisdom fully penetrates the great philosophical questions.

THE IDEAL AND THE MUNDANE

The lofty ideals, that is, the Platonic search for goodness and wisdom that I advocate for curriculum scholarship in the foregoing, are indeed serious. They make a claim that is similar to Broudy's in his critique of what professors of education profess.[9] He invoked Plato's *divided line* allegory (*The Republic*, Book VI), and argued that educational scholars seldom move beyond levels *two* and *three*, the levels of facts and hypothetical entities or models. It is, in fact, thought presumptuous for them to even claim investigations into level *four*, the realm of wisdom or intuition with the forms. Rarely, if ever, do curricularists, other educators, and scholars at large directly admit that they are engaged in the pursuit of wisdom, to usurp the title of Abraham Kaplan's book.[10] The job of curriculum scholars cannot stop short of this magnitude of inquiry. After all, one must go far to find an endeavor as worthy of seriousness as the study and development of the itineraries by which children and youth move toward adult social life.

The import of this endeavor is laudable, indeed admirable, and is, I believe, a subtle germ of inspiration that lingers in the hearts and minds of many in the curriculum professoriate. It is perhaps this germ of inspiration that enables curriculum professors to create amid some of the more debilitating characteristics of academe. These rather mundane characteristics, unmentioned thus far in this book, should be placed in juxtaposition to our loftiest ideals in order to provide a balanced view. Curriculum professors are expected to be first-class teachers, consultants, researchers, and authors. They are expected to compete in productivity with their colleagues in other disciplines, to have that productivity defined by these colleagues as publication rather than as direct service to the curricular journey of children and youth. Their work and their ability in the academic community carry a reputation of less than adequate. Moreover, curricularists' would-be clients in the schools often think of curriculum as dry and boring, largely due to its association with curriculum guides and similar documents. From yet another angle, one can scarcely pass over the public criticism that riddles the entire educational establishment from nursery to graduate school. Surely, curricularists are not immune to this phenomenon.

Clearly, there is no small hiatus between the ideal that motivates curriculum scholars and the worth of work attributed to them by colleagues, clients, and the public. A major problem, then, is to generate increased regard for the work of the curriculum professoriate. An important step can be made by applying curriculum inquiry to the wider domain from which it has grown, that is, to a holistic concern for the journey from birth through adulthood. Hopefully, this concern, which became professorial through the thrust of universal schooling, was only diverted and not expurgated by its necessary preoccupation with schooling. Today, I suggest that broader applications of curriculum inquiry are needed to include and go beyond schooling. I refer to one example as *non-school curricula* and to another as a *theory within persons*.

NON-SCHOOL CURRICULA

Curriculum books almost invariably attest to the near-universal emphasis on schooling by curriculum authors. Extricated from its social and cultural context, curriculum is addressed as only one of many forces in the journey that enables children to understand, function in, and contribute to adult life. That one force is schooling. Most any teacher will readily admit that forces beyond the control of schooling and outside of its purview have monumental influence on the child's view of the world. Quite obviously, homes, peer groups, formal youth organizations, jobs, and the media profoundly influence children and youth. I submit that these are curricula in their own right and should be studied as such by curriculum scholars.

Compared to the cumulative effect of these non-school curricula, the impact of school curriculum itself is dwarfed. It is doubtful that curriculum can be studied meaningfully today apart from full attention to the interdependent character of life's curricula. Each curriculum influences conceptions of self and others, hopes, ambitions, fears, insights, values, roles, rules, power hierarchies, and so on. The curriculum professoriate has accumulated a repertoire of analytic categories for the investigation of school curriculum. I suggest that these or similar categories can be used to map features of the journey of children and youth through the curricula of media, peer groups, jobs, organizations, and homes, that is, major domains of non-school curricula.

A "THEORY" WITHIN PERSONS

The non-school and school curricula shape a "theory" or worldview within children and youth. It is a theory that they are a living theory that guides their functioning, that embodies their information and misinformation about the world, how it works, and how to relate to it. Without knowledge of student knowledge, how can curriculum developers defensibly determine what is needed for subsequent stages of the journey of children and youth toward adulthood?[11] It is such knowledge of the journey that shapes human character and builds human ideals that must be addressed, in my estimation, if the spark that ignited perennial curriculum interest is to be kept alive. It was a similar spark that Jaeger sought when he described *paideia*, "the shaping of Greek character" (p. ix).[12] He described the unique purpose of his classic work as follows:

> Although many scholars have undertaken to describe the development of the state, the society, the literature, and religion, and the philosophy of the Greeks, no one seems to have attempted to explain the interaction between the historical process by which their character was formed and the intellectual process by which they constructed their ideal of human personality. (Jaeger, 1945, p. ix).

Characterizing *paideia* in every culture is, I suggest, important to any scholarly domain, foreign to none, and essential to the work of curriculum scholars. As we acquire a tighter grasp of the essence of our own *paideia*, we obtain a position from which we can more defensibly create curricular extensions of the journeys on which our children and youth continuously embark.

C H A P T E R   T W E L V E

Curriculum Literature and Its Authors

More Thoughts After
20 Additional Years of Pondering
(A Conclusion for the Second Edition)

After more than 20 years of work and reflection in curriculum studies, what can one say about the literature that has emerged? *Curriculum Books* began as a response to the problem of a lack of centralized resources that together define curriculum studies. As noted in the introduction, we assume that students of curriculum and seasoned scholars of curriculum studies could benefit from a listing and analysis of resources that make up the area to which they are developing their life's work. It seems increasingly evident that work in and reflection on curriculum studies over the years strangely clouds the possibility of definitive answers, perhaps shedding light on the depth and complexity of the questions. Even the matter of what constitutes resources is saturated with problems.

How does one make sense of the remarkable expansion of curriculum literature? No matter how one defines the literature, it must be concluded that unprecedented growth in scholarship has taken place from the early 1970s to the present, especially since the 1980s. The purpose of curriculum studies began to shift from the process of developing curriculum during and before the late 1960s and early 1970s toward understanding curricula as personal, cultural, and ideological phenomena in the 1980s and 1990s (see Pinar et al., 1995).

To identify the literature that best enables us to understand the broader and deeper significance of curriculum in culture, society, and individual life is a daunting task. Therefore, designating a book as curriculum literature has become more problematic than ever before, invoking various possibilities:

1. Should curriculum literature be defined simply as the writings produced by those who self-identify with the curriculum field **through**

membership in various institutional forums, that is, those who be-
long to one or more of the following organizations: Division B (Curriculum Studies) of the American Educational Research Association
(AERA); the Special Interest Group on Critical Issues in Curriculum
of AERA; Professors of Curriculum; the Curriculum Teachers Network of the Association for Supervision and Curriculum Development (ASCD); The Society for the Study of Curriculum History;
ASCD itself (though it now has some 200,000 members); those who
attend the JCT conferences (often referred to as Bergamo Conferences); a new organization called the American Association for Curriculum and Teaching started in the mid-1990s; the Annual
Conferences on Curriculum and Pedagogy; the World Council for
Curriculum and Instruction; and similar organizations of curricularists (mostly from universities) outside the United States?

2. Should curriculum literature be defined as **books with the label** *cur-
    riculum* in the title (either including or excluding specific subject
    matter specialties)?

3. What if curriculum literature were defined as that which is written by
    authors who frequent the pages of prominent **curriculum journals**:
    *Curriculum Inquiry, Journal of Curriculum Studies, JCT, Journal of Cur-
    riculum and Supervision, Curriculum and Teaching* (Australia), or *Curricu-
    lum* (Great Britain)?

4. Should curriculum scholarship also include **authors of literature fre-
    quently cited by members of such organizations**, in books labeled as
    curriculum, and in curriculum journals, yet who did not generally use
    any of these forums for conversation on curriculum (e.g., John
    Dewey, Jerome Bruner, Charles Silberman, Madeline Hunter,
    Jonathan Kozol, Sarah Lawrence Lightfoot, Deborah Meier, Paulo
    Freire, Howard Gardner, William Glasser, E. D. Hirsch, Alfie Kohn)
    or who have seldom frequented the officially designated curriculum
    circles, except perhaps to whisk in to make a keynote address and
    leave?

5. What if today's curriculum literature were defined through **intellec-
    tual genealogy**, that is, as writings produced by those who have
    studied with major curriculum writers of earlier decades of the twen-
    tieth century, regardless of whether the literature fits conventional
    conceptions of curriculum? Would this not provide a sense of new
    vistas (e.g., teaching, supervision, educational reform, the context of

curriculum, teaching, and reform) produced by those who began by serious study of the substantive materials of the curriculum field?

6. What if curriculum literature were defined as **whatever responds to what we have identified throughout this book as basic curriculum questions**: What is worth knowing, experiencing, doing, being, sharing, and contributing? Why? When? How? Where? For whom? With what consequences? Given this purpose, what authors scattered throughout the several subfields of education would need to be included?

7. Moving more deeply and broadly into these questions, would one not need to depart from mere inclusion of those who write about *curriculum* or schooling to identify philosophers, writers, humanitarians, scientists, religious leaders, artists, public intellectuals, and leaders in business, industry, technology, and media, **insightful persons from everyday life** who cannot be categorized easily?

Given the expansiveness of what we can legitimately name as curriculum literature, it only seems defensible to employ these multiple perspectives to address the question of what constitutes curriculum literature today. Moreover, the holding of multiple and simultaneous perspectives is commensurate with the emergent postmodern ethos in today's curriculum field. While space does not permit the full range of providing such perspectives, we can illustrate possibilities here.

Throughout the remainder of this chapter, we move out from the most narrow definition of curriculum literature—works specifically denoted as regarding curriculum, most often addressing its enactment in school settings—to the consideration of curriculum as books about the "courses" of living. We look at some of the new and old categories for classifying curriculum literature throughout the century (see Schubert & Lopez Schubert, 1980; Schubert, 1986; Jackson, 1992a; and Pinar et al., 1995). We also look at illustrative curriculum scholars and discuss how their work has expanded over the years. Further, we examine, genealogically, a small sample of mentor-student connections and the ways in which successive generations have moved with curriculum inquiry. Importantly, we also reexamine the basic curriculum questions and reflect on who has contributed meaningful responses to them, with attention to those who have been left out of the curriculum field. Finally, we ask where responses to basic curriculum questions reside in today's culture and society. In essence, who are the actual curricularists of today, in and out of school, and what is their relationship to the field of curriculum studies?

Along with this, we try to imagine something about the who and the what of curriculum studies in the future.

CONTEMPORARY OVERVIEWS ON THE CURRICULUM FIELD

The synoptic is still an emphasis as we move into a new century of curriculum—now becoming increasingly difficult as numbers of relevant sources increase tremendously. New synoptic texts include Marsh and Willis (1995), Longstreet and Shane (1993), Morrison (1993), Pratt (1994), Henson (1995), the synoptic handbook of curriculum research by Jackson (1992a), an edited synopsis of forms of curriculum inquiry (Short, 1991), an empirical presentation of a knowledge base for curriculum (Behar, 1994), the aforementioned elaborate exposition of new discourse texts in curriculum studies by Pinar et al. (1995), and an attempt to portray curriculum studies through a collage of commentary, interviews, contextual events, and stories (Marshall, Sears, & Schubert, 2000). New editions of longer-standing synoptic texts from previous decades include Doll (1996, ninth edition), Eisner (1994b, third edition), Print (1993, second edition), Wiles and Bondi (1998, fifth edition), Oliva (1997, fourth edition), McNeil (1996, fifth edition), Hass and Parkay (1993, sixth edition), Ornstein and Hunkins (1993, second edition), Posner (1995, second edition), Tanner and Tanner (1995, third edition), and a hoped-for revision of Schubert (1986). Many of these synoptic texts are geared to the master's degree or administrative certificate market, although Eisner, Tanner and Tanner, Marsh and Willis, Pinar et al., Marshall, Sears, and Schubert are clearly valuable to doctoral students as well.

Collections of previously published writings are another form of synoptic presentation that has portrayed the field for several decades; fewer of these were produced in the 1990s, perhaps due to rising costs of permissions to republish. Examples include Hollins (1996b), Ornstein and Behar (1994), and Flinders and Thornton (1997). Numerous original edited collections by Teachers College Press and the State University of New York Press contain chapters by several authors around a common theme, thus having a kind of bounded synoptic character. Similar, too, are ASCD Yearbooks, three of which in the 1990s exhibit curriculum themes: Cawelti (1993) on 50 years of innovation through ASCD; Beane (1995) on curriculum coherence or integration; and Elmore and Furhman (1994) on governance issues and curriculum.

NEW CURRICULUM DISCOURSES

One could conceive of new discourses on curriculum as topical areas within which curriculum scholars could be identified. Pinar, Reynolds, Slattery, and Taubman (1995) do this very well in more than a thousand pages. Suffice it to review their categories and to merely note a few recent examples of curriculum *texts* of evolving interest in the 1990s: *historical text* (Gibboney, 1994; Kliebard, 1995; Kridel, Bullough, & Shaker, 1996; Marshall, Sears, & Schubert, 2000; Spring, 1998a; Tanner, 1997; Willis, Schubert, Bullough, Kridel, and Holton, 1994;); *political text* (Anyon, 1997; Apple, 1996; Freire, 1996; Giroux, 1997b); *racial text* (McCarthy, 1990; Carger, 1996; Delpit, 1995; Fine, Weis, Powell, & Mun Wong, 1997); *gender text* (Britzman, 1991; Casey, 1993; Foster, 1997; Gaskell & Willinsky, 1995; Grumet, 1988; Lather, 1991; Miller, 1990; Noddings, 1992 and 1993; Pagano, 1990; Sears, 1992); *phenomenological text* (Berman, Hultgren, Lee, Rivken, & Roderick, 1991; Pinar & Reynolds, 1992; van Manen & Levering, 1996); *postmodern text* (Doll, 1993; Giroux, Lankshear, McLaren, & Peters, 1996; Stanley, 1992; Slattery, 1995; Lather & Smithies, 1997; McLaren, 1994b and 1996; Oliver & Gershman, 1989); *biographical and autobiographical text* (Goodson & Hargreaves, 1996; Graham, 1991; Kincheloe & Pinar, 1991; Kridel, Bullough, & Shaker, 1996; Miller, 1990); *aesthetic text* (Barone, 2000; Eisner, 1991 and 1994b; Greene, 1995); *theological text* (Purpel, 1989; Moffett, 1994; Freire, 1994 and 1996; Palmer, 1998; Miller, 2000); *international text* (Esteva & Prakash, 1998; Gutek, 1993). Much overlap exists, of course, among these new texts, and it must be remembered that the separation of "texts" is for purposes of organization, analysis, and interpretation.

In addition to the new texts, novel variations have occurred within the institutional text. Some of these trends are available under perennial category labels (e.g., curriculum change, organization, implementation, policy, evaluation and assessment, inquiry, research, conceptual frameworks, approaches and methods, processes, and the several subject areas) as represented in Jackson's (1992) *Handbook of Research on Curriculum* and the *International Encyclopedia of Curriculum* (Lewy, 1991). Some innovative new categories and variations that are included in both of these encyclopedic volumes and have emerged in the broader literature on education at large are worth noting separately. Examples include the following varieties that pertain to curriculum: Meier (1995) and Fliegel and MacGuire (1993) on curriculum in small schools; Ayers (1993, 1995, 1997; and Ayers & Ford, 1996) on teaching, teacher education, and curriculum in urban education; Ellsworth and Whatley (1990) on the hidden curriculum of media in classrooms; Giroux (1994a) on learning from popular culture; Egan (1992, 1997) on his new vision of developmental theory for curriculum and teaching; Noddings (1984, 1989, 1992, 1993) on developing caring and basic beliefs through schooling; John Nicholls (1989; Nicholls & Hazzard, 1993; Nicholls & Thorkildsen, 1995) on students as curriculum theorists; several perspectives on the doing, enactment, or implementation of curriculum (e.g., Ben-Peretz, 1990; Boomer, Lester, Onore, & Cook, 1992; Hawthorne, 1992; Paris, 1993; McCutcheon, 1995); several orientations to curriculum evaluation (e.g., Eisner, 1985b; Wiggins, 1993; Darling-Hammond, Ancess, & Falk, 1995); and varieties of reform efforts (e.g., Sizer, 1992; Hess, 1991; Comer, 1993; Hunter, 1994; Comer, Haynes, Joyner, & Ben-Avie, 1996; and Hirsch, 1996).

More themes exist and are presented below in discussions of other ways to determine what literature is curriculum literature. In the above we included literature that authors self-identified as *curriculum*, for the most part. Now we consider some additional ways to identify literature as curricular in character.

THE EXPANSION OF EMPHASIS IN WORK
BY KEY CURRICULUM SCHOLARS

As the work of curriculum scholars evolves, it often moves into new realms. Should those realms still be considered curriculum studies? To illustrate the expansion *within* the work of some of the main contributors to the curriculum field referred to earlier in this book, let us sample expansive moves by John Goodlad, Jerome Bruner, Arthur Wellesley Foshay, Maxine Greene, Louise Berman, Louis Rubin, Elliot Eisner, Dwayne Huebner, Michael Apple, Henry Giroux, William Pinar, and others. Goodlad began in the late 1950s by proposing a new nongraded solution to the problem of curriculum organization, proceeded to add theoretical dimensions to the Tyler Rationale in the 1960s, analyzed curriculum policy and practice in the wake of post-*Sputnik* reform in the 1970s, looked pervasively at schooling in the 1980s (Goodlad, 1984), and in the 1990s moved to analyses of the preparation and character of teachers (Goodlad, 1994a; Goodlad et al., 1993, 1994a), a reconsideration of educational purpose writ large (Goodlad, 1994b), and most recently the broad notion of education of the person in democracy and the ecosystem (Goodlad, 1997; Goodlad & McMannon, 1997).

While Jerome Bruner (1960, 1966) began by creating the intellectual seedbed for post-*Sputnik* curriculum reform, he branched to more broadly construed intellectual interests in the 1980s and 1990s, conveyed by such titles as *Actual Minds, Possible Worlds* (1986) and *Acts of Meaning* (1990). Although Maxine Greene (1965) began by exposing through literature the gulf between the public school and the private vision and the existential plight of teachers (1973), she recently focuses on great public issues such as freedom (1988) and the political or social imagination (1995). Louise Berman's powerful admonition in the late 1960s for schools to move beyond a traditional subject-oriented curriculum and embrace a curriculum of *new priorities* of caring, decision making, perceiving, valuing, and the like (Berman, 1968) has been expanded through many iterations. In the 1990s, she focuses collaboratively with colleagues on curriculum as a phenomenological search to interpret meanings of questioning, alienation, journey, detour, caring, and dwelling vis-à-vis life itself, not just school alone (Berman, Hultgren, Lee, Rivkin, Roderick, 1991). Louis Rubin's interest in the curriculum of schools in the 1950s through the 1970s moved into a concern for in-service education and the notion of artistry in teaching (Rubin, 1984) in the 1980s and 1990s. Wells Foshay's research on school curriculum and teaching from the 1940s through the 1960s evolved to the development of a matrix that shows the great complexity of curriculum designed to expand self-awareness and self-realization through six aspects of the self: intellectual, emotional, social, physical, aesthetic, and transcendent or spiritual (Foshay, 2000). Elliot Eisner began in the 1960s and 1970s by critiquing behavioral objectives, proposing expressive objectives, and offering a notion of evaluation that involved educational criticism and connoisseurship. He refined these aspects and many related ideas in synoptic form in *The Educational Imagination* (1979, 1985c, 1994b), and expanded his views throughout the 1990s, by advocating a broader array of ways of knowing applied to teaching and learning (Eisner, 1985b), relating curriculum to broader notions of cognition (1994a), and advocating an arts-based, imaginative orientation to educational research (1991). Dwayne Huebner, who in the 1960s and 1970s challenged curricularists with questions about classroom meanings and the need for new languages for expressing them, moved wholly toward an interest in the spiritual nature of life by moving from his professorial position at Teachers College, Columbia, to hold an appointment in the 1990s at the Yale Divinity School.

Huebner's most well-known student of curriculum, Michael Apple, opened up new languages of inquiry into the ideological ramifications of curriculum in schools (1979). Later, his inquiries explored broader spheres of the interplay of education and power in schools (1982b) and the political economy of texts (1986). In the 1990s, Apple sees the problem as even more pervasive, dealing with matters of official knowledge (1993) and cultural politics (1996) that actually create or subvert democratic education (Apple & Beane, 1995). Similarly, Henry Giroux's work in the late 1970s and early 1980s focused on the hidden curriculum of schools (1981; Giroux & Purpel, 1983) and ways to oppose its impositions (Giroux, 1983). In the late 1980s and 1990s, his work has moved to other educational venues of identity and culture, for example, work (1991), difference (1993), popular media (1994a), and cultural studies (Giroux & Shannon, 1997). William Pinar began in the

1970s to characterize the emergent reconceptualization of curriculum studies that would within a decade dominate curriculum theory. His own work focused on the identification and expansion of discourses (Pinar et al., 1995) that would expand the field in many different (often complementary and collaborative) directions—autobiographical, phenomenological, psychoanalytical, deconstructional (Pinar, 1988, 1994; Pinar & Reynolds, 1992; Kincheloe & Pinar, 1991).

The above authors were selected because the trends of their work extend over two or more decades, sometimes four or five. The point that clearly emerges here is that many of the key curriculum writers have widened the scope of their lens, progressing from focus on curriculum as a phenomenon of schooling to curriculum as a more pervasive social and cultural phenomenon. Many other authors, both seasoned and new to the field, would reveal a similar trend. Even a cursory glance at the foregoing sample of contributors to the curriculum field shows that the work carved out by curriculum scholars includes democracy, ideological analysis, the ecosystem, spirituality, meaning, imagination, autobiography, and more. This variety indicates that the curriculum field is not merely a subset of educational inquiry; neither is it only the concern of one institution—schools. Rather, the essence of curriculum studies lies at the heart of all cultural forms that educate. For example, while the senior author of this book began his career with publications on the curriculum field and its synoptic state, he expanded his interests to the arts as a neglected source of insight into what is worth knowing (Willis & Schubert, 1991), later explored teachers as bearers of experiential curriculum insights which he called *teacher lore* (Schubert & Ayers, 1992), moved to a similar treatment of student perspectives called *student lore*,[1] and more recently is rekindling a position that says we need to move to nonschool settings to understand what is worth knowing and experiencing (Schubert, 1981, 1982, 1986, 1994, 1995).[2] Such topics include the ways in which outlooks are formed and continuously re-formed by experience in homes, families, peer groups, non-school organizations, mass media, hobbies, jobs, and more.

Once again, should some of this expansion be seen as a moving away from curriculum studies, should it be considered a clear departure of interest, or is it better viewed as a reformulation of what constitutes meaningful curriculum inquiry?

FROM MENTOR TO STUDENT AND ONWARD

Another way to investigate curriculum literature is to look at mentor-student connections, what we have called curriculum genealogy.[3] In this case let us look at several mentor-student connections that have led to a proliferation of novel scholarly work in the 1990s; we begin with Elliot Eisner of Stanford, Paul Klohr of Ohio State University, William Pinar of Louisiana State University, and Michael Apple of the University of Wisconsin, noting the mentorship chain of each of these scholars, and briefly trace their students whose work is now well-known in the curriculum field of the 1990s.

Elliot Eisner studied with John Goodlad at the University of Chicago (who in turn studied there with Ralph Tyler); at Chicago, Eisner was also influenced by Joseph Schwab, Frank Chase, Philip Jackson, and Benjamin Bloom. Eisner's students were of course influenced by Eisner's emphasis on aesthetics, the educational imagination, criticism and connoisseurship as a basis for qualitative research, and so forth, the seedbed of which doubtless grew from the University of Chicago experience and the art communities in Chicago. Let us consider the examples of several of Eisner's most prominent students: Decker Walker, Gail McCutcheon, Elizabeth Vallance, Thomas Barone, Robert Donmoyer, James Henderson, Stephen Thornton, and David Flinders. Decker Walker remained at Stanford and is now a widely recognized senior professor there. He focused on the topic of curricular aims (Walker & Soltis, 1992) and prepared a synoptic text (Walker, 1990) patterned in some respects after the renowned text of Hilda Taba (1962). Walker offered an alternative model to the Tyler Rationale on how curriculum is formed (a naturalistic or political model),[4] and has been concerned with educational technology and curriculum (Hess & Walker, 1984). His practical work (Reid & Walker, 1975), associated with Schwab's practical deliberation and the work of Gail McCutcheon, both take the aesthetic perception of Eisner into problems of the institutionalized text in novel and enlightened ways. McCutcheon (1995) has focused primarily on collaborative curriculum making with schools. Vallance has focused on the hidden curriculum through application of perspectives drawn from educational criticism, and she eventually turned to education in the non-school sphere of the art museum (in St. Louis). Barone has refined a vision of educational criticism to form a literary nonfiction and even fictionalized (story and novel-like) writings about educational phenomena (Barone, 2000). Donmoyer has focused on a range of issues about educational research as feature editor of *Educational Researcher* in the 1990s, while his book-length treatments have dealt with policy matters such as the knowledge base for school administration (1995) and portraits of "at risk" students (1995). Henderson took his connoisseurship into reflective teaching (1992) and leadership (Henderson & Hawthorne, 1995). Thornton, while compiling with Flinders (Flinders & Thornton, 1997) a book of readings to depict some of the key publications on curriculum studies over the years, has turned much of his work toward social studies education. Flinders has worked with C. A. Bowers on several occasions to create responsive curriculum from a new ecological perspective (Bowers & Flinders, 1990, 1991). Eisner's contribution has been expanded by former students to include practical deliberation, collaboration in classrooms using educational criticism as a basis for evaluation, work in arts education from a non-school perspective, fictional and literary nonfictional writing about education, and ecological responsiveness to matters of curriculum and teaching.

A look at key students of Paul Klohr illustrates a proliferation of inquiry paths that move creatively apart from the traditional curriculum development emphasis of the field (the dominant mode until the 1970s). They include: Norman Overly, with whom both Patti Lather and James T. Sears studied; Paul Shaker; Robert Bullough, with whom Gary Knowles studied; Janet Miller; Lee Chairlotte; Craig Kridel; and William Pinar, with whom Madeleine Grumet, Ronald Padgham, Tony Whitson, William Reynolds, Patrick Slattery, and Peter Taubman studied. Overly (1970) pioneered the hidden curriculum in the early 1970s and throughout his career emphasized international perspectives on curriculum through the World Council for Curriculum and Instruction. Kridel focuses on curriculum artifacts, historical documents, history (1989), biography, and mentor-student connections (Kridel, Bullough, & Shaker, 1996). Bullough, too, is concerned with historical foundations of curriculum and particularly with the life history of teachers (e.g., Bullough, 1989, and Bullough, Knowles, & Crow, 1991). Janet Miller, too, has set her curriculum-derived interests in the lives of teachers (Miller, 1990) and has made marked contributions to the development of gender and autobiographical discourses (see Pinar et al., 1995, Chapters 7 and 10). Miller's organization of the JCT conferences has immeasurably furthered the reconceptualization of the curriculum field from the mid-1970s, through the 1980s and the 1990s. Finally, William Pinar (1974, 1975) set the tone for the reconceptualization of curriculum studies,[5] which fully proliferated in the 1990s, as revealed in *Understanding Curriculum* (Pinar, Reynolds, Slattery, & Taubman, 1995). Thus, from Klohr and from Klohr's close curriculum colleagues of his generation, James B. Macdonald and Dwayne Huebner (both of whom had studied with Virgil Herrick at the University of Wisconsin), we find his former students expanding the curriculum field to include exploration of the lives of teachers, mentors, and scholars through autobiography, biography, issues of identity, feminist scholarship, and critical questioning derived from literature, the arts, phenomenology, existentialism, depth psychology, radical psychoanalysis, and more. Klohr, who had studied with Harold Alberty (student of renowned philosopher of education Boyd Bode), had been immersed in the literature of the Eight Year Study and brought progressive perspectives to professional organizations such as ASCD. Klohr has been noted for his teaching and profound encouragement of doctoral students, and those he mentored went on to mentor others with similar inspiration.

Besides being influenced profoundly by Klohr, William Pinar is intellectually indebted to Dwayne Huebner and by James B. Macdonald (Macdonald's key works have been compiled in book form by his son; see Macdonald, 1995). Huebner, in *Curricular Language and Classroom Meanings*,[6] called for the curriculum field to move beyond preoccupation with technical and scientific languages to embrace new meanings through political, ethical, and aesthetic languages (a definitive collection of Huebner's work, edited by Hillis, was published in 1999). It can readily be seen that Pinar and his students have deeply embraced ethical and aesthetic languages. Madeleine Grumet has embodied aesthetic form and content in her writing and has provided a unique feminist and autobiographic literature of curriculum that draws from many sources—existential, phenomenological, and radical psychoanalytic, literary, and artistic (Grumet, 1988; and Pinar et al., 1995, Chapters 7, 8, 10, 11). Ronald Padgham made great strides to show how to build curriculum theory from immersion in twentieth century art and the issues surrounding it (see Pinar et al., 1995, Chapter 11), before his untimely death. Tony Whitson (1991) has drawn on his experience and knowledge as a lawyer and his immersion in semiotics and curriculum theory to provide an innovative interpretation of the U.S. Constitution and supreme court decisions. William Reynolds's work, in addition to his second authorship on *Understanding Curriculum*, has contributed to the understanding of curriculum as a hermeneutic, phenomenological, and deconstructed text (see Reynolds, 1989; Pinar & Reynolds, 1992), and he has brought curriculum perspectives to bear on larger educational issues (Martusewicz & Reynolds, 1994). Patrick Slattery, in addition to his contributions as third author of Pinar et al. (1995), drew from both theological and postmodern texts to create a postmodern perspective on *curriculum development* (Slattery, 1995), a term albeit reconceived but one from a previous incarnation that the emphasis on *understanding* sought to overcome. Peter Taubman (in addition to the synoptic work for Pinar et al., 1995) has contributed to the literatures on gender and identity in postmodern curriculum discourse (see Pinar et al., 1995, Chapters 7 and 9). Susan Edgerton (a former student of both Pinar and William Doll) has contributed to an integrated emphasis on identity through postmodern, racial, aesthetic, and gender texts (see Pinar et al., 1995, Chapters 6, 7, 9, 11). Thus, Pinar and his students have contributed markedly to contemporary curriculum theory, especially relative to gender, racial, autobiographical, aesthetic, postmodern (and identity), and theological discourses.

Michael Apple, mentored by Huebner in doctoral studies, built a world-wide sphere of influence through translations of his writings and those of his students, many of whom are at major universities. This work expands power-fully what Huebner called for as the political language for curriculum.[7] Among others, Apple's students include Landon Beyer, Andrew Gitlin, Joel Taxel, Jesse Goodman, Kathleen Casey, Cameron McCarthy, Daniel Liston, Linda Christian-Smith, Kenneth Teitlebaum, Dennis Carlson, Nancy King, Susan Jungck, and Linda Valli. As this group grows, the notion of ideological critique of curriculum expands. Beyer and Apple (1988) pushed frontiers of political analysis of curriculum, while Beyer, Feinberg, Pagano, and Whitson (1989) advocated critical educational studies that embraced the liberal arts in the curriculum of teacher education. With Daniel Liston, Beyer has provided a set of social visions for progressive education (Beyer & Liston, 1996), and he refined this in *Creating Democratic Classrooms* (Beyer, 1996) with practical proposals for blending theory and practice. Jesse Goodman (1991), too, writes persuasively of what democratic elementary schooling might be. Linda McNeil (1986) draws on ethnographic inquiry in classrooms to show ideological constraints that work against democratic experiences in the pursuits of learning as increased meaning, critique, and relevant action. Andrew Gitlin (1994) joins political activism and educational research, showing that advocacy is a part of inquiry itself. Clearly, through these writings, one is led to conclude that curriculum studies is more pervasive than deciding what to teach and learn, because it must address how to inquire or research what to teach and learn. Joel Taxel has furthered ideological critique into the area of children's literature, a realm that has been somewhat atheoretical, through his work as editor of the journal, *The New Advocate*, and in other writing. Cameron McCarthy and Warren Crichlow (1993) raise matters of race, identity, and representation—going beyond the canon—in an effort to add neglected breadth to curriculum studies. Kathleen Casey (1993) looks at teachers as embodiments of curricular assumptions as they devote their lives to their students in an effort to overcome constraints of control and competitiveness. Liston and Zeichner (1991) address relationships between teacher education and the social conditions of schooling, exploring what a social reconstruction-ist form of teacher education might be.

It is readily admitted that many more mentor-student connections exist in the curriculum field. For instance, more could be said about those who studied with James B. Macdonald (e.g., Esther Zaret, Alex Molnar, John Zahorik, David Purpel, Dale Brubaker, John [Steve] Mann). Esther Zaret and Bernice Wolfson joined Macdonald in authoring *Reschooling Society* (Macdonald, Wolfson, & Zaret, 1973), a demonstration of their faith in schools as an antidote to Ivan Illich's (1972) *Deschooling Society*. Purpel (1993) called for a remedy to the neglect of the spiritual in education at large. Brubaker has called through several decades for curriculum as a function of teachers and educational leaders. Steve Mann's mentorship (before leaving the curriculum field) of George Willis and William Doll can surely be considered a notable contribution. In the 1990s, Willis has furthered work on historical (Willis, et al., 1994), aesthetic (Willis & Schubert, 1991), and synoptic (Marsh & Willis, 1995) dimensions of curriculum, while Doll has presented a rendition of the postmodern for curriculum theory and practice, the latter being no mean feat indeed (Doll, 1993). Molnar (1997) has recently critiqued the massive influence of corporate business interests in schools.

Another major figure in curriculum in the 1990s is Daniel Tanner. Daniel and Laurel Tanner published the third edition of their famous *Curriculum Development: Theory into Practice* (Tanner & Tanner, 1995) on the heels of *History of the School Curriculum* (Tanner & Tanner, 1990). Their work on supervision links that topic with curriculum in ways that much technical supervision literature neglects, and they show the common historical roots of work on curriculum development and supervision. Independently, too, each of these coauthors has published widely. Daniel Tanner's earlier work in secondary education has been well regarded for more than two decades (see Tanner, 1971 and 1972), and his history of the John Dewey Society from its beginnings in 1935 to the early 1990s is a contribution that bears strongly on curriculum history, as well as the educational foundations generally. Laurel Tanner (1978) has placed the problem of school discipline in curriculum and historical contexts, and she has organized an examination of perennial curriculum development issues in the Eighty-seventh Yearbook of the National Society for the Study of Education (Tanner, 1988). Recently, her elaborate study of Dewey's Laboratory School documents provided the seedbed for a book (Tanner, 1997) that draws lessons for curriculum, teaching, supervision, and administration today. Interestingly, the Tanners' work draws heavily from Dewey and the progressive and social reconstructionist history of the first half of the twentieth century, but they have been critical of and seldom acknowledge contributions by curriculum scholars who are associated with the reconceptualizations of curriculum studies since the 1970s. Some of the principal viewpoints embedded within much of this reconceptualization are seen by many as kindred spirits to Dewey and other progressives (e.g., Jane Addams, Ella Flagg Young, Francis W. Parker, Carleton Washburne, Boyd Bode, Harold Rugg, William H. Kilpatrick, L. Thomas Hopkins, George S. Counts,

Caroline Pratt, Hollis Caswell, Stephen M. Corey, and Alice Miel). These scholars and much of the debate on curriculum from the late 1890s through mid-century is reflected in the work of the Tanners and is carried on by prominent students of Daniel Tanner, for example, Peter Hlebowitsh and William Wraga. Hlebowitsh (1993) raises numerous criticisms of the lines of scholarship represented by Macdonald, Huebner, Apple, Pinar, Giroux, and others of similar vein, using a context of progressive literature to do so. Wraga (1994) provides a treatment of the history of and possibilities of the comprehensive public high school as the source of potential for Deweyan progressive ideals in a democracy, and he has strongly critiqued reconceptualist sources in the *Educational Researcher*, which has led to a continuing exchange by William Pinar, James Henderson, and other authors in *ER* and other publications.[8]

Another network of curriculum scholars in Canada can be traced from Michael Connelly (student of Joseph Schwab and founding editor of *Curriculum Inquiry*), who developed a novel, practical connection between curriculum and the personal and practical thinking of teachers that is depicted in work with his student at OISE, Jean Clandinin (Connelly & Clandinin, 1988; Clandinin, Davies, Hogan, & Kennard, 1993; Clandinin & Connelly, 1995).

Many other students of Schwab, more recently Connelly, and most recently Clandinin could be traced as well, but those are additional stories of connection in the curriculum field, which could lead to a book-length treatment of curriculum genealogy. For example, one could elaborate the work of Ted Aoki at the University of Alberta, his students over many years, especially Max van Manen (see van Manen, 1990, 1991; van Manen & Levering, 1996), as well as that of van Manen's students, for example, David Smith, Stephen Smith, and others. Too, at Cornell University, George Posner (a former student of Mauritz Johnson) has made considerable strides through his work on curriculum analysis, curriculum reflection in field experience for preservice teachers, and course design (see Posner, 1996, and Posner & Rudnitsky, 1997), and Posner's students, Jean King, Deborah Trumbull, and others are extending this influence. At the University of Chicago, Philip Jackson's work has been respected for decades (e.g., Jackson, 1968, 1986, 1990, 1992a, 1992b); his philosophical discourses, often based on careful observation of teachers and classrooms, also focuses on, moral aspect of teaching (Jackson, Boostrom, & Hansen, 1993), and his synoptic editing of the state of perennial topics in curriculum as an institutional text, in the *Handbook of Research on Curriculum* (Jackson, 1992a), is a first of its kind in the curriculum field. His prominent students, Karen Zumwalt, former Dean of Teachers College, Columbia University, Lauren Sosniak (Anderson & Sosniak, 1994), David Hansen (1995), and many others, build on his work in curriculum. In England, starting at the University of East Anglia, work of the late Lawrence Stenhouse on teachers as researchers continues to be expanded by a coterie of British and Australian curriculum scholars including Jean Rudduck, Barry McDonald, Helen Simon, John Elliot, Stephen Kemmis, Robin McTaggart, Malcolm Skilbeck, and others.

An essential and interesting point about mentor-student connections is their complexity. Most scholars were influenced before, during, and especially after doctoral studies by a configuration of scholars in addition to their official mentors. One could argue, for instance, that sites of doctoral study are more important than specific mentors. Thus, students from the 1970s to the present at the University of Wisconsin in curriculum studies must have studied with Apple, Herbert Kliebard, Thomas Popkewitz, and Ken Zeichner, among others, while those at Stanford were doubtless influenced by Eisner, Nel Noddings, Larry Cuban, Decker Walker, Michael Kirst, D. C. Phillips, Lee Shulman, Lee Cronbach, and David Tyack; similarly those at Chicago experience the impact of Jackson, Benjamin Bloom, Joseph Schwab, Harold Dunkel, Herbert Thelen, and of course Ralph W. Tyler, even if most of them are no longer there and they are closing their department. Students at Ohio State today would be influenced by Patti Lather, Gail McCutcheon, Robert Donmoyer, Beverly Gordon, and more, while the diverse legacy of Paul Klohr, Jack Frymier, Alexander Frazier, Laura Zirbes, Harold and Elsie Alberty, and others can still be found. Today at Pennsylvania State University, any curriculum student would likely be affected by Dan Marshall, Henry Giroux, Murry Nelson, Madhu Prakash, Joe Kincheloe, Shirley Steinberg, and in the recent past Edmund C. Short. Today's curriculum student at Indiana University is mentored by Landon Beyer, Jesse Goodman, Kate Cruikshank, Stephen Thornton, David Flinders, Nancy Lesko, and Donald Warren, with recent past influences of Norman Overly, Harold Shane, Shirley Engle, and more. At the University of Illinois (Urbana-Champaign) current influences include Ian Westbury and Frederick Rodgers, and in the past Louis Rubin, J. Harlan Shores, B. Othanel Smith, Harry S. Broudy, Lawrence Metcalf, Joe R. Burnett, William O. Stanley, and more. At the University of South Carolina, Craig Kridel, Lorin Anderson, and James T. Sears are prominent influences in curriculum. Over the past few years at Louisiana State University, in addition to William Pinar, students have encountered William Doll, Tony Whitson, Wendi Kohli, Petra Munro, William Stanley, and Jacques Daignault. At the University of Illinois at Chicago, William H. Schubert, William Ayers, David Hansen, Caroline Heller, William H. Watkins, Herbert Walberg, Annette Henry, John Nicholls, Donald Hellison, Mark Smylie, Timothy Shanahan, Victoria Chou, Terri Thokildsen, Christine Pappas, Steven Tozer, Mark Smylie, Bernardo Gallegos, and others would be among the prominent influences. At the University of Maryland, one finds Louise Berman, Jessie Roderick, Steven Selden, Francine Hultgren, Diane Lee, and Mary Rivkin. At Harvard the curriculum student would doubtless have the impact of Donald Oliver, Sarah Lawrence Lightfoot, Robert Coles, Courtney Cazden, Roland Barth, Eleanor Duckworth, and the legacy of Israel Scheffler, Robert Ulich, Jeanne Chall, and other luminaries. At the University of Washington one finds such scholars as James Banks, Geneva Gay, John Goodlad, Francis Hunkins, Walter Parker, Nathalie Gehrke, and Kenneth Sirotnik. Teachers College, once a "mecca" of curriculum studies, has a history in curriculum-related scholars that includes Dewey, Thorndike, Rugg, Counts, Kilpatrick, L. Thomas Hopkins, Jesse Newlon, Patty Smith Hill, and Hollis Caswell—then more recently, Gordon MacKenzie, Alice Miel, Florence Stratemeyer, Philip Phenix, Arno Bellack, Arthur W. Foshay, Dwayne Huebner, Jonas Soltis, Ann Lieberman, Linda Darling-Hammond; and today Maxine Greene, Celia Oyler, Fran Bolin, Rene Arcilla, Janet Miller, Steve Thornton, David Hansen, Nancy Lesko, and Karen Zumwalt. Prominent faculty members move, often more quickly than one can publish their whereabouts, yet their legacy lives on at several stopping points.

These sets of mentor-student interests in curriculum scholarship and networks of scholars at noteworthy institutions, derived principally from genealogical linkages, demonstrate a vast expansion of interests that began in curriculum development and moved across generations of scholars to a whole range of attempts to understand, critique, and act educationally with large-scale curriculum questions in mind: What is worthwhile? Who says? Why? How is it acquired? What are its consequences? Whose interests are served?

CURRICULUM DEFINED SIMPLY BY THE QUESTIONS OF WORTH

The aforementioned questions may be the best guide to what should constitute the curriculum literature. In other words, whatever writings (whether recognized as part of the curriculum field or not) provide perspective on these questions should be considered curriculum literature. If this position were accepted, a much wider net would have to be cast throughout the wide range of writers in the field of education, not just those associated with accepted curriculum scholars and their scholarly or professional associations or those who publish in journals having *curriculum* on the masthead. In the past, for instance, the historical work of scholars outside the field of curriculum has had major impacts on those recognized as within the curriculum field, such as the history of Lawrence Cremin; the psychology of Jerome Bruner or Jean Piaget; the philosophy of Harry Broudy or Israel Scheffler; the sociology of

Willard Waller, James Coleman, or Robert Havighurst; the educational reform of Leo Tolstoy, Maria Montessori, or A. S. Neill; the revolutionary theory and practices of Ivan Illich or Paulo Freire; and many more. Today's curriculum scholars still frequently turn to these scholars. Leaders of curriculum practice and policymakers, however, now turn to a new generation of outsiders (though some hover between outsider and insider) for consultation: Howard Gardner, Alfie Kohn, David and Roger Johnson, E. D. Hirsch, Linda Darling-Hammond, William Bennett, William Glasser, Jonathan Kozol, Robert Sternberg, James Beane, Carl Glickman, Robert Coles. Additionally, a host of full-time consultants whose major commitment includes speaking and consulting about extant scholarly work, and publishing in the more popular professional and general public domains (e.g., Bruce Joyce, Daniel Goleman, Art Costa, Pat Wolfe, Heidi Hayes Jacobs, Spencer Kagan, William Daggett, Larry Lezotte, Roger Taylor) and dominate the upscale market of keynote speakers for educational institutes, conferences, and in-service programs. Indeed, it would be interesting to study exactly how the most "in-demand" speakers for educator audiences (including Madeline Hunter, Robert Mager, and others of the past as well as current big-time consultants) have influenced institutional practices.

Taking this line of thinking to its next level of expansion, if the curriculum field were based on the question of worth ("What is worth knowing and experiencing?") and its correlates as noted earlier, then it would seem that the whole world of insightful commentary on the human condition would need to be called curriculum studies—drawing from both past and contemporary philosophy, social sciences, psychology, religion and theology, chemistry and biology, other sciences, the arts, the humanities, and interdisciplinary discourses, both scholarly and popular. Clearly, within the curriculum literature today one can readily find frequent citations in curriculum theory writings to many who would not be considered within the field of education, such as Cornel West, Hannah Arendt, Richard Bernstein, Michel Foucault, Jacque Lacan, Richard Rorty, Pierre Bourdieu, Betty Friedan, Amy Gutmann, Sandra Harding, Mary Belenky, Carol Gilligan, bell hooks, Molefi Asante, Clifford Geertz, Jean Houston, Howard Zinn—to name only a few. Surely, a strong case can be made for the deeper domain of curriculum literature, as well, being embodied in powerful writings of human beings stretching back throughout ancient times and many cultures. This would include works of art and literature, not just nonfictional commentaries. Thus, great artists, musicians, playwrights, novelists, poets, and storywriters of all kinds (including the twentieth-century literatures of film and television) could be seen as sources of curriculum insight. Does this mean that they are curriculum writers? Is this out of the question? From Tolstoy to Toni Morrison, from Aristophenes to Camus, from Dante to Dickinson, from Aesop to James Baldwin, from Sappho to Dickens, from Confucius to Gandhi, from Shakespeare to Wole Soyinka, from Borges to Vonnegut, from Gabriel Garcia Marquez to Isabel Allende, from Mozart to Ella Fitzgerald, from da Vinci to Picasso—are they not all curricularists if they inspire their audience to reflect on what is worth knowing, experiencing, needing, being, doing, overcoming, and sharing?

THE EXPANDING CURRICULUM

One way to learn about this curriculum question is to ask others and ourselves what conditions and circumstances foster powerful learning. To listen carefully to our own stories and to those of others about the pathways or journeys that have brought about powerful learning experiences is one of the best (and sadly most neglected) ways to learn about curriculum. Within such stories we can ask: What was the environment like? The atmosphere or ambience? What were the social circumstances? Who helped and how did they treat you? Who determined the purposes and thought about the rationale for them?

When we engage our students in such reflection and storytelling we find that most of their powerful learning experiences have occurred outside of school. We wonder why, together with our students, only partially being able to set forth adequate explanations. Nevertheless, we go on to wonder whether the learners with whom we work (in our schools, classrooms, other formal educational settings, or informal settings outside of school) are able to experience the kinds of conditions we experienced to make our most powerful learnings emerge. Often participants sadly report that few opportunities for these powerful learning experiences exist in schools they know. We move ahead to ask what would need to be done to enable more conditions for powerful learning to exist in their schools or other educational settings in which they are involved.

Convinced that we should not ask of others what we do not ask of ourselves, we too reflect on these questions. The story of one of us (Bill Schubert) engaged in such reflection will illustrate the process in abbreviated form, and in similar fashion to the story set forth in *Turning Points in Curriculum* (Marshall, Sears, & Schubert, 2000):

When I think about the origins of the work that I do as a curriculum professor, I reflect on the skills, knowledge, and values that enable me to do this work. I think back to growing up on a farm in Indiana, an only child, a family of educators, small-town community life, a loving, nurturing family with high (but not too high) standards. I think of my parents, grandparents, and great-aunt, who conjured up stories and characters to imagine with me. Too, I reflect on the books, the movies, and the television shows that were sites of thinking aloud about the world and social life. I think about the sports we played and watched, the collections we made, the closeness to nature of farm life, cooperative work, the everyday problem solving, the fun and laughter, and the planning for and engaging in extensive travel during summer vacations, wherein we drove throughout all of the contiguous United States, much of Canada, and some of Mexico.

All of these experiences inspired my images of what is worth knowing, doing, pondering, being, overcoming, and sharing. These activities and the loving interest that accompanied them were my most important curriculum. I was a student in schools where my father was a respected administrator, and where my mother, grandmother, and great-aunt were recognized as excellent, dedicated teachers. More than any schooling, the informal experiences with family and friends are the seedbed for any skill, knowledge, or value that I could identify. (Marshall, Sears, & Schubert, 2000, pp. 232–233).

My stories, of course, include current family life—the innumerable ideas and experiences I have gleaned from my wife (Ann), children, and other family members as we have tried to orchestrate the resources of our home, city, and occasional travels to learn and grow.

This, however, is not to say that my formal education has been for naught. It has nevertheless been at its best for me when I engaged in self-designed study. The few independent studies or very small seminars in my bachelor's and master's work were of great value to me. My doctoral study was almost entirely seminars, conferences, and independent studies. I recall feeling in touch with scholars throughout the ages as I wandered amidst some 5 million books in stacks of the University of Illinois Library in Urbana. This kind of study was facilitated by J. Harlan Shores, my doctoral adviser, and others with whom I studied for the Ph.D. As a former elementary school teacher, I was intrigued by the question of what enabled teachers to be imaginative. I was convinced (and still am) that the imagination, grounded in philosophical reflection, is an indispensable resource for creating curriculum. This quest led me inward to reflect on my own teaching and learning experience, to compare what I have learned with relevant educational literature, to look for it through ethnography in classrooms, to search philosophical classics for insight on imagination, to do the same in literature and the arts, to learn from teaching teachers to be more imaginative, to juxtapose them with those not taught through comparative empirical study, to investigate progressive educational history and theory for understandings of imaginative teaching, to study the workings of imagination in my own teaching situation as a participant observer, and to relate what all of this taught me to the existing curriculum literature. Thus, my dissertation built on all of these inquiry modes and more. Beyond the dissertation, I thought that work should be done to show that imaginative curricula go far beyond that which can be written and packaged for mere implementation. Imaginative curricular experiences must grow out of the interaction of teachers and *learners—their environments, histories, anticipated futures, hopes, dreams, and immediate concerns. I saw this as the cutting edge of curriculum work. I wanted to play some part in helping to move toward adding this perspective to the curriculum field.*

When I accepted my first full-time university position in 1975, I wanted to continue to develop this work, but this didn't happen directly until considerably later. I learned that it is difficult for a beginning assistant professor to work at the cutting edge of the field. First one must prove oneself by making contributions that senior scholars in the field already appreciate. Therefore, I turned my attention to curriculum history, thinking that to centralize the field's resources would be a worthy accomplishment. Together with Ann Lopez, I focused on books, creating Curriculum Books: The First Eighty Years *(Schubert & Lopez Schubert, 1980), a modest attempt to capture an historical perspective on an essentially ahistorical field. After several years of teaching foundational master's and doctoral courses in curriculum, and always having more to relate than time permitted, I decided to write a book that was about the field as I saw it, thus authoring* Curriculum: Perspective, Paradigm, and Possibility *(Schubert, 1986). I wanted to present for graduate students a view of both perennial categories of curriculum studies and emergent perspectives that heretofore had been largely omitted from synoptic texts. I also worked into my text considerations that I had presented in articles and chapters over the years: the practical paradigm, the paradigm of critical praxis, the need to include teachers and learners in the configuration we call curriculum, the need to acknowledge the hidden and null curriculum, varieties of sources for understanding curricular consequences (e.g., science, art, philosophy, personal knowledge), the inequitable access to imaginative curriculum (due to race, class, gender, age, ethnicity, beliefs, health, ableness, and more), the need to attend to curricula implicit in non-school experiences (e.g., homes, families, churches, sports, clubs, television, film, popular music, jobs, hobbies), and the need to see an expansive curriculum that entails the many dimensions of life that have an impact on the outlooks of human beings.*

I began to join with colleagues to create books that provide more extensive treatment of some of these variations of expansion of the curriculum field. For instance, Edmund Short, George Willis, and I tried to summarize several of the ways the AERA SIG on Creation and Utilization of Curriculum Knowledge expanded curriculum knowledge from the mid-1970s to the mid-1980s (see Short, Willis, & Schubert, 1985*). Later, Willis and I also became convinced that many in the field had been influenced substantially by the arts (literature, art, music, theatre) and that these influences, in turn, had a big impact on the way they perceive curriculum and teaching. So we brought together 30-some curriculum scholars to write autobiographically about the ways in which a work of art, a genre, or a combination of artistic experiences have shaped their conception of curriculum, teaching, and related matters (*Willis & Schubert, 1991*). Together, we pointed to the expansion of curriculum inquiry.*

Growing from interactions with a study group of graduate students, which started in the mid-1980s to produce dissertations and articles based on the experiential knowledge of teachers, Bill Ayers and I developed the Teacher Lore Project (Schubert & Ayers, 1992). In the late 1980s, several curriculum colleagues and I worried about the fact that major curriculum documents were still relevant to current practical and theoretical discussions; however, they were no longer accessible. Therefore, we set out to provide an anthology that made relevant excerpts available (see Willis, Schubert, Bullough, Kridel, & Holton, 1992). We had been involved in initial years of the Society for the Study of Curriculum History, founded in 1977, so we saw this volume as extending our commitment to prevent curriculum from being unaware of its own history.

Focus on history, however, brought new concerns and wonders for me. What is the curriculum field, how is it conceived, and how should it be conceived? The need for expansion is surely borne out by the comments and contributions of those we interviewed for Turning Points in Curriculum *(Marshall, Sears, & Schubert, 2000). William Watkins, my former doctoral student, has helped us include more African American literatures,[9] and if we take seriously our basic curriculum questions of worth, we see blatantly that many non-white, non-male contributions to understanding what is worth knowing...have been grievously neglected. From another perspective, Alex Molnar has told us he learned from James Macdonald that curriculum, taken seriously, involves "study of how to have a world." Molnar went on to argue that he wants to address "ideas that are much more profound than can be expressed within the boundaries of the curriculum field," as it it currently conceived. We need, he admonishes, to give "attention to larger historical developments so that it is possible to express how [they]...manifest themselves in a place called school or in an institution called education."[10] I think that we must let the quest move beyond schooling and the usual confines of education to ask: What is it that enables the journey of growth to enhance human perspective? Whatever that is should be the most valuable subject matter to study as curricularists. As Molnar put it, "I thought that what I was part of and what I was experiencing was part of the evolution into the future....I was playing with ideas whose time was on the way." From a different perspective, one that looks back to ideological analysis as central to the concerns of curriculum study that embraces a broader politics of multicultural sources, Watkins says in his interview that curriculum studies today is "becoming so complicated and complex and multi-dimensional and chaotically postmodern that...it's not really going to be a field much longer, if it still is." As I see it, we may need to move beyond conceptualizing or even reconceptualizing ourselves as a field, but as strands of inquiry united only because of basic human concerns that lie beneath our hope for insight into fundamental curriculum questions about worthwhile lives. Giroux's sentiment is in many ways similar. "I was interested in combining a number of fields that simply could not be contained by curriculum theory....to me the field of curriculum theory is about theories of schooling...not about...broader issues...concerning the deconstruction...of popular media or popular culture." He goes on to say, "The more interesting people in curriculum theory had begun to move out....As long as curriculum theory defines itself as a field exclusively about schooling, it's a dead field....Curriculum theorists need to become less incestuous....They need to discover popular culture." Speaking of what he calls "disciplinary terrorism," Giroux adds, "We can only review a book if in fact it raises questions that legitimate our field....But what happens if you read a book that raises questions and in fact calls even the nature of the field into question? It doesn't get reviewed because people often either are not well read enough to review the book or terrified at reading such a book." To question the need for a field as it is may be so dreaded because it threatens our livelihood. Janet Miller, however, sees increased vitality in the expanding field. She says, "I think that the strength of what's happened in the last...twenty-five years in the field has permitted this variety and breadth and depth of perspective to be drawn in relation to the curriculum field per se." I vacillate on this. Perhaps the expansion is containable within a continuously reconstructed field, to use a Deweyan metaphor.*

Louis Rubin, reflecting on his long career, heavily influenced by a progressive ethos, reflects on the current political mood in educational policy and practice and laments, "I'm thoroughly pessimistic....Don't you think that the conservative mood has taken on the nation?" But he is not completely pessimistic, perhaps due to the ebbs and flows he has lived through as a professor and consultant since the 1950s. Thus, he adds, "I think that it simply has to play its way out." More tuned to benefits of theorizing for practice than some contemporary theorists, Rubin (who I remember for his penetrating questions in graduate school classes) causes me to wonder what may result when the current conservative mood does play itself out. Might it mean educational progressivism in schools as we know them or will it require some altogether different form? When I focus on responses to questions that I ask current teachers and administrators about their own most valuable educational experiences (a variation on teacher and student lore), they often highlight experiences that Foshay characterizes as spiritual or transcendent, ones that add the most to their self-realization. Further, their stories about origins of such transcending experiences rarely take place in schools.

Thus, in order to meet the deeply embedded inner needs of human beings in political contexts, I am increasingly convinced that we must prepare to think of curriculum in the world apart from the curriculum of schools. So, colleges of education need to be more than just colleges of schooling; they will have to deal with what I like to call the outside curricula in a much more substantial way. Mary Ellen Jacobs speaks to my concern here, by relating her greater sense of contribution through moving from curriculum studies to her more recent experience of teaching English at the community college level. She says, "I really love being connected with the discipline." It seems to be that through her love for literature and writing she can more fully come to grips with deeply human issues and wonderings than through preparing teachers for schools.

When Mike Apple looks at the future of the curriculum field, he says that we need to be fueled by the "question that...I've tried to transform, which is not what knowledge is most important but whose knowledge." I think both of these questions (what knowledge and whose knowledge) need to be asked; they check and balance each other. When Apple looks at the contributions of his students, he does not want them to be clones of himself. While he respects the field's history that came before him, noting, about his students, "They sit on my shoulders in the same way I sit on hundreds of other people's shoulders." Yet, he wants his students "to help reconstruct...that tradition," and he wants "to let them teach me, which is what they're doing now." Although Peter Hlebowitsh is critical of Apple, Pinar, Giroux, and others for arguing that curriculum development and design are no longer central, he raises a question that I feel needs to be carefully addressed when he says, "Every curricularist needs to think about...the act of design [and]...the ideal of practice." Hlebowitsh speaks of "a public mandate where...children learn about their differences and commonalties,...a comprehensive agenda,...vocational pursuits...with academic ones,...and ideas of tolerance and...mutuality...with the same critical minded-ness." So I wonder deeply about what kind of ideals of practice could emerge to provide a general public vision, if curriculum studies expand apart from schooling. What would be lost and gained? Petra Munro offers me an insight about this, saying, "My growth as a curriculum theorist has been my ability...to bring diverse threads together....that's what the agenda in curriculum history is all about." Here she speaks of a new kind of autobio-graphical, feminist, phenomenological, and postmodern history of curriculum that will surely and profoundly critique the kind of histories I have attempted to do. I look forward to learning more about this, as I began to do at the 1997 AERA meeting when I was invited to be a discussant for a session in which Janet Miller, Wendy Kohli, and Petra Munro presented such perspectives on curriculum history. What struck me most is that these histories are more about living and relating than about schooling. Thus, they spark my interest in expansion of the field in new ways. Susan Edgerton warns that "if we want to...survive institutionally, we might undermine the very kind of things that we really want to do." Her comments make me wonder: If we turn toward schools too fully will we undermine our attempt to theorize broadly enough, but if we separate from schools too fully how will we have a chance to reach any realm of practical experience? Will public and private resources be used to fund non-school curriculum efforts? Edgerton goes on to suggest that we might reach others more fully through performance, story, and art, more in the spirit of cultural studies than in multicultural schooling (see Edgerton, 1996). Tom Barone, too, calls for artistic renditions of curricular concerns, emphasizing that "how you view the world...depends almost entirely upon your own life story and especially upon the kind of stories you come into contact with in your life....So my hope...is that we...think about the field of curriculum more broadly than just...property of those people who are curriculum theorists....I think education generally, and certainly in the field of curriculum...we've just been...so very narrow and we speak only to ourselves, even as the major decisions about our lives are being made elsewhere....I think what we need to be doing is to be addressing a larger...group of people, and...I don't just mean practitioners, but I mean even the general public." I think here of Jim Henderson's frequent calls for educators to take on the role of public intellectuals.

To me, the central point is that many of today's key curriculum scholars (although they evolved within the curriculum field rather narrowly defined) perceive a need for that field to be more inclusive. This means that the field must accept scholars from all backgrounds, especially those neglected because of race and gender, who have addressed basic curriculum questions about worthwhile knowledge and lives. Such scholars ask who benefits, how, and why. So past responses to such questions must be rewritten, not just with the conclusions of African Americans, Latinos, Native Americans, women, children, youth, and other underrepresented groups included, but with an acceptance, too, of their manners of considering curriculum matters. A diversity of simultaneous histories (presents and futures, for that matter) should be created, portrayed, and performed. When I consult, for instance, I often act out the characters I write about as the major protagonists in curriculum work today: the intellectual traditionalist, the social behaviorist, the experientialist, and the critical reconstructionist.[11] I do not hold these positions to be comprehensive or all-inclusive; instead, I see them as an illustrative part of a much richer diversity than I can portray or fully comprehend.

I see that diversity moving far away from schooling while still including it (for some form of schooling will doubtless remain for some time if only to fulfill its custodial and sorting functions). I feel certain that there is a niche of possibility that I do not yet understand that educates a public from multiple vantage points. As I look at today's curriculum scene, I see the need for curriculum perspectives for what Cremin called "public education, writ large" (1976). My mind boggles when I attempt to comprehend the ways in which our collective and individual consciousness, character, and even conscience have been and are shaped by a broader form of education through families, homes, non-school organizations (such as scouts, clubs, churches, and gangs), jobs, hobbies, and the mass media (including the Internet, videogames, books, magazines, comic books, television, radio, popular music, movies, videos). All of these and many more events are the curricula that feed public interests daily. In a positive vein, our image of Louise Berman's (1968) "new priorities in curriculum" (perceiving, communicating, loving, knowing, decision making, patterning, creating, and valuing) are shaped more by the expanding context in which we live than by the admonishment and teachings of institutions called schools.

CONCLUSION

In conclusion, it seems clear that many key curriculum scholars assume that curriculum studies must be much greater in scope than inquiry that merely facilitates curriculum development to uncritically perpetuate society as it is. If personal meaning and the public good are at stake, as we contend they are, curriculum scholars need to study and inspire dialogue that brings new forms of personal and public growth. We need to look at the sources that shape the outlooks of our young—indeed, of us all. This means inquiry into the creators of popular movies, cartoons and comics, popular music, television, interactive computer media, web sites—whatever fashions our character and perspective. The authors of our outlooks on the world, those (including ourselves) who create our images of life, are the curricularists we need to join for mutual exploration of possibilities and for creation of defensible futures for us all. We cannot be content to be harbingers of what schools might be; rather, we need to expand our horizon to see curriculum as *whatever* brings us insight, meaning, and contributory action. We need to study these *whatevers*, learn from them, and inspire human growth through collaboration.

SOME QUESTIONS TO PONDER

Some of the questions we need to address, together with the several extant curricularists and children, youth, and parents, include the following:

1. What can be done to increase meaning, goodness, and happiness in the lives of young persons—of us all?

2. What is worthwhile? Worth knowing, experiencing, doing, needing, being, becoming, sharing, overcoming, contributing? How do and should we think about this?

3. Historically, what prevents focus on this, especially considering the several incarnations of resistance to ideals of progressive education, for example, behavioral objectives, state-mandated goals, high-stakes testing?

4. How do class, race, gender, ableness, health, membership, place, belief, religion, ethnicity, sexual orientation, status vis-à-vis marriage and parenting, age, nationality, appearance, reputation, and other factors influence education and opportunity?

5. How can alternative forms of inquiry and modes of expression provide insight about these matters?

6. How can the lore (experiential knowledge, stories, and insight) of educators (teachers, parents, educational leaders) and students themselves contribute to understanding of matters mentioned in these questions?

7. How can we better understand the explicit and implicit violence and oppression in curriculum, schooling, and society? Who benefits from it? How can it be overcome?

8. How can inquiry into the several kinds of curriculum (intended, taught, learned or embodied, null, hidden, and outside) provide better understanding of the above questions?

9. How can we focus more broadly on education, seeing schooling as one of several educative forces that constitute the curriculum of life, i.e., that which influences (even creates) who we become?

10. How can we infuse into this curriculum of life (at many junctures, including schooling) reflection on the following: What has been worthwhile? Why and how? What is worthwhile? Why and how? What will be worthwhile? Why and how?

A FINAL WONDER BY BILL SCHUBERT:
(HOW FINAL, IS THE QUESTION?!)

We recall that curriculum began as a formal area of study when universal schooling expanded to an extent that specialists were needed. Specialists were prepared in universities. Colleges of education in major universities are largely a phenomenon of the twentieth century, and departments of curriculum within colleges of education started in the mid-1930s with the establishment of the Department of Curriculum and Teaching under the leadership of Hollis Caswell at Teachers College, Columbia University. Today, we move to a new century and an era when schooling functions may be reclaimed by homes, mass media, tutorial centers, privatization efforts of many kinds, big business, and especially variations on distance learning, virtual realities (virtual schools), and quite simply the Internet. Many of these possible substitutes for schooling do not further the democratic prospect that founders of universal public schools had in mind. Maybe some have. However, it is fair to ask whether the democratic prospect has been furthered by public schools to date, or even whether the potential is there. Perhaps some combination of the above (and yet unrealized possibilities) could be a better means to achieve democratic ideals. Or maybe the very goal of democratic ideals needs to be revised as well.

In any case we need to address the value of continuing curriculum studies as a field or area of study. I recall a conversation I had with Ralph Tyler in the early 1990s, not long before his death. He related that Robert M. Hutchins advised that every 30 years institutions should be reviewed to determine if it made sense to continue their existence. Although I am not certain if any institution has followed this advice, self-preservation being so strong a motive, I wonder what would happen if we reconsidered whether curriculum studies should remain an area of study. To decide that it should not continue may seem blatantly self-destructive. However, I recall another story that may show a beneficial quality of dissolution. At the 1991 AERA meeting Philip L. Smith and I put together a symposium to address the question of whether there should be a new Division on Philosophy of Education. We invited a large number of scholars from the Foundations of Education area to speak to the matter—pro, con, or mixed. When Maxine Greene spoke, I was surprised and (at the time dismayed) that she spoke against the new division. I had hoped that the division would give greater visibility to philosophy of education and the cultural foundations of education in general. Professor Greene's argument, however, was that philosophy of education and cultural foundations should infuse all of AERA and not be relegated to a particular division. While I can think of counterarguments, the point remains that the efforts of philosophers of education should be to enhance the philosophical discourse on all educational matters.

In similar light, then, I wonder if the same should be said of curriculum studies—an area of inquiry born in philosophy of education and social foundations of education. Perhaps what we take to be a flight of scholarship away from curriculum design and development in the institutionalized curriculum is a deeper call to infuse basic curriculum questions in all aspects of education. This would point to the need to ask what is worth knowing, experiencing, needing, doing, being, overcoming, becoming, sharing, and contributing in all spheres of education. This, of course, pertains to schools as long as we have them, and it pertains to the whole range of forces and factors that educate in the whole of human endeavor—homes, non-school organizations, workplaces, peer relations, television, Internet, movies, other video, music, the arts, public spaces, and more. Perhaps, it is the great task remaining before any who consider themselves a part of curriculum studies to act on the obligation to keep alive the question of worth, for in that question is not only an individual or personal call for a worthwhile education, but also a call for continuously addressing the meaning and practice of a good, moral, and just life with others in our world.

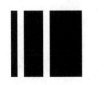

NOTES

PREFACE

1 This preface from the first edition of *Curriculum Books* was written in the late 1970s. In the past two decades much has been written to further curriculum history. The Society for the Study of Curriculum History, founded under the leadership of Laurel Tanner in 1977, continues to encourage work on the historical origins of our work in curriculum (see Kridel, 1988). Moreover, this revision attests to the important contributions made by Kliebard (1986, 1992), Franklin (1986), Goodson (1992, 1993, 1997), Kridel (2000), Tanner and Tanner (1990), Willis, Schubert, Bullough, Kridel, and Holton (1993), Marshall, Sears, and Schubert (2000), and many others listed throughout Chapters 9 and 10 of this edition.

2 Books that are included in the Bibliography of Curriculum Books section that concludes each chapter are not listed in a concluding bibliography. Readers may simply refer to the year indicated for complete citations. Other references and appended commentaries are included as footnotes.

3 Schubert, W. H. "The Literature of Curriculum Development: Toward Centralization and Analysis (Phase I)," 92 pages. A paper presented at the American Educational Research Association Annual Conference, San Francisco, April 22, 1976. This is now available from ERIC. Microfiche is listed in Resources in Education, and document is available from: ERIC Document Reproduction Service; P.O. Box 190; Arlington, Virginia 22210. (ED 163 617).

4 Schubert, W. H. "The Literature of Curriculum Development: Toward Centralization and Analysis (Phase II)." A paper presented at the American Educational Research Association Annual Conference, New York City, April 6, 1977.

5 Schubert, W. H. "A Chronology of Curriculum Development Literature." Printed and distributed by the American Educational Research Association Special Interest Group on the Creation and Utilization of Curriculum Knowledge, 1977.

INTRODUCTION

1   See Fadiman (1978) in dedication to Adler; cited in note 7 below.

2   Fleury, Claude. *The History of Choice and Method of Studies*, 1695.

3   Thomas, T. P. (1990). *The Ethical Dimensions of American Schooling: Curriculum Proposals and Programs for Moral Education, 1887–1966.* Unpublished Doctoral Dissertation at The University of Illinois at Chicago.

4   In 1976 Ann Fraley polled members of the Professors of Curriculum at their meeting during the Annual Conference of the Association for Supervision and Curriculum Development in Miami, Florida, and generated a list of 28 curriculum classics. The 14 classics listed from 1900 to 1940 were produced by nine authors: Dewey, Bagley, Bobbitt, Kilpatrick, Charters, Morrison, Counts, Caswell, and Campbell, and by two professional associations. It is rare to find substantial mention of the many other curriculum authors of this early period by writers in the fifties and sixties.

5   Ponder, G. A. "The Curriculum: Field Without a Past?" *Educational Leadership* (February 1974): 31, 461–464.

6   See, for example: L. Cremin, "Curriculum-making in the United States," *Teachers College Record*, (1971, 73 (2)): 207–220; A. Bellack, "History of Curriculum and Practice," *Review of Educational Research* (June 1969, 39): 283–92; H. Kliebard, "Persistent Curriculum Issues in Historical Perspective," in E.C. Short (Ed.) *A Search for Valid Content for Curriculum Development* (Toledo, OH: College of Education, University of Toledo, 1970); and D. Tanner and L. N. Tanner, *Curriculum Development: Theory into Practice* (historical sections), New York: Macmillan, 1980. These and other curriculum scholars called for serious inquiry into the curricular heritage.

7   Should the student desire to pursue curriculum thought prior to the twentieth century, I suggest Robert Ulich's *Three Thousand Years of Educational Wisdom* (Cambridge: Harvard University Press, 1954) and Ronald Gross's *The Teacher and the Taught* (New York: Delta, 1963) for samples of original writings by eminent philosophers and other scholars on educational topics. Students are also advised to see one or more of the good histories of education that explicate both scholarly ideas about education (thus curriculum to an extent) and practices that prevailed in schools and other educational endeavors throughout history. Examples of such histories include William Boyd's *The History of Western Education* (New York: Barnes and Noble, 1965), R. Freeman Butts's *A Cultural History of Education* (New York: McGraw-Hill, 1947), Lawrence Cremin's *The Transformation of the School* (New York: Alfred A. Knopf, 1961), *A Short History of Educational Thought* (London: University Tutorial Press, 1965) by S. J. Curtis and M. E. A. Boultwood, and Robert Ulich's *History of Educational Thought* (New York: American Book Company, 1950). These contain much that is relevant to curricular thought and descriptions of practice. Those who are interested in both literary and philosophical sources might start with Clifton Fadiman's *The Lifetime Reading Plan*

(New York: Crowell, 1978), or Abraham Kaplan's *In Pursuit of Wisdom* (New York: Glencoe Press, 1977), for an excellent introduction to countless curricular ideas, overt and covert, nestled within the pages of literary classics, ancient to contemporary.

8   Approximation of the number of curriculum books produced (by year and decade):

1900–2	1910–2	1920–8	
1901–1	1911–1	1921–5	
1902–3	1912–3	1922–5	
1903–1	1913–8	1923–9	
1904–1	1914–2	1924–14	
1905–5	1915–4	1925–12	
1906–3	1916–1	1926–18	
1907–1	1917–2	1927–24	
1908–1	1918–4	1928–14	
1909–1	1919–2	1929–18	
19	29	127	

1930–9	1940–14	1950–22	
1931–17	1941–8	1951–17	
1932–19	1942–13	1952–17	
1933–7	1943–10	1953–21	
1934–16	1944–6	1954–10	
1935–13	1945–5	1955–13	
1936–14	1946–16	1956–11	
1937–19	1947–11	1957–12	
1938–15	1948–12	1958–12	
1939–15	1949–8	1959–7	
144	102	142	

1960–27	1970–49	1980–80	1990–81
1961–24	1971–57	1981–93	1991–93
1962–20	1972–59	1982–78	1992–88
1963–26	1973–49	1983–90	1993–134
1964–35	1974–44	1984–79	1994–123
1965–24	1975–54	1985–75	1995–152
1966–42	1976–52	1986–82	1996–141
1967–41	1977–52	1987–75	1997–180
1968–36	1978–43	1988–85	1998–176
1969–49	1979–38	1989–58	1999–134
324	497	795	1302

Total=3481

CHAPTER ONE

1   This is the case with other chapters as well. Direct assertions of causation will rarely be advanced. The main purpose of presenting the Contextual Reminders section is to set highlights of the times before the reader. Hopefully, readers will identify interesting possible connections between curriculum thought and its context. Hopefully, too, readers will further curriculum understanding by investigating such relationships.

2   The National Education Association appointed the Committee of Ten on Secondary School Studies (chaired by Charles W. Eliot, then president of Harvard University) and the Committee of Fifteen in the 1890s. Their work geared much of the direction of school curriculum for decades to come toward the intellectual traditionalist orientation. For committee reports, see Willis, Schubert, Bullough, Kridel, and Holton (1993).

3   See Dunkel, H. B. (1984) for a detailed discussion of how Herbartians created an emphasis on lesson planning as a feature of Herbart's proposal for education. An examination of Herbart's writings evidenced that it was not a high priority in his own design for experienced-based education.

4   *The Child and the Curriculum* and *The School and Society* are often considered companion texts, as witnessed by their publication under the same cover by the University of Chicago Press (1956), with a new edition introduced by Philip Jackson in 1990.

5   Dewey's relevance to educational and social thought today is reflected in the scholarship that has been devoted to better understand and/or critique his ideas. See Boisvert, 1997; Cuffaro, 1995; Garrison, 1997; Paringer, 1990; Ryan, 1995; Simpson and Jackson, 1997; Laurel Tanner, 1997; and Westbrook, 1991.

CHAPTER TWO

1   Thanks are extended to Ralph Tyler for information concerning this conference, given to William Schubert during a May 18, 1979, interview with him.

2   For an engaging introduction to the person and ideas of Maria Montessori, see Hainstock, E. (1997). *The essential Montessori: An introduction to the woman, the writings, the method, and the movement* (Revised edition). New York: Plume.

3   See Cohen, R. D., & Mohl, R. A. (1979). *The paradox of progressive education: The Gary plan and urban schooling.* Port Washington, NY: Kennikat Press, for a discussion of the peculiar combinations of reform elements that constituted this experiment and Barrows's involvement.

4   The National Education Association appointed both the Committee of Ten on Secondary School Studies chaired by Charles W. Eliot, who was president of Harvard University, and the Committee of Fifteen on Elementary Education in the 1890s. Their work steered much of the direction of school curriculum for decades to come toward the intellectual traditionalist orientation.

CHAPTER THREE

1   Hopkins, L. T. (1931). Curriculum making: General, *Review of Educational Research* 1(1): 5.

2   Walker, D. F. (1975). The curriculum field in formation. *Curriculum Theory Network, 4* (4): 264.

CHAPTER FOUR

1   These three works are cited in the bibliographical sections of chapters for the decade in which they were published.

2   Schwab, J. J. "The Impossible Role of the Teacher in Progressive Education." *School Review*, (Summer, 1959): 67, 139–160.

CHAPTER FIVE

1   Information on the FBI's investigation of Counts and Rugg is included in "FBI Surveillance of Three Progressive Educators: Curricular Aspects," a paper presented to the Society for the Study of Curriculum History, Toronto, March 27, 1978, by M. R. Nelson and H. W. Singleton.

CHAPTER SIX

1   Tyler, R. W. (1977). Toward improved curriculum theory: The inside story. *Curriculum Inquiry* 6(4): 251-256. It should be noted that the remainder of the issue of *Curriculum Inquiry* containing these reflections was devoted to publication of proceedings of a 1976 curriculum conference held at the State University College of Arts and Science in Geneseo, New York, a conference designed to discuss the curriculum field's progress in the area of theory building.

CHAPTER SEVEN

1   See: Goodlad, J. I. (1964) in *School Curriculum Reform in the United States*; Goodlad and others (1966) in *The Changing School Curriculum*; Walker, D. F. & Schaffarzick, J. J. (Winter, 1974). Comparing Curricula, *Review of Educational Research*, (44): 83–111; and Schaffarzick, J. J. & Hampson, D. H. (1975).

2   Another means of acquiring curriculum perspectives within the larger arena of educational thought is to survey yearbooks and special publications of educational societies. Two societies that frequently provide direct contributions to curriculum are the Association for Supervision and Curriculum Development (ASCD) and the National Society for the Study of Education (NSSE). The yearbooks of each society portray major topical

concerns. Each of these and other societies (e.g., Phi Delta Kappa) publish special booklets, monographs, and paperback books. When such publications dealt directly with curriculum, they were included in the chronological bibliography presented in this book. Frequently, they are highlighted in the chapter discussions as well.

CHAPTER EIGHT

1   Theobald, R. (1976). *An alternative future for America's third century*. Chicago: The Swallow Press.

2   This question was used to focus much of the discussion on a *Nova* television special entitled "The Final Frontier."

3   See Dewey, J. (1933). First published in *New York Times*, 23 April 1933, Education section, page 7, from an address on 21 April 1933 to the Conference on the Educational Status of the Four- and Five-Year-Old Child at Teachers College, Columbia University. Also see commentary by W. H. Schubert in Ayers, Klonsky, and Lyon (2000).

4   Examples include Bowles, S., & Gintis, M. (1975). *Schooling in Capitalist America*. New York: Basic Books; Greer, C. (1972). *The Great School Legend*. New York: Basic Books; Karier, C. J., Violas, P., & Spring, J. (1973). *Roots of Crisis*. Chicago: Rand McNally; Katz, M. (1971). *Class, Bureaucracy, and Schools*. New York: Praeger; Sharp, R., & Green, A. (1975). *Education and Social Control*. London: Routledge and Kegan Paul; Spring, J. (1972). *Education and the Rise of the Corporate State*. Boston: Beacon. For a bit of counterpoint readers should see: Burnett, J. R. (1980). John Dewey and the Ploys of Revisionism. *Educational Considerations*, 7(2): 208.

5   Kuhn, T. S. (1970). *The Structure of Scientific Revolutions*. Chicago: University of Chicago Press.

6   The Practical: A Language for Curriculum. (Nov. 1969). *School Review* (78): 1–23.

7   See "The Practical: Arts of Eclectic." (1971). *School Review*, 79(4): 493–542; and "The Practical 3: Translation into Curriculum." (1973). *School Review*, 81(4): 501–22, both by Schwab. These and other essays by Schwab are presented by Westbury and Wilkof (1978) with an excellent introduction to Schwab's work. Schwab's perspective on research is related to similar orientations in: Schubert, W. H. (1980). "Recalibrating Educational Research Toward a Focus on Practice." *Educational Researcher*, 9(1): 17–24, 31, and in Schubert's (1986) *Curriculum: Perspectives, paradigms, and possibilities*.

8   See Pinar, W. F. (1978). "Notes on the Curriculum Field 1978." *Educational Researcher*, 7(8): 5–12. For a critical review of reconceptualist literature see: van Manen, M. (1978). "Reconceptualization in Curriculum Inquiry." *Curriculum Inquiry* 8(4): 365–375.

9   van Manen, M. (1978, March). "A Phenomenological Experiment in Educational Theory: The Utrecht School." Paper presented to the annual meeting of the American Educational Research Association, Toronto. Also note the many Dutch and German

sources mentioned in the bibliography of his paper. Subsequently revised and published as: "An experiment in educational theorizing: The Utrecht School, 1978–79." *Interchange*, 10(1): 48–66.

10 See discussions in the preface and introduction to this book, and note 5 in the introduction.

11 The Society for the Study of Curriculum History was founded in New York in 1977. Its first three annual meetings were held in Toronto in 1978, San Francisco in 1979, and Boston in 1980. Proceedings of these meetings have been discussed for publication.

12 Both were published in *Educational Researcher*, September 1978, 7(8): "Notes on the Curriculum Field, 1978," by William F. Pinar, and "Curriculum—A Field Shaped by Different Faces" by J. D. McNeil.

13 See: Decker Walker's "Toward Comprehension of Curricular Realities," a chapter in *Review of Research in Education*. (1976). (Edited by Lee Shulman). Itasca, IL: F. E. Peacock, 4, 268–308.

14 Jackson, P. (April 10, 1979). "The Curriculum and Its Discontents." Invited address for Division B (Curriculum and Objectives) of the American Educational Research Association, San Francisco.

15 In *Democracy and Education*, Dewey described education as follows: "We thus reach a technical definition of education: It is that reconstruction or reorganization of experience which adds to the meaning of experience, and which increases ability to direct the course of subsequent experience." Dewey, John. *Democracy and Education*. New York: Macmillan, 1916 and 1944, p. 76 of the 1966 Free Press paperbound edition.

CHAPTER TEN

1 In his review of Hirsch's text, Wallter Feinberg labeled the reform proposal the "new fundamentalism" and undertook to challenge the accuracy of Hirsch's chronicle of teaching in American public schools. See Feinberg, W. (1997). Educational manifestos and the new fundamentalism. *Educational Researcher* 26(8): 27–35. Hirsch's response is offered in Hirsch, E. D. (1998). Response to Professor Feinberg. *Educational Researcher* 27(2): 38-39.

2 Rifkin, J. (1995). *The end of work: The decline of the global labor force and the dawn of the post-market era*. New York: Tarcher/Putnam.

3 See Walker, D. F. (1971). "A naturalistic model for curriculum development." *School Review*, 80(1), 51-69.

CHAPTER ELEVEN

1 This observation was influenced by a viewpoint portrayed by Philip Jackson in a paper on values imposed on education by psychology. The paper was given at Session

4.14 of the Annual Conference of the American Educational Research Association, San Francisco, April 1979. He emphasized that the most important influences of psychology on education were not conveyed by overt values alone; instead, they were more *subtle, pervasive,* and *diffuse.*

2 A sizable portion of the conclusion is drawn from the following paper: Schubert, W. H. Frames of Curriculum Knowledge Production: Historical Review and Recommendations. Presented to the Annual Conference of the American Educational Research Association, San Francisco, April 1979. (Delivered in Session 16.26 to a symposium entitled Occupational Characteristics of the Curriculum Professoriate, organized by Stephen Hazlett.)

3 Schubert, W. H., & Posner, G. J. Toward a Genealogy of Curriculum Scholars. Presentation to the Society for the Study of Curriculum History, San Francisco, April 8, 1979. The research was also presented by Posner, G. J., & Schubert, W. H. A Genealogy of the Curriculum Field. Paper for the Annual Conference of the American Educational Research Association, San Francisco, April 12, 1979, Session 33.10. A further elaboration of this work is published in: Schubert, W. H., & Posner, G. J. Origins of the curriculum field based on a study of mentor-student relationships. *The Journal of Curriculum Theorizing,* 1980, 2(2).

4 Broudy, H. S. "What Do Professors of Education Profess?" Annual De Garmo Lecture to the Society of Professors of Education, Chicago, February 28, 1979. (Subsequently published by The Society.)

5 Readers will recall that Schwab (1970) criticized the epistemological base of educational research, labeled it *theoretic,* and advocated a move to the practical or quasi-practical. Similarly, Pinar (1975) criticized educational research of the social science ilk, labeled it *conceptual empiricist,* and advocated a move to reconceptualization and emancipation.

6 J. Fodor exemplifies the need to engage in serious speculation in a book-length essay that embraces psychology, linguistics, and philosophy of mind. See Fodor, J. *The Language of Thought.* New York: Crowell, 1975. The quotation was taken from p. vii.

7 This was a central purpose of a series of sessions at the 1979 Annual Conference of the American Educational Research Association, San Francisco, April, culminating in Session 12.01 chaired by Joseph Schwab, entitled Values Imposed by the Behavioral and Social Disciplines: Implications for Education Research and Development Policy. (This series included six sessions: 1.24, 4.14, 6.11, 8.17, 9.106, 11.30. It was organized by Hendrik Gideonse and Robert Koff.)

8 This challenge was communicated by Michael Scriven in his 1979 Presidential Address at the Annual Conference of the American Educational Research Association, San Francisco, April 10, 1979.

9 Broudy, H. S. What Do Professors of Education Profess? See note 4 above.

10 Kaplan, A. (1977). *In pursuit of wisdom.* London: Glencoe Press.

11   I briefly discussed this idea in: "Educational Knowledge about Student Knowledge."
     Insights. December 1978, 15(2), pp. 3-4. The *non-school curriculum* and *theory within per-
     sons* are current subjects of several pieces that are at different levels of preparation.

12   Jaeger, W. *Paideia: The Ideals of Greek Culture* (Volume I). New York: Oxford
     University Press, 1976 reprint of 1945 text, p. ix.

CHAPTER TWELVE

1   Schubert, W. H. (1993). Teacher and student lore: Their ways of looking at it.
     Contemporary Education 65(1), 42–46; Schubert, W. H. and Lopez, A. L. (1994).
     Students' curriculum experiences. In Husen, T., & Postlethwaite, N. T., Eds.,
     International encyclopedia of education, Second Edition, Oxford, UK: Pergamon, pp.
     5813–5818; Schubert, 1995.

2   Schubert, W. H. (1981). Knowledge about out-of -school curricula. *Educational Forum*
     45(2): 185–199; Schubert, W. H. (1982). The return of curriculum inquiry from
     schooling to education. *Curriculum Inquiry*, 12(2): 221–232.; Schubert, 1986; Schubert,
     W. H. (1994) Alternative curriculum designs. *Curriculum and Teaching* 9(1): 26–31;
     Schubert, W. H. (1995). Students as action researchers: Historical precedent and
     contradiction. *Curriculum and Teaching* 10(2): 3–14.

3   Schubert, W. H., Lopez-Schubert, A. L., Herzog, L. A., Posner, G. J., & Kridel, C.
     (1988). A genealogy of curriculum researchers. *The Journal of Curriculum Theorizing*
     8(1): 137–183.

4   Walker, D. F. (1971). A naturalistic model for curriculum development. *School Review*
     80(1): 51–69.

5   See also Pinar, W. F. (1978). Notes on the curriculum field. *Educational Researcher* 7(8):
     5–12.

6   In Macdonald & Leeper, 1966, pp. 8–26.

7   Huebner, D. (1967). Curriculum as concern for man's temporality. *Theory into Practice*
     6(4): 172-179.

8   Wraga, W. G. Extracting sun-beams out of cucumbers: The retreat from practice in
     reconceptualized curriculum studies. *Educational Researcher* 28(1): 4–13.

9   Watkins, W. (1993). Black curriculum orientations: A preliminary inquiry. *Harvard
     Educational Review* 63(3): 321–338.

10   The quotations of contemporary curriculum scholars included in this section are taken
     from transcripts of interviews that were conducted in the preparation of the text,
     Turning Points in Curriculum (Marshall, Sears, & Schubert, 2000). Other excerpts from
     these conversations are included in chapter 9 of *Turning Points*.

11 Schubert, W. H. (1996). Perspectives on four curriculum traditions. *Educational Horizons*,
     74(4): 169–176. (reprinted in *News and Views* (Hudson Institute) 15(11), November

1996, 25–32); Schubert, W. H. (1997). Character education from four perspectives on curriculum. In Molnar, A., Ed., *The construction of children's character*. (1997 NSSE Yearbook, Part II). Chicago: University of Chicago Press and the National Society for the Study of Education, pp. 17–30.

BIBLIOGRAPHIC INDEX

NAME INDEX

SUBJECT INDEX

Studies in the Postmodern Theory of Education

General Editors
Joe L. Kincheloe & Shirley R. Steinberg

Counterpoints publishes the most compelling and imaginative books being written in education today. Grounded on the theoretical advances in criticalism, feminism, and postmodernism in the last two decades of the twentieth century, Counterpoints engages the meaning of these innovations in various forms of educational expression. Committed to the proposition that theoretical literature should be accessible to a variety of audiences, the series insists that its authors avoid esoteric and jargonistic languages that transform educational scholarship into an elite discourse for the initiated. Scholarly work matters only to the degree it affects consciousness and practice at multiple sites. Counterpoints' editorial policy is based on these principles and the ability of scholars to break new ground, to open new conversations, to go where educators have never gone before.

For additional information about this series or for the submission of manuscripts, please contact:

> Joe L. Kincheloe & Shirley R. Steinberg
> c/o Peter Lang Publishing, Inc.
> 275 Seventh Avenue, 28th floor
> New York, New York 10001

To order other books in this series, please contact our Customer Service Department:

> (800) 770-LANG (within the U.S.)
> (212) 647-7706 (outside the U.S.)
> (212) 647-7707 FAX

Or browse online by series:

> www.peterlangusa.com